Life and Worklife Expectancies

Second Edition

Hugh Richards, M.S.
Michael Donaldson, Ph.D.

Contributing Authors

James Ciecka

Peter Ciecka

Frank Slesnick

Robert Thornton

Edward Timmons

 ® Lawyers & Judges
Publishing Company, Inc.

Tucson, Arizona

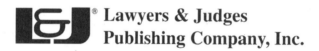 **Lawyers & Judges Publishing Company, Inc.**

P.O. Box 30040 • Tucson, AZ 85751-0040
(800) 209-7109 • FAX (800) 330-8795
e-mail: sales@lawyersandjudges.com
www.lawyersandjudges.com

Library of Congress Cataloging-in-Publication Data

Life and worklife expectancies / edited by Hugh Richards, Michael Donaldson ; contributing authors, James Ciecka ... [et al.]. -- 2nd ed.
    p. cm.
 Rev. ed. of: Life and worklife expectancies / Hugh Richards. c1999.
 Includes bibliographical references and index.
 ISBN-13: 978-1-933264-74-5 (hardcover : alk. paper)
 ISBN-10: 1-933264-74-8 (hardcover : alk. paper)
 1. Life expectancy--Statistics. 2. Occupational mortality--Statistics. I. Richards, Hugh. II. Donaldson, Michael, 1965- III. Richards, Hugh. Life and worklife expectancies.
 HB1322.3.R53 2009
 304.6'45021--dc22

                          2009043637

Printed in the United States of America
10 9 8 7 6 5 4 3 2 1

Dedication

To my family: Catherine, Max, and Ti, the three reasons I love to work at home.
—Michael Donaldson

Jamila and Juanito, you are the reason for everything,
and Erik, still depending on your computer.
—Hugh Richards

Contents

List of Tables

Acknowledgments

This work has depended upon the contributions to the literature of many people referenced throughout the book. It has also greatly benefited from the help of those not explicitly referenced. We want to express my deep thanks to these people.

Dr. Paul D. Sorlie, of the National Heart, Lung, and Blood Institute provided guidance in the initial phases of life expectancies by education, and *Dr. Norman J. Johnson* of the Bureau of the Census graciously responded to my many requests for information.

Jim Ciecka graciously provided help with several thorny problems in analysis of Years to Final Separation.

Our wives, *Jamila* and *Catherine*, helped keep body and soul together through the preparation of this book.

Finally, we want to thank the staff at Lawyers & Judges for patiently waiting for us to get this thing done—finally.

Part I: Life Expectancy

Chapter 1

Introduction

This second edition of *Life and Worklife Expectancies* updates the life and worklife tables but otherwise maintains much of what was in the first printing. Nevertheless, several changes have been made.

The most important is that standard errors for estimates are provided in Appendix tables. In all cases, except life expectancies by education, these have been calculated using bootstrapping sampling and Monte Carlos simulations.

Other major changes include the following: some tables are re-numbered; worklife expectancies by occupation are not included; and the chapter discussing Median Years to Retirement has been written by us. Because appropriate and more recent information is not available, the discussion and tables related to worklife expectancies by English language proficiency of Hispanics has not been revised. Chapter 3 (Life Expectancies and Properties of Survival Data) also remains unchanged.

1.1 Overview

Life and worklife tables and the underlying mortality and labor force participation data they contain are one of the foundations of almost all forensic economic analyses that involve lost earnings, non-market services, or valuation of pension benefits. This book has arisen out of a desire to collect this information into one reference.

The chapters in this book are separated into two parts. Part I is an introduction to life tables and life expectancy, and Part II discusses the duration of working life; both parts explain the methodology and data sources used to derive life and worklife tables. Detailed data are presented in the tables section following the text.

1.2 Introduction to Part I

Life tables are discussed in the six chapters of Part I. These chapters are meant to be practical rather than technical or theoretical. Although methodology is not the primary focus, it is described when necessary.

Life tables and their uses are not entirely straightforward:

- They may be constructed from "snapshot" data of an entire population during some short interval of time, or they may represent the mortality experience of a specific cohort followed through time from birth to death of all members (Chapter 2).

- The uses of life tables are varied. Probably the most commonly used data is average expected years of remaining life (i.e., "life expectancy"). Another measurement of longevity is typical, or "median," years of life—this is longer than "life expectancy" at young ages and shorter at old ages. Life tables also provide data to calculate probabilities of survival between any two ages. This information is especially pertinent to the Life-Participation-Employment method of estimating duration of economic life (Chapter 12).

- The probabilities that a given person will live exactly the number of years average for his or her cohort is quite small. Thus it is useful to know something about the variability of additional years of life and the shape of the distribution of life expectancies (Chapter 3).

- Life tables may reflect relative differences in mortality rates associated with factors such as race, ethnicity, education, tobacco use, medical risk conditions, etc. (Chapters 4, 5 and 6).

- It should be noted that life expectancies are affected by many lifestyle and socioeconomic factors. Education itself is not a determining factor; rather it is a proxy for the conditions that do affect life expectancy.

1.3 Use of Life Tables

Use of life tables involves several decisions: choice of the table that best characterizes the person in question; the age at which to estimate the additional duration of life; and whether to use earnings/retirement benefits/medical costs to a certain life expectancy or as annual mortality-adjusted dollar amounts.

Regarding the first decision, that is, which table to use, it is usually the case that less biased estimates are obtained for more narrowly specified characteristics. However, sampling errors usually increase as populations are disaggregated into smaller and smaller subpopulations. Thus, there is usually a tradeoff: less bias but larger possible error. This book indicates sampling variability for race/Hispanic origin and education. Note that estimates by educational level should be used whenever possible rather than estimates for populations of all educational levels combined (see Chapter 4).

Life expectancies by smoking status are presented only for all races combined. National Cancer Society research indicates that the effects of smoking on mortality rates are relatively consistent across races; thus life expectancies by smoking status and race can be estimated by following the procedure suggested at the end of Chapter 6. Be aware, though, that confounding factors will be larger for blacks and Hispanics than for whites, and that estimates of their life expectancies by smoking status will be less certain than for whites.

The choice of the age at which to determine life (and worklife) expectancy depends on the reason for the estimate. Economists and vocational and rehabilitation experts use life table information for two basic purposes: (a) estimates of lost earnings, non-market services, consumption, and retirement benefits, and (b) estimates of future medical expenses. In both cases, the age is chosen to fulfill the purpose of the tort, i.e., to make the affected party whole. Thus for lost earnings, etc., life expectancy should be based on the person's age at the date of the incident (to make him or her whole as of that moment). Medical expenses are a different situation. Funds must be sufficient to cover all estimated costs throughout life expectancy; because the injured person has already survived some additional years, his or her life expectancy is to an older age than it would have been at the date of the incident. Thus, life expectancy should be determined as of the date of the damage award.

Cases that incorporate medical risk conditions may involve both of these issues. Two general scenarios pertain: (1) persons with pre-existing medical risks with no subsequent increase in risk; and (2) those whose injuries caused or exacerbated medical risks. In the first case, medical risk factors should be applied to both pre- and post-incident life expectancy estimates. In the second case, the estimate of life expectancy without the injury should be based on pre-injury mortality rates, whereas the estimate of life expectancy with the injury should incorporate the additional medical risk factors. Both should be based on the age at injury. Life expectancy for the purpose of future medical or rehabilitation costs, however, should include the additional risk factors and be based on age at the date of report or trial.

Finally, some of the methods of dealing with the duration of working life (prime among which is the LPE model described in Chapter 12) are based on annual mortality-adjusted dollar amounts rather than on a life expectancy. Several economists have also demonstrated that future medical care costs and retirement benefits are more appropriately calculated this way (Eck, Baker and Davis, 1988; Fjeldsted, 1993).

Chapter 2

Overview of Life Expectancies

2.1 Current versus Cohort Life Tables

Life tables simply represent a summary of mortality rates (probabilities of death at each age) for a given population during some period of time. The tables are generated by exposing a hypothetical cohort of 100,000 persons at birth to these mortality rates.

Two methods are used to construct the tables. One is "cohort" or "generation." The other is "period" or "snapshot." "Current" life tables are "period" tables based on the most recently available data. "Cohort" and "period" life tables are distinguished from each other primarily by the period during which their mortality rates were observed.

A. Cohort Life Tables

Mortality rates used for construction of cohort life tables represent the experience of an actual cohort from birth through all subsequent ages. They may incorporate data from a series of historical "period" tables; they may make projections of mortality rates into the future based on current trends; or they may combine the two.

Because cohort life tables allow for decreases in age-specific mortality rates as the cohorts advance in age through time, this method is considered to forecast future life expectancies better than "current" tables. (As the next section explains, the "current" method assumes that age-specific mortality rates will remain as measured during the observed year.) The best known cohort tables in the U.S. are those produced by the Social Security Administration (SSA), the most recent of which include tables for ages zero through 119 by year of birth from 1900 to 2000 (in ten-year increments).

Projections of future mortality rates are based, at least partially, on past trends. Text Table 1 summarizes some his-torical trends in life expectancies. For projections of mortality rates into the future for the most recent SSA tables, the average annual percentage reduction in central death rates for those under 65 are projected to be relatively small compared with past reductions, whereas for older persons reductions are projected to continue at a relatively rapid pace. Mortality rates in the first year following 2001 were decreased by the entire projected rates. Thereafter, the annual decreases gradually become less, until after twenty-five years into the future, the rate of reduction in mortality was held constant at about one-third of the initial rate (SSA, 2005).

Specific age "cohort" life expectancies for U.S. Social Security areas by year of birth are presented in Text Table 2,[1] and for 2000 are compared with "current" life expectancies from the *U.S. Decennial Life Tables for 2000*. For males born in 2000, life expectancies from cohort tables are about 5.9 years longer than those from current tables for ages from birth through about 20. At older ages, the difference between cohort and current life expectancies gradually diminishes. For females the differences at the youngest ages are about 4.7 years.

How much better the "dynamic" forecasts of cohort tables are than the "static" data of current tables is a function of the validity of assumptions concerning the direction and extent of future trends in mortality, determined by factors such as:

> the development and application of new diagnostic, surgical and life sustaining techniques, the presence of environmental pollutants, improvements in exercise and nutrition, the incidence of violence, the isolation and treatment of causes of disease, the emergence of new forms of disease, improvements in prenatal care, the prevalence of cigarette smoking, the misuse of drugs (including alcohol), the extent to which people assume responsibility for their own health, education regarding health, and changes in our conception of the value of life. (SSA, 1992)

Text Table 1: U.S. life expectancies and rates of improvement; selected ages and periods, all races

Period	At Birth		Age 20		Age 40		Age 60	
	Males	Females	Males	Females	Males	Females	Males	Females
Life Expectancies								
1900-1902	47.88	50.70	42.03	43.60	27.65	29.08	14.33	15.21
1909-1911	49.86	53.24	42.48	44.66	27.32	29.15	13.95	14.90
1919-1921	55.50	57.40	44.99	45.63	29.63	30.58	15.22	15.87
1929-1931	57.71	60.90	44.88	47.21	28.68	30.86	14.62	15.94
1939-1941	61.60	65.89	46.91	50.37	29.57	32.68	14.99	16.92
1949-1951	65.47	70.96	48.92	53.73	30.79	35.06	15.68	18.50
1959-1961	66.80	73.24	49.77	55.60	31.42	36.61	15.94	19.52
1969-1971	67.04	74.64	49.54	56.59	31.48	37.64	15.99	20.60
1979-1981	70.11	77.62	51.88	58.98	33.64	39.80	17.46	22.29
1989-1991	71.83	78.81	53.25	59.87	35.09	40.65	18.53	22.90
2000	74.14	79.48	55.22	60.30	36.69	41.02	19.86	23.13
Compound Growth Rates								
Decades								
1901-1910	0.45%	0.54%	0.12%	0.27%	-0.13%	0.03%	-0.30%	-0.23%
1910-1920	1.08%	0.76%	0.58%	0.22%	0.81%	0.48%	0.88%	0.63%
1920-1930	0.39%	0.59%	-0.02%	0.34%	-0.33%	0.09%	-0.40%	0.04%
1930-1940	0.65%	0.79%	0.44%	0.65%	0.31%	0.57%	0.25%	0.60%
1940-1950	0.61%	0.74%	0.42%	0.65%	0.41%	0.71%	0.45%	0.90%
1950-1960	0.20%	0.32%	0.17%	0.34%	0.20%	0.43%	0.16%	0.54%
1960-1970	0.04%	0.19%	-0.05%	0.18%	0.02%	0.28%	0.03%	0.54%
1970-1980	0.45%	0.39%	0.46%	0.41%	0.67%	0.56%	0.88%	0.79%
1980-1990	0.24%	0.15%	0.26%	0.15%	0.42%	0.21%	0.60%	0.27%
1990-2000	0.32%	0.08%	0.36%	0.07%	0.45%	0.09%	0.69%	0.01%
Long Run								
1901-2000	0.44%	0.46%	0.28%	0.33%	0.29%	0.35%	0.33%	0.42%
1950-2000	0.25%	0.23%	0.24%	0.23%	0.35%	0.31%	0.47%	0.45%
1980-2000	0.28%	0.12%	0.31%	0.11%	0.43%	0.15%	0.65%	0.18%

Source: U.S. Department of Health and Human Services, National Center for Health Statistics, "Vital Statistics of the United States, 2000"

Text Table 2: Cohort life expectancies for U.S. Social Security Areas, selected birth cohorts and ages, all races

Year of Birth	Age					
	0	20	40	60	80	100
Males						
1900	51.52	47.28	31.20	16.34	6.86	1.97
1910	56.19	49.25	32.28	17.15	7.02	1.90
1920	61.77	51.52	33.80	18.41	7.26	2.02
1930	66.09	53.42	35.36	19.51	7.58	2.16
1940	69.55	55.15	37.08	20.56	7.96	2.30
1950	72.45	56.13	38.13	21.36	8.35	2.45
1960	73.88	57.19	39.14	22.06	8.72	2.59
1970	75.80	58.41	39.97	22.71	9.09	2.74
1980	77.60	59.41	40.78	23.33	9.44	2.89
1990	78.90	60.28	41.54	23.92	9.78	3.03
2000	80.01	61.09	42.26	24.48	10.11	3.18
2010	80.96	61.85	42.94	25.02	10.43	3.33
Females						
1900	58.28	53.38	37.64	21.58	8.93	2.25
1910	63.71	56.16	39.09	22.39	9.00	2.19
1920	69.22	58.01	39.66	22.67	8.91	2.32
1930	72.85	59.22	40.39	23.06	9.16	2.48
1940	75.75	60.36	41.36	23.63	9.57	2.64
1950	78.46	61.35	42.20	24.28	9.98	2.80
1960	79.58	62.12	42.94	24.94	10.38	2.97
1970	80.91	62.91	43.67	25.55	10.77	3.13
1980	82.27	63.65	44.37	26.14	11.14	3.29
1990	83.30	64.35	45.02	26.69	11.50	3.45
2000	84.19	65.02	45.64	27.22	11.84	3.61
2010	84.96	65.64	46.22	27.72	12.17	3.76
"Current" life expectancies from the Vital Statistics, 2000						
Male	74.14	55.22	36.69	19.86	7.63	2.41
Female	79.48	60.30	41.02	23.13	9.12	2.67
Difference (Cohort minus Current)						
Male	5.87	5.87	5.57	4.62	2.48	0.77
Female	4.71	4.72	4.62	4.09	2.72	0.94

Sources: U.S. Department of Health and Human Services, Social Security Administration, "Life Tables for the United States Social Security Area 1900-2100" and National Center for Health Statistics, National Vital Statistics Reports, Vol. 53, No. 6, November 10, 2004, "United States Life Tables, 2002."

On the positive side, many of the medical and informational factors listed above have shown steady improvement. But some trends are cause for concern. It is uncertain whether our society can afford to continue to attain the full benefits of medical research. In addition, the greatest increases in longevity over the past century have resulted not from improved medical care but from improvements in sanitation, nutrition, education, etc. Even today, many of the leading causes of premature death are best treated not by medicine but by improvements in lifestyle. Yet, it is unclear whether the population is living healthier lives. Tobacco use has increased in the last few years, particularly among teenagers. The proportion of overweight Americans has increased significantly in the last thirty years and is causing much concern about future life expectancies. Both show no indication of a diminution in the future. Finally, as will be discussed in Chapter 3, a portion of the increase in life expectancy over the last twenty-five years has been due to changes in the educational composition of the population rather than solely to decreases in mortality rates.

B. Current (Period) Life Tables

Period life tables are based on age-specific mortality rates as observed during a relatively brief period of time—usually one to three years. Period tables, as cohort tables, can incorporate changes in mortality rates over time, but they do it for a whole population rather than for each cohort as it moves through increasing age. In other words, the mortality data for current tables are taken as observed; they are not adjusted for future changes, and the tables are not forward-looking in the sense that future improvements in mortality are not incorporated.

The current life method assumes that as a hypothetical cohort moves through advancing ages it will experience the same age-specific death rates that were observed for those ages during the reference period. For example, the current life method (a) assumes that some young cohort in 2004 will be subject throughout its lifetime to the age-specific death rates existent in the actual population in 2004, and (b) applies these rates year by year to construct the life tables. Text Table 1 above represents a series of "period" tables for specific decades since 1990.

The most widely used current life tables are those published by the National Center for Health Statistics (NCHS), in *Vital Statistics of the United States*. The NCHS provides two sets of life tables: decennial and annual.

Decennial tables are based on actual census counts and three years of mortality data centered on the decennial census year. The most recent of these tables uses the 2000 Census of the Population and deaths during the period 1999-2001.

Annual tables are based on deaths in a single year and on postcensal estimates of population. They are calculated by abbreviated methods and are not quite as accurate as the decennial tables. As shown in Text Table 3, however, life expectancies in the 2000 annual tables are very close to those in the 1999–2001 decennial tables. Differences tend to be larger with advancing age, for males of all races than for females, and for blacks than for all races. For all races the largest differences are less than two tenths of a year (with the 2000 annual table greater than the decennial table). For blacks the largest differences are slightly more than three tenths of a year, with the annual estimates larger than the decennial data for males and the reverse for females. Because the differences are minor and the population estimates (upon which the annual tables are partially based) are projected only from the 2000 Census of the Population through 2004, updated annual tables can be considered sufficiently accurate for forensic purposes.

Text Table 3: Comparison of life expectancies at selected ages, Decennial 1999-2001 Life Tables versus annual 2000 Life Tables

Age	Male			Female		
	Decen'l	Annual	Diff	Decen'l	Annual	Diff
All Races						
0	74.10	74.14	-0.04	79.45	79.48	-0.03
20	55.17	55.22	-0.05	60.27	60.30	-0.03
40	36.58	36.69	-0.11	40.98	41.02	-0.04
60	19.71	19.86	-0.15	23.09	23.13	-0.04
80	7.44	7.63	-0.19	9.05	9.12	-0.07
Blacks						
0	68.09	68.19	-0.10	75.12	74.93	0.19
20	49.83	49.95	-0.12	56.48	56.31	0.17
40	32.10	32.26	-0.16	37.65	37.53	0.12
60	17.14	17.48	-0.34	21.18	20.99	0.19
80	7.12	7.34	-0.22	8.96	8.61	0.35

Sources: U.S. Department of Health and Human Services, National Center for Health Statistics, "U.S. Decennial Life Tables for 199-2001" and "Vital Statistics of the United States, 2000"

Other organizations have developed period life tables based on different sample populations. Insurance companies have developed several alternative sets of life tables based on their insured populations. "Select" life tables reflect the mortality experience of recently insured clients; "ultimate" tables exclude persons insured in the early years of the insurance contract; and "aggregate" tables include all who are insured. These life tables are biased upward because clients usually belong to higher socioeconomic groups (which have longer life expectancies) and must often pass medical examinations. The bias is particularly strong for the select tables because they are derived from the mortality data of those people who have most recently passed the medical examinations. Insurance companies also adjust their mortality rates, in what is called "margin," to provide a safety cushion for the companies. The indeterminate effects of the selection bias and the margin adjustments reduce the credibility of insurance life tables for courtroom use.

Current life tables are also produced by the Census Bureau using data from the U.S. National Longitudinal Mortality Study (NLMS). This is an important study because it demonstrates the relationships between mortality and a number of socioeconomic factors: geographic location, nativity, Hispanic status, education, income, household size, marital status, employment status, occupation, and industry. These data are used in this book to derive life tables by sex, race, Hispanic origin, and education. (Chapter 4)

C. Tables Presented in this Book

The tables in Part III present life tables for all ages from birth to age 85 for selected characteristics. Tables are provided by sex, race or Hispanic status, education, and cigarette smoking status (for 2004). This is not an exhaustive list of causative or correlated factors: others known to be relevant are listed in the paragraph above. For this book, the decision of which tables to include was based on several criteria: availability of data, relative effect of the characteristic, and stability across a hypothetical person's lifetime (marital status, income, occupation, etc., may vary considerably from one period in a person's life to another, whereas race and sex are stable). Several of the factors chosen for inclusion are relatively stable, but not immutable. For example, although tobacco is a strong addictant, people can change their use patterns; medical risks may change as medical technology improves; and educational attainment can increase.

The "current" life methodology is used for all the tables for the following reasons: (1) current life tables are updated every year (with a several year lag), (2) they are readily available—published in the *Vital Statistics of the United States*, on the internet at the NCHS and Social Security Administration home sites, and in many other publications such as the *Statistical Abstract of the United States*, (3) they can be modified easily to adjust for relative risks connected with factors such as education, tobacco use, medical conditions, etc., (4) they involve no speculative assumptions about future trends in longevity, (5) when decomposed into educational levels, they already implicitly include some of the trend factors by which cohort tables are generated, (6) compared to the cohort life tables they result in conservative estimates of remaining life, and (7) they are accepted in courts of law.[1]

Not all forensic economists agree that "current" life tables are appropriate to use. For example, Suyderhoud and Pollock (1990) argue that estimates of life expectancies should account for improvements in mortality that will probably occur between the date of the estimate and the projected death of the person in question. This, in their terms, is "ultimate" life expectancy. Practitioners who wish to use cohort tables can obtain them from the Social Security Administration.[2] The SSA tables present all of the information necessary for developing any of the measures of longevity described below. Data are available for persons born since 1900. (Text Table 2 summarizes some of the data.)

2.2 Measurements of Longevity

The most widely used measurement of longevity is the average number of years of life remaining, or "life expectancy." In the tables, these are presented in the "Expectation of Life" column. (In *Vital Statistics of the U.S.* life tables, these numbers are shown in the o_{e_x} column.) Average age at death is obtained by adding the age of the person in question with the corresponding "life expectancy."

In general, the following patterns occur: females have longer life expectancies than males; Hispanics have the longest life expectancies and blacks the shortest; longevity increases with educational attainment; nonsmokers live longer than smokers; longevity decreases with increasing extent of obesity, and increasing levels of medical risks decrease life expectancy. Although usually not relevant for forensic purposes, it should be noted that these patterns do not necessarily hold for the oldest age groups. Instead, for them, differences between all of the groups become small to nonexistent. Even though many blacks and less educated people die earlier, once they have reached 75 years of age or more, their average duration of remaining life is nearly the same as that of all other groups in the population.

A second measure of longevity is median duration of life or probable life expectancy. This is the age at which only half of the original cohort would remain alive. Median life expectancy for any age can be determined by finding the subsequent age at which the value in the column "Number Living at Beginning of Age Interval" (column *l* in *Vital Statistics of the U.S.* life tables) is exactly half that of the age in question. Because it is assumed that deaths are evenly distributed within each age interval, interpolation can be used to find values that fall between two integers for either average or median measures.

Median duration of life exceeds average duration at birth by about 3.3 years for white females, 3.4 for white males, 3.6 years for black males, and 3.7 years for black females. The differences grow gradually less with increasing age until the median becomes less than the average for ages greater than the early sixties for males and early seventies for females. These differences are caused by the skewed distribution of deaths. Although there are few deaths at young ages, they affect life expectancy relatively strongly because of the long period of time over which they factor into calculation of the averages.

A third measure of longevity is the probability of survival from an initial age to a given subsequent age. This is the measure used for mortality adjusted estimates and may be used to calculate the value of structured settlement annuities and medical/life care plans. It is also an important component for several of the methods used to estimate the length of working life. Among these are increment-decrement worklife tables, Life-Participation-Employment (LPE), and the Alter and Becker (1985) methodologies.

Two methods can be used to calculate survival probabilities. The simpler approach is to use the number of persons living at the beginning of the age. The probability of survival to a given age is obtained by dividing the number of persons in a cohort alive at the beginning of that age by the number living at the beginning of the initial age. For instance, using white, college-educated males, the probability of living from birth to age 40 equals the number living at the beginning of age 40 (i.e., 96,870 divided by the initial 100,000 assumed for the cohort at birth). The resulting prob-

ability is 0.96870. The probability of this male living to age 42 equals 96,611 divided by 96,870. The resulting probability is 0.99733. (See Table 1.)

Alternatively, probabilities of survival from each age to the next equal 1 minus the number in the column headed "Mortality Rates." To obtain the survival probability of living from the initial age to any given older age, multiply all of the intervening probabilities. Using the example of the 40-year-old male above, the proportion alive at the beginning of age 40 and dying before age 41 is 0.00126, and the proportion alive at age 41 and dying before age 42 is 0.00141. Thus, the survival probability from age 40 to 41 is 1.00000 minus 0.00126, which gives 0.99874; and from age 41 to 42 it is 1.00000 minus 0.00141, or 0.99859. The survival probability from age 40 to 42 is the product of 0.99874 and 0.99859. This equals the same 0.99733 calculated using the first method.

Endnotes

1. As stated on the end page of the *Vital Statistics,* "This document is hereby certified as an official Federal document and is fully admissible as evidence in Federal court. Under Federal Rule of Evidence 902: 'Self-authentication,' ... no extrinsic evidence of authenticity, that is seal or stamp, is required as a condition for admissibility of this document as evidence in court."

2. Complete tables are available from the U.S. Department of Health and Human Services, Social Security Administration, Office of the Actuary, Room 700, Altmeyer Building, Baltimore, MD 21235, Phone (410) 965-3015 or Fax (410) 965-6693 or on their website at www.ssa.gov/OACT/NOTES/as120/LifeTables_Body.html#wp1169372 and www.ssa.gov/OACT/NOTES/as120/LOT.html.

Chapter 3

Life Expectancy and the Properties of Survival Data*

James Ciecka and Peter Ciecka

By itself, life expectancy does not tell forensic economists about the variability of additional years of life for an individual or cohort, the shape of the distribution of additional years of life for an individual or cohort, or the range within which additional years of life will fall for an individual or cohort. Suppose life expectancy at age x is e_x. With a supposed 50% probability, are additional years of life equal to ex plus or minus 10%, 20%, or some other percentage? This chapter examines some properties of survival data and the behavior of additional-years-of-life data, and thereby increases the usefulness of the concept of life expectancy to forensic economists.

3.1 Life Expectancy Concepts

There are several ways to think of the concept of life expectancy. To explore these approaches, we specify a survival function for people who are exactly age x (London, 1988; Jordan, 1991). The survival function is denoted by $S(t;x)$, where $t \geq 0$ measures additional years of life. $S(t;x)$ is the probability that a person who is alive at age x will be alive after the passage of t additional years, and it has the following properties:

$$S(0;x) = 1, \tag{1a}$$
$$S(t;x) > S(t+\delta;x) \quad \text{for } \delta > 0 \tag{1b}$$
$$S(w;x) = 0 \quad \text{for large enough } w. \tag{1c}$$

Property (1a) holds because we are dealing with people who have survived to age x and are, therefore, alive at $t = 0$ years into the future. Property (1b) states that the probability of survival declines as time increases; and finally, (1c) states that the probability of survival is zero after the passage of a long enough period of time. The time $t = w$ denotes the shortest amount of time for which $S(t;x) = 0$, so it is also true that $S(t;x) = 0$ for $t > w$. Figures 1 and 2 illustrate survival functions for 30-year-old men and women using survival data from the *Vital Statistics of the U.S., Decennial Life Tables for 1989–91* (1997).

To calculate survival probabilities, let l_0 denote a cohort of newborns of which l_x survive to age x. The probability that a person age x will survive to age $x + t$ is

$$S(t;x) = \frac{l_{x+1}}{l_x} \tag{2}$$

Given that a person reaches a certain age, life expectancy is the sum of the probabilities that that person will be alive at successively higher ages. That is, life expectancy at age x is

$$e_x = \sum_{t=1}^{w} \frac{l_{x+1}}{l_x} \tag{3}$$

where t is additional years of life and $x + w$ is the age at which there are no survivors (i.e., $l_x + w = 0$).[1] For example, Figure 3 shows the cumulative probabilities that a 30-year-old male will be alive after the passage of a given number of years. The sum of these probabilities is the life expectancy of 44.1 years *(Vital Statistics of the U.S., Decennial Life Tables for 1989–91, 1997)*.

---

*This chapter is a reprint of an article by James Ciecka and Peter Ciecka published in *Litigation Economics Digest*, Volume I, No. 2, 1996. Reprinted with permission. It appears here without changes from the first edition.

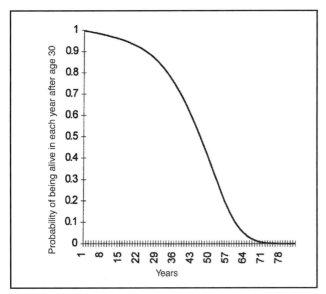

Figure 1 *Survival function for men age 30: S(t; 30)*

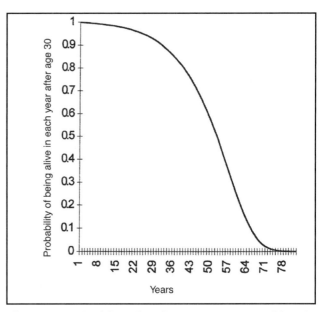

Figure 2 *Survival function for women age 30: S(t; 30)*

A second method for computing life expectancy involves starting with a cohort of l_x survivors who are age x, summing the years of life that that cohort will live, and then dividing by l_x. This approach yields a life expectancy of

$$e_x = \frac{1}{l_x} \sum_{t=1}^{w} l_{x+t} \tag{4}$$

It follows immediately that (3) and (4) yield identical life expectancies. For 30-year-old males, there are $l = 96,159$ survivors from an original cohort of $l_0 = 100,000$ births, and these survivors will collectively live 4,241,601 years of life (see Figure 4) before all members of the cohort die *(Vital Statistics of the U.S., 1990, 1994)*. The average number of years of life is 44.1 = (4,241,601/96,159).

Unfortunately, neither of the foregoing ways of viewing life expectancy is helpful if one wants to measure the variation in additional-years-of-life. With this end in mind, life expectancy can be viewed as the expected value of an additional-years-of-life random variable. The probability of living exactly t additional years, given a person is age x, is

$$p_{x+1} = \frac{l_{x+t} - l_{x+t+1}}{l_x} \tag{5}$$

and life expectancy is

$$e_x = \sum_{t=1}^{w} t p_{x+t} = \sum_{t=1}^{w} t \frac{(l_{x+t} - l_{x+t+1})}{l_x} \tag{6}$$

It is not immediately obvious that definition (6) yields the same value of life expectancy as (3) and (4); but, (6) can be rewritten as

$$e_x = \frac{1}{l_x}[(l_{x+1} - l_{x+2}) + 2(l_{x+2} - l_{x+3}) + 3(l_{x+3} - l_{x+4}) + ... + w(l_{x+w} - l_{x+w+1})]$$

$$= \frac{1}{l_x}[l_{x+1} + l_{x+2} + l_{x+3} + ... + l_{x+w} - wl_{x+w+1}]$$

$$= \frac{1}{l_x} \sum_{t=1}^{w} l_{x+1}, \text{since } l_{x+w+1} = 0$$

Figure 5 shows the probabilities of 30-year-old males living exactly t additional years. Life expectancy is the expected value of t, and it is once again 44.1 years for 30-year-old males. As mentioned above, the advantage of viewing life expectancy in this manner is that t is a random variable whose variance and standard deviation can be computed. The variance of additional years of life is

$$V[t] = \sum_{t=1}^{w} (t - e_x)^2 p_{x+t}. \tag{7}$$

The standard deviation for the length of life of a 30-year-old male is 15.5 years (see Text Table 4). In addition, it is clear from Figure 5 that the density function is skewed to the left, implying that the mean is less than the median, which is less than the modal number of additional years of life. For a 30-year-old male, the median number of additional years of life is 46.2 years, and the mode is 51 years.

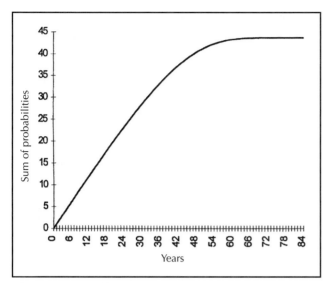

Figure 3 Sum of probabilities of 30-year-old males being alive after indicated number of years

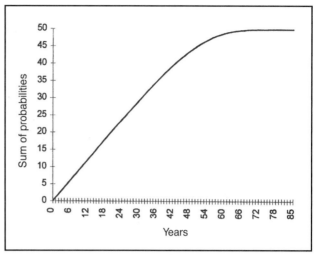

Figure 6 Sum of probabilities of 30-year-old females being alive after indicated number of years

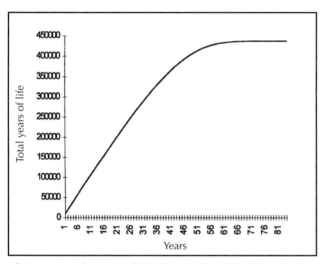

Figure 4 Total years of life live by l_{30} = 96,159 males after indicated number of years

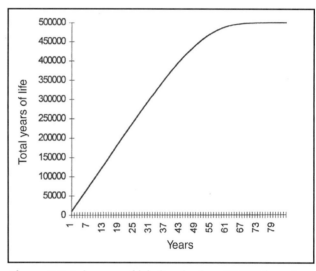

Figure 7 Total years of life live by l_{30} = 98,038 females after indicated number of years

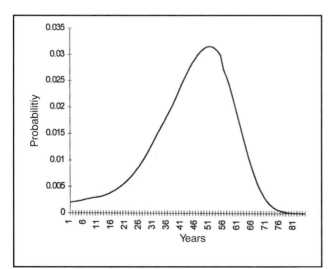

Figure 5 Probabilities of 30-year-old males living for exactly the number of years indicated

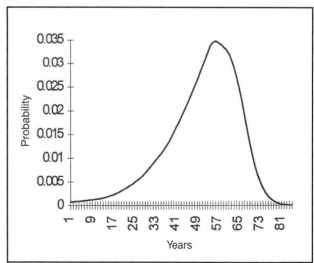

Figure 8 Probabilities of 30-year-old females living for exactly the number of years indicated

Text Table 4: Additional years of life for males and females, all races, 1990

Age	Men			Women		
	Life Expectancy	Standard Deviation	Median	Life Expectancy	Standard Deviation	Median
0	71.8	19.8	75.5	78.8	18.7	82.4
5	67.7	18.1	70.8	74.5	17.0	77.5
10	62.8	17.9	65.8	69.6	16.7	72.5
15	57.9	17.6	60.8	64.7	16.4	67.6
20	53.3	16.9	55.9	59.8	16.0	62.6
25	48.7	16.2	51.1	55.0	15.6	57.6
30	44.1	15.5	46.2	50.1	15.2	52.7
35	39.6	14.8	41.4	45.3	14.7	47.7
40	35.1	14.0	36.6	40.6	14.2	42.8
45	30.7	13.2	31.9	35.9	13.7	38.0
50	26.4	12.4	27.3	31.3	13.0	33.2
55	22.3	11.5	22.9	27.0	12.2	28.5
60	18.5	10.5	18.7	22.8	11.3	23.9
65	15.1	9.4	14.9	18.9	10.2	19.6
70	12.0	8.2	11.6	15.3	9.1	15.6

Source:
Life Expectancy column is from Vital Statistics of the U. S, 1990 (1994). Standard Deviation columns are calculated by taking the square root of (7). Median columns are calculated by solving for the value of t for which $l(x+1)/l(x) = 0.50$.

Figures 6–8 are for 30-year-old women; their life expectancy is 50.1 years with a standard deviation of 15.2 years. The additional-years-of-life variable in Figure 8 is skewed to the left, but it is less pronounced than for men. The median and modal values for additional years of life are 52.7 and 55 years, respectively.

3.2 Variation about Life Expectancy and Interval Estimates of Life Expectancy

Text Table 4 shows life expectancies and standard deviations for additional years of life at various ages between 0 and 70 for men and women. The basic data include the number of survivors l_x, at each age x. Chebychev's Inequality (DeGroot, 1989) can be used to calculate interval estimates of additional years of life. For example, the probability is at least 50% that the additional years of life will fall within the interval centered on e_x plus or minus 1.4 standard deviations of additional years of life.[2] For 30-year-old males, the probability is at least 50% that additional years of life are 44.1 ± (1.4 x 15.5), or between 22.4 years and 65.8 years. In other words, there is considerable variation around the mean years of life e. Text Table 4 also shows the median values for years

of life — values that always exceed e_x for women and exceed e_x for men age 62 and younger.

Chebychev's Inequality leads to very large, and therefore imprecise, interval estimates because it holds for all random variables regardless of their distributions. However, it is possible to get much more precise interval estimates of additional years of life. To this end, we proffer the following interval estimate: calculate the smallest interval estimate around life expectancy that includes at least 50% of the probability of additional years of life. That is, we wish to find the interval estimate about e_x that satisfies (8a)–(8c):

$$(t_1 \le e_x \le t_2), \tag{8a}$$

$$(t_2 - t_1) \text{ is minimized, and} \tag{8b}$$

$$\sum_{t=t_1}^{t_2} p_{x+1} = 0.50 \tag{8c}$$

where P_{x+t} is the probability of living exactly t additional years as defined in formula (5). Although life expectancy falls within this interval estimate, the interval is no longer necessarily centered on life expectancy as is the case with

Chebychev's Inequality. In addition, this interval estimate utilizes the actual probabilities of surviving exactly t years as calculated in formula (5). Text Table 5 shows these 50% interval estimates for men and women. As an example, a 30-year-old male has a life expectancy of 44.1 years, and the probability is 50% that he will live between 40.1 years and 57.1 years. In comparison to using Chebychev's Inequality, the interval estimates in Text Table 5 are much tighter because they are based on actual survival data and are not constrained to be symmetric about e_x. For males less than age 62 and for women of all ages in Text Table 5, the lower bounds of the intervals are closer to life expectancy than the upper bounds of the intervals. This occurs because the probabilities of dying in the years immediately prior to a person's life expectancy are smaller than the probabilities of dying in the years immediately after life expectancy. The reverse is true for males after age 62.

Fifty-percent interval estimates are the smallest intervals about life expectancy that include at least 50% of the probability of additional years of life. Lower and upper bounds are calculated in accordance with (8a)–(8c).

What does all of this mean in terms of present value calculations that are performed by forensic economists?

Consider the following hypothetical example: a 30-year-old male is injured; he will incur medical care costs for the rest of his life; care costs are projected to grow at a rate of 1% less than the rate of return on invested capital, implying a net real discount rate of 1%. Using a life expectancy of 44.1 years, the present value of one dollar of future care costs per year is $35.52, assuming care costs are incurred at the end of each year. From Text Table 5, 40.1 years is the lower bound estimate of additional years of life and 57.1 is the upper bound estimate. The corresponding lower bound estimate of present value of future expenditures is $32.90 and the upper bound is $43.34. The only number that forensic economists typically report is the point estimate of present value, or $35.52, in this hypothetical example. This is certainly a useful number, but the probability of it being exactly correct is practically zero. Therefore, it is also useful to know, in both direct testimony and in cross-examination, that the probability is 50% that the present value of future care costs is in the range of $32.90 to $43.34. Text Table 6 shows the present values of expenditures of one dollar per year for a person's life expectancy as well as the lower and upper bound estimates for various net real discount rates and ages.

Text Table 5: 50% interval estimates for additional years of life for males and females, all races, 1992

Age	Men			Women		
	Life Expectancy	50% Interval Estimate		Life Expectancy	50% Interval Estimate	
		Lower Bound	Upper Bound		Lower Bound	Upper Bound
0	71.8	69.8	87.8	78.8	76.8	92.8
5	67.7	65.7	82.7	74.5	72.5	88.5
10	62.8	60.8	77.8	69.6	67.6	83.6
15	57.9	54.9	71.9	64.7	62.7	78.7
20	53.3	50.3	67.3	59.8	56.8	72.8
25	48.7	45.7	62.7	55.0	52.0	68.0
30	44.1	40.1	57.1	50.1	47.1	63.1
35	39.6	35.6	52.6	45.3	43.3	58.3
40	35.1	31.1	47.1	40.6	38.6	53.6
45	10.7	26.7	42.7	35.9	32.9	47.9
50	26.4	21.4	36.4	31.3	28.3	43.3
55	22.3	16.3	31.3	27.0	23.0	38.8
60	18.5	12.5	26.5	22.8	18.8	32.8
65	15.1	8.1	20.1	18.9	13.9	26.9
70	12.0	4.0	14.0	15.3	10.3	22.3

Source:
Life Expectancy column is from Vital Statistics of the U. S., 1990 (1994).

Text Table 6: 50% interval estimates for present values

Age	Net Real Discount Rates		
	0%	1%	2%
Men			
20	($50.30, $53.30, $67.30)	($39.38, $41.16, $48.81)	($31.53, $32.60, $36.81)
30	($40.10, $44.10, $57.10)	($32.90, $35.52, $43.34)	($27.40, $29.12, $33.86)
40	($31.10, $35.10, $47.10)	($26.62, $29.48, $37.42)	($22.99, $25.05, $30.33)
50	($21.40, $26.40, $36.40)	($19.18, $23.10, $30.39)	($17.27, $20.36, $25.68)
60	($12.50, $18.50, $26.50)	($11.69, $16.81, $23.18)	($10.96, $15.34, $20.42)
Women			
20	($56.80, $59.80, $72.80)	($43.17, $44.85, $51.54)	($33.76, $34.70, $38.17)
30	($47.10, $50.10, $63.10)	($37.42, $39.26, $46.63)	($30.33, $31.46, $35.67)
40	($38.60, $40.60, $53.60)	($31.89, $33.23, $41.34)	($26.72, $27.62, $32.70)
50	($28.30, $31.30, $43.30)	($24.54, $26.76, $35.00)	($21.45, $23.10, $28.79)
60	($18.80, $22.80, $32.80)	($17.06, $20.30, $27.85)	($15.54, $18.17, $23.89)

Source:
For a zero percent net real discount rate, the entries in this table are the lower bound, life expectancy, and upper bound estimates from Table 2 expressed in dollar terms; that is, each cell in this table is ($t, $e, $t) when the net real discount rate is zero. For net real discount rates of l% and 2%, the present value of an annuity of one dollar is a[n, i] = (l/i)[l – 1/((1+i)(1+l))] where i = .0 1, .02 and n = t(1), e(x), t(2). Each cell in this table is (a[t(1), i], a[e(x) i], a[t(2), i] for i = .01, .02.

3.3 Conclusion

Life expectancy is a parameter, and the probability that a person will live exactly that number of years is very small. Therefore, it is useful to know something about the dispersion of additional years of life. The standard deviations reported in Text Table 4 provide such information; but, when they are used with Chebychev's Inequality, they lead to very large interval estimates of additional years of life, and hence large interval estimates of the present value of future expenditures or losses. The interval estimates in Text Table 5 are much tighter and potentially more useful to forensic economists because these estimates are more precise, and they are based on actual survival distributions.

References

DeGroot, Morris, *Probability and Statistics*, 2nd ed., Reading, Massachusetts: Addison Wesley, 1989, 227–229.

Fjelsted, Boyd, "The Significance of the Distinction Between a Life Annuity and an Annuity Certain for a Term Equal to Life Expectancy: A Note," *Journal of Forensic Economics*, 1993, 7(l) 125–127.

Hanson, Richard, "Future Transactions in Pension Valuation," *Journal of Legal Economics*, 1991, 1(2) 66–73.

Jordan Jr., Chester, *Society of Actuaries' Textbook on Life Contingencies*, Chicago: The Society of Actuaries, 1991, 3–7.

London, Dick, *Survival Models and Their Estimation*, Winsted and Avon, Connecticut: Actex Publication, 1988, 11–20.

Slesnick, Frank, and Robert Thornton, "Life Expectancies for Persons with Medical Risks," *Journal of Forensic Economics*, 1994, 7(2) 197–207.

U.S. Department of Health and Human Services, *Life Tables for the United States: 1900–2050*, Social Security Administration, SSA Publication No. II-1 1536, 1984, 46.

———,, *Vital Statistics of the United States, 1990*, Washington D.C.: U.S. Government Printing Office, 1994, 11–12.

———, *Vital Statistics of the United States, U.S. Decennial Life Tables for 1989–91*, Volume I, Number 1. DHHS Publication No. (PHS) 97-1150-1, Hyattsville, MD., 1997.

Notes

1. People who are alive at age x, but die before age $x + 1$, will have lived for varying amounts of time within the age interval from x to $x + 1$. It is common to assume that the typical person will die at the midpoint of age interval, that is, the typical person survives to age $x + 0.5$. The formulas in this chapter do not incorporate this assumption in order to reduce the amount of notation and the number of formulas. However, the empirical work does utilize this assumption.

2. A 50%-interval estimate relates to the standard of proof in many personal injury and wrongful death matters that requires expert testimony be accurate to within a reasonable degree of economic certainty or statistical certainty. This standard requires that expert opinions be more probably true than not true.

Chapter 4

Life Expectancies by Sex, Race, Hispanic Origin, and Education

4.1 Introduction

Over the course of the last several decades, many studies have shown that education has a strong relationship with life expectancy. Kitagawa and Hauser (1973) demonstrated that an inverse relationship exists between education and mortality rates. Since then, their results have consistently been corroborated by other researchers using different time periods and data sources, both for the U.S. and industrialized European countries (Duleep, 1989; Iams and McCoy, 1991; Rogot, Sorlie, and Johnson, 1992; Rogot, Sorlie, Johnson, and Schmitt, 1992; Kunst and Mackenbach, 1994; Sorlie, Backlund, and Keller, 1995; Lin, Rogot, Johnson, Sorlie, and Arias, 2003). Furthermore, the disparity in mortality rates between the less educated and the well educated in the United States appears to have increased since 1960 (Feldman et al., 1989 and Pappas et al., 1993).

    With several exceptions, these analyses dealt primarily with the direction and extent of the differences in life expectancies by education and placed lesser emphasis on the development of life tables. An extensive data set, now available from a match of the National Longitudinal Mortality Study (NLMS) and the National Death Index (NDI), allows "current" life tables to be created by sex, race, Hispanic origin, and educational attainment.

    This chapter discusses these tables for 2004 and shows that life expectancies have been consistently underestimated in the *Vital Statistics* tables. The appropriate measures for populations aggregated across educational levels are edu-

cationally weighted averages, which are longer than *Vital Statistics* data by about 0.9 year at birth for white females, at the low end, to about 1.5 years at birth for black males, at the high end.

4.2 Data Sources and Methods

The National Longitudinal Mortality Study (NLMS) is a large national study of the U.S. noninstitutionalized population spanning the period 1979 to the end of 1998. Twelve cohorts were initially surveyed; ten of these were used to compile mortality data. The ten cohorts were initially surveyed by the Current Population Surveys (CPS) of March 1979, April 1980, August 1980, December 1980, and March of the years 1981 through 1985. The CPS is a national survey of about 57,000 households conducted monthly on a rotating basis by the Census Bureau. It gathers extensive data on demographic, labor force, and income characteristics with occasional supplements focusing on special purposes. The samples in the NLMS were matched to the National Death Index (NDI) to determine deaths that occurred between 1979 and the end of 1998. The initial sample population for the ten cohorts was 1,046,959, and the number of matched deaths during the period was close to 255,000. (In the initial edition of this book deaths had been tabulated until 1989, at which time there were about 98,600 deaths.)

    The Census Bureau, Demographic Statistical Methods Division, used the NLMS mortality data to develop life tables by educational attainment for both sexes, blacks, whites, Hispanics, and all races combined. The educational categories are as follows: all educational levels combined, less than a high school degree, high school degree or GED, some college but not a graduate, a college graduate, and post-bachelor's education. For the black population, the last two educational categories were relatively small, so they were combined into a single group. For the Hispanic population, samples were even smaller and only three educational groupings were used: less than high school education, high school education,

Text Table 7: Age specific life expectancies and standard errors by years of education attainment from National Longitudinal Mortality Study and National Death Index Match

Age	Life Expectancy						Standard Error					
	All	0-11	12	13-15	16	17+	All	0-11	12	13-15	16	17+
Males of All Races												
25	50.75	47.65	50.59	51.80	54.15	55.58	0.04	0.13	0.09	0.12	0.14	0.17
45	32.16	29.96	32.22	33.08	34.97	36.35	0.04	0.07	0.07	0.11	0.13	0.15
65	16.11	15.14	16.30	16.83	17.79	18.77	0.03	0.05	0.06	0.10	0.12	0.14
White Males												
25	51.11	48.15	50.84	51.98	54.18	55.59	0.04	0.14	0.09	0.12	0.14	0.18
45	32.38	30.29	32.34	33.19	34.99	36.38	0.04	0.07	0.07	0.11	0.13	0.15
65	16.14	15.13	16.29	16.84	17.75	18.74	0.03	0.05	0.06	0.10	0.13	0.14
Black Males												
25	46.37	44.20	47.06	48.05	51.56		0.15	0.33	0.36	0.59	0.64	
45	28.93	27.62	29.67	30.07	32.81		0.14	0.20	0.32	0.54	0.63	
65	14.96	14.71	15.23	15.09	17.47		0.12	0.15	0.34	0.58	0.64	
Hispanic Males												
25	53.20	52.54	53.88	55.28			0.19	0.27	0.54	0.57		
45	34.70	34.16	35.54	36.38			0.19	0.23	0.51	0.57		
65	18.31	17.91	19.56	19.31			0.18	0.20	0.53	0.59		
Females of All Races												
25	56.48	54.14	56.90	57.82	58.84	59.48	0.04	0.11	0.07	0.11	0.15	0.25
45	37.28	35.4	37.76	38.53	39.38	40.19	0.04	0.07	0.06	0.11	0.15	0.19
65	20.17	19.34	20.49	21.01	21.40	22.02	0.03	0.05	0.06	0.10	0.13	0.18
White Females												
25	56.85	54.86	57.15	57.99	58.85	59.80	0.04	0.10	0.07	0.12	0.15	0.21
45	37.55	35.86	37.89	38.63	39.37	40.35	0.04	0.07	0.06	0.11	0.15	0.20
65	20.22	19.41	20.49	20.98	21.35	22.13	0.03	0.05	0.06	0.10	0.14	0.19
Black Females												
25	52.61	50.32	53.38	55.27	55.90		0.14	0.36	0.32	0.56	0.68	
45	34.19	32.76	35.00	36.61	37.15		0.14	0.20	0.29	0.52	0.55	
65	18.89	18.55	19.21	20.33	19.99		0.12	0.14	0.29	0.52	0.54	
Hispanic Females												
25	59.00	58.37	60.52	61.03			0.19	0.23	0.48	0.69		
45	39.63	39.04	41.23	41.40			0.18	0.22	0.48	0.69		
65	21.96	21.70	23.26	23.07			0.17	0.20	0.48	0.70		

Note: For blacks all persons with a college degree or more are included in the "16" years category, and for Hispanics all persons with a more than high school degree are included in "13-15" years.

and all others. (In the initial edition of this book a separate category for high school education was not available.)

Age-specific NLMS life expectancies and standard errors by sex, race, Hispanic origin, and education are shown in Text Table 7. Three general patterns are apparent: (a) Hispanics have the longest life expectancies and blacks the shortest, (b) the effect of education on life expectancy is stronger for males than for females, (c) the effect of education is stronger for blacks than for whites, and it is least strong for Hispanics (after accounting for population composition by education).

Concerning the effect of education on life expectancies of males as compared with females, males of all races with the highest education have life expectancies which are almost 8 years longer than those with lowest education (at age 25), while for females the difference is about 5.3 years. Regarding racial comparisons, the difference for white and black males in longevity between the highest and lowest educated is about 7.4 years; the difference for white females is 4.9 years, and for black females it is 5.6 years.

Hispanics require further discussion. Most notable is that their life expectancies are significantly longer than those of the general population. The difference is especially pronounced for Hispanics with less than a high school education. In fact, Hispanic males with less than a high school education can expect to live longer than males of the general population with some college education. Similarly, Hispanic females with less than a high school education can expect to live nearly as long as other females with a college degree.

The effects of education between the two sexes for Hispanics are quite similar. At age 25, the life expectancies of both Hispanic males and females with more than a high school degree or more is about 2.7 years longer than for those with less than a high school education. It appears that life expectancies of Hispanics are less sensitive to educational attainment than those of other racial/ethnic groups. For example, the life expectancy of high school graduate males of all races at age 25 is 2.9 years longer than for those with less than a high school education; for Hispanics the difference is only 1.3 years. For females the numbers are 2.8 and 2.1, respectively.

Text Table 8 compares NLMS life expectancies for the total male and female samples with those from the *Vital Statistics* of 2000. The life expectancies from the NLMS data are consistently greater than from the *Vital Statistics* except for middle-age and older males. The primary reason for the disparity is that the NLMS cohorts included only the noninstitutionalized population, which is generally healthier than the institutionalized population. Another, and probably minor, reason is that some deaths may not have been captured in the matching of the NLMS and the NDI (Rogot, Sorlie and Johnson 1992).

Text Table 8: Age-specific life expectancies: NLMS compared with "Vital Statistics, 2000"

Age	Males			Females		
	NLMS	U.S. 2000	Diff	NLMS	U.S. 2000	Diff
25	50.75	50.60	0.15	56.48	55.44	1.04
35	41.35	41.28	0.07	46.79	45.77	1.02
45	32.16	32.21	-0.05	37.28	36.35	0.93
55	23.54	23.76	-0.22	28.27	27.35	0.92
65	16.11	16.27	-0.16	20.17	19.16	1.01

Note: Data provided from Bureau of the Census were standardized to the 2000 Census of the Population.

To compensate for the discrepancies between the NLMS and *Vital Statistics* mortality rates, NLMS rates were scaled to the rates of the *Vital Statistics* life tables. Assuming that the rates between the institutionalized and the non-institutionalized populations vary consistently across education levels,

1) the NLMS mortality rate for any given sex, race, age and education level was divided by the NLMS mortality rate for the same sex, race and age for all education levels combined to obtain a "relative risk factor" for each age and category,

2) the relative risk factor was multiplied by the mortality rate from the *Vital Statistics* life tables for the given race, sex and age to obtain an education adjusted mortality rate for 2004 (mortality rates were smoothed across five years), and

3) life tables for the various racial and educational categories were derived using the standard "period" methodology with the adjusted mortality rates.

The same procedure was generally followed in regard to persons of Hispanic origin. However, because no Hispanic data are provided in the *Vital Statistics*, steps 1 and 2 were modified slightly. In step 1, the Hispanic NLMS mortality rate for each sex, age, and educational level was divided by the NLMS rate for *all races* and educational levels combined to derive a relative risk factor for Hispanics by education compared to the total U.S. population. In step 2, the relative risk factor was multiplied by the mortality rate from the *Vital Statistics* for the given sex and age of *all races* to obtain the educationally adjusted Hispanic mortality rate.

Because younger persons have not completed their education, the NLMS mortality data provided to me by education did not vary from the total population until age 25.

Text Table 9:
Age specific life expectancies, NLMS by educational attainment scaled to 2004 Vital Statistics Life Tables

Age	Years of Education Completed				
	0-11	12	13-15	16	17+
Males of All Races					
25	48.4	51.4	52.6	55.0	56.5
45	30.9	33.2	34.1	36.0	37.4
65	16.2	17.3	17.8	18.8	19.8
White Males					
25	49.0	51.7	52.9	55.1	56.6
45	31.3	33.4	34.3	36.1	37.5
65	16.2	17.3	17.9	18.8	19.8
Black Males					
25	44.6	47.4	48.5	51.8	
45	27.7	29.9	30.2	33.1	
65	14.9	15.5	15.4	17.6	
Hispanic Males					
25	53.4	54.9	56.2		
45	35.2	36.7	37.4		
65	19.0	20.6	20.4		
Females of All Races					
25	54.0	56.7	57.7	58.6	59.3
45	35.4	37.7	38.5	39.3	40.1
65	19.2	20.3	20.8	21.2	21.8
White Females					
25	54.6	56.9	57.7	58.6	59.5
45	35.8	37.8	38.5	39.2	40.2
65	19.3	20.3	20.8	21.1	21.9
Black Females					
25	50.8	53.5	55.4	56.0	
45	33.1	35.1	36.7	37.1	
65	18.3	19.0	20.1	19.6	
Hispanic Females					
25	58.2	60.2	60.7		
45	38.9	41.1	41.2		
65	21.5	23.0	22.8		

Note: See Text Table 4 regarding educational categories for blacks and Hispanics.

Text Table 9 shows scaled 2004 life expectancies for selected ages. The differences between educational life expectancies is probably slightly underestimated since some people moved to higher educational levels subsequent to the date of initial surveys. (The educational classifications of respondents were set at the date of the survey, but some of those classified in the lower educational categories would have moved to higher levels prior to the dates at which the follow-up tabulations were made. Because the mortality rates of better-educated individuals are lower, their improper inclusion in the less educated categories will make mortality rates appear lower than they actually are for the less educated populations.)

4.3 Bias of *Vital Statistics* Life Tables
A. Cause of Bias

As discussed in Chapter 2, "current" life tables are generated assuming that a hypothetical cohort will experience the same age-specific death rates that are observed for an actual population during some particular period. This methodology would provide correct estimates if all educational categories of the population at any age had the same mortality rates or if all ages had the same educational composition. As we have seen in Text Tables 7 and 9, however, educational attainment strongly affects life expectancy.

In addition, the educational composition of the population varies markedly across ages: the oldest cohorts are dominated by lower education levels; younger cohorts are better educated. For instance, the Current Population Survey microdata show that the percentage of males and females of all races with at least a high school degree was highest in the age interval 45 through 54 for males and 35 through 51 for females (over 88% and 89% of the total population, respectively). In contrast, it was only about 64% and 62% for ages 85 and over, respectively. Comparable numbers for those with a college degree or more are over 32% maximum for males in the age interval 50 through 58, dropping to about 19% for those 85 and older, and for females over 28% in the age interval 25 through 53 dropping to 12% for ages 85 and older.

Mortality rates for the general population at any age used in the *Vital Statistics* life tables are derived from people of all educational levels, and so for older ages, they are based on populations very heavily weighted toward lower educational levels. However, *ceteris paribus*, we know that when the current "middle age" cohorts reach 75 to 85 years of age they will be predominantly high-school educated with sizable proportions of college graduates. Therefore, when they reach these ages, the mortality of these cohorts will reflect *their* educational compositions, that is, their mortality rates will be *less* than those currently measured. Thus, basing life expectancies of current middle- and younger-aged persons on the mortality rates of the less well-educated oldest cohorts results in underestimated life expectancies for them.

B. Elimination of Bias

Differences in educational attainment can be incorporated into life tables for the total population aggregated across education levels by using weighted averages. These reflect the *actual educational composition at each age*, rather than the *composition of all subsequent ages*. Educationally weighted life expectancies are shown in Text Table 10.

Weighting is straightforward for older ages, being simply the sum of each educational life expectancy for that age multiplied by its proportion in the total population. Young cohorts, however, contain many members who have not reached their highest lifetime educational attainment. Assuming that historical patterns will remain constant, they

will eventually become at least as well educated as the cohort which currently exhibits the "highest" educational composition. Therefore, weighting factors for these younger cohorts should be based on the proportional composition of the population at the age which is currently best educated.

The educational composition which defines the "highest" educational level may not necessarily be the same for all sex and racial categories. For instance, it could be the point at which the lowest number of people have less than a high school education, or it could the point at which the highest number of people have more than a college education, etc. The "highest" educational composition is defined here as the age at which a proportion of those with at least some college education reached a maximum. The ages at which these maximum levels occurred, using three year running averages of population by educational attainment from the 2000 through 2006 Current Population Survey data, are as follows: males of all races, 34; white males, 34; black males, 35; Hispanic males, 52; females of all races, 31; white females, 34; black females, 31; and Hispanic females, 39.

Text Table 10: Age specific life expectancies for total populations: bias reduction by using educationally weighted averages, 2004

Age	Males			Females		
	Weighted Average	Vital Statistics Estimate	Bias	Weighted Average	Vital Statistics Estimate	Bias
	All Races			All Races		
0	76.1	75.2	1.0	81.4	80.4	1.1
25	52.6	51.6	1.0	57.4	56.3	1.1
45	34.1	33.1	1.0	38.2	37.2	1.0
65	17.7	17.1	0.6	20.4	20.0	0.4
	White			White		
0	76.5	75.7	0.8	81.7	80.8	0.9
25	52.8	52.0	0.8	57.6	56.6	0.9
45	33.5	32.5	1.0	38.3	37.4	0.9
65	17.7	17.1	0.6	20.4	20.0	0.4
	Black			Black		
0	71.0	69.5	1.5	77.8	76.3	1.5
25	48.3	46.7	1.5	54.4	52.8	1.6
45	30.2	29.1	1.1	35.7	34.3	1.4
65	15.5	15.2	0.4	19.0	18.6	0.4
	Hispanic			Hispanic		
0	78.2	77.6	0.7	83.5	82.6	0.9
25	54.7	54.1	0.7	59.7	58.7	0.9
45	36.3	35.7	0.6	40.3	39.5	0.8
65	19.7	19.3	0.4	22.1	21.7	0.4

The differences between life expectancies using weighted averages versus those from the *Vital Statistics* are, in general, small for the 65-year-old cohorts. The differences reach their maximum extent at the age of highest educational attainment, and then the differences remain relatively constant for all younger cohorts. Differences are greater for blacks than for whites and generally least for Hispanics. For example, from birth through early adulthood, weighted average life expectancies are longer by the following amounts: white males and females about 1.0 years, black males and females about 1.5 years, Hispanic males about 0.7 years and Hispanic females about 0.9 years.

The size of the difference is dependent on the relative effects of (a) the amount of the disparity in educational composition between a population's highest level and the level at older ages and (b) the difference between the mortality rates of the lowest and the highest educational levels.

C. Reduction of Bias versus Standard Error of the Estimator

It is important to determine whether the information gained from the reduction of bias is greater than that lost from an increase in the standard error. Because the life expectancy estimators from the NLMS have natural variability (the standard errors in Text Table 7), we have to show that the apparent reduction in bias gained above is not likely to be due to chance variation and that it is large compared to the standard error of the adjusted estimator.

Correcting for the education composition of each cohort will reduce bias. On the other hand, the standard error of the educationally weighted estimator will tend to be larger than that for the unweighted estimator because the former is based on subsamples of the cohort.

We are comparing two alternative estimators: $LE(x, race, sex)$, the life expectancy at age x not based on educational weightings; and $LE_w(x, race, sex)$, the life expectancy at age x which is based on educational weighting. If $w(E, x, race, sex)$ is the proportion of the population at age x that has or will eventually attain education level E, and $ELE(E, x, race, sex)$ is the life expectancy at age x for members of the population with educational level E and the given race and sex, the weighted estimator is

$$LE_w = (x, race, sex) = \sum_E w(E, x, race, sex) \ ELE \ (E, x, race, sex).$$

For example, using the data from the 2000–2006 CPS, 9.5% of 45-year-old white females have less than high school education, 31.9% have graduated from high school, 29.8% have some college, 19.6% have graduated from college, and 9.3% have some graduate degree. From the Census

Bureau life tables as shown in Text Table 7 (used for this example to avoid the complication of having to scale standard errors), the life expectancy of white females at these various education levels is: less than high school, 35.86 years; high school, 37.89 years; some college, 38.63 years; college degree, 39.37 years; and graduate degree, 40.35 years. The life expectancy of 45-year-old white females based on educational weighting is

$$LE_w = (x = 45, white, female) = (35.68 \times 0.095) + (37.89 \times 0.319) + (38.63 \times 0.298)$$
$$(39.37 \times 0.196) + (40.35 \times 0.093) = 38.44$$

The non-adjusted life expectancy from Text Table 7 is 37.55 years for 45-year-old white females. In this example, the adjustment adds about 0.9 years to the life expectancy. We determine whether or not the reduction in bias is significant by comparing it to the standard error of the difference of the two life expectancy estimates.

For 45-year-old white females, the standard error of the non-adjusted estimate is 0.04 years. Because the life expectancies for each educational level are independent (based on independent samples), we can easily find the standard error of the educationally weighted estimate:

$$se[LE_w(x, race, sex)] = \sqrt{\sum_E w^2(E, x, race, sex) + se^2[ELE \ (E, x, race, sex)]}.$$

Although the weights are samples from the CPS over the period 2000–2006, we consider them here as constants because of the large sample size and because the Bureau of the Census standardizes them against the latest census of the population.

Again, considering the 45-year-old white female, the quantities under the radical sign in the equation above are:

$$(0.095^2 \times 0.07^2 \ yr^2) + (0.319^2 \times 0.06^2 \ yr^2) + (0.298^2 \times 0.11^2 \ yr^2) + (0.196^2 \times 0.15^2 \ yr^2)$$
$$(0.093^2 + 0.20_2 \ yr^2) = 0.002692 \ yr^2$$

Therefore

$$se[LE_w(x, race, sex)] = se[LE_w(45, white, female)] = \sqrt{0.002692 \ yr^2} = 0.0519 \ yr$$

This is larger than the 0.04 year standard error for the unweighted life expectancy as shown in Text Table 7.

We can show that the bias in the unweighted estimator is large enough to justify using the weighted estimator by examining the ratio

$$\frac{LE(x, race, sex) - LE_w(x, race, sex)}{se[LE(x, race, sex) - LE_w(x, race, sex)]}.$$

Unfortunately, the two estimators are not independent because they are both based on the same data set. However, because the two estimators are certainly positively correlated, the standard error of the difference will be less than the standard error under independence. Under this assumption we get a conservative z-statistic using

$$Z = \frac{LE(x, race, sex) - LE_w(x, race, sex)}{\sqrt{se^2[LE(x, race, sex) + se^2[LE_w(x, race, sex)]]}}.$$

Considering again the 45-year-old white female, we find that $Z = 0.88/0.066 = 13.403$. This means that the estimated bias reduction is more than thirteen times as big as the variability of the estimated bias. The chance that an apparent bias reduction this large could occur by chance (assuming a roughly normal distribution for the life expectancy estimates) is almost

zero. Thus, the bias reduction is real for white females of this age, and the educationally weighted estimator should be used.

Text Table 11 summarizes comparisons of bias reduction to standard errors for all race and sex categories. All the bias adjustments, even with the conservative z-statistics, are seen to be significant at alpha 0.05 and almost all are significant at alpha 0.01.

Finally, although this discussion is based on the data presented in Text Table 7 without adjustment to *Vital Statistics* life expectancies, the life expectancy adjustment is applied to both the bias and the standard error. Therefore, the t-ratios in Text Table 11 data are the same as those of these data scaled to the *Vital Statistics* life expectancies.

Text Table 11: Statistical significance of bias reduction

Race	Gender	Age	Bias Reduction	Standard Errors			
				All	Joint	z- statistic	p-value
All Races	Females	25	1.07	0.04	0.11	9.362	0.00
		45	0.97	0.04	0.01	9.090	0.00
		65	0.39	0.03	0.08	4.786	0.00
	Male	25	0.99	0.04	0.11	8.776	0.00
		45	0.98	0.04	0.10	9.101	0.00
		65	0.58	0.03	0.07	7.632	0.00
White	Female	25	0.93	0.04	0.12	7.447	0.00
		45	0.88	0.04	0.10	7.846	0.00
		65	0.38	0.03	0.08	4.507	0.00
	Males	25	0.84	0.04	0.12	6.823	0.00
		45	0.95	0.04	0.10	8.644	0.00
		65	0.61	0.03	0.08	7.246	0.00
Black	Female	25	1.55	0.14	0.44	3.327	0.00
		45	1.36	0.14	0.39	3.286	0.00
		65	0.42	0.12	0.28	1.376	0.12
	Males	25	1.54	0.15	0.45	3.226	0.00
		45	1.14	0.14	0.40	2.704	0.01
		65	0.39	0.12	0.29	1.245	0.16
Hispanic	Female	25	0.91	0.19	0.30	2.587	0.01
		45	0.81	0.18	0.28	2.436	0.02
		65	0.40	0.17	0.21	1.501	0.01
	Males	25	0.68	0.19	0.26	2.126	0.03
		45	0.63	0.19	0.25	1.993	0.04
		65	0.40	0.18	0.22	1.418	0.11

Text Table 12: Comparisons of life expectancies between: 1980 vs 1990 and 1990 vs 2004

Age	(1)	(2)	(3)	(4)	(5)	(6)	(7)	(8)	(9)	(10)	(11)	(12)
	Vital Statistics			Weighted Averages #			Vital Statistics			Weighted Averages #		
	Period			Educational Comp of:		Effect of Ed *	Early	Later	Chng 1980 to 90	Educational Comp of:		Effect of Ed *
	Early	Later	Chng	Early	Later					Early	Later	
1980 Versus 1990												
	Males of All Races						Females of All Races					
45	29.1	30.7	1.6	31.2	31.7	0.5	35.0	35.9	0.9	36.1	36.5	0.4
55	21.0	22.3	1.3	22.5	22.9	0.4	26.3	27.0	0.7	27.1	27.3	0.2
65	14.1	15.1	1.0	15.1	15.4	0.3	18.3	18.9	0.6	18.9	19.1	0.2
75	8.8	9.4	0.5	9.3	9.4	0.1	11.5	12.0	0.5	12.0	12.0	0.1
	White Males						White Females					
45	29.4	31.1	1.6	31.6	32.1	0.5	35.4	36.2	0.8	36.5	36.8	0.3
55	21.2	22.5	1.4	22.8	23.1	0.4	26.5	27.2	0.7	27.3	27.6	0.2
65	14.2	15.2	1.1	15.3	15.5	0.3	18.5	19.1	0.6	19.1	19.3	0.2
75	8.8	9.4	0.6	9.3	9.5	0.1	11.5	12.0	0.5	12.1	12.1	0.1
	Black Males						Black Females					
45	25.2	26.2	1.0	26.6	27.1	0.6	31.4	32.4	1.0	32.8	33.4	0.6
55	18.4	19.0	0.6	19.2	19.5	0.3	23.4	24.2	0.8	24.3	24.7	0.4
65	12.9	13.2	0.3	13.3	13.4	0.1	16.5	17.2	0.6	17.2	17.3	0.1
75	8.3	8.6	0.3	8.7	8.7	0.1	10.7	11.2	0.5	11.2	11.2	0.0
1990 Versus 2004												
	Males of All Races						Females of All Races					
45	30.7	33.1	2.4	34.0	34.1	0.1	35.9	37.2	1.3	37.9	38.2	0.3
55	22.3	24.7	2.4	25.2	25.8	0.6	27.0	28.3	1.3	28.6	29.1	0.5
65	15.1	17.1	2.0	17.3	17.7	0.4	18.9	20.0	1.1	20.1	20.4	0.3
75	9.4	10.7	1.3	10.8	11.0	0.2	12.0	12.8	0.8	12.8	13.0	0.1
	White Males						White Females					
45	31.1	33.4	2.3	34.4	34.3	-0.0	36.2	37.4	1.2	38.1	38.3	0.2
55	22.5	24.9	2.4	25.4	25.9	0.5	27.2	28.4	1.2	28.7	29.2	0.5
65	15.2	17.2	2.0	17.4	17.7	0.3	19.1	20.0	0.9	20.2	20.4	0.2
75	9.4	10.7	1.3	10.8	11.0	0.3	12.0	12.8	0.8	12.8	12.9	0.1
	Black Males						Black Females					
45	26.2	29.1	2.9	29.7	30.2	0.6	32.4	34.3	1.9	35.2	35.7	0.5
55	19.0	21.5	2.5	21.8	22.4	0.6	24.2	26.0	1.8	26.4	27.0	0.6
65	13.2	15.2	2.0	15.2	15.5	0.3	17.2	18.6	1.4	18.7	19.0	0.3
75	8.6	9.9	1.3	10.0	10.1	0.1	11.2	12.2	1.0	12.3	12.4	0.1

Life expectancies by education are as of 1990 in the 1980 versus 1990 comparisons, and of 2004 in the 1990 versus 2004 comparisons; only the composition of the population by education is varied.

* Equals the weighted average based on the educational composition of the later period minus the weighted average based on the educational composition of the earlier period. Data for Hispanics not available from "Vital Statistics."

4.4 Educational Life Expectancies and Calculation of Retirement Benefits

Educational life expectancy data can affect calculation of retirement benefits in an injury or death case in two ways. For each of the following two hypothetical scenarios, it is assumed that: (a) the subject was 25 years old when injured or killed, (b) annual retirement payments are the same, (c) benefits ensue at age 65, (d) and discounting of the value of the benefits is not taken into account (discounting would somewhat reduce the effects discussed below). It should be noted that the age of the person at the time of the incident is relevant—effects would be greater for younger persons and less for older persons.

The first scenario deals with the bias corrections resulting from using *weighted average*. Data from the 2004 *Vital Statistics* indicate that a hypothetical white male would collect benefits from age 65 to his expected death at age 77.0 or for 12.0 years. However, the life expectancy of this white male at age 25 should actually be to age 77.8. This is about 0.8 years more than indicated by the U.S. Life Tables and represents an increase in estimated benefits of about 7% (0.8 years divided by 12.0 years). For black males, life expectancy in the *Vital Statistics* tables would be to age 71.7, the weighted average revision increases life expectancy to age 73.3, and the increase in total payment would be about 23%. For white females, life expectancy in the U.S. tables would be to age 81.6, the revision increases life expectancy by about 0.9 years, and the increase in total payment would be about 6%. For black females, life expectancy in the U.S. tables is 77.8, the revision increases life expectancy by about 1.6 years, and the increase in total payment would be about 12%.

The second scenario addresses differences in life expectancies *across educational levels*. Again referring to white males, those with less than a high school education would be expected to live to age 74.0 and collect Social Security benefits for 9.0 years. Those with more than a bachelor's degree would live to age 81.6 and collect benefits for 16.6 years; therefore, they would receive benefits almost twice as long as those males with less than a high school education. Black males with less than a high school education would, on average, live only long enough to collect benefits for about 4.6 years (life expectancy is to age 69.6). On the other hand, those with a bachelor's degree or more have a life expectancy to age 76.8 and would receive benefits for 11.8 years. White females with the highest education would collect benefits about 33% longer than white females with the lowest education. Black females with the highest education would collect benefits about 50% longer than black females with the lowest education.

4.5 *Vital Statistics* Overestimation of Historical Increases in Life Expectancy

Chapter 2 mentioned that "cohort" life tables are often considered better than "current" tables for forecasting life expectancies. However, determining the actual extent of the forecasting advantage is not as clear-cut as just comparing the life expectancies of the two methods.

For one thing, as shown earlier in this chapter, educational weighting corrects a downward bias in the *Vital Statistics* "current" life expectancies. Correcting for this bias reduces the 4.6-year apparent difference (from Text Table 2) between the two methods for females to 3.5 years. For males, educational weighting reduces the difference from the apparent 5.6 years to about 4.6 years.

The remainder of this chapter discusses another factor that may reduce the apparent forecasting advantage of the cohort method. This is the phenomenon that, without decomposition of mortality rates into educational components, the actual increases in life expectancy for any given hypothetical individual are not as great as indicated by tables from different periods of time. Rather, a large part of the apparent increase is due solely to replacement through time of lesser-educated with better-educated cohorts.

Text Table 12 indicates that *apparent* life expectancies, as measured by the *Vital Statistics*, would have changed between 1980 and 1990 and again between 1990 and 2004 even if underlying mortality rates had remained constant. In the top section of this table, all educationally weighted averages were calculated using 1990 mortality rates by education; in the lower half, by 2004 mortality rates by education. The only difference in the top portion of the table is that the educational composition of the population in 1980 is used as weighting factors for the 1980 averages, whereas the 1990 composition is used for the 1990 weighted averages. Similarly, the lower portion of the table uses 1990 and 2000–2006 educational compositions. Changes resulting purely from compositional effects are thus shown in columns (6) and (12).[1]

For example, the *Vital Statistics* life tables indicate that the life expectancy of 45-year-old white males increased by about 1.6 years between 1980 and 1990. However, about 0.5 years (30%) of that apparent increase was due solely to changes in the educational composition of the population as better educated cohorts replaced lesser educated cohorts with the passage of time. The obvious corollary is that only about 70% of that apparent increase was due to decreases in mortality rates. In other words, under the assumption that all educational levels had identical changes in mortality over these ten years,[2] the increase in life expectancy for any hypothetical white male would be about 1.1 years instead of the apparent 1.6 years. For white females, only about 60% of the apparent increase in life expectancies was due to decreasing mortality rates, and for blacks of both sexes it was about 60%. Between 1990 and the early years of the first decade of the twenty-first century educational attainment has risen as rapidly as in previous decades and the highly educated cohorts are growing older. Thus, in general, smaller proportions of the increase in life expectancy have been due to an educational composition.

For their "cohort" tables, the SSA projects past decreases in mortality rates into the future (see Chapter 2). The rates were determined for ten categories of cause of death. To the extent that prevalence of disease and death is correlated with education, historical data regarding decreases in mortality rates are realistic predictors of the future. However, to the extent that disease and death are not correlated with education, it is probable that the SSA has projected mortality rates that are too low into the future. They may, therefore, be overestimating life expectancies for cohorts living past the present time. If so, the differences between the "cohort" and "current" life expectancies would be even less than the 3.5 years for females and the 4.6 years for males described above.[3]

Notes

1. These data are approximations. A more rigorous analysis, incorporating all the confounding factors, would provide slightly different results.

2. Several studies indicate that the disparity in mortality rates by education level has increased since 1960 (Feldman et al., 1989, and Pappas et al., 1993). If so, the confounding factor of educational composition would be magnified, and real decreases in mortality rates would be even less than indicated above.

3. Health care researchers are raising alarms that current trends in longevity may be severely impacted by an obesity epidemic in the U.S. Indeed, a recent analysis of county-wide data show that life expectancies are actually decreasing in many counties across the rural south, primarily caused by chronic diseases related to smoking, obesity, and high blood pressure (Ezzati et al., 2008).

Chapter 5

Life Expectancies for Persons with Medical Risks

Frank Slesnick, Robert Thornton, and Edward Timmons[1]

5.1 Introduction

In calculating lost earnings in personal injury and wrongful death cases, economic experts usually rely on mortality and life expectancy data published by the U.S. Government. Either the interest is on average life expectancy (ALE) or on survival probabilities at various ages. In either case, though, the assumption is that the person in question could be expected to live (or to have lived) an average life span and that his or her health/medical/survival status is no different from that of an "average" individual.

But what about the situation where an individual, for whatever reason, would not be expected to have an average life expectancy? For example, the *Wall Street Journal* (Gevelin, 1992) reported that a mechanic suing for lost future earnings was ordered to undergo testing for the AIDS virus to help determine how long he might live, and thus how much compensation he should receive. Or consider the case of a woman who had previously suffered a stroke before an injury rendered her permanently disabled. Clearly, as a stroke victim her life expectancy even before the injury would not be expected to be as high as that for an "average" individual in the population.

In using average life expectancy data for persons with serious health/medical problems, many economic experts render themselves vulnerable to defense objections that they have exaggerated the life expectancy for the case in question. In such cases, a common explanation given by the expert is:

> "The data used for calculating an average life expectancy *does* include people with various infirmities," or

> "Unfortunately, disease-specific life expectancy tables are generally unavailable."

The trouble with the first response is that even though life expectancy data include individuals with various medical problems, such people are likely to constitute only a very tiny percentage of the group sampled. Thus, the problem of the ALE not being a representative statistic still exists.

As far as the second problem—the unavailability of such information—is concerned, insurance companies do collect information; but it is generally proprietary and not available to experts on request. Instead, medical doctors are sometimes asked to render an opinion on life expectancy, which the expert can then use as the basis for the loss calculations. However, as we discuss below, other data sources and methods are available.

In this chapter, we provide an explanation of how experts can compute estimates of life expectancies for those with specific diseases or afflictions, as well as which experts are best suited to make these estimates. We also discuss the data sources which can be used to calculate such life expectancies. We then offer several examples which will indicate how such life expectancies can be utilized, and explain how a reduced life expectancy will likely affect the estimate of economic loss. The relative simplicity of the technique and the greater accessibility of survival/mortality data can serve to broaden the scope of the forensic economist while giving further precision to calculations of economic losses. We then discuss some important issues concerning the calculation and use of life expectancy in the context of litigation, issues such as the constancy of relative mortality ratios over time, who may be qualified to construct and apply life expectancy estimates, and the relationship between life expectancy and worklife expectancy. Finally we provide a set of life expectancy tables broken down by age, race, gender, and relative mortality ratios.

5.2 Calculating Average Life Expectancies
A. General Concepts

The notion of average life expectancy for a given group of individuals at age t is simply the number of aggregate person-years that the group could expect to survive divided by the initial number of persons in the group. For example, assume a group of 10 individuals is alive at exact age 80. Suppose that 9 survive the first year, 5 the second year, and 3 the third year, but that after the third year there are no survivors left. The average life expectancy (ALE) would then equal the sum of the total person-years survived (9 + 5 + 3 = 17) divided by the initial number of persons (10)—or 1.7 years.

We now develop some general notation and demonstrate the concepts with a slightly more complicated example. Let l_t be the number of people alive at exact age t, and d_t be the number who die between exact ages t and t+1. Then $q_t = d_t/l_t$ is the percentage who die between ages t and t+1. Further,

$$l_{t+1} = l_t - d_t = l_t - q_t l_t = l_t(1 - q_t). \qquad (1)$$

From equation (1) above, we can determine average life expectancy beginning with equation (2):

$$T_t = \sum_{j=t+1}^{N} l_j \qquad (2)$$

where T_t is the number of person-years remaining for those alive at exact age t and N represents the age beyond which there are no survivors. Average life expectancy at age t (e_t) can then be defined as follows:

$$e_t = T_t / l_t \qquad (3)$$

There is an alternative but equivalent method for calculating average life expectancy, which utilizes probabilities. Define $p_t(m)$ to be the probability that a person lives from exact age t to exact age m. This probability can also be expressed as $p_t(m) = l_m/l_t$. It can easily be shown that:

$$e_t = \sum_{j=t+1}^{N} p_t(j) \qquad (4)$$

In other words, the average life expectancy for a person of a given age t can also be calculated as the sum of the probabilities of a person surviving from that age to each year in the future. This is so since

$$e_t = p_t(t+1) + p_t(t+2) + \ldots + p_t(N) \qquad (5)$$
$$= l_{t+1}/l_t + l_{t+2}/l_t + \ldots + l_N/l_t$$
$$= T_t / l_t,$$

which is the same definition for average life expectancy as in equation (3) above.[2]

A simple numerical example illustrating these concepts is shown in Text Table 13. Assume that a cohort of 1,000 people is born (age 0). The death rate (q_t) in column (3) determines the number of deaths (d_t) occurring at each age, as given in column (4). Subtracting deaths from the number alive (l_t) at exact age t yields the number alive at exact age t+1 in column (2). Note that N, the age beyond which there are no survivors, is 19. T_t, the number of person-years remaining for persons alive at exact age t, is shown in column (5). For example, at T_0, 9,500 represents the expected number of person-years left for the 1,000 individuals born in year 0. This is determined by summing l_t from age 1 to the end of the second column. Equation (3) provides an estimate of average life expectancy for any given age. For example, as shown in the table average life expectancy at age 0 is 9500/1000 = 9.5 years. The average life expectancy for age 5 would be 5250/750 = 7 years.

Column (6) calculates average life expectancy for age 0 by using the alternative sum-of-survival probabilities approach, as explained previously with equations (4) and (5). Each entry in column (6) represents the probability of a person living from exact age 0 to exact age t, and is calculated by dividing the appropriate entry in column (2) by l_0 (which is equal to 1,000). Equivalently, each probability in column (6) may also be thought of as the product of all the year-to-year survival probabilities from the beginning age to the age in question. For example, $p_0(2)$ is equal to (950/1000) x (900/950) = 0.9.

Summing all the probabilities in column (6) yields the ALE for persons at exact age 0 (9.5 years). It should be noted that the ALEs for persons of exact age 0 is the same as determined by the aggregate person-years approach.

In the above example, we have assumed that all deaths in a given year occur immediately after the year begins. For instance, the ALE of a person who is exactly 19 is seen to be zero years. However, under the more reasonable assumption that deaths occur uniformly throughout any year, the ALE of a person this age should actually be one-half year. Determining the number alive at the midpoint of each age and calculating ALE using these values rather than values of l_t can easily correct the error. This is, in fact, the way U.S. Life Tables are routinely calculated. However, using beginning-of-year values makes the ALE easier to explain and to calculate. Further, the error can be corrected by simply adding one-half year to any ALE estimated in the above manner.

Text Table 13:
Example: General Life Expectancy Calculations

(1) Age	(2) l_t	(3) q_t	(4) d_t	(5) T_t	(6) $p_0(t)$
0	1000	0.0500	50	9500	0.95
1	950	0.0526	50	8550	0.90
2	900	0.0556	50	7650	0.85
3	850	0.0588	50	6800	0.80
4	800	0.0625	50	6000	0.75
5	750	0.0667	50	5250	0.70
6	700	0.0714	50	4550	0.65
7	650	0.0769	50	3900	0.60
8	600	0.0833	50	3300	0.55
9	550	0.0909	50	2750	0.50
10	500	0.1000	50	2250	0.45
11	450	0.1111	50	1800	0.40
12	400	0.1250	50	1400	0.35
13	350	0.1429	50	1050	0.30
14	300	0.1667	50	750	0.25
15	250	0.2000	50	500	0.20
16	200	0.2500	50	300	0.15
17	150	0.3333	50	150	0.10
18	100	0.5000	50	20	0.05
19	50	1.0000	50	0	0.00
20	0		0		
					9.50

$e_0 = 9500/1000 = 9.5$ years

Column (2) is the number alive at beginning of period.
Column (3) is the percentage who die during period. It is assumed all deaths occur at the beginning of period.
Column (4) is the number who die each period.
Column (5) is the total person-years left for those alive at beginning of period and who do not immediately die.
Column (6) are survival probabilities from period 0 to period t.

As a final measure of average life expectancy, Ciecka and Ciecka (1996) developed what they termed an additional-years-of-life (AYL) variable which measures the probability of living exactly j more years given one is alive at age t. For example, if t is equal to 50, then one can estimate the probability of living exactly one more year, two more years, etc. By estimating these probabilities up to some maximum age such as 115, the result will be a probability distribution where it is possible to estimate various statistics such as the mean (average life expectancy), standard deviation, variance, and percentiles. Ciecka and Ciecka also calculate the minimum interval that a) contains the average life expectancy and b) contains 50% of the probability distribution. As an example, based upon their calculations the average life expectancy of a 30-year-old male is 44.1 years while the 50% interval is 40.1 years to 57.1 years—an obviously non-symmetrical interval. The economist can testify that the probability of living from 40.1 years to 57.1 years is approximately 50%, which corresponds to the more-likely-than-not rule. The economist could then match, e.g., the estimated future medical costs with this range to get an interval estimate for the cost of a life care plan.

Text Table 14:
Example: Reduced Life Expectancy Calculations for a Relative Mortality Ratio = 1.5

(1) Age	(2) l_t	(3) q_t	(4) d_t	(5) q_{dt} (RMR=1.5)	(6) l_{dt}	(7) T_{dt}	(8) $p_0(dt)$
0	1000	0.0500	50	0.0750	1000	7401.29	
1	950	0.0526	50	0.0789	925	6476.29	0.9250
2	900	0.0556	50	0.0833	851.97	5624.31	0.8520
3	850	0.0588	50	0.0882	780.98	4843.34	0.7810
4	800	0.0625	50	0.0938	712.07	4131.27	0.7121
5	750	0.0667	50	0.1000	645.31	3485.96	0.6453
6	700	0.0714	50	0.1071	580.78	2905.18	0.5808
7	650	0.0769	50	0.1154	518.55	2386.63	0.5186
8	600	0.0833	50	0.1250	458.72	1927.91	0.4587
9	550	0.0909	50	0.1364	401.38	1526.53	0.4014
10	500	0.1000	50	0.1500	346.65	1179.88	0.3466
11	450	0.1111	50	0.1667	294.65	885.23	0.2946
12	400	0.1250	50	0.1875	245.54	639.69	0.2455
13	350	0.1429	50	0.2143	199.50	440.19	0.1995
14	300	0.1667	50	0.2500	156.75	283.44	0.1568
15	250	0.2000	50	0.3000	117.56	165.88	0.1176
16	200	0.2500	50	0.3750	82.29	83.58	0.0823
17	150	0.3333	50	0.5000	51.43	32.15	0.0514
18	100	0.5000	50	0.7500	25.72	6.43	0.0257
19	50	1.0000	50	1.0000	6.43		
20	0		0		0.00		
			1000				7.3949

$e_0 = 7401.29/1000 = 7.4013$

Columns (1) – (4) are the same as in Text Table 13.
Column (5) increases values in column 3 by a factor of 1.5 (except for age 19).
Remaining columns are the same as in Text Table 13 but applied to case where RMR = 1.5 rather than 1.0.

B. Relative Mortality Ratios

The methods above can be used to calculate life expectancies for the general population. But to calculate life expectancies for persons with various medical problems, we can make use of relative mortality ratios.

Again let q_t represent the probability of a person in the general population dying over the year beginning at exact age t. We will similarly define q_{dt} as the probability of a person with a specific disease or infirmity d (e.g., stroke, heart disease, cancer, etc.) dying during the year beginning at age t. Now let the relative mortality ratio R_{dt} for persons with this infirmity d at age t be defined as:

$$R_{dt} = q_{dt}/q_t. \qquad (6)$$

In other words, the relative mortality ratio is a ratio that denotes how much more likely individuals in one group are to die at a certain age than individuals in the general population. For example, if the relative mortality ratio of stroke victims at age 40 is 7 (sometimes written as 700%), it means that a 40-year-old stroke victim is 7 times more likely to die during this year than a person in the general population. Or if the relative mortality ratio for psoriasis sufferers is 1, it means that psoriasis sufferers need concern themselves only with the "heartbreak" of their disease—they're just as likely to survive as persons in the general population.

Of what use are mortality ratios? By rearranging the terms in equation (6), the probability of an individual with a specific infirmity, d, dying over the age interval t to t+1 is equal to the product of the relative mortality ratio and the probability of a person in the general population dying, or

$$q_{dt} = R_{dt}q_t. \qquad (7)$$

By using q_{dt} rather than q_t in ALE calculations, one can thus calculate a set of adjusted person-year values, l_{dt}, representing the number of individuals with infirmity d who are alive at exact age t. Or alternatively one can calculate a set of adjusted survival probabilities, $p_{dt}(t+j)$, for calculating the probability of a person with a certain infirmity surviving from year t to year t + j. These adjusted values can then be utilized in precisely the same manner as described earlier to estimate the average life expectancy of a person with a given infirmity at a certain age.

An example using a constant relative mortality ratio of 1.50 is given in Text Table 14. Columns (1) through (4) are identical to the corresponding columns in Text Table 13. Column (5) contains q_{dt}, the adjusted mortality rate for each age t and is derived by multiplying the death rates of the general population, q_t, by the relative mortality ratio, R_{dt}.

These adjusted death rates listed in column (5) are used to determine the numbers alive at exact age t, l_{dt}, as indicated in column (6). T_{dt}, the number of person-years remaining for persons alive at exact age t is shown in column (7). Entries in column (8) represent the probability of a person living from exact age 0 to exact age t, and the ALE can be calculated by simply summing the entries in the column as indicated by equation (4). It should be noted that the slight discrepancy in the ALEs calculated by the two approaches is simply due to rounding error.

Before concluding this section, several additional points should be noted. Our examples have implicitly assumed both that the relative mortality ratio is the best measure for estimating the relative mortality of individuals with different medical risks and that the ratio is constant as a person ages. Neither of these assumptions is necessarily correct. First, there is another measure—the excess death rate (EDR)—that is sometimes used for estimating the relative mortality of individuals with different medical risks. In contrast to the relative mortality ratio, which is defined as q_{dt}/q_t, the excess death rate is defined as $(q_{dt} - q_t)$. As pointed out by Anderson (2002, Chapter 7), in some circumstances the EDR may be a better measure of relative mortality risk than the RMR. As an example, suppose that the subject of study is 10-year-old boys with a certain medical condition. Suppose also that the death rate for persons with this condition at this age, compared to that of the general population, rises from .000138 to .000276. Thus, the RMR is equal to 2 while the EDR is equal to .000138. If it is assumed that the RMR is constant, then for 70 year-old males, the death rate would rise from .026257 to .052514. However, if a constant EDR is a more accurate indication of relative risk, the probability of death for 70-year-old males would rise only from .026257 to .026395. Thus, if one began with a study of younger individuals and applied a constant RMR when a constant EDR was more appropriate, the life expectancy (ALE) of older individuals would be significantly understated.

In addition, it is often the case that by either measure relative mortality risk does change as a person with a certain medical condition ages. In fact, a common pattern is that both the RMR and EDR associated with certain medical conditions may fall with age. This happens because the most aggressive forms of a disease may cause early death, and patients who have the best defenses display survival of the fittest (Anderson, Chapter 5).

C. Relative Mortality Information Sources

Mortality rates for the general population and by race and gender are available annually from the U.S. Department of Health and Human Services (HHS) in its National Vital Statistics Reports.[3] With such information, one can easily set up a table similar to Text Tables 13 and 14 and then use a spreadsheet that automatically calculates average life expectancy for any age. The National Vital Statistics Reports themselves present ALEs by age for the general population.

It might be noted that the year-to-year mortality data for the general population in the National Vital Statistics Reports are provided only up to age 100. (Before 1997, the cut-off age was 85.) Ignoring ages beyond 100 in the calculations is not desirable, of course, since the result will be an ALE which is downward biased. Several possible remedies exist. One possibility is to request unpublished yearly mortality data for ages beyond 100 from the Department of HHS.[4] Or one can instead use the *U.S. Decennial Life Tables*, which present yearly mortality rates for ages beyond 100. At the time of this writing, however, the Decennial Life Tables based on the 2000 Census were still not available.

The survival and mortality data in the sources noted above are for the general population. For relative mortality ratio data, some forensic economists have used a two-volume study by Lew and Gajewski, *Medical Risks: Trends in Mortality by Age and Time Elapsed* (1990). The volumes provide a compendious review of medical, statistical, and actuarial studies of persons with various medical problems (e.g., stroke, heart disease, etc.). The Lew-Gajewski volume is based on over 1,000 articles in medical journals as well as numerous mortality studies published in the actuarial, statistical, and public health literature (p. VIII). Also included are results from much unpublished literature. From these studies (many of which are abstracted), a number of life table concepts are then derived, including observed deaths, expected deaths, and—most importantly for our purpose—relative mortality ratios for various diseases and medical impairments. Nevertheless, the information is still by no means everywhere complete and definitive, and usually the studies are limited to particular time-periods, age ranges, and countries. Unfortunately, the Lew-Gajewski work is now over 15 years old; and with the death of Edward Lew in 1996, it is unclear whether it will be updated. In addition to the Lew-Gajewski study, of course, the professional journals carried in any medical library contain mortality studies of persons with various medical impairments.

There are also several articles in the forensic economics literature that focus upon average life expectancy of individuals with specific medical impairments. (See Slesnick (1990), Slesnick and Thornton (1994), Ciecka and Goldman (1995), Lewis (1995), Thornton and Slesnick (1997), and Huttner and Alhajii (1998).) The main focus of these articles is to examine the medical literature and show how reduced life expectancy can impact the present value of future medical costs. The medical studies upon which these articles are based can be found in a number of sources, but a particularly good starting point is the website of David Strauss and Robert Shavelle at www.lifeexpectancy.com/index.shtml. The studies cited cover a wide range of illnesses including cerebral palsy, spinal cord injury, and traumatic brain injury. In addition, Anderson (2002) explores the literature for individuals with cerebral palsy, traumatic brain injury, and tetraplegia.

Text Table 15:
Average Remaining Life Expectancies (Years) for Males by Selected
Ages and Various Relative Mortality Ratios (R), 2003

Age	R=1	R=2	R=3	R=4	R=5	R=10	R=15	R=20
20	55.8	47.5	42.6	39.2	36.5	28.2	23.6	20.4
25	51.2	43.1	38.5	35.2	32.7	25.1	21.0	18.2
30	46.5	38.7	34.2	31.1	28.7	21.7	18.0	15.5
35	41.9	34.2	29.9	27.0	24.7	18.2	14.8	12.6
40	37.3	29.9	25.8	23.0	20.9	14.9	11.8	9.9
45	32.8	25.7	21.9	19.2	17.3	11.9	9.2	7.6
50	28.5	21.8	18.2	15.9	14.1	9.4	7.1	5.7
55	24.4	18.1	14.9	12.8	11.2	7.2	5.3	4.2
60	20.4	14.7	11.8	9.9	8.6	5.2	3.7	2.9
65	16.8	11.6	9.1	7.5	6.4	3.7	2.6	1.9
70	13.5	8.9	6.8	5.5	4.6	2.5	1.6	1.2

It needs to be emphasized again that large-scale studies often show that after a certain age the RMR declines while the EDR will either stay relatively constant or actually rise. This last situation can happen with certain chronic diseases such as diabetes or with smoking. There are also patterns of declining RMR and EDR, such as immediately after an event such as an accident. If one had accurate data for all ages, then it would not make any difference whether one used the RMR or EDR as long as the risk adjustment was done properly. However, most studies are not large-scale but rather more commonly focus on certain population groups. In that case, the analyst must often make an "educated" guess whether to use the RMR or EDR and how to adjust it for different age groups. (See Anderson, Chapter 11.)

5.3 Concerns, Critiques, and Controversies

David Strauss and Robert Shavelle have published a number of articles that directly relate to the topic of this chapter. Their critique of current practices with regards to calculating life expectancy is far-ranging, and we discuss some of their concerns in this section.[5]

A. The Quality of Care and Life Expectancy

One issue relating to ALE applications concerns the quality of care. It is, of course, reasonable to assume that better care will normally increase life expectancy. But some plaintiff's attorneys will argue that with good (expensive) care, a reduction in life expectancy will not occur. This is, of course, an empirical question with the answer varying according to the type and severity of the condition and the quality of care considered.

A related issue (Strauss, 2003) is whether life expectancies are increasing over time. The plaintiff's side may argue that computed ALEs are based upon historical data and hence do not reflect future improvements in health care. It should be noted that this same argument can be applied to the general life tables, which are based upon cross-section data. The question of whether life expectancies are increasing generally, as pointed out in the article, is uncertain. As an example, the authors report the following with regards to cerebral palsy: "The University of California Life Expectancy Project reported substantially improved survival of infants with extremely severe disabilities (the so-called 'vegetative state')—and there may be some evidence for improved survival in children with very severe disabilities. For higher-functioning children, and for all adults, however, careful examination of the data has revealed no evidence of a trend. Published studies from Britain and Australia also failed to detect a trend." (p. 4)

B. Who Should Determine Life Expectancy?

Another question regarding ALE applications that Strauss and Shavelle discuss is that of who should actually perform calculations of ALE and survival probabilities. In their view, physicians should not usually do so on their own (Strauss and Shavelle, 1998). Yet, despite weak or nonexistent training in statistics, physicians are often called upon to estimate life expectancies. As Strauss and Shavelle state, "Witnesses lacking statistical or actuarial training are frequently unable to define life expectancy, compute it in a simple case, or distinguish it from the median survival time." (p. 2) One who does so can either rely on published studies or on his or her own judgment. If the physician relies on published studies, they are often of limited scope and may not apply closely to the plaintiff being considered. If the physician relies on his own experience, then according to the authors he is even more vulnerable. How many patients did he examine that closely resemble the plaintiff? Did he follow up the patients over time? Has he kept up with the literature on statistical methods concerning survival probabilities? These and other questions suggested that physicians, by themselves, cannot accurately estimate life expectancy.

Strauss and Shavelle argue that two experts are needed in court. A qualified medical specialist would provide detailed information about the plaintiff. A qualified analyst, who must possess training in medical statistics, would then take this information and calculate a life expectancy. What is important is that the person doing the calculations have access to a sufficiently large database to handle the information provided by the medical specialist.

C. The Role of Life Annuities and Structured Settlements

There is another important issue closely related to the question of who is best suited to calculate life expectancy—namely, what is the role that life annuities and structured settlements might have in a trial? Riccardi (2005) discusses this issue at length, with focus on the State of New York. In New York as elsewhere, the level of damages involving catastrophic injury is influenced by the jury's determination of a life expectancy. But as Riccardi points out, the difficult issues faced by a jury having to make this decision, often with widely diverse input from the plaintiff and defense side, may be totally avoided if a life annuity were to be considered. "The jury would determine the starting amount for life-care payments and the rate at which the jury says they should increase. The defendant would then solicit bids and purchase a life annuity from a qualified life insurance company. Since the life insurance company would then be responsible for payments for the rest of the woman's life, it would not matter how long the jury thought the woman would live." (p. 18) It is important for the insurance company to accurately estimate the life expectancy of the plaintiff, for it has a self-interest in doing so.

5.4 Some Applications and Additional Implications

Having discussed some of the major problems and concerns with estimating and using life expectancies in litigation, we now turn to some applications. A forensic economist may find it appropriate to make adjustments to a life table for the general population for two reasons. First, and most obviously, an otherwise healthy individual may have a shortened life expectancy as a *result* of an injury. Second, an individual who has been injured may have had a medical condition *prior* to the injury. For example, the person may have suffered from heart disease, diabetes, or have been a heavy smoker.

When the tort itself has caused the lower life expectancy, estimates of future medical costs may be affected but *not* estimates of pre-injury potential wages or household services. Interestingly, life care planners hired by plaintiff attorneys will sometimes fail to reduce life expectancy when estimating future medical costs. However, when determining the future employability of an injured individual, vocational experts will often argue that the injured party now faces the prospect of reduced income as a result of lower wages and a lower probability of labor force participation. Although it is possible for certain injuries to affect employability but not life expectancy, often these two factors are related.

A common example of a precondition that would affect life expectancy even in the absence of a litigated tort is that of smoking. Lew and Gajewski (1990, pp. 3-7 to 3-11 and 3-76 to 3-100) provide substantial evidence that the death rate for smokers is far higher than that for nonsmokers. They also point out that cigarette smoking is not only the major cause of lung cancer in the United States, but that it is also linked to other types of cancers (e.g., oral, laryngeal, and stomach). The authors report the results of numerous studies and find that in most such studies relative mortality ratios for smokers lie in the range of 1.5 to 2.5. This means that the annual death rate of smokers is 1.5 to 2.5 times that of the general population. It should be noted that some of the studies examined by Lew and Gajewski compare the mortality rates of smokers with those of nonsmokers. However, for purposes of calculating ALE, the forensic expert should keep in mind that the proper comparison group is that of *all individuals* regardless of smoking habits. This is so because the general life tables themselves include smokers.

What is the impact on estimated losses if a reduced life expectancy is incorporated in the estimates rather than the life expectancy pertaining to the general population? Surprisingly, as it turns out, the answer depends upon whether the reduced life expectancy was caused by the tort or existed prior to the tort. If the life expectancy was reduced as a result of the tort, then the lower life expectancy should be applied to estimated future medical costs and to the post-injury earnings and household-service-generating potential. However, the lower life expectancy should *not* be applied to the earnings and household-service-generating potential which would have existed had it not been for the injury. In this case, then, it is uncertain whether total economic losses estimated with a reduced life expectancy will be higher or lower than estimates based on the ALE of the general population. It ultimately depends on the relative importance of medical costs on the one hand and the earnings and household-services losses on the other hand.

Another possible scenario is where the reduced life expectancy relates to a prior condition, but where the injury itself does not have an impact upon life expectancy. In this case, the economic loss estimates based on the reduced life expectancy would be lower than those based on the life expectancy of the general population. For example, assume that a person who has been a smoker for several years is injured in an auto accident, but that the accident itself has no impact on life expectancy. Medical costs *specifically related to the injury* should properly reflect the reduced life expectancy given that the person is a smoker. Further, both the pre-injury and post-injury estimates of earnings potential and household-service-generating potential should be based upon the lower life expectancy of a smoker.

A third and quite complicated case arises when the tort aggravates a medical condition that was already present. Conceptually, this is similar to the first case where the lower life expectancy was caused by the tort. Thus, the effect of incorporating a reduced life expectancy is again uncertain, depending as it does upon the relative importance of medical costs vs. earnings and household services losses. The only difference is that even prior to the tort the individual possessed a reduced life expectancy. Here the tort has lowered life expectancy even further. An example would be the case of a smoker who was exposed to asbestos over a number of years. If the suit is against the asbestos manufacturer, then the proper measurement would be one based on the incremental economic loss caused by exposure to asbestos.

Text Table 16:
Average Remaining Life Expectancies (Years) for Females by
Selected Ages and Various Relative Mortality Ratios (R), 2003

Age	R=1	R=2	R=3	R=4	R=5	R=10	R=15	R=20
20	60.9	53.3	48.8	45.6	43.1	35.4	31.0	27.9
25	56.0	48.5	44.1	41.0	38.6	31.2	27.1	24.2
30	51.2	43.8	39.5	36.4	34.1	27.0	23.1	20.4
35	46.4	39.1	34.9	31.9	29.7	23.0	19.3	16.8
40	41.6	34.5	30.4	27.6	25.5	19.2	15.8	13.6
45	37.0	30.1	26.2	23.5	21.5	15.7	12.7	10.7
50	32.4	25.8	22.2	19.7	17.8	12.6	10.0	8.3
55	28.0	21.7	18.3	16.0	14.4	9.7	7.5	6.1
60	23.8	17.9	14.8	12.7	11.2	7.3	5.4	4.3
65	19.8	14.4	11.6	9.8	8.6	5.3	3.8	3.0
70	16.0	11.2	8.8	7.3	6.3	3.7	2.5	1.9

Text Table 17:
Average Remaining Life Expectancies (Years) for White Males by
Selected Ages and Various Relative Mortality Ratios (R), 2003

Age	R=1	R=2	R=3	R=4	R=5	R=10	R=15	R=20
20	56.3	48.1	43.4	40.0	37.3	29.2	24.5	21.3
25	51.6	43.7	39.2	35.9	33.4	26.0	21.8	19.0
30	46.9	39.2	34.8	31.8	29.4	22.4	18.6	16.1
35	42.2	34.7	30.5	27.6	25.3	18.8	15.4	13.1
40	37.6	30.4	26.3	23.5	21.4	15.4	12.3	10.4
45	33.1	26.2	22.3	19.7	17.8	12.4	9.7	8.0
50	28.8	22.2	18.6	16.3	14.5	9.8	7.5	6.1
55	24.6	18.4	15.2	13.0	11.5	7.5	5.6	4.4
60	20.6	14.9	12.0	10.1	8.8	5.4	3.9	3.0
65	16.9	11.8	9.2	7.7	6.6	3.8	2.6	2.0
70	13.5	9.0	6.7	5.6	4.7	2.6	1.7	1.2

Text Table 18:
Average Remaining Life Expectancies (Years) for White Females by
Selected Ages and Various Relative Mortality Ratios (R), 2003

Age	R=1	R=2	R=3	R=4	R=5	R=10	R=15	R=20
20	61.2	53.8	49.4	46.3	43.9	36.4	32.0	28.9
25	56.3	49.0	44.8	41.7	39.4	32.2	28.0	25.2
30	51.5	44.3	40.1	37.1	34.8	27.9	24.0	21.4
35	46.6	39.5	35.4	32.6	30.4	23.7	20.1	17.6
40	41.9	34.9	30.9	28.2	26.1	19.8	16.5	14.2
45	37.2	30.4	26.6	24.0	22.0	16.3	13.3	11.3
50	32.6	26.1	22.5	20.1	18.2	13.0	10.4	8.7
55	28.1	21.9	18.6	16.3	14.6	10.0	7.8	6.4
60	23.8	18.0	15.0	12.9	11.4	7.5	5.6	4.5
65	19.8	14.5	11.7	10.0	8.7	5.4	3.9	3.0
70	16.0	11.2	8.9	7.4	6.4	3.7	2.6	1.9

Text Table 19:
Average Remaining Life Expectancies (Years) for Black Males by
Selected Ages and Various Relative Mortality Ratios (R), 2003

Age	R=1	R=2	R=3	R=4	R=5	R=10	R=15	R=20
20	50.7	41.4	36.2	32.7	30.0	22.0	17.8	14.9
25	46.3	37.3	32.4	29.1	26.6	19.4	15.6	13.2
30	41.8	33.2	28.5	25.4	23.1	16.7	13.4	11.3
35	37.3	29.0	24.6	21.7	19.5	13.7	10.8	9.0
40	32.9	24.9	20.8	18.0	16.1	10.8	8.3	6.8
45	28.7	21.1	17.2	14.7	12.9	8.2	6.1	4.9
50	24.8	17.6	14.1	11.8	10.2	6.2	4.4	3.4
55	21.2	14.6	11.5	9.5	8.1	4.7	3.3	2.5
60	17.9	11.9	9.1	7.4	6.2	3.4	2.3	1.7
65	14.9	9.6	7.2	5.8	4.8	2.6	1.7	1.2
70	12.1	7.5	5.4	4.3	3.5	1.8	1.1	0.7

5.5 Life Expectancy Tables by Various Relative Mortality Ratios

In Text Tables 15 through 20 we have presented remaining life expectancies for individuals at 5-year age intervals from ages 20 through 70. The Text Tables are based upon 2003 data from the U.S. Department of Health and Human Services (HHS) in its National Vital Statistics Reports. The life expectancies are given for selected relative mortality ratios ranging from R = 1 to R = 20. Interpolations across age and relative-mortality-ratio levels can be done with minor loss of accuracy. The life expectancies given in the R = 1 column are, of course, identical to those given in the general life

tables. It is important to note that the RMRs are assumed to be constant and, as pointed out earlier, such an assumption may not always be realistic.

The ALEs presented in the tables can ordinarily be used in a straightforward fashion. The situation becomes more complicated, however, when an adjusted life expectancy is used as part of an estimate of worklife expectancy. It may be incorrect to argue that a lower life expectancy will have no impact on worklife as long as the years of life expectancy still exceed those given in the general worklife tables. For example, assume that a 50 year-old male, who happens to be a heavy smoker, is injured. Suppose that smoking reduces his

Text Table 20:
Average Remaining Life Expectancies (Years) for Black Females by
Selected Ages and Various Relative Mortality Ratios (R), 2003

Age	R=1	R=2	R=3	R=4	R=5	R=10	R=15	R=20
20	57.4	48.5	43.5	40.0	37.3	29.4	25.2	22.3
25	52.6	43.8	38.9	35.5	32.9	25.4	21.4	18.8
30	47.8	39.2	34.4	31.1	28.6	21.5	17.8	15.4
35	43.1	34.7	30.0	26.9	24.5	17.8	14.4	12.2
40	38.6	30.4	25.9	22.9	20.7	14.5	11.4	9.5
45	34.1	26.3	22.1	19.3	17.3	11.7	9.0	7.3
50	29.9	22.5	18.6	16.0	14.2	9.2	6.9	5.6
55	25.9	19.0	15.4	13.1	11.5	7.2	5.3	4.1
60	22.1	15.6	12.4	10.4	9.0	5.4	3.8	2.9
65	18.5	12.7	9.9	8.2	7.0	4.0	2.8	2.0
70	15.3	10.1	7.6	6.2	5.2	2.8	1.9	1.3

life expectancy by five years, from age 80 to age 75. Suppose also that the expected remaining *worklife* for the general population of males of his age is 12 years (to age 62). It would not necessarily be correct for the forensic economist to claim that, because life expectancy is reduced only to age 75, there is no impact on worklife expectancy. The reason is that the survival probabilities are lower in *each* year. And since the worklife tables themselves are also based on yearly survival probabilities, higher relative mortality ratios will also affect worklife expectancies. Put another way, the effects of a reduction in life expectancy do not simply materialize "all at once" at the end. Ciecka and Goldman (1995) directly incorporate a reduced life expectancy into a standard increment-decrement worklife model to determine the reduced expected worklife of smokers. For forensic economists who use the so-called LPE (life-participation-employment) model, incorporation of reduced life expectancy is straightforward. The economist need simply reduce the L (life) column appropriately to calculate the revised estimate of worklife.

5.6 Conclusions

Using appropriate life expectancy tables is extremely important when calculating economic losses whether one is considering medical costs, lost wages, or lost household services. The life expectancy of a particular individual may be different than that indicated in the general life tables either because of the tort itself or due to a medical condition present prior to the tort. A competent physician or other medical expert can often provide such evidence, but it is argued here that it may be necessary to obtain the input of a qualified statistician/actuary/economist who is familiar with the ap-

propriate databases. If necessary, a range of economic losses can be estimated based upon various mortality rate assumptions.

Obviously, there are uncertainties associated with such estimates. For example, how will the estimated relative mortality ratio change as a person ages? Will advances in technology result in a lowering of relative mortality ratios in the future for people with certain afflictions? Despite these and other uncertainties, it is the opinion of the authors that in many cases the alternative approach—the reliance on general population life tables—is clearly inappropriate. It must be remembered that in any estimate of future economic losses by a forensic expert, a prediction of the future is made. And if the general life tables are used for a person suffering from a spinal cord injury or for a person who is a heavy smoker, that itself is an implicit prediction of the future.

References

Anderson, T.W., Life Expectancy in Court, A Textbook for Doctors and Lawyers, Vancouver, Canada: Teviot Press, 2002.

Ciecka, James, and Peter Ciecka, "Life Expectancy and the Properties of Survival Data." Litigation Economics Digest, Spring 1996 1(2),19-33.

Ciecka, James, and Jerry Goldman, "A Markov Process Model for Worklife Expectancies of Smokers and Non-smokers," Journal of Forensic Economics, Winter 1995, 8(1), 1-12.

DeVivo, Michael, "Life Expectancy and Causes of Death for Persons with Spinal Cord Injuries," Research Update. Medical Rehabilitation Research and Training Center, University of Alabama at Birmingham, 1990.

Geyelin, Milo, "Judge Orders Injury Plaintiff Tested for HIV," Wall Street Journal, May 6, 1992, B1.

Huettner, David, and Anas Alhajji, "Economic Damages due to Spinal Cord Injuries: Trends and Policy Implications," Journal of Forensic Economics, Spring-Summer 1998, 11(2), 121-26.

Lew, Edward, and Jerzy Gajewski, eds., Medical Risks: Trends in Mortality by Age and Time Elapsed, New York: Praeger, 1990.

Lewis, Cris, "Measuring the Effect of Preexisting Health Conditions on Expected Economic Loss," Journal of Legal Economics, 1995, 5(2), 33-42.

Riccardi, Anthony, "The Impact of a Reduced Life Expectancy on the Recovery of Life Care Expenses," The Earnings Analyst, 2005, 7, 15-32.

Slesnick, Frank, "Forecasting Medical Costs in Tort Cases: The Role of the Economist," Journal of Forensic Economics, Winter 1990, 4(1) 83-100.

Slesnick, Frank, and Robert Thornton, "Life Expectancies for Persons with Medical Risks," Journal of Forensic Economics, Spring/Summer, 1994, 7(2), 197-207.

Strauss, David, "Longer Life?" Personal Injury Law Journal, February 2003, 2-5.

Strauss, David, and Robert Shavelle, "Doctors Are Not Experts on Life Expectancy," The Expert Witness Newsletter, Economica LTD, Summer 1998, 3(2), 1-4.

Strauss, David; Robert Shavelle; Christopher Pflaum; and Christopher Bruce, "Discounting the Cost of Future Care for Persons with Disabilities, Journal of Forensic Economics, Winter 2001, 14(1), 79-87.

Thornton, Robert, and Frank Slesnick, "New Estimates of Life Expectancies for Persons with Medical Risks," Journal of Forensic Economics, Fall 1997, 10 (3), 285-90.

U.S. Department of Health and Human Services, National Center for Health Statistics, National Vital Statistics Reports. United States Life Tables, 2003. 54 (14), April 19, 2006.

Endnotes

1. The authors are, respectively, Professor Emeritus of Economics at Bellarmine University, Professor of Economics at Lehigh University, and Assistant Professor of Economics at St. Francis University. This chapter draws heavily on two articles by Frank Slesnick and Robert Thornton in the *Journal of Forensic Economics,* Vol. 7, No. 2, 1994, and Vol. 10, No. 3, 1997.

2. For the purpose of our example, deaths at any age are assumed to occur immediately after the person attains that age.

3. At the time of this writing (2006), the latest Report uses mortality data for 2003. See Elizabeth Arias, "United States Life Tables, 2003," National Vital Statistics Reports, US Department of Health and Human Services, National Center for Health Statistics.

4. We wish to thank Elizabeth Arias for making such data available to us for the year 2003.

5. In a 2001 article dealing with the estimation of damages, Strauss, Shavelle, Pflaum and Bruce also evaluate three common methods of estimating and applying a survival function (year-by-year probabilities of surviving) for a given ALE, rather than calculating an ALE as is the scope of this chapter. The first method is the "ratio method," which determines a fixed RMR that will generate the given life expectancy. A second approach is one that estimates future damages with certainty for the average life expectancy calculated. In essence, the survival probabilities of the person for whom damages are being calculated are assumed to be unity until the ALE is reached, after which they fall to zero. A third method, called "rating up," is commonly used by the insurance industry. For example, assume that Johnny is 10 years old but that, due to severe injuries, an actuary determines that his life expectancy is now only 20 years. Twenty years is also the life expectancy of a 63 year-old male, so the insurance company might then "rate up" Johnny from age 10 to age 63. The article then compares the above three approaches, along with an empirical model that generates a survival probability function, with respect to the present values of the costs of a hypothetical life care plan that each would generate.

Chapter 6

Effects of Cigarette Smoking on Life Expectancy

6.1 Introduction

Cigarette smoking is the most preventable cause of death in this country. It is currently related to one in five premature deaths the United States (CDC, 2006).[1] Approximately 21% of the population smoked in 2004. This is down markedly from over 40% in 1965. Rates for young persons have varied markedly recently. The percentage of 18- through 25-year-old smokers was at a low of about 23% in 1991, had risen to about 28.5% in 2002, and by 2004 had fallen again to about 23.6% (CDC, Office on Smoking and Health).

Males have a higher prevalence of smoking than females (23.4% and 18.5%, respectively—all percentages are as of 2004 from CDC, 2005); smoking is indirectly related to educational attainment (26.2% of those with less than a high school education smoke versus 8.0% of those with a college degree or more); blacks have a slightly lower prevalence than whites; and Hispanics have the lowest (22.2%, 20.2% and 15.0%, respectively). Males smoke more cigarettes per day than females; whites more than Hispanics; and blacks less than any category except non-Hispanic Asians and Pacific Islanders (CDC, Office on Smoking and Health, 1995). From 1993 through 2004 the prevalence of heavy smokers (more than 24 cigarettes per day) decreased steadily from 19.1% to 122.1%, but the prevalence of lighter smokers has increased. The number of cigarettes smoked per day has decreased—males from 21.3 per day in 1993 to 17.8 in 2004, and females from 17.8 to 15.3.

It was not until the fifties that major epidemiological studies began to demonstrate the clear link between cigarette smoking and diseases. The first studies showed differences between the two sexes in risk of disease associated with cigarette smoking. For instance, male smokers had a tenfold greater risk of developing lung cancer than male never-smokers, whereas the increased risk was only two-fold for females. However, as these and subsequent studies came to demonstrate, these differences are related to lifelong smoking behavior—males had begun smoking at earlier ages, smoked more cigarettes per day, were more likely to inhale deeply, and used fewer filter cigarettes than females. In other words, differences in cigarette-induced mortality are strongly dependent on behavior, rather than biological susceptibility (NIH Pub. No. 97-4213, 1997 and Rogers and Powell-Griner, 1991).

6.2 Life Tables by Smoking Status

Many studies have dealt with increased risk of disease related to cigarette smoking, but less effort has been made to develop life tables by smoking status. One of the first was a set of life tables produced from the blended mortality experience of five insurance companies during the period 1973–78 (Marion, 1983). These tables are now dated and have several other limitations: (a) only insured persons were included (producing possible health, income, and education biases), (b) mortality estimates may have been affected by non-uniform definitions of smoking status (three companies included substantial numbers of nonsmokers in the smoking group), (c) extensive actuarial adjustments were made, (d) female tables were mainly based on estimated and assumed relationships to males (due to smaller female sample sizes), and (e) the tables include insurance "margin" adjustments.

Rogers and Powell-Griner, 1991, used data from a match of the 1985 and 1987 National Health Interview Surveys (NHIS) and the 1986 National Mortality Followback Survey (NMFS) to develop life tables for white U.S. smokers and nonsmokers. They developed life expectancies for nonsmokers, former smokers, and smokers. Recently Hummer, Nam and Rodgers (1998) further categorized smokers between light (fewer than 25 cigarettes per day) and heavy (more than 25 per day).

This book uses mortality data from the American Cancer Society's second Cancer Prevention Study (CPS-II). The CPS-II data have the following advantages compared to the NMFS data: (a) the data reflect the experience of all races rather than just whites, (b) the sample is markedly larger (56,000 versus 18,733 deaths), and (c) multivariate analyses, which have been conducted on this data set, have shown that (other than age and sex) factors such as race, education, dietary and alcohol use patterns, marital status, etc., have very little net impact on estimates of relative risk for similar patterns of cigarette consumption (Thun et al., 2000).

6.3 Data
The CPS-II consisted of 1,185,106 Americans age 30 years or older enrolled by volunteers in the fall of 1982. Participants consisted mostly of friends, neighbors, and acquaintances of the volunteers. As such, participants were older and were more likely to be white (93%), better educated, married, and part of the middle class than the general population. The sample consisted of 228,682 current cigarette smokers (smoke at least one cigarette per day for one year or more), 482,681 lifelong never-smokers, and 262,790 former smokers. Because of incomplete data or of being pipe or cigar smokers, 210,953 persons were excluded from the analyses.

Participants completed a four-page questionnaire in which they detailed many personal characteristics. In addition to current smoking status, the number of cigarettes typically smoked per day, and the number of years smoked, the data included demographic, socioeconomic, marital, and lifestyle factors.

> Compared to the never-smokers, current smokers were on average 3–4 years younger, less educated, less likely to be currently employed (if male), slightly more likely to have held a 'blue collar' job and to report ever being exposed to asbestos, more likely to consume a diet low in vegetables and high in fat, more likely to drink alcohol and not to take vitamin supplements, and less physically active. (Thun, ibid.)

The volunteers followed participants in the survey through personal contact every two years for six years. By the end of the six years 79,802 participants (6.7%) had died, 1,083,600 (91.4%) were alive, and 21,704 (1.8%) were lost to follow-up.

Information on the composition of the U.S. population by smoking status, age, and education was derived from the Tobacco Use Supplements of the CPS for the months of January and May of 2000, June and November of 2001, February of 2002, and February, June and November of 2003. The CPS of these months included not only the basic sociodemographic and economic data collected in each CPS, but also a Smoking Supplement with extensive information on smoking behavior.

6.4 Relative Risk Factors and Methodology
Mortality data by smoking status from the CPS-II are shown in Text Table 21. For each category, the mortality rate was calculated as the ratio of deaths to the number of person-years, expressed per 100,000 person-years. The relative risks are of "current" and "former" users compared to "never-smokers."[2] These relative risks, however, cannot be used to create life tables (as discussed in the preceding chapter) without the additional adjustments discussed in the following paragraphs. (Although there is a strong correlation between smoking duration and increased mortality, this analysis is based only on current activity because dealing with multiple factors is extremely complex and would require many overlapping tables.)

An important consideration in calculating mortality rates for subpopulations is whether the population is homogeneous or heterogeneous in regard to the effects in question. Specifically, since we are disaggregating the population by educational attainment, the question is two-fold: (1) do people of different educational levels experience the same health effects from given levels of cigarette consumption, and (2) does the prevalence of cigarette consumption vary between the various educational populations? Data indicate that the first criterion is met—i.e., the effects of tobacco use are homogeneous across educational categories (Thun, ibid.). We are left then with the second question—does cigarette consumption vary with educational attainment?

Text Table 22 shows the percentage of persons in the 2000 through 2003 CPS sample by five-year age groupings and by education in each smoking category. Reading across the table shows how smoking composition varies by education. For instance, 25% of the *total* male population ages 35 to 39 were current smokers. When considered by educational category, however, the prevalence of current smokers varied from about 37% of those with less than a high school education level to about 7% of those with a graduate education. Thus a strong negative relationship exists between smoking cigarettes and educational level—the higher the education, the less likely to smoke. For females the same pattern exists but the correlation is not so strong and the overall prevalence of smoking is markedly less (except for the youngest age categories).

Text Table 21: Mortality and relative risks (compared to nonsmokers) by smoking status, CPS-II

Age	Nonsmoker			Current Smoker			Former Smoker			Relative Rates to Nonsmoker	
	Deaths	P-Years	Rate	Deaths	P-Years	Rate	Deaths	P-Years	Rate	Current	Former
Males											
30-34	14	9,189	152	11	6,203	177	2	2,817	71	1.16	0.47
35-39	16	21,944	73	37	16,869	219	10	9,049	111	3.01	1.52
40-44	21	22,407	94	65	21,408	304	25	14,645	171	3.24	1.82
45-49	102	67,204	152	268	62,754	427	125	56,454	221	2.81	1.46
50-54	283	127,821	221	800	117,909	679	461	125,515	367	3.06	1.66
55-59	487	132,430	368	1,367	126,134	1,084	958	160,475	597	2.95	1.62
60-64	815	121,174	673	1,925	105,519	1,824	1,780	162,796	1,093	2.71	1.63
65-69	1,120	102,124	1,097	1,984	68,771	2,885	2,326	128,491	1,810	2.63	1.65
70-74	1,321	71,536	1,847	1,760	37,732	4,665	2,548	86,889	2,933	2.53	1.59
75-79	1,389	40,362	3,441	1,113	15,201	7,322	2,084	44,237	4,711	2.13	1.37
80-84	981	17,945	5,467	434	4,154	10,448	1,125	15,346	7,331	1.91	1.34
85+	899	8,069	11,141	135	979	13,790	556	4,853	11,457	1.24	1.03
Females											
30-34	20	17,549	114	12	8,077	149	3	5,007	60	1.30	0.53
35-39	40	49,633	81	22	24,784	89	13	17,192	76	1.10	0.94
40-44	93	85,111	109	50	45,081	111	43	37,702	114	1.02	1.04
45-49	255	208,331	122	256	101,349	253	151	87,622	172	2.06	1.41
50-54	564	309,700	182	501	143,772	349	285	125,642	227	1.91	1.25
55-59	927	345,629	268	874	145,951	599	467	134,956	346	2.23	1.29
60-64	1,401	340,560	411	1,140	121,752	936	677	121,378	558	2.28	1.36
65-69	1,871	280,728	667	1,243	81,048	1,534	832	90,165	923	2.30	1.38
70-74	2,216	206,345	1,074	1,020	45,801	2,227	844	58,430	1,445	2.07	1.35
75-79	2,487	135,257	1,839	658	19,252	3,418	734	27,966	2,625	1.86	1.43
80-84	2,245	71,175	3,154	285	5,747	4,959	360	8,996	4,002	1.57	1.27
85+	3,331	41,281	8,069	171	1,601	10,681	254	2,941	8,637	1.32	1.07

Sources: Unpublished data from CPS-II and NIH Publication No. 97-4213.

Age standardized relative mortality rates for current-smoker males and females are 2.07 and 1.74, respectively. The 95% confident intervals of these RRs are (1.98, 2.17) and (1.66, 1.82), respectively.

Text Table 22: Smoking status prevalence by sex and educational attainment, all races, 2000 through 2003

Age	All	< HS	HS	Some Col	Col	Grad	All	< HS	HS	Some Col	Col	Grad
	Males						Females					
Current Smokers												
35 to 39	25%	37%	34%	24%	12%	7%	22%	33%	30%	23%	9%	7%
40 to 44	26%	40%	36%	26%	13%	7%	23%	32%	31%	23%	11%	6%
45 to 49	27%	40%	35%	28%	14%	10%	20%	29%	27%	21%	11%	7%
50 to 54	24%	37%	32%	27%	15%	9%	18%	27%	23%	19%	11%	8%
55 to 59	22%	35%	27%	22%	14%	8%	17%	23%	21%	18%	10%	8%
60 to 64	19%	29%	22%	19%	12%	9%	15%	20%	17%	14%	9%	7%
65 to 69	14%	19%	16%	13%	10%	6%	12%	14%	12%	12%	8%	8%
70 to 74	11%	16%	11%	12%	7%	5%	10%	10%	10%	10%	8%	7%
75 to 79	7%	10%	8%	6%	4%	3%	7%	8%	7%	7%	5%	6%
80+	5%	6%	6%	3%	4%	2%	4%	3%	5%	4%	4%	3%
Never-Smokers												
35 to 39	61%	49%	51%	60%	76%	81%	65%	60%	56%	62%	78%	80%
40 to 44	55%	45%	46%	53%	71%	78%	61%	58%	53%	57%	72%	78%
45 to 49	50%	42%	41%	46%	63%	69%	61%	61%	55%	57%	70%	75%
50 to 54	46%	41%	37%	41%	54%	65%	61%	59%	57%	58%	69%	69%
55 to 59	41%	35%	33%	36%	49%	57%	57%	58%	56%	55%	62%	63%
60 to 64	39%	36%	34%	34%	47%	54%	58%	60%	57%	54%	62%	63%
65 to 69	38%	36%	34%	36%	42%	53%	60%	62%	60%	56%	60%	61%
70 to 74	38%	35%	37%	34%	43%	51%	62%	66%	64%	56%	60%	61%
75 to 79	39%	37%	40%	36%	39%	48%	67%	70%	67%	62%	62%	71%
80+	47%	45%	46%	47%	48%	60%	75%	81%	73%	72%	68%	70%
Former Smokers												
35 to 39	15%	14%	15%	17%	13%	12%	13%	7%	13%	16%	13%	13%
40 to 44	18%	15%	19%	21%	17%	15%	17%	10%	17%	20%	17%	16%
45 to 49	23%	18%	24%	26%	23%	21%	19%	11%	18%	22%	19%	18%
50 to 54	30%	22%	30%	32%	31%	27%	21%	14%	20%	23%	21%	23%
55 to 59	38%	30%	40%	42%	37%	35%	25%	19%	24%	28%	28%	30%
60 to 64	42%	35%	45%	47%	42%	38%	27%	20%	27%	32%	29%	31%
65 to 69	48%	45%	49%	51%	48%	41%	29%	25%	28%	32%	33%	32%
70 to 74	51%	49%	52%	55%	50%	44%	28%	25%	26%	35%	33%	33%
75 to 79	54%	53%	52%	58%	57%	49%	27%	23%	26%	32%	33%	24%
80+	48%	49%	47%	51%	48%	39%	21%	16%	22%	24%	28%	27%

Source:
Current Population Survey, Tobacco Use Supplements, January 2000 through November 2003.
Slightly less than 25% of CPS respondents did not provide enough information to determine smoking status: prevalence rates are derived from only persons who provided full information. Prevalence rates of current smokers derived from the CPS microdata are slightly lower than rates published by the Centers for Disease Control.

The relevance of this can perhaps be most easily understood by looking at the life expectancies of the least and most highly educated males. As discussed in Chapter 4, the life expectancy of the male population with graduate degrees is much higher than that of those with less than a high school education. Numerous factors probably contribute to the higher mortality risks associated with low educational attainment: more dangerous occupations, less access to medical care, and so forth. In addition, what we see from Text Table 22 is a much higher prevalence of cigarette consumption. Therefore, part of the higher mortality of males with less than a high school education already accounts for cigarette consumption. Alternatively, with only about 7% of all males with a graduate education being smokers, much of their low mortality is due to low incidence of smoking.

It is therefore inappropriate to assume that the relative risk factors experienced due to smoking are the same for all educational levels when compared to each of their baseline mortality rates. The added relative risk due to smoking compared with the educationally specific baseline risk for those least educated should be less than that of the population as a whole because their baseline risk already incorporates the effects of high incidence of smoking. Conversely, the relative risk of smoking compared with the educationally specific baseline risk of those most educated should be more than that of the population as a whole because their baseline risk incorporates only the low prevalence of smoking.

Because of these differences across education and because the CPS-II sample differed from the demographic and socioeconomic structure of the U.S. population as a whole, age-specific probabilities of death had to be standardized to the U.S. rates. This was done for each five-year age group, beginning at age 35, using the following procedure: (1) relative risks of smokers and former smokers compared to never-smokers were calculated (the relative risk of nonsmokers is initially set equal to 1.00), (2) these relative risks were multiplied by the proportion of the U.S. population in the respective three smoking-status categories and by a constant (representing the death rate among never-smokers) so that their sum equaled the 2004 U.S. death rate during the appropriate five-year age category (in other words, the weighted average of the three death rates was set equal to the 2004 U.S. death rate), (3) the equation was solved for the constant, i.e. the death rate among never-smokers, and (4) this rate was multiplied by the relative risk factors for the other two smoking statuses to determine their probabilities of death (Thun et al., 1997, and Thun personal communication, 1998). Relative risks compared with the population as a whole by educational category are shown in Text Table 23.

As expected, relative risk factors of current smokers are less for the lower education levels and greater for the higher education levels. They are smaller for females than for males because the duration, amount consumed, degree of inhalation, and use of nonfilter tipped products has been less for females than for males. Adjustments are also somewhat smaller and more uniform across educational categories at older ages. This is, in the most part, due to the "cohort" effect resulting from the fact that smoking patterns were more uniform thirty or forty years ago regardless of educational category and, in lesser degree, due to premature removal from the population through death of those who had been smokers. Note that these relative risks do not incorporate possible confounding factors. For example, if smoking behavior, such as amount consumed, degree of inhalation, duration, etc., varies extensively between different educational groupings, then those with more intensive use will have higher relative risks than shown in Text Table 23, and vice versa.

The CPS-II also contains information on mortality by the number of cigarettes smoked. The National Cancer Institute designated five categories of daily consumption of cigarettes (1–9, 10–19, 20–39, 40, and 41+). Relative mortality risks of persons in each of these categories (compared to never-smokers) are shown in Text Table 24. In addition, the CPS-II data were consolidated into three groups to obtain larger sample sizes: "light" (1–19), "medium" (20), and "heavy" (more than 20).[3]

Text Table 24 also compares the CPS-II relative risks by consumption levels with those developed by Hummer, Nam and Rogers (1998) from the NHIS/NMFS data set. The two data sets provide generally similar relative risks, but there are some differences. For males, relative risks of smoking appear greater in the CPS-II study. For females with low levels of consumption, the CPS-II study also indicates slightly higher relative mortality than the NHIS/NMFS data; but at high levels of consumption, the NHIS/NMFS relative risks are much higher than those of the CPS-II. These differences may only reflect sampling variability since sample sizes in both studies are relatively small.

6.5 Life Tables by Smoking Status

Text Table 25 presents age-specific life expectancies for all persons, never-smokers, and current smokers. Tables are created only for all races. Three patterns are apparent.

First, differences in life expectancies between smokers and never-smokers are much larger for males than for females. For instance at age 25, the difference between smoker and never-smoker life expectancies for males with a high school degree is 9.0 years whereas for females the difference is 6.4 years. For those with graduate degrees, the differences are 7.9 and 5.5 years, respectively.

Text Table 23: Relative mortality risk by sex, age, and education

Age	Male					Female				
	Less Than HS	HS	Some Col	Col	Grad	Less Than HS	HS	Some Col	Col	Grad
Never-Smokers										
35 to 39	0.55	0.57	0.64	0.77	0.83	0.97	0.98	0.99	1.00	1.00
40 to 44	0.49	0.51	0.57	0.70	0.78	0.99	0.99	0.99	0.99	0.99
45 to 49	0.55	0.57	0.61	0.74	0.79	0.74	0.74	0.76	0.84	0.87
50 to 54	0.52	0.54	0.57	0.66	0.74	0.78	0.79	0.81	0.87	0.89
55 to 59	0.53	0.56	0.59	0.67	0.73	0.75	0.76	0.77	0.83	0.85
60 to 64	0.58	0.61	0.62	0.69	0.72	0.75	0.76	0.77	0.82	0.84
65 to 69	0.62	0.63	0.65	0.68	0.73	0.79	0.79	0.78	0.82	0.82
70 to 74	0.65	0.68	0.67	0.71	0.75	0.84	0.83	0.82	0.84	0.85
75 to 79	0.76	0.78	0.78	0.80	0.82	0.86	0.85	0.84	0.84	0.87
80 to 84	0.82	0.82	0.83	0.83	0.87	0.94	0.92	0.92	0.91	0.92
Current Smokers										
35 to 39	1.66	1.72	1.93	2.32	2.49	1.07	1.08	1.09	1.10	1.10
40 to 44	1.60	1.66	1.84	2.28	2.52	1.01	1.00	1.00	1.01	1.01
45 to 49	1.56	1.61	1.73	2.08	2.21	1.53	1.52	1.57	1.73	1.79
50 to 54	1.61	1.64	1.73	2.03	2.26	1.50	1.52	1.56	1.67	1.70
55 to 59	1.57	1.66	1.74	1.97	2.15	1.67	1.69	1.72	1.85	1.89
60 to 64	1.58	1.65	1.67	1.86	1.96	1.72	1.74	1.76	1.86	1.91
65 to 69	1.64	1.66	1.70	1.79	1.93	1.81	1.82	1.80	1.88	1.89
70 to 74	1.65	1.72	1.68	1.80	1.89	1.74	1.73	1.70	1.73	1.75
75 to 79	1.62	1.65	1.66	1.70	1.75	1.60	1.59	1.56	1.57	1.62
80 to 84	1.56	1.57	1.59	1.59	1.66	1.48	1.45	1.44	1.43	1.45
Former Smokers										
35 to 39	0.83	0.86	0.97	1.17	1.26	0.91	0.92	0.93	0.94	0.94
40 to 44	0.90	0.93	1.04	1.28	1.42	1.03	1.03	1.03	1.03	1.04
45 to 49	0.81	0.84	0.90	1.08	1.15	1.05	1.04	1.07	1.18	1.22
50 to 54	0.87	0.89	0.94	1.01	1.22	0.97	0.99	1.01	1.08	1.11
55 to 59	0.87	0.92	0.96	1.08	1.18	0.96	0.98	0.99	1.07	1.09
60 to 64	0.95	0.99	1.00	1.12	1.18	1.02	1.04	1.05	1.11	1.14
65 to 69	1.03	1.04	1.07	1.12	1.21	1.09	1.09	1.09	1.13	1.13
70 to 74	1.04	1.08	1.06	1.13	1.19	1.13	1.12	1.10	1.12	1.14
75 to 79	1.04	1.06	1.07	1.09	1.13	1.23	1.22	1.20	1.20	1.24
80 to 84	1.01	1.10	1.12	1.12	1.17	1.20	1.17	1.16	1.15	1.17

NOTE: The relative risks are compared to all persons regardless of smoking status of the specified educational level.

Text Table 24: Relative rates of current smokers to nonsmokers by number of cigarettes smoked per day, CPS-II and Hummer, Nam and Rodgers

Age	CPS-II									Hummer	
	1-9	10-19	20	21-39	40	41+	1-19	20	21+	1-25	26+
Males											
35-39	4.5	1.0	3.1	3.4	3.2	2.9	2.4	3.1	3.3	2.0	2.2
40-44	1.1	1.5	3.5	2.4	5.3	5.6	1.3	3.5	3.9		
45-49	3.1	2.4	2.5	2.1	3.6	4.2	2.7	2.5	3.0	2.3	2.9
50-54	2.5	3.4	2.8	2.9	3.4	3.6	3.1	2.8	3.2		
55-59	2.5	2.5	3.0	2.7	3.4	3.6	2.5	3.0	3.1	1.3	2.6
60-64	2.1	2.4	2.8	2.7	3.2	2.7	2.3	2.8	2.9		
65-69	2.1	2.2	2.8	2.6	2.9	3.4	2.1	2.8	2.8	1.3	3.0
70-74	2.1	2.5	2.6	2.5	2.9	2.3	2.3	2.6	2.6		
75-79	1.8	1.9	2.2	2.4	2.5	2.7	1.8	2.2	2.5		
80-84	1.8	1.8	2.2	1.8	1.7	1.7	1.8	2.2	1.7		
85+	1.2	1.2	1.3	2.1	na	0.8	1.2	1.3	1.6		
Females											
35-39	1.3	0.9	1.6	na	na	na	1.1	1.6	na	1.4	2.2
40-44	1.3	0.7	0.9	1.1	0.9	3.2	0.9	0.9	1.2		
45-49	1.7	1.5	2.2	1.9	3.3	3.4	1.6	2.2	2.5	1.5	4.2
50-54	1.2	1.7	1.9	2.1	2.5	4.1	1.5	1.9	2.4		
55-59	1.5	1.9	2.3	2.7	3.2	3.0	1.7	2.3	2.9	1.5	3.7
60-64	1.4	2.0	2.5	2.6	3.1	3.1	1.8	2.5	2.8		
65-69	2.7	2.1	2.6	2.6	2.4	3.5	2.3	2.6	2.6	1.3	4.8
70-74	1.4	1.9	2.4	2.4	2.9	2.0	1.7	2.4	2.5		
75-79	1.6	1.6	2.0	2.4	2.5	1.9	1.6	2.0	2.4		
80-84	1.1	1.6	1.8	2.2	2.0	1.6	1.4	1.8	2.1		
85+	0.9	1.3	1.8	1.5	1.4	na	1.1	1.8	1.5		

Sources: NIH Pub. No. 97-4213 and Hummer et al., 1998.

Text Table 25: Age specific life expectancies by smoking status, all races, CPS II relative risk factors applied to 2004 mortality rates

Age	Males					Females				
	< HS	HS	Some Col	Col	Grad	< HS	HS	Some Col	Col	Grad
All Persons										
25	48.4	51.4	52.6	55.0	56.5	54.0	56.7	57.7	58.6	59.3
35	39.6	42.2	43.2	45.4	46.9	44.5	47.1	48.0	48.9	49.7
45	30.9	33.2	34.1	36.0	37.4	35.4	37.7	38.5	39.3	40.1
55	23.2	24.9	25.6	27.0	28.3	26.9	28.7	29.3	30.0	30.6
65	16.2	17.3	17.8	18.8	19.8	19.2	20.3	20.8	21.2	21.8
75	10.3	10.9	11.1	11.6	12.5	12.5	12.9	13.3	13.4	13.7
Never-Smokers										
25	53.0	55.2	56.0	57.3	58.3	56.6	59.1	59.9	60.6	61.1
35	44.3	46.0	46.5	47.7	48.7	46.2	48.5	49.2	49.8	50.5
45	35.1	36.6	37.1	38.2	39.1	37.1	39.1	39.7	40.3	40.9
55	26.4	27.6	28.1	28.9	29.8	28.3	29.9	30.5	30.9	31.4
65	18.3	19.2	19.6	20.2	21.0	20.1	21.1	21.7	21.9	22.4
75	11.3	11.8	11.9	12.3	13.1	12.9	13.4	13.7	13.9	14.0
Current Smokers										
25	43.1	46.2	47.2	49.3	50.4	49.3	52.6	53.7	54.7	55.6
35	34.1	36.9	37.6	39.6	40.7	39.8	43.0	44.0	44.9	45.9
45	26.0	28.3	29.1	30.7	31.8	30.6	33.5	34.5	35.3	36.3
55	18.9	20.6	21.2	22.6	23.5	22.5	24.9	25.7	26.4	27.1
65	12.7	13.9	14.4	15.3	16.0	15.7	17.2	18.0	18.4	19.1
75	8.1	8.8	8.8	9.5	10.1	10.6	11.2	11.7	11.9	12.1

Second, the relationship between life expectancies of the total population compared with never-smokers or smokers varies from one education level to another because of the compositional effects discussed above. Consider first males with less than a high school education. The life expectancy at age 25 of a never-smoker is about 4.6 years longer than average for all males with less than a high school education while for current smokers it is about 5.3 years less. On the other hand, corresponding differences for males with a graduate education are 1.8 years longer for never-smokers and 6.2 years shorter for current smokers. Similar patterns exist for females, but the differences are smaller and smoking is associated with a smaller relative reduction in life expectancy across all education levels. For instance considering females with less than a high school education, the life

expectancy of never-smokers at age 25 is about 2.3 years longer than average while that of current smokers is about 4.1 years shorter. For females with graduate degrees, the differences are about 1.8 and 3.8 years, respectively.

Third, at least part of the difference in life expectancies between males and females is explained by smoking patterns—prevalence, duration, degree of inhalation, etc. For instance, the difference in life expectancies between the two sexes at age 25 for all persons with less than a high school education is 5.6 years. This gap narrows to 3.6 years when only never-smokers are compared. Conversely, it widens to 6.2 years for current smokers (males smoke more cigarettes, inhale more deeply, and on average have smoked more years). For those with a graduate education, the differences are 2.8 years (all persons), 2.8 years (never-smokers), and 5.2 years (current smokers).

Text Table 26: Age specific life expectancies by daily consumption of cigarettes, all races, 2004, CPS II relative risk factors applied to 2004 mortality rates

Age	Males					Females				
	< HS	HS	Some Col	Col	Grad	< HS	HS	Some Col	Col	Grad
Light Smokers (1 to 19 cigarettes per day)										
25	45.1	48.0	49.0	50.9	52.0	51.2	54.4	55.6	56.5	57.3
35	36.0	38.7	39.4	41.1	42.3	41.6	44.7	45.8	46.7	47.6
45	27.2	29.5	30.2	31.9	32.9	32.5	35.3	36.3	37.1	38.0
55	20.2	21.9	22.5	23.8	24.7	24.2	26.4	27.3	28.0	28.7
65	13.7	14.8	15.3	16.2	16.8	16.8	18.4	19.1	19.5	20.2
75	8.7	9.3	9.4	10.0	10.7	11.8	12.4	12.8	13.1	13.2
Medium Smokers (20 cigarettes per day)										
25	42.9	45.9	46.9	49.0	50.0	48.2	51.5	52.6	53.6	54.4
35	33.8	36.5	37.3	39.2	40.3	38.6	41.8	42.8	43.8	44.7
45	25.8	28.1	28.8	30.4	31.5	29.5	32.4	33.3	34.1	35.1
55	18.5	20.2	20.8	22.1	22.9	21.4	23.7	24.5	25.3	25.9
65	12.2	13.3	13.9	14.7	15.4	14.5	16.0	16.7	17.1	17.8
75	7.6	8.3	8.3	9.0	9.6	9.6	10.1	10.5	10.8	11.0
Heavy Smokers (more than 20 cigarettes per day)										
25	42.3	45.4	46.4	48.5	49.5	47.1	50.5	51.6	52.7	53.6
35	33.2	36.0	36.8	38.8	39.8	37.4	40.8	41.8	42.8	43.8
45	25.3	27.7	28.4	30.1	31.1	28.4	31.5	32.4	33.2	34.3
55	18.3	20.0	20.6	21.9	22.8	20.6	23.0	23.7	24.5	25.2
65	12.2	13.3	13.8	14.7	15.4	14.1	15.6	16.4	16.8	17.6
75	7.5	8.1	8.2	8.9	9.4	9.1	9.7	10.2	10.5	10.8

Age-specific life expectancies are presented in Text Table 26 for "light" smokers (less than 20 cigarettes per day), "medium" smokers (20 per day), and "heavy" smokers (more than 20 per day). When consumption levels are included in the analyses of the previous paragraph, the differences in life expectancies between male and female smokers are even smaller. For example, for "heavy" smokers the difference between life expectancies of males versus females with less than a high school education is 4.7 years compared to 5.6 years for all smokers (at age 25). At the graduate level, the difference reduces to 4.1 years compared to 2.8 years for all smokers.

Differences between life expectancies of "medium" and "heavy" smokers appear to be relatively small in Text Table 26. This, however, is mostly a factor of the small number of "very heavy" smokers within the "heavy" category. The relative risks associated with the highest levels of cigarette consumption for both males and females are markedly higher than at the medium level (approximately 25% higher for males and nearly 50% higher for females). Unfortunately, the samples are too small to derive statistically significant mortality data at the highest consumption levels.

6.6 Former Smokers

Life tables are not developed here for former smokers. On average, their life expectancies differ only slightly from those of the total population. For an individual, though, relative risk depends on the joint effects of the duration of prior smoking, the number of cigarettes consumed per day, depth of inhalation, and the length of time since cessation of smoking.

Based on data from the U.S. Veterans study, male smokers do not experience any appreciable reduction in risk for the first five years after cessation (NIH, 1997). After 20 years of nonsmoking, previous light smokers attain mortality rates about 10% greater than those of never-smokers. Previous very heavy smokers reduce their risk from more than 300% that of never-smokers at the time of quitting down to about 40% greater after 20 years. Results of other epidemiological studies show similar patterns for females.

6.7 Confounding Factors

The final question to be addressed is whether impairments in health resulting from a given consumption pattern are stable across demographic and socioeconomic characteristics. This was the assumption in all the life expectancies by smoking status and education derived for these tables. For instance, it was assumed that male smokers with a graduate degree experience the same biological effects from smoking as do male smokers with very little education.

Thun (ibid.) examined this question. A multivariate analysis of the CPS-II data which adjusted for occupation (blue collar vs. white collar), marital status, race, education, and various lifestyle and dietary patterns showed that "adjusting the RR [relative risk] estimates associated with cigarette smoking for multiple other demographic and behavioral characteristics had minimal impact on the RR estimates adjusted only for age [and sex]." Thus the assumption that relative risks are stable across education levels for similar consumption patterns appears to be relatively robust.

Relative risk analyses and life tables can theoretically be developed for whites, blacks, and Hispanics by smoking status. However, black and Hispanic smokers consume fewer cigarettes per day than whites do, and it is probable that their "current smoker" relative risks (without cross-tabulating by number of cigarettes smoked) would be somewhat less than average for all races. Because prevalence by age and education needs to be known, development of life tables by smoking status for blacks and Hispanics will have to wait for much larger, or race specific, epidemiological studies. In the interim, the following method is suggested to scale race and Hispanic estimates by smoking status.

6.8 Estimates by Race

Life expectancies by race or ethnicity and smoking status can be closely estimated using the following steps: (1) determine the appropriate life expectancy for the specific sex, race, and education, (2) subtract the estimate regardless of smoking status from the estimate by smoking status for all races combined (when known use estimates by daily consumption), and (3) add this difference to the result obtained in step 1.

Assume a 45-year-old, white, high school educated male is a heavy smoker. His life expectancy, regardless of smoking status, is an additional 33.4 years. The life expectancy at age 45 for a high school educated male *of all races* regardless of smoking status is an additional 33.2 years whereas for a heavy smoker it is 27.7. Thus the estimated life expectancy for the heavy smoking, white male is an additional 27.9 years {33.4 + (27.7 − 33.2) = 27.9}.

When information on the daily consumption level of the person in question is not known, estimates derived from scaling will probably be quite good for whites (since they compose such a high percentage of the total population). However, results for blacks and Hispanics may or may not be so reliable.

Compared to males of all races, black males have a slightly higher prevalence of smoking and of low educational attainment. Scaling provides reliable estimates for blacks to the extent that their higher incidence of smoking is correlated with their educational composition. If composition totally accounts for higher prevalences of smoking, then scaling produces good estimates. If black males smoke more at all education levels, scaled estimates for smokers are too low and for nonsmokers, they are too high. The opposite is true for black females, but the effects would be quite small because the prevalence of black female smokers is only slightly less than for the population as a whole.

Interestingly, Hispanics have the lowest prevalence of smokers *and* the lowest educational composition. Therefore, scaling which does not account for daily consumption levels probably overestimates the life expectancies of Hispanic smokers and underestimates the life expectancies of Hispanics who have never smoked. Sufficient data is not available to refine the procedure precisely, but the prevalence of smokers in the male Hispanic population is about the average of the prevalence of smokers in the some-college and college educated portion of the general population. For Hispanic females it is approximately the same as the prevalence of all races college educated females. It might be preferable, therefore, to scale Hispanic estimates by the smoking status differences that exist within these educational categories for all races.

Notes

1. Because health risks associated with cigarette smoking are greater and have been more accurately quantified than those resulting from use of cigars and smokeless tobacco products, this chapter deals only with the mortality effects of cigarette use. Cigars and smokeless tobacco, however, *are* associated with increased mortality rates from cancers and other nicotine-induced diseases (NIH Pub No 86-2874). For example, a recent study showed that cigar smoking increases a man's risk of coronary heart disease by about 30% and roughly doubles the probability of developing cancer in the mouth, throat, esophagus, or lungs (Iribarren et al., 1999). Although not negligible, it should be noted that these risks are only a half (heart disease) to a tenth (lung cancer) of those associated with cigarette smoking.

2. The CPS-II contains data for the age category 30–34, but they were not used in this study because the low number of deaths in some smoking categories caused unreliable mortality rate estimates.

3. For ages prior to 60, the prevalence of each of these categories is approximately as follows: half of male smokers were in the "heavy" category and the remainder were about equally divided between "light" and "medium"; females were equally proportioned among all three categories. After age 60, the percentage in the "light" class grows increasingly larger for both sexes with most of the reduction occurring in the "heavy" category.

Part II: Duration of Working Life

Chapter 7

Introduction to Estimates of Working Life

Estimates of working life are the counterpart to the various measures of life expectancy except that, rather than estimating the number of years of remaining life, they estimate the cumulative duration of remaining activity in the labor force.

Estimates of working life duration can be broken into two broad categories: (1) those that attempt to describe the period during which a person is *capable* of working (capacity), and (2) those that attempt to describe the period during which an average person could be *expected* to be working (expectancy). In general terms, capacity assumes continuous participation until some date of final exit, while expectancy reduces the period of working life to account for the amount of time that the *average* person is not in the labor force. Even though in many jurisdictions capacity is the legal measure to be used, nearly three quarters of forensic economists usually use expectancy measures.

7.1 Capacity

At the extreme, worklife capacity would be equal to life expectancy minus non-voluntary absences from the labor force. However, capacity is almost universally given a stricter interpretation—usually the number of uninterrupted years until retirement. The most commonly used measures of capacity are as follows:[1]

- The number of years to a designated retirement age: This might be the normal age of retirement in defined benefit pension plans, an age for Social Security benefits, or a person's intended retirement age.
- Median years to final separation from the labor force: First developed by Richard Nelson (1983), this is the number of years that elapse until one half

of those in the base age would have become separated from the labor force for good. Whereas Nelson used cross-sectional information, Smith (1985) derived median years to separation based on transition probabilities using the Markov model.

- Mean years to final separation from the labor force: Frasca and Winger (1989) criticized the median years to final separation method for, among other reasons, not providing information on the number of years of accrued earning capacity before or after the median age of final separation. Mean years to final separation, which rectifies this problem, differs slightly from the median years to final separation method, being less at younger ages and more at older ages. Skoog and Ciecka (2003) have updated and expanded on these methods extensively (see Chapter 13).

The first of these capacity measures is developed according to individual characteristics of the person in question. The second and third are based on statistical data.

7.2 Expectancy

Expectancy is also variously described. In general, expectancy attempts to estimate the total number of years that the *average* person (by sex, race, education, etc.) *would actually be in the labor force*. The most common measures of expectancy are briefly described below. The first of these implicitly assumes, as do capacity measures, that all periods of inactivity will occur at the end of the worklife period rather than at various times during the interval. This assumption usually results in overestimates of the net present value of losses because all earnings are assumed to occur when discounting is least heavy. All the other expectancy measures spread inactivity across all ages.

- Worklife expectancy: Worklife expectancy tables provide the number of years, from the base age, that the average person would spend in the labor

2

force. Labor force activity is assumed to occur continuously with no periods of inactivity. Worklife expectancies have been presented in a decades-long series of Bureau of Labor Statistics tables. Initially basing the tables on what in this book is called the "conventional" model, the BLS switched in the early 1980s to the "increment-decrement" model because it improved some of the estimates. Ciecka, Donley and Goldman (1995, 1997, and 2000) updated "increment-decrement" tables using 1992–93, 1994–95, and 1997-98 data. Ciecka, Donley, Epstein and Goldman (1998) have also modified increment-decrement tables by incorporating mortality rates by smoking status. Skoog (2001), Skoog and Ciecka (2004), Krueger (2004) and Krueger et al. (2006) have extended the analysis of the increment-decrement model to include multiple statistics on worklife expectancies, to examine full-time and part-time, incorporate inter-year labor force status, etc. Milliment et al. (2003) derived worklife expectancies (defined narrowly as only periods of actually working) using an econometric analysis of March Annual Demographic Surveys in the CPS. This book uses 2000–2006 CPS monthly data and incorporates mortality rates by educational attainment. Chapter 8 describes estimates derived using the Markov Model. Chapters 9–11 discuss "conventional" model tables that incorporate the effects of education, Hispanic status, and smoking behavior.

- Modified Worklife Expectancy: Earnings are evenly distributed over the years remaining until final separation from the labor force by assigning to each year a probability of being in the labor force equal to the number of years of worklife expectancy divided by the years to final separation (Boudreaux, 1983).
- Year-by-Year Losses: Losses in each year of remaining life are calculated using a formula that accounts for probabilities of survival and transition into and out of the labor force at the midpoint of each age (Becker and Alter, 1985).
- Simplified Year-by-Year Losses: Similar to Year-by-Year Losses but reduces the complexity of the formula by assuming that all changes occur at the beginning of the year.
- Life–Participation–Employment (LPE): The LPE method calculates earnings for each age, adjusting for the joint probabilities of living through that age (L), of participating in the labor force (P), and of being employed (E) [Chapter 12].

7.3 Choice of Tables

In addition to capacity/expectancy distinctions, there may be more than one table from which one can obtain a worklife expectancy estimate for an individual. For example, one might choose between a number of methodologies such as increment-decrement, conventional, LPE, and so forth for the expectancy measures. If we restrict ourselves to increment-decrement tables, we can use a table based on all active males, on active white males, or on active college-educated males. Some considerations include:

Match of cohort to individual: Data for an individual should be derived from the table most representative of the person's characteristics. For instance, data *should always be race/Hispanic origin and education specific*. In some instances, other characteristics might be quite important. Disability status, especially of those severely disabled, is a strong determinant of working behavior. Smoking status can also have significant impacts on worklife expectancies. Note, however, that estimates based on small sample sizes may have large standard errors, and confounding factors may reduce the reliability of both life and worklife estimates by smoking status for black and Hispanics.

Reliability of the sampled data to represent future trends (i.e. stability of the data): If there are strong indications that the sampled data for a subgroup of the population will not reflect their future experience, it might be preferable to use a larger, aggregated group. This issue is discussed at length in Chapter 15.

Reliability of the sampled data to represent a specific individual: As with life expectancies, education works as a proxy for various factors that influence worklife expectancies. Some individuals certainly are not well-represented by educational worklife expectancies.

Standard error: If the sample size is too small, the standard errors could become large enough to eliminate the advantages of using a model based on a small subpopulation.

Poorly defined cohort: Characteristics such as race and sex do not change over a lifetime, but other characteristics are less fixed. Examples are smoking status, not being disabled, English language proficiency of Hispanics, etc. Estimates based on characteristics that are not stable might potentially have problems. Significant crossover within the observed samples from one status to another may bias estimates; samples may not represent working patterns that will remain stable into the future. The practitioner has to be aware that using these data carries the implicit assumption that the individual in question will not change to another status.

The following chapters examine various estimates and aspects of duration of working life. Chapter 8 deals with the "increment-decrement" worklife expectancy model. Chapters 9 through 11 describe "conventional" model estimates, which deal with the effects of characteristics such as detailed educational levels, Hispanic origin, and smoking status. Chapter 12 discusses the LPE model. This is followed by the only capacity measure presented in this book—a chapter on mean years to retirement.

The concluding chapters examine other topics affecting the duration of working life. Chapter 14 deals with a variety of issues: capacity versus expectancy, female labor force patterns, disability, and possible trends in future labor force participation. Strengths and weaknesses of some of the methodologies are presented in Chapter 15. Finally, Chapter 15 also develops and compares some sample earnings estimates using each of the methodologies described above.

Notes

1. The various measures of duration of working life below are those described in "A Survey of the Structure and Duration of Time Periods for Lost Earnings Calculations," by James Ciecka (1994). Mathematical formulas for present values of estimated earnings are in Chapter 15.

Chapter 8

Increment-Decrement Worklife Expectancies

8.1 Introduction

"Worklife expectancy" is usually defined as the statistically average remaining years of participation in the labor force for a person of given age and demographic characteristics. Participation includes a) those who are working plus b) those who are unemployed but either expecting to be called back to work or actively seeking employment, i.e., those who are described by the BLS as being "in the labor force."

In "real life," many people take breaks from periods of employment to further their education, raise families, recuperate from severe illnesses, or temporarily drop out for other voluntary and involuntary reasons. Worklife expectancies, however, combine all expected periods of future participation into a single number. This "front-loads" estimates of earnings losses somewhat, and, through the effects of discounting, causes moderate overestimation of losses, especially for persons without an established history of strong labor force attachment (see Chapter 15). Worklife expectancies are easy to use, though, and avoid significant computational complications that can exist in some expectancy measures when retirement benefits are included. Furthermore, they are easily understood by juries. Consequently, they are used by a much higher percentage of forensic economists than any of the other alternatives for estimating duration of working life: 54% used worklife expectancies, 13% used a fixed time period, 11% used LPE, and 21% used a combination of these methods (Brookshire et al., 2006).

Three main methods have been used to derive worklife expectancies—the increment-decrement (Markov) model, what is called the conventional model in this book, and an econometric approach. The conventional and increment-decrement models are developed in this book: each has strengths, and they can complement each other. This chapter deals with increment-decrement model estimates; the next, with the conventional model. Worklife expectancies derived from the econometric approach are discussed in an article by Daniel Millimet et al. (Millimet et al., 2003). Worklife expectancies for various categories of disabled persons are presented in *The New Worklife Expectancy Tables* (Gamboa and Gibson, 2006). It is important to note that the Millimet and Gamboa worklife expectancies are defined differently than most others in that they exclude periods of unemployment. Also Gamboa's tables have come under criticism by some in the forensic economic community over the question of whether the CPS captures usable disability labor force data (See Chapter 15).

8.2 Data and Methodology

Upon its introduction by the BLS in 1982, the increment-decrement methodology became the accepted standard. It has advantages over the conventional model in that, being based on dynamic changes in labor force participation patterns, it provides better estimates for populations which enter and leave the labor force often (for example, females). It also allows explicit estimation of worklife expectancies of those initially "active" or "inactive" as of the date of injury, death, etc.

Briefly, increment-decrement estimates are derived from the rates of change (transition probabilities) between three states: being economically active (being in the labor force), being economically inactive, and leaving the population through death. A cohort at any given age experiences change as it moves to the next age. Some who were initially active remain active, and some become inactive. Some who were initially inactive remain inactive, and some become active. And some from both groups die and are removed from the population. The proportion of those who are active in the second period (i.e., the next year of age) depends on the rates of change between the various states. This process continues in the model as the cohort moves through each subsequent age until it reaches the end of any significant labor force activity (or the age at which data are no longer available). Worklife expectancies are derived from the cumulative pattern of labor force involvement.

A detailed description of the increment-decrement methodology and its advantages compared with the older "conventional" methodology can be found in Smith (1982 and 1986), Foster and Skoog (2004), and Skoog and Ciecka (2004). In recent years research has expanded the amount of statistical information that can be derived from this model. Skoog and Ciecka used probability mass functions to derive mean, mode, median, standard deviation, skewness, kurtosis, and probability intervals for worklife expectancies (2001a and b); they show that the conventional and LPE models are also Markov models with restricted transition probabilities (2004); they use the model to determine the amount of working life a railroad worker might spend in this occupation versus moving to other occupations (2006a); and they provide information to assist in correcting for the "front-loading" bias of worklife expectancies (2006b). Krueger published data to assist the calculation of labor force participation probabilities by age so that lifetime earnings can better be estimated, and he also provides an excellent discussion of the history of life and worklife tables and the source of the data used to derive labor force transition rates (2004). Krueger, Skoog, and Ciecka explored issues of part-time and full-time in regard to worklife expectancies (2006).

The primary purpose of this book is to provide worklife expectancy and standard error tables. It derives these data using the methodology suggested by Smith and the bootstrap technique (see below for a more detailed description of these calculations).

A. Data

Two types of data at each age are necessary to develop increment-decrement worklife expectancies. One is rates of change between states of labor market activity. The other is mortality. Together they describe the possible "transition probabilities." Because mortality rates are more straightforward, they are discussed first.

Most increment-decrement worklife tables have been derived using mortality rates specific only to age, sex, and race. This analysis also incorporates mortality rates by educational attainment and by Hispanic ethnicity. These rates

are derived from the *Vital Statistics of the United States, 1994 Life Tables*, and from Bureau of the Census, Demographic Statistical Methods Division data, based on the National Longitudinal Mortality Study. Detailed descriptions of data sources and methodology can be found in Chapter 4.

Data for labor activity transition probabilities are derived from the Current Population Survey (CPS). The CPS gathers a wide range of socioeconomic data, including demographic, educational, and labor force characteristics from the civilian, non-institutionalized population. It is a rotating, monthly survey of 50,000 residences (rather than individuals). Each month, a new set of residences, comprising one twelfth of the 50,000, is added to the sample. Inhabitants are interviewed for four consecutive months, left alone for eight months, interviewed again for another four consecutive months, and then dropped from the sample. Thus, a year separates the first and second set of interviews for each residence.

Transition probabilities are derived only for people who remain in the survey from one year to the next. Because the survey follows residences rather than people, it is possible that the follow-up data of the second four-month period do not represent the same people originally surveyed. Therefore, it is necessary to restrict the sample to persons who can be matched from one year to the next. Matched samples are derived using an algorithm which compares household identification number, household serial prefix, household replacement number, person line number, sex, age (from no change to plus two), sampling month, year, and education. Transition probabilities are calculated between month-in-sample four (MIS4) and month-in-sample eight (MIS8) for two reasons: 1) the person weighting factors in MIS4 and MIS8 represent the U.S. population better than the other MIS samples, and 2) they have the smallest month-in-sample biases compared with the other MIS matches (see Chapter 15).

B. Period of Data Observation

The period over which data are observed has always been an important issue. As Shirley Smith wrote:

> The multistate working life table model is extremely sensitive to rapid changes in rates of labor force entry or withdrawal. Tables based on a recessionary period, during which labor force exits increase, present a very bleak picture of lifetime labor force involvement. Conversely, those calculated during periods of rapid recovery or expansion tend to overstate the average degree of lifetime labor force attachment. (1986)

Thus, increment-decrement worklife expectancies should be derived using data from periods which represent "normal" periods of economic activity, periods during which changes in participation are representative of historical patterns.

We have derived our transition probabilities from CPS surveys from July 1999 through June 2007. This was a period with both expansions and contractions. The long expansion of the 1990s was beginning to level out by 1999, reaching a peak in March 2001. The economy then contracted for half a year. The trough occurred in November 2001, following which the economy was relatively flat for about a year and a half and then expanded for the remainder of the period surveyed in this book. The length of the contraction in this period was less than the historical average since World War II (about 9.5% of this period versus 16.7% over the post World War II period), but the recovery following the trough in November 2001 was much more sluggish than usual, with nearly no expansion for over a year and then a smaller degree of expansion than normal.

In short, this period contains both expansions and contractions and is the most recent full business cycle. It is difficult to know at this time, however, whether it will turn out to be a good representation of future labor force patterns, producing accurate worklife expectancies.

This period of observation allows us to use data for seven full years. Those initially surveyed in the final six months of 1999 are resampled in the final six months of 2000, and those initially surveyed in the first six months of 2006 are resurveyed in the first six months of 2007. The only persons not captured are those initially surveyed in the final six months of 2006.

An advantage of using seven years is that the number of observations in the matched samples is large. The samples for this analysis consist of 319,431 males and 368,318 females eighteen years of age and older. Larger sample sizes generally reduce sampling errors and allow worklife expectancies to be derived for more population groups. Thus, increment-decrement worklife estimates by education are disaggregated into five groups for whites and for all races combined: less than high school, high school or GED, some college, bachelor's degree, and graduate degree. For Blacks four categories are estimated: less than high school, high school or GED, some college, and bachelor's degree and more. And for Hispanics three categories are estimated: less than high school, high school or GED, and some college and higher.

Note, however, that for blacks and Hispanics sample sizes at older ages are quite small and sampling errors are large. It is thus especially important for these groups to cross reference increment-decrement estimates with conventional estimates, and if large differences exist fall back on the conventional model estimates.

C. Transition Probabilities

Transition probabilities (p) for actives to actives and for inactives to inactives were derived from the matched BLS microdata samples. In each case, the weighted number of individuals who were observed to have remained in a given activity status was divided by the number initially observed in that status.

Within any cohort, let $^{a,i}N_x^{a,i}$ represent the weighted population who were active (a) or inactive (i) in both age x and $x + 1$, and let $^{a,i}N_x$ be the weighted population of actives (inactives) at time x. To adjust for the fact that reported ages in the CPS are on average a half year older than exact ages, transition probabilities for exact ages were calculated as the average of the reported age and a year younger. Thus:

$$^a p_x^a = \left[\left(\frac{^a N_x^a}{^a N_x}\right) + \left(\frac{^a N_{x-1}^a}{^a N_{x-1}}\right)\right] \div 2 \qquad (1)$$

(i.e., transition probabilities from active to active)

and

$$^i p_x^i = \left[\left(\frac{^i N_x^i}{^i N_x}\right) + \left(\frac{^i N_{x-1}^i}{^i N_{x-1}}\right)\right] \div 2 \qquad (2)$$

(i.e., transition probability from inactive to inactive).

These are conditional on survival from age x to $x + 1$ (the matched population from which they were derived consists only of people who did not die). As all people in an activity status in one period (who do not die) must either remain in the same status or switch to the opposite status in the next period, we can calculate the probabilities of transition from active to inactive and from inactive to active as follow:

$$^a p_x^i = 1 - {}^a p_x^a \quad \text{and} \quad ^i p_x^a = 1 - {}^i p_x^i \qquad (3)$$

Since the transition probabilities have some sampling variability from one age to the next, they were smoothed using running five-year unweighted averages. (Transition probabilities provided in Table 3, Part III represent only the relevant exact age; that is, they are not averages of several years.) For the most part, smoothing has little effect on worklife estimates; but, it eliminates some instances where one-year decreases in age would have had anomalous decreases in worklife expectancy.

The transition probabilities defined above were used in the Alter and Becker method to calculate worklife expectancies. As noted above, these transition probabilities are conditional on survival from one age to the next. Transition probabilities, however, are often shown inclusive of survival probabilities. Expressed mathematically, letting the transition probabilities above be $\cdot p_x^{\cdot}$, where the "·" can represent any activity status, then

$$^i p_x^a = {}^i p_x^{a'}(1 - p_x^d)$$
$$^i p_x^i = {}^i p_x^{i'}(1 - p_x^d)$$
$$^a p_x^i = {}^a p_x^{i'}(1 - p_x^d), \text{ and}$$
$$^a p_x^a = {}^a p_x^{a'}(1 - p_x^d)$$

For consistency with Smith in her BLS publications of 1982 and 1986, this is the way the 2000–2006 transition probabilities in Table 3, Part III, are presented.

D. Methodology for Calculating Worklife Expectancies

Two general methods are available to calculate increment-decrement worklife expectancies.

The first method, used by Smith (1982 and 1986) and by Ciecka et al. (1995, 1996 and 1997), uses transition probabilities to derive probabilities of being in the labor force during the initial and all subsequent ages. The stable living population at each age (found in life tables) is then multiplied by the probability of being in the labor force to determine person-years of labor force activity at that age (i.e., the stable active population). Stable active populations for the current and all subsequent ages are summed to derive total person-years of remaining activity as of the age. Finally, worklife expectancies are calculated as this total divided by the number of people alive at the beginning of the age.

The other method, proposed by Alter and Becker (1985), is similar to the first except that it uses mortality rates rather than stationary populations. The two methods are equivalent mathematically and provide identical estimates. The second method is used for this book.

Using the notations above for transition probabilities that are conditional on survival, and letting l_x represent the number of survivors at age x, the number of active and inactive survivors at age $x + 1$ (i.e., ${}^a l_{x+1}$ and ${}^i l_{x+1}$) can be defined as:

$$^i l_{x+1} = (1 - p_x^d)({}^i p_x^i \, {}^i l_x + {}^a p_x^i \, {}^a l_x)$$
$$\text{and} \tag{4}$$
$$^a l_{x+1} = (1 - p_x^d)({}^a p_x^a \, {}^a l_x + {}^i p_x^a \, {}^i l_x)$$

The conditions $l_x = {}^a l_x + {}^i l_x$ and $l_{x+1} = l_x(1 - p_x^d)$ hold, where $(1 - p_x^d)$ is the probability that the individual will survive from age x to age $x + 1$. In this analysis p_x^d is specific to sex, race/Hispanic origin, and education, and it is independent of labor force status.

Worklife expectancy (w) for persons at age x is calculated as:

$$w = \left(\frac{1}{l_x}\right)\sum_{n=0}^{m}[(1 - p_{x+n}^d)({}^a l_{x+n} \, {}^a p_{x+n}^a + 0.5\, {}^a l_{x+n} \, {}^a p_{x+n}^i + 0.5\, {}^i l_{x+n} \, {}^i p_{x+n}^a)$$
$$+ 0.5\, {}^a l_{x+n} \, {}^a p_{x+n}^d \tag{5}$$

where the cohort dies out after $x + m + 1$ years. For these tables, termination was assumed after age eighty-five. As a practical matter, continuation after this age, even if sample populations were large enough to perform the calculations, would make almost no difference in estimated worklife expectancies.

The above equation consists of four terms (excluding $1 - p_{x+n}^d$, which reduces the following three terms for mortality), each of which captures a portion of the probability of participation in any given year. The first three address persons who survive to the next year of age: the first refers to the accumulated active years of persons who remain active for the entire year between age $x + n$ and age $x + n + 1$, and the second and third terms refer to persons who move from active to inactive or from inactive to active status. The fourth term refers to persons who are active at the beginning of the year, but die during the year. The final three terms assume that transitions from one state to the other occur in the middle of the year and contribute half a year of activity.

Worklife expectancies for the active population are calculated assuming that ${}^a l_x$ comprised the total population at age x, and those for the inactive population are calculated assuming that ${}^i l_x$ comprised the total population at age x. In this analysis, the initial populations (${}^a l_x$ and ${}^i l_x$) were set at 100,000, but any other number could have been used without affecting the results.

Worklife expectancies for the general population were calculated as weighted averages of the active and inactive groups. Weighting factors were BLS rates of participation, r_x (for actives) and $1 - r_x$ (for inactives). Worklife expectancies for the general populations could alternatively be calculated using the methodology described above, where ${}^a l_x$ and ${}^i l_x$ would equal $l_x \times r_x$ and $l_x \times (1 - r_x)$, respectively.

Text Table 27: Effect of mortality rates by education on increment-decrement worklife expectancies, active males and females, all races and blacks, 2000-2006

Age	< HS	HS/ GED	Some College	College Degree	Grad Degreee	< HS	HS/ GED	Some College	College Degree +
	Males of All Races					Black Males			
	Mortality rates by education								
25	28.6	33.0	34.9	38.3	40.0	21.1	28.1	31.4	35.7
35	20.8	24.5	26.0	28.9	30.5	15.6	21.0	23.4	26.7
45	13.7	16.3	17.3	19.6	21.1	11.4	14.0	15.3	18.0
55	7.8	9.0	9.6	11.1	12.2	6.9	7.8	9.1	10.0
65	3.8	4.2	4.6	5.2	5.7	3.6	3.6	4.6	4.4
	Mortality rates for the total population								
25	29.5	33.2	34.7	37.2	38.5	21.8	28.0	30.7	33.9
35	21.5	24.6	25.9	28.1	29.3	16.1	20.8	23.0	25.4
45	14.2	16.3	17.1	19.0	20.1	11.7	13.9	15.0	17.1
55	8.0	9.0	9.5	10.7	11.7	7.0	7.7	8.9	9.5
65	3.9	4.1	4.5	5.0	5.4	3.6	3.6	4.6	4.1
	Amount of bias correction								
25	-0.9	-0.2	0.2	1.1	1.5	-0.6	0.1	0.7	1.8
35	-0.7	-0.1	0.2	0.8	1.2	-0.5	0.2	0.4	1.3
45	-0.4	-0.0	0.1	0.6	1.0	-0.3	0.2	0.3	1.0
55	-0.2	0.0	0.1	0.4	0.6	-0.1	0.1	0.2	0.5
65	-0.1	0.0	0.1	0.2	0.3	-0.0	0.0	0.0	0.3
	Females of All Races					Black Females			
	Mortality rates by education								
25	19.6	28.4	31.4	32.3	35.1	18.9	27.1	29.6	34.8
35	14.9	21.9	24.2	24.8	27.1	13.5	20.2	21.8	26.2
45	10.1	14.9	16.5	17.2	18.8	9.4	13.3	14.2	17.5
55	6.2	8.4	9.4	9.6	10.4	6.0	7.3	7.7	9.2
65	3.2	4.2	4.5	4.6	5.0	3.5	3.4	3.7	3.9
	Mortality rates for the total population								
25	19.9	28.4	31.2	31.8	34.6	19.3	27.0	29.2	34.0
35	15.2	21.9	24.0	24.4	26.5	13.8	20.1	21.3	25.4
45	10.3	14.8	16.3	16.9	18.3	9.6	13.2	13.9	17.0
55	6.3	8.3	9.3	9.4	10.1	6.1	7.3	7.6	9.0
65	3.3	4.2	4.4	4.5	4.9	3.6	3.4	3.6	3.8
	Amount of bias correction								
25	-0.3	0.0	0.2	0.4	0.6	-0.4	0.1	0.4	0.8
35	-0.3	0.0	0.2	0.4	0.6	-0.3	0.1	0.4	0.8
45	-0.2	0.0	0.2	0.3	0.5	-0.2	0.1	0.3	0.6
55	-0.1	0.0	0.1	0.2	0.3	-0.1	0.1	0.1	0.3
65	-0.0	0.0	0.1	0.1	0.1	-0.0	0.0	0.1	0.1

NOTE: Estimates for blacks may have large sampling errors because of very small sample sizes.

8.3 Results and Discussion
A. Worklife Expectancies by Education
Worklife is directly correlated with education, i.e., as educational attainment increases so does worklife expectancy (Text Table 27). For instance, at age 25, initially active males with less than a high school education have worklife expectancies of 28.6 years; those with a high school degree have worklife expectancies of 33.0 years; and so on, until worklife expectancies are 40.0 years for those with a graduate degree. This is a range of 11.4 years from the least to most educated groups. Worklife expectancies of females show an even stronger direct relationship with education. Those with a graduate degree have worklife expectancies which are 15.5 years longer than those with less than a high school education. Differences between individual education levels also vary by sex. The greatest increase in worklife expectancy for both sexes occurs with attainment of a high school degree: 4.4 years for males and 8.8 years for females, at age 25. From high school to graduate educational levels, the sexes have nearly equal ranges, but the jump is larger for males from some college to a college degree, while the jump from a bachelor's to a graduate degree is larger for females.

Estimates for blacks were derived for inclusion in Text Table 27 so that several issues could be examined. As noted above, sample sizes by educational attainment are quite small. This is especially true for black males, whose sample sizes are about 4,900 for less than high school, 9,100 for high school, 6,300 for some college and 4,000 for bachelor's or more. For females samples range from approximately a 33% to 55% higher, i.e., 6,500, 12,000, 9,900, and 6,100, respectively. These estimates therefore are subject to large sampling errors. See Appendix Table 3.

With this caveat in mind, worklife expectancies for blacks are also directly correlated with education. At age 25, for example, the worklife expectancy of initially active black males with less than a high school education is 21.1 years; with a high school degree, 28.1; with some college education, 31.4 years; and with a college degree or more, 35.7 years. The fact that this range (14.5 years) is greater than that for all males highlights the importance of using education-specific worklife expectancies for blacks. A similar pattern occurs for black females, except that their worklife expectancies differ but little from those of all females. Similarly, the range between education levels is about the same as for all females.

B. Effect of Mortality Rates by Educational Attainment
Text Table 27 also provides data to show the effects of using mortality rates by education. Most increment-decrement worklife expectancies have been derived using mortality rates for the general population. As discussed in Chapter 4, however, mortality rates are not constant across educational levels, but instead are indirectly related. Thus, increment-decrement worklife expectancies calculated using mortality rates for the total population are biased for many educational groups—upward for those with less than a high school education, downward for well-educated persons.

Several patterns are apparent. First, as expected, bias corrections are directly related to educational attainment. Worklife expectancies of those with the least education are decreased, and expectancies of those with the most education are increased. Bias corrections are relatively large at the highest and lowest educational levels, and they are small to negligible for modal educational categories. For example, incorporating mortality by education reduces worklife expectancies of initially active males of all races with less than a high school education by almost a year at age 25; it increases expectancies of males with a graduate degree by a year and a half; but it has almost no effect on worklife expectancies of those with a high school or some college education. Similar patterns exist for blacks.

Second, bias corrections are larger for males than for females. For example, estimates at age 25 for initially active males with a graduate degree are increased 1.5 years through incorporation of mortality by education, but estimates for females are increased only 0.6 years. This follows the pattern that mortality rates vary much more across educational categories for males than for females.

C. Weighted Averages, Bias, and Estimates for All Education Levels Combined
The importance of using educationally weighted averages for derivation of estimates for total populations was discussed in Chapter 4 in regard to life expectancies. The situation is analogous for worklife expectancies, i.e., estimates derived from aggregate data are biased downward.

Text Table 28 shows that weighted averaging corrects biases for females of all races more than for males of all races and that the reverse pertains to blacks. Further, bias corrections are more for blacks. Referring back to Chapter 4, the amount of bias correction resulting from educational weighting depends primarily upon two factors: the differences of worklife estimates across educational categories and the differences in educational composition of the population across age cohorts.

The data shown in Text Tables 27 and 28 are important for several reasons. First, worklife is highly correlated with education, and estimates by educational attainment should be used whenever possible. Second, worklife estimates for total populations derived from aggregated data are biased, the extent of which cannot reliably be established for some populations. And third, worklife expectancies for populations aggregated across all education levels can be driven down (or, theoretically, up) solely by educational composition characteristics of the population. Although these factors are of little consequence for all races and whites, for whom sample sizes are large enough to calculate estimates by education, they are important for blacks and Hispanics. Worklife expectancies for some educational categories for these groups cannot be accurately estimated, and estimates for total populations are biased. To ignore these problems is to estimate duration of working life incorrectly. This issue is addressed in Chapter 15.

D. Historic Trends in Worklife Expectancies

A selected history of increment-decrement worklife expectancies by educational attainment from their earliest publication by Smith (using 1979-1980 data) to those published in this book is presented in Text Table 29(a). Most of these estimates are not directly comparable, however, because the researchers have used different educational definitions or, in the case of data generated by Richards (1999) and in this publication, the worklife expectancies incorporate mortality rates by education.

Text Table 28: Bias reduction by use of educationally weighted averages, increment-decrement model, all races and blacks, 2000-2006

Age	Wgt Ave	Aggr'd Data		Wgt Ave	Aggr'd Data	
		All	Bias		All	Bias
	Males of All Races			Black Males		
25	34.5	34.3	0.2	29.4	28.4	0.9
35	25.7	25.6	0.2	21.7	21.0	0.7
45	17.0	16.8	0.1	13.9	13.4	0.5
55	9.1	8.7	0.3	7.2	6.7	0.5
65	2.7	2.649	0.1	2.1	2.0	0.1
	Females of All Races			Black Females		
25	29.4	28.9	0.5	28.3	27.7	0.6
35	22.2	21.8	0.4	20.7	20.1	0.6
45	14.8	14.5	0.3	13.2	12.7	0.5
55	7.541	7.242	0.3	6.3	6.0	0.2
65	1.930	1.896	0.0	1.601	1.509	0.1

Note: Biases for blacks are approximate due to very small sample sizes by educational attainment.

Text Table 29(b) attempts to make the estimates more comparable. High school and some college worklives for both Smith and Ciecka et al. are approximated from their aggregated estimates by assuming the same relationship existed between them as existed in the 1996-98 estimates for high school and some college categories. Where appropriate, college and graduate degree expectancies are combined, and all estimates are based on non-education specific mortality rates.

It appears that worklife expectancies of males decreased during the 1980s, with the exception of those with high school or some college education, which appear to have increased a little at younger ages. Worklife expectancies for most females increased fairly substantially. However, expectancies for females with less than a high school education decreased on the order of about one year.

Between 1992-93 and 1996-98 the pattern for males was reversed, i.e., expectancies for those with less than a high school education and those with at least a college degree increased, and the two middle educational groups decreased. Females experienced a similar pattern, i.e., increases for the least and best educated and decreases for the middle educational categories. It should be noted, though, that these comparisons are rough approximations. Both the Smith and Ciecka et al. estimates were derived from quite small sample sizes—vulnerable to sampling error and to possible biases resulting from the economic conditions during the years surveyed.

The more recent analyses indicate increasing worklife expectancies for almost all groups. Krueger's estimates using 1998-2004 data were greater than Richards' using 1996-98. The estimates in this publication are within tenths of a year of Krueger, with the exception of young females without a high school degree which are almost a year less.

In summary, assuming that the early estimates are not substantially biased by small sample sizes or abnormal economic conditions, worklife expectancies for males decreased between 1979-80 and 1996-98, and in general for females they increased. It appears that worklife expectancies for both sexes and all educational categories have subsequently increased. Note, though, that some of this apparent increase may be due to the use of different month-in-sample matches (see Chapter 15).

Text Table 29 (a): Historical trends of increment-decrement worklife expectancies, initially active

Age	< HS	HS	Some College	College Degree	Grad Degree	< HS	HS	Some College	College Degree	Grad Degree
	Males					Females				
1979-1980 Data (Smith, 1986)										
25	29.80	34.10		36.60		18.90	25.30		28.60	
35	22.00	25.40		27.70		14.80	19.20		21.70	
45	14.30	16.80		18.80		10.50	13.00		14.40	
55	7.50	9.00		10.70		6.30	7.70		7.80	
65	3.60	4.30		5.40		3.50	4.00		4.10	
1992-1993 Data (Ciecka, Donley and Goldman, 1995)										
25	26.70	34.70		35.70		17.90	29.10		31.80	
35	19.80	26.10		26.90		14.00	22.20		23.90	
45	13.00	17.40		17.90		9.70	15.10		15.80	
55	7.00	9.10		9.60		5.50	8.50		7.90	
65	3.30	4.00		4.50		3.20	3.60		3.10	
1996-1998 Data (Richards, 1999)										
25	27.49	32.79	34.13	37.01	39.38	19.96	27.89	30.07	31.54	34.69
35	19.97	24.09	25.27	27.83	30.16	14.82	20.94	22.43	23.91	26.57
45	13.20	15.94	16.60	18.63	20.74	9.90	13.82	14.52	15.88	18.14
55	7.05	8.51	8.84	10.01	11.90	6.01	7.31	7.52	8.05	9.78
65	3.34	3.77	4.17	4.28	6.13	2.93	3.18	3.28	3.51	4.36
1998-2004 Data (Krueger, 2005)										
25	29.49	32.86	34.44	37.53		20.82	28.67	31.22	32.58	
35	21.53	24.34	25.59	28.45		15.73	21.88	23.79	24.87	
45	14.38	16.06	16.88	19.41		10.57	14.76	16.14	17.08	
55	8.11	8.73	9.24	11.00		6.35	8.16	9.19	9.31	
65	3.85	3.98	4.28	5.11		3.30	4.15	4.35	4.37	
2000-2006 Data (Richards and Donaldson, this publication)										
25	28.62	32.98	34.89	38.26	39.98	19.60	28.39	31.43	32.27	35.12
35	20.80	24.55	26.01	28.92	30.53	14.89	21.92	24.16	24.83	27.08
45	13.75	16.28	17.26	19.65	21.01	10.14	14.89	16.49	17.18	18.77
55	7.78	9.01	9.63	11.08	12.24	6.19	8.37	9.44	9.59	10.40
65	3.84	4.16	4.59	5.18	5.69	3.22	4.21	4.48	4.59	5.02

Data are not directly comparable. Smith combined two years of college with high school for one category and everything above for the highest educational category. Ciecka, Donley, and Goldman combined high school with some college, and bachelor's and graduate degrees. Krueger combined bachelor's and graduate degrees. Only the expectancies by Richards (1999) and those in this publication incorporate mortality rates by educational attainment.

Text Table 29 (b): Historical trends of increment-decrement worklife expectancies, currently active, data interpolated to four educational categories with none using educational mortality rates

Age	< HS	HS	Some College	College Degree	< HS	HS	Some College	College Degree
	Males				Females			
1979-1980 Data (Smith, 1986)								
25	29.80	33.55	34.69	36.60	18.90	24.29	26.20	28.60
35	22.00	24.84	25.94	27.70	14.80	18.53	19.83	21.70
45	14.30	16.50	17.10	18.80	10.50	12.70	13.35	14.40
55	7.50	8.88	9.17	10.70	6.30	7.62	7.84	7.80
65	3.60	4.14	4.55	5.40	3.50	3.97	4.06	4.10
1992-1993 Data (Ciecka, Donley and Goldman, 1995)								
25	26.70	34.14	35.31	35.70	17.90	27.94	30.14	31.80
35	19.80	25.52	26.65	26.90	14.00	21.42	22.93	23.90
45	13.00	17.09	17.71	17.90	9.70	14.76	15.51	15.80
55	7.00	8.98	9.27	9.60	5.50	8.41	8.66	7.90
65	3.30	3.85	4.23	4.50	3.20	3.58	3.65	3.10
1996-1998 Data (Richards, 1999)								
25	28.36	32.79	33.92	36.19	20.25	27.79	29.97	31.56
35	20.56	24.08	25.14	27.62	15.04	20.86	22.33	24.41
45	13.55	15.88	16.45	18.81	10.04	13.74	14.45	16.55
55	7.20	8.45	8.73	10.38	6.08	7.27	7.47	8.59
65	3.40	3.74	4.11	4.82	2.95	3.17	3.24	3.76
1998-2004 Data (Krueger, 2005)								
25	29.49	32.86	34.44	37.53	20.82	28.67	31.22	32.58
35	21.53	24.34	25.59	28.45	15.73	21.88	23.79	24.87
45	14.38	16.06	16.88	19.41	10.57	14.76	16.14	17.08
55	8.11	8.73	9.24	11.00	6.35	8.16	9.19	9.31
65	3.85	3.98	4.28	5.11	3.30	4.15	4.35	4.37
2000-2006 Data (Richards and Donaldson, this publication)								
25	29.55	33.15	34.66	37.35	19.93	28.37	31.22	32.23
35	21.46	24.64	25.85	28.47	15.16	21.88	23.97	25.08
45	14.19	16.32	17.12	19.40	10.32	14.85	16.34	17.33
55	7.98	8.99	9.53	11.11	6.28	8.33	9.35	9.72
65	3.91	4.15	4.52	5.21	3.26	4.19	4.43	4.65

Data for high school and some college categories for Smith and Ciecka et al., assume same relationship as exist in Richards, 1999. College degree for Smith still includes all persons with more than 14 year education.

Chapter 9

Conventional Model Worklife Estimates by Education

9.1 Introduction

The previous chapter of this book discussed worklife expectancies derived from the increment-decrement methodology. This chapter discusses worklife expectancies derived from an older methodology, in this book to be labeled the "conventional" model. Both models have strengths and weaknesses, and the best worklife expectancy data is probably obtained by combining results from the two models.

As discussed in Chapter 8, increment-decrement worklife expectancies are derived from a sample of the CPS. This sample contains significantly fewer observations than the sample which can be used for conventional model estimates.[1] With its larger sample sizes, conventional model worklife expectancies can be derived for more subpopulations than with the increment-decrement model, especially by more disaggregated educational levels. This is one of the major advantages of this model. It can also be used to derive worklife expectancies by smoking status and other medical conditions where sufficiently robust relative risk factors are known. Additionally, worklife expectancies for disabled persons are published periodically by Vocational Econometrics, Inc. These are not duplicated in this book. (Note, among the forensic economics community there has been much hesitation to use CPS labor force data by disability status because it is felt that the CPS does not measure disability accurately for this purpose) (see Chapter 14).

A disadvantage of the conventional model is that, in contrast to the increment-decrement model, it does not provide good estimates by a person's initial activity status. Therefore, all conventional model estimates in this book are for persons regardless of initial activity status.

This chapter discusses worklife expectancies for males and females by *race* and *education* based on 2000 through 2006 CPS data. (Subsequent chapters deal with smoking status and Hispanics by language proficiency.)

Females warrant special attention. Use of worklife expectancies for all women, regardless of marital or parental status, underestimates worklife *capacity* of women, because statistical data reflect extensive time voluntarily absent from the labor force for child care, homemaking, and so forth. Female *capacity* is more accurately measured by estimates for childless, never-married women whose incentives for labor force participation are more similar to those of males. In fact, 1970 BLS estimates for single females were close to those of men across all but the oldest age groups (1977). In addition, Corcione and Thornton (1991) developed measures of female worklife expectancies based on potential, rather than actual, labor force participation patterns. They demonstrated that, once voluntary non-participation in the labor force was accounted for, potential worklife expectancies of women do not vary much from those of men.

To deal with these issues, forensic economists have often used male data to estimate worklife expectancies for females. This book additionally presents data specifically for childless, never-married females by race and education.

9.2 Data Sources and Methods
A. Data Sources

As with the increment-decrement tables, mortality data are from the *Vital Statistics of the United States, Life Tables,* and the National Longitudinal Mortality Study (see Chapter 4). Mortality rates are by the following educational levels for all races and whites of both sexes and for never-married females all races: all educational levels combined, less than a high school degree, high school degree or GED, some college or associate degree, college graduate, and post-bachelor's education. For the black population, the last two educational categories are combined into a single category (college graduate and more); for the Hispanic population, everything above a high school degree is combined into a single category (some college and more).

Current Population Survey monthly microdata samples for the years 2000 through 2006 are used for labor force data (see Chapter 8). In contrast to the CPS data used in Chapter 8, the entire sample, rather than just a matched sample, is used to derive labor force participation rates for the conventional model, and as such consisted of about 9.7 million observations, representing about 1.6 million persons (about 763,000 males and 847,000 females). The CPS sample population is drawn only from the civilian, non-institutionalized population, i.e., it excludes military personnel and persons in penal, mental, and old age institutions. The sample for childless, never-married females (henceforth referred to as single females) was restricted to women who met the following characteristics: (a) those who had never been married, (b) those who had never given birth, and (c) women who did not live with any family member.[2] This sample is about 350,000 observations, representing about 58,000 women.

Labor force participation consists of persons who worked, those who were on layoff or temporarily absent from work, and those who were unemployed but had been looking and available for work during the last four weeks. Labor force participation rates are calculated as the ratio of persons in the labor force to the total population at each age, sex, race/Hispanic origin, and education level. The rates are smoothed using a five-year running average with the following exceptions: the first year is not smoothed, the second year is a three-year average, and the rate for age 85 is the average for ages 85 plus.[3]

B. Conventional Model

A brief explanation of the conventional worklife methodology is that, at each age, average labor force participation rates are multiplied by the stationary population living at that age to determine the stationary population which is in the labor force (i.e., person-years of labor force activity at that age). The stationary labor force population in the given age is added to those of all subsequent ages to obtain the total person-years in the labor force from that age forth. This total is divided by the

number living at the beginning of the age to derive the number of expected years of worklife, i.e. average years remaining in the labor force (see U.S. Department of Labor, Bureau of Labor Statistics, "Length of Working Life for Men and Women, 1970", Special Labor Force Report 187, Revised, 1977).

Worklife expectancies for all races and for whites are derived for the following educational categories: less than high school, high school degree or GED, some college education (disaggregated into those with an associate degree and those with some college but no degree), bachelor's degree, and graduate degree (disaggregated into those with a master's degree and those with a doctorate or professional degree). For blacks the highest educational level contains master's degree and higher; for Hispanics, bachelor's degree and higher. Worklife estimates for total populations (including all educational levels) are calculated two ways: (1) from mortality and labor force participation rates for the total population, and (2) as weighted averages of their component educational estimates (derived using education-specific mortality and labor force participation rates).

9.3 Empirical Findings
A. Worklife Expectancies by Education

As with increment-decrement estimates, conventional model worklife expectancies are directly correlated with education, as shown in Text Table 30.[4] For example, worklife expectancies of males with some college education increase by about a year and a half at younger ages over having only a high school degree; moving to an associate degree has relatively minimal effect, while obtaining a bachelor's degree increases estimates another two and a half years. Females experience a much larger increase in worklife expectancy through obtaining some college education (about two and a half years at younger ages) and again almost two more years by getting an associate degree. On the other hand, worklives of females with a bachelor's degree are actually slightly less than for those with an associate degree.

Males with a master's degree have only slightly longer worklife expectancies than do those with a bachelor's, but moving to a Ph.D. or professional degree leads to a little more than a three year increase. For females, moving to a master's increases worklife expectancy more than two and a half years at younger ages, while obtaining an advanced degree results in a smaller increase (less than two years).

These data indicate that wherever possible one should attempt to use the most specific education of the person in question when estimating worklife expectancies.

Text Table 30: Conventional model worklife expectancies by age, sex, race, Hispanic ethnicity and education, 2000-2006, selected ages

Age	All Ed Levels		<HS	HS	Some College			College Degree	Graduate Degree		
	Aggr't Data*	Wgt Ave**			All	No Degree	Assoc Degree		All	Master's	Phd/ Prof'l
Males											
All Races											
25	34.6	35.1	29.6	33.6	35.4	35.1	35.9	38.3	39.9	38.5	41.6
40	21.4	21.8	17.5	20.6	21.9	21.8	22.2	24.4	26.1	24.8	27.8
55	9.0	9.5	7.2	8.5	9.3	9.3	9.4	10.9	12.4	11.1	14.0
White											
25	35.2	35.5	30.0	34.2	35.8	35.7	36.2	38.5		38.8	41.2
40	21.8	22.0	17.6	20.9	22.3	22.2	22.4	24.5		24.8	27.2
55	9.1	9.6	6.9	8.6	9.5	9.5	9.5	11.0		11.1	13.4
Black											
25	29.6	30.8	23.1	29.6	31.8			36.1	36.9		
40	13.8	14.5	10.6	14.1	14.9			18.1	19.1		
55	6.9	7.5	5.3	7.3	7.7			10.1	10.7		
Hispanic *											
25	34.7	35.6	33.4	35.4	37.1			39.7			
40	21.2	22.2	20.0	22.0	23.7			25.9			
55	9.0	9.8	8.1	9.9	11.1			13.0			
Females											
All Races											
25	29.0	29.7	19.9	28.2	31.2	30.6	32.3	32.1	35.2	34.8	36.5
40	18.0	18.6	12.0	17.6	19.7	19.3	20.3	20.3	22.9	22.5	24.1
55	7.0	7.5	4.3	6.8	8.1	7.9	8.4	8.4	10.3	9.8	11.4
White											
25	29.2	29.7	19.8	28.3	31.2	30.5	32.4	32.1		35.2	36.7
40	18.2	18.7	12.1	17.7	19.8	19.4	20.5	20.1		22.6	24.1
55	7.1	7.6	4.4	6.9	8.1	7.9	8.5	8.3		9.9	11.4
Black											
25	28.4	29.7	20.2	27.8	31.5			34.8	35.2		
40	16.9	18.1	11.6	16.7	19.4			21.9	22.1		
55	6.3	6.9	4.2	6.5	8.0			9.2	8.9		
Hispanic *											
25	25.2	26.2	19.9	27.1	31.3			33.1			
40	15.6	16.6	12.4	17.1	20.1			21.4			
55	5.8	6.3	4.1	6.9	8.8			9.4			
Single Females, All Races											
25	33.0	34.5	19.9	30.0	34.5	33.8	36.1	37.0	38.6	38.3	39.8
40	20.1	20.9	11.6	18.3	21.5	21.0	22.8	23.2	24.7	24.4	26.1
55	8.4	9.1	4.7	7.7	9.5	9.2	10.4	10.2	11.0	10.8	12.3

* Hispanic worklife expectancies in the College Degree category are for college degree and higher.

B. Worklife Expectancies of Single Females

With the exception of less than a high school education and a high school degree, worklife expectancies of single females are much closer to those of males than of all females (Text Table 30). Single females have nearly identical worklife expectancies as all females. At the high school level, the worklife expectancy at age 25 of single females is about 3.6 years less than that of males and 1.9 years greater than females of all marital statuses. Worklife expectancies of single females remain lower than males at the higher education level (0.8 years for some college; 1.3 years for bachelor's degree; and about 1.3 years for graduate degree) but they become much higher than those of all females (3.3, 4.9, and 3.3 years, respectively).[5]

C. Increment-Decrement Model Compared with the Conventional Model Estimates

Conventional model worklife expectancies are compared with those of the increment-decrement model (regardless of initial activity status) in Text Table 31. For males, the conventional model produces higher estimates than does the increment-decrement model for all educational levels and ages. For females, conventional model estimates are markedly larger at the lowest and highest educational levels, while at middle ages the estimates show minor differences.

The smaller increment-decrement estimates may be due in part to slightly decreasing labor force participation rates in the early years of the 2000-2006 period. Rates were decreasing or relatively stable for ages 25 through 55, the ages of heaviest participation, but for both older men and women participation rates were increasing during this period. Two other possible reasons for lower increment-decrement estimates are discussed in more detail in Chapter 15.

9.4 Need to Use Education-Specific Worklife Estimates

Two potential problems exist with using worklife estimates not specific to race and education. First, estimates calculated from data aggregated across educational groups are biased downward due to cohort compositional effects (see Chapter 8). Second, relative differences across educational levels are not constant from one race to another. For instance, black male worklife expectancies are more sensitive to education than those of all races combined.

Race and education-specific data should always be used, but this creates a conundrum. Increment-decrement estimates are not available for all race and detailed education categories, while conventional model estimates do not reflect the dynamic nature of labor force involvement, thus providing no information on initial activity status. To address this situation, three alternatives are available: (1) use increment-decrement estimates, (2) use conventional model estimates, or (3) use a combination of both to take advantage of the strengths of each. The authors recommend the third approach. Specifically, conventional model estimates can be scaled by their appropriate increment-decrement counterpart. This is a necessity if one wishes to obtain increment-decrement equivalent estimates by some of the education levels (associate degree, some college but no degree, master's, and Ph.D./professional degrees) For blacks and Hispanics, specific education levels not included in their conventional model tables can be extrapolated from all races data. (For more discussion see Chapter 15.)

Two examples using this method are presented below. The first is for initially "active" black males at age 25 with less than high school and the second is for the same male but with a Ph.D./professional degree. (All data come from Tables 4 and 5 in Part III.) Differences, rather than ratios, should be used. Ratios produce nearly similar results during young age, but beginning in the late fifties (as the denominator grows increasingly smaller) they become increasingly inaccurate.

First, consider those with less than a high school education. Step 1—from Table 5 determine that the conventional model worklife for these black males is 33.1 years. Step 2—from Table 4 determine that the worklife expectancy of those initially active is 0.4 years longer than the general population. Step 3—add the 0.4 to the 33.1 to get a worklife expectancy of 33.5 years for a black male with less than a high school education who is initially active.

Next, consider the somewhat more complicated process for black males with a doctorate or professional degree. Because the conventional model estimates do not distinguish beyond all graduates, several additional steps are required. Step 1—using Table 5 for black males find that the worklife expectancy for black males with a graduate degree at 25 years of age is 37.0 years. Step 2—using the same table for all males determine that the worklife expectancy for all males with a graduate degree is 1.7 years less than for those with a Ph.D./professional degree (41.6 minus 39.9) Step 3—add 1.7 years to 37.0 years to obtain a 38.7 year worklife for all black males with a Ph.D./professional degree. Step 4—from Table 4 determine that the worklife expectancy of all males with a graduate degree initially active is 0.2 years longer than the general population. Finally, step 5—add the 0.2 to the 38.7 to get a worklife expectancy of 38.9 years for a black male with a Ph.D./professional degree who is initially active. Although this description appears somewhat complicated, the practice is relatively simple.

Text Table 31: Comparison of worklife expectancies—conventional model versus increment-decrement model (regardless of initial activity state), all races by sex and education

Age	< HS	HS/ GED	Some College	College Degree	Grad Degree	< HS	HS/ GED	Some College	College Degree	Grad Degree
			All Males					All Females		
			Conventional Model Worklife Expectancies							
25	29.00	33.58	35.37	38.36	39.86	19.84	28.19	31.27	32.21	35.23
35	20.90	24.92	26.46	29.15	30.77	14.74	21.23	23.62	24.16	26.93
45	13.21	16.38	17.61	19.86	21.46	9.24	13.94	15.84	16.48	18.78
55	6.69	8.55	9.41	11.00	12.42	4.34	6.90	8.20	8.57	10.28
65	2.03	2.78	3.19	4.01	5.04	1.18	1.95	2.55	2.64	3.62
			Increment-Decrement Worklife Expectancies (regardless of initial activity state)							
25	28.34	32.78	34.71	38.10	39.83	18.55	27.81	31.01	31.95	34.78
35	20.39	24.32	25.87	28.87	30.49	13.79	21.11	23.56	24.02	26.52
45	12.68	15.82	16.96	19.54	21.01	8.72	13.94	15.83	16.55	18.29
55	6.18	8.03	8.84	10.59	11.87	4.18	6.80	8.21	8.62	9.77
65	1.80	2.34	2.86	3.43	4.19	0.95	1.78	2.21	2.34	3.08
			Amount that Conventional Worklives are greater than Increment-Decrement Worklives							
25	0.67	0.80	0.66	0.26	0.03	1.29	0.38	0.27	0.26	0.46
35	0.51	0.60	0.59	0.27	0.28	0.95	0.13	0.06	0.13	0.41
45	0.53	0.56	0.65	0.32	0.45	0.52	0.01	0.00	-0.07	0.49
55	0.51	0.52	0.56	0.41	0.55	0.17	0.01	-0.01	-0.05	0.51
65	0.23	0.44	0.33	0.58	0.85	0.23	0.17	0.34	0.30	0.54

The methodology for single females is the same as described above, except that scaling should be done to increment-decrement worklife expectancies of males rather than females because the labor participation patterns of single women are more like those of males than those of the total female population.

Notes

1. Samples upon which increment-decrement estimates are based lose data points in two ways: a) as discussed in the preceding chapter, losses occur making matches of persons from one year to the next, and b) each person in the (reduced) matched sample provides only one data point. In contrast, the conventional model estimates in this book are based on nearly every record in the CPS from 2000 through 2006. The only records not used are those with non-identified labor force participation status or weighting factors.

2. Four definitions of relationships in the CPS data are included in the never-married women sample: reference person without relatives, unmarried partner without relatives, housemate/roommate without relatives, and roomer/boarder without relatives.

3. Beginning in 2003, the CPS microdata samples do not contain information for ages above 80, other than that age 80 is the sum of it and all subsequent ages. Calculations of worklife expectancies which are truncated for all ages over 80 result in slight underestimates, i.e. about one tenth of a year for educational attainments up to a bachelor's degree, about two tenths of a year for bachelor's and master's, and about three tenths of a year for Ph.D./professional degrees (males of all races). The estimates in this book carry the calculations through to age 85 by extrapolating from the 2000 through 2002 data for the oldest ages through the remaining three years. It is possible that these worklife expectations are slightly underestimated if the labor force participation of those 80 to 85 during 2003 through 2006 increased as it did for others over the age of 60.

4. Note that mortality rates by educational attainment are used in the calculation of all estimates. As discussed in Chapter 8, compared with using mortality rates from U.S. life tables (i.e., regardless of educational attainment) this results in reducing worklives for persons with less than a high school education (up to a year for all males at age 25), very little change for those with a high school degree, and significant increases for those with the highest educational attainments (more than two years for black males with at least a bachelor's degree).

5. Sample sizes in the CPS microdata are not large enough to calculate worklife expectancies by race for single females. The microdata from the 2000 Census of the Population appear not to be usable for the purpose of calculating worklife expectancies due to discrepancies between its labor force data versus those of the more reliable CPS data, and therefore it is not possible to take advantage of its much larger sample sizes. In the previous edition of this book, however, the 1990 Census of the Population was used and it was possible to observe that race has a much smaller effect on worklife expectancies of single females than it does for males. For example, using the 1990 data, the worklife expectancy of 25-year-old black males with a high school education is 5.6 years less than that of white males, but the difference between black versus white single females is only 2.2 years. At the college level the difference by race for males is 3.2 years while the difference for single females is only 0.3 year, and at the graduate level the differences are 3.4 and 0.8, respectively.

Chapter 10

Hispanic Worklife Expectancies by Education and English Language Proficiency*

10.1 Introduction

Persons of Hispanic origin represent one of the fastest growing working groups in the United States. With a rate of growth nearly four times greater than other segments of the U.S. work force during the 1980s and early 1990s, the Hispanic labor force is projected to exceed that of blacks by 2006 (Fullerton, 1997).

Although often treated as a distinct ethnic category, "Hispanic" represents a very heterogeneous population including Mexicans, Cubans, Puerto Ricans, persons from Spain, persons from Central and South American countries, and persons from the Dominican Republic. Each has its own demographic and labor force characteristics. Mexicans are both the youngest and least well educated; Cubans are the oldest and best educated. Central and South American Hispanics, along with Mexicans, tend to have the highest labor force participation rates; Cubans are about average for the country as a whole; and Hispanics from Puerto Rico are about five percentage points below average. Nevertheless, because many cultural similarities define a Hispanic or Latino identity, the U.S. government presents statistics for them as a separate ethnic group (Cattan, 1993).

Many characteristics of the Hispanic population affect estimates of their earnings loss: Hispanics have longer life expectancies than the general population; at most education levels their worklife expectancies are longer; their average annual earnings are less; and their rates of unemployment are greater. In addition, fluency in English is strongly correlated with many factors of Hispanic market success: unemployment rates and average annual earnings are positively correlated with English proficiency, but, perhaps surprisingly, at the lowest education levels worklife expectancies are negatively correlated with proficiency (McManus, Gould, and Welch, 1983; Grenier, 1984; Tainer, 1988; Richards, 1998; Mora and Davila, 1998).

10.2 Data Sources and Methods

As described in the previous chapters, mortality data are from the National Longitudinal Mortality Study and the *Vital Statistics of the United States, 1990*. All other data are from the 1990 U.S. Decennial Census of the Population 5% "Public Use Microdata Samples" (PUMS). The samples included Hispanic persons 18 years of age and older and consisted of 336,896 females and 336,645 males.

The PUMS designated five categories of English language proficiency. Respondents could report speaking "not at all," "not well," "well," "very well," or "only English" "if they spoke only English at home." The Hispanic population is strongly skewed toward low educational attainment (Text Table 32). Approximately half of all Hispanics have less than a high school education, while for the U.S. in general only about a quarter have less than a high school education. Similarly, the percentage of Hispanics with a college education or more is only half that of the overall population. Regarding fluency within educational categories, Hispanics with less than a high school education have a very high percentage of persons with poor English fluency (about 40% speak English poorly or not at all). In all other education levels, most Hispanics speak English "well" or better, with "very well" modal in all cases.[1]

---

*This chapter and Table 7 in Part III have not been revised because valid updated data are not available. Note that most data and discussions in this chapter refer to data from the 1990 Census of the Population.

Text Table 32: Estimated Hispanic population composition by sex, education, and English fluency, 1990 Census of the Population

Level of English Proficiency	All	<HS	HS	Some College	College Degree	Grad Degree
Males						
Estimated Population						
No English	570,101	488,707	48,764	23,412	5,553	3,665
Speak Poorly	1,208,318	919,136	160,083	95,171	20,052	13,876
Speak Well	1,396,687	812,781	292,411	216,470	44,479	30,546
Speak Very Well	2,659,906	989,760	693,900	673,767	187,960	114,519
Speak Primarily English	1,338,591	381,557	384,313	402,674	115,084	54,963
All Levels	**7,173,603**	**3,591,941**	**1,579,471**	**1,411,494**	**373,128**	**217,569**
% by Education of All		50.1%	22.0%	19.7%	5.2%	3.0%
Percentage by English Proficiency						
No English	7.9%	13.6%	3.1%	1.7%	1.5%	1.7%
Speak Poorly	16.8%	25.6%	10.1%	6.7%	5.4%	6.4%
Speak Well	19.5%	22.6%	18.5%	15.3%	11.9%	14.0%
Speak Very Well	37.1%	27.6%	43.9%	47.7%	50.4%	52.6%
Speak Primarily English	18.7%	10.6%	24.3%	28.5%	30.8%	25.3%
All Levels	**100.0%**	**100.0%**	**100.0%**	**100.0%**	**100.0%**	**100.0%**
Females						
Estimated Population						
No English	750,961	647,821	63,738	27,725	6,782	4,895
Speak Poorly	1,110,689	823,526	166,121	87,805	21,921	11,316
Speak Well	1,186,074	630,585	288,158	200,470	45,022	21,839
Speak Very Well	2,674,669	928,142	745,791	728,094	187,384	85,258
Speak Primarily English	1,298,625	366,907	394,499	403,283	98,969	34,967
All Levels	**7,021,018**	**3,396,981**	**1,658,307**	**1,447,377**	**360,078**	**158,275**
% by Education of All		48.4%	23.6%	20.6%	5.1%	2.3%
Percentage by English Proficiency						
No English	10.7%	19.1%	3.8%	1.9%	1.9%	3.1%
Speak Poorly	15.8%	24.2%	10.0%	6.1%	6.1%	7.1%
Speak Well	16.9%	18.6%	17.4%	13.9%	12.5%	13.8%
Speak Very Well	38.1%	27.3%	45.0%	50.3%	52.0%	53.9%
Speak Primarily English	18.5%	10.8%	23.8%	27.9%	27.5%	22.1%
All Levels	**100.0%**	**100.0%**	**100.0%**	**100.0%**	**100.0%**	**100.0%**

Source: 1990 Census of the Population, United States.

Fluency designations have the limitations that they were self-reported and referred only to speaking—not reading, writing, or comprehension. It is probable that responses were not totally consistent across respondents. In addition, because the fluency of immigrants can improve with length of residency, this characteristic is probably not stable through time.[2] Nevertheless, the problem of stability may not be too severe if age-specific labor force participation rates of immigrants remain relatively constant with current rates. Factors related to culture, economic necessity, and habit increase the probability of this happening.

As discussed in previous chapters, worklife expectancies for the total population are educationally weighted averages. In contrast to the other groups in Chapters 8 and 9, bias corrections for the Hispanic population are slightly larger.

10.3 Discussion

As with other segments of the population, Hispanic worklife expectancies were directly related to educational attainment (Text Table 33). However, the relatively long worklife of Hispanic males with less than a high school education causes a much smaller range between education levels than for the total male population. Hispanic females, on the other hand, have a slightly larger range than females of all races.

Text Table 34 shows that at age 25 the worklife expectancies of Hispanic males and females were longer than those of the general population for nearly all education levels, with the difference greater for males than females. Hispanic males with less than a high school education have much longer worklife expectancies than the general population (3.8 years, 13.5% longer). The difference drops to a little more than a year for high school graduates and some college (3.3% and 3.6%, respectively), and then to hardly any difference at all for those with the most education. Hispanic females closely approximate the general population at the upper and lower levels of educational attainment while those with some college or a bachelor's degree have worklife expectancies about one to one and a half years longer (3.7% and 5.0%, respectively).

Regarding English language proficiency, the longest worklife expectancies of Hispanic males in most educational categories occur for those who speak English "well" or "very well" rather than "primarily." Several anomalies exist however. Those with a high school education who speak "well" have the longest worklives (about 0.8 year more than average) while those who speak "very well" appear to have the shortest worklives (about 0.4 years less than average).

The longest worklives for Hispanic males with some college education occur for those who speak "well" or "very well," but the difference is quite small (about 0.3 year more than average); in addition, the shortest worklives occur for the highest fluency level (about 0.5 year less than average).

For females, the pattern is different. A relatively strong direct relationship exists between fluency and worklife expectancy for both high school graduates and those with some college education. At age 25, females with a high school education who speak English poorly have worklives almost 4.0 years less than average while the difference for those with some college education is almost 6.9 years. At the highest fluency levels (including both "very well" and "primarily English"), worklife expectancies are about 1.0 year above average for both education levels.

Interestingly, both Hispanic males and females with less than a high school education show unusual relationships between fluency and worklife expectancy. For males, those who speak English poorly have the longest worklives (about 1.0 year longer than average for the educational level), and those who cannot speak English at all have the second longest worklives (about 0.6 year longer than average). For all higher levels of fluency, a strong inverse relationship exists. Those who speak primarily English have worklives about 2.5 years less than average.

Text Table 33: Hispanic age specific worklife expectancies by sex and education, 1990 Census of the Population

Age	All*	<HS	HS or GED	Some College	College Degree	Grad Degree
Male						
25	34.5	32.1	34.9	36.6	38.4	39.8
35	26.1	24.2	26.2	27.8	29.4	31.2
45	17.7	16.1	18.0	19.3	20.7	22.6
55	9.4	8.4	9.9	11.0	12.1	14.1
65	3.0	2.5	3.5	4.1	4.9	6.5
Female						
25	26.0	19.9	27.0	31.2	32.6	35.8
35	19.4	14.8	20.5	23.7	24.6	27.9
45	12.1	9.3	13.4	16.0	16.5	19.2
55	5.7	4.4	6.7	8.5	8.5	10.6
65	1.5	1.1	2.1	2.9	2.8	3.9

* Educationally weighted averages.

Text Table 34: Hispanic worklife expectancies compared with all races at age 25 by selected levels of English language proficiency, 1990 Census of the Population

	All*	<HS	HS or GED	Some College	College Degree	Grad Degree
Male						
Hispanic (of all proficiencies)	34.5	32.1	34.9	36.6	38.4	39.8
All Races	35.1	28.3	33.8	35.3	38.1	40.0
Hispanic Minus All Races	-0.6	3.8	1.1	1.3	0.3	-0.2
Hispanic % of All Races	98.2%	113.5%	103.3%	103.6%	100.7%	99.6%
Hispanic by English Proficiency						
Speak No English		32.7				
Speak Poorly		33.1	34.7	36.2		
Speak Well		32.4	35.7	36.8		
Speak Very Well		31.4	34.5	36.9		
Speak English Primarily		29.6	35.0	36.1		
Female						
Hispanic (of all proficiencies)	26.0	19.9	27.0	31.2	32.6	35.8
All Races	28.4	20.0	26.9	30.1	31.0	35.3
Hispanic Minus All Races	-2.4	-0.1	0.1	1.1	1.6	0.5
Hispanic % of All Races	91.5%	99.3%	100.3%	103.7%	105.0%	101.4%
Hispanic by English Proficiency						
Speak No English		17.1				
Speak Poorly		20.4	23.1	24.3		
Speak Well		21.2	26.8	30.3		
Speak Very Well		20.6	28.0	32.3		
Speak English Primarily		19.7	27.8	32.1		

* Educationally weighted averages. Whereas the Hispanic worklife expectancies for nearly all educational categories are greater than those for all races, the weighted averages for all Hispanics are less because their population is heavily skewed toward lower education levels.

The reason for these anomalous and rather unexpected results may lie in immigration patterns and incentives. The least fluent populations may have higher numbers of recent immigrants, who came to the U.S. to better their lives economically and consequently tend to participate at high levels. Conversely, the most fluent Hispanics are likely to have been born in this country and to have labor force patterns closer to those of average Americans.

The pattern for females with less than a high school education differs from that of males. Those with moderate fluency have the longest worklife expectancies (about 1.3 years longer than average) while those at both extremes of fluency have the shortest (about 2.8 years less for non English speakers and about 0.2 year less for primarily English speakers).

Notes

1. Worklife expectancies by English proficiency are calculated only for categories with large enough samples or significant differences between worklife expectancies.

2. Mora and Davila (1998) showed that those who participate in the labor market increase their English proficiency.

Chapter 11

Worklife Expectancies by Education and Cigarette Smoking Status

11.1 Introduction

As discussed in Chapter 4, cigarette smoking reduces average life expectancies of males by up to ten years and of females by up to six years. All other things being equal, shorter life expectancies alone cause shorter worklife expectancies. In addition, cigarette smoking might also affect or be related to other factors that affect labor force participation. The direction and degree of such a correlation is not obvious *a priori*, however. On the one hand, cigarette smoking is linked with increased susceptibility to diseases that may cause temporary or long-term absences from the labor force. On the other hand, smokers may have personality traits, such as propensity toward risk taking, that are related to increased labor force participation.

The effect of *mortality* alone on worklife expectancies by smoking status was analyzed by Ciecka and Goldman (1995). Incorporating smoking status mortality rates in the increment-decrement model (with labor force transition probabilities for all persons regardless of smoking status), they found that worklife expectancies of non-smoking males were a little more than two years longer than those of male smokers (for ages in the twenties and thirties). For females the difference was smaller—a little over half a year. In a follow-up study, Ciecka, Donley, Epstein, and Goldman (1998) incorporated mortality rates by *consumption* levels. This indicated that male heavy smokers experience another half-year decrease in worklife expectancies compared with all smokers (during their twenties). The effect on female heavy smokers is more pronounced—an additional year decrease compared to all female smokers.

The following discussion updates Richards (1999), using larger samples and more recent data: both *mortality* and *labor force participation rates* by smoking status are used, estimates are derived for five levels of educational attainment, and the conventional model is used, so that labor force participation rates by smoking status can be incorporated in the model.

11.2 Data and Methodology

Mortality data are from the American Cancer Society's second Cancer Prevention Study (CPS-II) (see Chapter 6). Labor force participation rates and demographic information are from Tobacco Use Supplements of the Current Population Surveys (CPS) for the months of January and May of 2000, June and November of 2001, February of 2002, and February, June and November of 2003 (these are all of the CPS surveys of tobacco use which occurred during the years 2000–2006).

The Tobacco Use Supplements collected detailed cigarette smoking information for persons 15 years of age and older, and summarized the data into the following categories: "not in the universe," "indeterminate status," "never-smoker," "everyday smoker," "some days smoker," and "former smoker." In this analysis, the "everyday smoker" and "some days smoker" categories are combined and defined as being current smokers. Those defined as "not in the universe" or "indeterminate status" are not included in the analysis by smoking status; but for the purpose of deriving estimates for the total population, the entire sample is used.

Total sample observations (18 years of age or older) for males are 379,847 (of whom 293,842 were placed by the CPS into a definite smoking status) and for females, 423,701 (of whom 331,423 were in a definite smoking status). Samples by smoking status are as follows: male never-smokers, 154,705; male current smokers, 65,831; male former smokers, 73,306; female never-smokers, 210,906; female current smokers, 59,911; and female former smokers, 60,606.

Text Table 35 (A): Labor force participation rates by smoking status and education, males, 2000-2003

Age	Labor Force Participation Rates					Difference (Smoking Status minus All)				
	<HS	HS	Some Col	Col	Grad	<HS	HS	Some Col	Col	Grad
All Males Regardless of Smoking Status										
18 to 24	69.2%	82.9%	71.0%	85.4%	77.9%					
25 to 34	87.0%	92.0%	93.5%	94.8%	94.9%					
35 to 44	82.6%	91.2%	93.6%	96.7%	96.9%					
45 to 54	73.3%	85.9%	89.1%	94.5%	95.7%					
55 to 64	52.5%	64.9%	70.3%	76.5%	81.0%					
65+	11.7%	16.6%	19.4%	24.3%	29.2%					
25 to 64	75.4%	85.6%	88.8%	92.7%	92.5%					
Never-Smokers										
18 to 24	65.6%	80.9%	68.6%	84.9%	71.3%	-3.5%	-1.9%	-2.4%	-0.5%	-6.6%
25 to 34	88.5%	92.8%	94.7%	95.5%	95.7%	1.5%	0.8%	1.3%	0.7%	0.7%
35 to 44	84.6%	92.8%	95.5%	97.7%	97.9%	2.0%	1.7%	1.9%	1.0%	1.0%
45 to 54	77.7%	88.8%	92.0%	96.2%	97.1%	4.4%	2.9%	2.9%	1.7%	1.4%
55 to 64	55.9%	67.4%	73.5%	79.3%	82.1%	3.4%	2.5%	3.2%	2.8%	1.1%
65+	11.0%	17.0%	19.6%	23.4%	30.3%	-0.7%	0.4%	0.1%	-0.8%	1.1%
25 to 64	79.8%	88.8%	92.1%	94.7%	94.4%	4.4%	3.1%	3.3%	2.0%	1.8%
Current Smokers										
18 to 24	80.2%	89.3%	84.9%	92.6%	87.0%	11.0%	6.5%	13.9%	7.2%	9.1%
25 to 34	86.5%	92.7%	93.7%	95.2%	94.5%	-0.5%	0.6%	0.3%	0.4%	-0.4%
35 to 44	80.5%	90.7%	91.8%	95.5%	94.6%	-2.2%	-0.5%	-1.8%	-1.2%	-2.3%
45 to 54	69.5%	83.7%	84.9%	90.6%	92.2%	-3.9%	-2.2%	-4.2%	-3.9%	-3.4%
55 to 64	50.2%	62.7%	68.0%	73.3%	73.6%	-2.2%	-2.2%	-2.3%	-3.2%	-7.4%
65+	13.1%	18.8%	20.7%	23.8%	27.7%	1.4%	2.1%	1.3%	-0.4%	-1.6%
25 to 64	73.8%	85.8%	87.2%	90.9%	89.1%	-1.6%	0.2%	-1.6%	-1.8%	-3.4%

Source: BLS, Current Population Surveys, January 2000 through November 2003.

Worklife estimates are derived using the "conventional" model. For calculation of current smoker worklife estimates, mortality and labor force participation rates are those for all smokers (without distinguishing between level or duration of cigarette consumption). Never-smoker mortality rates are applied to never-smoker labor force participation rates.

Estimates are calculated for five levels of educational attainment: less than high school, high school diploma or GED, some college or associate degree, bachelor's degree, and graduate degree. Estimates for all education levels combined by smoking status are not derived because weighting would have been compounded by changing prevalences in both education and smoking status by age, and, therefore, such estimates would have been extremely difficult to derive.

11.3 Discussion

The effects of cigarette-smoking behavior on worklife expectancies are examined here in two stages. The first deals with the relationship, if any, between smoking and labor force participation. The second incorporates the effects of mortality by smoking status.

Text Tables 35 (A) and (B) and Table 11 in the Tables Section of the book show 2000–03 labor force participation rates by smoking status for males and females of all races. (For the following discussion, the age category 18–24 is ignored because of confounding compositional effects.)[1] For males, never-smoker labor force participation rates are higher than those of the population as a whole, and current smoker rates are lower, with the difference possibly increas-

Text Table 35 (B): Labor force participation rates by smoking status and education, females, 2000–2003

Age	Labor Force Participation Rates					Difference (Smoking Status minus All)				
	<HS	HS	Some Col	Col	Grad	<HS	HS	Some Col	Col	Grad
All Females Regardless of Smoking Status										
18 to 24	52.0%	71.4%	70.9%	83.3%	80.4%					
25 to 34	53.6%	72.6%	79.1%	81.8%	84.0%					
35 to 44	59.2%	75.8%	80.5%	78.8%	85.1%					
45 to 54	52.2%	75.1%	79.8%	82.1%	88.7%					
55 to 64	33.4%	52.8%	59.9%	63.7%	72.4%					
65+	5.4%	10.1%	12.8%	13.9%	19.6%					
25 to 64	49.8%	70.1%	76.8%	78.8%	83.7%					
Never-Smokers										
18 to 24	49.2%	69.2%	68.5%	82.5%	79.2%	-2.8%	-2.2%	-2.5%	-0.8%	-1.3%
25 to 34	51.0%	72.5%	78.9%	81.5%	83.8%	-2.5%	-0.1%	-0.1%	-0.3%	-0.1%
35 to 44	58.5%	76.5%	80.9%	78.1%	85.4%	-0.6%	0.7%	0.4%	-0.7%	0.3%
45 to 54	54.4%	74.9%	81.3%	82.6%	89.4%	2.2%	-0.2%	1.5%	0.5%	0.8%
55 to 64	33.2%	52.4%	59.8%	64.5%	72.5%	-0.2%	-0.4%	-0.1%	0.8%	0.1%
65+	4.5%	9.3%	11.6%	12.0%	17.3%	-1.0%	-0.7%	-1.2%	-1.8%	-2.3%
25 to 64	49.4%	70.0%	77.4%	79.0%	84.3%	-0.4%	-0.1%	0.7%	0.2%	0.6%
Current Smokers										
18 to 24	63.6%	81.9%	83.9%	92.5%	93.3%	11.6%	10.4%	12.9%	9.2%	12.8%
25 to 34	61.4%	75.6%	82.8%	91.7%	93.6%	7.9%	3.0%	3.8%	9.9%	9.6%
35 to 44	59.6%	76.1%	81.3%	89.4%	86.2%	0.4%	0.3%	0.8%	10.7%	1.1%
45 to 54	50.6%	75.1%	78.4%	83.3%	88.8%	-1.6%	0.0%	-1.4%	1.2%	0.1%
55 to 64	35.9%	54.3%	60.5%	63.0%	71.2%	2.5%	1.5%	0.6%	-0.8%	-1.2%
65+	8.1%	13.8%	14.1%	12.3%	15.2%	2.6%	3.8%	1.3%	-1.5%	-4.5%
25 to 64	53.0%	72.4%	78.5%	85.4%	85.9%	3.3%	2.3%	1.7%	6.6%	2.2%

Source: BLS, Current Population Surveys, January 2000 through November 2003.

ing with age through the period of the normal working life. Never-smoking tends to show a greater effect on labor force participation rates for lower educational levels. For females, the correlation between smoking and labor force appears to be opposite that of males; that is, current smokers have higher participation rates than the total population, and never-smokers have slightly lower rates.[2] The negative correlation is particularly strong for college graduates.[3]

Worklife expectancies are calculated by incorporating both labor force participation and mortality rates by smoking status. Results are shown in Text Tables 36 (A) and (B). It is important to note that, although conventional model worklife expectancies of the total population of males and females are discussed in Chapter 9 and presented in Table 5 in the Tables Section, they are also calculated from the Tobacco Supplement data. This is necessary because these supplements surveyed only selected months and occurred only during the period 2000 through 2003, rather than extending through 2006.

For never-smokers, worklife expectancies for the lesser educated males at age 45 and younger are up to two years greater than for the total population. For the most educated males worklife expectancies of never-smokers are a little less than a year greater.[4] Conversely, worklife expectancies of male current smokers are reduced approximately two years for the lower educational levels and almost four years for those with a graduate education.

The effects are much less for females. Mortality factors almost compensate for lower labor force participation rates of never-smokers. Worklife expectancies for current smokers of lower educational attainment vary but little from the total population; for women with some college education they are reduced by almost a year during the middle working ages; and for the highest education levels they are in general reduced by a year and more.

11.4 Scaling of Smoker Worklife Estimates

It is recommended that these estimates be scaled to those of the increment-decrement model or where more disaggregated educational attainment is desired to conventional model estimates derived from the full 2000 through 2006 data (see Chapters 9 and 15). The method is similar to that suggested for the other conventional model estimates but an important difference in this case is that smoking adjustment factors should all be derived from Table 8 (Part III). For example, from Table 8 (Part III), the 2000-03 worklife expectancy of male current smokers with a college education at age 35 is 26.3, and that for males regardless of smoking status with a college education is 29.0 years. The difference between the two (26.3 − 29.0 = −2.7) is added to the 2000-06 increment-decrement estimate (from Table 4) for all males with a college education (29.1 years). The result is a scaled estimate of 26.4 years of additional worklife.

It seems reasonable that scaling can also be used for whites, blacks, and Hispanics. As discussed in Chapter 6, Thun et al. (2000) examined possible confounding factors in regard to mortality and concluded that "adjusting the RR [relative risk] estimates associated with cigarette smoking for multiple other demographic and behavioral characteristics had minimal impact on the RR estimates adjusted only for age [and sex]." Confounding might be slightly more for labor force participation. For instance, prevalence of smoking is higher than average for black males and lower than average for Hispanics. Thus, the reduction in worklives of black smokers might be less than for all races and increases in worklives of black never-smokers might be greater. These correlations might be reversed for Hispanics.

Notes

1. At age 18, there are few current smokers proportional to the total population; labor force participation rates are also quite low. At age 24, both the prevalence of current smokers and labor force participation rates are much higher. Mathematically, weighted average labor force participation rates of current smokers, for the entire age group 18 to 24 can be higher than for the total population, even if this is not true for any or all of the individual ages.

2. Similarly, unemployment rates are lower for male never-smokers and higher for female never-smokers.

3. Correlation does not imply causation. Personalities of female smokers may incline them to participate more in the labor force. Alternatively, causation may lie in workplace factors that induce smoking.

4. In part, these patterns result from compositional effects. Because the prevalence of smokers is very low at high education levels, never-smokers lie close to the mean and current smokers diverge from it. The opposite is true for low education levels.

Text Table 36 (A): Male age-specific worklife expectancies by smoking status

Age	Worklife Expectancies					Difference (Smoking Status minus All)				
	<HS	HS	Some Col	Col Deg	Grad Deg	<HS	HS	Some Col	Col Deg	Grad Deg
All Males Regardless of Smoking Status										
25	28.9	33.6	35.4	38.2	40.0					
35	20.8	24.9	26.4	29.0	30.9					
45	13.2	16.3	17.5	19.7	21.5					
55	6.7	8.4	9.3	10.7	12.4					
65	2.0	2.6	3.1	3.9	5.0					
Never-Smokers										
25	30.9	35.4	37.1	39.4	41.0	2.1	1.8	1.7	1.2	1.0
35	22.8	26.6	28.0	30.1	31.7	2.0	1.7	1.6	1.1	0.9
45	14.7	17.6	18.7	20.6	22.2	1.5	1.3	1.2	0.9	0.7
55	7.4	9.2	10.0	11.4	12.9	0.7	0.8	0.7	0.6	0.5
65	2.1	3.0	3.3	4.1	5.3	0.1	0.3	0.2	0.2	0.3
Current Smokers										
25	26.8	31.8	32.9	35.5	36.1	-2.1	-1.8	-2.5	-2.7	-3.9
35	18.7	23.0	23.9	26.3	26.9	-2.1	-1.9	-2.5	-2.7	-4.0
45	11.6	14.7	15.5	17.4	18.1	-1.6	-1.6	-2.0	-2.3	-3.4
55	5.8	7.4	8.0	9.3	9.7	-0.9	-1.0	-1.2	-1.5	-2.7
65	1.6	2.2	2.4	3.1	3.3	-0.4	-0.4	-0.6	-0.8	-1.7

Sources: BLS, Current Population Surveys, January 2000 through November 2003, Tobacco Supplements; CDC, National Vital Statistics Report, Number 56, "United States Life Tables, 2004"; and unpublished data from CPS-II and NIH Publication Number 97-4213.

Text Table 36 (B): Female age-specific worklife expectancies by smoking status

Age	Worklife Expectancies					Difference (Smoking Status minus All)				
	<HS	HS	Some Col	Col Deg	Grad Deg	<HS	HS	Some Col	Col Deg	Grad Deg
All Females Regardless of Smoking Status										
25	20.0	28.3	31.1	32.0	35.2					
35	14.8	21.2	23.3	23.9	27.0					
45	9.1	13.9	15.5	16.2	18.7					
55	4.2	6.7	7.8	8.3	10.1					
65	1.1	1.8	2.3	2.5	3.4					
Never-Smokers										
25	19.9	28.5	31.3	31.9	35.0	-0.1	0.1	0.2	-0.1	-0.2
35	15.0	21.4	23.5	23.9	26.8	0.2	0.1	0.2	-0.1	-0.2
45	9.4	14.0	15.7	16.2	18.4	0.3	0.1	0.2	-0.0	-0.3
55	4.2	6.8	7.8	8.2	9.7	-0.0	0.0	-0.0	-0.1	-0.4
65	1.0	1.8	2.2	2.2	3.0	-0.1	-0.0	-0.1	-0.2	-0.4
Current Smokers										
25	20.5	28.5	30.7	33.1	34.9	0.5	0.2	-0.4	1.1	-0.4
35	14.5	21.1	22.5	24.0	25.7	-0.3	-0.1	-0.8	0.1	-1.3
45	8.8	13.7	14.6	15.3	17.3	-0.3	-0.2	-0.8	-1.0	-1.4
55	4.3	6.7	7.3	7.4	8.8	0.0	-0.0	-0.6	-1.0	-1.3
65	1.1	1.9	1.9	1.8	2.3	0.1	0.1	-0.4	-0.7	-1.1

Sources: BLS, Current Population Surveys, January 2000 through November 2003, Tobacco Supplements; CDC, National Vital Statistics Report, Number 56, "United States Life Tables, 2004"; and unpublished data from CPS-II and NIH Publication Number 97-4213.

Chapter 12

The Life, Participation, Employment Method

12.1 Introduction

Michael Brookshire and William Cobb proposed the LPE method of determining earnings losses in 1983. The LPE approach sums *probable* earnings across all remaining years of a person's life expectancy. In contrast to worklife expectancy and capacity measures, the LPE methodology adjusts for expected periods of labor force inactivity in each year.

In the LPE methodology, estimated earnings at each age are dependent on three conditions: whether the person would have been alive, whether he or she would have been willing and able to work, and whether he or she would have actually been employed. These are described as the following probabilities:

- Probability of life (L): probability that a person will survive through a subsequent age from the initial age.
- Probability of labor force participation (P): percentage of living persons who are either employed or actively seeking work (i.e., the labor force participation rate for the appropriate sex, age, race, education, etc.).
- Probability of employment (E): the percentage of persons in the labor force who are actually working (equivalent to one minus the unemployment rate).

These three probabilities when multiplied together provide a joint Life-Participation-Employment (LPE) probability. Expected earnings at each age are estimated as this joint probability multiplied by an earnings amount (which, for instance, can be based on projections of past earnings, statistical data, etc.). The present value of expected lifetime earnings is the summation of the present values for all ages.

Although in theory earnings should be summed throughout the entire life expectancy, 75 has often been taken as the ending age, based on the assumption that probable earnings for subsequent ages are insignificant. This assumption is relatively accurate for estimates which begin at young ages, but it is increasingly violated the older the person is at the time of injury or death. For instance, when not continued beyond age 75, the LPE method truncates losses by about 1% for 30-year-old males and about 7% for 60-year-old males. Female losses are not affected quite as heavily, about half a percent and 5%, respectively.

12.2 Sample Calculation

Assume a 33-year-old male with a high school education. Survival probabilities (L) are from Table 1 (Part III) and labor force participation rates (P) and probabilities of employment (E) are from Table 9. Earnings are assumed constant at $30,000 per year, and earnings are discounted at a net rate of 2.0%.

| Age | Average Annual Earnings | Probabilities | | | | Expected Annual Earnings |
		(L) Life	(P) Participation	(E) Employment	(LPE) Joint	
33	$30,000	0.998389	0.922	0.948	0.87271	$25,668
34	$30,000	0.99669	0.922	0.948	0.87123	$25,122
35	$30,000	0.99507	0.915	0.953	0.86718	$24,506
36	$30,000	0.99339	0.915	0.953	0.86572	$23,994
37	$30,000	0.91733	0.915	0.953	0.86427	$23,484
38	...	...	...	...	...	...
39	...	...	...	...	...	...
						Lifetime Total

The model can be refined in several ways. Earnings can be varied with age. Probabilities of participation and employment can be set to 100% during initial years for persons who have demonstrated a long period of continuous employment. Conversely, they can be set lower than average for persons who have been employed only sporadically. Probabilities of receiving retirement benefits in addition to or instead of continued earnings can be built into more complicated models. Retirement benefits may also require different net discount rates from those of earnings, and in some cases different components of the retirement benefits have different net discount rates.

The probability of working full-time decreases with advancing age, and use of full-time earnings data may overestimate losses. CPS Annual Social and Economic (ASEC) Supplement 2006 data for males show a decrease of full-time employment from 78% between ages 55–64 to 52% for ages 65–74, and 38% for ages over 75. For females of similar ages the percentages of full-time employment were 66%, 41%, and 31% for ages 55–64, 65–74 and over 75, respectively. Additionally, hourly earnings are usually lower for older persons.

These problems can be dealt with beginning at, for example, age 65 by using "all workers" rather than "full-time" earnings data and not reducing earnings to reflect the probability of being employed. For active, full-time persons whose death or injury occurred at older ages, full-time earnings should usually be continued for some period of time. A possible choice would be to continue full-time earnings at least through the worklife expectancy.

Employee benefits are also typically lower for part-time employees. For instance, Lettau and Buchmueller (1999) showed that part-time employees receive non-mandated fringe benefits only about 40% as often as full-time employees. However, although methodologically rigorous, inclusion of properly reduced fringe benefits would have small effects on most LPE estimates.

12.3 Data for Probabilities of Life (L), Participation (P) and Employment (E)

Probability of survival (L) data by race and all educational levels combined are available in the *Vital Statistics of the United States* and online at *www.cdc.gov/nchswww*. Table 1 (Part III) provides mortality data by sex, race/Hispanic origin, and educational attainment, and Table 2 provides mortality data by smoking status and education. It should be noted that, as discussed in Chapter 4, mortality by education corrects for biases in data from the *Vital Statistics of the United States*. Probabilities of participation (P) and employment (E) are published by the BLS in *Employment and Earnings* and are available online at *www.bls.gov*. Data disaggregated by sex, race, education, and ten-year age groupings can be obtained from the BLS by special request at (202) 606-6378. In addition, this book provides data by education and 5-year age groupings for many demographic characteristics over the period 2000 through 2006 and for smoking status for 2000 through 2003.

For many decades probabilities of labor force participation (P) have typically been decreasing for males and increasing for females. For demographic groups whose trends have been steadily up or down it is best to use the most recent participation rates—in the past data that were not current would have overestimated male losses and underestimated female losses. Data from the CPS show, however, that not all demographic groups have experienced smooth trends. This was especially true for demographic groups with relatively small populations. However, recently participation rates for both sexes at most educational levels have become, and are expected to remain, more stable. The exception is persons of older ages whose participation has recently begun to increase and is projected by the BLS to continue increasing for some time.

Probabilities of employment (E) should be long-term historical averages to mitigate the effects of economic business cycles on employment and to reduce sampling errors, which are relatively large for CPS samples when disaggregated by age and education. Finally, although it is preferable to use the most recent mortality data, survival probabilities change only slowly, and several year old data will only minimally bias earnings estimates.

To assist in deriving LPE estimates, Tables 9 through 11 (Part III) provide probabilities of participation (P) and employment (E) by 5-year age groupings. (The information is presented as *unemployment*, but conversion is simple: one minus unemployment rates equal probabilities of employment.) The data in these tables (with the exception of Table 11) are averaged across 2000 through 2006, thus covering a period which is about average for the length of an economic cycle. Participation (P) and employment (E) are available for the following characteristics by sex, age, and education:

- All races, whites, black and Hispanics
- Single females of all races
- Smoking status: never-smokers, current smokers, and former smokers

Data sources and methodologies used to derive the participation probabilities for these characteristics are described in Chapters 9–11. Employment probabilities are derived from the same data sources and are defined as the percentage of employed persons divided by the number of persons in the labor force (of the given subpopulation).

Chapter 13

Mean Years to Final Separation

13.1 Introduction

Years to final separation (YFS) provides estimates of the number of years remaining before final (permanent) separation from the labor force, *irrespective of the number and length of inactive and active periods*. This is in contrast to worklife expectancy and LPE methods which estimate only the expected number of years a worker will be *actively participating* in the labor force from a given age.

13.2 Brief History

Nelson (1983) introduced the concept of years to final separation by calculating median age at final separation[1] using data from the Bureau of Labor Statistics' 1977 increment-decrement working life tables. The Nelson median is the number of years that pass before the labor force declines to one-half of the original base age size. Smith updated Nelson's results using 1979-80 data, but did not publish her results. Frasca and Winger (1989) published Smith's tables and made a distinction between the "Nelson Median" and "True Median." They argued that the true median can only be determined using data from longitudinal studies and that Nelson's estimates had the potential to deviate from the true median because he did not distinguish between permanent and temporary separations. Frasca and Winger also proposed a method for estimating mean years to final separation using transition probabilities from CPS data matched across two years to determine means indirectly. Their definition of the mean is the sum of "total years to final separation for all labor force participants…(divided by)…the size of the labor force at the age."

The most recent and extensive analyses of mean and median years to final separation come from the work of Skoog and Ciecka (2003, 2004a). Building on Frasca and Winger, they formalized the probabilistic foundations for mean and median YFS by developing a set of recursive formulae to generate explicit probability distributions of years to final separation. They also calculated many other measures of central tendency (median, mode, standard deviation, skewness, kurtosis, and probability intervals) and showed that the shape of the probability distribution changes depending on the base age.[2]

13.3 Data and Methodology

Data are derived from the Current Population Survey and the National Mortality Study. Transition probabilities used in this chapter are identical to those discussed and used in calculations of increment-decrement worklife expectancies. See Chapter 8 for more detail.

The mathematical basis for the methodology used in this book is the same as described by Frasca and Winger (1989) and Skoog and Ciecka (2003). The only difference is that the increment-decrement model was *implicit* in their calculations whereas the approach here uses the Markov increment-decrement model *explicitly*. Our method produces the same numerical results, but the method described below provides the additional heuristic value of illustrating how the estimates are generated.

Mortality rates and transition probabilities from the increment-decrement model predict that in every age after the beginning age (BA) there will be some probability of exiting the labor force through death or permanent inactivity.[3] Permanent inactivity can arise for reasons such as permanent total disability, voluntary retirement, involuntary retirement for family reasons, etc. These we term "live exit." Death from an active state and "live exit" followed by death constitute the only two ways to permanently exit the labor force. The age at which this occurs is termed the age of final separation.

The probability of exiting at the beginning age, x, is equal to the probability of death at age x plus the probability of becoming inactive and dying during age $x + 1$, plus the probability of remaining inactive through periods $x + 1$ and $x + 2$ and then dying, plus the probability of remaining inactive through periods $x + 1$ through $x + 3$ and then dying, etc., until all persons are dead. Note that this provides *only* the probability of the person exiting in age x. The probability of exiting at age $x + 1$ is calculated in the same fashion with the exception that the beginning population at age $x + 1$ depends upon the increment-decrement transitions of age x. Again note that following this procedure provides the probability of the person exiting only in age $x + 1$. The same process is followed for all remaining years of life to determine the probability of exiting at each of those given ages (or number of years after the beginning age). Combining all of these probabilities produces the probability distribution that predicts the likelihood that a person at beginning age x, will experience final separation in each subsequent age. (Another way of considering this procedure is by tracking changes in a population. If we assume a population of 100,000, all active in age x, age $x + 1$ and all following years will have different portions of the initial 100,000 active, inactive, and dead.)

We present the following visualization of the process as the population moves age by succeeding age through the increment-decrement transitions. We examine it in several distinct steps. The first step is how the population changes age by age. The second step is how probabilities of being removed from the population by death for each age following the beginning age are developed. The third is how the probability of live exit for age x is derived from the preceding increment-decrement transitions. And, finally, how the mean years to final separation are calculated based on the preceding steps.

As the first step in visualizing the process, Figure 9 shows how the population changes with age. Starting with all persons active at the beginning age (*BA*) there are three possible transitions to the next older age, *BA* + 1. The first possibility is to remain active (move from *a* to *a*), the second to become inactive (move from *a* to *i*), and the third possibility is death (moving from *a* to *ad*). Graphically, deaths are represented on the right-half of Figure 9, and those remaining alive are represented on the left. Thus, the only way for the person at *BA* to experience certain final separation from the labor force is to die. We assume mid-year transitions, so the age of final separation for those that die between *BA* and *BA* + 1 is *BA* + 0.5. Those who become inactive between *BA* and *BA* + 1 could potentially remain permanently inactive until death at some future age. These individuals would be credited with exiting the labor force as a live exit at *age BA + 0.5 because their final separation from the labor force occurred at the age when they transitioned from active to inactive, not when they died.*

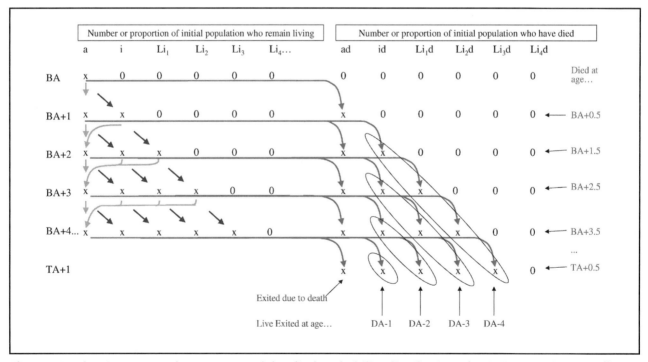

Figure 9 *Markov increment-decrement model to find probability distributions for AFS, assuming initially active. Legend: a = active; i = inactive; Li=long-term inactive; d = dead; TA = Truncation age (last possible living age for the population)*

At the next age, *BA* + 1, the population now has both actives and inactives. Between *BA* + 1 and *BA* + 2 some remain or become active (remaining at or moving to *a*), some become inactive (moving from *a* to *i*), and some of the inactives die (moving to *id*). As above, note that inactives who die at age *BA* + 1.5 actually exited the labor force at *BA* + 0.5. Some of the inactives, however, remain inactive and move to *Li₁*. These are *potentially* live exits for age *BA* + 0.5, because at this point, they have already experienced one full year of inactivity. However, they must be tracked through future ages until death to determine the proportion (or number) that actually remained permanently inactive versus those who returned to an active state in some future year. Moving from age to age, these are called long-term inactives (labeled as *Li₁*, *Li₂*, *Li₃*, etc.) and represent those who have not returned to active status.

The pattern repeats for the transitions between *BA* + 2 and *BA* + 3. Some remain or become active, some of the actives become inactive (moving to *i* in the 4th row of Figure 9), some of the actives die (moving from *a* to *ad* between the 3rd and 4th rows of Figure 9 and therefore having an age of final separation of *BA* + 2.5*), and some of the inactives die (moving to *id* in row *BA* + 3). Unlike the actives who died in this age interval, however, the age at final separation for these live exits is determined by the inactive state from which they transitioned as live exits (i.e., *Li₁*, *Li₂*, *Li₃*, etc.). At this point, there is only one long-term inactive state *Li₁* and the proportion of them that die at age *BA* + 2.5 (moving to *Li₁d*) actually separated at age *BA* + 0.5. This process continues as we move through *BA* + 4, *BA* + 5, etc. until the age at which the entire population has died, i.e., *TA* + 1.[4]

The next step is to examine how the probabilities of live exit are calculated at each subsequent age. (Note that we are referring only to the contribution that each successive age along the Markov tree makes to the overall probability of live exit at *BA* + 0.5.) Final separation due to death for each age is accounted for in the "*ad*" column of Figure 9. Final separation due to live exit is tracked separately in the remaining right-hand columns of Figure 9. By the beginning of *BA* + 1 a proportion of the original population will have become inactive. Some of these will die between *BA* + 1 and *BA* + 2. The probability of this happening equals the transition probability of active to inactive (from *BA* to *BA* + 1) multiplied by the probability of dying between *BA* + 1 and *BA* + 2. Again, it is important to understand that this is the contribution that age *BA* + 1 makes to the probability of live exit for age *BA* + 0.5. At the beginning of *BA* + 2 a proportion of the original population will have remained inactive for 1.5 years. Some of these will die between *BA* + 2 and *BA* + 3 (i.e., move from *Li₁* to *Li₁d* and then die).

This probability equals the transition probability of active to inactive (from *BA* to *BA* + 1) multiplied by the transition probability of inactive to inactive (from *BA* + 1 to *BA* + 2) multiplied by the probability of dying between *BA* + 2 and *BA* + 3. As above, note that this is the contribution age *BA* + 2 makes to the probability of live exit at *BA* + 0.5. At the beginning of *BA* + 3 a proportion of the original population will have remained inactive for 2.5 years. Some of these will die between *BA* + 3 and *BA* + 4 (i.e., move from *Li₂* to *Li₂d* and experience final exit). This probability equals the transition probability of active to inactive (from *BA* to *BA* + 1) multiplied by the transition probability of inactive to inactive (from *BA* + 1 to *BA* + 2) multiplied by the transition probability of inactive to inactive (from *BA* + 2 to *BA* + 3) multiplied by the probability of dying in *BA* + 3 to *BA* + 4. This process continues as we move through all ages to the truncation age plus one. Each represents the probability of having remained *consistently* inactive after becoming inactive at age *BA* + 0.5 multiplied by the mortality rate of its age. These portions of the population, given a starting population of 100,000, are represented as the right-most number at each age following *BA* moving down the diagonal in Figure 9, i.e., within the right-most circled diagonal.

Finally, the probability for a person at *BA* to have *live exit* at age *BA*+0.5 is the sum of the probabilities of the right most diagonal in Figure 9, i.e., the diagonal *id* to *Li₁₁₀₋ᵦₐd*, *and the probability of final separation at BA+0.5 is the sum of all* numbers along the diagonal (i.e., including *ad* at age *BA* + 1). For instance, for a person 20 years old this gives us the probability that this person will experience final separation at age 20.5. It is still necessary, however, to determine what are the probabilities of remaining inactive and dying during ages 21, 22, 23, and so forth. These probabilities are generated by the same increment-decrement tree shown in Figure 9 for the remaining ages (i.e., BA + 1, BA + 2, BA + 3, etc.). The only difference is that the starting population is taken to be composed of actives, inactives, and deceased as determined by all increment-decrement transitions to that age. For example, the probability of final separation at age *BA* + 2.5 is the probability of exit due to death (column *ad* for age *BA* + 3) plus the sum of the diagonal starting at *id* for *BA* + 4 and ending at *Li₁₀₇₋ᵦₐd* (i.e., the sum of probabilities within the third diagonal from the left). Compiled for all ages, these sums describe the probabilities that a person at age *BA* will experience final separation at age *BA* + 0.5. (See Figures 10 and 11.)

For younger ages, the probabilities of live exit along the diagonals are products of relatively small numbers and, therefore, become vanishingly small as they progress down the diagonal. Thus, the probability of final separation remains small for young ages (dominated by mortality rates), rises sharply to a peak in the sixties (dominated by live exits), and then declines steadily (due to the small numbers of those remaining active at older ages). (See Figure 10 for an initially active cohort beginning at age 20.) For older initially active beginning ages the probability of permanent separation is large and then declines steadily for latter ages. (See Figure 11 for an initially active cohort beginning at age 60.)

The final step is to combine the probability distribution with the years past BA associated with each probability. Specifically, mean years to final separation is the weighted average calculated by multiplying the probabilities of final separation at every year past *BA* by the number of years past *BA*. For example, for the 20 year old, mean years to final separation is the sum of the probability of exiting at age 20.5 multiplied by 0.5, plus the probability of exiting at age 21.5 multiplied by 1.5, plus the probability of exiting at age 22.5

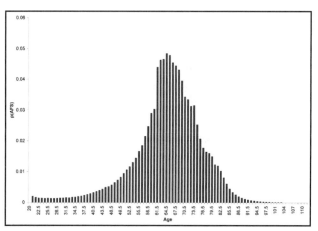

Figure 10 *Probability distribution, age of final separation, males all education levels, beginning age 20.*

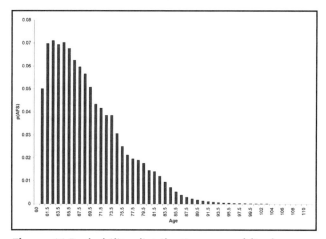

Figure 11 *Probability distribution, age of final separation, males all education levels, beginning age 65.*

multiplied by 2.5,...plus the probability of exiting at age 60.5 multiplied by 40.5,...plus the probability of exiting at age 110.5 multiplied by 90.5. Note that these probabilities of exiting are shown graphically for each age in the probability distributions such as those in Figures 10 and 11.

Using the mathematical notation of Skoog and Ciecka (2003), the formula is:

$$\overline{YFS} = E(s_{x,m}) = \sum_{s-0}^{TA-x} s \cdot p_{YFS}(x,m,s)$$

Where s = years, x = beginning age, m = initial state (active or inactive), and *TA* = truncation age (i.e., age at which the total population is assumed to have died).

13.4 Differences Between Initially Actives and Initially Inactives

We present tables in this book both for those beginning active and for those beginning inactive. Differences are slight for younger ages but greater for older ages. For initially actives, all workers accrue a minimum of 0.5 years of worklife regardless of beginning age. Thus the probability of zero years of activity for initially actives is zero. For initially inactives, however, there is *non-zero* probability of accruing zero years of activity—that is, never entering the work force (see the furthest-right diagonal of Figure 12). For an initially active 18 year old, this probability is a nominal amount, but for older beginning ages it becomes *substantial*. Thus, means for initially inactives in late middle ages become increasingly less than for initially actives.

13.5 Results

Figure 13 and Text Table 37 present summaries of Mean Years to Final Separation by sex, race, education, and initial activity status. YFS is greater for higher education levels for both sexes and all racial/ethnicity categories (with the exception of white females with a graduate education), and it is greater for males than for females. Initial activity state has almost no effect on YFS at younger ages regardless of education, sex, or race. For older ages, however, initial activity state does have an effect. For example, at 65 years of age, white males and females with less than a high school education who are initially inactive have YFSs which are 2.2 and 2.3 years, respectively, less than those who are initially active. For 65-year-old white males the difference remains relatively constant across all education levels. The effect of initial activity state across education levels differs, however, for other groups. It generally increases with education for white females, decreases for black males and females, and decreases for Hispanic males but increases for Hispanic females.

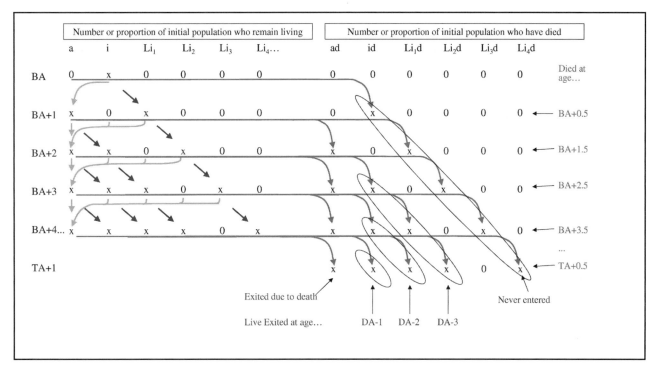

Figure 12 *Markov increment-decrement model to find probability distributions for AFS, assuming initially inactive.*

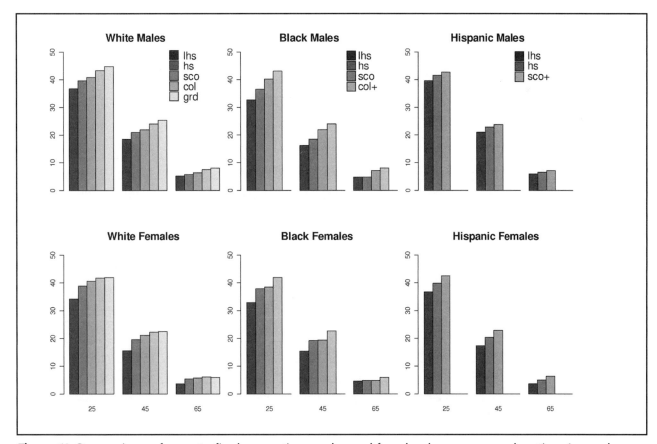

Figure 13 *Comparison of years to final separation, males and females, by age, race, education. Legend: lhs=less than high school, hs=high school, sco=some college, col=college degree, grd=graduate degree.*

Text Table 37: Mean years to final separation, initially active vs. initially inactive

Age	< HS	HS	Some College	College Degree	Grad Degree	< HS	HS	Some College	College Degree	Grad Degree
			Initially Active					Initially Inactive		
					Males					
					All Races					
25	36.14	39.45	40.78	43.22	44.89	36.12	39.44	40.78	43.21	44.89
45	18.12	20.76	21.90	23.96	25.47	16.82	20.09	21.44	23.79	25.38
65	5.15	5.75	6.41	7.49	8.13	2.99	3.80	4.47	5.41	6.14
					White					
25	36.75	39.76	40.91	43.36	44.97	36.74	39.75	41	43.35	44.97
45	18.49	20.98	21.98	24.11	25.56	17.09	20.30	21.50	23.92	25.44
65	5.23	5.82	6.43	7.58	8.19	3.01	3.88	4.43	5.45	6.19
					Black					
25	32.71	36.68	40.22	43.13		32.69	36.67	40.21	43.13	
45	16.19	18.63	21.97	24.14		14.87	18.03	21.66	24.06	
65	4.84	4.81	7.20	8.12		2.86	2.99	6.35	7.07	
					Hispanic					
25	39.72	41.58	42.83			39.72	41.57	42.83		
45	21.06	22.91	23.88			20.76	22.62	23.71		
65	6.10	6.63	7.18			3.86	5.42	5.92		
					Females					
					All Races					
25	34.01	38.78	40.38	42.03	41.88	33.99	38.77	40.38	42.02	41.87
45	15.50	19.63	21.05	22.50	22.37	14.67	18.87	20.53	22.22	22.11
65	3.99	5.29	5.64	6.37	5.85	1.67	2.69	3.11	4.04	3.19
					White					
25	34.26	38.97	40.66	41.90	42.08	34.24	38.96	41	41.89	42.07
45	15.67	19.77	21.33	22.38	22.50	14.87	18.97	20.78	22.06	22.25
65	3.83	5.41	5.80	6.30	6.08	1.53	2.69	3.18	3.88	3.24
					Black					
25	33.05	38.06	38.60	41.92		33.03	38.06	38.60	41.92	
45	15.40	19.26	19.48	22.72		14.44	18.67	19.07	22.59	
65	4.63	4.92	4.82	6.15		2.29	3.28	3.01	4.61	
					Hispanic					
25	36.74	39.87	42.52			36.73	39.86	42.52		
45	17.49	20.49	22.94			17.17	20.06	22.72		
65	3.83	5.06	6.49			2.18	3.05	4.27		

Note: For Blacks the College Degree category includes Bachelor's and Graduate degrees, and for Hispanics the Some College category includes everything over a high school degree

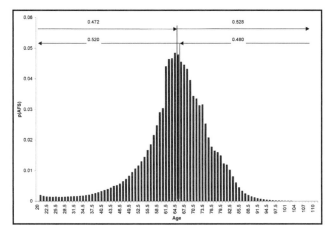

Figure 14 *Probability distribution, 20-year-old initially active males, summing the probabilities from young to older versus old to younger.*

Notably, mean years to final separation is less sensitive to educational attainment than worklife expectancy, especially for females (see Text Table 27 for a comparison). For example, the difference between worklife expectancy for a 25-year-old male (all races) with less than high school education versus one with a graduate degree is 11.4 years, whereas the difference for YFS is 8.8 years. For females the comparable figures are 15.5 and 7.9 years, respectively. For black males, 14.5 and 10.4 years; and for black females, 15.9 and 8.9 years, respectively.

13.6 The Problem with Median YFS

Unlike mean YFS, median YFS does not have a simple solution. Its practical definition is simple and on the surface appears to be a straightforward calculation, i.e., the number of years that pass before the labor force declines to one-half of the original base age size. Finding the median according to the practical definition would simply involve summing the probabilities and finding the point at which the cumulative sum crosses the 50% threshold. As this usually occurs between two discrete ages the exact 50% value would be found by interpolation. However, unlike the mean, whose practical solution is exactly equal to the mathematical solution, the practical solution for median is not mathematically correct because of the discrete nature of the variable *age*. As Figure 14 shows, we find that a different threshold is obtained if cumulative probabilities are calculated from young to older versus old to younger (for the 20-year-old cohort discussed above). Accumulating from young to older ages, the 50%

break point lies between YFS 64.5 and 65.5 (65.1 by interpolation). However, accumulating from old to younger ages, the 50% break point lies between YFS 66.5 and 65.5 (66.1 by interpolation). One possible "exact" median would be the average of the two. However, this is somewhat arbitrary, and other criteria could affect the final number (see Skoog and Ciecka, 2003, for additional details). Therefore, we do not include median YFS estimates in our tables.

Notes

1. Final separation occurs when a worker leaves the labor force never to reenter. In this chapter we use the terms *years to final separation* (YFS) and *age at final separation* (AFS) interchangeably. AFS is the expected age of final separation for a given beginning age (BA). Years to final separation is simply AFS – BA.

2. The distribution is bell-shaped for younger ages and highly skewed to the left for older ages (see Figures 10 and 11). This makes intuitive sense: at young beginning ages the probability of final separation is very small for many years, while at beginning ages in the sixties and older the probability of immediate final separation is quite high and remains so for several years before gradually decreasing with advancing age.

3. Note that the random variables YFS and AFS depend upon a great number of possible worklife paths that any given individual may follow in a Markov chain. A key assumption for any random variable is that the underlying probabilities are independent of one another. It is not feasible, however, to assume that the 20-year-old worker who experiences 30 years of inactivity would do so for 29 independent reasons. Rather, it is more likely that continued inactivity would result from a single (or few) underlying cause(s). Thus, YFS and AFS do not theoretically qualify as fully random variables in the strictest sense. Therefore statistical statements made about them must be carefully evaluated for error.

4. Using the same methods as Skoog and Ciecka (2003), we assume truncation age at 110 and estimate transition probabilities and mortality rates past 80. That is, we assume active-to-active probability declines at a rate of $^a p_x^a = 0.9 \, (^a p_{x-1}^a)$ to age 109 and then = 0 for age 110. We assume inactive to inactive increases at a rate of $^i p_x^i = (^i p_{x-1}^i)$ to age 109 and = 1 at age 110. We extrapolate mortality rates at a rate of $p_x^d = 1.065 \, (p_{x-1}^d)$ to age 109 and $p_x^d = 1$ for age 110.

Chapter 14

Issues in Estimations of Worklife

14.1 Capacity versus Expectancy

The first decision regarding determination of duration of working life is whether to use a "capacity" or an "expectancy" measure. The choice is usually based on legal standards, relevance to an individual person, ease of explanation to a jury, or other details of a particular case.

For the following discussion of working life duration, "capacity" is defined as the "reasonable" period during which a person is *capable* of working whether he or she might choose to or not.[1] Capacity estimators *do not reduce* worklife estimates for periods of inactivity. "Expectancy" is defined as a measure of the amount of time that the average person is in the labor force and *does reduce* duration of working life for statistically average periods of inactivity.

In actual practice, the distinction between these two methods is not always clear, and what are really expectancy measures are often used even when capacity is the legal standard.

A. Capacity

Theoretically, at the extreme, capacity would extend throughout life expectancy, diminished only by average work-limiting disability and other nonvoluntary absences from the labor force. In practice, it is usually taken as the number of uninterrupted years remaining from the age at injury or death until retirement. This meets the general legal standard that testimony not be arbitrary—that it is instead "reasonably certain" (Horner and Slesnick, 1999). In some cases, a specific age is chosen. Some examples include: the normal age of retirement in a defined benefit pension plan, an age for Social Security benefits, or a person's intended

retirement age. In other cases, retirement age is statistically derived; Years to Final Separation (YFS) is an example discussed in this book.

Capacity measures are especially appropriate for persons who (a) were in a defined retirement benefit plan with mandated retirement age for eligibility of full benefits, (b) have a history of high attachment to the labor force, or (c) can demonstrate their intention to work to a chosen retirement age.

The arguments for use of Years to Final Separation (YFS) capacity measures can be summarized as follows:

- Even YFS may be conservative as a true capacity measure to the extent that people voluntarily retire while still having earning capacity.
- Expectancy measures may not adjust for sick pay, unemployment insurance, and disability income.
- Using plaintiff's historical average earnings already incorporates their periods of temporary absences from the labor force and use of worklife expectancy would double count these periods.

Another argument for capacity measures is the economic theory of "opportunity cost." In the context of labor force participation, the opportunity cost concept is the recognition that the value of an activity chosen in lieu of working for money is at least as high to the person as the amount of money that might have been earned. Otherwise, the person would have chosen to work for money. If a worker chooses to leave the labor force for a period of time (for childcare, additional education, etc.), the voluntary substitution of this activity should be valued at the same rate as the earnings which are foregone. If, as a result of the wrongful actions of the tort feasor, the injured party no longer has the *opportunity* to make such a choice, the person should be compensated for both lost earnings *and* the time he or she may have spent in an equally valued alternative activity. Therefore, basing duration of working life on data that reflects only actual levels of participation in the labor force *under-compensates* injured parties.

In practice, the issue is not so clear. A significant proportion of voluntary absences from the labor market are devoted to activities that are intended to increase future earnings potential. For example, of those voluntarily not in the labor force and not retired, nearly 40% of males and 10% of females attend school. Others are voluntarily absent to achieve optimal search duration for better employment. To include these periods in estimates of lost earnings that also incorporate increases in earnings with age would be to double count: the absence itself partially results in the subsequent earnings increases.

A practical problem with use of a retirement age, such as one designated in a defined benefit pension plan, is that it does not account for the probabilities of becoming disabled or of not surviving to that date. In addition, it does not account for the probability of choosing to continue work for another employer or in another field afterward.

B. Expectancy

Even when "capacity" is the legal standard, "expectancy" estimators are often used. As Lewis (1987) argues, "It simply is not reasonable to fail to adjust the appraisal of lost earnings to reflect the probability of occurrences of disability or voluntary separation from the labor force regardless of what some court would have ruled." The majority of forensic economists appear to concur with Lewis' view of "reasonable certainty" requirements. In a survey of "prevailing practice," Brookshire et al. (2006) reported that slightly more than two-thirds of forensic economists use methods that reduce working lives to account for periods of inactivity, and a high percentage of those remaining use these methods in combination with others to achieve similar results.

The most common measure of expectancy, used by about half of forensic economists, is the number of expected years of remaining worklife, that is, worklife expectancy (Brookshire et al., 2006).

Use of data from "worklife expectancy" tables implicitly assumes that all periods of inactivity will occur at the end of the worklife period rather than at various times during the interval. This results in overestimated net present value of losses because earnings are assumed to occur during periods that are less heavily discounted.

Other "worklife expectancy" methodologies attempt to correct for the "discounting bias" by spreading out periods of inactivity. The two most popular are the Life-Participation-Employment (LPE) method described in Chapter 12, and spreading remaining years of worklife expectancy estimates out proportionally over a longer time period as discussed by Skoog (2001 and 2002), and Skoog and Ciecka (2006). These and others, such as those suggested by Boudreaux (1983) and Becker and Alter (1985), are briefly discussed and compared in Chapter 16.

14.2 Female Labor Force Patterns

For females the expectancy/capacity distinction is especially troublesome, and the opportunity cost argument is especially strong. Married women or single women with children may be voluntarily absent from the labor market for extended periods for childcare and other household services. Because labor force participation statistics do not include work at home, they underestimate female participation in value producing activities. Because of this and the fact that a 1977 BLS study showed that worklife expectancies of single females (i.e., those with minimal need or incentive to remain out of the labor force) were very similar to those of males, many forensic economists have used worklife statistics of males as a proxy for capacity of females. To address this issue, worklife expectancies specific to single females are presented in this book (see Chapter 9 and Table 6).

In addition to the opportunity cost concept, two dominant aspects of women's labor force patterns are important in considering their lifetime working patterns. The first is that female participation in the labor force, after a long, steady increase beginning with World War II, reached a peak in 1999 at about 60 percent and appears to have been decreasing slightly since then. The participation of married mothers with young children appears to have reached a peak in 1997 and 1998 and has since decreased about 4 percentage points. The BLS projects that female participation rates will remain flat in the future, except for moderately increasing rates at older ages.

The second is that women tend to be quite persistent in their work habits: those who do not work usually continue not to work, and those who do work usually continue to work (Heckman and Willis, 1977; Long and Jones, 1980; Shaw, 1994). In fact, previous work behavior is a stronger predictor of future female work patterns than any other personal characteristic. For instance, for a 40-year-old, married, white female with a high school degree, the probability of labor force participation if employed in the previous year is 25 percentage points greater than indicated by average BLS participation rates, and it would take about 12 years to decrease to average rates (Capozza, Nakamura and Bloss, 1989). Recent research using the Early Childhood Longitudinal Study-Birth Cohort supports these conclusions (Han et al., 2008).

Patterns of persistence (both activity rates and number of hours worked) develop before marriage and extend into the married years. Thus, labor force participation of females had increased during the last decades not so much because persistence has changed, but rather because the number of persistent workers increased. In addition, the duration and extent of reduced hours relative to average life-cycle patterns are less pronounced than in the past; that is, one year's decline is less likely to cause the next year to remain below lifetime averages (Shaw, 1994).

In short, given opportunity cost factors, trends in female labor force participation rates, and the persistence of their work patterns, it is inappropriate in most cases to use worklife expectancies for all females regardless of marital status for determining worklife expectancies of females unless a loss estimate for a particular woman includes a high dollar amount for the value of remaining at home for childcare and other services to the family.

14.3 Disabled Persons

This book has not addressed the question of worklife statistics for disabled persons because these data can be purchased from Vocational Econometrics.[2] This is the only source currently available for these data. However, a vociferous debate has raged between Vocational Econometrics (Gibson, 2000) and many members of the forensic economic community regarding the credibility of these worklife estimates (Ciecka, 2001; Skoog, 2002). The following summarizes some of the perceived problems. Note, though, that some of these problems have become reduced or moot as the Census has changed its survey instruments and Vocational Econometrics has added information from the American Community Survey to its calculations. See the end of this section.

The primary reason so many forensic economists have not trusted Vocational Econometrics' worklife expectancies is that the definitions of disabled in the Current Population Surveys upon which their tables are based, have not been sufficient to distinguish adequately between disabled persons who may have work limitations and those who do not. Additionally, the CPS has not provided enough information to address varying degrees of work limitations. Most researchers appear to agree that the data have been adequate for identifying trends but not for how various impairments limit major activities and more specifically, labor force participation (among others: Barnow, 2008; Hale, 2001; Rones, 1981).

Disability data in general are problematic in how to measure the effects of disability on labor force participation accurately. Nonworkers often have unobserved economic or psychological reasons to overstate the extent of their disability. Among these are guilt, self-justification, and fear of loss of benefits (Stern, 1989).

The employment dynamics of the disabled are also not well known. Social Security Disability Insurance (SSDI) and other disability-related compensation programs provide the primary data for labor force participation patterns after onset of disability, but these data are incomplete because not all those who are eligible for these programs apply, and not all those who are rejected go back to work (Yelin and Katz, 1994).

Data from the SSDI show that demographic characteristics are strongly correlated with whether beneficiaries work after becoming disabled. For example, education is positively related: less than 10% of those with less than nine years of school do some work after becoming disabled, compared to about 35% of those with more than a high school education. The percentage of never-married recipients who do some work is twice that of those who were ever-married (41% versus 20%), and the percentage decreases sharply with age (about 60% for those less than 25 years of age versus less than 15% for those 45 to 54 years of age). Overall, financial need is the dominant reason for return to work, for the number of hours worked per week, and for number of years worked since disability (Schechter, 1997). This kind of information can be useful in determining whether or which disability worklife table is relevant for a particular case.

Persons with nonstrenuous employment are less likely to incur or report disabilities, and, partially because of the ability to meet job demands even with disabilities, they are less likely to report work limitations resulting from disabilities. In the nonphysical occupations (defined as managerial/professional, sales and clerical) approximately 14% of men and women reported a work limitation, while in the physical occupations, 23% of men and 26% of women reported work limitations. Perhaps because they tend to work fewer hours, married women experienced the smallest effect of disability on their participation (Loprest et al., 1995).

People with disabilities may be enabled by developments in computer hardware and software in the future to become competitive in the labor market and increase their labor force participation. If so, projecting today's data into the future is problematic.

Another weakness of the Vocational Econometric tables is that they do not incorporate mortality data by educational level or labor force participation status (the inactive population faces greater risk of dying than the active population) (Rogot et al., 1992 and Sorlie et al., 1995). Possible future research may allow determination of relative mortality risks by degree of disability.

Nevertheless, it is demonstrably a fact that disabled persons as a whole have lower labor force participation rates than those not disabled. By definition, worklife expectancies of those unable to participate in the labor force are reduced, either in full or in part. The devil lies in the details: whether a particular person falls in a category, which category, for how long, and whether worklife expectancies based on the CPS surveys can adequately measure any of these. Purists say no; some believe that even possibly flawed worklife tables are better than none; and others attempt to work with vocational experts to tailor occupational and worklife plans for individual persons as best as possible.

Other research shows that knowing the labor force status of people with disabilities is itself misleading, because they are more likely to be in "nonstandard jobs" (Schur, 2002). About twice as many people with disabilities as without disabilities voluntarily work in part-time and/or temporary jobs and choose to be independent contractors because these allow them to manage their health conditions better. These jobs typically pay lower wages and offer less generous fringe benefits.

Finally, several task forces, established in the late 1990s, were tasked with the development of accurate and reliable measures of the employment rate of people with disabilities. The American Community Survey implemented its improved question set in 2008 stating that it will "be able to give an acceptable estimate of the population of persons with disabilities, as defined by a person's risk of participation limitation when he or she has a functional limitation or impairment" (Brault and Stern, 2007). The Current Population Survey has also been working to improve its disability questions, and according to Mr. McMenamin, BLS Division of Labor Force Statistics, the CPS measures disability well enough now in regard to capacity and actual labor force participation.

14.4 Factors Influencing Future Trends of Labor Force Participation

All methods of estimating worklife expectancies depend on data observed during a particular past period. Conventional model worklife expectancies for males and females of all races with either a high school or bachelor's degree using data over the eleven-year period 1996 through 2006 are shown in Text Table 38 and Figures 15 and 16. At 35 years of age the worklife of males with a high school education has fluctuated slightly around 25 additional years, whereas it has exhibited a small, steady increase for those with a bachelor's degree. For females, worklife expectancies of both educational levels have gradually increased, although with periods of little change. At 55 years of age male worklife expectancies have increased only slightly, whereas females expectancies have experienced much larger increases at both educational levels. For blacks with a high school education, the worklife expectancies of males either 35 or 55 have remained relatively stable, whereas for black females they have increased.

Estimates would obviously be improved if future work behavior could be predicted. Although this is not possible, we can look at some of the forces that may shape future labor force patterns and may give a hint of future trends in worklife expectancies.

As noted above, historical patterns may be in a period of transition. Although average number of years spent by males in the labor force has steadily declined for many decades and increased for females, the BLS projects relative stabilization of participation for both sexes. For those less than 25, participation rates have been steadily falling (for males from 73.0% in 1986 to 63.3% in 2006, and for females from 64.3% to 57.9%) and both are projected to continue to decrease through 2016—an additional 4.0 per-

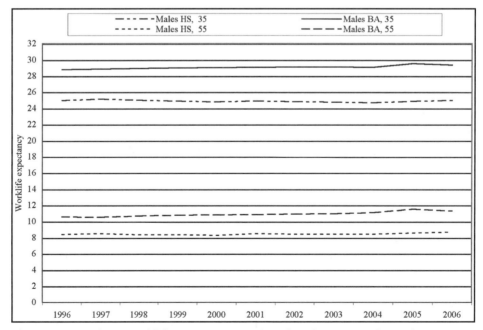

Figure 15 *Trends in worklife expectancy, using data from 1996 through 2006, males of all races, high school and college degrees.*

centage points for males and 3.1 percentage points for females (Toossi, 2007). Toossi projects continual decreases at slower rates through 2050 (Toossi, 2006). For those in prime working ages (25-54), male participation rates are projected to continue their long decline, although at a much slower rate. Females in these ages are projected to fluctuate slightly around their 2000 level, i.e., between 76 and 77%. It is at older ages that the greatest changes are expected to occur.

For many years in the past, most incentives encouraged permanent retirement at earlier and earlier ages. Attractive early retirement packages were common. Social Security encouraged retirement: it replaced nearly 50% of the income of nearly two-thirds of all workers; it penalized recipients for earning more than specified amounts; and it actuarially encouraged retirement before age 65 (Herz and Rones, 1989). Workers were forced to choose between continued full-time employment at the cost of lost pension benefits, part-time employment for low wages, or complete retirement. Most workers faced with these limitations and incentives exited the labor force permanently.

Text Table 38: Worklife Expectancy Trend: 1996 to 2006, using conventional model, all races

Age	1996	1997	1998	1999	2000	2001	2002	2003	2004	2005	2006	
Males of All Races with a High School Education Worklife Expectancies												
25	33.8	33.9	33.8	33.7	33.6	33.6	33.5	33.4	33.3	33.5	33.5	
35	25.0	25.1	25.0	24.9	24.8	24.9	24.8	24.7	24.7	24.8	24.9	
45	16.4	16.5	16.4	16.3	16.1	16.3	16.3	16.2	16.2	16.4	16.5	
55	8.4	8.5	8.4	8.4	8.3	8.5	8.4	8.4	8.4	8.6	8.7	103.3%
65	2.5	2.5	2.4	2.5	2.6	2.7	2.6	2.6	2.7	2.8	3.0	121.4%
Males of All Races with a Bachelor's Degree Worklife Expectancies												
25	38.1	38.2	38.2	38.3	38.4	38.3	38.4	38.3	38.3	38.7	38.6	
35	28.8	28.9	28.9	29.0	29.1	29.1	29.1	29.1	29.1	29.5	29.4	
45	19.5	19.5	19.6	19.7	19.7	19.8	19.8	19.8	19.9	20.3	20.1	
55	10.6	10.6	10.7	10.8	10.8	10.9	10.9	11.0	11.1	11.5	11.3	106.8%
65	3.7	3.6	3.7	3.9	4.0	3.9	4.0	4.1	4.2	4.4	4.2	113.7%
Females of All Races with a High School Education Worklife Expectancies												
25	27.9	28.1	28.0	28.1	28.2	28.3	28.3	28.3	28.1	28.0	28.1	
35	20.7	20.9	20.8	20.9	21.0	21.1	21.3	21.4	21.3	21.3	21.3	
45	13.3	13.4	13.3	13.5	13.6	13.7	13.9	14.2	14.1	14.1	14.2	
55	6.2	6.4	6.4	6.4	6.5	6.7	6.9	7.0	7.0	7.1	7.2	115.2%
65	1.6	1.6	1.6	1.7	1.7	1.8	1.9	2.0	2.1	2.1	2.2	137.3%
Females of All Races with a Bachelor's Degree Worklife Expectancies												
25	31.8	32.1	32.1	32.1	32.1	31.9	31.9	32.1	32.1	32.4	32.4	
35	23.5	23.8	23.9	23.9	23.9	23.8	23.8	24.1	24.1	24.4	24.4	
45	15.5	15.8	16.0	15.9	16.1	16.1	16.1	16.4	16.5	16.7	16.7	
55	7.6	7.8	8.0	8.0	8.2	8.3	8.2	8.5	8.6	8.8	8.8	115.4%
65	2.2	2.2	2.3	2.4	2.5	2.5	2.4	2.6	2.7	2.8	2.8	127.6%

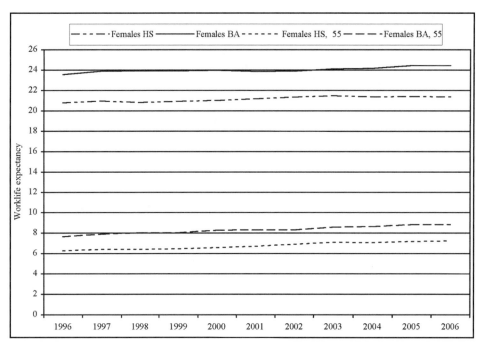

Figure 16 *Trends in worklife expectancy, using data from 1996 through 2006, females of all races, high school and college graduates.*

Recently, however, many institutional and economic factors have begun to provide incentives for older workers to remain in the labor force:

- Social Security: beginning in 2000 the age for full retirement benefits gradually increases to 67 and the penalty for early retirement increases from 20% to 30%; the delayed retirement credit will be increased; the withholding rate will decrease from $1 of every $2 earned above exempt levels to $1 of every $3; and, as SS replaces a smaller percentage of income (as average earnings increase), the opportunity cost of early retirement becomes greater (Herz and Rones, 1989, and Best and Kale, 1996). These changes are expected to decrease part-time employment, increase full-time employment, and modestly increase the age of retirement (Gustman and Steinmeier, 1985, and Fields and Mitchell, 1987).
- Cost of Living Allowances (COLAs) and ad hoc increases in pension benefits are not as common as in the past. Plans granting increases at least once in the previous five years decreased from 51% in 1983 to 6% in 1993, and only 4% of private plans contain automatic COLAs (Herz, 1995).
- Because health has increased, retirees are able to work longer, and savings must be spread over longer years of retirement.

- Although early retirement packages are incentives for early retirement from one job, the effect might be mitigated by return to work of those who would have chosen a later age for retirement (Herz, 1995).
- The shift to defined contribution plans may result in lower overall benefits. Also, most pre-retirement lump-sum distributions have not been retained for the retirement period: less than half of persons aged 45 to 55 put lump-sum distributions entirely into savings (Herz, 1995; Costo, 2006).
- Reduction in retiree health coverage provides an incentive to continue employment (Herz, 1995).
- Changes in work, such as enhanced job satisfaction, cleaner and safer work sites, easing by computers of physical demands, etc., may encourage older workers to remain active (Best and Kale, 1996).
- Rising divorce rates are forcing more people to care for themselves on smaller incomes (Best and Kale, 1996).
- Decreases in savings rates may necessitate continued labor market participation.
- Age discrimination in the past appears to have been a factor in some early exits from the labor force (Herz and Rones, 1989).

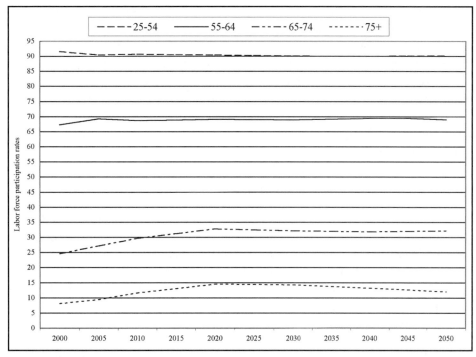

Figure 17 *Labor force participation rates 2000 to 2008 and projected to 2050, males of all races*

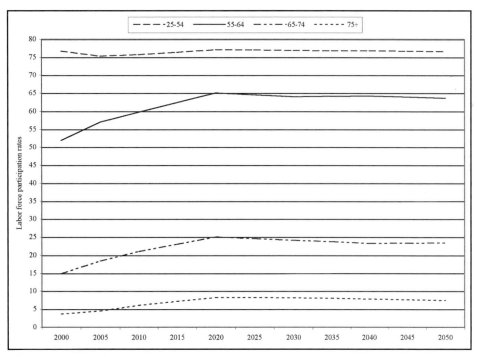

Figure 18 *Labor force participation rates 2000 to 2008 and projections to 2050, females of all races*

- The labor market itself may provide incentives for employers to encourage continued participation of older workers as the baby boomer generation passes its high participation years and the economy requires more workers. As an example, service sector employment often allows for flexible working schedules (Herz, 1995).
- The 2008 crash of the housing and stock markets has decimated the retirement savings of many people and may force many workers close to retirement to work more years and/or bring retired persons back into the labor force.

As a consequence of these and other factors, labor force participation of the older population has begun to increase and is projected to continue to do so. Participation of males 55 to 64 increased by 2.3 percentage points between 2000 and 2006 (to 69.6%). Toossi projects that their participation rates may reach 70% by 2016 but will remain thereafter at about 69%. Participation rates of males 65 to 74 have increased 4.2 percentage points since 2000 (to 28.8% in 2006) and are projected to reach a maximum of nearly 35% by 2016 before stabilizing around 32% for the next three decades. Males 75 years of age and older have had and are projected to have a similar, although slightly flatter, pattern. See Figure 17.

In contrast to younger females, participation rates of females 55 to 64 increased dramatically between 2000 and 2006 (6.3 percentage points, from 51.9% to 58.2%). Toossi projects that their participation rates will continue to increase significantly, reaching a peak of about 65% by 2020 and then decreasing slightly for the next three decades. Participation rates of females 65 to 74 have increased 4.3 percentage points since 2000 (to 19.2% in 2006) and are projected to reach a maximum of about 25% by 2016 before decreasing very slightly during the next three decades. Females 75 years of age and older have had and are projected to have a similar, although slightly flatter, pattern. See Figure 18.

In addition, the prevalence of full-time work among these groups has increased markedly. For instance, for ages 66 to 69 full-time participation for males has increased about 18% (67.6% working full-time in 2007), and for females it has increased about 16% (49.2% working full-time in 2007).

Notes

1. See Stephen Horner and Frank Slesnick's discussion of many aspects of earning capacity in the *Journal of Forensic Economics*, Vol. XII (1) 1999.

2. Vocational Econometrics, Inc., 1 Riverfront Plaza Building, Suite 2100, Louisville, Kentucky 40202, (800) 227–0198.

Chapter 15

Comparisons of Methods

This chapter is broken into three sections. The first deals with pros and cons, advantages and disadvantages, and strengths and weaknesses of the more common methods of estimating duration of working life. The second provides some examples to show relative differences in loss estimates resulting from each of seven methods. Finally, the third section is a brief overall summary.

15.1 Pros and Cons, Advantages and Disadvantages, Strengths and Weaknesses
A. Increment-Decrement Model

The increment-decrement, or Markov process, methodology of estimating worklife expectancies has been a widely accepted standard since the BLS first introduced it in 1982 to replace what is called in this book the "conventional" model (Smith, 1982). The BLS updated these tables in 1986, based on 1979–80 labor force patterns (Smith, 1986). Subsequently, Ciecka et al. updated the tables for data from 1992–93, 1994–95, 1997-98 (1995, 1996 and 2000); Richards provided tables based on 1996-98 data (1999) and discussed whether increment-decrement estimates for the population regardless of initial activity status are biased downward; Krueger updated the tables for 1998-2004 data (2004) and with Ciecka and Skoog examined issues of worklife expectancies with full- or part-time employment (Krueger et al., 2006); and

Skoog and Ciecka applied a competing risk/multiple decrement increment-decrement model to worklife expectancies for railroad workers (2006). This book contains tables based on July 1999 through June 2007 data (thus providing estimates based on seven years of matches), and differs from most estimates in that (a) mortality rates are by educational attainment, (b) estimates are derived for more education categories, and (c) estimates are derived for Blacks and Hispanics by several educational categories (see Chapter 8). The reader is advised that Skoog, Ciecka, and Krueger have expanded the theoretical basis for the increment-decrement model, provided many statistical parameters not previously available and not included in this book, and have written very completely and well about their work.

The BLS switched from the conventional methodology because it did not deal realistically with some labor force patterns and produced questionable estimates for persons who are "currently active" and "currently inactive" as of the age the worklife is estimated. The conventional model required the unrealistic assumption that all persons other than those in the labor force at the age of peak labor force participation would be lifetime inactives. In reality, however, many people enter and leave the labor force multiple times. Turnover rates are especially high for women. The conventional model for "initially actives," therefore, underestimated the portion of the population that would be active during some part of their lives. The mathematical consequence was overestimation of worklife expectancies of those currently active.[1]

The increment-decrement model does not make this assumption. By using transition probabilities observed directly from the population, it explicitly incorporates the effects of multiple entries and exits and allows for direct estimation of the worklife expectancies of the currently "active" and "inactive" populations.

Shortly after the BLS introduced the increment-decrement methodology, John Finch (1983) described an apparent inconsistency in its results when compared to actual labor force participation rates. While agreeing that the increment-decrement model is a useful tool for distinguishing between worklife expectancies of those currently "active" or "inactive," he showed that if the same data were used, worklife expectancies of the general population (i.e., including all persons, starting active and inactive) should be identical mathematically whether calculated using the conventional or the increment-decrement methodology. Comparisons of worklife expectancies from the two methods, however, show that this has never been the case. Increment-decrement estimates have been consistently less than those of the conventional model for men and usually less for women. Finch further contended that since the two methods do not provide identical results, even with the same database, either (a) the transition probabilities are not correct (possibly because of transitory turnovers or matching biases), or (b) sampling error is magnified by the iterative computations of the model.

In her rejoinder, Shirley Smith (1983) agreed that the two models would give identical results for populations which include both starting active and inactive if the populations were stable and if age-specific labor force participation rates did not change from year to year. But when rates are changing, the participation rate at time $t + 1$ for a group at age x is a function of its experience at age x, not a function of the age group $x + 1$ at time t. Thus, labor force participation rates at time $t + 1$ derived from transition probabilities between age x and $x + 1$ will not necessarily be the same as those observed for age $x + 1$ at time t. The more rapidly activity rates change, the greater the difference between the two. This effect continues through all ages since the "increment-decrement" methodology calculates the lifetime implications of transition rates observed in the sample year.

The practical difference between the two models (for estimates of the general population) is that the conventional model produces "period" worklife expectancies, i.e., those for a population assuming constant participation rates as of the period of sample observation, while the increment-decrement model produces "cohort" worklife expectancies, i.e., as they would exist for participation rates of a hypothetical person advancing through older ages.

As an example, let us assume that between age x and $x + 1$ the average participation rate for every age cohort experiences a one percent increase over its level at the initial time t. The conventional model, using time $t + 1$ data, would reflect labor force participation rates for all ages as of that exact date (i.e., a "period" tables which is "current" as of time $t + 1$). For increment-decrement estimates, however, the estimated active population (or alternatively the implicit labor force participation rate) for age $x + 1$ would reflect the

one percent participation rate increase between ages x and $x + 1$. The estimated active population for age $x + 2$ would reflect the increase already calculated for age $x + 1$ as well as another one-percent-participation rate increase between ages $x + 1$ and $x + 2$. This would continue through all remaining ages. The effects of the one percent increases in participation would become less with each additional x_n but would be cumulative across all ages (i.e., a "cohort" estimate). As Smith stated:

The multistate working life table model is extremely sensitive to rapid changes in rates of labor force entry or withdrawal. Tables based on a recessionary period, during which labor force exits increase, present a very bleak picture of lifetime labor force involvement. Conversely, those calculated during periods of rapid recovery or expansion tend to overstate the average degree of lifetime labor force attachment (1986).

Therefore, observation periods should be chosen to avoid data exclusively from a period of expansion or contraction. This book uses July 1999 through June 2007 over which to measure transition probabilities. This period contains months of economic contraction and of growth which are about average for U. S. business cycles since World War II. The use of a period this long also increases sample sizes so that worklife expectancies can be derived for multiple educational attainments. Nevertheless, fewer educational categories are estimated for blacks and Hispanics, and sampling errors for these smaller populations can be fairly large.

It is problematic that estimates cannot be derived across all educational categories for all racial/ethnicity groups because worklife expectancies do not vary consistently across educational levels for all groups. (See Chapters 8 and 9.) For example, worklife expectancies of black males are more strongly correlated with education than those of all races combined; the correlation is not very strong for Hispanic males; but it is strong for black and Hispanic females.

Skoog and Ciecka in a detailed analysis concluded that the conventional model (which they term the demographic or actuarial model) is itself a Markov model, but with restrictions (2004). It must rely upon unreasonable assumptions to derive worklife expectancies for "initially actives." They did not attempt to examine the conventional model for populations regardless of initial activity status, presuming that such numbers would be useless to forensic economists, who always would know the initial activity state of the person in question. We believe, however, that conventional model estimates are valuable for several reasons: (a) for all races they can be derived for more educational groups, (b) estimates for blacks and Hispanics can be derived by educational levels, and (c) they provide a check on possible data or methodological problems with the Markov estimates.

In fact, as shown in Text Table 31, Chapter 9, most increment-decrement estimates (regardless of initial activity status) are lower than conventional estimates. For males all increment-decrement estimates are markedly lower. The difference tends to lessen with age for the lower educational attainment and to be greater with age for college and graduate degrees. For females the largest discrepancies are at the lowest and highest educational groups, while only minor differences exist between the two models in the mid-educational categories. The next few paragraphs explore this incongruity, showing that much of the differences are caused by (a) the ages at which the two models "close" calculations, and (b) month-in-sample biases within the CPS data.

1. Closing Age

Prior to 2003 the CPS files available for researchers contained information by age through 89 and totals for persons age 90 and above. Since 2003 the CPS provides data by age only through 79, with sums for 80 and above and 85 and above. Following the lead of Krueger, the increment-decrement estimates in this book close at age 80. On the other hand, data by age to 90 are available from the surveys of 2000 through 2002 (i.e., half the period used in this book for conventional model estimates). It is assumed in this book that the 2000-2002 data can be extrapolated to the remaining survey years for persons age 80-85. Thus, conventional model estimates of this book close at age 85.[2]

Text Table 39 shows that closing conventional model estimates at age 80, rather than 85, biases worklife expectancies for both sexes and all education levels upwards. The size of the bias is directly related to educational attainment. Biases are less than a tenth of a year at the lower educational attainments, but at the highest levels they reach three tenths of a year or more. Thus, not closing conventional model estimates until age 85 is important.

Text Table 39: Effect on convention model estimates of truncating at age 80 rather than age 85

Age	< HS	HS	Some College	College Degree	Grad Degree	< HS	HS	Some College	College Degree	Grad Degree
	Males					Females				
Calculations to age 80 (using 2000-06 data)										
25	29.05	33.65	35.50	38.56	40.16	19.89	28.27	31.38	32.32	35.44
35	20.95	24.99	26.59	29.34	31.08	14.78	21.32	23.72	24.26	27.14
45	13.26	16.46	17.75	20.06	21.77	9.28	14.03	15.94	16.59	18.99
55	6.74	8.63	9.55	11.21	12.74	4.39	6.98	8.31	8.68	10.49
65	2.09	2.87	3.35	4.23	5.39	1.23	2.05	2.67	2.76	3.84
Calculations to age 85 (using 2000-06 data)										
25	29.00	33.58	35.37	38.36	39.86	19.84	28.19	31.27	32.21	35.23
35	20.90	24.92	26.46	29.15	30.77	14.74	21.23	23.62	24.16	26.93
45	13.21	16.38	17.61	19.86	21.46	9.24	13.94	15.84	16.48	18.78
55	6.69	8.55	9.41	11.00	12.42	4.34	6.90	8.20	8.57	10.28
65	2.03	2.78	3.19	4.01	5.04	1.18	1.95	2.55	2.64	3.62
Amount estimates calculated to 85 are smaller than those calculated to age 80										
25	0.05	0.07	0.13	0.20	0.30	0.04	0.08	0.10	0.10	0.20
35	0.05	0.07	0.13	0.20	0.31	0.04	0.08	0.10	0.10	0.21
45	0.05	0.07	0.14	0.20	0.31	0.04	0.09	0.11	0.11	0.21
55	0.05	0.08	0.14	0.21	0.32	0.05	0.09	0.11	0.11	0.21
65	0.06	0.09	0.16	0.22	0.35	0.05	0.09	0.12	0.11	0.22

Text Table 40: Effect on increment-decrement model estimates of truncating at age 80 rather than age 85 and on conventional model estimates of truncating at age 85 rather than 90

Age	< HS	HS	Some College	College Degree	Grad Degree	< HS	HS	Some College	College Degree	Grad Degree
			Males					Females		
Increment-decrement Model Worklife Estimates										
Calculations to age 85 (using 1996-98 data for all persons regardless of initial activity state)										
25	25.94	32.69	34.00	36.99	39.20	19.22	27.47	29.80	31.32	34.51
35	17.07	23.92	25.17	27.79	30.12	13.83	20.36	21.88	23.35	26.18
45	8.56	15.47	16.33	18.51	20.67	8.51	12.97	13.99	15.41	17.84
55	3.20	7.76	8.20	9.61	11.52	3.88	5.97	6.48	7.20	9.19
65	0.93	2.00	2.44	2.70	4.39	0.79	1.31	1.61	1.68	2.38
Calculations to age 80 (using 1996-98 data for all persons regardless of initial activity state)										
25	25.91	32.65	33.94	36.90	39.06	19.21	27.45	29.76	31.31	34.35
35	17.04	23.87	25.11	27.70	29.98	13.81	20.34	21.85	23.34	26.03
45	8.53	15.42	16.27	18.42	20.53	8.50	12.95	13.96	15.40	17.69
55	3.17	7.72	8.14	9.52	11.38	3.86	5.94	6.45	7.19	9.04
65	0.89	1.95	2.37	2.60	4.23	0.77	1.28	1.57	1.68	2.21
Amount estimates calculated to 80 are smaller than those calculated to age 85										
25	0.03	0.04	0.05	0.09	0.14	0.01	0.02	0.03	0.01	0.15
35	0.03	0.04	0.05	0.09	0.14	0.01	0.02	0.04	0.01	0.15
45	0.04	0.04	0.06	0.09	0.14	0.01	0.02	0.04	0.01	0.15
55	0.04	0.05	0.06	0.09	0.15	0.02	0.02	0.04	0.01	0.16
65	0.05	0.05	0.07	0.10	0.16	0.02	0.02	0.04	0.01	0.17
Conventional Model Worklife Estimates										
Calculations to age 90 (using 2000-06 data for all persons regardless of initial activity state)										
25	29.00	33.57	35.37	38.36	39.87	19.84	28.17	31.22	32.21	35.27
35	20.90	24.91	26.46	29.14	30.78	14.73	21.22	23.57	24.15	26.96
45	13.21	16.37	17.61	19.86	21.47	9.23	13.93	15.79	16.48	18.81
55	6.69	8.54	9.41	10.99	12.43	4.34	6.88	8.15	8.57	10.32
65	2.03	2.77	3.19	4.00	5.05	1.17	1.94	2.50	2.64	3.66
Calculations to age 85 (using 2000-06 data for all persons regardless of initial activity state)										
25	29.00	33.58	35.37	38.36	39.86	19.84	28.19	31.27	32.21	35.23
35	20.90	24.92	26.46	29.15	30.77	14.74	21.23	23.62	24.16	26.93
45	13.21	16.38	17.61	19.86	21.46	9.24	13.94	15.84	16.48	18.78
55	6.69	8.55	9.41	11.00	12.42	4.34	6.90	8.20	8.57	10.28
65	2.03	2.78	3.19	4.01	5.04	1.18	1.95	2.55	2.64	3.62
Amount estimates calculated to 85 are smaller than those calculated to age 90										
25	0.00	-0.01	0.00	-0.01	0.01	-0.01	-0.01	-0.05	-0.00	0.03
35	0.00	-0.01	0.00	-0.01	0.01	-0.01	-0.01	-0.05	-0.00	0.03
45	0.00	-0.01	0.00	-0.01	0.01	-0.01	-0.01	-0.05	-0.00	0.03
55	0.00	-0.00	0.00	-0.01	0.01	-0.01	-0.01	-0.05	-0.00	0.03
65	0.00	-0.01	0.00	-0.01	0.01	-0.01	-0.01	-0.05	-0.01	0.03

Text Table 40 examines the effect of closing increment-decrement estimates at 80 rather than 85 and of closing conventional estimates at 85 rather than 90. Based on data from 1996-98 (years the CPS provided information to age 90), the increment-decrement model does not appear to be very sensitive to closing at 80 versus 85. It is only at high educational attainment that small biases appear, i.e., one to two tenths of a year. Similarly, (using 2000 through 2002 data) the conventional model shows only very small biases resulting from closing at age 85 rather than 90.

In short, closing increment-decrement estimates at age 80 underestimates worklife expectancies for only some educational groups, and then only by one to two tenths of a year. Closing the conventional models at age 85 has almost no biasing effect on estimates, but closing at 80 would result in overestimates of up to several tenths at high educational attainment.

2. Month-in-Sample

As discussed in Chapter 8, the CPS is a rotating, monthly survey with interviews for four consecutive months, an interim of eight months with no interviews, and then another four consecutive months of interviews. The first month is labeled "month-in-sample one" (MIS1); the second, MIS2; etc., to MIS8. The BLS uses averages of all MISs to derive its published labor force participation rates. However, participation rates do not remain constant from one MIS to the next. Rather, as shown in Text Table 41, participation declines on average from MIS1 through MIS4 and from MIS5 through MIS8. Additionally, participation rates for MIS1 through MIS4 are higher than for MIS5 through MIS8.

Increment-decrement worklife estimates are based on labor force transition probabilities. Transition probabilities, however, appear to be biased because of the month-in-sample phenomenon—probabilities for becoming or remaining active, downward and/or for becoming or remaining inactive, upward. On average, biases would be greatest for MIS1 – MIS5 matches and smallest for MIS4 – MIS8 matches. Until the recent work of Krueger (2004) researchers have not indicated which MIS matches were used to derive transition probabilities. Krueger correctly used MIS4 and MIS8 and mentioned the month-in-sample problem, but he seems not to have addressed it further.

In an attempt to determine the effect of this month-in-sample phenomenon we make here a first approximation of worklife expectancies derived from transition probabilities adjusted for the month-in-sample bias. At each age we have divided the labor force participation rates of MIS4 by those of MIS8. The percentage difference between the two

is multiplied by the active to active transition probability for the age, already calculated from the original matches. New worklife expectancies are calculated using these adjusted transition probabilities. (Note that in this first approximation, probabilities of remaining or becoming inactive are not adjusted. Further research may provide more sophisticated adjustments.)

Text Table 42 indicates that the extent of the MIS effect is up to a year at younger ages for males with lower education levels and slightly less for females. The effect is much smaller for males with a bachelor's degree or more, whereas for females with a graduate degree it is relatively large. Referring back to Text Table 31, MIS adjustments greatly reduce the differences between male conventional and increment-decrement estimates for most educational levels at young ages. At older ages the MIS effect is much smaller. Males with a graduate degree are exceptions, with the unadjusted increment-decrement worklife expectancies closer to (but still less than) the conventional estimates.

For females, the adjustment has a substantial effect at younger ages on worklives for the lower educational categories. In contrast to males, effects on worklives of those with a graduate degree are relatively large. The effect of making these adjustments brings the increment-decrement estimates for females at highest and lowest levels of education closer to conventional model estimates, but for those in middle educational levels the results are much smaller and may or may not narrow the differences between increment-decrement and conventional model estimates for populations regardless of initial activity status.

3. Joint Effects of Month-in-Sample and Closing Age

Accounting for the MIS effect almost totally eliminates differences between estimates of the two models for males with less than a high school education and substantially reduces differences for the other education levels up to age 55. An exception is males with a graduate degree, for whom the MIS adjustment has negligible effects. For females, accounting for the MIS effect substantially reduces differences between worklife expectancies of the two models for those with less than a high school education, but has limited effect on other education levels up to graduate degree, for whom it reduces differences at younger ages.[3]

Accounting additionally for closing age makes nearly all MIS-adjusted increment-decrement estimates larger than conventional estimates at younger ages and reduces the gap at older ages, especially at medium to high educational levels for males and females with a graduate degree.

Text Table 41: Month in sample labor force participation rates, males and females with a high school degree

Age	1st	2nd	3rd	4th	5th	6th	7th	8th
\multicolumn{9}{Males with a High School Degree / GED}								
\multicolumn{9}{Labor Force Participation Rates by Month-in-Sample}								
25	92.41%	92.21%	91.56%	92.04%	90.58%	90.78%	91.42%	91.31%
35	92.66%	92.22%	91.93%	90.85%	92.08%	92.29%	92.18%	92.10%
45	90.00%	88.83%	89.00%	89.09%	88.50%	88.45%	88.67%	87.62%
55	80.44%	79.64%	79.76%	80.00%	79.87%	79.74%	78.76%	79.36%
65	34.61%	32.52%	32.41%	32.30%	31.16%	30.71%	31.00%	31.81%
\multicolumn{9}{Difference Between Labor Force Participation of MIS and Previous MIS}								
25		-0.19%	-0.65%	0.48%	-1.47%	0.21%	0.64%	-0.11%
35		-0.43%	-0.29%	-1.08%	1.23%	0.21%	-0.11%	-0.08%
45		-1.17%	0.18%	0.09%	-0.59%	-0.05%	0.22%	-1.05%
55		-0.80%	0.12%	0.24%	-0.12%	-0.14%	-0.97%	0.60%
65		-2.09%	-0.11%	-0.11%	-1.14%	-0.44%	0.29%	0.81%
25-64		-0.42%	-0.17%	-0.20%	0.05%	-0.22%	-0.02%	-0.09%
\multicolumn{9}{Differences: (5 year ave centered at age)}								
	1st to 5th	2nd to 6th	3rd to 7th	4th to 8th				
25	-0.58%	-0.53%	-0.47%	-0.60%				
35	-0.48%	-0.34%	-0.25%	0.16%				
45	-0.72%	-0.46%	-0.32%	-0.60%				
55	-0.60%	-0.45%	-1.05%	-0.87%				
65	-2.08%	-1.56%	-0.76%	-0.76%				
25 to 64	-0.75%	-0.54%	-0.40%	-0.29%				
\multicolumn{9}{Females with a High School Degree / GED}								
\multicolumn{9}{Labor Force Participation Rates by Month-in-Sample}								
25	73.18%	72.01%	71.03%	70.95%	73.20%	71.69%	72.42%	70.54%
35	76.06%	73.90%	73.87%	72.65%	74.61%	74.32%	73.83%	74.19%
45	77.76%	77.80%	78.42%	77.57%	77.17%	76.25%	76.17%	76.70%
55	65.48%	65.21%	64.63%	64.53%	65.27%	64.48%	65.60%	64.95%
65	24.87%	24.20%	23.52%	23.75%	24.36%	23.92%	24.80%	24.88%
\multicolumn{9}{Difference Between Labor Force Participation of MIS and Previous MIS}								
25		-1.17%	-0.98%	-0.08%	2.24%	-1.51%	0.73%	-1.88%
35		-2.15%	-0.04%	-1.22%	1.96%	-0.30%	-0.49%	0.36%
45		0.04%	0.62%	-0.85%	-0.40%	-0.91%	-0.09%	0.53%
55		-0.26%	-0.58%	-0.11%	0.74%	-0.79%	1.12%	-0.65%
65		-0.67%	-0.69%	0.23%	0.60%	-0.44%	0.88%	0.07%
25-64		-0.53%	-0.20%	-0.19%	-0.29%	-0.32%	-0.01%	0.07%
\multicolumn{9}{Differences: (5 year ave centered at age)}								
	1st to 5th	2nd to 6th	3rd to 7th	4th to 8th				
25	-1.11%	-1.18%	-0.52%	-0.34%				
35	-1.25%	-1.18%	-0.81%	-0.08%				
45	-1.18%	-0.80%	-1.19%	-1.04%				
55	-1.12%	-1.23%	-0.27%	-0.15%				
65	-1.94%	-1.23%	-0.94%	-0.71%				
25 to 64	-1.20%	-1.00%	-0.81%	-0.56%				

Text Table 42: Effect on Markov model estimates of Month in Sample Bias and comparison with conventional model estimates

Age	< HS	HS	Some College	College Degree	Grad Degree	< HS	HS	Some College	College Degree	Grad Degree
	All Males					All Females				
Markov estimates without MIS adjustment										
25	28.34	32.78	34.71	38.10	39.83	18.55	27.81	31.01	31.95	34.78
35	20.39	24.32	25.87	28.87	30.49	13.79	21.11	23.56	24.02	26.52
45	12.68	15.82	16.96	19.54	21.01	8.72	13.94	15.83	16.55	18.29
55	6.18	8.03	8.84	10.59	11.87	4.18	6.80	8.21	8.62	9.77
65	1.80	2.34	2.86	3.43	4.19	0.95	1.78	2.21	2.34	3.08
Markov estimates with MIS adjustment										
25	29.05	33.81	35.67	38.41	39.72	19.44	28.42	31.45	32.28	35.40
35	20.87	25.01	26.58	29.07	30.45	14.65	21.39	23.70	24.06	26.89
45	13.15	16.29	17.58	19.66	20.96	9.11	13.95	15.81	16.33	18.63
55	6.74	8.33	9.22	10.60	11.71	4.31	6.67	7.96	8.26	9.80
65	2.03	2.44	2.85	3.43	4.22	1.03	1.71	2.17	2.18	2.89
Extent of adjustment (MIS-adjusted worklife minus without MIS adjustment)										
25	0.72	1.02	0.96	0.31	-0.10	0.89	0.61	0.44	0.33	0.62
35	0.47	0.70	0.70	0.20	-0.03	0.86	0.28	0.15	0.03	0.36
45	0.47	0.47	0.62	0.12	-0.06	0.39	0.01	-0.03	-0.23	0.34
55	0.56	0.30	0.38	0.01	-0.16	0.13	-0.13	-0.25	-0.36	0.03
65	0.23	0.01	-0.00	-0.00	0.02	0.08	-0.07	-0.05	-0.16	-0.19
Conventional Model Worklife Expectancies										
25	29.00	33.58	35.37	38.36	39.86	19.84	28.19	31.27	32.21	35.23
35	20.90	24.92	26.46	29.15	30.77	14.74	21.23	23.62	24.16	26.93
45	13.21	16.38	17.61	19.86	21.46	9.24	13.94	15.84	16.48	18.78
55	6.69	8.55	9.41	11.00	12.42	4.34	6.90	8.20	8.57	10.28
65	2.03	2.78	3.19	4.01	5.04	1.18	1.95	2.55	2.64	3.62
Difference (Conventional model minus MIS-adjusted Markov model estimates)										
25	-0.05	-0.23	-0.30	-0.05	0.14	0.41	-0.23	-0.17	-0.07	-0.16
35	0.04	-0.09	-0.12	0.08	0.32	0.09	-0.16	-0.08	0.10	0.04
45	0.06	0.09	0.03	0.20	0.50	0.12	-0.01	0.03	0.16	0.15
55	-0.05	0.22	0.19	0.40	0.71	0.04	0.23	0.24	0.31	0.48
65	0.00	0.35	0.34	0.58	0.82	0.15	0.25	0.39	0.46	0.73

To summarize, the strength of the increment-decrement model lies in two areas. First, it can measure the effect of trends in labor force participation through time. Second, it measures working life by current labor force activity status. On the other hand, estimates by education are somewhat limited by CPS sample sizes, especially for blacks and Hispanics. Additionally, it is important to realize that increment-decrement transition probabilities are based on only two years' observation for any given person. Persons with long-term continuous participation in the labor force will not be well represented by these transition probabilities. They would probably remain in the labor force longer than indicated by worklife expectancies, and vice versa for those with sporadic or minimal labor force participation.

B. Conventional Model

In her 1982 introduction to the BLS implementation of the increment-decrement model, Shirley Smith set out the three main limitations of the conventional model. The following paragraphs present these points and discuss their relative importance so far as data in this book is concerned.

- Because it assumes continuous labor force attachment, the conventional model upwardly biases worklife expectancies of the *active* population. This problem is especially severe for women, who typically have multiple exits and entries, often of a seasonal nature. Response: This publication does not attempt to estimate conventional model worklife expectancies for the currently "active" or "inactive" populations. For the general population, the conventional model is not biased by the assumption of continuous labor force attachment, and this limitation is not relevant.
- The conventional model assumes constant participation rates over time. Response: This was more problematic historically when the rates for men were falling steadily while those of women were rising. The BLS projects much smaller changes in participation in the next decades (with the exception of older persons).
- The conventional model for *active* women must be broken into different categories such as single, separated, divorced, and ever-married without children to be meaningful. Response: As discussed above, the conventional model *is inappropriate* for estimating worklife expectancies of the active population, and no attempt is made to do so.

The conventional model has the following advantages over the increment-decrement model:

- Larger sample sizes allow disaggregation into more educational levels for all main racial/Hispanic status groups.
- Worklife estimates by smoking status reflect the effects of both mortality and labor force participation patterns for smokers, former smokers, and nonsmokers.
- For corresponding racial/educational groups standard errors are smaller.

Given that both the increment-decrement and conventional models have strengths and weaknesses the question is which one to use? One choice is to use increment-decrement estimates as is, accepting slight underestimates for most categories and incomplete information by education. Another choice is to use conventional model worklife expectancies. We believe, though, that scaling of conventional model estimates to those of the increment-decrement model combines the best of both models.

15.2 Scaling Conventional to Increment-Decrement Worklife Estimates

Merging increment-decrement and conventional model estimates can take advantage of the strengths of each. Conventional model estimates by demographic, smoking, or marital status can be scaled to the appropriate increment-decrement counterpart. Combining the two is a necessity if one wishes to obtain increment-decrement equivalent estimates by some of the education levels (associate degree, some college but no degree, master's, and Ph.D./professional degrees). It is a necessity for many education levels for blacks and Hispanics.

Due to the closing age and month-in-sample issues discussed above, the preference of the authors of this book for determining worklife expectancies is as follows: use conventional model tables to derive the base worklife expectancy, and use the increment-decrement tables to adjust for the effect of initial activity state. For blacks and Hispanics, specific education levels not included in any of the tables in this book can be extrapolated using data from the All Races tables.

Two examples using this method are presented below. The first is for initially "active" black males at age 25 with less than high school and the second is for the same male but with a Ph.D./professional degree. (All data come from Tables 4 and 5 in Part III.) Differences, rather than ratios, should be used. Ratios produce nearly similar results during young age, but beginning in the late fifties (as the denominator grows increasingly smaller) they become increasingly inaccurate.

First, consider those with less than a high school education. Step 1—from Table 5 determine that the conventional model worklife for these black males is 23.1 years. Step 2—from Table 4 determine that the worklife expectancy of those initially active is 0.4 years longer than the general population. Step 3—add the 0.4 to the 23.1 to get a worklife expectancy of 23.5 years for a black male with less than a high school education who is initially active.

Next, consider the somewhat more complicated process for black males with a doctorate or professional degree. Because the conventional model estimates for black males do not distinguish between graduate degrees, several additional steps are required. Step 1—using Table 5 for black males find that the worklife expectancy for black males with a graduate degree at 25 years of age is 37.0 years. Step 2—using the same table for all males determine that the worklife expectancy for all males with a Ph.D./professional degree is 1.7 years greater than for those with any graduate degree (41.6 minus 39.9). Step 3—add 1.7 years to 37.0 years to obtain a 38.7 year worklife for all black males with a Ph.D./professional degree. Step 4—from Table 4 determine that the worklife expectancy of all males with a graduate degree initially active is 0.2 years longer than the general population. Finally, step 5—add the 0.2 to the 38.7 to get a worklife expectancy of 38.9 years for a black male with a Ph.D./professional degree who is initially active. Although this description appears somewhat complicated, the practice is relatively simple.

The methodology for single females is the same as described above, except that scaling should be done to increment-decrement worklife expectancies of males rather than females because the labor participation patterns of single women are more like those of males than those of the total female population.

Adjustment factors by smoking status should be derived only from Table 8. For example, consider the black male with less than a high school education discussed above. Should he be a current smoker, an additional step would be taken. Using data from Table 7 determine that for 25-year-old males with less than a high school education the worklife expectancy of current smokers (26.8 years) is 2.1 years less than for those regardless of smoking status (28.9 years). The 2.1 years is subtracted from the worklife expectancy determined from Tables 3 and 4 (as discussed above) to factor in the effect of smoking. In this case, 2.1 is subtracted from 23.5 to derive a worklife expectancy of 21.4 years.

15.3 Modified Worklife Expectancy

Worklife expectancy tables provide the number of years, from the base age, that the average person would spend in the labor force. Labor force activity is assumed to occur continuously with no periods of inactivity. If used in economic loss calculations, this "forcing" of all periods of inactivity to the post-worklife ages is likely to overestimate losses because all earnings take place during the least heavily discounted periods. This is termed "front loading."

Boudreaux (1983) proposed that years of working life be spread evenly from commencement to some age of retirement (e.g., age for full Social Security benefits, the mean or median age of retirement, etc.). For example, assume an active, high school graduate, 25-year-old male with a worklife expectancy of 34 additional years who will be eligible to receive full SS benefits at age 67. On average, he will be separated from the labor for about 19% of the time between age 25 and age 67. His earnings, thus, are calculated by extending his working life to age 67, but reducing each year's earnings by 19% to account for periods of separation.

In reality, the probability of being out of the labor force is higher at the youngest ages and at ages nearing normal retirement ages. Similarly, earnings are lower at younger ages, generally rising with age until gradually declining near or after the age of normal retirement. Hence, putting the time out of the labor force at the "back end" may be as reasonable as spreading it out. Whether spreading earnings evenly over a time to retirement results in more accurate estimates of economic loss is an empirical question addressed later in this chapter.

15.4 Life, Participation, Employment

The final method of estimating duration of working life to be discussed here is the LPE method.[4] It is considered to have the following advantages:

- A strong theoretical advantage lies in discounting. By spreading expected earnings proportionally over many years rather than concentrating them in the earliest periods, it subjects them to more appropriate discounting.
- Probabilities of participation (P) data are available with very little time lag. In contrast, worklife tables are compiled only periodically and often are based on older data.
- The LPE method has been able to use more race and education specific information than was previously available in worklife tables. The worklife tables in this book, however, minimize this advantage of the LPE.

- LPE has been credited as the only model that explicitly reduces earnings estimates for periods of unemployment. Such an adjustment, however, can easily be made in estimates derived using the other worklife models.
- Finally, the LPE model is easy to explain to juries.

On the other hand, the LPE methodology has been criticized as having the following flaws:

- By explicitly addressing expectancy, it is not appropriate when capacity is the legal standard.
- Reduction of earnings for all periods of unemployment may be inappropriate since voluntary unemployment is a choice of allocation of time rather than a diminishment in capacity to work (see Chapter 14).
- The LPE method fails to distinguish properly between whether a person is currently active or inactive and treats all workers as having equal probabilities of working in any subsequent year. This is not of major importance for younger workers who have relatively high mobility between active and inactive periods, but it becomes critical for older people (Frasca and Hadley, 1987). For example, the probabilities that an active 55-year-old white male would be in the labor force at age 60 would be about 74%, and at age 65 about 42%. For those initially inactive the probabilities would be about 38.2% and 31.3%, respectively, and for the total population, about 67% and 35.7%, respectively. Thus, total population labor force participation rates underestimate the actual P for initially active older males and overestimates them for initially inactive older males. The effect is stronger for women and occurs at earlier ages.
- The corollary to the above paragraph is that the LPE underestimates losses which begin at middle ages or older unless they incorporate E and P probabilities based on the person's past patterns, i.e., not on statistical averages.
- The LPE model can also create severe computational complications for estimating retirement benefits (Romans and Floss, 1993).

15.5 Sample Calculations and Comparisons

This section derives and compares several examples of present values of earnings losses.[5] First, brief mathematical descriptions of the models are presented. Following these are

estimates from each of the models for males and females with a high school and a college education assuming that the loss began at ages 30, 45, and 60.

A. Models

Conventions used for notation throughout the remainder of this chapter are as follows:

A person's age when injury or wrongful death occurred.

t time index for yearly period, $t = A, A + 1,...$

E_t lost earnings in year t (inclusive of age-earnings adjustments but exclusive of inflation).

r net real discount rate (difference between the gross discount rate and the growth rate of earnings).

$^a p^i_t$ transition probability that a person who is active a in the labor force at the start of year t will be inactive i at the end of year t, inclusive of survival probabilities.

$^i p^a_t$ transition probability that a person who is inactive in the labor force at the start of year t will be active at the end of year t, inclusive of survival probabilities.

$^a p^a_t$ transition probability that a person who is active in the labor force at the start of year t will be active at the end of year t, inclusive of survival probabilities.

$^i p^i_t$ transition probability that a person who is inactive in the labor force at the start of year t will be inactive at the end of year t, inclusive of survival probabilities.

p^d_t probability of dying in year t.

l_A number of people in the cohort at age A (usually assumed to be 100,000).

$_a l_t$ number of people in l_t who are active in year t.

$_i l_t$ number of people in l_t who are inactive in year t.

P_{et} probability of being employed in year t.

The following equations hold:

$^a p^a_t + {}^a p^i_t + p^d_t = 1$ and $^i p^i_t + {}^i p^a_t + p^d_t = 1$ (i.e., a person who is active at the beginning of a year will either remain active, become inactive, or die by the end of the year, and similarly a person who is inactive at the beginning of a year will either remain inactive, become active, or die.)

$_a l_t + {}_i l_t = l_t$ (i.e., the number of people active in the labor force plus the number inactive equals the number who are alive in year t.)

Model 1: Years to Retirement: This is the simplest of the capacity measures: losses are assumed to occur from age A until a projected retirement age, in R years. The age of retirement could relate to the terms of a defined benefit retirement plan, a person's stated intentions, or eligibility for Social Security benefits. The age of full SS benefits, i.e. 65, is assumed for the purpose of these analyses. (Models 1 through 3 assume continuous labor force participation.) The present value of lost earnings for *R* years is given in equation 1.

$$PV_R = \sum_{j=1}^{R} E_{j+A}(1+r)^{(-j+0.5)} \qquad (1)$$

Model 2: Years to Final Separation (YFS): Described in Chapter 13 with data by age and sex from Table 12. The present value of lost earnings for *M* years is given in equation 2.

$$PV_{YFS} = \sum_{j=1}^{YFS} E_{j+A}(1+r)^{(-j+0.5)} \qquad (2)$$

Model 3: Worklife Expectancy: Described in Chapter 8 and based on increment-decrement data by age and sex from Table 4. The present value of lost earnings for *e* years is given in equation 3.

$$PV_M = \sum_{j=1}^{M} E_{j+A}(1+r)^{(-j+0.5)} \qquad (3)$$

Model 4: Modified Worklife Expectancy: Provides for periods of inactivity by evenly spreading years of activity over total years of assumed capacity (Boudreaux 1983, Smith 1983). The present value of lost earnings for *K* years (where *K = R* or *M*, or any number of years appropriate for a specific person and *K>e*) is given in equation 4.

$$PV_e = \sum_{j=1}^{e} E_{j+A}P_{j+A}(1+r)^{(-j+0.5)} \qquad (4)$$

***

In the remaining estimates the timing of labor force activity is not combined into a single number; the expected value of earnings year by year to some old age is estimated.

Model 5: Year to Year Losses: Introduced by Alter and Becker in 1985, the present value of lost earnings to age 80 is given in equation 5, where mortality data are from Table 1 and transition probabilities are from Table 3 in Part III of this book.

$$PV_{YY} = \left(\frac{1}{l_A}\right)\sum_{j=0}^{85-A} E_{j+A}P_{E,j+A}\left(\begin{array}{c}{}^a l_{j+A}{}^a p_{j+A}^a + 0.5{}^a l_{j+A}{}^a p_{j+A}^i \\ +0.5{}^i l_{j+A}{}^i p_{j+A}^a + 0.5{}^a l_{j+A} p_{j+A}^d\end{array}\right)(1+r)^{-(j+0.5)} \qquad (5)$$

Lost earnings (E_{j+A}) are multiplied by the sum of four terms, each of which is a transition probability multiplied by the percentage of the population to which it applies. Term one captures the probability of staying active; term two, of moving from active to inactive; term three, of moving from inactive to active; and term four, of remaining active but dying at mid-year. The transition in each of the terms two through four is assumed to occur at mid-year.

Model 6: Simplified Year to Year Losses: Simplifies equation 5 by assuming a full year of earnings for years in which a person becomes active and zero earnings when they become inactive or die. The present value of lost earnings to age 85 is given in equation 6.

$$PV_{SYY} = \left(\frac{1}{l_A}\right)\sum_{j=0}^{85-A} E_{j+A}P_{E,j+A}\left({}^a l_{j+A}{}^a p_{j+A}^a + {}^i l_{j+A}{}^i p_{j+A}^a\right)(1+r)^{-(j+0.5)} \qquad (6)$$

Model 7: Life, Participation, Employment: Described in Chapter 12, lost earnings (E_{j+A}) are multiplied by the joint probabilities of survival from age *A* ($P_{l,t}$), participating in the labor force ($P_{p,t}$), and being employed ($P_{e,t}$). The probability of survival is conditioned on being alive at age *A*, but the other two probabilities are not conditioned on any previous labor force or employment status. The present value of lost earnings to age 85 is given in equation 7.

$$PV_{LPE} = \sum_{j=0}^{85-A} E_{j+A}P_{L,(j+A)}P_{P,(j+A)}P_{E,(j+A)}(1+r)^{-(j+0.5)} \qquad (7)$$

B. Sample Calculations and Comparisons

The size of awards for personal injury or death obtained by employing some of the methods described above have been examined by Alter and Becker (1985), Schieren (1993), and Bell and Taub (1998). Of primary concern in these analyses were differences in losses between the year to year method versus worklife expectancies. They also examined effects of different net discount rates. Ciecka (1994) compared all the main methods, in the approach adopted here. Recently Skoog and Ciecka (2006) have provided a series of nonograms for forensic economists to use to correct the front loading of worklife expectancies and the effect of uniformly spreading a worklife expectancy to age 66.

This analysis calculates present values for active males and females with a high school and a bachelor's degree assuming ages at the time of death or injury to be 30, 45, and 60. Earnings are for full-time, year-round workers in 2007 (Bureau of the Census, 2008). Fringe benefits are not included. Earnings and probabilities of employment (i.e., one minus unemployment rates) are by five-year age categories except for the oldest ages, where they are for ages 75 and over. Earnings during ages over 65 are not adjusted for the probability of working part- rather than full-time. Data show that full-time work becomes much less prevalent for older workers, but the effect of the assumption of full-time earnings is offset by the fact that no retirement benefits have been estimated in any of the models.

For Model 1 (years to retirement) and Model 4 (modified worklife expectancy) it is assumed that retirement occurs at age 65, with the exception that modified worklife expectancies are set equal to worklife expectancy when worklife extends beyond age 65. Calculations terminate at age 80 for the year to year, simplified year to year, and LPE models. (When these methods do not continue beyond age 75 they truncate lifetime earnings by the following percentages for the examples presented here: males with a high school degree—loss beginning at age 30, 0.6%; at age 45, 1.2%; and at age 60, 6.4%; males with a college degree—0.9%, 1.8%, and 7.8%, respectively; females with a high school degree—0.5%, 0.9%, and 4.9%, respectively; and females with a college degree—0.5%, 1.0%, and 6.0%, respectively.)

For purposes of comparison, female lifetime losses are calculated using data for females of all marital states. As discussed above, though, where capacity is the standard, duration of working life, earnings, and employment probabilities should be based on data for single women.

Finally, estimates are discounted at a real net rate of 2.0%. Differences between calculated losses would be less with lower discount rates, and vice versa.

Text Table 43 presents the results. Estimates derived from the year to year method may be the most methodologically accurate of the expectancy measures, and they are taken as the standard in this table against which other methods are compared.[6] Three general patterns exist. First, the choice of method makes a larger difference in estimates of loss for females than for males. (Differences would be smaller for single women.) Second, the choice of method has a larger impact on estimates of those less well educated. And third, differences between methods expressed in dollar amounts decline with age of onset of the loss, but in most cases percentage differences increase.

The capacity measures (i.e. retirement at age 65 and YFS) provide the largest estimates of loss. This is especially true for females, since all the other methods reflect the significant absences from the labor force which are average for women. Especially at older ages of onset of loss, the YFS method provides estimates significantly higher than any other method. Assuming losses continue to 65, however, results in some of the lower estimates for groups which have relatively high labor force attachment, i.e., well-educated males and females.

Worklife expectancies provide the next largest estimates. As a percentage of year to year losses, worklife expectancy estimates diverge slightly more with age for males and slightly less for females. Given the assumptions in these scenarios, use of worklife expectancy produces losses between 5% and 10% larger than those of the year to year method.

Modified worklife expectancies and the LPE method are quite close to the year to year method at young ages for males and females. Modified worklife expectancies and the LPE method have the advantage of being easier to calculate

and explain than year to year losses, but they diverge from year to year losses with advancing age of injury or death. Modified worklife expectancies produce slightly larger estimates, gradually approaching those of worklife expectancies. LPE estimates produce smaller estimates and in nearly all cases significantly underestimate remaining lifetime earnings at advanced ages of onset of loss.

15.6 Summary

No single method of determining the duration of working life is appropriate for all situations, and no model is without problems. The strict capacity measures (Models 1 and 2) may best represent the future working life of people who have established a very strong attachment to the labor force, who are covered by a retirement plan which has a defined date of retirement, or who have definite plans for a retirement age. Also they would be appropriate if capacity, regardless of the person's past labor force history or of statistical averages for the population as a whole, is at issue.

The main advantage of worklife expectancy (Model 3) is ease of use and explanation to a jury. Worklife expectancies that are derived from conventional estimates scaled to those of the increment-decrement model provide data for many characteristics, allow consideration of pre-injury or pre-death activity states, and may be relatively insensitive to data instabilities. Calculation of retirement benefits is also straightforward. The primary disadvantage of worklife expectancies is that loss estimates are front-loaded by having all losses occur during an uninterrupted period immediately subsequent to the onset of loss. Thus, they usually produce moderate overestimates of loss.

The modified worklife expectancy method (Model 4) has the same advantages as worklife expectancies and, by spreading earnings out over more years, has heavier discounting. It differs from worklife expectancies more for women than for men because (on average) women have more entries and exits, with shorter duration for each period of activity. Note, though, that averages may hide patterns of strong female labor force persistence, so that it is important to examine each case carefully. For females, expectancies for single females should be used.

The year to year approach is probably the most theoretically correct expectancy model. It has several disadvantages, though. It is computationally cumbersome and difficult to explain to a jury. It is limited to demographic groups for which transition probability data are available. Where a retirement plan is an important component of the estimate, computations of the dependent probabilities of continuing to work versus those of receiving retirement benefits could get quite complex.

Text Table 43: Comparison of present value of losses for different methods of estimating duration of working life, active males and females, high school and college degree, by selected age at onset of loss

	High School or GED			Bachelor's Degree		
	Age 30	Age 45	Age 60	Age 30	Age 45	Age 60
Males						
Estimated loss						
Years to Final Separation	1,099,048	800,034	360,265	2,186,551	1,645,889	826,035
To Age 65	1,105,935	777,999	262,451	2,050,063	1,430,462	603,761
Worklife Expectancy	949,845	654,666	262,451	1,990,493	1,409,560	603,761
Modified Worklife	911,048	633,356	262,451	1,970,767	1,405,087	603,761
Year by Year	907,442	618,893	242,455	1,925,466	1,343,166	554,045
Simplified Year by Year	894,856	602,577	223,034	1,905,112	1,316,329	521,198
LPE	912,848	610,208	190,769	1,914,953	1,331,506	477,052
Percentage Loss Compared with "Year to Year" Method						
Years to Final Separation	121.1%	129.3%	148.6%	113.6%	122.5%	149.1%
To Age 65	121.9%	125.7%	108.2%	106.5%	106.5%	109.0%
Worklife Expectancy	104.7%	105.8%	108.2%	103.4%	104.9%	109.0%
Modified Worklife	100.4%	102.3%	108.2%	102.4%	104.6%	109.0%
Year by Year	100.0%	100.0%	100.0%	100.0%	100.0%	100.0%
Simplified Year by Year	98.6%	97.4%	92.0%	98.9%	98.0%	94.1%
LPE	100.6%	98.6%	78.7%	99.5%	99.1%	86.1%
Females						
Estimated loss						
Years to Final Separation	753,691	524,618	226,310	1,435,129	981,263	427,589
To Age 65	771,855	532,606	172,552	1,386,758	902,976	315,359
Worklife Expectancy	599,636	417,013	172,552	1,203,359	802,210	315,359
Modified Worklife	556,592	396,423	172,552	1,126,942	775,546	315,359
Year by Year	556,365	392,753	163,774	1,104,270	749,762	290,547
Simplified Year by Year	547,056	381,027	150,107	1,089,735	731,777	269,720
LPE	543,446	364,315	107,190	1,086,168	713,885	213,528
Percentage Loss Compared with "Year to Year" Method						
Years to Final Separation	135.5%	133.6%	138.2%	130.0%	130.9%	147.2%
To Age 65	138.7%	135.6%	105.4%	125.6%	120.4%	108.5%
Worklife Expectancy	107.8%	106.2%	105.4%	109.0%	107.0%	108.5%
Modified Worklife	100.0%	100.9%	105.4%	102.1%	103.4%	108.5%
Year by Year	100.0%	100.0%	100.0%	100.0%	100.0%	100.0%
Simplified Year by Year	98.3%	97.0%	91.7%	98.7%	97.6%	92.8%
LPE	97.7%	92.8%	65.5%	98.4%	95.2%	73.5%

The simplified year to year is not quite as complicated as the year to year approach. However, it underestimates the probability of participation during each age and the slight increase in simplicity is offset by loss of accuracy.

The life-participation-employment method can incorporate up-to-date information, provides for theoretically appropriate discounting, and is much easier to implement than the year to year method. As with the modified worklife approach, LPE estimates reflect the fact that women have more entries, exits, and shorter durations for each period of activity than men. It is important, though, to consider work history of women carefully because their past patterns are very good predictors of probable future participation. In general, because the LPE model does not take into consideration preinjury or pre-death activity patterns, it increasingly underestimates losses for active people whose onset of loss is at older ages. Finally, as with the year to year method, calculation of defined benefit retirement payments is problematic.

Notes

1. At any age, the sum of persons ever-active in subsequent ages is the denominator in calculations of active worklife expectancies.

2. Given the recent trend in higher participation rates for older cohorts, it is likely that, if anything, labor force participation rates for ages 80 through 85 are somewhat underestimated by this process, and worklife expectancies are slightly too short.

3. It is, of course, possible that rather than increment-decrement estimates being biased downward, conventional estimates are biased upward. Such would be the case if the latter MISs are more accurate representations of "actual" labor force participation rates than all MISs combined so that labor force participation rates averaged across the entire CPS sample would be greater than "actual" rates. If so, conventional model estimates would be biased upward.

    The MIS phenomenon has been recognized and researched for many years. Mansur and Bac (2003) determined that the unemployment rate measured by the CPS is best represented either by MIS1 or the average of all MISs. In personal communication, Mansur has written that this is also true for labor force participation rates. (Note that the average of participation rates from all MISs are the data published by the BLS.) Thus conventional model estimates appear relatively unbiased.

4. In the final section of this chapter, several other methods are analyzed in regard to relative sizes of loss estimates. These are variants of the methods already presented and/or use information derived from the other methods and are not discussed until Section 15.5.

5. These notations and much of this section owe much to, and in some cases are copied directly from (by permission of the author), the excellent article "A Survey of the Structure and Duration of Time Periods for Lost Earnings Calculations," by James Ciecka (1994).

6. Note, though, that, as discussed above, the month-in-sample phenomenon causes year by year losses to be biased downward for some educational categories.

Part III: Tables

For sources of data used in the following tables, refer to the relevant chapters in Part I and Part II.

Table 1: Mortality rates, number living at beginning of age (out of 100,000 born alive), and expectations of remaining years of life, 2004—All Races Males

	Mortality Rates—All Races Males					Number Living at Beginning of Age Interval					Expectation of Life—All Races Males					
Age	<HS	High School	Some College	College Degree	Graduate Degree	<HS	High School	Some College	College Degree	Graduate Degree	All Ed Levels *	<HS	High School	Some College	College Degree	Grad Degree
0	0.00747	0.00747	0.00747	0.00747	0.00747	100,000	100,000	100,000	100,000	100,000	76.1	72.0	75.0	76.2	78.6	80.0
1	0.00051	0.00051	0.00051	0.00051	0.00051	99,253	99,253	99,253	99,253	99,253	75.7	71.6	74.6	75.8	78.2	79.6
2	0.00033	0.00033	0.00033	0.00033	0.00033	99,202	99,202	99,202	99,202	99,202	74.8	70.6	73.6	74.8	77.2	78.7
3	0.00025	0.00025	0.00025	0.00025	0.00025	99,170	99,170	99,170	99,170	99,170	73.8	69.6	72.6	73.9	76.2	77.7
4	0.00021	0.00021	0.00021	0.00021	0.00021	99,145	99,145	99,145	99,145	99,145	72.8	68.6	71.6	72.9	75.3	76.7
5	0.00019	0.00019	0.00019	0.00019	0.00019	99,124	99,124	99,124	99,124	99,124	71.8	67.7	70.7	71.9	74.3	75.7
6	0.00018	0.00018	0.00018	0.00018	0.00018	99,106	99,106	99,106	99,106	99,106	70.8	66.7	69.7	70.9	73.3	74.7
7	0.00017	0.00017	0.00017	0.00017	0.00017	99,087	99,087	99,087	99,087	99,087	69.8	65.7	68.7	69.9	72.3	73.7
8	0.00015	0.00015	0.00015	0.00015	0.00015	99,070	99,070	99,070	99,070	99,070	68.8	64.7	67.7	68.9	71.3	72.8
9	0.00013	0.00013	0.00013	0.00013	0.00013	99,055	99,055	99,055	99,055	99,055	67.9	63.7	66.7	67.9	70.3	71.8
10	0.00011	0.00011	0.00011	0.00011	0.00011	99,043	99,043	99,043	99,043	99,043	66.9	62.7	65.7	66.9	69.3	70.8
11	0.00011	0.00011	0.00011	0.00011	0.00011	99,033	99,033	99,033	99,033	99,033	65.9	61.7	64.7	65.9	68.3	69.8
12	0.00016	0.00016	0.00016	0.00016	0.00016	99,022	99,022	99,022	99,022	99,022	64.9	60.7	63.7	65.0	67.3	68.8
13	0.00027	0.00027	0.00027	0.00027	0.00027	99,006	99,006	99,006	99,006	99,006	63.9	59.7	62.7	64.0	66.4	67.8
14	0.00043	0.00043	0.00043	0.00043	0.00043	98,978	98,978	98,978	98,978	98,978	62.9	58.8	61.8	63.0	65.4	66.8
15	0.00061	0.00061	0.00061	0.00061	0.00061	98,936	98,936	98,936	98,936	98,936	61.9	57.8	60.8	62.0	64.4	65.8
16	0.00078	0.00078	0.00078	0.00078	0.00078	98,876	98,876	98,876	98,876	98,876	61.0	56.8	59.8	61.1	63.4	64.9
17	0.00093	0.00093	0.00093	0.00093	0.00093	98,799	98,799	98,799	98,799	98,799	60.0	55.9	58.9	60.1	62.5	63.9
18	0.00106	0.00106	0.00106	0.00106	0.00106	98,706	98,706	98,706	98,706	98,706	59.1	54.9	57.9	59.2	61.5	63.0
19	0.00117	0.00117	0.00117	0.00117	0.00117	98,601	98,601	98,601	98,601	98,601	58.1	54.0	57.0	58.2	60.6	62.1
20	0.00127	0.00127	0.00127	0.00127	0.00127	98,486	98,486	98,486	98,486	98,486	57.2	53.0	56.1	57.3	59.7	61.1
21	0.00136	0.00136	0.00136	0.00136	0.00136	98,362	98,362	98,362	98,362	98,362	56.3	52.1	55.1	56.4	58.8	60.2
22	0.00142	0.00142	0.00142	0.00142	0.00142	98,228	98,228	98,228	98,228	98,228	55.4	51.2	54.2	55.4	57.8	59.3
23	0.00188	0.00161	0.00137	0.00115	0.00115	98,089	98,089	98,089	98,089	98,089	54.4	50.2	53.3	54.5	56.9	58.4
24	0.00234	0.00163	0.00124	0.00104	0.00157	97,904	97,931	97,954	97,976	97,976	53.5	49.3	52.4	53.6	56.0	57.4
25	0.00266	0.00168	0.00112	0.00075	0.00126	97,676	97,771	97,833	97,874	97,823	52.6	48.4	51.4	52.6	55.0	56.5
26	0.00269	0.00166	0.00102	0.00069	0.00103	97,416	97,606	97,724	97,801	97,700	51.7	47.6	50.5	51.7	54.1	55.6
27	0.00294	0.00173	0.00089	0.00045	0.00083	97,154	97,444	97,624	97,734	97,599	50.7	46.7	49.6	50.8	53.1	54.7
28	0.00272	0.00162	0.00096	0.00060	0.00093	96,868	97,276	97,537	97,689	97,518	49.8	45.8	48.7	49.8	52.1	53.7
29	0.00247	0.00169	0.00102	0.00054	0.00040	96,605	97,119	97,443	97,631	97,427	48.9	45.0	47.8	48.9	51.2	52.8
30	0.00229	0.00163	0.00111	0.00070	0.00043	96,367	96,955	97,344	97,578	97,388	47.9	44.1	46.9	47.9	50.2	51.8
31	0.00239	0.00168	0.00118	0.00064	0.00043	96,146	96,796	97,236	97,509	97,346	47.0	43.2	45.9	47.0	49.2	50.8
32	0.00228	0.00167	0.00134	0.00079	0.00045	95,916	96,633	97,121	97,447	97,305	46.0	42.3	45.0	46.0	48.3	49.8
33	0.00229	0.00171	0.00136	0.00083	0.00044	95,697	96,472	96,991	97,370	97,260	45.1	41.4	44.1	45.1	47.3	48.8
34	0.00231	0.00176	0.00148	0.00090	0.00050	95,478	96,307	96,859	97,289	97,217	44.2	40.5	43.2	44.1	46.3	47.9
35	0.00246	0.00184	0.00162	0.00096	0.00074	95,257	96,138	96,716	97,202	97,169	43.2	39.6	42.2	43.2	45.4	46.9
36	0.00272	0.00198	0.00176	0.00102	0.00086	95,023	95,961	96,559	97,108	97,097	42.3	38.7	41.3	42.3	44.4	45.9
37	0.00306	0.00213	0.00188	0.00111	0.00098	94,765	95,771	96,389	97,009	97,014	41.3	37.8	40.4	41.3	43.5	45.0
38	0.00333	0.00233	0.00203	0.00118	0.00118	94,476	95,568	96,208	96,901	96,918	40.4	36.9	39.5	40.4	42.5	44.0
39	0.00373	0.00249	0.00224	0.00132	0.00116	94,161	95,345	96,013	96,787	96,804	39.5	36.0	38.6	39.5	41.6	43.1
40	0.00401	0.00277	0.00232	0.00150	0.00119	93,809	95,108	95,798	96,659	96,691	38.6	35.1	37.7	38.6	40.6	42.1
41	0.00436	0.00294	0.00247	0.00164	0.00134	93,433	94,845	95,576	96,515	96,576	37.7	34.3	36.8	37.7	39.7	41.2
42	0.00477	0.00316	0.00263	0.00178	0.00143	93,026	94,566	95,339	96,356	96,447	36.8	33.4	35.9	36.8	38.7	40.2
43	0.00525	0.00343	0.00286	0.00205	0.00161	92,582	94,267	95,088	96,185	96,309	35.9	32.6	35.0	35.9	37.8	39.3
44	0.00568	0.00375	0.00310	0.00230	0.00181	92,096	93,944	94,817	95,987	96,154	35.0	31.7	34.1	35.0	36.9	38.3
45	0.00639	0.00405	0.00343	0.00241	0.00192	91,573	93,592	94,523	95,767	95,980	34.1	30.9	33.2	34.1	36.0	37.4
46	0.00669	0.00441	0.00381	0.00276	0.00204	90,988	93,213	94,199	95,536	95,796	33.3	30.1	32.4	33.2	35.1	36.5
47	0.00693	0.00486	0.00431	0.00289	0.00224	90,379	92,802	93,840	95,273	95,600	32.4	29.3	31.5	32.3	34.2	35.5
48	0.00752	0.00529	0.00466	0.00293	0.00234	89,752	92,351	93,436	94,997	95,386	31.6	28.5	30.7	31.4	33.3	34.6
49	0.00820	0.00565	0.00491	0.00306	0.00267	89,078	91,863	93,000	94,719	95,163	30.8	27.7	29.8	30.6	32.4	33.7
50	0.00846	0.00625	0.00532	0.00338	0.00282	88,347	91,343	92,544	94,429	94,909	29.9	27.0	29.0	29.7	31.4	32.8
51	0.00911	0.00678	0.00557	0.00354	0.00311	87,600	90,772	92,052	94,110	94,642	29.1	26.2	28.2	28.9	30.6	31.9
52	0.00986	0.00708	0.00586	0.00400	0.00338	86,801	90,157	91,539	93,778	94,347	28.3	25.4	27.3	28.1	29.7	31.0
53	0.01032	0.00740	0.00640	0.00444	0.00360	85,946	89,518	91,002	93,402	94,029	27.4	24.7	26.5	27.2	28.8	30.1
54	0.01079	0.00778	0.00682	0.00473	0.00381	85,058	88,856	90,420	92,988	93,690	26.6	23.9	25.7	26.4	27.9	29.2
55	0.01146	0.00793	0.00735	0.00506	0.00434	84,141	88,165	89,803	92,548	93,333	25.8	23.2	24.9	25.6	27.0	28.3
56	0.01208	0.00830	0.00794	0.00521	0.00474	83,177	87,466	89,143	92,080	92,928	24.9	22.4	24.1	24.8	26.2	27.4
57	0.01261	0.00891	0.00852	0.00565	0.00514	82,172	86,740	88,436	91,601	92,488	24.1	21.7	23.3	23.9	25.3	26.5
58	0.01349	0.00959	0.00919	0.00615	0.00550	81,136	85,967	87,682	91,083	92,013	23.3	21.0	22.5	23.1	24.4	25.7
59	0.01429	0.01059	0.01009	0.00675	0.00607	80,042	85,142	86,876	90,523	91,507	22.4	20.2	21.7	22.4	23.6	24.8
60	0.01563	0.01172	0.01077	0.00760	0.00620	78,898	84,241	86,000	89,912	90,951	21.6	19.5	21.0	21.6	22.7	24.0
61	0.01703	0.01280	0.01159	0.00864	0.00694	77,665	83,253	85,074	89,228	90,388	20.8	18.8	20.2	20.8	21.9	23.1
62	0.01838	0.01417	0.01237	0.00969	0.00740	76,343	82,187	84,088	88,457	89,760	20.0	18.2	19.5	20.1	21.1	22.3
63	0.01963	0.01540	0.01306	0.01102	0.00825	74,939	81,023	83,047	87,600	89,096	19.2	17.5	18.7	19.3	20.3	21.4
64	0.02116	0.01640	0.01380	0.01196	0.00911	73,468	79,775	81,963	86,635	88,361	18.4	16.8	18.0	18.5	19.5	20.6
65	0.02231	0.01776	0.01486	0.01287	0.01045	71,914	78,466	80,832	85,599	87,556	17.7	16.2	17.3	17.8	18.8	19.8
66	0.02365	0.01948	0.01600	0.01416	0.01128	70,310	77,073	79,630	84,497	86,641	16.9	15.5	16.6	17.1	18.0	19.0
67	0.02542	0.02104	0.01740	0.01516	0.01292	68,647	75,571	78,356	83,300	85,663	16.2	14.9	15.9	16.3	17.2	18.2
68	0.02740	0.02272	0.01951	0.01626	0.01454	66,902	73,981	76,993	82,038	84,556	15.5	14.3	15.3	15.6	16.5	17.4
69	0.02953	0.02456	0.02177	0.01811	0.01585	65,069	72,300	75,491	80,704	83,327	14.8	13.7	14.6	14.9	15.8	16.7
70	0.03192	0.02647	0.02401	0.01961	0.01711	63,147	70,525	73,848	79,242	82,006	14.2	13.1	14.0	14.2	15.1	16.0
71	0.03464	0.02813	0.02658	0.02095	0.01904	61,132	68,658	72,075	77,688	80,603	13.5	12.5	13.3	13.6	14.3	15.2
72	0.03755	0.03076	0.02849	0.02320	0.02097	59,014	66,726	70,159	76,060	79,068	12.9	11.9	12.7	12.9	13.6	14.5
73	0.04121	0.03348	0.03126	0.02529	0.02320	56,798	64,674	68,160	74,296	77,410	12.2	11.4	12.1	12.3	13.0	13.8
74	0.04521	0.03638	0.03449	0.02856	0.02591	54,458	62,509	66,030	72,417	75,614	11.6	10.8	11.5	11.7	12.3	13.1
75	0.04920	0.03940	0.03801	0.03222	0.02882	51,996	60,235	63,752	70,349	73,655	11.0	10.3	10.9	11.1	11.6	12.5
76	0.05230	0.04364	0.04292	0.03550	0.03180	49,437	57,862	61,329	68,082	71,532	10.4	9.8	10.3	10.5	11.0	11.8
77	0.05651	0.04701	0.04843	0.03970	0.03467	46,852	55,337	58,696	65,665	69,257	9.9	9.3	9.8	9.9	10.4	11.2
78	0.06088	0.05241	0.05223	0.04431	0.03924	44,204	52,736	55,854	63,058	66,855	9.4	8.9	9.2	9.4	9.8	10.6
79	0.06586	0.05845	0.05778	0.04859	0.04405	41,513	49,972	52,936	60,264	64,232	8.8	8.4	8.7	8.9	9.2	10.0
80	0.07132	0.06479	0.06423	0.05487	0.05028	38,779	47,051	49,877	57,336	61,402	8.3	8.0	8.2	8.4	8.7	9.4
81	0.07797	0.07090	0.06937	0.06224	0.05597	36,013	44,002	46,674	54,190	58,315	7.9	7.5	7.8	8.0	8.1	8.9
82	0.08458	0.07789	0.07492	0.06722	0.06335	33,205	40,883	43,436	50,817	55,051	7.4	7.1	7.3	7.5	7.6	8.4
83	0.09134	0.08348	0.08419	0.07576	0.06879	30,397	37,698	40,181	47,401	51,563	7.0	6.7	6.9	7.1	7.2	7.9
84	0.09910	0.09167	0.08993	0.07968	0.07527	27,620	34,551	36,799	43,810	48,016	6.6	6.4	6.5	6.7	6.7	7.5
85	1.00000	1.00000	1.00000	1.00000	1.00000	24,883	31,384	33,489	40,319	44,402	6.2	6.0	6.1	6.3	6.2	7.0

* Weighted average by education.

Table 1: Mortality rates, number living at beginning of age (out of 100,000 born alive), and expectations of remaining years of life, 2004, continued—All Races Females

Age	Mortality Rates—All Races Females					Number Living at Beginning of Age Interval					Expectation of Life—All Races Females					
	<HS	High School	Some College	College Degree	Graduate Degree	<HS	High School	Some College	College Degree	Graduate Degree	All Ed Levels*	<HS	High School	Some College	College Degree	Grad Degree
0	0.00609	0.00609	0.00609	0.00609	0.00609	100,000	100,000	100,000	100,000	100,000	81.4	78.1	80.8	81.7	82.7	83.3
1	0.00046	0.00046	0.00046	0.00046	0.00046	99,391	99,391	99,391	99,391	99,391	80.9	77.6	80.3	81.2	82.2	82.8
2	0.00027	0.00027	0.00027	0.00027	0.00027	99,346	99,346	99,346	99,346	99,346	80.0	76.6	79.3	80.2	81.2	81.8
3	0.00020	0.00020	0.00020	0.00020	0.00020	99,319	99,319	99,319	99,319	99,319	79.0	75.6	78.3	79.2	80.2	80.9
4	0.00017	0.00017	0.00017	0.00017	0.00017	99,300	99,300	99,300	99,300	99,300	78.0	74.6	77.4	78.3	79.3	79.9
5	0.00015	0.00015	0.00015	0.00015	0.00015	99,283	99,283	99,283	99,283	99,283	77.0	73.6	76.4	77.3	78.3	78.9
6	0.00014	0.00014	0.00014	0.00014	0.00014	99,268	99,268	99,268	99,268	99,268	76.0	72.6	75.4	76.3	77.3	77.9
7	0.00013	0.00013	0.00013	0.00013	0.00013	99,254	99,254	99,254	99,254	99,254	75.0	71.7	74.4	75.3	76.3	76.9
8	0.00012	0.00012	0.00012	0.00012	0.00012	99,241	99,241	99,241	99,241	99,241	74.0	70.7	73.4	74.3	75.3	75.9
9	0.00011	0.00011	0.00011	0.00011	0.00011	99,229	99,229	99,229	99,229	99,229	73.1	69.7	72.4	73.3	74.3	74.9
10	0.00011	0.00011	0.00011	0.00011	0.00011	99,218	99,218	99,218	99,218	99,218	72.1	68.7	71.4	72.3	73.3	73.9
11	0.00011	0.00011	0.00011	0.00011	0.00011	99,208	99,208	99,208	99,208	99,208	71.1	67.7	70.4	71.3	72.3	72.9
12	0.00014	0.00014	0.00014	0.00014	0.00014	99,196	99,196	99,196	99,196	99,196	70.1	66.7	69.4	70.3	71.3	71.9
13	0.00018	0.00018	0.00018	0.00018	0.00018	99,183	99,183	99,183	99,183	99,183	69.1	65.7	68.4	69.3	70.3	71.0
14	0.00024	0.00024	0.00024	0.00024	0.00024	99,165	99,165	99,165	99,165	99,165	68.1	64.7	67.4	68.4	69.4	70.0
15	0.00031	0.00031	0.00031	0.00031	0.00031	99,142	99,142	99,142	99,142	99,142	67.1	63.7	66.5	67.4	68.4	69.0
16	0.00037	0.00037	0.00037	0.00037	0.00037	99,112	99,112	99,112	99,112	99,112	66.1	62.8	65.5	66.4	67.4	68.0
17	0.00042	0.00042	0.00042	0.00042	0.00042	99,075	99,075	99,075	99,075	99,075	65.2	61.8	64.5	65.4	66.4	67.0
18	0.00045	0.00045	0.00045	0.00045	0.00045	99,033	99,033	99,033	99,033	99,033	64.2	60.8	63.5	64.4	65.4	66.1
19	0.00045	0.00045	0.00045	0.00045	0.00045	98,989	98,989	98,989	98,989	98,989	63.2	59.8	62.6	63.5	64.5	65.1
20	0.00046	0.00046	0.00046	0.00046	0.00046	98,944	98,944	98,944	98,944	98,944	62.2	58.9	61.6	62.5	63.5	64.1
21	0.00046	0.00046	0.00046	0.00046	0.00046	98,899	98,899	98,899	98,899	98,899	61.3	57.9	60.6	61.5	62.5	63.1
22	0.00047	0.00047	0.00047	0.00047	0.00047	98,853	98,853	98,853	98,853	98,853	60.3	56.9	59.6	60.6	61.6	62.2
23	0.00069	0.00060	0.00056	0.00038	0.00091	98,807	98,807	98,807	98,807	98,807	59.3	55.9	58.7	59.6	60.6	61.2
24	0.00078	0.00057	0.00048	0.00034	0.00103	98,739	98,748	98,751	98,769	98,716	58.4	55.0	57.7	58.6	59.6	60.3
25	0.00097	0.00056	0.00052	0.00040	0.00095	98,662	98,691	98,704	98,735	98,615	57.4	54.0	56.7	57.7	58.6	59.3
26	0.00095	0.00058	0.00054	0.00039	0.00088	98,566	98,636	98,653	98,695	98,521	56.4	53.1	55.8	56.7	57.7	58.4
27	0.00103	0.00060	0.00055	0.00037	0.00086	98,472	98,579	98,599	98,657	98,434	55.5	52.1	54.8	55.7	56.7	57.4
28	0.00091	0.00051	0.00045	0.00040	0.00049	98,371	98,520	98,545	98,620	98,350	54.5	51.2	53.8	54.7	55.7	56.5
29	0.00096	0.00060	0.00057	0.00045	0.00039	98,281	98,469	98,500	98,581	98,301	53.5	50.2	52.9	53.8	54.7	55.5
30	0.00077	0.00067	0.00056	0.00039	0.00052	98,187	98,409	98,444	98,536	98,263	52.6	49.3	51.9	52.8	53.7	54.5
31	0.00103	0.00074	0.00055	0.00037	0.00063	98,111	98,343	98,389	98,498	98,212	51.6	48.3	50.9	51.8	52.8	53.6
32	0.00121	0.00079	0.00060	0.00037	0.00067	98,011	98,271	98,335	98,462	98,149	50.6	47.4	50.0	50.9	51.8	52.6
33	0.00124	0.00082	0.00067	0.00050	0.00056	97,892	98,193	98,276	98,425	98,084	49.6	46.4	49.0	49.9	50.8	51.6
34	0.00128	0.00089	0.00074	0.00045	0.00053	97,770	98,112	98,210	98,376	98,029	48.7	45.5	48.1	48.9	49.8	50.7
35	0.00156	0.00095	0.00078	0.00044	0.00054	97,645	98,024	98,138	98,332	97,977	47.7	44.5	47.1	48.0	48.9	49.7
36	0.00165	0.00101	0.00085	0.00052	0.00060	97,493	97,931	98,061	98,289	97,924	46.7	43.6	46.1	47.0	47.9	48.7
37	0.00166	0.00110	0.00088	0.00062	0.00065	97,332	97,833	97,977	98,237	97,865	45.7	42.7	45.2	46.0	46.9	47.7
38	0.00189	0.00125	0.00095	0.00066	0.00067	97,170	97,725	97,891	98,176	97,801	44.8	41.7	44.2	45.1	45.9	46.8
39	0.00212	0.00135	0.00106	0.00084	0.00080	96,987	97,604	97,798	98,112	97,736	43.8	40.8	43.3	44.1	45.0	45.8
40	0.00232	0.00150	0.00118	0.00103	0.00090	96,781	97,472	97,694	98,030	97,657	42.9	39.9	42.3	43.2	44.0	44.8
41	0.00251	0.00165	0.00132	0.00113	0.00095	96,557	97,325	97,579	97,929	97,570	41.9	39.0	41.4	42.2	43.0	43.9
42	0.00281	0.00179	0.00143	0.00127	0.00111	96,314	97,165	97,450	97,819	97,478	41.0	38.1	40.5	41.3	42.1	42.9
43	0.00307	0.00195	0.00161	0.00133	0.00102	96,044	96,991	97,311	97,694	97,370	40.1	37.2	39.5	40.3	41.1	42.0
44	0.00338	0.00210	0.00166	0.00154	0.00113	95,749	96,802	97,155	97,564	97,270	39.1	36.3	38.6	39.4	40.2	41.0
45	0.00371	0.00231	0.00176	0.00157	0.00113	95,425	96,599	96,993	97,414	97,161	38.2	35.4	37.7	38.5	39.3	40.1
46	0.00407	0.00246	0.00193	0.00174	0.00114	95,071	96,375	96,823	97,261	97,050	37.3	34.6	36.8	37.5	38.3	39.1
47	0.00437	0.00261	0.00214	0.00182	0.00125	94,684	96,139	96,636	97,092	96,940	36.4	33.7	35.9	36.6	37.4	38.1
48	0.00466	0.00271	0.00231	0.00198	0.00146	94,270	95,888	96,430	96,915	96,819	35.5	32.8	35.0	35.7	36.4	37.2
49	0.00479	0.00291	0.00254	0.00204	0.00150	93,830	95,628	96,207	96,724	96,678	34.5	32.0	34.1	34.7	35.5	36.2
50	0.00503	0.00307	0.00270	0.00221	0.00155	93,381	95,349	95,963	96,526	96,532	33.6	31.1	33.2	33.8	34.6	35.3
51	0.00511	0.00331	0.00298	0.00234	0.00176	92,911	95,056	95,704	96,313	96,383	32.7	30.3	32.3	32.9	33.7	34.3
52	0.00532	0.00364	0.00309	0.00242	0.00191	92,435	94,742	95,419	96,087	96,213	31.8	29.5	31.4	32.0	32.7	33.4
53	0.00571	0.00390	0.00316	0.00289	0.00211	91,943	94,397	95,124	95,854	96,029	30.9	28.6	30.5	31.1	31.8	32.5
54	0.00631	0.00415	0.00350	0.00291	0.00220	91,419	94,029	94,823	95,578	95,827	30.0	27.8	29.6	30.2	30.9	31.5
55	0.00669	0.00453	0.00372	0.00315	0.00257	90,842	93,639	94,492	95,299	95,616	29.1	26.9	28.7	29.3	30.0	30.6
56	0.00729	0.00489	0.00401	0.00330	0.00293	90,234	93,214	94,141	94,999	95,370	28.2	26.1	27.8	28.4	29.1	29.7
57	0.00789	0.00519	0.00464	0.00358	0.00314	89,576	92,758	93,763	94,686	95,090	27.3	25.3	27.0	27.5	28.2	28.8
58	0.00848	0.00567	0.00517	0.00370	0.00346	88,869	92,277	93,328	94,346	94,792	26.4	24.5	26.1	26.7	27.3	27.9
59	0.00918	0.00613	0.00556	0.00428	0.00438	88,116	91,754	92,846	93,998	94,464	25.5	23.7	25.3	25.8	26.4	27.0
60	0.01009	0.00662	0.00651	0.00466	0.00467	87,307	91,191	92,330	93,595	94,050	24.6	22.9	24.4	24.9	25.5	26.1
61	0.01103	0.00730	0.00713	0.00525	0.00539	86,426	90,587	91,729	93,159	93,610	23.7	22.2	23.6	24.1	24.6	25.2
62	0.01216	0.00801	0.00742	0.00593	0.00602	85,472	89,926	91,075	92,670	93,106	22.9	21.4	22.7	23.3	23.7	24.3
63	0.01304	0.00872	0.00820	0.00657	0.00667	84,433	89,205	90,399	92,121	92,545	22.0	20.7	21.9	22.4	22.9	23.5
64	0.01395	0.00956	0.00885	0.00688	0.00642	83,332	88,428	89,658	91,515	91,928	21.2	19.9	21.1	21.6	22.0	22.6
65	0.01489	0.01047	0.00920	0.00763	0.00724	82,169	87,582	88,864	90,885	91,338	20.4	19.2	20.3	20.8	21.2	21.8
66	0.01609	0.01143	0.01006	0.00830	0.00754	80,945	86,665	88,046	90,192	90,676	19.6	18.5	19.5	20.0	20.3	20.9
67	0.01711	0.01258	0.01150	0.00917	0.00831	79,643	85,675	87,160	89,443	89,993	18.8	17.8	18.7	19.2	19.5	20.1
68	0.01876	0.01368	0.01247	0.01027	0.00878	78,280	84,597	86,158	88,623	89,244	18.0	17.1	18.0	18.4	18.7	19.2
69	0.02028	0.01489	0.01372	0.01199	0.01032	76,811	83,440	85,084	87,713	88,461	17.2	16.4	17.2	17.6	17.9	18.4
70	0.02186	0.01632	0.01515	0.01385	0.01100	75,253	82,197	83,917	86,661	87,548	16.5	15.7	16.5	16.9	17.1	17.6
71	0.02336	0.01801	0.01689	0.01595	0.01153	73,608	80,856	82,646	85,461	86,585	15.7	15.1	15.7	16.1	16.3	16.8
72	0.02551	0.01976	0.01777	0.01771	0.01362	71,889	79,400	81,249	84,099	85,587	15.0	14.4	15.0	15.4	15.6	16.0
73	0.02753	0.02199	0.01945	0.01981	0.01586	70,055	77,831	79,806	82,609	84,421	14.3	13.8	14.3	14.7	14.8	15.2
74	0.02969	0.02437	0.02159	0.02272	0.01820	68,126	76,120	78,253	80,973	83,082	13.6	13.1	13.6	14.0	14.1	14.4
75	0.03184	0.02697	0.02344	0.02447	0.02192	66,103	74,265	76,564	79,133	81,570	13.0	12.5	12.9	13.3	13.4	13.7
76	0.03454	0.02920	0.02566	0.02559	0.02571	63,999	72,262	74,770	77,197	79,782	12.3	11.9	12.3	12.6	12.8	13.0
77	0.03721	0.03229	0.02948	0.02840	0.02629	61,788	70,152	72,851	75,221	77,730	11.7	11.3	11.6	11.9	12.1	12.3
78	0.04084	0.03585	0.03339	0.03147	0.02951	59,489	67,887	70,703	73,084	75,687	11.0	10.8	11.0	11.2	11.4	11.6
79	0.04527	0.04060	0.03684	0.03350	0.03249	57,059	65,453	68,342	70,785	73,453	10.4	10.2	10.4	10.6	10.8	11.0
80	0.05026	0.04525	0.04163	0.03584	0.03470	54,476	62,795	65,824	68,414	71,067	9.8	9.7	9.8	10.0	10.1	10.3
81	0.05455	0.05069	0.04669	0.04168	0.03827	51,739	59,954	63,084	65,962	68,601	9.3	9.1	9.3	9.4	9.5	9.7
82	0.05935	0.05640	0.05255	0.04753	0.04456	48,916	56,914	60,139	63,213	65,976	8.7	8.6	8.7	8.8	8.9	9.0
83	0.06469	0.06269	0.06096	0.05319	0.05024	46,013	53,705	56,979	60,208	63,036	8.2	8.2	8.2	8.3	8.3	8.4
84	0.07055	0.06940	0.07076	0.06573	0.05698	43,036	50,338	53,505	57,005	59,869	7.7	7.7	7.8	7.8	7.8	7.8
85	1.00000	1.00000	1.00000	1.00000	1.00000	40,000	46,845	49,720	53,258	56,458	7.3	7.2	7.3	7.3	7.3	7.3

* Weighted average by education.

Table 1: Mortality rates, number living at beginning of age (out of 100,000 born alive), and expectations of remaining years of life, 2004, continued—White Males

Age	Mortality Rates—White Males					Number Living at Beginning of Age Interval					Expectation of Life—White Males					
	<HS	High School	Some College	College Degree	Graduate Degree	<HS	High School	Some College	College Degree	Graduate Degree	All Ed Levels *	<HS	High School	Some College	College Degree	Grad Degree
0	0.00622	0.00622	0.00622	0.00622	0.00622	100,000	100,000	100,000	100,000	100,000	76.5	72.7	75.4	76.6	78.8	80.2
1	0.00046	0.00046	0.00046	0.00046	0.00046	99,378	99,378	99,378	99,378	99,378	76.0	72.1	74.9	76.1	78.3	79.7
2	0.00030	0.00030	0.00030	0.00030	0.00030	99,333	99,333	99,333	99,333	99,333	75.0	71.2	73.9	75.1	77.3	78.8
3	0.00022	0.00022	0.00022	0.00022	0.00022	99,303	99,303	99,303	99,303	99,303	74.0	70.2	73.0	74.1	76.3	77.8
4	0.00020	0.00020	0.00020	0.00020	0.00020	99,281	99,281	99,281	99,281	99,281	73.1	69.2	72.0	73.1	75.4	76.8
5	0.00017	0.00017	0.00017	0.00017	0.00017	99,262	99,262	99,262	99,262	99,262	72.1	68.2	71.0	72.2	74.4	75.8
6	0.00017	0.00017	0.00017	0.00017	0.00017	99,244	99,244	99,244	99,244	99,244	71.1	67.2	70.0	71.2	73.4	74.8
7	0.00016	0.00016	0.00016	0.00016	0.00016	99,228	99,228	99,228	99,228	99,228	70.1	66.2	69.0	70.2	72.4	73.8
8	0.00014	0.00014	0.00014	0.00014	0.00014	99,212	99,212	99,212	99,212	99,212	69.1	65.2	68.0	69.2	71.4	72.8
9	0.00011	0.00011	0.00011	0.00011	0.00011	99,198	99,198	99,198	99,198	99,198	68.1	64.3	67.0	68.2	70.4	71.9
10	0.00001	0.00001	0.00001	0.00001	0.00001	99,187	99,187	99,187	99,187	99,187	67.1	63.3	66.0	67.2	69.4	70.9
11	0.00010	0.00010	0.00010	0.00010	0.00010	99,177	99,177	99,177	99,177	99,177	66.1	62.3	65.0	66.2	68.4	69.9
12	0.00015	0.00015	0.00015	0.00015	0.00015	99,167	99,167	99,167	99,167	99,167	65.1	61.3	64.1	65.2	67.4	68.9
13	0.00026	0.00026	0.00026	0.00026	0.00026	99,152	99,152	99,152	99,152	99,152	64.1	60.3	63.1	64.2	66.5	67.9
14	0.00041	0.00041	0.00041	0.00041	0.00041	99,126	99,126	99,126	99,126	99,126	63.2	59.3	62.1	63.2	65.5	66.9
15	0.00059	0.00059	0.00059	0.00059	0.00059	99,085	99,085	99,085	99,085	99,085	62.2	58.3	61.1	62.3	64.5	65.9
16	0.00075	0.00075	0.00075	0.00075	0.00075	99,027	99,027	99,027	99,027	99,027	61.2	57.4	60.1	61.3	63.5	65.0
17	0.00090	0.00090	0.00090	0.00090	0.00090	98,953	98,953	98,953	98,953	98,953	60.3	56.4	59.2	60.4	62.6	64.0
18	0.00102	0.00102	0.00102	0.00102	0.00102	98,865	98,865	98,865	98,865	98,865	59.3	55.5	58.2	59.4	61.6	63.1
19	0.00111	0.00111	0.00111	0.00111	0.00111	98,764	98,764	98,764	98,764	98,764	58.4	54.5	57.3	58.5	60.7	62.1
20	0.00120	0.00120	0.00120	0.00120	0.00120	98,655	98,655	98,655	98,655	98,655	57.4	53.6	56.4	57.5	59.8	61.2
21	0.00128	0.00128	0.00128	0.00128	0.00128	98,537	98,537	98,537	98,537	98,537	56.5	52.6	55.4	56.6	58.8	60.3
22	0.00133	0.00133	0.00133	0.00133	0.00133	98,411	98,411	98,411	98,411	98,411	55.6	51.7	54.5	55.7	57.9	59.4
23	0.00200	0.00156	0.00121	0.00107	0.00107	98,280	98,280	98,280	98,280	98,280	54.7	50.8	53.6	54.7	57.0	58.4
24	0.00251	0.00155	0.00112	0.00099	0.00156	98,084	98,126	98,161	98,175	98,175	53.7	49.9	52.6	53.8	56.1	57.5
25	0.00280	0.00159	0.00101	0.00071	0.00127	97,838	97,974	98,052	98,077	98,021	52.8	49.0	51.7	52.9	55.1	56.6
26	0.00289	0.00157	0.00097	0.00068	0.00106	97,564	97,818	97,953	98,008	97,897	51.9	48.1	50.8	51.9	54.1	55.7
27	0.00310	0.00163	0.00086	0.00046	0.00089	97,282	97,665	97,857	97,941	97,794	50.9	47.3	49.9	51.0	53.2	54.7
28	0.00267	0.00149	0.00101	0.00059	0.00100	96,980	97,505	97,773	97,896	97,706	50.0	46.4	49.0	50.0	52.2	53.8
29	0.00240	0.00160	0.00103	0.00054	0.00038	96,721	97,360	97,674	97,838	97,608	49.1	45.5	48.0	49.1	51.2	52.8
30	0.00217	0.00155	0.00112	0.00071	0.00041	96,488	97,204	97,573	97,785	97,571	48.1	44.6	47.1	48.1	50.3	51.8
31	0.00220	0.00160	0.00110	0.00065	0.00039	96,279	97,053	97,464	97,716	97,530	47.2	43.7	46.2	47.2	49.3	50.9
32	0.00211	0.00160	0.00125	0.00080	0.00042	96,067	96,897	97,357	97,652	97,492	46.2	42.8	45.3	46.2	48.3	49.9
33	0.00210	0.00163	0.00123	0.00086	0.00041	95,864	96,742	97,235	97,574	97,451	45.3	41.9	44.3	45.3	47.4	48.9
34	0.00205	0.00165	0.00136	0.00091	0.00051	95,663	96,585	97,115	97,490	97,411	44.4	41.0	43.4	44.3	46.4	47.9
35	0.00225	0.00175	0.00151	0.00095	0.00074	95,466	96,425	96,982	97,401	97,361	43.4	40.1	42.5	43.4	45.5	46.9
36	0.00239	0.00188	0.00172	0.00100	0.00088	95,252	96,256	96,836	97,308	97,289	42.5	39.2	41.6	42.5	44.5	46.0
37	0.00268	0.00200	0.00184	0.00111	0.00102	95,023	96,076	96,669	97,211	97,203	41.5	38.3	40.6	41.5	43.5	45.0
38	0.00288	0.00219	0.00203	0.00119	0.00121	94,768	95,883	96,491	97,103	97,104	40.6	37.4	39.7	40.6	42.6	44.1
39	0.00327	0.00236	0.00225	0.00135	0.00120	94,496	95,673	96,295	96,987	96,986	39.7	36.5	38.8	39.7	41.6	43.1
40	0.00359	0.00261	0.00229	0.00155	0.00126	94,187	95,447	96,079	96,856	96,870	38.8	35.6	37.9	38.8	40.7	42.2
41	0.00401	0.00275	0.00244	0.00169	0.00141	93,849	95,198	95,858	96,706	96,748	37.9	34.7	37.0	37.9	39.8	41.2
42	0.00437	0.00297	0.00258	0.00182	0.00148	93,472	94,936	95,625	96,543	96,611	37.0	33.9	36.1	37.0	38.8	40.3
43	0.00484	0.00325	0.00275	0.00203	0.00165	93,064	94,655	95,379	96,367	96,468	36.1	33.0	35.2	36.1	37.9	39.3
44	0.00517	0.00356	0.00294	0.00228	0.00185	92,614	94,347	95,117	96,171	96,309	35.2	32.2	34.3	35.2	37.0	38.4
45	0.00570	0.00386	0.00323	0.00238	0.00196	92,135	94,011	94,836	95,952	96,131	34.3	31.3	33.4	34.3	36.1	37.5
46	0.00593	0.00423	0.00357	0.00269	0.00204	91,610	93,648	94,530	95,724	95,942	33.5	30.5	32.6	33.4	35.1	36.5
47	0.00610	0.00463	0.00405	0.00280	0.00224	91,066	93,252	94,193	95,467	95,747	32.6	29.7	31.7	32.5	34.2	35.6
48	0.00671	0.00501	0.00436	0.00286	0.00231	90,511	92,820	93,812	95,200	95,533	31.8	28.9	30.8	31.6	33.3	34.7
49	0.00736	0.00532	0.00462	0.00297	0.00263	89,904	92,355	93,402	94,927	95,312	31.0	28.1	30.0	30.7	32.4	33.8
50	0.00759	0.00592	0.00501	0.00320	0.00269	89,242	91,864	92,970	94,645	95,061	30.1	27.3	29.1	29.9	31.5	32.9
51	0.00823	0.00635	0.00532	0.00339	0.00296	88,565	91,320	92,504	94,342	94,806	29.3	26.5	28.3	29.0	30.6	32.0
52	0.00908	0.00659	0.00566	0.00372	0.00320	87,836	90,741	92,012	94,022	94,525	28.5	25.7	27.5	28.2	29.7	31.1
53	0.00953	0.00685	0.00619	0.00419	0.00342	87,039	90,143	91,491	93,672	94,222	27.6	24.9	26.7	27.3	28.8	30.1
54	0.01002	0.00724	0.00652	0.00449	0.00358	86,209	89,525	90,925	93,279	93,900	26.8	24.2	25.9	26.5	27.9	29.2
55	0.01064	0.00737	0.00705	0.00481	0.00418	85,345	88,877	90,332	92,861	93,563	25.9	23.4	25.0	25.7	27.1	28.4
56	0.01123	0.00778	0.00748	0.00495	0.00463	84,437	88,221	89,696	92,414	93,173	25.1	22.6	24.2	24.9	26.2	27.5
57	0.01170	0.00845	0.00794	0.00547	0.00495	83,488	87,535	89,024	91,956	92,741	24.2	21.9	23.4	24.1	25.3	26.6
58	0.01253	0.00914	0.00871	0.00590	0.00535	82,512	86,795	88,317	91,454	92,282	23.4	21.1	22.6	23.2	24.5	25.7
59	0.01321	0.01018	0.00975	0.00650	0.00591	81,478	86,001	87,548	90,914	91,788	22.5	20.4	21.8	22.4	23.6	24.9
60	0.01454	0.01131	0.01053	0.00742	0.00604	80,401	85,126	86,695	90,324	91,245	21.7	19.7	21.0	21.7	22.8	24.0
61	0.01580	0.01247	0.01144	0.00859	0.00680	79,232	84,164	85,782	89,653	90,694	20.9	19.0	20.3	20.9	21.9	23.1
62	0.01707	0.01388	0.01240	0.00962	0.00719	77,980	83,114	84,801	88,883	90,078	20.1	18.2	19.5	20.1	21.1	22.3
63	0.01837	0.01512	0.01295	0.01093	0.00801	76,649	81,961	83,750	88,028	89,430	19.3	17.6	18.8	19.4	20.3	21.5
64	0.02002	0.01605	0.01362	0.01189	0.00887	75,241	80,722	82,665	87,066	88,714	18.5	16.9	18.1	18.6	19.5	20.6
65	0.02127	0.01739	0.01451	0.01276	0.01019	73,735	79,426	81,539	86,031	87,928	17.7	16.2	17.3	17.9	18.8	19.8
66	0.02275	0.01909	0.01559	0.01398	0.01098	72,166	78,044	80,356	84,933	87,032	17.0	15.6	16.6	17.1	18.0	19.0
67	0.02464	0.02067	0.01687	0.01491	0.01274	70,525	76,555	79,103	83,746	86,076	16.3	14.9	16.0	16.4	17.2	18.2
68	0.02667	0.02233	0.01902	0.01611	0.01436	68,787	74,972	77,769	82,498	84,979	15.6	14.3	15.3	15.6	16.5	17.4
69	0.02887	0.02421	0.02124	0.01789	0.01575	66,953	73,298	76,289	81,169	83,759	14.9	13.6	14.6	14.9	15.8	16.7
70	0.03131	0.02610	0.02342	0.01957	0.01708	65,020	71,524	74,669	79,717	82,440	14.2	13.0	14.0	14.3	15.0	15.9
71	0.03411	0.02779	0.02593	0.02091	0.01903	62,985	69,656	72,920	78,157	81,032	13.5	12.4	13.3	13.6	14.3	15.2
72	0.03712	0.03039	0.02787	0.02338	0.02074	60,836	67,720	71,029	76,523	79,491	12.9	11.9	12.7	12.9	13.6	14.5
73	0.04087	0.03321	0.03058	0.02534	0.02292	58,578	65,663	69,050	74,733	77,842	12.2	11.3	12.1	12.3	12.9	13.8
74	0.04500	0.03609	0.03368	0.02875	0.02562	56,184	63,482	66,938	72,840	76,058	11.6	10.8	11.5	11.7	12.3	13.1
75	0.04897	0.03917	0.03743	0.03229	0.02822	53,656	61,190	64,684	70,745	74,109	11.0	10.2	10.9	11.1	11.6	12.4
76	0.05204	0.04335	0.04246	0.03526	0.03124	51,028	58,794	62,263	68,461	72,018	10.4	9.7	10.3	10.5	11.0	11.8
77	0.05630	0.04673	0.04784	0.03933	0.03450	48,373	56,245	59,619	66,047	69,768	9.9	9.3	9.8	9.9	10.4	11.2
78	0.06072	0.05226	0.05176	0.04413	0.03902	45,649	53,617	56,766	63,449	67,361	9.3	8.8	9.2	9.4	9.8	10.5
79	0.06574	0.05861	0.05779	0.04843	0.04388	42,877	50,815	53,828	60,649	64,733	8.8	8.3	8.7	8.9	9.2	9.9
80	0.07139	0.06517	0.06440	0.05473	0.05042	40,058	47,837	50,717	57,712	61,892	8.3	7.9	8.2	8.4	8.6	9.4
81	0.07830	0.07140	0.06970	0.06295	0.05600	37,199	44,719	47,451	54,554	58,771	7.8	7.4	7.7	7.9	8.1	8.8
82	0.08509	0.07875	0.07590	0.06767	0.06326	34,286	41,526	44,144	51,119	55,480	7.3	7.0	7.3	7.5	7.6	8.3
83	0.09214	0.08428	0.08555	0.07621	0.06909	31,369	38,256	40,793	47,660	51,970	6.9	6.6	6.9	7.0	7.1	7.9
84	0.10007	0.09266	0.09177	0.08028	0.07553	28,478	35,031	37,304	44,028	48,379	6.5	6.2	6.5	6.6	6.7	7.4
85	1.00000	1.00000	1.00000	1.00000	1.00000	25,629	31,785	33,880	40,494	44,725	6.1	5.9	6.1	6.3	6.2	7.0

* Weighted average by education.

Table 1: Mortality rates, number living at beginning of age (out of 100,000 born alive), and expectations of remaining years of life, 2004, continued—White Females

Age	Mortality Rates—White Females					Number Living at Beginning of Age Interval					Expectation of Life—White Females					
	<HS	High School	Some College	College Degree	Graduate Degree	<HS	High School	Some College	College Degree	Graduate Degree	All Ed Levels *	<HS	High School	Some College	College Degree	Grad Degree
0	0.00507	0.00507	0.00507	0.00507	0.00507	100,000	100,000	100,000	100,000	100,000	81.7	78.8	81.1	81.9	82.7	83.7
1	0.00042	0.00042	0.00042	0.00042	0.00042	99,493	99,493	99,493	99,493	99,493	81.1	78.2	80.5	81.3	82.2	83.1
2	0.00023	0.00023	0.00023	0.00023	0.00023	99,452	99,452	99,452	99,452	99,452	80.2	77.3	79.5	80.3	81.2	82.1
3	0.00018	0.00018	0.00018	0.00018	0.00018	99,429	99,429	99,429	99,429	99,429	79.2	76.3	78.5	79.4	80.2	81.2
4	0.00015	0.00015	0.00015	0.00015	0.00015	99,412	99,412	99,412	99,412	99,412	78.2	75.3	77.6	78.4	79.2	80.2
5	0.00013	0.00013	0.00013	0.00013	0.00013	99,397	99,397	99,397	99,397	99,397	77.2	74.3	76.6	77.4	78.2	79.2
6	0.00012	0.00012	0.00012	0.00012	0.00012	99,383	99,383	99,383	99,383	99,383	76.2	73.3	75.6	76.4	77.2	78.2
7	0.00012	0.00012	0.00012	0.00012	0.00012	99,371	99,371	99,371	99,371	99,371	75.2	72.3	74.6	75.4	76.3	77.2
8	0.00011	0.00011	0.00011	0.00011	0.00011	99,359	99,359	99,359	99,359	99,359	74.2	71.3	73.6	74.4	75.3	76.2
9	0.00001	0.00001	0.00001	0.00001	0.00001	99,349	99,349	99,349	99,349	99,349	73.2	70.3	72.6	73.4	74.3	75.2
10	0.00009	0.00009	0.00009	0.00009	0.00009	99,339	99,339	99,339	99,339	99,339	72.2	69.3	71.6	72.4	73.3	74.2
11	0.00001	0.00001	0.00001	0.00001	0.00001	99,330	99,330	99,330	99,330	99,330	71.2	68.3	70.6	71.4	72.3	73.2
12	0.00012	0.00012	0.00012	0.00012	0.00012	99,320	99,320	99,320	99,320	99,320	70.3	67.3	69.6	70.5	71.3	72.2
13	0.00017	0.00017	0.00017	0.00017	0.00017	99,308	99,308	99,308	99,308	99,308	69.3	66.4	68.6	69.5	70.3	71.2
14	0.00023	0.00023	0.00023	0.00023	0.00023	99,292	99,292	99,292	99,292	99,292	68.3	65.4	67.6	68.5	69.3	70.3
15	0.00031	0.00031	0.00031	0.00031	0.00031	99,269	99,269	99,269	99,269	99,269	67.3	64.4	66.7	67.5	68.3	69.3
16	0.00038	0.00038	0.00038	0.00038	0.00038	99,238	99,238	99,238	99,238	99,238	66.3	63.4	65.7	66.5	67.4	68.3
17	0.00043	0.00043	0.00043	0.00043	0.00043	99,200	99,200	99,200	99,200	99,200	65.3	62.4	64.7	65.5	66.4	67.3
18	0.00045	0.00045	0.00045	0.00045	0.00045	99,157	99,157	99,157	99,157	99,157	64.4	61.5	63.7	64.6	65.4	66.3
19	0.00045	0.00045	0.00045	0.00045	0.00045	99,113	99,113	99,113	99,113	99,113	63.4	60.5	62.8	63.6	64.4	65.4
20	0.00044	0.00044	0.00044	0.00044	0.00044	99,068	99,068	99,068	99,068	99,068	62.4	59.5	61.8	62.6	63.5	64.4
21	0.00044	0.00044	0.00044	0.00044	0.00044	99,024	99,024	99,024	99,024	99,024	61.4	58.5	60.8	61.6	62.5	63.4
22	0.00044	0.00044	0.00044	0.00044	0.00044	98,981	98,981	98,981	98,981	98,981	60.5	57.6	59.8	60.7	61.5	62.5
23	0.00056	0.00056	0.00047	0.00035	0.00035	98,937	98,937	98,937	98,937	98,937	59.5	56.6	58.9	59.7	60.5	61.5
24	0.00048	0.00053	0.00038	0.00033	0.00050	98,882	98,882	98,891	98,902	98,902	58.5	55.6	57.9	58.7	59.6	60.5
25	0.00066	0.00053	0.00041	0.00044	0.00042	98,834	98,830	98,853	98,870	98,852	57.6	54.6	56.9	57.7	58.6	59.5
26	0.00065	0.00054	0.00040	0.00045	0.00034	98,769	98,778	98,813	98,826	98,811	56.6	53.7	56.0	56.8	57.6	58.6
27	0.00073	0.00055	0.00045	0.00044	0.00032	98,705	98,724	98,773	98,781	98,777	55.6	52.7	55.0	55.8	56.6	57.6
28	0.00063	0.00045	0.00043	0.00047	0.00059	98,634	98,670	98,729	98,738	98,746	54.6	51.7	54.0	54.8	55.7	56.6
29	0.00083	0.00053	0.00055	0.00048	0.00045	98,572	98,626	98,686	98,691	98,688	53.7	50.8	53.0	53.8	54.7	55.6
30	0.00065	0.00057	0.00057	0.00038	0.00051	98,490	98,573	98,632	98,643	98,643	52.7	49.8	52.1	52.9	53.7	54.7
31	0.00084	0.00064	0.00057	0.00034	0.00063	98,426	98,517	98,575	98,606	98,593	51.7	48.9	51.1	51.9	52.7	53.7
32	0.00097	0.00071	0.00058	0.00035	0.00066	98,344	98,455	98,519	98,572	98,531	50.7	47.9	50.1	50.9	51.8	52.7
33	0.00099	0.00075	0.00064	0.00045	0.00055	98,248	98,385	98,462	98,538	98,466	49.8	46.9	49.2	50.0	50.8	51.8
34	0.00104	0.00083	0.00069	0.00044	0.00049	98,151	98,311	98,398	98,493	98,412	48.8	46.0	48.2	49.0	49.8	50.8
35	0.00126	0.00091	0.00074	0.00043	0.00060	98,048	98,229	98,330	98,450	98,364	47.8	45.0	47.2	48.0	48.8	49.8
36	0.00135	0.00095	0.00084	0.00049	0.00066	97,925	98,139	98,258	98,408	98,305	46.8	44.1	46.3	47.1	47.8	48.8
37	0.00134	0.00103	0.00088	0.00060	0.00073	97,793	98,046	98,175	98,360	98,240	45.9	43.2	45.3	46.1	46.9	47.9
38	0.00166	0.00116	0.00091	0.00065	0.00071	97,661	97,945	98,089	98,301	98,168	44.9	42.2	44.4	45.1	45.9	46.9
39	0.00186	0.00124	0.00101	0.00087	0.00087	97,500	97,832	97,999	98,236	98,098	44.0	41.3	43.4	44.2	44.9	45.9
40	0.00199	0.00135	0.00110	0.00105	0.00094	97,318	97,710	97,900	98,151	98,013	43.0	40.4	42.5	43.2	44.0	45.0
41	0.00214	0.00145	0.00127	0.00117	0.00097	97,125	97,579	97,792	98,049	97,921	42.1	39.4	41.5	42.3	43.0	44.0
42	0.00247	0.00155	0.00136	0.00127	0.00104	96,917	97,437	97,668	97,934	97,825	41.1	38.5	40.6	41.3	42.1	43.1
43	0.00262	0.00174	0.00155	0.00135	0.00093	96,677	97,286	97,535	97,810	97,724	40.2	37.6	39.7	40.4	41.1	42.1
44	0.00294	0.00185	0.00164	0.00158	0.00099	96,424	97,117	97,383	97,678	97,633	39.2	36.7	38.7	39.4	40.2	41.1
45	0.00329	0.00207	0.00172	0.00157	0.00102	96,141	96,937	97,224	97,523	97,536	38.3	35.8	37.8	38.5	39.2	40.2
46	0.00359	0.00225	0.00185	0.00173	0.00100	95,824	96,736	97,056	97,369	97,436	37.4	34.9	36.9	37.6	38.3	39.2
47	0.00374	0.00242	0.00204	0.00185	0.00117	95,480	96,519	96,876	97,201	97,339	36.5	34.1	36.0	36.6	37.3	38.3
48	0.00414	0.00247	0.00220	0.00199	0.00134	95,123	96,285	96,679	97,021	97,225	35.6	33.2	35.0	35.7	36.4	37.3
49	0.00418	0.00270	0.00241	0.00191	0.00141	94,729	96,047	96,466	96,828	97,095	34.7	32.3	34.1	34.8	35.5	36.4
50	0.00438	0.00281	0.00258	0.00211	0.00149	94,332	95,787	96,234	96,643	96,958	33.7	31.5	33.2	33.9	34.6	35.4
51	0.00443	0.00303	0.00279	0.00226	0.00168	93,919	95,518	95,986	96,439	96,813	32.8	30.6	32.3	33.0	33.6	34.5
52	0.00460	0.00336	0.00289	0.00233	0.00186	93,503	95,228	95,718	96,221	96,651	31.9	29.7	31.4	32.1	32.7	33.5
53	0.00497	0.00364	0.00298	0.00276	0.00210	93,073	94,908	95,441	95,996	96,471	31.0	28.9	30.5	31.1	31.8	32.6
54	0.00555	0.00391	0.00334	0.00294	0.00214	92,611	94,562	95,156	95,731	96,268	30.1	28.0	29.6	30.2	30.9	31.6
55	0.00596	0.00433	0.00353	0.00317	0.00245	92,097	94,193	94,839	95,450	96,063	29.2	27.2	28.7	29.3	30.0	30.7
56	0.00653	0.00471	0.00384	0.00330	0.00287	91,548	93,785	94,504	95,148	95,828	28.2	26.3	27.9	28.4	29.1	29.8
57	0.00722	0.00503	0.00440	0.00359	0.00299	90,951	93,343	94,142	94,834	95,553	27.3	25.5	27.0	27.5	28.1	28.9
58	0.00779	0.00554	0.00493	0.00365	0.00333	90,294	92,873	93,728	94,494	95,267	26.4	24.7	26.1	26.7	27.2	28.0
59	0.00853	0.00603	0.00525	0.00422	0.00424	89,591	92,359	93,265	94,149	94,950	25.5	23.9	25.3	25.8	26.3	27.1
60	0.00940	0.00653	0.00624	0.00463	0.00467	88,826	91,802	92,776	93,752	94,548	24.6	23.1	24.4	24.9	25.4	26.2
61	0.01037	0.00721	0.00690	0.00523	0.00532	87,991	91,203	92,197	93,318	94,106	23.8	22.3	23.6	24.1	24.6	25.3
62	0.01141	0.00795	0.00733	0.00587	0.00606	87,078	90,545	91,561	92,830	93,606	22.9	21.5	22.7	23.2	23.7	24.4
63	0.01233	0.00862	0.00804	0.00664	0.00659	86,085	89,826	90,889	92,285	93,039	22.1	20.7	21.9	22.4	22.8	23.6
64	0.01322	0.00943	0.00882	0.00686	0.00642	85,023	89,051	90,159	91,671	92,426	21.2	20.0	21.1	21.6	22.0	22.7
65	0.01415	0.01034	0.00921	0.00756	0.00711	83,899	88,212	89,364	91,042	91,833	20.4	19.3	20.3	20.8	21.1	21.9
66	0.01540	0.01131	0.01000	0.00820	0.00727	82,712	87,300	88,541	90,354	91,180	19.6	18.5	19.5	20.0	20.3	21.0
67	0.01651	0.01244	0.01140	0.00897	0.00812	81,438	86,312	87,656	89,613	90,517	18.8	17.8	18.7	19.2	19.4	20.2
68	0.01809	0.01360	0.01254	0.01004	0.00860	80,094	85,238	86,657	88,809	89,783	18.0	17.1	18.0	18.4	18.6	19.3
69	0.01966	0.01489	0.01360	0.01181	0.01006	78,645	84,079	85,570	87,917	89,011	17.2	16.4	17.2	17.6	17.8	18.5
70	0.02125	0.01637	0.01497	0.01369	0.01046	77,099	82,827	84,406	86,879	88,115	16.5	15.7	16.4	16.8	17.0	17.7
71	0.02273	0.01803	0.01688	0.01600	0.01107	75,460	81,471	83,143	85,689	87,193	15.7	15.1	15.7	16.1	16.2	16.9
72	0.02502	0.01975	0.01773	0.01788	0.01303	73,745	80,003	81,739	84,318	86,228	15.0	14.4	15.0	15.4	15.5	16.0
73	0.02714	0.02193	0.01942	0.02008	0.01487	71,900	78,423	80,291	82,810	85,104	14.3	13.7	14.3	14.6	14.8	15.2
74	0.02935	0.02420	0.02171	0.02307	0.01729	69,948	76,703	78,731	81,148	83,839	13.6	13.1	13.6	13.9	14.1	14.5
75	0.03148	0.02680	0.02353	0.02457	0.02134	67,895	74,847	77,022	79,276	82,389	12.9	12.5	12.9	13.2	13.4	13.7
76	0.03430	0.02901	0.02568	0.02536	0.02477	65,758	72,841	75,210	77,328	80,631	12.3	11.9	12.3	12.5	12.7	13.0
77	0.03686	0.03219	0.02958	0.02815	0.02559	63,503	70,728	73,279	75,367	78,634	11.6	11.3	11.6	11.8	12.0	12.3
78	0.04050	0.03586	0.03344	0.03132	0.02912	61,162	68,452	71,111	73,245	76,622	11.0	10.7	11.0	11.2	11.4	11.6
79	0.04515	0.04055	0.03686	0.03353	0.03208	58,685	65,997	68,733	70,951	74,390	10.4	10.1	10.4	10.5	10.7	11.0
80	0.05020	0.04519	0.04199	0.03638	0.03411	56,035	63,321	66,200	68,572	72,004	9.8	9.6	9.8	9.9	10.1	10.3
81	0.05450	0.05069	0.04702	0.04230	0.03761	53,222	60,460	63,420	66,077	69,548	9.2	9.1	9.2	9.3	9.4	9.6
82	0.05941	0.05629	0.05293	0.04829	0.04369	50,322	57,395	60,438	63,282	66,933	8.7	8.6	8.7	8.8	8.8	9.0
83	0.06489	0.06272	0.06145	0.05349	0.04872	47,332	54,164	57,239	60,227	64,009	8.2	8.1	8.2	8.2	8.2	8.4
84	0.07097	0.06956	0.07104	0.06571	0.05511	44,261	50,767	53,722	57,005	60,890	7.7	7.6	7.7	7.7	7.7	7.8
85	1.00000	1.00000	1.00000	1.00000	1.00000	41,119	47,235	49,905	53,259	57,535	7.2	7.1	7.2	7.3	7.2	7.2

* Weighted average by education.

Table 1: Mortality rates, number living at beginning of age (out of 100,000 born alive), and expectations of remaining years of life, 2004, continued—Black Males

Age	Mortality Rates—Black Males					Number Living at Beginning of Age Interval					Expectation of Life—Black Males					
	<HS	High School	Some College	College Degree	Graduate Degree	<HS	High School	Some College	College Degree	Graduate Degree	All Ed Levels *	<HS	High School	Some College	College Degree	Grad Degree
0	0.01525	0.01525	0.01525	0.01525	0.01525	100,000	100,000	100,000	100,000	100,000	71.0	67.5	70.2	71.2	74.5	74.5
1	0.00076	0.00076	0.00076	0.00076	0.00076	98,475	98,475	98,475	98,475	98,475	71.1	67.5	70.3	71.3	74.7	74.7
2	0.00047	0.00047	0.00047	0.00047	0.00047	98,400	98,400	98,400	98,400	98,400	70.2	66.6	69.4	70.3	73.7	73.7
3	0.00039	0.00039	0.00039	0.00039	0.00039	98,354	98,354	98,354	98,354	98,354	69.2	65.6	68.4	69.4	72.8	72.8
4	0.00031	0.00031	0.00031	0.00031	0.00031	98,315	98,315	98,315	98,315	98,315	68.2	64.6	67.4	68.4	71.8	71.8
5	0.00028	0.00028	0.00028	0.00028	0.00028	98,285	98,285	98,285	98,285	98,285	67.2	63.6	66.4	67.4	70.8	70.8
6	0.00026	0.00026	0.00026	0.00026	0.00026	98,257	98,257	98,257	98,257	98,257	66.3	62.7	65.5	66.4	69.8	69.8
7	0.00024	0.00024	0.00024	0.00024	0.00024	98,231	98,231	98,231	98,231	98,231	65.3	61.7	64.5	65.5	68.8	68.8
8	0.00021	0.00021	0.00021	0.00021	0.00021	98,208	98,208	98,208	98,208	98,208	64.3	60.7	63.5	64.5	67.9	67.9
9	0.00017	0.00017	0.00017	0.00017	0.00017	98,188	98,188	98,188	98,188	98,188	63.3	59.7	62.5	63.5	66.9	66.9
10	0.00015	0.00015	0.00015	0.00015	0.00015	98,171	98,171	98,171	98,171	98,171	62.3	58.7	61.5	62.5	65.9	65.9
11	0.00016	0.00016	0.00016	0.00016	0.00016	98,156	98,156	98,156	98,156	98,156	61.3	57.7	60.5	61.5	64.9	64.9
12	0.00022	0.00022	0.00022	0.00022	0.00022	98,141	98,141	98,141	98,141	98,141	60.3	56.7	59.5	60.5	63.9	63.9
13	0.00035	0.00035	0.00035	0.00035	0.00035	98,119	98,119	98,119	98,119	98,119	59.4	55.7	58.5	59.5	62.9	62.9
14	0.00055	0.00055	0.00055	0.00055	0.00055	98,084	98,084	98,084	98,084	98,084	58.4	54.8	57.6	58.5	61.9	61.9
15	0.00077	0.00077	0.00077	0.00077	0.00077	98,030	98,030	98,030	98,030	98,030	57.4	53.8	56.6	57.6	61.0	61.0
16	0.00100	0.00100	0.00100	0.00100	0.00100	97,955	97,955	97,955	97,955	97,955	56.5	52.8	55.6	56.6	60.0	60.0
17	0.00123	0.00123	0.00123	0.00123	0.00123	97,856	97,856	97,856	97,856	97,856	55.5	51.9	54.7	55.7	59.1	59.1
18	0.00144	0.00144	0.00144	0.00144	0.00144	97,736	97,736	97,736	97,736	97,736	54.6	50.9	53.8	54.7	58.2	58.2
19	0.00163	0.00163	0.00163	0.00163	0.00163	97,595	97,595	97,595	97,595	97,595	53.7	50.0	52.8	53.8	57.2	57.2
20	0.00182	0.00182	0.00182	0.00182	0.00182	97,436	97,436	97,436	97,436	97,436	52.7	49.1	51.9	52.9	56.3	56.3
21	0.00200	0.00200	0.00200	0.00200	0.00200	97,259	97,259	97,259	97,259	97,259	51.8	48.2	51.0	52.0	55.4	55.4
22	0.00215	0.00215	0.00215	0.00215	0.00215	97,064	97,064	97,064	97,064	97,064	50.9	47.3	50.1	51.1	54.5	54.5
23	0.00180	0.00230	0.00275	0.00180	0.00180	96,856	96,856	96,856	96,856	96,856	50.1	46.4	49.2	50.2	53.7	53.7
24	0.00219	0.00224	0.00237	0.00139	0.00139	96,682	96,633	96,589	96,682	96,682	49.2	45.5	48.3	49.4	52.8	52.8
25	0.00291	0.00263	0.00195	0.00095	0.00095	96,470	96,416	96,361	96,548	96,548	48.3	44.6	47.4	48.5	51.8	51.8
26	0.00273	0.00260	0.00151	0.00048	0.00048	96,189	96,162	96,173	96,456	96,456	47.4	43.7	46.6	47.6	50.9	50.9
27	0.00324	0.00266	0.00123	0.00000	0.00000	95,926	95,912	96,027	96,410	96,410	46.5	42.8	45.7	46.6	49.9	49.9
28	0.00415	0.00262	0.00042	0.00045	0.00045	95,615	95,657	95,909	96,410	96,410	45.5	41.9	44.8	45.7	48.9	48.9
29	0.00382	0.00279	0.00056	0.00098	0.00098	95,218	95,407	95,869	96,366	96,366	44.6	41.1	43.9	44.7	47.9	47.9
30	0.00331	0.00251	0.00102	0.00098	0.00098	94,854	95,140	95,815	96,272	96,272	43.7	40.3	43.1	43.7	47.0	47.0
31	0.00375	0.00254	0.00166	0.00137	0.00137	94,540	94,902	95,717	96,177	96,177	42.8	39.4	42.2	42.8	46.0	46.0
32	0.00334	0.00251	0.00202	0.00153	0.00153	94,185	94,660	95,558	96,045	96,045	41.9	38.6	41.3	41.9	45.1	45.1
33	0.00328	0.00246	0.00231	0.00130	0.00130	93,870	94,423	95,365	95,899	95,899	41.0	37.7	40.4	40.9	44.2	44.2
34	0.00352	0.00267	0.00268	0.00129	0.00129	93,562	94,191	95,145	95,774	95,774	40.1	36.8	39.5	40.0	43.2	43.2
35	0.00383	0.00259	0.00261	0.00168	0.00168	93,233	93,939	94,890	95,651	95,651	39.1	35.9	38.6	39.1	42.3	42.3
36	0.00437	0.00284	0.00243	0.00151	0.00151	92,876	93,696	94,642	95,490	95,490	38.2	35.1	37.7	38.2	41.3	41.3
37	0.00496	0.00312	0.00254	0.00152	0.00152	92,470	93,430	94,412	95,345	95,345	37.3	34.2	36.8	37.3	40.4	40.4
38	0.00542	0.00350	0.00252	0.00174	0.00174	92,011	93,139	94,173	95,200	95,200	36.3	33.4	35.9	36.4	39.5	39.5
39	0.00579	0.00358	0.00283	0.00161	0.00161	91,512	92,812	93,935	95,034	95,034	35.5	32.6	35.0	35.5	38.5	38.5
40	0.00562	0.00419	0.00318	0.00174	0.00174	90,982	92,480	93,670	94,881	94,881	34.6	31.8	34.1	34.6	37.6	37.6
41	0.00585	0.00438	0.00338	0.00216	0.00216	90,471	92,093	93,372	94,716	94,716	33.7	30.9	33.3	33.7	36.6	36.6
42	0.00646	0.00454	0.00365	0.00250	0.00250	89,941	91,690	93,056	94,511	94,511	32.8	30.1	32.4	32.8	35.7	35.7
43	0.00709	0.00462	0.00430	0.00332	0.00332	89,360	91,274	92,716	94,275	94,275	31.9	29.3	31.6	32.0	34.8	34.8
44	0.00800	0.00500	0.00505	0.00355	0.00355	88,727	90,852	92,318	93,962	93,962	31.1	28.5	30.7	31.1	33.9	33.9
45	0.00962	0.00516	0.00583	0.00368	0.00368	88,017	90,398	91,852	93,629	93,629	30.2	27.7	29.9	30.2	33.1	33.1
46	0.01010	0.00559	0.00694	0.00434	0.00434	87,171	89,931	91,316	93,285	93,285	29.4	27.0	29.0	29.4	32.2	32.2
47	0.01083	0.00639	0.00775	0.00433	0.00433	86,291	89,428	90,682	92,880	92,880	28.6	26.3	28.2	28.6	31.3	31.3
48	0.01169	0.00722	0.00840	0.00400	0.00400	85,356	88,857	89,979	92,478	92,478	27.8	25.6	27.4	27.8	30.4	30.4
49	0.01287	0.00809	0.00824	0.00454	0.00454	84,358	88,215	89,223	92,108	92,108	27.0	24.9	26.5	27.1	29.6	29.6
50	0.01365	0.00878	0.00874	0.00600	0.00600	83,272	87,501	88,488	91,690	91,690	26.2	24.2	25.8	26.3	28.7	28.7
51	0.01451	0.01044	0.00807	0.00643	0.00643	82,135	86,733	87,715	91,140	91,140	25.4	23.5	25.0	25.5	27.9	27.9
52	0.01486	0.01175	0.00792	0.00870	0.00870	80,943	85,828	87,007	90,554	90,554	24.7	22.8	24.2	24.7	27.0	27.0
53	0.01537	0.01265	0.00923	0.00895	0.00895	79,740	84,820	86,318	89,766	89,766	23.9	22.2	23.5	23.9	26.3	26.3
54	0.01600	0.01310	0.01089	0.00970	0.00970	78,515	83,747	85,521	88,962	88,962	23.1	21.5	22.8	23.1	25.5	25.5
55	0.01681	0.01373	0.01215	0.01034	0.01034	77,259	82,650	84,590	88,099	88,099	22.4	20.9	22.1	22.4	24.8	24.8
56	0.01800	0.01403	0.01493	0.01005	0.01005	75,960	81,515	83,562	87,188	87,188	21.7	20.2	21.4	21.7	24.0	24.0
57	0.01938	0.01430	0.01711	0.01027	0.01027	74,593	80,371	82,314	86,312	86,312	20.9	19.6	20.7	21.0	23.2	23.2
58	0.02048	0.01605	0.01595	0.01143	0.01143	73,147	79,222	80,906	85,426	85,426	20.2	18.9	20.0	20.3	22.5	22.5
59	0.02170	0.01757	0.01528	0.01365	0.01365	71,649	77,950	79,615	84,449	84,449	19.5	18.3	19.3	19.7	21.7	21.7
60	0.02324	0.01949	0.01515	0.01331	0.01331	70,094	76,581	78,399	83,297	83,297	18.8	17.7	18.7	19.0	21.0	21.0
61	0.02522	0.02015	0.01615	0.01433	0.01433	68,465	75,089	77,211	82,188	82,188	18.1	17.1	18.0	18.2	20.3	20.3
62	0.02722	0.02117	0.01507	0.01689	0.01689	66,738	73,576	75,964	81,010	81,010	17.5	16.6	17.4	17.5	19.6	19.6
63	0.02833	0.02276	0.01843	0.01857	0.01857	64,922	72,018	74,820	79,642	79,642	16.8	16.0	16.7	16.8	18.9	18.9
64	0.02992	0.02428	0.02114	0.01688	0.01688	63,083	70,379	73,441	78,163	78,163	16.2	15.5	16.1	16.1	18.3	18.3
65	0.03066	0.02645	0.02499	0.01938	0.01938	61,195	68,670	71,888	76,844	76,844	15.5	14.9	15.5	15.4	17.6	17.6
66	0.03192	0.02839	0.02730	0.02049	0.02049	59,319	66,854	70,092	75,355	75,355	14.9	14.4	14.9	14.8	16.9	16.9
67	0.03349	0.02975	0.03129	0.02108	0.02108	57,426	64,956	68,178	73,810	73,810	14.3	13.8	14.3	14.2	16.3	16.3
68	0.03567	0.03235	0.03263	0.02165	0.02165	55,502	63,023	66,045	72,254	72,254	13.8	13.3	13.8	13.7	15.6	15.6
69	0.03796	0.03416	0.03673	0.02410	0.02410	53,523	60,984	63,890	70,690	70,690	13.2	12.8	13.2	13.1	14.9	14.9
70	0.04059	0.03782	0.04089	0.02175	0.02175	51,491	58,901	61,543	68,986	68,986	12.6	12.3	12.7	12.6	14.3	14.3
71	0.04326	0.04025	0.04477	0.02380	0.02380	49,401	56,674	59,026	67,486	67,486	12.1	11.8	12.1	12.1	13.6	13.6
72	0.04633	0.04429	0.04448	0.02497	0.02497	47,264	54,393	56,384	65,880	65,880	11.6	11.3	11.6	11.6	12.9	12.9
73	0.05002	0.04532	0.04950	0.03211	0.03211	45,074	51,984	53,876	64,235	64,235	11.1	10.8	11.1	11.2	12.2	12.2
74	0.05343	0.05095	0.06015	0.03397	0.03397	42,820	49,628	51,209	62,173	62,173	10.6	10.3	10.6	10.7	11.6	11.6
75	0.05865	0.05345	0.05951	0.03945	0.03945	40,532	47,099	48,129	60,061	60,061	10.1	9.9	10.2	10.4	11.0	11.0
76	0.06289	0.05872	0.06170	0.04864	0.04864	38,154	44,582	45,265	57,691	57,691	9.7	9.5	9.7	10.0	10.4	10.4
77	0.06706	0.06358	0.07534	0.04965	0.04965	35,755	41,964	42,472	54,885	54,885	9.3	9.1	9.3	9.6	9.9	9.9
78	0.07168	0.06709	0.08136	0.05114	0.05114	33,357	39,296	39,272	52,160	52,160	8.9	8.7	8.9	9.4	9.4	9.4
79	0.07679	0.07087	0.06892	0.05986	0.05986	30,966	36,660	36,077	49,492	49,492	8.5	8.3	8.5	9.1	8.9	8.9
80	0.08130	0.07085	0.07616	0.07056	0.07056	28,588	34,062	33,591	46,530	46,530	8.1	8.0	8.1	8.8	8.5	8.5
81	0.08676	0.07579	0.07938	0.06330	0.06330	26,264	31,649	31,032	43,247	43,247	7.8	7.6	7.7	8.5	8.1	8.1
82	0.09219	0.07718	0.06306	0.08491	0.08491	23,985	29,250	28,569	40,509	40,509	7.4	7.3	7.3	8.2	7.6	7.6
83	0.09788	0.07909	0.06159	0.09090	0.09090	21,774	26,992	26,768	37,070	37,070	7.0	7.0	6.9	7.7	7.2	7.2
84	0.10464	0.08605	0.04602	0.09472	0.09472	19,643	24,858	25,119	33,700	33,700	6.7	6.7	6.4	7.1	6.9	6.9
85	1.00000	1.00000	1.00000	1.00000	1.00000	17,587	22,719	23,963	30,508	30,508	6.3	6.4	6.0	6.5	6.6	6.6

* Weighted average by education.

Table 1: Mortality rates, number living at beginning of age (out of 100,000 born alive), and expectations of remaining years of life, 2004, continued—Black Females

Age	Mortality Rates—Black Females					Number Living at Beginning of Age Interval					Expectation of Life—Black Females					
	<HS	High School	Some College	College Degree	Graduate Degree	<HS	High School	Some College	College Degree	Graduate Degree	All Ed Levels *	<HS	High School	Some College	College Degree	Grad Degree
0	0.01237	0.01237	0.01237	0.01237	0.01237	100,000	100,000	100,000	100,000	100,000	77.8	74.2	77.0	78.8	79.3	79.3
1	0.00066	0.00066	0.00066	0.00066	0.00066	98,763	98,763	98,763	98,763	98,763	77.7	74.1	77.0	78.8	79.2	79.2
2	0.00041	0.00041	0.00041	0.00041	0.00041	98,698	98,698	98,698	98,698	98,698	76.8	73.1	76.0	77.8	78.3	78.3
3	0.00030	0.00030	0.00030	0.00030	0.00030	98,657	98,657	98,657	98,657	98,657	75.8	72.2	75.0	76.9	77.3	77.3
4	0.00025	0.00025	0.00025	0.00025	0.00025	98,627	98,627	98,627	98,627	98,627	74.8	71.2	74.1	75.9	76.3	76.3
5	0.00024	0.00024	0.00024	0.00024	0.00024	98,603	98,603	98,603	98,603	98,603	73.9	70.2	73.1	74.9	75.4	75.4
6	0.00021	0.00021	0.00021	0.00021	0.00021	98,579	98,579	98,579	98,579	98,579	72.9	69.2	72.1	73.9	74.4	74.4
7	0.00019	0.00019	0.00019	0.00019	0.00019	98,558	98,558	98,558	98,558	98,558	71.9	68.2	71.1	72.9	73.4	73.4
8	0.00018	0.00018	0.00018	0.00018	0.00018	98,539	98,539	98,539	98,539	98,539	70.9	67.3	70.1	71.9	72.4	72.4
9	0.00018	0.00018	0.00018	0.00018	0.00018	98,521	98,521	98,521	98,521	98,521	69.9	66.3	69.1	71.0	71.4	71.4
10	0.00018	0.00018	0.00018	0.00018	0.00018	98,503	98,503	98,503	98,503	98,503	68.9	65.3	68.1	70.0	70.4	70.4
11	0.00019	0.00019	0.00019	0.00019	0.00019	98,485	98,485	98,485	98,485	98,485	67.9	64.3	67.2	69.0	69.5	69.5
12	0.00021	0.00021	0.00021	0.00021	0.00021	98,466	98,466	98,466	98,466	98,466	67.0	63.3	66.2	68.0	68.5	68.5
13	0.00024	0.00024	0.00024	0.00024	0.00024	98,445	98,445	98,445	98,445	98,445	66.0	62.3	65.2	67.0	67.5	67.5
14	0.00027	0.00027	0.00027	0.00027	0.00027	98,422	98,422	98,422	98,422	98,422	65.0	61.3	64.2	66.0	66.5	66.5
15	0.00031	0.00031	0.00031	0.00031	0.00031	98,396	98,396	98,396	98,396	98,396	64.0	60.4	63.2	65.1	65.5	65.5
16	0.00036	0.00036	0.00036	0.00036	0.00036	98,365	98,365	98,365	98,365	98,365	63.0	59.4	62.2	64.1	64.5	64.5
17	0.00041	0.00041	0.00041	0.00041	0.00041	98,330	98,330	98,330	98,330	98,330	62.1	58.4	61.3	63.1	63.6	63.6
18	0.00046	0.00046	0.00046	0.00046	0.00046	98,290	98,290	98,290	98,290	98,290	61.1	57.4	60.3	62.1	62.6	62.6
19	0.00051	0.00051	0.00051	0.00051	0.00051	98,245	98,245	98,245	98,245	98,245	60.1	56.4	59.3	61.1	61.6	61.6
20	0.00056	0.00056	0.00056	0.00056	0.00056	98,195	98,195	98,195	98,195	98,195	59.1	55.5	58.3	60.2	60.6	60.6
21	0.00062	0.00062	0.00062	0.00062	0.00062	98,139	98,139	98,139	98,139	98,139	58.2	54.5	57.4	59.2	59.7	59.7
22	0.00068	0.00068	0.00068	0.00068	0.00068	98,078	98,078	98,078	98,078	98,078	57.2	53.5	56.4	58.2	58.7	58.7
23	0.00149	0.00096	0.00129	0.00204	0.00204	98,012	98,012	98,012	98,012	98,012	56.2	52.6	55.4	57.3	57.8	57.8
24	0.00199	0.00087	0.00122	0.00202	0.00202	97,866	97,918	97,886	97,813	97,813	55.3	51.6	54.5	56.4	56.9	56.9
25	0.00236	0.00085	0.00147	0.00199	0.00199	97,672	97,833	97,766	97,615	97,615	54.4	50.8	53.5	55.4	56.0	56.0
26	0.00235	0.00091	0.00174	0.00196	0.00196	97,442	97,750	97,622	97,420	97,420	53.5	49.9	52.6	54.5	55.1	55.1
27	0.00243	0.00100	0.00167	0.00207	0.00207	97,212	97,661	97,453	97,229	97,229	52.6	49.0	51.6	53.6	54.2	54.2
28	0.00193	0.00077	0.00087	0.00017	0.00017	96,976	97,563	97,290	97,028	97,028	51.6	48.1	50.7	52.7	53.3	53.3
29	0.00174	0.00110	0.00010	0.00062	0.00062	96,789	97,489	97,206	97,012	97,012	50.7	47.2	49.7	51.7	52.3	52.3
30	0.00130	0.00132	0.00070	0.00082	0.00082	96,620	97,381	97,109	96,951	96,951	49.7	46.3	48.8	50.8	51.4	51.4
31	0.00184	0.00136	0.00054	0.00097	0.00097	96,495	97,252	97,041	96,872	96,872	48.8	45.3	47.8	49.8	50.4	50.4
32	0.00227	0.00142	0.00080	0.00082	0.00082	96,317	97,120	96,989	96,778	96,778	47.8	44.4	46.9	48.8	49.4	49.4
33	0.00209	0.00144	0.00092	0.00112	0.00112	96,099	96,982	96,912	96,699	96,699	46.9	43.5	46.0	47.9	48.5	48.5
34	0.00202	0.00145	0.00118	0.00066	0.00066	95,898	96,843	96,823	96,591	96,591	45.9	42.6	45.0	46.9	47.5	47.5
35	0.00250	0.00142	0.00131	0.00065	0.00065	95,705	96,702	96,709	96,528	96,528	45.0	41.7	44.1	46.0	46.6	46.6
36	0.00256	0.00159	0.00129	0.00080	0.00080	95,465	96,564	96,582	96,465	96,465	44.0	40.8	43.2	45.0	45.6	45.6
37	0.00271	0.00172	0.00130	0.00094	0.00094	95,221	96,411	96,457	96,388	96,388	43.1	39.9	42.2	44.1	44.6	44.6
38	0.00286	0.00202	0.00153	0.00078	0.00078	94,963	96,245	96,332	96,297	96,297	42.1	39.0	41.3	43.2	43.7	43.7
39	0.00327	0.00219	0.00174	0.00083	0.00083	94,692	96,050	96,185	96,223	96,223	41.2	38.1	40.4	42.2	42.7	42.7
40	0.00396	0.00251	0.00203	0.00105	0.00105	94,382	95,840	96,017	96,143	96,143	40.2	37.2	39.5	41.3	41.7	41.7
41	0.00427	0.00298	0.00203	0.00098	0.00098	94,009	95,599	95,822	96,041	96,041	39.3	36.4	38.6	40.4	40.8	40.8
42	0.00435	0.00337	0.00217	0.00190	0.00190	93,607	95,315	95,627	95,947	95,947	38.4	35.5	37.7	39.5	39.8	39.8
43	0.00509	0.00354	0.00208	0.00191	0.00191	93,200	94,994	95,420	95,764	95,764	37.5	34.7	36.8	38.5	38.9	38.9
44	0.00525	0.00409	0.00182	0.00239	0.00239	92,726	94,657	95,222	95,581	95,581	36.6	33.9	35.9	37.6	38.0	38.0
45	0.00541	0.00445	0.00196	0.00254	0.00254	92,239	94,270	95,049	95,352	95,352	35.7	33.1	35.1	36.7	37.1	37.1
46	0.00594	0.00450	0.00231	0.00301	0.00301	91,740	93,850	94,862	95,110	95,110	34.8	32.2	34.2	35.8	36.2	36.2
47	0.00682	0.00472	0.00269	0.00229	0.00229	91,196	93,428	94,643	94,824	94,824	33.9	31.4	33.4	34.8	35.3	35.3
48	0.00672	0.00516	0.00326	0.00272	0.00272	90,573	92,987	94,389	94,607	94,607	33.0	30.6	32.6	33.9	34.3	34.3
49	0.00737	0.00524	0.00356	0.00322	0.00322	89,965	92,506	94,082	94,350	94,350	32.2	29.8	31.7	33.1	33.4	33.4
50	0.00790	0.00583	0.00344	0.00308	0.00308	89,302	92,022	93,747	94,046	94,046	31.3	29.1	30.9	32.2	32.5	32.5
51	0.00823	0.00622	0.00452	0.00279	0.00279	88,597	91,485	93,424	93,757	93,757	30.4	28.3	30.1	31.3	31.6	31.6
52	0.00888	0.00645	0.00479	0.00290	0.00290	87,868	90,916	93,002	93,495	93,495	29.6	27.5	29.2	30.4	30.7	30.7
53	0.00932	0.00678	0.00492	0.00373	0.00373	87,087	90,329	92,557	93,224	93,224	28.7	26.7	28.4	29.6	29.8	29.8
54	0.00100	0.00701	0.00553	0.00329	0.00329	86,275	89,717	92,101	92,877	92,877	27.9	26.0	27.6	28.7	28.9	28.9
55	0.01048	0.00706	0.00680	0.00397	0.00397	85,413	89,088	91,592	92,571	92,571	27.0	25.3	26.8	27.9	28.0	28.0
56	0.01134	0.00722	0.00699	0.00464	0.00464	84,518	88,459	90,970	92,204	92,204	26.2	24.5	26.0	27.0	27.1	27.1
57	0.01162	0.00770	0.00826	0.00577	0.00577	83,559	87,820	90,334	91,776	91,776	25.3	23.8	25.2	26.2	26.3	26.3
58	0.01246	0.00824	0.00879	0.00593	0.00593	82,588	87,143	89,588	91,246	91,246	24.5	23.1	24.4	25.4	25.4	25.4
59	0.01328	0.00848	0.00960	0.00719	0.00719	81,559	86,425	88,801	90,705	90,705	23.7	22.3	23.6	24.7	24.6	24.6
60	0.01417	0.00943	0.01059	0.00682	0.00682	80,476	85,692	87,949	90,053	90,053	22.9	21.6	22.8	23.9	23.7	23.7
61	0.01509	0.01048	0.01044	0.00802	0.00802	79,336	84,884	87,017	89,439	89,439	22.1	20.9	22.0	23.1	22.9	22.9
62	0.01661	0.01114	0.00972	0.00856	0.00856	78,139	83,994	86,109	88,722	88,722	21.3	20.3	21.2	22.4	22.1	22.1
63	0.01734	0.01232	0.01174	0.00929	0.00929	76,841	83,058	85,272	87,963	87,963	20.5	19.6	20.5	21.6	21.3	21.3
64	0.01818	0.01409	0.01122	0.00966	0.00966	75,508	82,035	84,270	87,146	87,146	19.8	18.9	19.7	20.9	20.5	20.5
65	0.01906	0.01558	0.01110	0.01167	0.01167	74,136	80,879	83,325	86,304	86,304	19.0	18.3	19.0	20.1	19.6	19.6
66	0.02007	0.01631	0.01337	0.01334	0.01334	72,723	79,618	82,400	85,296	85,296	18.3	17.6	18.3	19.3	18.9	18.9
67	0.02082	0.01815	0.01564	0.01527	0.01527	71,264	78,319	81,298	84,158	84,158	17.6	17.0	17.6	18.6	18.1	18.1
68	0.02290	0.01878	0.01486	0.01585	0.01585	69,780	76,898	80,027	82,873	82,873	16.9	16.3	16.9	17.8	17.4	17.4
69	0.02445	0.01942	0.01941	0.01802	0.01802	68,182	75,454	78,838	81,560	81,560	16.2	15.7	16.2	17.1	16.7	16.7
70	0.02644	0.01996	0.02166	0.02105	0.02105	66,515	73,988	77,308	80,090	80,090	15.5	15.1	15.5	16.4	16.0	16.0
71	0.02840	0.02242	0.02246	0.01996	0.01996	64,756	72,511	75,633	78,404	78,404	14.9	14.5	14.8	15.8	15.3	15.3
72	0.03058	0.02458	0.02407	0.02145	0.02145	62,917	70,886	73,935	76,839	76,839	14.2	13.9	14.1	15.1	14.6	14.6
73	0.03258	0.02820	0.02488	0.02610	0.02610	60,993	69,143	72,155	75,191	75,191	13.6	13.3	13.5	14.5	13.9	13.9
74	0.03525	0.03227	0.02351	0.02865	0.02865	59,005	67,193	70,360	73,228	73,228	13.0	12.7	12.9	13.9	13.3	13.3
75	0.03797	0.03578	0.02734	0.03186	0.03186	56,925	65,025	68,706	71,130	71,130	12.4	12.2	12.3	13.2	12.6	12.6
76	0.04010	0.03981	0.03218	0.04244	0.04244	54,764	62,699	66,827	68,864	68,864	11.8	11.6	11.7	12.5	12.0	12.0
77	0.04388	0.04250	0.03320	0.04107	0.04107	52,568	60,203	64,677	65,941	65,941	11.3	11.1	11.2	11.9	11.6	11.6
78	0.04760	0.04485	0.04084	0.04163	0.04163	50,261	57,644	62,529	63,233	63,233	10.7	10.6	10.6	11.3	11.0	11.0
79	0.05122	0.05182	0.04422	0.04029	0.04029	47,869	55,059	59,976	60,601	60,601	10.2	10.1	10.1	10.8	10.5	10.5
80	0.05594	0.05735	0.04216	0.04057	0.04057	45,417	52,206	57,324	58,159	58,159	9.7	9.6	9.6	10.3	9.9	9.9
81	0.06123	0.05948	0.04373	0.04367	0.04367	42,876	49,212	54,907	55,799	55,799	9.2	9.1	9.2	9.7	9.3	9.3
82	0.06524	0.06668	0.04825	0.05638	0.05638	40,251	46,285	52,506	53,362	53,362	8.8	8.7	8.8	9.1	8.7	8.7
83	0.06996	0.06943	0.05285	0.07775	0.07775	37,625	43,198	49,972	50,354	50,354	8.3	8.3	8.3	8.6	8.2	8.2
84	0.07541	0.07141	0.06229	0.09642	0.09642	34,992	40,199	47,331	46,439	46,439	7.9	7.9	7.9	8.0	7.8	7.8
85	1.00000	1.00000	1.00000	1.00000	1.00000	32,354	37,328	44,382	41,961	41,961	7.5	7.5	7.5	7.5	7.6	7.6

* Weighted average by education.

Table 1: Mortality rates, number living at beginning of age (out of 100,000 born alive), and expectations of remaining years of life, 2004, continued—Hispanic Males

Age	Mortality Rates—Hispanic Males					Number Living at Beginning of Age Interval					Expectation of Life—Hispanic Males					
	<HS	High School	Some College	College Degree	Graduate Degree	<HS	High School	Some College	College Degree	Graduate Degree	All Ed Levels *	<HS	High School	Some College	College Degree	Grad Degree
0	0.00761	0.00761	0.00761	0.00761	0.00761	100,000	100,000	100,000	100,000	100,000	78.2	76.9	78.3	79.7	79.7	79.7
1	0.00052	0.00052	0.00052	0.00052	0.00052	99,239	99,239	99,239	99,239	99,239	77.8	76.5	77.9	79.3	79.3	79.3
2	0.00038	0.00038	0.00038	0.00038	0.00038	99,188	99,188	99,188	99,188	99,188	76.9	75.6	76.9	78.3	78.3	78.3
3	0.00031	0.00031	0.00031	0.00031	0.00031	99,150	99,150	99,150	99,150	99,150	75.9	74.6	76.0	77.4	77.4	77.4
4	0.00022	0.00022	0.00022	0.00022	0.00022	99,119	99,119	99,119	99,119	99,119	74.9	73.6	75.0	76.4	76.4	76.4
5	0.00021	0.00021	0.00021	0.00021	0.00021	99,097	99,097	99,097	99,097	99,097	73.9	72.6	74.0	75.4	75.4	75.4
6	0.00019	0.00019	0.00019	0.00019	0.00019	99,076	99,076	99,076	99,076	99,076	72.9	71.6	73.0	74.4	74.4	74.4
7	0.00017	0.00017	0.00017	0.00017	0.00017	99,057	99,057	99,057	99,057	99,057	72.0	70.7	72.0	73.4	73.4	73.4
8	0.00012	0.00012	0.00012	0.00012	0.00012	99,040	99,040	99,040	99,040	99,040	71.0	69.7	71.1	72.5	72.5	72.5
9	0.00009	0.00009	0.00009	0.00009	0.00009	99,028	99,028	99,028	99,028	99,028	70.0	68.7	70.1	71.5	71.5	71.5
10	0.00009	0.00009	0.00009	0.00009	0.00009	99,020	99,020	99,020	99,020	99,020	69.0	67.7	69.1	70.5	70.5	70.5
11	0.00011	0.00011	0.00011	0.00011	0.00011	99,011	99,011	99,011	99,011	99,011	68.0	66.7	68.1	69.5	69.5	69.5
12	0.00013	0.00013	0.00013	0.00013	0.00013	99,000	99,000	99,000	99,000	99,000	67.0	65.7	67.1	68.5	68.5	68.5
13	0.00030	0.00030	0.00030	0.00030	0.00030	98,987	98,987	98,987	98,987	98,987	66.0	64.7	66.1	67.5	67.5	67.5
14	0.00050	0.00050	0.00050	0.00050	0.00050	98,958	98,958	98,958	98,958	98,958	65.0	63.7	65.1	66.5	66.5	66.5
15	0.00067	0.00067	0.00067	0.00067	0.00067	98,908	98,908	98,908	98,908	98,908	64.1	62.8	64.1	65.5	65.5	65.5
16	0.00084	0.00084	0.00084	0.00084	0.00084	98,842	98,842	98,842	98,842	98,842	63.1	61.8	63.2	64.6	64.6	64.6
17	0.00107	0.00107	0.00107	0.00107	0.00107	98,759	98,759	98,759	98,759	98,759	62.2	60.8	62.2	63.6	63.6	63.6
18	0.00121	0.00121	0.00121	0.00121	0.00121	98,653	98,653	98,653	98,653	98,653	61.2	59.9	61.3	62.7	62.7	62.7
19	0.00133	0.00133	0.00133	0.00133	0.00133	98,534	98,534	98,534	98,534	98,534	60.3	59.0	60.4	61.8	61.8	61.8
20	0.00128	0.00128	0.00128	0.00128	0.00128	98,402	98,402	98,402	98,402	98,402	59.4	58.1	59.5	60.9	60.9	60.9
21	0.00127	0.00127	0.00127	0.00127	0.00127	98,276	98,276	98,276	98,276	98,276	58.4	57.1	58.5	59.9	59.9	59.9
22	0.00122	0.00122	0.00122	0.00122	0.00122	98,151	98,151	98,151	98,151	98,151	57.5	56.2	57.6	59.0	59.0	59.0
23	0.00114	0.00086	0.00212	0.00086	0.00086	98,032	98,032	98,032	98,032	98,032	56.6	55.3	56.7	58.1	58.1	58.1
24	0.00125	0.00111	0.00188	0.00096	0.00096	97,920	97,947	97,824	97,947	97,947	55.7	54.3	55.8	57.1	57.1	57.1
25	0.00141	0.00180	0.00169	0.00080	0.00080	97,798	97,838	97,640	97,853	97,853	54.7	53.4	54.9	56.2	56.2	56.2
26	0.00140	0.00192	0.00160	0.00060	0.00060	97,660	97,662	97,475	97,774	97,774	53.8	52.5	54.0	55.2	55.2	55.2
27	0.00142	0.00188	0.00169	0.00031	0.00031	97,523	97,475	97,319	97,716	97,716	52.9	51.6	53.1	54.3	54.3	54.3
28	0.00142	0.00208	0.00067	0.00050	0.00050	97,385	97,292	97,154	97,685	97,685	51.9	50.7	52.2	53.3	53.3	53.3
29	0.00139	0.00204	0.00113	0.00028	0.00028	97,246	97,089	97,089	97,636	97,636	51.0	49.8	51.2	52.3	52.3	52.3
30	0.00136	0.00157	0.00160	0.00036	0.00036	97,111	96,891	96,980	97,608	97,608	50.1	48.9	50.3	51.3	51.3	51.3
31	0.00142	0.00143	0.00163	0.00059	0.00059	96,980	96,739	96,825	97,573	97,573	49.1	48.0	49.3	50.4	50.4	50.4
32	0.00130	0.00133	0.00142	0.00073	0.00073	96,842	96,601	96,667	97,515	97,515	48.2	47.0	48.4	49.4	49.4	49.4
33	0.00135	0.00144	0.00165	0.00077	0.00077	96,716	96,472	96,530	97,444	97,444	47.2	46.1	47.5	48.4	48.4	48.4
34	0.00138	0.00129	0.00165	0.00093	0.00093	96,586	96,334	96,370	97,368	97,368	46.3	45.2	46.6	47.5	47.5	47.5
35	0.00144	0.00132	0.00150	0.00133	0.00133	96,453	96,209	96,212	97,278	97,278	45.4	44.2	45.6	46.5	46.5	46.5
36	0.00152	0.00140	0.00184	0.00136	0.00136	96,314	96,082	96,067	97,149	97,149	44.4	43.3	44.7	45.6	45.6	45.6
37	0.00189	0.00199	0.00218	0.00168	0.00168	96,168	95,947	95,891	97,017	97,017	43.5	42.3	43.8	44.6	44.6	44.6
38	0.00214	0.00217	0.00239	0.00200	0.00200	95,985	95,757	95,682	96,853	96,853	42.6	41.4	42.9	43.7	43.7	43.7
39	0.00237	0.00242	0.00242	0.00240	0.00240	95,780	95,549	95,453	96,659	96,659	41.7	40.5	42.0	42.8	42.8	42.8
40	0.00247	0.00252	0.00258	0.00216	0.00216	95,553	95,317	95,222	96,427	96,427	40.8	39.6	41.1	41.9	41.9	41.9
41	0.00279	0.00310	0.00254	0.00263	0.00263	95,317	95,077	94,976	96,219	96,219	39.8	38.7	40.2	41.0	41.0	41.0
42	0.00299	0.00308	0.00282	0.00285	0.00285	95,051	94,782	94,735	95,966	95,966	39.0	37.8	39.3	40.1	40.1	40.1
43	0.00324	0.00332	0.00339	0.00295	0.00295	94,767	94,490	94,468	95,692	95,692	38.1	36.9	38.4	39.2	39.2	39.2
44	0.00364	0.00391	0.00387	0.00293	0.00293	94,460	94,177	94,148	95,410	95,410	37.2	36.1	37.5	38.3	38.3	38.3
45	0.00410	0.00438	0.00427	0.00343	0.00343	94,116	93,808	93,783	95,131	95,131	36.3	35.2	36.7	37.4	37.4	37.4
46	0.00449	0.00472	0.00513	0.00346	0.00346	93,730	93,397	93,382	94,805	94,805	35.5	34.3	35.8	36.5	36.5	36.5
47	0.00457	0.00473	0.00554	0.00328	0.00328	93,309	92,956	92,903	94,477	94,477	34.6	33.5	35.0	35.7	35.7	35.7
48	0.00459	0.00504	0.00508	0.00332	0.00332	92,882	92,516	92,389	94,167	94,167	33.8	32.7	34.2	34.8	34.8	34.8
49	0.00478	0.00504	0.00554	0.00352	0.00352	92,456	92,050	91,919	93,854	93,854	32.9	31.8	33.4	33.9	33.9	33.9
50	0.00523	0.00536	0.00637	0.00374	0.00374	92,013	91,586	91,410	93,524	93,524	32.1	31.0	32.6	33.0	33.0	33.0
51	0.00545	0.00546	0.00642	0.00438	0.00438	91,532	91,095	90,828	93,174	93,174	31.2	30.1	31.8	32.1	32.1	32.1
52	0.00595	0.00616	0.00602	0.00543	0.00543	91,034	90,597	90,244	92,767	92,767	30.4	29.3	31.0	31.3	31.3	31.3
53	0.00636	0.00663	0.00640	0.00568	0.00568	90,492	90,039	89,702	92,263	92,263	29.6	28.5	30.2	30.4	30.4	30.4
54	0.00674	0.00730	0.00603	0.00617	0.00617	89,917	89,442	89,128	91,739	91,739	28.7	27.7	29.3	29.6	29.6	29.6
55	0.00704	0.00785	0.00567	0.00659	0.00659	89,311	88,789	88,590	91,173	91,173	27.9	26.9	28.5	28.8	28.8	28.8
56	0.00717	0.00807	0.00618	0.00600	0.00600	88,682	88,091	88,088	90,572	90,572	27.1	26.1	27.7	28.0	28.0	28.0
57	0.00749	0.00830	0.00741	0.00541	0.00541	88,047	87,380	87,543	90,028	90,028	26.3	25.3	26.8	27.2	27.2	27.2
58	0.00766	0.00838	0.00781	0.00550	0.00550	87,387	86,655	86,894	89,541	89,541	25.4	24.5	26.0	26.3	26.3	26.3
59	0.00772	0.00814	0.00815	0.00601	0.00601	86,717	85,929	86,215	89,048	89,048	24.6	23.7	25.2	25.4	25.4	25.4
60	0.00819	0.00860	0.00878	0.00617	0.00617	86,048	85,230	85,513	88,513	88,513	23.7	22.9	24.4	24.6	24.6	24.6
61	0.00900	0.00955	0.00997	0.00597	0.00597	85,343	84,496	84,762	87,967	87,967	22.9	22.1	23.7	23.7	23.7	23.7
62	0.00978	0.01023	0.01066	0.00720	0.00720	84,576	83,689	83,917	87,442	87,442	22.1	21.3	22.9	22.9	22.9	22.9
63	0.01110	0.01181	0.01114	0.00847	0.00847	83,748	82,834	83,022	86,813	86,813	21.3	20.5	22.1	22.0	22.0	22.0
64	0.01211	0.01297	0.01215	0.00891	0.00891	82,819	81,855	82,097	86,077	86,077	20.5	19.7	21.4	21.2	21.2	21.2
65	0.01275	0.01357	0.01221	0.01025	0.01025	81,816	80,793	81,099	85,310	85,310	19.7	19.0	20.6	20.4	20.4	20.4
66	0.01317	0.01398	0.01140	0.01225	0.01225	80,773	79,697	80,109	84,435	84,435	19.0	18.3	19.9	19.6	19.6	19.6
67	0.01460	0.01548	0.01260	0.01372	0.01372	79,709	78,583	79,195	83,401	83,401	18.2	17.5	19.1	18.9	18.9	18.9
68	0.01616	0.01714	0.01416	0.01445	0.01445	78,545	77,367	78,198	82,257	82,257	17.5	16.8	18.3	18.1	18.1	18.1
69	0.01827	0.01931	0.01702	0.01533	0.01533	77,276	76,041	77,090	81,069	81,069	16.7	16.1	17.6	17.4	17.4	17.4
70	0.02077	0.02179	0.02147	0.01522	0.01522	75,864	74,572	75,778	79,826	79,826	16.0	15.4	16.9	16.6	16.6	16.6
71	0.02363	0.02510	0.02224	0.01829	0.01829	74,288	72,947	74,151	78,611	78,611	15.3	14.7	16.3	15.9	15.9	15.9
72	0.02542	0.02739	0.02335	0.01822	0.01822	72,533	71,116	72,502	77,173	77,173	14.6	14.1	15.6	15.2	15.2	15.2
73	0.02684	0.02838	0.02626	0.01959	0.01959	70,689	69,168	70,809	75,767	75,767	14.0	13.4	15.0	14.4	14.4	14.4
74	0.02911	0.03128	0.02706	0.01978	0.01978	68,792	67,205	68,950	74,283	74,283	13.3	12.8	14.4	13.7	13.7	13.7
75	0.03187	0.03453	0.02679	0.02252	0.02252	66,790	65,103	67,084	72,814	72,814	12.7	12.2	13.8	13.0	13.0	13.0
76	0.03551	0.03867	0.03095	0.02155	0.02155	64,661	62,855	65,287	71,174	71,174	12.1	11.6	13.1	12.3	12.3	12.3
77	0.03938	0.04224	0.03267	0.02951	0.02951	62,365	60,425	63,266	69,640	69,640	11.4	11.1	12.5	11.5	11.5	11.5
78	0.04554	0.04865	0.03489	0.03864	0.03864	59,909	57,872	61,199	67,585	67,585	10.9	10.6	11.9	10.9	10.9	10.9
79	0.05173	0.05388	0.03880	0.05468	0.05468	57,181	55,057	59,064	64,973	64,973	10.3	10.1	11.3	10.3	10.3	10.3
80	0.05810	0.05915	0.04333	0.06976	0.06976	54,223	52,090	56,772	61,420	61,420	9.9	9.6	10.8	9.9	9.9	9.9
81	0.06146	0.06213	0.04409	0.07586	0.07586	51,072	49,009	54,313	57,135	57,135	9.5	9.2	10.2	9.6	9.6	9.6
82	0.06668	0.06757	0.04893	0.08037	0.08037	47,933	45,964	51,918	52,801	52,801	8.9	8.8	9.7	9.3	9.3	9.3
83	0.07013	0.07215	0.04948	0.07611	0.07611	44,737	42,858	49,378	48,557	48,557	8.5	8.4	9.2	9.1	9.1	9.1
84	0.07023	0.07396	0.04826	0.06485	0.06485	41,599	39,766	46,934	44,862	44,862	8.2	8.0	8.6	8.8	8.8	8.8
85	1.00000	1.00000	1.00000	1.00000	1.00000	38,678	36,825	44,669	41,952	41,952	7.8	7.6	8.0	8.3	8.3	8.3

* Weighted average by education.

Table 1: Mortality rates, number living at beginning of age (out of 100,000 born alive), and expectations of remaining years of life, 2004, continued—Hispanic Females

Age	Mortality Rates—Hispanic Females					Number Living at Beginning of Age Interval					Expectation of Life—Hispanic Females					
	<HS	High School	Some College	College Degree	Graduate Degree	<HS	High School	Some College	College Degree	Graduate Degree	All Ed Levels *	<HS	High School	Some College	College Degree	Grad Degree
0	0.00838	0.00838	0.00838	0.00838	0.00838	100,000	100,000	100,000	100,000	100,000	83.5	82.1	84.1	84.6	84.6	84.6
1	0.00063	0.00063	0.00063	0.00063	0.00063	99,162	99,162	99,162	99,162	99,162	83.3	81.8	83.8	84.3	84.3	84.3
2	0.00028	0.00028	0.00028	0.00028	0.00028	99,099	99,099	99,099	99,099	99,099	82.3	80.8	82.9	83.4	83.4	83.4
3	0.00013	0.00013	0.00013	0.00013	0.00013	99,072	99,072	99,072	99,072	99,072	81.3	79.9	81.9	82.4	82.4	82.4
4	0.00012	0.00012	0.00012	0.00012	0.00012	99,059	99,059	99,059	99,059	99,059	80.3	78.9	80.9	81.4	81.4	81.4
5	0.00017	0.00017	0.00017	0.00017	0.00017	99,047	99,047	99,047	99,047	99,047	79.3	77.9	79.9	80.4	80.4	80.4
6	0.00015	0.00015	0.00015	0.00015	0.00015	99,030	99,030	99,030	99,030	99,030	78.4	76.9	78.9	79.4	79.4	79.4
7	0.00014	0.00014	0.00014	0.00014	0.00014	99,015	99,015	99,015	99,015	99,015	77.4	75.9	77.9	78.4	78.4	78.4
8	0.00013	0.00013	0.00013	0.00013	0.00013	99,001	99,001	99,001	99,001	99,001	76.4	74.9	76.9	77.4	77.4	77.4
9	0.00009	0.00009	0.00009	0.00009	0.00009	98,988	98,988	98,988	98,988	98,988	75.4	73.9	75.9	76.5	76.5	76.5
10	0.00007	0.00007	0.00007	0.00007	0.00007	98,979	98,979	98,979	98,979	98,979	74.4	72.9	75.0	75.5	75.5	75.5
11	0.00010	0.00010	0.00010	0.00010	0.00010	98,973	98,973	98,973	98,973	98,973	73.4	71.9	74.0	74.5	74.5	74.5
12	0.00009	0.00009	0.00009	0.00009	0.00009	98,962	98,962	98,962	98,962	98,962	72.4	70.9	73.0	73.5	73.5	73.5
13	0.00015	0.00015	0.00015	0.00015	0.00015	98,953	98,953	98,953	98,953	98,953	71.4	69.9	72.0	72.5	72.5	72.5
14	0.00018	0.00018	0.00018	0.00018	0.00018	98,939	98,939	98,939	98,939	98,939	70.4	69.0	71.0	71.5	71.5	71.5
15	0.00019	0.00019	0.00019	0.00019	0.00019	98,921	98,921	98,921	98,921	98,921	69.4	68.0	70.0	70.5	70.5	70.5
16	0.00018	0.00018	0.00018	0.00018	0.00018	98,903	98,903	98,903	98,903	98,903	68.5	67.0	69.0	69.5	69.5	69.5
17	0.00029	0.00029	0.00029	0.00029	0.00029	98,885	98,885	98,885	98,885	98,885	67.5	66.0	68.0	68.5	68.5	68.5
18	0.00030	0.00030	0.00030	0.00030	0.00030	98,857	98,857	98,857	98,857	98,857	66.5	65.0	67.0	67.5	67.5	67.5
19	0.00028	0.00028	0.00028	0.00028	0.00028	98,827	98,827	98,827	98,827	98,827	65.5	64.0	66.1	66.6	66.6	66.6
20	0.00038	0.00038	0.00038	0.00038	0.00038	98,799	98,799	98,799	98,799	98,799	64.5	63.1	65.1	65.6	65.6	65.6
21	0.00041	0.00041	0.00041	0.00041	0.00041	98,762	98,762	98,762	98,762	98,762	63.5	62.1	64.1	64.6	64.6	64.6
22	0.00048	0.00048	0.00048	0.00048	0.00048	98,721	98,721	98,721	98,721	98,721	62.6	61.1	63.1	63.6	63.6	63.6
23	0.00052	0.00043	0.00043	0.00043	0.00043	98,674	98,674	98,674	98,674	98,674	61.6	60.1	62.2	62.7	62.7	62.7
24	0.00060	0.00041	0.00062	0.00041	0.00041	98,623	98,632	98,632	98,632	98,632	60.6	59.2	61.2	61.7	61.7	61.7
25	0.00053	0.00028	0.00050	0.00028	0.00028	98,564	98,592	98,571	98,592	98,592	59.7	58.2	60.2	60.7	60.7	60.7
26	0.00047	0.00017	0.00039	0.00017	0.00017	98,512	98,564	98,522	98,564	98,564	58.7	57.2	59.3	59.7	59.7	59.7
27	0.00043	0.00024	0.00040	0.00000	0.00000	98,465	98,548	98,483	98,548	98,548	57.7	56.2	58.3	58.7	58.7	58.7
28	0.00042	0.00038	0.00054	0.00008	0.00008	98,423	98,524	98,444	98,548	98,548	56.7	55.2	57.3	57.7	57.7	57.7
29	0.00044	0.00052	0.00049	0.00023	0.00023	98,382	98,486	98,391	98,540	98,540	55.7	54.2	56.3	56.7	56.7	56.7
30	0.00046	0.00060	0.00062	0.00037	0.00037	98,339	98,435	98,343	98,517	98,517	54.7	53.3	55.4	55.8	55.8	55.8
31	0.00049	0.00069	0.00076	0.00040	0.00040	98,293	98,376	98,282	98,480	98,480	53.8	52.3	54.4	54.8	54.8	54.8
32	0.00053	0.00058	0.00081	0.00048	0.00048	98,245	98,308	98,207	98,441	98,441	52.8	51.3	53.4	53.8	53.8	53.8
33	0.00056	0.00050	0.00075	0.00061	0.00061	98,192	98,251	98,127	98,394	98,394	51.8	50.4	52.5	52.8	52.8	52.8
34	0.00055	0.00050	0.00065	0.00051	0.00051	98,138	98,202	98,054	98,334	98,334	50.9	49.4	51.5	51.9	51.9	51.9
35	0.00055	0.00057	0.00060	0.00047	0.00047	98,084	98,153	97,990	98,284	98,284	49.9	48.4	50.5	50.9	50.9	50.9
36	0.00070	0.00069	0.00063	0.00063	0.00063	98,029	98,098	97,932	98,237	98,237	48.9	47.4	49.6	49.9	49.9	49.9
37	0.00067	0.00068	0.00056	0.00067	0.00067	97,961	98,030	97,870	98,175	98,175	48.0	46.5	48.6	48.9	48.9	48.9
38	0.00081	0.00087	0.00095	0.00043	0.00043	97,896	97,963	97,815	98,110	98,110	47.0	45.5	47.6	48.0	48.0	48.0
39	0.00093	0.00105	0.00099	0.00056	0.00056	97,816	97,877	97,722	98,068	98,068	46.0	44.5	46.7	47.0	47.0	47.0
40	0.00118	0.00130	0.00137	0.00052	0.00052	97,725	97,774	97,625	98,013	98,013	45.1	43.6	45.7	46.0	46.0	46.0
41	0.00122	0.00156	0.00141	0.00044	0.00044	97,609	97,647	97,492	97,962	97,962	44.1	42.6	44.8	45.1	45.1	45.1
42	0.00143	0.00181	0.00150	0.00063	0.00063	97,490	97,495	97,354	97,919	97,919	43.1	41.7	43.9	44.1	44.1	44.1
43	0.00142	0.00175	0.00136	0.00094	0.00094	97,351	97,318	97,209	97,857	97,857	42.2	40.8	42.9	43.1	43.1	43.1
44	0.00165	0.00175	0.00177	0.00143	0.00143	97,213	97,147	97,077	97,765	97,765	41.2	39.9	42.0	42.1	42.1	42.1
45	0.00181	0.00194	0.00188	0.00146	0.00146	97,052	96,978	96,905	97,626	97,626	40.3	38.9	41.1	41.2	41.2	41.2
46	0.00207	0.00200	0.00228	0.00185	0.00185	96,876	96,789	96,722	97,483	97,483	39.3	38.0	40.1	40.3	40.3	40.3
47	0.00220	0.00230	0.00228	0.00172	0.00172	96,676	96,596	96,501	97,303	97,303	38.4	37.1	39.2	39.3	39.3	39.3
48	0.00245	0.00302	0.00201	0.00167	0.00167	96,463	96,374	96,282	97,135	97,135	37.5	36.2	38.3	38.4	38.4	38.4
49	0.00241	0.00325	0.00193	0.00099	0.00099	96,226	96,083	96,089	96,973	96,973	36.6	35.3	37.4	37.5	37.5	37.5
50	0.00253	0.00333	0.00178	0.00166	0.00166	95,995	95,771	95,903	96,877	96,877	35.7	34.4	36.5	36.5	36.5	36.5
51	0.00267	0.00352	0.00183	0.00175	0.00175	95,752	95,452	95,732	96,716	96,716	34.7	33.5	35.5	35.6	35.6	35.6
52	0.00275	0.00320	0.00244	0.00201	0.00201	95,496	95,116	95,557	96,547	96,547	33.8	32.6	34.6	34.6	34.6	34.6
53	0.00292	0.00309	0.00287	0.00252	0.00252	95,234	94,812	95,323	96,353	96,353	32.8	31.7	33.7	33.7	33.7	33.7
54	0.00319	0.00349	0.00296	0.00256	0.00256	94,955	94,519	95,050	96,110	96,110	31.9	30.8	32.8	32.8	32.8	32.8
55	0.00317	0.00354	0.00301	0.00205	0.00205	94,652	94,189	94,769	95,864	95,864	31.0	29.9	31.9	31.8	31.8	31.8
56	0.00333	0.00371	0.00309	0.00212	0.00212	94,352	93,857	94,483	95,668	95,668	30.1	29.0	30.9	30.9	30.9	30.9
57	0.00392	0.00467	0.00308	0.00224	0.00224	94,037	93,509	94,191	95,465	95,465	29.2	28.1	30.0	30.0	30.0	30.0
58	0.00422	0.00502	0.00332	0.00245	0.00245	93,669	93,072	93,901	95,251	95,251	28.2	27.3	29.1	29.0	29.0	29.0
59	0.00477	0.00563	0.00367	0.00285	0.00285	93,273	92,606	93,589	95,018	95,018	27.3	26.4	28.2	28.1	28.1	28.1
60	0.00569	0.00667	0.00422	0.00374	0.00374	92,829	92,084	93,246	94,747	94,747	26.4	25.5	27.3	27.2	27.2	27.2
61	0.00648	0.00759	0.00475	0.00453	0.00453	92,300	91,470	92,853	94,393	94,393	25.5	24.7	26.4	26.3	26.3	26.3
62	0.00670	0.00771	0.00496	0.00494	0.00494	91,702	90,776	92,411	93,965	93,965	24.7	23.9	25.6	25.4	25.4	25.4
63	0.00751	0.00850	0.00621	0.00491	0.00491	91,087	90,076	91,953	93,501	93,501	23.8	23.1	24.7	24.5	24.5	24.5
64	0.00790	0.00866	0.00694	0.00558	0.00558	90,403	89,311	91,383	93,042	93,042	22.9	22.3	23.8	23.7	23.7	23.7
65	0.00833	0.00891	0.00746	0.00654	0.00654	89,689	88,537	90,749	92,523	92,523	22.1	21.5	23.0	22.8	22.8	22.8
66	0.00919	0.00989	0.00804	0.00698	0.00698	88,942	87,749	90,071	91,918	91,918	21.3	20.6	22.2	21.9	21.9	21.9
67	0.01009	0.01070	0.00843	0.00938	0.00938	88,125	86,881	89,347	91,276	91,276	20.4	19.8	21.4	21.1	21.1	21.1
68	0.01127	0.01203	0.00931	0.01020	0.01020	87,235	85,951	88,594	90,420	90,420	19.6	19.1	20.5	20.3	20.3	20.3
69	0.01328	0.01451	0.00947	0.01201	0.01201	86,252	84,917	87,770	89,497	89,497	18.8	18.3	19.7	19.5	19.5	19.5
70	0.01504	0.01621	0.01160	0.01320	0.01320	85,107	83,685	86,939	88,423	88,423	18.1	17.5	18.9	18.7	18.7	18.7
71	0.01578	0.01666	0.01354	0.01299	0.01299	83,827	82,328	85,930	87,256	87,256	17.3	16.8	18.1	18.0	18.0	18.0
72	0.01802	0.01898	0.01601	0.01379	0.01379	82,504	80,956	84,766	86,122	86,122	16.5	16.1	17.4	17.2	17.2	17.2
73	0.01948	0.02013	0.01713	0.01889	0.01889	81,017	79,420	83,409	84,935	84,935	15.8	15.4	16.6	16.4	16.4	16.4
74	0.02076	0.02072	0.02152	0.01894	0.01894	79,439	77,822	81,981	83,331	83,331	15.1	14.7	15.9	15.7	15.7	15.7
75	0.02261	0.02273	0.02328	0.01891	0.01891	77,789	76,210	80,216	81,752	81,752	14.4	14.0	15.3	15.0	15.0	15.0
76	0.02389	0.02476	0.02158	0.01798	0.01798	76,030	74,477	78,349	80,206	80,206	13.7	13.3	14.6	14.3	14.3	14.3
77	0.02674	0.02767	0.02499	0.01855	0.01855	74,214	72,633	76,658	78,763	78,763	13.0	12.6	13.9	13.5	13.5	13.5
78	0.02997	0.03215	0.02569	0.01341	0.01341	72,230	70,623	74,743	77,302	77,302	12.3	12.0	13.3	12.8	12.8	12.8
79	0.03447	0.03686	0.02767	0.02098	0.02098	70,066	68,352	72,822	76,265	76,265	11.7	11.4	12.6	12.0	12.0	12.0
80	0.03744	0.04020	0.02912	0.02224	0.02224	67,650	65,833	70,808	74,665	74,665	11.0	10.8	11.9	11.2	11.2	11.2
81	0.04494	0.04687	0.03520	0.04195	0.04195	65,117	63,186	68,745	73,004	73,004	10.4	10.2	11.3	10.5	10.5	10.5
82	0.04848	0.05076	0.03399	0.05058	0.05058	62,191	60,225	66,325	69,942	69,942	9.9	9.7	10.7	9.9	9.9	9.9
83	0.05351	0.05556	0.03509	0.06434	0.06434	59,176	57,168	64,071	66,404	66,404	9.4	9.2	10.0	9.4	9.4	9.4
84	0.06265	0.06415	0.03657	0.09448	0.09448	56,010	53,992	61,823	62,132	62,132	8.9	8.7	9.4	9.0	9.0	9.0
85	1.00000	1.00000	1.00000	1.00000	1.00000	52,501	50,529	59,562	56,262	56,262	8.4	8.3	8.7	8.9	8.9	8.9

* Weighted average by education.

Table 2: Mortality rates, number living at beginning of age (out of 100,000 born alive), and expectations of remaining years of life by smoking status, 2004— All Races Males, Never Smokers

Age	Mortality Rates—Male Never Smokers					Number Living at Beginning of Age Interval					Expectation of Life—Male Never Smokers					
	<HS	High School	Some College	College Degree	Graduate Degree	<HS	High School	Some College	College Degree	Graduate Degree	All Ed Levels *	<HS	High School	Some College	College Degree	Grad Degree
0	0.00747	0.00747	0.00747	0.00747	0.00747	100,000	100,000	100,000	100,000	100,000	79.3	76.5	78.6	79.5	80.8	81.8
1	0.00051	0.00051	0.00051	0.00051	0.00051	99,253	99,253	99,253	99,253	99,253	78.9	76.1	78.2	79.1	80.4	81.4
2	0.00033	0.00033	0.00033	0.00033	0.00033	99,202	99,202	99,202	99,202	99,202	78.0	75.1	77.3	78.1	79.5	80.4
3	0.00025	0.00025	0.00025	0.00025	0.00025	99,170	99,170	99,170	99,170	99,170	77.0	74.1	76.3	77.1	78.5	79.4
4	0.00021	0.00021	0.00021	0.00021	0.00021	99,145	99,145	99,145	99,145	99,145	76.0	73.2	75.3	76.1	77.5	78.5
5	0.00019	0.00019	0.00019	0.00019	0.00019	99,124	99,124	99,124	99,124	99,124	75.0	72.2	74.3	75.2	76.5	77.5
6	0.00018	0.00018	0.00018	0.00018	0.00018	99,106	99,106	99,106	99,106	99,106	74.0	71.2	73.3	74.2	75.6	76.5
7	0.00017	0.00017	0.00017	0.00017	0.00017	99,087	99,087	99,087	99,087	99,087	73.0	70.2	72.4	73.2	74.6	75.5
8	0.00015	0.00015	0.00015	0.00015	0.00015	99,070	99,070	99,070	99,070	99,070	72.1	69.2	71.4	72.2	73.6	74.5
9	0.00013	0.00013	0.00013	0.00013	0.00013	99,055	99,055	99,055	99,055	99,055	71.1	68.2	70.4	71.2	72.6	73.5
10	0.00011	0.00011	0.00011	0.00011	0.00011	99,043	99,043	99,043	99,043	99,043	70.1	67.2	69.4	70.2	71.6	72.5
11	0.00011	0.00011	0.00011	0.00011	0.00011	99,033	99,033	99,033	99,033	99,033	69.1	66.2	68.4	69.2	70.6	71.5
12	0.00016	0.00016	0.00016	0.00016	0.00016	99,022	99,022	99,022	99,022	99,022	68.1	65.3	67.4	68.2	69.6	70.5
13	0.00027	0.00027	0.00027	0.00027	0.00027	99,006	99,006	99,006	99,006	99,006	67.1	64.3	66.4	67.2	68.6	69.6
14	0.00043	0.00043	0.00043	0.00043	0.00043	98,978	98,978	98,978	98,978	98,978	66.1	63.3	65.4	66.3	67.7	68.6
15	0.00061	0.00061	0.00061	0.00061	0.00061	98,936	98,936	98,936	98,936	98,936	65.1	62.3	64.5	65.3	66.7	67.6
16	0.00078	0.00078	0.00078	0.00078	0.00078	98,876	98,876	98,876	98,876	98,876	64.2	61.3	63.5	64.3	65.7	66.6
17	0.00093	0.00093	0.00093	0.00093	0.00093	98,799	98,799	98,799	98,799	98,799	63.2	60.4	62.6	63.4	64.8	65.7
18	0.00106	0.00106	0.00106	0.00106	0.00106	98,706	98,706	98,706	98,706	98,706	62.3	59.4	61.6	62.4	63.8	64.8
19	0.00117	0.00117	0.00117	0.00117	0.00117	98,601	98,601	98,601	98,601	98,601	61.4	58.5	60.7	61.5	62.9	63.8
20	0.00127	0.00127	0.00127	0.00127	0.00127	98,486	98,486	98,486	98,486	98,486	60.4	57.6	59.7	60.6	62.0	62.9
21	0.00136	0.00136	0.00136	0.00136	0.00136	98,362	98,362	98,362	98,362	98,362	59.5	56.7	58.8	59.6	61.1	62.0
22	0.00142	0.00142	0.00142	0.00142	0.00142	98,228	98,228	98,228	98,228	98,228	58.6	55.7	57.9	58.7	60.1	61.1
23	0.00188	0.00161	0.00137	0.00115	0.00115	98,089	98,089	98,089	98,089	98,089	57.7	54.8	57.0	57.8	59.2	60.2
24	0.00234	0.00163	0.00124	0.00104	0.00157	97,904	97,931	97,954	97,976	97,976	56.8	53.9	56.1	56.9	58.3	59.2
25	0.00266	0.00168	0.00112	0.00075	0.00126	97,676	97,771	97,833	97,874	97,823	55.8	53.0	55.2	56.0	57.3	58.3
26	0.00269	0.00166	0.00102	0.00069	0.00103	97,416	97,606	97,724	97,801	97,700	54.9	52.2	54.3	55.0	56.4	57.4
27	0.00294	0.00173	0.00089	0.00045	0.00083	97,154	97,444	97,624	97,734	97,599	54.0	51.3	53.3	54.1	55.4	56.4
28	0.00272	0.00162	0.00096	0.00060	0.00093	96,868	97,276	97,537	97,689	97,518	53.1	50.5	52.4	53.1	54.5	55.5
29	0.00247	0.00169	0.00102	0.00054	0.00040	96,605	97,119	97,443	97,631	97,427	52.1	49.6	51.5	52.2	53.5	54.5
30	0.00229	0.00163	0.00111	0.00070	0.00043	96,367	96,955	97,344	97,578	97,388	51.2	48.7	50.6	51.2	52.5	53.6
31	0.00239	0.00168	0.00118	0.00064	0.00043	96,146	96,796	97,236	97,509	97,346	50.3	47.8	49.7	50.3	51.5	52.6
32	0.00228	0.00167	0.00134	0.00079	0.00045	95,916	96,633	97,121	97,447	97,305	49.3	46.9	48.8	49.3	50.6	51.6
33	0.00229	0.00171	0.00136	0.00083	0.00044	95,697	96,472	96,991	97,370	97,260	48.4	46.1	47.9	48.4	49.6	50.6
34	0.00231	0.00176	0.00148	0.00090	0.00050	95,478	96,307	96,859	97,289	97,217	47.5	45.2	46.9	47.5	48.7	49.7
35	0.00135	0.00105	0.00104	0.00074	0.00061	95,257	96,138	96,716	97,202	97,169	46.5	44.3	46.0	46.5	47.7	48.7
36	0.00149	0.00113	0.00113	0.00079	0.00071	95,129	96,037	96,616	97,130	97,109	45.6	43.3	45.1	45.6	46.7	47.7
37	0.00168	0.00121	0.00120	0.00086	0.00081	94,986	95,929	96,506	97,053	97,040	44.6	42.4	44.1	44.6	45.8	46.7
38	0.00183	0.00133	0.00130	0.00091	0.00098	94,827	95,812	96,390	96,970	96,961	43.6	41.5	43.2	43.7	44.8	45.8
39	0.00206	0.00142	0.00144	0.00102	0.00096	94,653	95,685	96,265	96,882	96,866	42.7	40.5	42.2	42.8	43.9	44.8
40	0.00198	0.00142	0.00132	0.00105	0.00093	94,458	95,549	96,126	96,783	96,773	41.8	39.6	41.3	41.8	42.9	43.9
41	0.00215	0.00151	0.00141	0.00116	0.00104	94,271	95,413	96,000	96,681	96,683	40.8	38.7	40.3	40.9	41.9	42.9
42	0.00235	0.00162	0.00150	0.00126	0.00111	94,068	95,270	95,864	96,570	96,583	39.9	37.8	39.4	39.9	41.0	42.0
43	0.00259	0.00176	0.00163	0.00144	0.00125	93,847	95,116	95,721	96,448	96,476	38.9	36.9	38.5	39.0	40.0	41.0
44	0.00280	0.00192	0.00177	0.00162	0.00141	93,604	94,949	95,565	96,309	96,355	38.0	36.0	37.5	38.1	39.1	40.1
45	0.00353	0.00232	0.00210	0.00178	0.00151	93,341	94,767	95,396	96,153	96,219	37.1	35.1	36.6	37.1	38.2	39.1
46	0.00370	0.00253	0.00234	0.00204	0.00160	93,011	94,547	95,196	95,982	96,074	36.2	34.2	35.7	36.2	37.2	38.2
47	0.00383	0.00278	0.00265	0.00214	0.00176	92,667	94,307	94,973	95,786	95,920	35.3	33.3	34.8	35.3	36.3	37.2
48	0.00416	0.00303	0.00286	0.00217	0.00184	92,312	94,045	94,721	95,581	95,751	34.4	32.4	33.9	34.4	35.4	36.3
49	0.00453	0.00324	0.00302	0.00227	0.00210	91,928	93,759	94,450	95,374	95,575	33.5	31.6	33.0	33.5	34.5	35.4
50	0.00443	0.00335	0.00301	0.00224	0.00208	91,511	93,455	94,165	95,158	95,375	32.6	30.7	32.1	32.6	33.5	34.4
51	0.00478	0.00363	0.00315	0.00234	0.00230	91,106	93,142	93,882	94,945	95,176	31.7	29.8	31.2	31.7	32.6	33.5
52	0.00516	0.00380	0.00331	0.00265	0.00249	90,671	92,803	93,587	94,722	94,958	30.9	29.0	30.3	30.8	31.7	32.6
53	0.00541	0.00397	0.00362	0.00294	0.00266	90,202	92,451	93,277	94,471	94,721	30.0	28.1	29.4	29.9	30.8	31.7
54	0.00565	0.00417	0.00385	0.00313	0.00281	89,714	92,084	92,939	94,193	94,469	29.1	27.3	28.5	29.0	29.9	30.7
55	0.00611	0.00448	0.00434	0.00337	0.00316	89,207	91,700	92,581	93,898	94,204	28.2	26.4	27.6	28.1	28.9	29.8
56	0.00645	0.00469	0.00469	0.00348	0.00345	88,662	91,289	92,179	93,581	93,906	27.3	25.6	26.8	27.2	28.0	28.9
57	0.00673	0.00503	0.00504	0.00377	0.00374	88,090	90,861	91,746	93,256	93,582	26.4	24.7	25.9	26.3	27.1	28.0
58	0.00720	0.00542	0.00544	0.00410	0.00400	87,497	90,404	91,284	92,905	93,233	25.5	23.9	25.0	25.5	26.2	27.1
59	0.00763	0.00598	0.00596	0.00451	0.00442	86,868	89,915	90,788	92,523	92,859	24.6	23.1	24.1	24.6	25.3	26.2
60	0.00913	0.00711	0.00665	0.00522	0.00448	86,205	89,377	90,246	92,106	92,449	23.7	22.3	23.3	23.7	24.5	25.3
61	0.00995	0.00777	0.00716	0.00593	0.00502	85,418	88,742	89,646	91,626	92,035	22.8	21.5	22.5	22.9	23.6	24.4
62	0.01074	0.00860	0.00764	0.00665	0.00535	84,568	88,052	89,005	91,083	91,573	22.0	20.7	21.6	22.1	22.7	23.6
63	0.01147	0.00934	0.00806	0.00756	0.00597	83,660	87,295	88,325	90,477	91,083	21.1	19.9	20.8	21.2	21.9	22.7
64	0.01236	0.00995	0.00852	0.00820	0.00659	82,700	86,480	87,613	89,793	90,539	20.3	19.1	20.0	20.4	21.0	21.8
65	0.01391	0.01119	0.00961	0.00875	0.00767	81,678	85,619	86,866	89,056	89,943	19.4	18.3	19.2	19.6	20.2	21.0
66	0.01475	0.01227	0.01035	0.00963	0.00828	80,542	84,661	86,031	88,277	89,253	18.6	17.6	18.4	18.7	19.4	20.1
67	0.01585	0.01326	0.01125	0.01030	0.00948	79,354	83,622	85,141	87,428	88,514	17.8	16.9	17.6	17.9	18.6	19.3
68	0.01708	0.01431	0.01262	0.01105	0.01067	78,096	82,513	84,183	86,527	87,675	17.1	16.1	16.9	17.1	17.8	18.5
69	0.01842	0.01547	0.01408	0.01231	0.01162	76,762	81,332	83,121	85,571	86,740	16.3	15.4	16.1	16.3	16.9	17.7
70	0.02086	0.01798	0.01600	0.01400	0.01281	75,348	80,074	81,950	84,517	85,732	15.5	14.7	15.3	15.6	16.1	16.9
71	0.02264	0.01911	0.01771	0.01495	0.01426	73,776	78,634	80,639	83,334	84,633	14.8	14.0	14.6	14.8	15.4	16.1
72	0.02455	0.02089	0.01899	0.01656	0.01570	72,106	77,131	79,211	82,088	83,427	14.0	13.3	13.9	14.1	14.6	15.3
73	0.02694	0.02274	0.02083	0.01805	0.01737	70,336	75,520	77,708	80,729	82,117	13.3	12.6	13.2	13.3	13.8	14.5
74	0.02955	0.02472	0.02298	0.02039	0.01940	68,441	73,803	76,089	79,272	80,691	12.6	11.9	12.5	12.6	13.1	13.8
75	0.03750	0.03063	0.02967	0.02570	0.02377	66,418	71,979	74,341	77,655	79,125	11.9	11.3	11.8	11.9	12.3	13.1
76	0.03986	0.03393	0.03351	0.02832	0.02623	63,927	69,774	72,135	75,660	77,244	11.2	10.7	11.1	11.2	11.7	12.4
77	0.04307	0.03655	0.03781	0.03167	0.02859	61,379	67,406	69,718	73,517	75,219	10.6	10.1	10.5	10.6	11.0	11.7
78	0.04640	0.04075	0.04077	0.03534	0.03236	58,735	64,943	67,082	71,189	73,068	10.0	9.6	9.9	10.0	10.3	11.0
79	0.05020	0.04545	0.04511	0.03876	0.03632	56,010	62,297	64,347	68,673	70,704	9.4	9.0	9.3	9.4	9.7	10.4
80	0.05827	0.05314	0.05357	0.04567	0.04377	53,198	59,465	61,444	66,011	68,135	8.8	8.5	8.7	8.8	9.1	9.7
81	0.06370	0.05815	0.05785	0.05180	0.04871	50,099	56,306	58,153	62,997	65,153	8.2	7.9	8.2	8.3	8.5	9.1
82	0.06910	0.06388	0.06248	0.05595	0.05514	46,907	53,032	54,789	59,733	61,979	7.7	7.5	7.6	7.8	7.9	8.6
83	0.07462	0.06846	0.07020	0.06306	0.05988	43,666	49,644	51,366	56,391	58,562	7.2	7.0	7.1	7.3	7.3	8.1
84	0.08096	0.07518	0.07500	0.06632	0.06552	40,408	46,245	47,760	52,836	55,055	6.7	6.5	6.6	6.8	6.8	7.5
85	1.00000	1.00000	1.00000	1.00000	1.00000	37,136	42,769	44,178	49,332	51,448	6.2	6.0	6.1	6.3	6.2	7.0

* Weighted average by education.

Table 2: Mortality rates, number living at beginning of age (out of 100,000 born alive), and expectations of remaining years of life by smoking status, 2004, continued—All Races Males, Current Smokers

Age	Mortality Rates—Male Current Smokers					Number Living at Beginning of Age Interval					Expectation of Life—Male Current Smokers					
	<HS	High School	Some College	College Degree	Graduate Degree	<HS	High School	Some College	College Degree	Graduate Degree	All Ed Levels *	<HS	High School	Some College	College Degree	Grad Degree
0	0.00747	0.00747	0.00747	0.00747	0.00747	100,000	100,000	100,000	100,000	100,000	70.7	66.8	69.8	70.9	72.9	74.0
1	0.00051	0.00051	0.00051	0.00051	0.00051	99,253	99,253	99,253	99,253	99,253	70.3	66.3	69.4	70.4	72.5	73.5
2	0.00033	0.00033	0.00033	0.00033	0.00033	99,202	99,202	99,202	99,202	99,202	69.3	65.3	68.4	69.4	71.5	72.6
3	0.00025	0.00025	0.00025	0.00025	0.00025	99,170	99,170	99,170	99,170	99,170	68.3	64.4	67.4	68.4	70.5	71.6
4	0.00021	0.00021	0.00021	0.00021	0.00021	99,145	99,145	99,145	99,145	99,145	67.3	63.4	66.4	67.5	69.5	70.6
5	0.00019	0.00019	0.00019	0.00019	0.00019	99,124	99,124	99,124	99,124	99,124	66.4	62.4	65.5	66.5	68.6	69.6
6	0.00018	0.00018	0.00018	0.00018	0.00018	99,106	99,106	99,106	99,106	99,106	65.4	61.4	64.5	65.5	67.6	68.6
7	0.00017	0.00017	0.00017	0.00017	0.00017	99,087	99,087	99,087	99,087	99,087	64.4	60.4	63.5	64.5	66.6	67.7
8	0.00015	0.00015	0.00015	0.00015	0.00015	99,070	99,070	99,070	99,070	99,070	63.4	59.4	62.5	63.5	65.6	66.7
9	0.00013	0.00013	0.00013	0.00013	0.00013	99,055	99,055	99,055	99,055	99,055	62.4	58.4	61.5	62.5	64.6	65.7
10	0.00011	0.00011	0.00011	0.00011	0.00011	99,043	99,043	99,043	99,043	99,043	61.4	57.4	60.5	61.5	63.6	64.7
11	0.00011	0.00011	0.00011	0.00011	0.00011	99,033	99,033	99,033	99,033	99,033	60.4	56.4	59.5	60.5	62.6	63.7
12	0.00016	0.00016	0.00016	0.00016	0.00016	99,022	99,022	99,022	99,022	99,022	59.4	55.5	58.5	59.5	61.6	62.7
13	0.00027	0.00027	0.00027	0.00027	0.00027	99,006	99,006	99,006	99,006	99,006	58.4	54.5	57.5	58.5	60.6	61.7
14	0.00043	0.00043	0.00043	0.00043	0.00043	98,978	98,978	98,978	98,978	98,978	57.4	53.5	56.5	57.6	59.7	60.7
15	0.00061	0.00061	0.00061	0.00061	0.00061	98,936	98,936	98,936	98,936	98,936	56.5	52.5	55.6	56.6	58.7	59.8
16	0.00078	0.00078	0.00078	0.00078	0.00078	98,876	98,876	98,876	98,876	98,876	55.5	51.5	54.6	55.6	57.7	58.8
17	0.00093	0.00093	0.00093	0.00093	0.00093	98,799	98,799	98,799	98,799	98,799	54.5	50.6	53.6	54.7	56.8	57.8
18	0.00106	0.00106	0.00106	0.00106	0.00106	98,706	98,706	98,706	98,706	98,706	53.6	49.6	52.7	53.7	55.8	56.9
19	0.00117	0.00117	0.00117	0.00117	0.00117	98,601	98,601	98,601	98,601	98,601	52.7	48.7	51.8	52.8	54.9	56.0
20	0.00127	0.00127	0.00127	0.00127	0.00127	98,486	98,486	98,486	98,486	98,486	51.7	47.7	50.8	51.8	53.9	55.0
21	0.00136	0.00136	0.00136	0.00136	0.00136	98,362	98,362	98,362	98,362	98,362	50.8	46.8	49.9	50.9	53.0	54.1
22	0.00142	0.00142	0.00142	0.00142	0.00142	98,228	98,228	98,228	98,228	98,228	49.8	45.9	48.9	50.0	52.1	53.2
23	0.00188	0.00161	0.00137	0.00115	0.00115	98,089	98,089	98,089	98,089	98,089	48.9	44.9	48.0	49.0	51.1	52.2
24	0.00234	0.00163	0.00124	0.00104	0.00157	97,904	97,931	97,954	97,976	97,976	48.0	44.0	47.1	48.1	50.2	51.3
25	0.00266	0.00168	0.00112	0.00075	0.00126	97,676	97,771	97,833	97,874	97,823	47.1	43.1	46.2	47.2	49.3	50.4
26	0.00269	0.00166	0.00102	0.00069	0.00103	97,416	97,606	97,724	97,801	97,700	46.1	42.2	45.2	46.2	48.3	49.4
27	0.00294	0.00173	0.00089	0.00045	0.00083	97,154	97,444	97,624	97,734	97,599	45.2	41.3	44.3	45.3	47.3	48.5
28	0.00272	0.00162	0.00096	0.00060	0.00093	96,868	97,276	97,537	97,689	97,518	44.2	40.4	43.4	44.3	46.3	47.5
29	0.00247	0.00169	0.00102	0.00054	0.00040	96,605	97,119	97,443	97,631	97,427	43.3	39.6	42.5	43.3	45.4	46.6
30	0.00229	0.00163	0.00111	0.00070	0.00043	96,367	96,955	97,344	97,578	97,388	42.4	38.7	41.5	42.4	44.4	45.6
31	0.00239	0.00168	0.00118	0.00064	0.00043	96,146	96,796	97,236	97,509	97,346	41.4	37.7	40.6	41.4	43.4	44.6
32	0.00228	0.00167	0.00134	0.00079	0.00045	95,916	96,633	97,121	97,447	97,305	40.5	36.8	39.7	40.5	42.5	43.6
33	0.00229	0.00171	0.00136	0.00083	0.00044	95,697	96,472	96,991	97,370	97,260	39.5	35.9	38.7	39.5	41.5	42.6
34	0.00231	0.00176	0.00148	0.00090	0.00050	95,478	96,307	96,859	97,289	97,217	38.6	35.0	37.8	38.6	40.5	41.7
35	0.00407	0.00316	0.00313	0.00224	0.00185	95,257	96,138	96,716	97,202	97,169	37.6	34.1	36.9	37.6	39.6	40.7
36	0.00450	0.00339	0.00340	0.00237	0.00214	94,870	95,834	96,414	96,985	96,990	36.7	33.2	36.0	36.8	38.6	39.8
37	0.00506	0.00365	0.00362	0.00257	0.00245	94,443	95,509	96,086	96,755	96,782	35.8	32.4	35.1	35.9	37.7	38.8
38	0.00552	0.00399	0.00391	0.00273	0.00295	93,965	95,160	95,738	96,506	96,545	34.9	31.5	34.2	35.0	36.8	37.9
39	0.00618	0.00427	0.00432	0.00307	0.00289	93,447	94,780	95,364	96,242	96,260	34.1	30.7	33.4	34.1	35.9	37.1
40	0.00641	0.00459	0.00428	0.00341	0.00300	92,869	94,375	94,951	95,947	95,981	33.2	29.9	32.5	33.3	35.0	36.2
41	0.00697	0.00488	0.00456	0.00375	0.00337	92,274	93,942	94,545	95,620	95,693	32.4	29.1	31.7	32.4	34.2	35.3
42	0.00763	0.00523	0.00486	0.00407	0.00359	91,630	93,483	94,114	95,261	95,371	31.5	28.3	30.8	31.6	33.3	34.4
43	0.00839	0.00569	0.00527	0.00468	0.00406	90,931	92,994	93,657	94,874	95,028	30.7	27.5	30.0	30.7	32.4	33.5
44	0.00909	0.00621	0.00572	0.00524	0.00455	90,169	92,465	93,164	94,430	94,643	29.9	26.7	29.1	29.9	31.6	32.6
45	0.00995	0.00653	0.00592	0.00501	0.00425	89,349	91,891	92,630	93,935	94,212	29.1	26.0	28.3	29.1	30.7	31.8
46	0.01041	0.00712	0.00658	0.00575	0.00451	88,461	91,290	92,082	93,464	93,812	28.2	25.2	27.5	28.2	29.9	30.9
47	0.01079	0.00784	0.00745	0.00602	0.00495	87,540	90,640	91,476	92,926	93,388	27.5	24.5	26.7	27.4	29.1	30.1
48	0.01170	0.00854	0.00806	0.00610	0.00517	86,595	89,930	90,794	92,367	92,926	26.7	23.7	25.9	26.6	28.2	29.2
49	0.01276	0.00913	0.00849	0.00637	0.00591	85,583	89,162	90,063	91,804	92,445	25.9	23.0	25.1	25.8	27.4	28.3
50	0.01359	0.01028	0.00921	0.00685	0.00637	84,491	88,348	89,299	91,219	91,899	25.1	22.3	24.3	25.1	26.6	27.5
51	0.01464	0.01114	0.00965	0.00718	0.00703	83,342	87,440	88,476	90,594	91,314	24.4	21.6	23.6	24.3	25.8	26.7
52	0.01583	0.01164	0.01016	0.00813	0.00764	82,123	86,466	87,622	89,943	90,672	23.6	20.9	22.8	23.5	24.9	25.9
53	0.01658	0.01216	0.01108	0.00901	0.00814	80,823	85,460	86,732	89,212	89,979	22.9	20.2	22.1	22.7	24.1	25.1
54	0.01732	0.01279	0.01181	0.00960	0.00861	79,483	84,421	85,771	88,408	89,246	22.1	19.6	21.4	22.0	23.4	24.3
55	0.01802	0.01319	0.01280	0.00994	0.00931	78,106	83,341	84,759	87,559	88,478	21.4	18.9	20.6	21.2	22.6	23.5
56	0.01900	0.01381	0.01383	0.01024	0.01017	76,699	82,241	83,673	86,688	87,654	20.6	18.2	19.9	20.5	21.8	22.7
57	0.01984	0.01482	0.01485	0.01111	0.01102	75,242	81,106	82,516	85,801	86,763	19.9	17.6	19.2	19.8	21.0	21.9
58	0.02121	0.01596	0.01602	0.01210	0.01180	73,750	79,903	81,290	84,847	85,807	19.1	16.9	18.5	19.1	20.2	21.2
59	0.02248	0.01762	0.01758	0.01329	0.01302	72,185	78,628	79,988	83,821	84,794	18.4	16.3	17.8	18.4	19.5	20.4
60	0.02477	0.01929	0.01803	0.01415	0.01216	70,563	77,243	78,582	82,707	83,690	17.6	15.7	17.1	17.7	18.7	19.7
61	0.02699	0.02107	0.01941	0.01608	0.01362	68,815	75,753	77,165	81,537	82,673	16.9	15.0	16.4	17.0	18.0	18.9
62	0.02914	0.02332	0.02072	0.01804	0.01451	66,958	74,157	75,667	80,226	81,547	16.2	14.4	15.7	16.4	17.3	18.2
63	0.03111	0.02535	0.02187	0.02051	0.01618	65,007	72,428	74,100	78,779	80,364	15.5	13.9	15.1	15.7	16.6	17.4
64	0.03353	0.02700	0.02311	0.02225	0.01788	62,985	70,592	72,479	77,164	79,063	14.8	13.3	14.5	15.0	15.9	16.7
65	0.03659	0.02943	0.02529	0.02301	0.02017	60,873	68,686	70,804	75,447	77,650	14.2	12.7	13.9	14.4	15.3	16.0
66	0.03879	0.03228	0.02722	0.02532	0.02178	58,645	66,664	69,014	73,711	76,084	13.6	12.2	13.3	13.7	14.6	15.3
67	0.04170	0.03488	0.02960	0.02710	0.02493	56,370	64,512	67,135	71,844	74,427	13.0	11.7	12.7	13.1	14.0	14.6
68	0.04494	0.03766	0.03319	0.02907	0.02806	54,020	62,263	65,148	69,897	72,571	12.4	11.2	12.1	12.5	13.4	14.0
69	0.04844	0.04070	0.03704	0.03238	0.03058	51,592	59,918	62,985	67,865	70,535	11.8	10.7	11.6	11.9	12.8	13.4
70	0.05270	0.04542	0.04041	0.03536	0.03236	49,093	57,479	60,652	65,668	68,378	11.2	10.2	11.1	11.3	12.2	12.8
71	0.05719	0.04827	0.04473	0.03777	0.03601	46,505	54,869	58,202	63,346	66,165	10.7	9.7	10.6	10.8	11.6	12.2
72	0.06201	0.05277	0.04796	0.04183	0.03966	43,846	52,220	55,598	60,953	63,783	10.2	9.3	10.1	10.3	11.0	11.6
73	0.06804	0.05744	0.05260	0.04559	0.04387	41,127	49,465	52,932	58,404	61,253	9.7	8.9	9.6	9.8	10.5	11.1
74	0.07465	0.06243	0.05805	0.05150	0.04901	38,329	46,623	50,148	55,741	58,566	9.2	8.5	9.2	9.3	10.0	10.6
75	0.07979	0.06518	0.06313	0.05468	0.05057	35,467	43,713	47,236	52,870	55,696	8.8	8.1	8.8	8.8	9.5	10.1
76	0.08481	0.07219	0.07129	0.06025	0.05580	32,637	40,864	44,254	49,979	52,879	8.4	7.8	8.3	8.4	9.0	9.6
77	0.09164	0.07776	0.08044	0.06738	0.06083	29,869	37,914	41,099	46,968	49,929	8.0	7.4	7.9	8.0	8.6	9.2
78	0.09873	0.08669	0.08675	0.07519	0.06885	27,132	34,966	37,793	43,803	46,891	7.6	7.1	7.6	7.6	8.1	8.7
79	0.10680	0.09670	0.09597	0.08246	0.07728	24,453	31,934	34,515	40,509	43,663	7.3	6.9	7.2	7.3	7.8	8.3
80	0.11136	0.10155	0.10237	0.08728	0.08365	21,842	28,847	31,203	37,169	40,288	7.0	6.6	7.0	7.1	7.4	8.0
81	0.12174	0.11113	0.11056	0.09900	0.09310	19,409	25,917	28,008	33,925	36,918	6.7	6.4	6.7	6.8	7.1	7.7
82	0.13205	0.12209	0.11941	0.10692	0.10539	17,047	23,037	24,912	30,566	33,481	6.5	6.2	6.5	6.6	6.8	7.4
83	0.14262	0.13084	0.13417	0.12051	0.11443	14,795	20,225	21,937	27,298	29,953	6.3	6.1	6.3	6.4	6.6	7.2
84	0.15473	0.14368	0.14333	0.12675	0.12521	12,685	17,578	18,994	24,008	26,525	6.2	6.0	6.2	6.3	6.4	7.1
85	1.00000	1.00000	1.00000	1.00000	1.00000	10,723	15,053	16,271	20,965	23,204	6.2	6.0	6.1	6.3	6.2	7.0

* Weighted average by education.

Table 2: Mortality rates, number living at beginning of age (out of 100,000 born alive), and expectations of remaining years of life by smoking status, 2004, continued—All Races Females, Never Smokers

Age	Mortality Rates—Female Never Smokers					Number Living at Beginning of Age Interval					Expectation of Life—Female Never Smokers					
	<HS	High School	Some College	College Degree	Graduate Degree	<HS	High School	Some College	College Degree	Graduate Degree	All Ed Levels *	<HS	High School	Some College	College Degree	Grad Degree
0	0.00609	0.00609	0.00609	0.00609	0.00609	100,000	100,000	100,000	100,000	100,000	82.6	79.7	82.1	82.9	83.7	84.1
1	0.00046	0.00046	0.00046	0.00046	0.00046	99,391	99,391	99,391	99,391	99,391	82.1	79.2	81.6	82.5	83.2	83.6
2	0.00027	0.00027	0.00027	0.00027	0.00027	99,346	99,346	99,346	99,346	99,346	81.2	78.2	80.7	81.5	82.2	82.6
3	0.00020	0.00020	0.00020	0.00020	0.00020	99,319	99,319	99,319	99,319	99,319	80.2	77.2	79.7	80.5	81.2	81.7
4	0.00017	0.00017	0.00017	0.00017	0.00017	99,300	99,300	99,300	99,300	99,300	79.2	76.3	78.7	79.5	80.2	80.7
5	0.00015	0.00015	0.00015	0.00015	0.00015	99,283	99,283	99,283	99,283	99,283	78.2	75.3	77.7	78.5	79.3	79.7
6	0.00014	0.00014	0.00014	0.00014	0.00014	99,268	99,268	99,268	99,268	99,268	77.2	74.3	76.7	77.6	78.3	78.7
7	0.00013	0.00013	0.00013	0.00013	0.00013	99,254	99,254	99,254	99,254	99,254	76.3	73.3	75.7	76.6	77.3	77.7
8	0.00012	0.00012	0.00012	0.00012	0.00012	99,241	99,241	99,241	99,241	99,241	75.3	72.3	74.7	75.6	76.3	76.7
9	0.00011	0.00011	0.00011	0.00011	0.00011	99,229	99,229	99,229	99,229	99,229	74.3	71.3	73.7	74.6	75.3	75.7
10	0.00011	0.00011	0.00011	0.00011	0.00011	99,218	99,218	99,218	99,218	99,218	73.3	70.3	72.8	73.6	74.3	74.7
11	0.00011	0.00011	0.00011	0.00011	0.00011	99,208	99,208	99,208	99,208	99,208	72.3	69.3	71.8	72.6	73.3	73.7
12	0.00014	0.00014	0.00014	0.00014	0.00014	99,196	99,196	99,196	99,196	99,196	71.3	68.3	70.8	71.6	72.3	72.8
13	0.00018	0.00018	0.00018	0.00018	0.00018	99,183	99,183	99,183	99,183	99,183	70.3	67.3	69.8	70.6	71.3	71.8
14	0.00024	0.00024	0.00024	0.00024	0.00024	99,165	99,165	99,165	99,165	99,165	69.3	66.4	68.8	69.6	70.3	70.8
15	0.00031	0.00031	0.00031	0.00031	0.00031	99,142	99,142	99,142	99,142	99,142	68.3	65.4	67.8	68.6	69.4	69.8
16	0.00037	0.00037	0.00037	0.00037	0.00037	99,112	99,112	99,112	99,112	99,112	67.4	64.4	66.8	67.7	68.4	68.8
17	0.00042	0.00042	0.00042	0.00042	0.00042	99,075	99,075	99,075	99,075	99,075	66.4	63.4	65.9	66.7	67.4	67.8
18	0.00045	0.00045	0.00045	0.00045	0.00045	99,033	99,033	99,033	99,033	99,033	65.4	62.4	64.9	65.7	66.4	66.9
19	0.00045	0.00045	0.00045	0.00045	0.00045	98,989	98,989	98,989	98,989	98,989	64.4	61.5	63.9	64.7	65.5	65.9
20	0.00046	0.00046	0.00046	0.00046	0.00046	98,944	98,944	98,944	98,944	98,944	63.5	60.5	62.9	63.8	64.5	64.9
21	0.00046	0.00046	0.00046	0.00046	0.00046	98,899	98,899	98,899	98,899	98,899	62.5	59.5	62.0	62.8	63.5	64.0
22	0.00047	0.00047	0.00047	0.00047	0.00047	98,853	98,853	98,853	98,853	98,853	61.5	58.6	61.0	61.8	62.6	63.0
23	0.00069	0.00060	0.00056	0.00038	0.00091	98,807	98,807	98,807	98,807	98,807	60.6	57.6	60.0	60.9	61.6	62.0
24	0.00078	0.00057	0.00048	0.00034	0.00103	98,739	98,748	98,751	98,769	98,716	59.6	56.6	59.1	59.9	60.6	61.1
25	0.00097	0.00056	0.00052	0.00040	0.00095	98,662	98,691	98,704	98,735	98,615	58.6	55.7	58.1	58.9	59.6	60.1
26	0.00095	0.00058	0.00054	0.00039	0.00088	98,566	98,636	98,653	98,695	98,521	57.7	54.7	57.1	58.0	58.6	59.2
27	0.00103	0.00060	0.00055	0.00037	0.00086	98,472	98,579	98,599	98,657	98,434	56.7	53.8	56.2	57.0	57.7	58.2
28	0.00091	0.00051	0.00045	0.00040	0.00049	98,371	98,520	98,545	98,620	98,350	55.7	52.8	55.2	56.0	56.7	57.3
29	0.00096	0.00060	0.00057	0.00045	0.00039	98,281	98,469	98,500	98,581	98,301	54.7	51.9	54.2	55.0	55.7	56.3
30	0.00077	0.00067	0.00056	0.00039	0.00052	98,187	98,409	98,444	98,536	98,263	53.8	50.9	53.3	54.1	54.7	55.3
31	0.00103	0.00074	0.00055	0.00037	0.00063	98,111	98,343	98,389	98,498	98,212	52.8	50.0	52.3	53.1	53.8	54.4
32	0.00121	0.00079	0.00060	0.00037	0.00067	98,011	98,271	98,335	98,462	98,149	51.8	49.0	51.3	52.1	52.8	53.4
33	0.00124	0.00082	0.00067	0.00050	0.00056	97,892	98,193	98,276	98,425	98,084	50.9	48.1	50.4	51.2	51.8	52.4
34	0.00128	0.00089	0.00074	0.00045	0.00053	97,770	98,112	98,210	98,376	98,029	49.9	47.1	49.4	50.2	50.8	51.5
35	0.00151	0.00093	0.00077	0.00044	0.00054	97,645	98,024	98,138	98,332	97,977	48.9	46.2	48.5	49.2	49.8	50.5
36	0.00160	0.00098	0.00084	0.00052	0.00060	97,497	97,933	98,062	98,289	97,924	48.0	45.3	47.5	48.3	48.9	49.5
37	0.00161	0.00107	0.00087	0.00062	0.00065	97,341	97,837	97,979	98,237	97,865	47.0	44.3	46.5	47.3	47.9	48.6
38	0.00183	0.00122	0.00093	0.00066	0.00067	97,183	97,732	97,894	98,177	97,801	46.0	43.4	45.6	46.4	46.9	47.6
39	0.00206	0.00132	0.00104	0.00084	0.00080	97,005	97,613	97,802	98,112	97,735	45.1	42.5	44.6	45.4	46.0	46.6
40	0.00230	0.00148	0.00117	0.00102	0.00089	96,805	97,484	97,700	98,030	97,657	44.1	41.6	43.7	44.4	45.0	45.7
41	0.00249	0.00163	0.00131	0.00112	0.00094	96,583	97,339	97,586	97,930	97,570	43.2	40.7	42.8	43.5	44.0	44.7
42	0.00278	0.00177	0.00141	0.00126	0.00110	96,343	97,181	97,459	97,821	97,479	42.2	39.8	41.8	42.6	43.1	43.7
43	0.00304	0.00193	0.00159	0.00132	0.00101	96,075	97,009	97,321	97,698	97,372	41.3	38.9	40.9	41.6	42.1	42.8
44	0.00335	0.00208	0.00164	0.00153	0.00112	95,783	96,822	97,167	97,569	97,273	40.4	38.0	40.0	40.7	41.2	41.8
45	0.00276	0.00170	0.00134	0.00131	0.00099	95,461	96,621	97,007	97,420	97,164	39.5	37.1	39.1	39.7	40.3	40.9
46	0.00302	0.00181	0.00147	0.00146	0.00099	95,198	96,456	96,878	97,292	97,068	38.5	36.2	38.1	38.8	39.3	39.9
47	0.00325	0.00192	0.00162	0.00153	0.00108	94,911	96,282	96,736	97,150	96,972	37.6	35.3	37.2	37.9	38.4	39.0
48	0.00346	0.00199	0.00176	0.00166	0.00127	94,602	96,098	96,579	97,002	96,867	36.7	34.4	36.3	36.9	37.4	38.0
49	0.00356	0.00214	0.00193	0.00171	0.00130	94,275	95,906	96,409	96,841	96,744	35.7	33.6	35.3	36.0	36.5	37.0
50	0.00394	0.00244	0.00220	0.00193	0.00137	93,939	95,700	96,223	96,675	96,618	34.8	32.7	34.4	35.0	35.5	36.1
51	0.00400	0.00262	0.00242	0.00204	0.00156	93,569	95,467	96,011	96,489	96,485	33.9	31.8	33.5	34.1	34.6	35.1
52	0.00417	0.00288	0.00251	0.00211	0.00170	93,195	95,217	95,779	96,292	96,335	33.0	30.9	32.6	33.2	33.7	34.2
53	0.00447	0.00309	0.00257	0.00251	0.00187	92,806	94,943	95,538	96,089	96,171	32.0	30.1	31.7	32.3	32.8	33.3
54	0.00494	0.00329	0.00284	0.00254	0.00195	92,392	94,649	95,292	95,848	95,991	31.1	29.2	30.8	31.4	31.8	32.3
55	0.00499	0.00343	0.00287	0.00262	0.00218	91,936	94,338	95,021	95,605	95,804	30.2	28.3	29.9	30.5	30.9	31.4
56	0.00544	0.00369	0.00309	0.00274	0.00248	91,477	94,014	94,749	95,355	95,595	29.3	27.5	29.0	29.5	30.0	30.4
57	0.00588	0.00392	0.00358	0.00297	0.00266	90,979	93,667	94,456	95,094	95,358	28.3	26.6	28.1	28.6	29.1	29.5
58	0.00632	0.00429	0.00398	0.00307	0.00293	90,444	93,299	94,118	94,811	95,104	27.4	25.8	27.2	27.7	28.2	28.6
59	0.00685	0.00464	0.00429	0.00355	0.00371	89,872	92,899	93,743	94,520	94,825	26.5	24.9	26.3	26.8	27.2	27.7
60	0.00761	0.00506	0.00502	0.00382	0.00392	89,257	92,468	93,341	94,184	94,473	25.6	24.1	25.4	26.0	26.3	26.8
61	0.00832	0.00558	0.00550	0.00430	0.00452	88,578	92,000	92,872	93,825	94,103	24.7	23.3	24.6	25.1	25.4	25.9
62	0.00917	0.00612	0.00573	0.00485	0.00505	87,840	91,487	92,362	93,422	93,678	23.8	22.5	23.7	24.2	24.5	25.0
63	0.00984	0.00666	0.00633	0.00538	0.00559	87,035	90,927	91,833	92,968	93,205	22.9	21.7	22.8	23.4	23.7	24.1
64	0.01052	0.00731	0.00683	0.00564	0.00538	86,178	90,321	91,252	92,468	92,683	22.1	20.9	22.0	22.5	22.8	23.3
65	0.01170	0.00827	0.00722	0.00623	0.00594	85,271	89,660	90,628	91,947	92,185	21.2	20.1	21.1	21.7	21.9	22.4
66	0.01264	0.00902	0.00789	0.00677	0.00618	84,274	88,919	89,974	91,374	91,637	20.3	19.3	20.3	20.8	21.1	21.5
67	0.01345	0.00993	0.00902	0.00748	0.00681	83,208	88,117	89,265	90,755	91,071	19.5	18.6	19.5	20.0	20.2	20.6
68	0.01474	0.01080	0.00977	0.00838	0.00719	82,089	87,242	88,460	90,076	90,451	18.7	17.8	18.7	19.1	19.3	19.8
69	0.01594	0.01176	0.01076	0.00978	0.00846	80,879	86,300	87,595	89,321	89,800	17.9	17.1	17.9	18.3	18.5	18.9
70	0.01839	0.01362	0.01238	0.01157	0.00929	79,591	85,286	86,653	88,447	89,040	17.1	16.3	17.1	17.5	17.7	18.1
71	0.01965	0.01503	0.01381	0.01332	0.00975	78,127	84,124	85,580	87,424	88,213	16.3	15.6	16.3	16.7	16.9	17.2
72	0.02146	0.01649	0.01453	0.01480	0.01151	76,592	82,860	84,398	86,259	87,353	15.6	14.9	15.6	16.0	16.1	16.4
73	0.02316	0.01835	0.01591	0.01655	0.01340	74,949	81,494	83,172	84,982	86,347	14.8	14.3	14.8	15.2	15.3	15.6
74	0.02497	0.02033	0.01765	0.01898	0.01538	73,213	79,999	81,848	83,576	85,190	14.1	13.6	14.1	14.4	14.6	14.8
75	0.02742	0.02302	0.01963	0.02064	0.01908	71,385	78,372	80,404	81,989	83,880	13.4	12.9	13.4	13.7	13.9	14.0
76	0.02975	0.02491	0.02149	0.02159	0.02237	69,427	76,568	78,826	80,297	82,280	12.7	12.3	12.7	12.9	13.1	13.3
77	0.03205	0.02755	0.02469	0.02396	0.02288	67,362	74,661	77,132	78,564	80,439	12.0	11.6	12.0	12.2	12.4	12.6
78	0.03518	0.03059	0.02796	0.02654	0.02567	65,202	72,603	75,227	76,682	78,599	11.3	11.0	11.3	11.5	11.7	11.9
79	0.03899	0.03464	0.03085	0.02825	0.02827	62,909	70,382	73,124	74,647	76,581	10.6	10.4	10.6	10.8	11.0	11.2
80	0.04734	0.04163	0.03820	0.03262	0.03191	60,455	67,944	70,868	72,538	74,416	10.0	9.8	10.0	10.2	10.3	10.5
81	0.05139	0.04663	0.04284	0.03794	0.03519	57,593	65,115	68,161	70,172	72,042	9.4	9.3	9.4	9.5	9.7	9.8
82	0.05591	0.05188	0.04822	0.04327	0.04098	54,634	62,079	65,241	67,510	69,506	8.8	8.7	8.9	8.9	9.0	9.1
83	0.06094	0.05767	0.05593	0.04842	0.04620	51,579	58,858	62,095	64,589	66,658	8.3	8.2	8.3	8.4	8.4	8.5
84	0.06646	0.06384	0.06493	0.05983	0.05239	48,436	55,464	58,622	61,461	63,578	7.8	7.7	7.8	7.8	7.8	7.9
85	1.00000	1.00000	1.00000	1.00000	1.00000	45,217	51,923	54,816	57,784	60,247	7.3	7.2	7.3	7.3	7.3	7.3

* Weighted average by education.

Table 2: Mortality rates, number living at beginning of age (out of 100,000 born alive), and expectations of remaining years of life by smoking status, 2004, continued—All Races Females, Current Smokers

Age	Mortality Rates—Female Current Smokers					Number Living at Beginning of Age Interval					Expectation of Life—Female Current Smokers					
	<HS	High School	Some College	College Degree	Graduate Degree	<HS	High School	Some College	College Degree	Graduate Degree	All Ed Levels *	<HS	High School	Some College	College Degree	Grad Degree
0	0.00609	0.00609	0.00609	0.00609	0.00609	100,000	100,000	100,000	100,000	100,000	77.4	73.4	76.7	77.8	78.8	79.6
1	0.00046	0.00046	0.00046	0.00046	0.00046	99,391	99,391	99,391	99,391	99,391	76.9	72.9	76.2	77.3	78.3	79.1
2	0.00027	0.00027	0.00027	0.00027	0.00027	99,346	99,346	99,346	99,346	99,346	76.0	71.9	75.2	76.3	77.3	78.1
3	0.00020	0.00020	0.00020	0.00020	0.00020	99,319	99,319	99,319	99,319	99,319	75.0	70.9	74.3	75.4	76.4	77.1
4	0.00017	0.00017	0.00017	0.00017	0.00017	99,300	99,300	99,300	99,300	99,300	74.0	69.9	73.3	74.4	75.4	76.1
5	0.00015	0.00015	0.00015	0.00015	0.00015	99,283	99,283	99,283	99,283	99,283	73.0	69.0	72.3	73.4	74.4	75.2
6	0.00014	0.00014	0.00014	0.00014	0.00014	99,268	99,268	99,268	99,268	99,268	72.0	68.0	71.3	72.4	73.4	74.2
7	0.00013	0.00013	0.00013	0.00013	0.00013	99,254	99,254	99,254	99,254	99,254	71.0	67.0	70.3	71.4	72.4	73.2
8	0.00012	0.00012	0.00012	0.00012	0.00012	99,241	99,241	99,241	99,241	99,241	70.0	66.0	69.3	70.4	71.4	72.2
9	0.00011	0.00011	0.00011	0.00011	0.00011	99,229	99,229	99,229	99,229	99,229	69.0	65.0	68.3	69.4	70.4	71.2
10	0.00011	0.00011	0.00011	0.00011	0.00011	99,218	99,218	99,218	99,218	99,218	68.1	64.0	67.3	68.4	69.4	70.2
11	0.00011	0.00011	0.00011	0.00011	0.00011	99,208	99,208	99,208	99,208	99,208	67.1	63.0	66.3	67.4	68.4	69.2
12	0.00014	0.00014	0.00014	0.00014	0.00014	99,196	99,196	99,196	99,196	99,196	66.1	62.0	65.3	66.4	67.5	68.2
13	0.00018	0.00018	0.00018	0.00018	0.00018	99,183	99,183	99,183	99,183	99,183	65.1	61.0	64.3	65.5	66.5	67.2
14	0.00024	0.00024	0.00024	0.00024	0.00024	99,165	99,165	99,165	99,165	99,165	64.1	60.0	63.4	64.5	65.5	66.2
15	0.00031	0.00031	0.00031	0.00031	0.00031	99,142	99,142	99,142	99,142	99,142	63.1	59.0	62.4	63.5	64.5	65.3
16	0.00037	0.00037	0.00037	0.00037	0.00037	99,112	99,112	99,112	99,112	99,112	62.1	58.1	61.4	62.5	63.5	64.3
17	0.00042	0.00042	0.00042	0.00042	0.00042	99,075	99,075	99,075	99,075	99,075	61.1	57.1	60.4	61.5	62.5	63.3
18	0.00045	0.00045	0.00045	0.00045	0.00045	99,033	99,033	99,033	99,033	99,033	60.2	56.1	59.4	60.5	61.6	62.3
19	0.00045	0.00045	0.00045	0.00045	0.00045	98,989	98,989	98,989	98,989	98,989	59.2	55.1	58.5	59.6	60.6	61.4
20	0.00046	0.00046	0.00046	0.00046	0.00046	98,944	98,944	98,944	98,944	98,944	58.2	54.2	57.5	58.6	59.6	60.4
21	0.00046	0.00046	0.00046	0.00046	0.00046	98,899	98,899	98,899	98,899	98,899	57.2	53.2	56.5	57.6	58.6	59.4
22	0.00047	0.00047	0.00047	0.00047	0.00047	98,853	98,853	98,853	98,853	98,853	56.3	52.2	55.5	56.7	57.7	58.4
23	0.00069	0.00060	0.00056	0.00038	0.00091	98,807	98,807	98,807	98,807	98,807	55.3	51.2	54.6	55.7	56.7	57.5
24	0.00078	0.00057	0.00048	0.00034	0.00103	98,739	98,748	98,751	98,769	98,716	54.3	50.3	53.6	54.7	55.7	56.5
25	0.00097	0.00056	0.00052	0.00040	0.00095	98,662	98,691	98,704	98,735	98,615	53.4	49.3	52.6	53.7	54.7	55.6
26	0.00095	0.00058	0.00054	0.00039	0.00088	98,566	98,636	98,653	98,695	98,521	52.4	48.4	51.7	52.8	53.8	54.6
27	0.00103	0.00060	0.00055	0.00037	0.00086	98,472	98,579	98,599	98,657	98,434	51.4	47.4	50.7	51.8	52.8	53.7
28	0.00091	0.00051	0.00045	0.00040	0.00049	98,371	98,520	98,545	98,620	98,350	50.4	46.4	49.7	50.8	51.8	52.7
29	0.00096	0.00060	0.00057	0.00045	0.00039	98,281	98,469	98,500	98,581	98,301	49.5	45.5	48.7	49.8	50.8	51.7
30	0.00077	0.00067	0.00056	0.00039	0.00052	98,187	98,409	98,444	98,536	98,263	48.5	44.5	47.8	48.9	49.8	50.8
31	0.00103	0.00074	0.00055	0.00037	0.00063	98,111	98,343	98,389	98,498	98,212	47.5	43.6	46.8	47.9	48.9	49.8
32	0.00121	0.00079	0.00060	0.00037	0.00067	98,011	98,271	98,335	98,462	98,149	46.5	42.6	45.8	46.9	47.9	48.8
33	0.00124	0.00082	0.00067	0.00050	0.00056	97,892	98,193	98,276	98,425	98,084	45.6	41.7	44.9	46.0	46.9	47.9
34	0.00128	0.00089	0.00074	0.00045	0.00053	97,770	98,112	98,210	98,376	98,029	44.6	40.7	43.9	45.0	45.9	46.9
35	0.00167	0.00102	0.00085	0.00049	0.00060	97,645	98,024	98,138	98,332	97,977	43.6	39.8	43.0	44.0	44.9	45.9
36	0.00177	0.00108	0.00093	0.00057	0.00066	97,482	97,924	98,054	98,284	97,918	42.6	38.8	42.0	43.1	44.0	44.9
37	0.00178	0.00118	0.00096	0.00068	0.00072	97,310	97,818	97,963	98,228	97,854	41.7	37.9	41.0	42.1	43.0	44.0
38	0.00202	0.00134	0.00103	0.00072	0.00074	97,137	97,702	97,869	98,161	97,783	40.7	37.0	40.1	41.1	42.0	43.0
39	0.00227	0.00146	0.00115	0.00092	0.00089	96,941	97,571	97,768	98,090	97,711	39.8	36.0	39.1	40.2	41.0	42.0
40	0.00233	0.00150	0.00118	0.00103	0.00090	96,720	97,429	97,656	97,999	97,625	38.8	35.1	38.2	39.2	40.1	41.1
41	0.00252	0.00166	0.00133	0.00113	0.00095	96,495	97,283	97,540	97,898	97,537	37.8	34.2	37.3	38.3	39.1	40.1
42	0.00282	0.00179	0.00143	0.00128	0.00111	96,251	97,121	97,411	97,787	97,444	36.9	33.3	36.3	37.3	38.2	39.1
43	0.00308	0.00196	0.00161	0.00134	0.00103	95,979	96,947	97,272	97,662	97,335	36.0	32.4	35.4	36.4	37.2	38.2
44	0.00340	0.00211	0.00166	0.00155	0.00113	95,683	96,758	97,115	97,532	97,235	35.0	31.5	34.5	35.4	36.3	37.2
45	0.00569	0.00351	0.00276	0.00271	0.00203	95,358	96,554	96,953	97,380	97,125	34.1	30.6	33.5	34.5	35.3	36.3
46	0.00623	0.00373	0.00303	0.00301	0.00204	94,815	96,215	96,686	97,116	96,927	33.2	29.8	32.6	33.6	34.4	35.3
47	0.00670	0.00396	0.00335	0.00315	0.00224	94,224	95,856	96,393	96,824	96,729	32.3	28.9	31.8	32.7	33.5	34.4
48	0.00714	0.00412	0.00363	0.00342	0.00262	93,593	95,477	96,070	96,519	96,513	31.5	28.1	30.9	31.8	32.6	33.5
49	0.00735	0.00442	0.00398	0.00353	0.00269	92,924	95,084	95,721	96,189	96,260	30.6	27.3	30.0	30.9	31.7	32.6
50	0.00754	0.00466	0.00420	0.00369	0.00263	92,241	94,663	95,340	95,849	96,001	29.7	26.5	29.1	30.0	30.8	31.7
51	0.00766	0.00501	0.00464	0.00390	0.00299	91,546	94,222	94,940	95,496	95,748	28.8	25.7	28.3	29.1	30.0	30.7
52	0.00797	0.00552	0.00481	0.00404	0.00325	90,845	93,750	94,499	95,124	95,462	27.9	24.9	27.4	28.3	29.1	29.8
53	0.00855	0.00592	0.00493	0.00481	0.00358	90,121	93,233	94,045	94,739	95,152	27.1	24.1	26.6	27.4	28.2	28.9
54	0.00945	0.00629	0.00544	0.00485	0.00374	89,350	92,681	93,582	94,284	94,811	26.2	23.3	25.7	26.5	27.3	28.0
55	0.01115	0.00766	0.00640	0.00584	0.00487	88,506	92,097	93,073	93,826	94,457	25.3	22.5	24.9	25.7	26.4	27.1
56	0.01214	0.00825	0.00690	0.00611	0.00554	87,520	91,392	92,477	93,278	93,997	24.5	21.8	24.1	24.9	25.6	26.3
57	0.01313	0.00876	0.00799	0.00664	0.00594	86,457	90,638	91,839	92,709	93,476	23.6	21.0	23.3	24.0	24.8	25.4
58	0.01412	0.00958	0.00889	0.00685	0.00654	85,322	89,844	91,105	92,093	92,921	22.8	20.3	22.5	23.2	23.9	24.5
59	0.01529	0.01036	0.00958	0.00793	0.00829	84,117	88,984	90,295	91,463	92,314	21.9	19.6	21.7	22.4	23.1	23.7
60	0.01732	0.01152	0.01143	0.00869	0.00892	82,831	88,063	89,430	90,737	91,548	21.1	18.9	20.9	21.6	22.3	22.9
61	0.01895	0.01270	0.01251	0.00978	0.01029	81,397	87,048	88,408	89,948	90,732	20.3	18.2	20.1	20.9	21.4	22.1
62	0.02088	0.01394	0.01303	0.01105	0.01149	79,854	85,943	87,301	89,069	89,798	19.5	17.6	19.4	20.1	20.7	21.3
63	0.02239	0.01517	0.01441	0.01225	0.01273	78,187	84,745	86,164	88,085	88,767	18.8	16.9	18.7	19.4	19.9	20.6
64	0.02395	0.01664	0.01554	0.01283	0.01225	76,436	83,459	84,923	87,006	87,637	18.0	16.3	17.9	18.7	19.1	19.8
65	0.02693	0.01902	0.01660	0.01434	0.01366	74,606	82,071	83,603	85,890	86,563	17.3	15.7	17.2	18.0	18.4	19.1
66	0.02909	0.02076	0.01816	0.01559	0.01421	72,597	80,510	82,214	84,659	85,381	16.6	15.1	16.6	17.2	17.6	18.3
67	0.03094	0.02285	0.02075	0.01722	0.01568	70,484	78,839	80,722	83,339	84,167	15.9	14.6	15.9	16.6	16.9	17.6
68	0.03392	0.02485	0.02249	0.01929	0.01656	68,304	77,037	79,047	81,904	82,847	15.3	14.0	15.3	15.9	16.2	16.9
69	0.03667	0.02705	0.02475	0.02251	0.01946	65,987	75,123	77,269	80,324	81,475	14.6	13.5	14.6	15.2	15.5	16.1
70	0.03813	0.02824	0.02568	0.02399	0.01928	63,567	73,091	75,357	78,516	79,890	14.0	13.0	14.0	14.6	14.8	15.4
71	0.04074	0.03116	0.02865	0.02763	0.02021	61,144	71,027	73,421	76,632	78,350	13.4	12.5	13.4	14.0	14.2	14.7
72	0.04450	0.03420	0.03013	0.03069	0.02388	58,652	68,814	71,318	74,515	76,766	12.8	12.0	12.8	13.4	13.6	14.0
73	0.04803	0.03805	0.03299	0.03432	0.02779	56,042	66,461	69,170	72,228	74,933	12.3	11.5	12.3	12.8	13.0	13.4
74	0.05178	0.04217	0.03660	0.03936	0.03190	53,351	63,931	66,888	69,749	72,851	11.7	11.1	11.7	12.2	12.4	12.7
75	0.05098	0.04278	0.03648	0.03836	0.03546	50,588	61,236	64,439	67,003	70,527	11.2	10.6	11.2	11.7	11.9	12.1
76	0.05530	0.04631	0.03995	0.04012	0.04158	48,009	58,616	62,089	64,433	68,026	10.7	10.2	10.7	11.1	11.4	11.6
77	0.05958	0.05122	0.04589	0.04453	0.04252	45,355	55,902	59,608	61,848	65,198	10.2	9.7	10.2	10.5	10.8	11.0
78	0.06539	0.05687	0.05198	0.04933	0.04772	42,652	53,038	56,873	59,094	62,425	9.7	9.3	9.7	10.0	10.3	10.5
79	0.07248	0.06440	0.05734	0.05251	0.05254	39,863	50,022	53,916	56,179	59,446	9.3	8.9	9.3	9.5	9.8	10.0
80	0.07444	0.06545	0.06005	0.05129	0.05017	36,974	46,801	50,825	53,229	56,323	8.9	8.6	8.9	9.1	9.3	9.5
81	0.08080	0.07332	0.06736	0.05965	0.05533	34,222	43,738	47,772	50,499	53,497	8.5	8.3	8.5	8.6	8.8	9.0
82	0.08790	0.08157	0.07581	0.06802	0.06443	31,457	40,531	44,555	47,487	50,537	8.1	7.9	8.1	8.2	8.3	8.5
83	0.09581	0.09067	0.08794	0.07613	0.07264	28,692	37,225	41,177	44,257	47,281	7.8	7.7	7.8	7.8	7.9	8.1
84	0.10449	0.10038	0.10208	0.09407	0.08238	25,943	33,850	37,556	40,887	43,847	7.5	7.4	7.5	7.5	7.5	7.7
85	1.00974	0.99873	1.01173	0.96352	0.87960	23,232	30,452	33,722	37,041	40,235	7.3	7.2	7.3	7.3	7.3	7.3

* Weighted average by education.

Table 3: Transition probabilities by sex, race, Hispanic origin, and education, July 1999 through June 2007

Age	Males—All Education Levels (All Races)					Females—All Education Levels (All Races)				
	Living to Dead	Inactive to Inactive	Inactive to Active	Active to Inactive	Active to Active	Living to Dead	Inactive to Inactive	Inactive to Active	Active to Inactive	Active to Active
18	0.00106	0.65535	0.34359	0.22870	0.77024	0.00045	0.67976	0.31980	0.23671	0.76284
19	0.00117	0.64107	0.35777	0.17912	0.81971	0.00045	0.65495	0.34460	0.20565	0.79390
20	0.00127	0.63406	0.36468	0.14205	0.85668	0.00046	0.64238	0.35716	0.18295	0.81659
21	0.00136	0.63090	0.36774	0.11856	0.88008	0.00046	0.64652	0.35302	0.16698	0.83256
22	0.00142	0.62022	0.37836	0.09629	0.90229	0.00047	0.66290	0.33663	0.15006	0.84947
23	0.00143	0.61654	0.38203	0.07646	0.92211	0.00048	0.68411	0.31541	0.13173	0.86779
24	0.00142	0.61751	0.38107	0.06097	0.93762	0.00049	0.70092	0.29859	0.11480	0.88471
25	0.00139	0.60560	0.39301	0.05016	0.94845	0.00051	0.71258	0.28692	0.10426	0.89524
26	0.00137	0.58050	0.41814	0.04396	0.95467	0.00052	0.72332	0.27616	0.10038	0.89909
27	0.00134	0.56296	0.43570	0.03856	0.96010	0.00054	0.73930	0.26016	0.09915	0.90030
28	0.00134	0.58980	0.40886	0.03342	0.96524	0.00056	0.74956	0.24987	0.09568	0.90376
29	0.00134	0.63184	0.36682	0.02864	0.97002	0.00059	0.75500	0.24440	0.09091	0.90849
30	0.00135	0.65631	0.34233	0.02643	0.97222	0.00063	0.75542	0.24395	0.08926	0.91011
31	0.00137	0.65648	0.34215	0.02647	0.97216	0.00067	0.76225	0.23708	0.08868	0.91065
32	0.00141	0.66108	0.33751	0.02553	0.97306	0.00071	0.76719	0.23210	0.08683	0.91246
33	0.00147	0.66193	0.33660	0.02510	0.97343	0.00076	0.77200	0.22723	0.08432	0.91491
34	0.00155	0.66713	0.33132	0.02469	0.97376	0.00082	0.77721	0.22196	0.08012	0.91906
35	0.00165	0.67204	0.32631	0.02393	0.97442	0.00089	0.78221	0.21689	0.07517	0.92394
36	0.00177	0.68119	0.31704	0.02336	0.97487	0.00097	0.78438	0.21465	0.07146	0.92756
37	0.00191	0.69310	0.30498	0.02317	0.97492	0.00107	0.78870	0.21023	0.06875	0.93018
38	0.00207	0.70204	0.29588	0.02306	0.97487	0.00119	0.79311	0.20570	0.06571	0.93310
39	0.00225	0.71504	0.28270	0.02304	0.97470	0.00132	0.79453	0.20415	0.06266	0.93601
40	0.00244	0.73382	0.26374	0.02351	0.97406	0.00145	0.79554	0.20300	0.06059	0.93795
41	0.00263	0.74549	0.25188	0.02392	0.97344	0.00159	0.79741	0.20101	0.05863	0.93979
42	0.00285	0.75558	0.24156	0.02486	0.97228	0.00173	0.79738	0.20089	0.05623	0.94205
43	0.00311	0.77411	0.22277	0.02564	0.97124	0.00188	0.79806	0.20006	0.05464	0.94348
44	0.00341	0.79018	0.20640	0.02525	0.97134	0.00205	0.80471	0.19323	0.05418	0.94377
45	0.00373	0.79509	0.20118	0.02526	0.97101	0.00224	0.81167	0.18609	0.05361	0.94414
46	0.00407	0.80018	0.19575	0.02594	0.96998	0.00244	0.81666	0.18090	0.05253	0.94503
47	0.00443	0.80733	0.18824	0.02647	0.96911	0.00263	0.82384	0.17353	0.05307	0.94430
48	0.00481	0.80776	0.18743	0.02786	0.96733	0.00282	0.83208	0.16511	0.05475	0.94243
49	0.00521	0.81371	0.18109	0.03046	0.96433	0.00301	0.83823	0.15877	0.05587	0.94113
50	0.00565	0.82852	0.16583	0.03274	0.96161	0.00320	0.84452	0.15227	0.05683	0.93997
51	0.00612	0.84031	0.15357	0.03501	0.95887	0.00343	0.85302	0.14354	0.05915	0.93742
52	0.00659	0.84985	0.14355	0.03785	0.95556	0.00370	0.86099	0.13531	0.06231	0.93400
53	0.00705	0.86025	0.13271	0.04080	0.95215	0.00400	0.86778	0.12822	0.06654	0.92946
54	0.00749	0.86627	0.12624	0.04441	0.94810	0.00435	0.87320	0.12246	0.07131	0.92435
55	0.00795	0.87079	0.12126	0.04913	0.94293	0.00473	0.88026	0.11501	0.07570	0.91958
56	0.00846	0.87695	0.11459	0.05484	0.93670	0.00514	0.88914	0.10572	0.08061	0.91425
57	0.00906	0.88281	0.10813	0.06193	0.92900	0.00559	0.89720	0.09721	0.08587	0.90854
58	0.00981	0.88951	0.10068	0.06931	0.92088	0.00611	0.90526	0.08863	0.09180	0.90209
59	0.01071	0.89725	0.09204	0.08320	0.90609	0.00670	0.91419	0.07911	0.10490	0.88840
60	0.01176	0.90520	0.08304	0.10311	0.88513	0.00739	0.92161	0.07100	0.12399	0.86862
61	0.01293	0.91266	0.07441	0.12065	0.86641	0.00817	0.92666	0.06517	0.14098	0.85086
62	0.01416	0.91916	0.06668	0.13975	0.84609	0.00898	0.93219	0.05883	0.16294	0.82809
63	0.01536	0.92370	0.06093	0.16181	0.82282	0.00978	0.93775	0.05248	0.18698	0.80324
64	0.01656	0.92532	0.05812	0.17734	0.80610	0.01058	0.94202	0.04740	0.19994	0.78948
65	0.01785	0.92542	0.05674	0.18713	0.79503	0.01147	0.94589	0.04264	0.20686	0.78167
66	0.01933	0.92530	0.05537	0.20114	0.77953	0.01250	0.94958	0.03792	0.21635	0.77115
67	0.02099	0.92606	0.05295	0.21216	0.76685	0.01366	0.95243	0.03391	0.21993	0.76641
68	0.02286	0.92747	0.04967	0.21606	0.76108	0.01497	0.95470	0.03033	0.21828	0.76675
69	0.02492	0.92923	0.04585	0.21981	0.75527	0.01641	0.95680	0.02679	0.22134	0.76225
70	0.02707	0.93218	0.04076	0.22597	0.74696	0.01795	0.95833	0.02372	0.22521	0.75685
71	0.02936	0.93490	0.03574	0.23537	0.73527	0.01962	0.95955	0.02083	0.23025	0.75013
72	0.03203	0.93601	0.03196	0.24475	0.72322	0.02150	0.95998	0.01851	0.24521	0.73328
73	0.03518	0.93606	0.02876	0.24759	0.71723	0.02364	0.96000	0.01636	0.25761	0.71876
74	0.03873	0.93638	0.02489	0.24578	0.71549	0.02599	0.95980	0.01421	0.26573	0.70829
75	0.04241	0.93562	0.02197	0.24198	0.71561	0.02836	0.95942	0.01222	0.27681	0.69483
76	0.04617	0.93376	0.02006	0.24013	0.71370	0.03085	0.95881	0.01034	0.28022	0.68893
77	0.05033	0.93124	0.01844	0.24497	0.70470	0.03382	0.95765	0.00853	0.28314	0.68304
78	0.05508	0.92895	0.01596	0.25678	0.68814	0.03748	0.95569	0.00683	0.29414	0.66838
79	0.06050	0.92501	0.01449	0.28319	0.65631	0.04179	0.95277	0.00544	0.30476	0.65344
80	0.06656	0.91942	0.01403	0.29982	0.63362	0.04646	0.94909	0.00445	0.27893	0.67461

Mortality is from Table 1; mortality-adjusted, exact-age transition probabilities are from CPS microdata samples, July 1999 through June 2007

Table 3: Transition probabilities by sex, race, Hispanic origin, and education, July 1999 through June 2007, continued

Age	Males—Less than High School (All Races)					Females—Less than High School (All Races)				
	Living to Dead	Inactive to Inactive	Inactive to Active	Active to Inactive	Active to Active	Living to Dead	Inactive to Inactive	Inactive to Active	Active to Inactive	Active to Active
18	0.00106	0.61466	0.38427	0.26275	0.73618	0.00045	0.72863	0.27093	0.33504	0.66451
19	0.00117	0.62914	0.36970	0.22243	0.77640	0.00045	0.72453	0.27501	0.29241	0.70714
20	0.00127	0.63551	0.36322	0.16186	0.83687	0.00046	0.72882	0.27072	0.25776	0.74178
21	0.00136	0.65112	0.34752	0.12291	0.87573	0.00046	0.74147	0.25807	0.23823	0.76131
22	0.00142	0.66141	0.33717	0.10281	0.89577	0.00047	0.76646	0.23307	0.24346	0.75607
23	0.00188	0.66889	0.32923	0.08993	0.90819	0.00069	0.79243	0.20689	0.23673	0.76258
24	0.00234	0.67949	0.31817	0.08039	0.91728	0.00078	0.81107	0.18815	0.21573	0.78349
25	0.00266	0.65795	0.33940	0.07049	0.92685	0.00097	0.82410	0.17493	0.19482	0.80421
26	0.00269	0.62323	0.37408	0.05778	0.93953	0.00095	0.81405	0.18500	0.18942	0.80963
27	0.00294	0.63347	0.36359	0.04680	0.95025	0.00103	0.80332	0.19565	0.19757	0.80140
28	0.00272	0.69708	0.30021	0.03942	0.95786	0.00091	0.79281	0.20628	0.20697	0.79212
29	0.00247	0.75191	0.24562	0.03625	0.96129	0.00096	0.79177	0.20727	0.21110	0.78794
30	0.00229	0.75481	0.24290	0.04222	0.95549	0.00077	0.79365	0.20558	0.20820	0.79103
31	0.00239	0.74914	0.24847	0.04502	0.95259	0.00103	0.79953	0.19945	0.19164	0.80734
32	0.00228	0.74304	0.25468	0.04625	0.95147	0.00121	0.79605	0.20273	0.18050	0.81828
33	0.00229	0.73734	0.26037	0.04825	0.94946	0.00124	0.79720	0.20155	0.17300	0.82576
34	0.00231	0.73714	0.26055	0.04692	0.95077	0.00128	0.80246	0.19626	0.16637	0.83235
35	0.00246	0.73392	0.26362	0.04330	0.95425	0.00156	0.80953	0.18891	0.16017	0.83827
36	0.00272	0.73756	0.25973	0.04343	0.95385	0.00165	0.81758	0.18077	0.15861	0.83974
37	0.00306	0.75170	0.24524	0.04593	0.95101	0.00166	0.82991	0.16843	0.15850	0.83984
38	0.00333	0.76541	0.23126	0.04754	0.94913	0.00189	0.84216	0.15595	0.15316	0.84495
39	0.00373	0.78309	0.21318	0.04816	0.94811	0.00212	0.84826	0.14962	0.14485	0.85303
40	0.00401	0.80650	0.18949	0.04947	0.94652	0.00232	0.84552	0.15215	0.14012	0.85756
41	0.00436	0.82201	0.17363	0.05078	0.94486	0.00251	0.83748	0.16001	0.13880	0.85869
42	0.00477	0.83262	0.16261	0.05176	0.94347	0.00281	0.83624	0.16095	0.13228	0.86491
43	0.00525	0.84953	0.14522	0.05109	0.94366	0.00307	0.83382	0.16311	0.12571	0.87122
44	0.00568	0.86255	0.13177	0.04863	0.94569	0.00338	0.83187	0.16474	0.12821	0.86841
45	0.00639	0.86325	0.13036	0.04959	0.94401	0.00371	0.84017	0.15611	0.13216	0.86413
46	0.00669	0.86351	0.12980	0.05082	0.94249	0.00407	0.85377	0.14216	0.12793	0.86800
47	0.00693	0.86525	0.12781	0.04981	0.94325	0.00437	0.86185	0.13378	0.12685	0.86877
48	0.00752	0.86008	0.13241	0.05166	0.94082	0.00466	0.86970	0.12564	0.13413	0.86121
49	0.00820	0.86218	0.12963	0.05497	0.93683	0.00479	0.88166	0.11354	0.13709	0.85812
50	0.00846	0.87905	0.11248	0.05772	0.93382	0.00503	0.89267	0.10230	0.13640	0.85857
51	0.00911	0.88999	0.10089	0.06294	0.92795	0.00511	0.90058	0.09430	0.13943	0.85546
52	0.00986	0.89093	0.09922	0.06974	0.92040	0.00532	0.90432	0.09035	0.14300	0.85168
53	0.01032	0.89437	0.09530	0.07320	0.91647	0.00571	0.90859	0.08571	0.14065	0.85364
54	0.01079	0.89746	0.09175	0.07568	0.91354	0.00631	0.91309	0.08060	0.13570	0.85799
55	0.01146	0.90044	0.08811	0.07772	0.91083	0.00669	0.91326	0.08004	0.13527	0.85803
56	0.01208	0.90403	0.08390	0.07906	0.90886	0.00729	0.91575	0.07696	0.13679	0.85592
57	0.01261	0.91122	0.07617	0.08333	0.90406	0.00789	0.92417	0.06794	0.13977	0.85234
58	0.01349	0.92110	0.06542	0.08839	0.89812	0.00848	0.93297	0.05855	0.14619	0.84533
59	0.01429	0.92575	0.05996	0.10652	0.87919	0.00918	0.93691	0.05391	0.16608	0.82474
60	0.01563	0.92565	0.05872	0.13832	0.84605	0.01009	0.94004	0.04987	0.18750	0.80241
61	0.01703	0.93025	0.05273	0.16506	0.81791	0.01103	0.94340	0.04557	0.20686	0.78211
62	0.01838	0.93673	0.04488	0.19034	0.79127	0.01216	0.94651	0.04133	0.23425	0.75359
63	0.01963	0.93953	0.04085	0.21797	0.76241	0.01304	0.95028	0.03668	0.25693	0.73003
64	0.02116	0.94038	0.03846	0.23044	0.74841	0.01395	0.95387	0.03218	0.25919	0.72686
65	0.02231	0.93982	0.03788	0.23053	0.74717	0.01489	0.95896	0.02614	0.25863	0.72648
66	0.02365	0.93883	0.03753	0.22981	0.74654	0.01609	0.96252	0.02139	0.27526	0.70865
67	0.02542	0.93642	0.03815	0.22921	0.74537	0.01711	0.96386	0.01903	0.28031	0.70257
68	0.02740	0.93556	0.03704	0.22720	0.74541	0.01876	0.96235	0.01889	0.27088	0.71036
69	0.02953	0.93756	0.03291	0.23135	0.73911	0.02028	0.96136	0.01836	0.27820	0.70152
70	0.03192	0.93908	0.02900	0.24274	0.72534	0.02186	0.96066	0.01748	0.28986	0.68828
71	0.03464	0.93804	0.02733	0.25999	0.70537	0.02336	0.96042	0.01622	0.27251	0.70413
72	0.03755	0.93832	0.02413	0.27879	0.68366	0.02551	0.96015	0.01434	0.27052	0.70397
73	0.04121	0.93795	0.02084	0.28259	0.67620	0.02753	0.96039	0.01208	0.30237	0.67010
74	0.04521	0.93553	0.01926	0.27820	0.67659	0.02969	0.96071	0.00960	0.33062	0.63970
75	0.04920	0.93414	0.01666	0.25814	0.69266	0.03184	0.96012	0.00804	0.34862	0.61954
76	0.05230	0.93323	0.01447	0.24502	0.70268	0.03454	0.95892	0.00654	0.38010	0.58536
77	0.05651	0.92873	0.01476	0.25250	0.69099	0.03721	0.95745	0.00534	0.41103	0.55176
78	0.06088	0.92528	0.01384	0.27442	0.66470	0.04084	0.95521	0.00395	0.40292	0.55623
79	0.06586	0.92102	0.01312	0.31789	0.61625	0.04527	0.95133	0.00340	0.40280	0.55193
80	0.07132	0.91659	0.01209	0.34392	0.58476	0.05026	0.94710	0.00264	0.39419	0.55555

Mortality is from Table 1; mortality-adjusted, exact-age transition probabilities are from CPS microdata samples, July 1999 through June 2007

Table 3: Transition probabilities by sex, race, Hispanic origin, and education, July 1999 through June 2007, continued

Age	Males—High School Degree / GED (All Races)					Females—High School Degree / GED (All Races)				
	Living to Dead	Inactive to Inactive	Inactive to Active	Active to Inactive	Active to Active	Living to Dead	Inactive to Inactive	Inactive to Active	Active to Inactive	Active to Active
18	0.00106	0.58722	0.41172	0.14361	0.85532	0.00045	0.59959	0.39997	0.20102	0.79853
19	0.00117	0.53132	0.46752	0.12165	0.87719	0.00045	0.56523	0.43431	0.18077	0.81878
20	0.00127	0.51760	0.48113	0.09964	0.89910	0.00046	0.56959	0.42996	0.16081	0.83873
21	0.00136	0.54105	0.45759	0.08451	0.91413	0.00046	0.60771	0.39183	0.14644	0.85310
22	0.00142	0.57739	0.42119	0.07406	0.92452	0.00047	0.66961	0.32992	0.14111	0.85841
23	0.00161	0.61142	0.38697	0.06666	0.93173	0.00060	0.71166	0.28774	0.14266	0.85674
24	0.00163	0.64903	0.34934	0.05816	0.94021	0.00057	0.72203	0.27740	0.14180	0.85763
25	0.00168	0.66362	0.33470	0.05076	0.94756	0.00056	0.71210	0.28734	0.13420	0.86524
26	0.00166	0.64268	0.35566	0.04856	0.94978	0.00058	0.71544	0.28399	0.12611	0.87332
27	0.00173	0.60605	0.39223	0.04620	0.95207	0.00060	0.74734	0.25206	0.12095	0.87845
28	0.00162	0.61419	0.38419	0.04283	0.95555	0.00051	0.76804	0.23144	0.11811	0.88138
29	0.00169	0.65160	0.34671	0.03713	0.96117	0.00060	0.76746	0.23193	0.11079	0.88861
30	0.00163	0.68691	0.31146	0.03260	0.96577	0.00067	0.75546	0.24387	0.10297	0.89635
31	0.00168	0.67961	0.31870	0.03276	0.96556	0.00074	0.76129	0.23798	0.10091	0.89835
32	0.00167	0.68432	0.31400	0.03150	0.96683	0.00079	0.76768	0.23153	0.09646	0.90274
33	0.00171	0.68708	0.31121	0.03072	0.96757	0.00082	0.77708	0.22210	0.09172	0.90745
34	0.00176	0.69038	0.30786	0.03061	0.96763	0.00089	0.78237	0.21674	0.08688	0.91223
35	0.00184	0.69725	0.30091	0.03006	0.96810	0.00095	0.78475	0.21430	0.08172	0.91733
36	0.00198	0.71159	0.28644	0.02906	0.96896	0.00101	0.78159	0.21740	0.07684	0.92216
37	0.00213	0.72164	0.27624	0.02852	0.96935	0.00110	0.77753	0.22138	0.07385	0.92506
38	0.00233	0.72277	0.27491	0.02828	0.96939	0.00125	0.77518	0.22358	0.07187	0.92689
39	0.00249	0.72738	0.27013	0.02832	0.96919	0.00135	0.77349	0.22516	0.06853	0.93011
40	0.00277	0.74180	0.25544	0.02904	0.96820	0.00150	0.77765	0.22085	0.06635	0.93215
41	0.00294	0.75153	0.24553	0.02912	0.96794	0.00165	0.78588	0.21247	0.06542	0.93293
42	0.00316	0.76000	0.23684	0.03035	0.96649	0.00179	0.79162	0.20660	0.06281	0.93541
43	0.00343	0.78082	0.21575	0.03152	0.96505	0.00195	0.79844	0.19960	0.06054	0.93751
44	0.00375	0.80029	0.19596	0.03094	0.96531	0.00210	0.81195	0.18595	0.05990	0.93800
45	0.00405	0.80976	0.18619	0.03112	0.96484	0.00231	0.82263	0.17506	0.05823	0.93946
46	0.00441	0.81476	0.18082	0.03207	0.96351	0.00246	0.82906	0.16848	0.05572	0.94182
47	0.00486	0.82311	0.17203	0.03210	0.96304	0.00261	0.83801	0.15938	0.05593	0.94146
48	0.00529	0.82716	0.16755	0.03369	0.96102	0.00271	0.84735	0.14994	0.05918	0.93811
49	0.00565	0.82972	0.16462	0.03711	0.95723	0.00291	0.85571	0.14138	0.06158	0.93550
50	0.00625	0.83719	0.15655	0.03923	0.95452	0.00307	0.86190	0.13503	0.06227	0.93466
51	0.00678	0.84829	0.14494	0.04149	0.95174	0.00331	0.86671	0.12999	0.06406	0.93264
52	0.00708	0.85990	0.13301	0.04497	0.94795	0.00364	0.87241	0.12395	0.06704	0.92932
53	0.00740	0.86780	0.12481	0.04826	0.94434	0.00390	0.87813	0.11796	0.07104	0.92506
54	0.00778	0.87481	0.11741	0.05207	0.94015	0.00415	0.88048	0.11537	0.07683	0.91902
55	0.00793	0.88172	0.11035	0.05777	0.93431	0.00453	0.88708	0.10838	0.08245	0.91302
56	0.00830	0.88665	0.10505	0.06290	0.92880	0.00489	0.89811	0.09700	0.08767	0.90744
57	0.00891	0.88880	0.10229	0.06922	0.92187	0.00519	0.90700	0.08782	0.09429	0.90052
58	0.00959	0.89372	0.09669	0.07650	0.91391	0.00567	0.91414	0.08019	0.09970	0.89463
59	0.01059	0.90070	0.08872	0.09310	0.89631	0.00613	0.92262	0.07125	0.11102	0.88285
60	0.01172	0.90610	0.08218	0.11877	0.86951	0.00662	0.92904	0.06434	0.12940	0.86398
61	0.01280	0.91313	0.07407	0.14289	0.84431	0.00730	0.93321	0.05949	0.14749	0.84521
62	0.01417	0.91980	0.06602	0.16720	0.81863	0.00801	0.93808	0.05391	0.16959	0.82240
63	0.01540	0.92371	0.06089	0.19191	0.79269	0.00872	0.94260	0.04868	0.19384	0.79744
64	0.01640	0.92636	0.05724	0.20765	0.77594	0.00956	0.94616	0.04428	0.21037	0.78007
65	0.01776	0.92687	0.05536	0.21516	0.76708	0.01047	0.94952	0.04001	0.22035	0.76918
66	0.01948	0.92489	0.05563	0.22597	0.75455	0.01143	0.95284	0.03573	0.22706	0.76151
67	0.02104	0.92559	0.05337	0.23262	0.74633	0.01258	0.95535	0.03207	0.22559	0.76183
68	0.02272	0.92760	0.04968	0.23915	0.73813	0.01368	0.95746	0.02886	0.21714	0.76918
69	0.02456	0.92812	0.04732	0.24770	0.72774	0.01489	0.95947	0.02564	0.20596	0.77914
70	0.02647	0.93057	0.04296	0.25102	0.72251	0.01632	0.96145	0.02223	0.19983	0.78385
71	0.02813	0.93564	0.03622	0.25491	0.71696	0.01801	0.96234	0.01966	0.20513	0.77686
72	0.03076	0.93781	0.03144	0.26299	0.70626	0.01976	0.96279	0.01745	0.21757	0.76267
73	0.03348	0.93891	0.02761	0.25043	0.71610	0.02199	0.96334	0.01467	0.23097	0.74704
74	0.03638	0.94167	0.02194	0.23062	0.73299	0.02437	0.96306	0.01257	0.24269	0.73294
75	0.03940	0.94325	0.01735	0.22824	0.73236	0.02697	0.96202	0.01101	0.25013	0.72290
76	0.04364	0.94145	0.01491	0.23467	0.72169	0.02920	0.96169	0.00912	0.24967	0.72113
77	0.04701	0.93917	0.01383	0.24597	0.70702	0.03229	0.95985	0.00785	0.25131	0.71639
78	0.05241	0.93574	0.01185	0.25681	0.69079	0.03585	0.95723	0.00691	0.26800	0.69615
79	0.05845	0.92925	0.01229	0.29055	0.65099	0.04060	0.95363	0.00577	0.28788	0.67152
80	0.06479	0.92114	0.01407	0.27751	0.65770	0.04525	0.95071	0.00404	0.22337	0.73138

Mortality is from Table 1; mortality-adjusted, exact-age transition probabilities are from CPS microdata samples, July 1999 through June 2007

Table 3: Transition probabilities by sex, race, Hispanic origin, and education, July 1999 through June 2007, continued

Age	Males—Some College Education (All Races)					Females—Some College Education (All Races)				
	Living to Dead	Inactive to Inactive	Inactive to Active	Active to Inactive	Active to Active	Living to Dead	Inactive to Inactive	Inactive to Active	Active to Inactive	Active to Active
18	0.00106	0.68509	0.31385	0.20968	0.78925	0.00045	0.63705	0.36250	0.18174	0.81781
19	0.00117	0.68922	0.30962	0.19156	0.80727	0.00045	0.64724	0.35231	0.18481	0.81474
20	0.00127	0.67580	0.32294	0.17092	0.82781	0.00046	0.64630	0.35325	0.18373	0.81582
21	0.00136	0.65669	0.34195	0.14654	0.85210	0.00046	0.63720	0.36234	0.17145	0.82808
22	0.00142	0.63037	0.36821	0.11652	0.88206	0.00047	0.62493	0.37459	0.15063	0.84890
23	0.00137	0.59881	0.39982	0.08591	0.91272	0.00056	0.61829	0.38115	0.12882	0.87062
24	0.00124	0.57247	0.42629	0.06202	0.93674	0.00048	0.62442	0.37510	0.11002	0.88950
25	0.00112	0.54340	0.45548	0.04869	0.95019	0.00052	0.64893	0.35054	0.10097	0.89851
26	0.00102	0.52084	0.47815	0.04530	0.95368	0.00054	0.68465	0.31481	0.09681	0.90265
27	0.00089	0.50946	0.48964	0.04243	0.95667	0.00055	0.71302	0.28643	0.09362	0.90582
28	0.00096	0.54516	0.45388	0.03629	0.96275	0.00045	0.72318	0.27637	0.08860	0.91095
29	0.00102	0.58570	0.41328	0.02858	0.97041	0.00057	0.72771	0.27172	0.08386	0.91557
30	0.00111	0.60832	0.39058	0.02367	0.97522	0.00056	0.73501	0.26443	0.08440	0.91503
31	0.00118	0.63550	0.36332	0.02516	0.97366	0.00055	0.73708	0.26237	0.08569	0.91377
32	0.00134	0.64216	0.35650	0.02420	0.97446	0.00060	0.73855	0.26085	0.08449	0.91491
33	0.00136	0.64950	0.34914	0.02386	0.97477	0.00067	0.73800	0.26134	0.08165	0.91768
34	0.00148	0.66025	0.33827	0.02418	0.97434	0.00074	0.73631	0.26295	0.07652	0.92274
35	0.00162	0.65979	0.33859	0.02351	0.97487	0.00078	0.73843	0.26079	0.06989	0.92933
36	0.00176	0.64984	0.34840	0.02202	0.97622	0.00085	0.74308	0.25607	0.06367	0.93547
37	0.00188	0.64855	0.34957	0.02155	0.97657	0.00088	0.75478	0.24433	0.05881	0.94031
38	0.00203	0.65592	0.34205	0.02105	0.97692	0.00095	0.76298	0.23607	0.05520	0.94386
39	0.00224	0.66900	0.32876	0.02044	0.97732	0.00106	0.76735	0.23159	0.05286	0.94608
40	0.00232	0.68346	0.31422	0.02047	0.97721	0.00118	0.77499	0.22383	0.05187	0.94695
41	0.00247	0.69935	0.29818	0.02135	0.97618	0.00132	0.78100	0.21768	0.05105	0.94763
42	0.00263	0.71946	0.27790	0.02231	0.97505	0.00143	0.78202	0.21655	0.05009	0.94848
43	0.00286	0.73933	0.25781	0.02407	0.97308	0.00161	0.78625	0.21214	0.04920	0.94920
44	0.00310	0.75169	0.24520	0.02563	0.97127	0.00166	0.79448	0.20386	0.04936	0.94898
45	0.00343	0.75253	0.24404	0.02606	0.97051	0.00176	0.79547	0.20278	0.04929	0.94896
46	0.00381	0.76338	0.23281	0.02655	0.96965	0.00193	0.79579	0.20229	0.04909	0.94898
47	0.00431	0.77851	0.21718	0.02815	0.96754	0.00214	0.80297	0.19489	0.05074	0.94712
48	0.00466	0.78265	0.21269	0.02979	0.96555	0.00231	0.81146	0.18623	0.05187	0.94582
49	0.00491	0.79841	0.19668	0.03187	0.96322	0.00254	0.81504	0.18243	0.05158	0.94589
50	0.00532	0.82201	0.17267	0.03478	0.95989	0.00270	0.82343	0.17388	0.05273	0.94457
51	0.00557	0.83471	0.15972	0.03799	0.95644	0.00298	0.83852	0.15850	0.05661	0.94042
52	0.00586	0.84288	0.15126	0.04113	0.95301	0.00309	0.84896	0.14796	0.06039	0.93652
53	0.00640	0.85693	0.13668	0.04409	0.94951	0.00316	0.85778	0.13905	0.06473	0.93210
54	0.00682	0.86434	0.12884	0.04854	0.94464	0.00350	0.86713	0.12938	0.06781	0.92870
55	0.00735	0.86964	0.12301	0.05459	0.93806	0.00372	0.87428	0.12200	0.06844	0.92784
56	0.00794	0.87567	0.11639	0.06157	0.93049	0.00401	0.87997	0.11602	0.06963	0.92637
57	0.00852	0.88113	0.11035	0.06906	0.92241	0.00464	0.88497	0.11039	0.07231	0.92305
58	0.00919	0.88865	0.10216	0.07830	0.91251	0.00517	0.89019	0.10464	0.07728	0.91756
59	0.01009	0.89741	0.09250	0.09356	0.89636	0.00556	0.90016	0.09428	0.08999	0.90445
60	0.01077	0.90860	0.08064	0.10909	0.88015	0.00651	0.91090	0.08259	0.11025	0.88324
61	0.01159	0.91813	0.07028	0.11936	0.86904	0.00713	0.91718	0.07569	0.12718	0.86569
62	0.01237	0.92518	0.06245	0.13564	0.85199	0.00742	0.92254	0.07004	0.14802	0.84456
63	0.01306	0.92835	0.05859	0.15940	0.82754	0.00820	0.92805	0.06374	0.17367	0.81813
64	0.01380	0.92439	0.06181	0.17607	0.81013	0.00885	0.93098	0.06017	0.18789	0.80326
65	0.01486	0.92138	0.06376	0.18737	0.79776	0.00920	0.93317	0.05762	0.19294	0.79786
66	0.01600	0.92154	0.06246	0.20894	0.77506	0.01006	0.93840	0.05154	0.19742	0.79252
67	0.01740	0.92139	0.06121	0.22978	0.75283	0.01150	0.94395	0.04455	0.19734	0.79116
68	0.01951	0.92124	0.05925	0.23289	0.74761	0.01247	0.94973	0.03781	0.20084	0.78670
69	0.02177	0.92441	0.05382	0.22604	0.75219	0.01372	0.95417	0.03212	0.21161	0.77467
70	0.02401	0.93156	0.04443	0.22856	0.74743	0.01515	0.95619	0.02867	0.22088	0.76397
71	0.02658	0.93504	0.03839	0.22806	0.74537	0.01689	0.95725	0.02585	0.23938	0.74372
72	0.02849	0.93626	0.03524	0.22167	0.74983	0.01777	0.95977	0.02247	0.27607	0.70617
73	0.03126	0.93730	0.03144	0.22970	0.73904	0.01945	0.95977	0.02077	0.29004	0.69051
74	0.03449	0.93873	0.02678	0.23804	0.72746	0.02159	0.95904	0.01937	0.29001	0.68840
75	0.03801	0.93530	0.02669	0.24862	0.71337	0.02344	0.96125	0.01531	0.29824	0.67833
76	0.04292	0.93092	0.02615	0.25841	0.69867	0.02566	0.96242	0.01191	0.28712	0.68722
77	0.04843	0.92936	0.02221	0.25765	0.69392	0.02948	0.96054	0.00998	0.27257	0.69795
78	0.05223	0.92925	0.01851	0.26907	0.67870	0.03339	0.95876	0.00785	0.27669	0.68991
79	0.05778	0.92709	0.01513	0.28169	0.66053	0.03684	0.95827	0.00489	0.28423	0.67893
80	0.06423	0.92422	0.01155	0.23345	0.70232	0.04163	0.95153	0.00685	0.41348	0.54489

Mortality is from Table 1; mortality-adjusted, exact-age transition probabilities are from CPS microdata samples, July 1999 through June 2007

Table 3: Transition probabilities by sex, race, Hispanic origin, and education, July 1999 through June 2007, continued

Age	Males—Bachelor's Degree (All Races)					Females—Bachelor's Degree (All Races)				
	Living to Dead	Inactive to Inactive	Inactive to Active	Active to Inactive	Active to Active	Living to Dead	Inactive to Inactive	Inactive to Active	Active to Inactive	Active to Active
18	0.001	0.000	0.999	0.000	0.999	0.000	1.000	0.000	0.358	0.642
19	0.001	0.641	0.358	0.000	0.999	0.001	0.879	0.121	0.186	0.813
20	0.001	0.862	0.137	0.037	0.962	0.001	0.693	0.307	0.109	0.890
21	0.001	0.725	0.274	0.057	0.941	0.001	0.541	0.459	0.080	0.920
22	0.001	0.578	0.421	0.075	0.923	0.001	0.529	0.470	0.111	0.889
23	0.001	0.570	0.429	0.055	0.944	0.000	0.595	0.405	0.091	0.908
24	0.001	0.593	0.406	0.050	0.949	0.000	0.646	0.353	0.075	0.925
25	0.001	0.582	0.418	0.043	0.957	0.000	0.674	0.325	0.068	0.932
26	0.001	0.550	0.449	0.032	0.967	0.000	0.693	0.306	0.072	0.928
27	0.001	0.518	0.481	0.023	0.977	0.000	0.701	0.299	0.076	0.924
28	0.001	0.514	0.486	0.019	0.981	0.000	0.715	0.284	0.072	0.928
29	0.001	0.515	0.484	0.019	0.980	0.001	0.736	0.263	0.067	0.933
30	0.001	0.528	0.471	0.020	0.980	0.000	0.750	0.250	0.067	0.933
31	0.001	0.531	0.469	0.017	0.983	0.000	0.769	0.231	0.069	0.930
32	0.001	0.532	0.467	0.015	0.984	0.000	0.782	0.217	0.070	0.929
33	0.001	0.526	0.473	0.013	0.986	0.001	0.791	0.208	0.070	0.930
34	0.001	0.515	0.484	0.012	0.987	0.000	0.802	0.198	0.066	0.933
35	0.000	0.502	0.497	0.013	0.986	0.000	0.808	0.191	0.062	0.937
36	0.001	0.522	0.477	0.013	0.986	0.001	0.813	0.187	0.060	0.939
37	0.001	0.562	0.437	0.013	0.986	0.001	0.819	0.180	0.059	0.940
38	0.001	0.585	0.414	0.014	0.985	0.001	0.824	0.176	0.058	0.942
39	0.001	0.602	0.396	0.014	0.984	0.001	0.822	0.178	0.055	0.944
40	0.001	0.626	0.373	0.015	0.984	0.001	0.813	0.186	0.053	0.946
41	0.002	0.629	0.370	0.015	0.983	0.001	0.807	0.192	0.049	0.950
42	0.002	0.613	0.386	0.016	0.982	0.001	0.798	0.200	0.046	0.953
43	0.002	0.619	0.379	0.016	0.982	0.001	0.787	0.211	0.045	0.953
44	0.002	0.652	0.345	0.014	0.984	0.002	0.787	0.211	0.044	0.954
45	0.002	0.670	0.328	0.013	0.984	0.002	0.792	0.206	0.044	0.955
46	0.003	0.666	0.332	0.014	0.983	0.002	0.790	0.208	0.044	0.954
47	0.003	0.659	0.338	0.016	0.981	0.002	0.788	0.210	0.044	0.954
48	0.003	0.673	0.324	0.018	0.980	0.002	0.792	0.207	0.044	0.954
49	0.003	0.689	0.308	0.020	0.977	0.002	0.793	0.205	0.046	0.952
50	0.003	0.716	0.280	0.023	0.974	0.002	0.795	0.203	0.048	0.950
51	0.004	0.750	0.247	0.025	0.972	0.002	0.802	0.196	0.051	0.947
52	0.004	0.786	0.210	0.027	0.969	0.002	0.813	0.184	0.054	0.944
53	0.004	0.807	0.189	0.031	0.965	0.003	0.820	0.177	0.059	0.938
54	0.005	0.812	0.183	0.034	0.961	0.003	0.827	0.170	0.065	0.932
55	0.005	0.817	0.178	0.037	0.957	0.003	0.840	0.157	0.070	0.927
56	0.005	0.830	0.165	0.043	0.951	0.003	0.856	0.141	0.075	0.922
57	0.006	0.849	0.146	0.050	0.944	0.004	0.871	0.126	0.080	0.916
58	0.006	0.861	0.133	0.056	0.938	0.004	0.887	0.109	0.087	0.909
59	0.007	0.872	0.122	0.066	0.928	0.004	0.898	0.097	0.099	0.896
60	0.008	0.891	0.101	0.080	0.912	0.005	0.907	0.089	0.116	0.880
61	0.009	0.906	0.086	0.094	0.898	0.005	0.913	0.082	0.128	0.867
62	0.001	0.911	0.079	0.108	0.882	0.006	0.919	0.075	0.143	0.851
63	0.011	0.916	0.073	0.125	0.864	0.007	0.926	0.067	0.159	0.835
64	0.012	0.923	0.065	0.140	0.848	0.007	0.935	0.058	0.164	0.829
65	0.013	0.924	0.063	0.150	0.837	0.008	0.939	0.053	0.173	0.820
66	0.014	0.923	0.063	0.166	0.820	0.008	0.942	0.050	0.192	0.800
67	0.015	0.929	0.056	0.179	0.806	0.009	0.945	0.046	0.208	0.782
68	0.016	0.936	0.048	0.187	0.797	0.010	0.948	0.042	0.217	0.773
69	0.018	0.938	0.044	0.201	0.781	0.012	0.950	0.038	0.240	0.748
70	0.020	0.940	0.041	0.213	0.767	0.014	0.953	0.033	0.252	0.734
71	0.021	0.945	0.034	0.225	0.754	0.016	0.956	0.028	0.252	0.732
72	0.023	0.943	0.034	0.237	0.740	0.018	0.956	0.026	0.267	0.716
73	0.025	0.939	0.036	0.251	0.724	0.020	0.955	0.025	0.265	0.715
74	0.029	0.939	0.033	0.247	0.724	0.023	0.955	0.023	0.258	0.719
75	0.032	0.938	0.030	0.232	0.736	0.024	0.955	0.021	0.277	0.699
76	0.036	0.936	0.028	0.235	0.730	0.026	0.954	0.020	0.291	0.683
77	0.040	0.935	0.025	0.247	0.714	0.028	0.956	0.016	0.298	0.674
78	0.044	0.933	0.022	0.237	0.719	0.031	0.956	0.013	0.334	0.635
79	0.049	0.930	0.021	0.270	0.682	0.033	0.957	0.001	0.354	0.612
80	0.055	0.919	0.026	0.270	0.675	0.036	0.958	0.006	0.306	0.658

Mortality is from Table 1; mortality-adjusted, exact-age transition probabilities are from CPS microdata samples, July 1999 through June 2007

Table 3: Transition probabilities by sex, race, Hispanic origin, and education, July 1999 through June 2007, continued

Age	Males—All Graduate Degrees (All Races)					Females—All Graduate Degrees (All Races)				
	Living to Dead	Inactive to Inactive	Inactive to Active	Active to Inactive	Active to Active	Living to Dead	Inactive to Inactive	Inactive to Active	Active to Inactive	Active to Active
18										
19										
20										
21						0.00046	0.55129	0.44825	0.00000	0.99954
22	0.00115	0.82552	0.17334	0.12418	0.87467	0.00047	0.63967	0.35986	0.00000	0.99953
23	0.00157	0.63158	0.36685	0.08512	0.91332	0.00091	0.74716	0.25193	0.00770	0.99139
24	0.00126	0.45684	0.54191	0.03042	0.96832	0.00103	0.73901	0.25996	0.01561	0.98336
25	0.00103	0.44631	0.55266	0.01554	0.98343	0.00095	0.68410	0.31494	0.03065	0.96840
26	0.00083	0.44967	0.54949	0.01931	0.97986	0.00088	0.62837	0.37075	0.04287	0.95625
27	0.00093	0.48467	0.51440	0.01723	0.98184	0.00086	0.61281	0.38633	0.05583	0.94331
28	0.00040	0.57110	0.42850	0.01283	0.98677	0.00049	0.64583	0.35368	0.06094	0.93856
29	0.00043	0.58889	0.41068	0.01224	0.98733	0.00039	0.70224	0.29736	0.06260	0.93700
30	0.00043	0.48622	0.51335	0.01322	0.98635	0.00052	0.73129	0.26819	0.06563	0.93385
31	0.00045	0.46394	0.53560	0.01380	0.98575	0.00063	0.72831	0.27106	0.06239	0.93697
32	0.00044	0.42380	0.57575	0.01540	0.98415	0.00067	0.74179	0.25754	0.05971	0.93962
33	0.00050	0.42139	0.57812	0.01463	0.98487	0.00056	0.74053	0.25890	0.05885	0.94058
34	0.00074	0.44188	0.55738	0.01366	0.98560	0.00053	0.75721	0.24226	0.05527	0.94420
35	0.00086	0.48580	0.51334	0.01365	0.98549	0.00054	0.77393	0.22553	0.05086	0.94860
36	0.00098	0.51491	0.48411	0.01201	0.98701	0.00060	0.77208	0.22733	0.05034	0.94906
37	0.00118	0.54267	0.45615	0.00993	0.98889	0.00065	0.76448	0.23486	0.04792	0.95143
38	0.00116	0.57960	0.41924	0.00910	0.98974	0.00067	0.76901	0.23032	0.04161	0.95772
39	0.00119	0.59950	0.39931	0.00888	0.98992	0.00080	0.77426	0.22494	0.03799	0.96121
40	0.00134	0.59668	0.40198	0.00830	0.99036	0.00090	0.77864	0.22047	0.03545	0.96365
41	0.00143	0.59201	0.40656	0.00930	0.98928	0.00095	0.78365	0.21541	0.03131	0.96774
42	0.00161	0.58418	0.41421	0.01054	0.98785	0.00111	0.77601	0.22288	0.02934	0.96955
43	0.00181	0.58201	0.41618	0.01075	0.98744	0.00102	0.76974	0.22924	0.02905	0.96993
44	0.00192	0.62754	0.37054	0.01113	0.98695	0.00113	0.77622	0.22265	0.02687	0.97200
45	0.00204	0.66971	0.32825	0.01181	0.98615	0.00113	0.78052	0.21834	0.02618	0.97269
46	0.00224	0.70638	0.29139	0.01179	0.98597	0.00114	0.78130	0.21756	0.02757	0.97129
47	0.00234	0.71044	0.28723	0.01284	0.98482	0.00125	0.79368	0.20507	0.02903	0.96973
48	0.00267	0.72045	0.27688	0.01519	0.98214	0.00146	0.80220	0.19634	0.02998	0.96855
49	0.00282	0.74124	0.25594	0.01702	0.98016	0.00150	0.79310	0.20540	0.03103	0.96747
50	0.00311	0.73648	0.26041	0.01832	0.97857	0.00155	0.78036	0.21809	0.03155	0.96690
51	0.00338	0.75140	0.24522	0.01953	0.97709	0.00176	0.78629	0.21195	0.03086	0.96738
52	0.00360	0.79240	0.20400	0.02106	0.97534	0.00191	0.79896	0.19913	0.03286	0.96523
53	0.00381	0.81644	0.17976	0.02412	0.97208	0.00211	0.80574	0.19216	0.03838	0.95951
54	0.00434	0.81844	0.17722	0.02866	0.96700	0.00220	0.81555	0.18225	0.04545	0.95235
55	0.00474	0.83414	0.16112	0.03491	0.96035	0.00257	0.83512	0.16231	0.05512	0.94230
56	0.00514	0.83755	0.15731	0.04275	0.95212	0.00293	0.84889	0.14818	0.06604	0.93104
57	0.00550	0.83944	0.15506	0.04919	0.94531	0.00314	0.84850	0.14836	0.07087	0.92599
58	0.00607	0.85430	0.13963	0.05599	0.93794	0.00346	0.85531	0.14124	0.07422	0.92233
59	0.00620	0.86840	0.12540	0.06618	0.92762	0.00438	0.86978	0.12583	0.08599	0.90962
60	0.00694	0.87311	0.11995	0.07801	0.91504	0.00467	0.88278	0.11255	0.10241	0.89292
61	0.00740	0.88147	0.11113	0.09159	0.90101	0.00539	0.89249	0.10212	0.11574	0.87887
62	0.00825	0.89433	0.09742	0.10755	0.88420	0.00602	0.90723	0.08675	0.13668	0.85730
63	0.00911	0.89855	0.09233	0.12378	0.86710	0.00667	0.91828	0.07505	0.16376	0.82957
64	0.01045	0.90477	0.08478	0.14158	0.84797	0.00642	0.92440	0.06918	0.17345	0.82013
65	0.01128	0.91468	0.07404	0.16120	0.82752	0.00724	0.93130	0.06146	0.17217	0.82059
66	0.01292	0.91835	0.06873	0.17423	0.81285	0.00754	0.93492	0.05754	0.17783	0.81463
67	0.01454	0.92049	0.06497	0.17474	0.81072	0.00831	0.93686	0.05483	0.18937	0.80232
68	0.01585	0.92383	0.06032	0.17284	0.81132	0.00878	0.94468	0.04655	0.20276	0.78846
69	0.01711	0.92620	0.05669	0.17801	0.80487	0.01032	0.95267	0.03701	0.21933	0.77035
70	0.01904	0.92726	0.05370	0.19846	0.78250	0.01100	0.95701	0.03199	0.23442	0.75458
71	0.02097	0.93161	0.04741	0.21638	0.76265	0.01153	0.96389	0.02457	0.24004	0.74843
72	0.02320	0.93472	0.04209	0.22877	0.74803	0.01362	0.96291	0.02347	0.22949	0.75689
73	0.02591	0.93550	0.03858	0.25016	0.72392	0.01586	0.95899	0.02515	0.21515	0.76900
74	0.02882	0.93550	0.03567	0.25840	0.71278	0.01820	0.96014	0.02166	0.20958	0.77222
75	0.03180	0.93452	0.03368	0.23577	0.73242	0.02192	0.95750	0.02057	0.20727	0.77080
76	0.03467	0.93558	0.02974	0.22665	0.73868	0.02571	0.95283	0.02146	0.20019	0.77411
77	0.03924	0.93636	0.02440	0.24805	0.71271	0.02629	0.95839	0.01532	0.19804	0.77566
78	0.04405	0.93879	0.01716	0.24678	0.70917	0.02951	0.96072	0.00977	0.20277	0.76773
79	0.05028	0.93947	0.01025	0.28667	0.66305	0.03249	0.95546	0.01205	0.18868	0.77883
80						0.03470	0.95725	0.00806	0.23889	0.72641

Mortality is from Table 1; mortality-adjusted, exact-age transition probabilities are from CPS microdata samples, July 1999 through June 2007

Table 3: Transition probabilities by sex, race, Hispanic origin, and education, July 1999 through June 2007, continued

Age	White Males—All Education Levels					White Females—All Education Levels				
	Living to Dead	Inactive to Inactive	Inactive to Active	Active to Inactive	Active to Active	Living to Dead	Inactive to Inactive	Inactive to Active	Active to Inactive	Active to Active
18	0.00102	0.63233	0.36665	0.19858	0.80041	0.00045	0.64922	0.35033	0.20974	0.78981
19	0.00111	0.62808	0.37082	0.15661	0.84228	0.00045	0.63615	0.36340	0.18733	0.81222
20	0.00120	0.62997	0.36883	0.12585	0.87296	0.00044	0.63333	0.36623	0.16854	0.83102
21	0.00128	0.62816	0.37056	0.10473	0.89399	0.00044	0.64551	0.35405	0.15428	0.84528
22	0.00133	0.60519	0.39349	0.08254	0.91613	0.00044	0.66861	0.33095	0.13955	0.86001
23	0.00134	0.58518	0.41348	0.06317	0.93549	0.00044	0.69368	0.30588	0.12416	0.87539
24	0.00131	0.57376	0.42493	0.04993	0.94876	0.00045	0.71264	0.28691	0.10880	0.89075
25	0.00128	0.56780	0.43093	0.04130	0.95742	0.00046	0.72485	0.27469	0.09798	0.90157
26	0.00124	0.55129	0.44747	0.03597	0.96279	0.00047	0.73916	0.26037	0.09499	0.90454
27	0.00122	0.54228	0.45651	0.03133	0.96746	0.00048	0.75755	0.24197	0.09527	0.90425
28	0.00121	0.57637	0.42242	0.02705	0.97174	0.00050	0.76737	0.23213	0.09371	0.90579
29	0.00121	0.62572	0.37307	0.02346	0.97533	0.00053	0.76875	0.23072	0.08998	0.90949
30	0.00123	0.65815	0.34062	0.02242	0.97635	0.00056	0.76601	0.23343	0.08824	0.91120
31	0.00125	0.66337	0.33539	0.02238	0.97637	0.00059	0.77153	0.22788	0.08789	0.91152
32	0.00128	0.66467	0.33404	0.02160	0.97711	0.00063	0.77539	0.22398	0.08639	0.91297
33	0.00135	0.66232	0.33634	0.02114	0.97751	0.00068	0.78041	0.21891	0.08409	0.91522
34	0.00143	0.66745	0.33112	0.02059	0.97798	0.00074	0.78639	0.21287	0.07991	0.91935
35	0.00153	0.66714	0.33134	0.01975	0.97872	0.00081	0.79180	0.20740	0.07449	0.92470
36	0.00164	0.67548	0.32288	0.01944	0.97892	0.00088	0.79396	0.20515	0.07011	0.92901
37	0.00178	0.69407	0.30415	0.01960	0.97862	0.00097	0.79751	0.20152	0.06700	0.93202
38	0.00194	0.70660	0.29146	0.01965	0.97841	0.00108	0.80094	0.19798	0.06362	0.93530
39	0.00212	0.71843	0.27945	0.01968	0.97821	0.00119	0.80035	0.19846	0.06029	0.93852
40	0.00230	0.73473	0.26298	0.02020	0.97750	0.00130	0.79954	0.19916	0.05835	0.94035
41	0.00249	0.74159	0.25592	0.02040	0.97711	0.00142	0.80156	0.19702	0.05646	0.94212
42	0.00269	0.74703	0.25027	0.02102	0.97629	0.00155	0.80129	0.19716	0.05378	0.94467
43	0.00293	0.76467	0.23240	0.02178	0.97529	0.00169	0.80013	0.19818	0.05188	0.94643
44	0.00320	0.78189	0.21492	0.02170	0.97510	0.00185	0.80437	0.19378	0.05113	0.94702
45	0.00348	0.79078	0.20573	0.02201	0.97450	0.00203	0.80963	0.18834	0.05029	0.94769
46	0.00378	0.79886	0.19736	0.02272	0.97349	0.00221	0.81401	0.18377	0.04923	0.94855
47	0.00411	0.80879	0.18710	0.02321	0.97269	0.00239	0.82125	0.17636	0.04997	0.94764
48	0.00445	0.81027	0.18528	0.02449	0.97106	0.00256	0.83094	0.16651	0.05185	0.94559
49	0.00481	0.81518	0.18000	0.02678	0.96840	0.00272	0.84013	0.15716	0.05346	0.94383
50	0.00522	0.82877	0.16601	0.02898	0.96580	0.00289	0.84807	0.14904	0.05479	0.94232
51	0.00566	0.83938	0.15496	0.03146	0.96289	0.00309	0.85565	0.14125	0.05672	0.94019
52	0.00609	0.84726	0.14664	0.03433	0.95958	0.00334	0.86340	0.13326	0.05918	0.93748
53	0.00652	0.85816	0.13532	0.03734	0.95614	0.00364	0.86979	0.12657	0.06278	0.93358
54	0.00694	0.86519	0.12787	0.04100	0.95206	0.00399	0.87384	0.12217	0.06715	0.92886
55	0.00737	0.87065	0.12198	0.04578	0.94685	0.00437	0.88018	0.11545	0.07128	0.92435
56	0.00786	0.87873	0.11342	0.05196	0.94018	0.00479	0.88890	0.10632	0.07634	0.91887
57	0.00844	0.88481	0.10674	0.05928	0.93228	0.00524	0.89670	0.09806	0.08254	0.91222
58	0.00917	0.88997	0.10086	0.06682	0.92401	0.00576	0.90461	0.08964	0.08866	0.90559
59	0.01006	0.89715	0.09279	0.08152	0.90842	0.00634	0.91357	0.08009	0.10040	0.89326
60	0.01111	0.90573	0.08316	0.10197	0.88692	0.00703	0.92137	0.07160	0.11905	0.87392
61	0.01228	0.91386	0.07386	0.11940	0.86832	0.00780	0.92687	0.06533	0.13620	0.85600
62	0.01350	0.92105	0.06545	0.13882	0.84768	0.00860	0.93259	0.05881	0.15752	0.83387
63	0.01469	0.92609	0.05923	0.16118	0.82414	0.00939	0.93810	0.05252	0.18235	0.80827
64	0.01586	0.92795	0.05619	0.17595	0.80819	0.01017	0.94226	0.04757	0.19585	0.79398
65	0.01714	0.92760	0.05526	0.18507	0.79779	0.01104	0.94661	0.04235	0.20159	0.78737
66	0.01863	0.92688	0.05449	0.19938	0.78199	0.01206	0.95056	0.03737	0.21023	0.77770
67	0.02031	0.92732	0.05237	0.21098	0.76872	0.01323	0.95328	0.03349	0.21268	0.77409
68	0.02219	0.92808	0.04973	0.21446	0.76335	0.01454	0.95594	0.02952	0.20901	0.77645
69	0.02427	0.92912	0.04661	0.21786	0.75786	0.01599	0.95842	0.02559	0.21139	0.77263
70	0.02643	0.93204	0.04153	0.22295	0.75062	0.01754	0.95963	0.02283	0.21647	0.76599
71	0.02874	0.93492	0.03634	0.23017	0.74109	0.01922	0.96054	0.02024	0.22220	0.75858
72	0.03143	0.93573	0.03284	0.23697	0.73160	0.02112	0.96100	0.01788	0.23601	0.74287
73	0.03459	0.93586	0.02955	0.23851	0.72689	0.02326	0.96082	0.01592	0.24893	0.72781
74	0.03817	0.93657	0.02526	0.23780	0.72403	0.02562	0.96032	0.01406	0.25758	0.71680
75	0.04184	0.93589	0.02227	0.23672	0.72144	0.02798	0.96001	0.01201	0.26800	0.70403
76	0.04558	0.93391	0.02051	0.23693	0.71748	0.03046	0.95954	0.01000	0.27148	0.69807
77	0.04976	0.93163	0.01860	0.24338	0.70686	0.03345	0.95835	0.00820	0.27558	0.69097
78	0.05462	0.92944	0.01594	0.25777	0.68761	0.03717	0.95619	0.00665	0.28906	0.67378
79	0.06020	0.92509	0.01471	0.28312	0.65667	0.04156	0.95316	0.00529	0.30222	0.65622
80	0.06648	0.91905	0.01447	0.30019	0.63334	0.04630	0.94925	0.00445	0.28665	0.66705

Mortality is from Table 1; mortality-adjusted, exact-age transition probabilities are from CPS microdata samples, July 1999 through June 2007

Table 3: Transition probabilities by sex, race, Hispanic origin, and education, July 1999 through June 2007, continued

Age	White Males—Less than High School					White Females—Less than High School				
	Living to Dead	Inactive to Inactive	Inactive to Active	Active to Inactive	Active to Active	Living to Dead	Inactive to Inactive	Inactive to Active	Active to Inactive	Active to Active
18	0.00102	0.57561	0.42338	0.22223	0.77675	0.00045	0.76137	0.23818	0.31766	0.68189
19	0.00111	0.58936	0.40953	0.18868	0.81021	0.00045	0.72056	0.27899	0.25682	0.74273
20	0.00120	0.59898	0.39982	0.13005	0.86876	0.00044	0.72902	0.27054	0.23055	0.76900
21	0.00128	0.62137	0.37735	0.09865	0.90007	0.00044	0.74274	0.25682	0.22644	0.77312
22	0.00133	0.62473	0.37394	0.08577	0.91290	0.00044	0.77854	0.22102	0.24660	0.75296
23	0.00200	0.61716	0.38084	0.07777	0.92023	0.00056	0.80904	0.19040	0.25017	0.74927
24	0.00251	0.62659	0.37091	0.06709	0.93040	0.00048	0.82271	0.17682	0.23282	0.76670
25	0.00280	0.61466	0.38254	0.05398	0.94322	0.00066	0.83155	0.16779	0.20914	0.79020
26	0.00289	0.58579	0.41132	0.04224	0.95487	0.00065	0.82991	0.16945	0.19849	0.80086
27	0.00310	0.60923	0.38767	0.03487	0.96202	0.00073	0.82340	0.17587	0.20481	0.79446
28	0.00267	0.68426	0.31306	0.03115	0.96618	0.00063	0.80836	0.19102	0.21498	0.78440
29	0.00240	0.75652	0.24107	0.02917	0.96843	0.00083	0.79855	0.20062	0.22075	0.77842
30	0.00217	0.77129	0.22654	0.03777	0.96006	0.00065	0.79975	0.19960	0.21646	0.78289
31	0.00220	0.75246	0.24533	0.04149	0.95630	0.00084	0.80287	0.19629	0.19891	0.80025
32	0.00211	0.74026	0.25763	0.04370	0.95419	0.00097	0.80030	0.19873	0.18753	0.81150
33	0.00210	0.72395	0.27395	0.04534	0.95256	0.00099	0.80183	0.19717	0.17932	0.81969
34	0.00205	0.70922	0.28873	0.04156	0.95639	0.00104	0.80651	0.19245	0.17001	0.82895
35	0.00225	0.70152	0.29623	0.03628	0.96147	0.00126	0.81297	0.18578	0.16181	0.83693
36	0.00239	0.70487	0.29274	0.03539	0.96221	0.00135	0.82182	0.17683	0.15903	0.83962
37	0.00268	0.72342	0.27390	0.03665	0.96066	0.00134	0.83329	0.16536	0.15729	0.84136
38	0.00288	0.74358	0.25354	0.03828	0.95884	0.00166	0.84399	0.15435	0.15157	0.84677
39	0.00327	0.76972	0.22700	0.03971	0.95702	0.00186	0.84882	0.14933	0.14498	0.85316
40	0.00359	0.79652	0.19989	0.04154	0.95487	0.00199	0.84393	0.15408	0.14136	0.85665
41	0.00401	0.81250	0.18349	0.04321	0.95278	0.00214	0.83431	0.16355	0.13856	0.86848
42	0.00437	0.82341	0.17222	0.04521	0.95043	0.00247	0.83490	0.16262	0.12905	0.87557
43	0.00484	0.83920	0.15597	0.04518	0.94998	0.00262	0.83210	0.16528	0.12181	0.87300
44	0.00517	0.84826	0.14657	0.04310	0.95173	0.00294	0.82627	0.17079	0.12406	0.87078
45	0.00570	0.85085	0.14345	0.04455	0.94975	0.00329	0.83526	0.16144	0.12593	0.87365
46	0.00593	0.85742	0.13664	0.04599	0.94807	0.00359	0.85126	0.14515	0.12276	0.87112
47	0.00610	0.86457	0.12933	0.04388	0.95002	0.00374	0.85745	0.13881	0.12514	0.86378
48	0.00671	0.86587	0.12742	0.04377	0.94952	0.00414	0.86589	0.12997	0.13208	0.86079
49	0.00736	0.87151	0.12113	0.04599	0.94666	0.00418	0.88142	0.11439	0.13503	0.86083
50	0.00759	0.88841	0.10400	0.04886	0.94355	0.00438	0.89257	0.10306	0.13479	0.85834
51	0.00823	0.89825	0.09351	0.05492	0.93684	0.00443	0.89904	0.09652	0.13723	0.85823
52	0.00908	0.89782	0.09311	0.06282	0.92810	0.00460	0.90418	0.09122	0.13717	0.86526
53	0.00953	0.90116	0.08931	0.06759	0.92288	0.00497	0.90899	0.08604	0.12977	0.87136
54	0.01002	0.90344	0.08653	0.07054	0.91944	0.00555	0.91303	0.08142	0.12309	0.87293
55	0.01064	0.90532	0.08403	0.07192	0.91743	0.00596	0.91318	0.08086	0.12112	0.87319
56	0.01123	0.90864	0.08012	0.07206	0.91671	0.00653	0.91491	0.07856	0.12028	0.86729
57	0.01170	0.91451	0.07379	0.07499	0.91331	0.00722	0.92233	0.07045	0.12550	0.85619
58	0.01253	0.92080	0.06667	0.08087	0.90660	0.00779	0.92938	0.06283	0.13602	0.83685
59	0.01321	0.92331	0.06347	0.10217	0.88462	0.00853	0.93187	0.05960	0.15462	0.81210
60	0.01454	0.92537	0.06009	0.13615	0.84931	0.00940	0.93659	0.05401	0.17850	0.78391
61	0.01580	0.93212	0.05208	0.16723	0.81697	0.01037	0.94123	0.04840	0.20572	0.75017
62	0.01707	0.93888	0.04405	0.19754	0.78539	0.01141	0.94483	0.04376	0.23843	0.72129
63	0.01837	0.94192	0.03971	0.22436	0.75727	0.01233	0.95005	0.03762	0.26638	0.71321
64	0.02002	0.94363	0.03635	0.23471	0.74527	0.01322	0.95458	0.03220	0.27357	0.71457
65	0.02127	0.94183	0.03690	0.23526	0.74347	0.01415	0.95992	0.02593	0.27128	0.70424
66	0.02275	0.93998	0.03727	0.23129	0.74596	0.01540	0.96390	0.02070	0.28036	0.70462
67	0.02464	0.93826	0.03710	0.22473	0.75063	0.01651	0.96526	0.01823	0.27887	0.71413
68	0.02667	0.93725	0.03608	0.22020	0.75313	0.01809	0.96433	0.01758	0.26778	0.70978
69	0.02887	0.93847	0.03267	0.22396	0.74717	0.01966	0.96403	0.01631	0.27056	0.69792
70	0.03131	0.93943	0.02927	0.23286	0.73583	0.02125	0.96304	0.01571	0.28083	0.71244
71	0.03411	0.93845	0.02744	0.24782	0.71807	0.02273	0.96233	0.01493	0.26482	0.71498
72	0.03712	0.93834	0.02453	0.26228	0.70060	0.02502	0.96165	0.01333	0.26000	0.68576
73	0.04087	0.93756	0.02157	0.26434	0.69479	0.02714	0.96147	0.01138	0.28710	0.65303
74	0.04500	0.93531	0.01969	0.25990	0.69510	0.02935	0.96173	0.00893	0.31763	0.62500
75	0.04897	0.93443	0.01660	0.23951	0.71152	0.03148	0.96149	0.00704	0.34353	0.59020
76	0.05204	0.93354	0.01442	0.22612	0.72184	0.03430	0.96062	0.00508	0.37550	0.55622
77	0.05630	0.92923	0.01446	0.23914	0.70455	0.03686	0.95949	0.00365	0.40693	0.55160
78	0.06072	0.92601	0.01327	0.26935	0.66993	0.04050	0.95664	0.00285	0.40790	0.55075
79	0.06574	0.92145	0.01282	0.31378	0.62049	0.04515	0.95205	0.00280	0.40410	0.54960
80	0.07139	0.91641	0.01220	0.34619	0.58242	0.05020	0.94752	0.00229	0.40020	0.54960

Mortality is from Table 1; mortality-adjusted, exact-age transition probabilities are from CPS microdata samples, July 1999 through June 2007

Table 3: Transition probabilities by sex, race, Hispanic origin, and education, July 1999 through June 2007, continued

Age	White Males—High School Degree / GED					White Females—High School Degree / GED				
	Living to Dead	Inactive to Inactive	Inactive to Active	Active to Inactive	Active to Active	Living to Dead	Inactive to Inactive	Inactive to Active	Active to Inactive	Active to Active
18	0.00102	0.54416	0.45482	0.11132	0.88766	0.00045	0.55812	0.44143	0.18319	0.81636
19	0.00111	0.51662	0.48228	0.09556	0.90333	0.00045	0.55448	0.44507	0.16572	0.83383
20	0.00120	0.52268	0.47612	0.08102	0.91779	0.00044	0.57494	0.42462	0.14422	0.85534
21	0.00128	0.54325	0.45547	0.07013	0.92859	0.00044	0.62434	0.37522	0.12987	0.86969
22	0.00133	0.55860	0.44007	0.06130	0.93737	0.00044	0.68888	0.31068	0.13021	0.86935
23	0.00156	0.57564	0.42280	0.05276	0.94568	0.00056	0.72919	0.27025	0.13889	0.86055
24	0.00155	0.60636	0.39209	0.04347	0.95498	0.00053	0.73811	0.26136	0.13740	0.86208
25	0.00159	0.63721	0.36120	0.03741	0.96101	0.00053	0.73079	0.26869	0.12321	0.87626
26	0.00157	0.62718	0.37125	0.03582	0.96260	0.00054	0.74217	0.25729	0.11480	0.88466
27	0.00163	0.58951	0.40886	0.03596	0.96241	0.00055	0.77327	0.22618	0.11508	0.88437
28	0.00149	0.59080	0.40770	0.03561	0.96290	0.00045	0.78634	0.21321	0.11641	0.88314
29	0.00160	0.62333	0.37507	0.03290	0.96549	0.00053	0.78152	0.21795	0.10625	0.89322
30	0.00155	0.65775	0.34070	0.02941	0.96904	0.00057	0.76797	0.23146	0.09550	0.90393
31	0.00160	0.66628	0.33212	0.02914	0.96926	0.00064	0.76819	0.23117	0.09663	0.90274
32	0.00160	0.67225	0.32615	0.02721	0.97119	0.00071	0.77279	0.22650	0.09334	0.90595
33	0.00163	0.67990	0.31847	0.02575	0.97262	0.00075	0.78283	0.21642	0.09107	0.90817
34	0.00165	0.70146	0.29689	0.02514	0.97321	0.00083	0.78900	0.21017	0.08627	0.91290
35	0.00175	0.71094	0.28731	0.02416	0.97410	0.00091	0.79257	0.20652	0.07918	0.91991
36	0.00188	0.72519	0.27293	0.02305	0.97507	0.00095	0.79087	0.20819	0.07405	0.92500
37	0.00200	0.74598	0.25202	0.02267	0.97533	0.00103	0.78573	0.21324	0.07141	0.92756
38	0.00219	0.74759	0.25021	0.02293	0.97488	0.00116	0.78080	0.21804	0.06930	0.92954
39	0.00236	0.73982	0.25783	0.02357	0.97407	0.00124	0.77647	0.22229	0.06658	0.93218
40	0.00261	0.74516	0.25224	0.02446	0.97293	0.00135	0.77977	0.21888	0.06497	0.93369
41	0.00275	0.75155	0.24570	0.02408	0.97317	0.00145	0.78975	0.20880	0.06364	0.93491
42	0.00297	0.75495	0.24209	0.02472	0.97231	0.00155	0.79610	0.20235	0.05995	0.93849
43	0.00325	0.77290	0.22386	0.02574	0.97101	0.00174	0.80100	0.19726	0.05588	0.94239
44	0.00356	0.79640	0.20004	0.02574	0.97069	0.00185	0.81217	0.18597	0.05461	0.94354
45	0.00386	0.81279	0.18335	0.02685	0.96929	0.00207	0.82115	0.17678	0.05336	0.94457
46	0.00423	0.81776	0.17801	0.02857	0.96720	0.00225	0.82735	0.17040	0.05079	0.94695
47	0.00463	0.82434	0.17103	0.02924	0.96612	0.00242	0.83689	0.16069	0.05157	0.94601
48	0.00501	0.82817	0.16682	0.03079	0.96421	0.00247	0.84646	0.15107	0.05641	0.94112
49	0.00532	0.82966	0.16502	0.03400	0.96067	0.00270	0.85684	0.14046	0.05990	0.93740
50	0.00592	0.83479	0.15929	0.03584	0.95824	0.00281	0.86472	0.13247	0.06142	0.93577
51	0.00635	0.84360	0.15005	0.03751	0.95614	0.00303	0.86676	0.13021	0.06338	0.93359
52	0.00659	0.85521	0.13820	0.04073	0.95268	0.00336	0.87160	0.12504	0.06511	0.93153
53	0.00685	0.86567	0.12747	0.04426	0.94889	0.00364	0.87912	0.11724	0.06798	0.92838
54	0.00724	0.87349	0.11926	0.04811	0.94465	0.00391	0.88139	0.11470	0.07301	0.92307
55	0.00737	0.88154	0.11108	0.05367	0.93896	0.00433	0.88741	0.10826	0.07751	0.91816
56	0.00778	0.88921	0.10301	0.05974	0.93248	0.00471	0.89902	0.09627	0.08243	0.91286
57	0.00845	0.89151	0.10004	0.06640	0.92515	0.00503	0.90833	0.08664	0.09034	0.90463
58	0.00914	0.89495	0.09591	0.07366	0.91720	0.00554	0.91593	0.07853	0.09630	0.89817
59	0.01018	0.90165	0.08817	0.09113	0.89869	0.00603	0.92500	0.06897	0.10702	0.88695
60	0.01131	0.90713	0.08156	0.11815	0.87054	0.00653	0.93124	0.06223	0.12556	0.86791
61	0.01247	0.91382	0.07371	0.14269	0.84484	0.00721	0.93569	0.05710	0.14322	0.84956
62	0.01388	0.92163	0.06449	0.16782	0.81830	0.00795	0.94043	0.05162	0.16378	0.82827
63	0.01512	0.92649	0.05839	0.19447	0.79042	0.00862	0.94355	0.04783	0.18799	0.80339
64	0.01605	0.92822	0.05573	0.20949	0.77446	0.00943	0.94644	0.04413	0.20353	0.78704
65	0.01739	0.92809	0.05452	0.21525	0.76736	0.01034	0.95042	0.03925	0.21044	0.77922
66	0.01909	0.92577	0.05514	0.22591	0.75500	0.01131	0.95367	0.03501	0.21718	0.77150
67	0.02067	0.92536	0.05397	0.23305	0.74628	0.01244	0.95594	0.03162	0.21622	0.77134
68	0.02233	0.92644	0.05123	0.23865	0.73902	0.01360	0.95856	0.02784	0.20716	0.77924
69	0.02421	0.92697	0.04883	0.24608	0.72971	0.01489	0.96077	0.02434	0.19854	0.78657
70	0.02610	0.93017	0.04372	0.24778	0.72611	0.01637	0.96262	0.02101	0.19603	0.78760
71	0.02779	0.93647	0.03574	0.25005	0.72216	0.01803	0.96351	0.01846	0.19976	0.78221
72	0.03039	0.93890	0.03071	0.25653	0.71309	0.01975	0.96382	0.01643	0.20757	0.77268
73	0.03321	0.93981	0.02698	0.24257	0.72422	0.02193	0.96400	0.01408	0.21986	0.75822
74	0.03609	0.94287	0.02103	0.22585	0.73806	0.02420	0.96345	0.01235	0.23037	0.74544
75	0.03917	0.94392	0.01691	0.22747	0.73336	0.02680	0.96222	0.01099	0.23705	0.73615
76	0.04335	0.94125	0.01540	0.23561	0.72103	0.02901	0.96178	0.00921	0.24047	0.73052
77	0.04673	0.93870	0.01457	0.24851	0.70476	0.03219	0.95984	0.00797	0.25072	0.71710
78	0.05226	0.93513	0.01261	0.26229	0.68545	0.03586	0.95711	0.00703	0.27276	0.69138
79	0.05861	0.92809	0.01330	0.29500	0.64639	0.04055	0.95341	0.00604	0.29941	0.66004
80	0.06517	0.91959	0.01523	0.28164	0.65319	0.04519	0.95057	0.00425	0.24058	0.71424

Mortality is from Table 1; mortality-adjusted, exact-age transition probabilities are from CPS microdata samples, July 1999 through June 2007

Table 3: Transition probabilities by sex, race, Hispanic origin, and education, July 1999 through June 2007, continued

Age	White Males—Some College Education					White Females—Some College Education				
	Living to Dead	Inactive to Inactive	Inactive to Active	Active to Inactive	Active to Active	Living to Dead	Inactive to Inactive	Inactive to Active	Active to Inactive	Active to Active
18	0.00102	0.66256	0.33642	0.19576	0.80322	0.00045	0.57941	0.42014	0.15522	0.84432
19	0.00111	0.67888	0.32001	0.18042	0.81847	0.00045	0.61413	0.38542	0.16837	0.83118
20	0.00120	0.67197	0.32683	0.16123	0.83758	0.00044	0.62801	0.37155	0.17196	0.82760
21	0.00128	0.65402	0.34470	0.13416	0.86456	0.00044	0.63112	0.36844	0.16031	0.83925
22	0.00133	0.61853	0.38014	0.10065	0.89802	0.00044	0.62495	0.37461	0.13838	0.86118
23	0.00121	0.57148	0.42732	0.07039	0.92841	0.00047	0.62861	0.37093	0.11597	0.88356
24	0.00112	0.52427	0.47461	0.05172	0.94717	0.00038	0.63867	0.36095	0.09922	0.90040
25	0.00101	0.49323	0.50576	0.04235	0.95663	0.00041	0.65937	0.34022	0.09379	0.90580
26	0.00097	0.47412	0.52491	0.03889	0.96014	0.00040	0.69245	0.30715	0.09345	0.90615
27	0.00086	0.47527	0.52387	0.03434	0.96480	0.00045	0.72468	0.27487	0.09135	0.90820
28	0.00101	0.52203	0.47695	0.02720	0.97178	0.00043	0.74746	0.25211	0.08788	0.91169
29	0.00103	0.56951	0.42946	0.02084	0.97813	0.00055	0.75155	0.24790	0.08497	0.91448
30	0.00112	0.61332	0.38556	0.01816	0.98072	0.00057	0.75310	0.24633	0.08558	0.91385
31	0.00110	0.66052	0.33839	0.01830	0.98060	0.00057	0.75717	0.24226	0.08738	0.91205
32	0.00125	0.66444	0.33431	0.01811	0.98064	0.00058	0.75698	0.24244	0.08592	0.91351
33	0.00123	0.66901	0.32975	0.01809	0.98067	0.00064	0.75411	0.24524	0.08219	0.91717
34	0.00136	0.67090	0.32773	0.01870	0.97994	0.00069	0.75153	0.24778	0.07730	0.92201
35	0.00151	0.65705	0.34144	0.01899	0.97949	0.00074	0.75194	0.24732	0.06969	0.92957
36	0.00172	0.65260	0.34568	0.01912	0.97916	0.00084	0.75542	0.24375	0.06124	0.93792
37	0.00184	0.66658	0.33158	0.01953	0.97863	0.00088	0.76527	0.23385	0.05544	0.94368
38	0.00203	0.68718	0.31080	0.01923	0.97874	0.00091	0.77341	0.22568	0.05174	0.94735
39	0.00225	0.70665	0.29110	0.01849	0.97926	0.00101	0.77965	0.21934	0.04870	0.95028
40	0.00229	0.71819	0.27952	0.01839	0.97931	0.00110	0.78677	0.21213	0.04756	0.95133
41	0.00244	0.71710	0.28046	0.01925	0.97832	0.00127	0.78925	0.20948	0.04732	0.95141
42	0.00258	0.72237	0.27505	0.01995	0.97747	0.00136	0.78787	0.21077	0.04662	0.95202
43	0.00275	0.73467	0.26258	0.02137	0.97588	0.00155	0.79045	0.20800	0.04594	0.95250
44	0.00294	0.74038	0.25668	0.02289	0.97417	0.00164	0.79466	0.20370	0.04597	0.95239
45	0.00323	0.74150	0.25527	0.02344	0.97333	0.00172	0.79217	0.20611	0.04612	0.95216
46	0.00357	0.75673	0.23970	0.02341	0.97302	0.00185	0.79358	0.20457	0.04631	0.95184
47	0.00405	0.77839	0.21757	0.02422	0.97174	0.00204	0.80229	0.19566	0.04780	0.95016
48	0.00436	0.78425	0.21139	0.02562	0.97002	0.00220	0.81228	0.18553	0.04881	0.94899
49	0.00462	0.80013	0.19525	0.02719	0.96819	0.00241	0.82030	0.17729	0.04912	0.94847
50	0.00501	0.82338	0.17161	0.02958	0.96541	0.00258	0.83150	0.16593	0.05006	0.94736
51	0.00532	0.83400	0.16068	0.03292	0.96176	0.00279	0.84450	0.15271	0.05284	0.94437
52	0.00566	0.83822	0.15612	0.03630	0.95804	0.00289	0.85308	0.14402	0.05660	0.94051
53	0.00619	0.85277	0.14104	0.03954	0.95427	0.00298	0.86035	0.13667	0.06062	0.93639
54	0.00652	0.86422	0.12926	0.04405	0.94943	0.00334	0.86619	0.13047	0.06334	0.93332
55	0.00705	0.87241	0.12054	0.05039	0.94257	0.00353	0.87106	0.12541	0.06474	0.93174
56	0.00748	0.88193	0.11059	0.05840	0.93412	0.00384	0.87676	0.11940	0.06677	0.92940
57	0.00794	0.88839	0.10367	0.06687	0.92519	0.00440	0.88205	0.11355	0.06982	0.92578
58	0.00871	0.89362	0.09767	0.07671	0.91459	0.00493	0.88743	0.10763	0.07412	0.92095
59	0.00975	0.90020	0.09004	0.09385	0.89640	0.00525	0.89829	0.09646	0.08513	0.90962
60	0.01053	0.91019	0.07928	0.11076	0.87871	0.00624	0.90975	0.08401	0.10446	0.88930
61	0.01144	0.91999	0.06857	0.11970	0.86886	0.00690	0.91655	0.07655	0.12091	0.87219
62	0.01240	0.92803	0.05957	0.13417	0.85343	0.00733	0.92243	0.07024	0.13999	0.85268
63	0.01295	0.93208	0.05497	0.15613	0.83092	0.00804	0.92837	0.06359	0.16342	0.82855
64	0.01362	0.92979	0.05660	0.17189	0.81449	0.00882	0.93100	0.06018	0.17634	0.81484
65	0.01451	0.92797	0.05752	0.18433	0.80116	0.00921	0.93337	0.05742	0.18306	0.80773
66	0.01559	0.92699	0.05741	0.20980	0.77460	0.01000	0.93876	0.05124	0.19012	0.79988
67	0.01687	0.92563	0.05750	0.23472	0.74841	0.01140	0.94376	0.04484	0.19202	0.79659
68	0.01902	0.92373	0.05725	0.23901	0.74197	0.01254	0.94906	0.03840	0.19612	0.79134
69	0.02124	0.92513	0.05363	0.23397	0.74479	0.01360	0.95381	0.03259	0.20647	0.77992
70	0.02342	0.93173	0.04485	0.23628	0.74030	0.01497	0.95556	0.02947	0.21515	0.76988
71	0.02593	0.93438	0.03970	0.23414	0.73993	0.01688	0.95667	0.02645	0.23411	0.74901
72	0.02787	0.93525	0.03688	0.22549	0.74664	0.01773	0.96024	0.02203	0.27218	0.71010
73	0.03058	0.93696	0.03246	0.23483	0.73459	0.01942	0.96047	0.02012	0.29093	0.68966
74	0.03368	0.93822	0.02810	0.24351	0.72281	0.02171	0.95929	0.01900	0.29359	0.68470
75	0.03743	0.93382	0.02875	0.25399	0.70859	0.02353	0.96184	0.01463	0.29682	0.67965
76	0.04246	0.92942	0.02812	0.26465	0.69289	0.02568	0.96315	0.01117	0.28494	0.68938
77	0.04784	0.92897	0.02319	0.26173	0.69043	0.02958	0.96073	0.00969	0.26771	0.70271
78	0.05176	0.92945	0.01879	0.27145	0.67679	0.03344	0.95897	0.00759	0.26492	0.70163
79	0.05779	0.92748	0.01472	0.28004	0.66216	0.03686	0.95910	0.00404	0.27541	0.68773
80	0.06440	0.92466	0.01094	0.23169	0.70391	0.04199	0.95138	0.00663	0.40498	0.55303

Mortality is from Table 1; mortality-adjusted, exact-age transition probabilities are from CPS microdata samples, July 1999 through June 2007

Table 3: Transition probabilities by sex, race, Hispanic origin, and education, July 1999 through June 2007, continued

Age	White Males—Bachelor's Degree					White Females—Bachelor's Degree				
	Living to Dead	Inactive to Inactive	Inactive to Active	Active to Inactive	Active to Active	Living to Dead	Inactive to Inactive	Inactive to Active	Active to Inactive	Active to Active
18										
19	0.00111					0.00045	0.85173	0.14782	0.29366	0.70589
20	0.00120	0.53080	0.46801	0.03549	0.96331	0.00044	0.65906	0.34050	0.12585	0.87371
21	0.00128	0.54628	0.45244	0.05649	0.94223	0.00044	0.47817	0.52139	0.07252	0.92704
22	0.00133	0.55494	0.44373	0.07313	0.92554	0.00044	0.48534	0.51422	0.10076	0.89880
23	0.00107	0.55057	0.44836	0.05318	0.94575	0.00035	0.55783	0.44182	0.08330	0.91634
24	0.00099	0.57155	0.42746	0.04719	0.95182	0.00033	0.63984	0.35983	0.06897	0.93070
25	0.00071	0.56837	0.43092	0.04128	0.95801	0.00044	0.67844	0.32112	0.06407	0.93549
26	0.00068	0.55782	0.44151	0.03243	0.96690	0.00045	0.69619	0.30336	0.06897	0.93058
27	0.00046	0.54965	0.44988	0.02277	0.97676	0.00044	0.70800	0.29156	0.07383	0.92573
28	0.00059	0.56706	0.43235	0.01715	0.98226	0.00047	0.72314	0.27638	0.07026	0.92926
29	0.00054	0.59115	0.40832	0.01583	0.98363	0.00048	0.74682	0.25270	0.06687	0.93264
30	0.00071	0.60978	0.38951	0.01527	0.98402	0.00038	0.75900	0.24063	0.06721	0.93242
31	0.00065	0.60111	0.39824	0.01361	0.98574	0.00034	0.77613	0.22353	0.06718	0.93247
32	0.00080	0.59423	0.40498	0.01213	0.98708	0.00035	0.78876	0.21090	0.06786	0.93180
33	0.00086	0.56463	0.43450	0.01119	0.98795	0.00045	0.79656	0.20299	0.06672	0.93282
34	0.00091	0.53756	0.46152	0.01138	0.98770	0.00044	0.80612	0.19344	0.06399	0.93557
35	0.00095	0.50783	0.49121	0.01152	0.98753	0.00043	0.81418	0.18539	0.06166	0.93791
36	0.00100	0.50625	0.49275	0.01166	0.98734	0.00049	0.81843	0.18108	0.06010	0.93941
37	0.00111	0.53144	0.46745	0.01209	0.98679	0.00060	0.82471	0.17469	0.05922	0.94017
38	0.00119	0.55230	0.44651	0.01202	0.98679	0.00065	0.83028	0.16907	0.05680	0.94255
39	0.00135	0.56901	0.42964	0.01175	0.98690	0.00087	0.82591	0.17323	0.05400	0.94514
40	0.00155	0.59630	0.40215	0.01223	0.98622	0.00105	0.81526	0.18369	0.05199	0.94697
41	0.00169	0.60149	0.39683	0.01251	0.98580	0.00117	0.81230	0.18653	0.04882	0.95001
42	0.00182	0.59183	0.40635	0.01274	0.98544	0.00127	0.80526	0.19347	0.04645	0.95228
43	0.00203	0.61740	0.38056	0.01293	0.98504	0.00135	0.79293	0.20572	0.04688	0.95177
44	0.00228	0.66701	0.33072	0.01207	0.98565	0.00158	0.79394	0.20447	0.04607	0.95235
45	0.00238	0.68865	0.30898	0.01121	0.98642	0.00157	0.79878	0.19965	0.04448	0.95395
46	0.00269	0.68667	0.31064	0.01185	0.98546	0.00173	0.79230	0.20597	0.04420	0.95407
47	0.00280	0.68230	0.31490	0.01363	0.98358	0.00185	0.78953	0.20862	0.04380	0.95435
48	0.00286	0.68434	0.31280	0.01565	0.98149	0.00199	0.79761	0.20040	0.04280	0.95521
49	0.00297	0.69016	0.30686	0.01826	0.97877	0.00191	0.80135	0.19675	0.04409	0.95400
50	0.00320	0.71398	0.28282	0.02135	0.97544	0.00211	0.80432	0.19357	0.04638	0.95151
51	0.00339	0.74998	0.24663	0.02397	0.97265	0.00226	0.81599	0.18175	0.04852	0.94921
52	0.00372	0.78450	0.21177	0.02611	0.97017	0.00233	0.82857	0.16910	0.05120	0.94647
53	0.00419	0.80221	0.19359	0.02921	0.96659	0.00276	0.83245	0.16479	0.05704	0.94020
54	0.00449	0.80709	0.18843	0.03245	0.96306	0.00294	0.83919	0.15788	0.06337	0.93369
55	0.00481	0.81376	0.18143	0.03542	0.95976	0.00317	0.85336	0.14347	0.06796	0.92887
56	0.00495	0.82821	0.16684	0.04102	0.95403	0.00330	0.86677	0.12993	0.07466	0.92204
57	0.00547	0.84738	0.14715	0.04805	0.94648	0.00359	0.87898	0.11743	0.08144	0.91497
58	0.00590	0.85993	0.13417	0.05306	0.94104	0.00365	0.89331	0.10304	0.08779	0.90856
59	0.00650	0.87281	0.12069	0.06173	0.93177	0.00422	0.90307	0.09271	0.09685	0.89893
60	0.00742	0.89523	0.09735	0.07559	0.91698	0.00463	0.91013	0.08524	0.11135	0.88402
61	0.00859	0.91031	0.08110	0.08825	0.90317	0.00523	0.91443	0.08034	0.12272	0.87205
62	0.00962	0.91458	0.07580	0.10276	0.88762	0.00587	0.92000	0.07412	0.13750	0.85662
63	0.01093	0.91962	0.06945	0.12143	0.86764	0.00664	0.92733	0.06603	0.15672	0.83664
64	0.01189	0.92690	0.06121	0.13663	0.85148	0.00686	0.93506	0.05807	0.16503	0.82811
65	0.01276	0.92621	0.06103	0.14455	0.84269	0.00756	0.94010	0.05234	0.17425	0.81819
66	0.01398	0.92486	0.06116	0.15847	0.82755	0.00820	0.94426	0.04754	0.19516	0.79664
67	0.01491	0.93307	0.05202	0.17321	0.81188	0.00897	0.94789	0.04314	0.20738	0.78365
68	0.01611	0.93962	0.04428	0.17935	0.80455	0.01004	0.95082	0.03913	0.20917	0.78079
69	0.01789	0.93935	0.04275	0.19184	0.79027	0.01181	0.95331	0.03488	0.23194	0.75625
70	0.01957	0.94073	0.03970	0.20916	0.77127	0.01369	0.95437	0.03193	0.24280	0.74351
71	0.02091	0.94479	0.03430	0.22330	0.75579	0.01600	0.95620	0.02780	0.24056	0.74344
72	0.02338	0.94076	0.03586	0.23332	0.74330	0.01788	0.95650	0.02562	0.25475	0.72737
73	0.02534	0.93685	0.03780	0.24503	0.72962	0.02008	0.95624	0.02368	0.25305	0.72687
74	0.02875	0.93752	0.03373	0.23825	0.73300	0.02307	0.95498	0.02195	0.24547	0.73146
75	0.03229	0.93724	0.03048	0.22247	0.74524	0.02457	0.95526	0.02018	0.26803	0.70740
76	0.03526	0.93592	0.02882	0.22571	0.73903	0.02536	0.95621	0.01843	0.28815	0.68649
77	0.03933	0.93470	0.02597	0.23384	0.72683	0.02815	0.95710	0.01475	0.29822	0.67363
78	0.04413	0.93327	0.02260	0.22345	0.73242	0.03132	0.95633	0.01234	0.33654	0.63214
79	0.04843	0.92983	0.02175	0.25621	0.69537	0.03353	0.95721	0.00926	0.35960	0.60687
80	0.05473	0.91842	0.02685	0.25968	0.68559	0.03638	0.95729	0.00633	0.35066	0.61296

Mortality is from Table 1; mortality-adjusted, exact-age transition probabilities are from CPS microdata samples, July 1999 through June 2007

Table 3: Transition probabilities by sex, race, Hispanic origin, and education, July 1999 through June 2007, continued

Age	White Males—All Graduate Degrees					White Females—All Graduate Degrees				
	Living to Dead	Inactive to Inactive	Inactive to Active	Active to Inactive	Active to Active	Living to Dead	Inactive to Inactive	Inactive to Active	Active to Inactive	Active to Active
18										
19										
20										
21										
22	0.00133	0.65421	0.34446	0.08117	0.91750	0.00044	0.67159	0.32797	0.00000	0.99956
23	0.00107	0.47969	0.51924	0.03278	0.96615	0.00035	0.74194	0.25771	0.00942	0.99023
24	0.00156	0.43448	0.56396	0.02487	0.97356	0.00050	0.60185	0.39764	0.01880	0.98070
25	0.00127	0.38693	0.61181	0.01853	0.98020	0.00042	0.60982	0.38976	0.03201	0.96757
26	0.00106	0.36475	0.63419	0.01263	0.98631	0.00034	0.56684	0.43282	0.03933	0.96034
27	0.00089	0.40682	0.59228	0.01104	0.98806	0.00032	0.57129	0.42839	0.04743	0.95225
28	0.00100	0.44632	0.55267	0.00986	0.98913	0.00059	0.62105	0.37836	0.05248	0.94693
29	0.00038	0.43586	0.56376	0.00980	0.98982	0.00045	0.68098	0.31856	0.05825	0.94130
30	0.00041	0.41411	0.58547	0.01013	0.98945	0.00051	0.70195	0.29754	0.06596	0.93353
31	0.00039	0.39989	0.59972	0.01028	0.98933	0.00063	0.71572	0.28365	0.06328	0.93608
32	0.00042	0.36636	0.63321	0.01072	0.98886	0.00066	0.73140	0.26794	0.06262	0.93673
33	0.00041	0.34946	0.65013	0.01165	0.98794	0.00055	0.74756	0.25189	0.06224	0.93721
34	0.00051	0.38247	0.61701	0.01108	0.98840	0.00049	0.77921	0.22030	0.05888	0.94064
35	0.00074	0.41579	0.58347	0.01056	0.98870	0.00060	0.79855	0.20084	0.05471	0.94469
36	0.00088	0.46974	0.52938	0.01108	0.98803	0.00066	0.79315	0.20619	0.05351	0.94583
37	0.00102	0.48993	0.50905	0.01050	0.98848	0.00073	0.78554	0.21373	0.05011	0.94916
38	0.00121	0.50904	0.48975	0.00922	0.98957	0.00071	0.78952	0.20977	0.04262	0.95667
39	0.00120	0.53056	0.46823	0.00876	0.99004	0.00087	0.78499	0.21414	0.03691	0.96222
40	0.00126	0.54167	0.45707	0.00868	0.99006	0.00094	0.78423	0.21483	0.03316	0.96590
41	0.00141	0.55569	0.44289	0.00779	0.99080	0.00097	0.79165	0.20738	0.02916	0.96986
42	0.00148	0.57337	0.42515	0.00835	0.99017	0.00104	0.78165	0.21731	0.02766	0.97130
43	0.00165	0.58504	0.41331	0.00950	0.98886	0.00093	0.77060	0.22848	0.02780	0.97127
44	0.00185	0.60600	0.39216	0.00922	0.98894	0.00099	0.77318	0.22583	0.02609	0.97292
45	0.00196	0.65626	0.34178	0.00920	0.98884	0.00102	0.77215	0.22682	0.02531	0.97367
46	0.00204	0.70154	0.29642	0.00970	0.98827	0.00100	0.76971	0.22929	0.02667	0.97233
47	0.00224	0.74645	0.25131	0.00990	0.98786	0.00117	0.78223	0.21661	0.02802	0.97081
48	0.00231	0.73521	0.26248	0.01125	0.98644	0.00134	0.79337	0.20529	0.02882	0.96984
49	0.00263	0.72695	0.27042	0.01369	0.98368	0.00141	0.79208	0.20651	0.03092	0.96767
50	0.00269	0.74895	0.24836	0.01602	0.98129	0.00149	0.78461	0.21390	0.03292	0.96559
51	0.00296	0.75594	0.24109	0.01792	0.97912	0.00168	0.79365	0.20467	0.03273	0.96559
52	0.00320	0.76545	0.23135	0.01914	0.97765	0.00186	0.80721	0.19092	0.03466	0.96348
53	0.00342	0.79731	0.19927	0.02053	0.97605	0.00210	0.80839	0.18951	0.03992	0.95798
54	0.00358	0.81862	0.17780	0.02372	0.97270	0.00214	0.81167	0.18620	0.04630	0.95156
55	0.00418	0.82133	0.17450	0.02856	0.96726	0.00245	0.82994	0.16761	0.05525	0.94230
56	0.00463	0.83405	0.16132	0.03512	0.96026	0.00287	0.84371	0.15342	0.06543	0.93171
57	0.00495	0.84194	0.15311	0.04278	0.95227	0.00299	0.84414	0.15287	0.07037	0.92664
58	0.00535	0.84490	0.14975	0.04966	0.94498	0.00333	0.85302	0.14365	0.07458	0.92209
59	0.00591	0.85862	0.13547	0.05598	0.93811	0.00424	0.86662	0.12914	0.08637	0.90939
60	0.00604	0.87045	0.12351	0.06377	0.93019	0.00467	0.87977	0.11556	0.10224	0.89309
61	0.00680	0.87662	0.11658	0.07384	0.91936	0.00532	0.89101	0.10367	0.11590	0.87879
62	0.00719	0.88570	0.10711	0.08626	0.90655	0.00606	0.90535	0.08859	0.13786	0.85609
63	0.00801	0.89490	0.09709	0.10125	0.89075	0.00659	0.91813	0.07529	0.16691	0.82651
64	0.00887	0.89843	0.09270	0.11721	0.87392	0.00642	0.92664	0.06694	0.17853	0.81505
65	0.01019	0.90356	0.08626	0.13312	0.85669	0.00711	0.93579	0.05710	0.17324	0.81965
66	0.01098	0.91266	0.07636	0.14959	0.83943	0.00727	0.94003	0.05271	0.17295	0.81979
67	0.01274	0.91579	0.07147	0.16424	0.82302	0.00812	0.94150	0.05039	0.17865	0.81323
68	0.01436	0.91813	0.06751	0.17124	0.81441	0.00860	0.94920	0.04220	0.17946	0.81194
69	0.01575	0.92253	0.06172	0.17491	0.80934	0.01006	0.95696	0.03298	0.18694	0.80300
70	0.01708	0.92484	0.05808	0.17395	0.80898	0.01046	0.96024	0.02929	0.20461	0.78493
71	0.01903	0.92482	0.05616	0.18034	0.80064	0.01107	0.96488	0.02405	0.21983	0.76910
72	0.02074	0.92929	0.04997	0.19146	0.78780	0.01303	0.96210	0.02488	0.21816	0.76882
73	0.02292	0.93401	0.04307	0.20512	0.77196	0.01487	0.95738	0.02775	0.21129	0.77384
74	0.02562	0.93565	0.03873	0.23364	0.74074	0.01729	0.95896	0.02375	0.20837	0.77434
75	0.02822	0.93766	0.03412	0.25695	0.71484	0.02134	0.95551	0.02315	0.19905	0.77961
76	0.03124	0.93804	0.03072	0.24214	0.72662	0.02477	0.95048	0.02474	0.17685	0.79837
77	0.03450	0.93785	0.02765	0.23517	0.73033	0.02559	0.95699	0.01743	0.16325	0.81117
78	0.03902	0.93898	0.02199	0.26409	0.69689	0.02912	0.96064	0.01023	0.17343	0.79744
79	0.04388	0.93735	0.01877	0.26921	0.68691	0.03208	0.95546	0.01246	0.16265	0.80527
80	0.05042	0.93326	0.01632	0.26831	0.68127	0.03411	0.95770	0.00819	0.22622	0.73968

Mortality is from Table 1; mortality-adjusted, exact-age transition probabilities are from CPS microdata samples, July 1999 through June 2007

Table 3: Transition probabilities by sex, race, Hispanic origin, and education, July 1999 through June 2007, continued

Age	Black Males—All Education Levels					Black Females—All Education Levels				
	Living to Dead	Inactive to Inactive	Inactive to Active	Active to Inactive	Active to Active	Living to Dead	Inactive to Inactive	Inactive to Active	Active to Inactive	Active to Active
18	0.00144	0.69674	0.30182	0.40789	0.59067	0.00046	0.72838	0.27116	0.39168	0.60786
19	0.00163	0.65222	0.34616	0.31412	0.68425	0.00051	0.67724	0.32225	0.31283	0.68666
20	0.00182	0.62261	0.37558	0.23767	0.76051	0.00056	0.64935	0.35009	0.26013	0.73930
21	0.00200	0.61984	0.37815	0.19545	0.80255	0.00062	0.63673	0.36265	0.22617	0.77321
22	0.00215	0.63674	0.36112	0.17300	0.82485	0.00068	0.62627	0.37305	0.19735	0.80197
23	0.00225	0.66727	0.33048	0.15478	0.84298	0.00072	0.62581	0.37346	0.16762	0.83165
24	0.00231	0.68658	0.31111	0.12941	0.86828	0.00077	0.62388	0.37535	0.14281	0.85642
25	0.00237	0.66712	0.33051	0.10618	0.89146	0.00083	0.62788	0.37129	0.13001	0.86916
26	0.00242	0.63738	0.36020	0.09834	0.89924	0.00089	0.60128	0.39783	0.12154	0.87757
27	0.00246	0.62757	0.36997	0.09104	0.90649	0.00095	0.60524	0.39381	0.11322	0.88583
28	0.00249	0.65845	0.33906	0.07886	0.91865	0.00101	0.61725	0.38174	0.10133	0.89766
29	0.00250	0.68471	0.31279	0.06217	0.93533	0.00107	0.63508	0.36385	0.09331	0.90563
30	0.00251	0.68870	0.30879	0.05448	0.94301	0.00113	0.64669	0.35218	0.09117	0.90770
31	0.00253	0.67663	0.32084	0.05761	0.93986	0.00121	0.66885	0.32995	0.08766	0.91113
32	0.00257	0.68831	0.30912	0.05776	0.93967	0.00129	0.67719	0.32153	0.08481	0.91390
33	0.00264	0.70852	0.28884	0.05998	0.93738	0.00137	0.68308	0.31554	0.08003	0.91860
34	0.00274	0.71809	0.27917	0.06095	0.93631	0.00147	0.67766	0.32087	0.07783	0.92070
35	0.00286	0.73326	0.26388	0.05906	0.93808	0.00158	0.67405	0.32438	0.07632	0.92210
36	0.00301	0.73890	0.25809	0.05587	0.94112	0.00170	0.67479	0.32350	0.07401	0.92429
37	0.00320	0.72841	0.26839	0.05340	0.94340	0.00187	0.69186	0.30627	0.07416	0.92397
38	0.00341	0.72252	0.27407	0.05120	0.94538	0.00210	0.71792	0.27998	0.07392	0.92399
39	0.00366	0.73451	0.26183	0.04958	0.94676	0.00235	0.74190	0.25575	0.07043	0.92722
40	0.00391	0.76002	0.23608	0.05085	0.94524	0.00262	0.76443	0.23295	0.06830	0.92908
41	0.00419	0.78450	0.21131	0.05353	0.94228	0.00288	0.77572	0.22140	0.06873	0.92839
42	0.00456	0.80496	0.19048	0.05549	0.93995	0.00314	0.77664	0.22022	0.06807	0.92879
43	0.00504	0.81758	0.17738	0.05631	0.93865	0.00342	0.78804	0.20854	0.06850	0.92808
44	0.00563	0.82496	0.16942	0.05389	0.94048	0.00371	0.80696	0.18934	0.07111	0.92518
45	0.00627	0.81976	0.17397	0.05086	0.94288	0.00402	0.81949	0.17649	0.07359	0.92239
46	0.00693	0.81770	0.17536	0.05022	0.94285	0.00434	0.82772	0.16794	0.07364	0.92202
47	0.00764	0.81876	0.17359	0.05084	0.94152	0.00469	0.83577	0.15954	0.07413	0.92118
48	0.00839	0.81876	0.17284	0.05309	0.93852	0.00506	0.83624	0.15870	0.07554	0.91940
49	0.00919	0.82745	0.16336	0.05804	0.93277	0.00545	0.83244	0.16211	0.07421	0.92034
50	0.01006	0.84227	0.14767	0.06178	0.92815	0.00587	0.83409	0.16004	0.07142	0.92271
51	0.01100	0.85623	0.13276	0.06397	0.92502	0.00633	0.84201	0.15167	0.07185	0.92182
52	0.01193	0.86540	0.12267	0.06841	0.91966	0.00678	0.84712	0.14610	0.07447	0.91874
53	0.01281	0.86684	0.12036	0.07194	0.91525	0.00724	0.85618	0.13658	0.07799	0.91478
54	0.01365	0.86601	0.12034	0.07486	0.91150	0.00770	0.86633	0.12597	0.08455	0.90775
55	0.01454	0.86698	0.11849	0.07991	0.90555	0.00820	0.87562	0.11618	0.09468	0.89712
56	0.01553	0.86490	0.11957	0.08406	0.90041	0.00877	0.88937	0.10186	0.10215	0.88907
57	0.01661	0.87211	0.11128	0.09153	0.89186	0.00940	0.90244	0.08815	0.10656	0.88403
58	0.01778	0.88605	0.09616	0.09840	0.88381	0.01011	0.90963	0.08026	0.11755	0.87235
59	0.01907	0.89721	0.08372	0.10875	0.87218	0.01089	0.91667	0.07244	0.14261	0.84650
60	0.02050	0.90348	0.07602	0.12921	0.85029	0.01177	0.92281	0.06543	0.17875	0.82505
61	0.02206	0.90863	0.06931	0.14812	0.82983	0.01274	0.92535	0.06191	0.20651	0.80851
62	0.02368	0.91124	0.06508	0.16549	0.81082	0.01376	0.92916	0.05708	0.22286	0.77973
63	0.02528	0.91316	0.06155	0.19074	0.78398	0.01479	0.93468	0.05053	0.22983	0.76235
64	0.02684	0.91122	0.06194	0.21422	0.75895	0.01583	0.93887	0.04530	0.24731	0.75434
65	0.02838	0.90925	0.06237	0.22840	0.74322	0.01691	0.93812	0.04496	0.24652	0.73578
66	0.03002	0.91434	0.05564	0.21941	0.75058	0.01809	0.93964	0.04228	0.25957	0.73539
67	0.03183	0.91542	0.05275	0.23097	0.73720	0.01940	0.94021	0.04039	0.27895	0.72103
68	0.03396	0.91593	0.05011	0.24703	0.71901	0.02089	0.94196	0.03715	0.28690	0.70016
69	0.03641	0.91629	0.04730	0.26385	0.69974	0.02258	0.94340	0.03402	0.30602	0.69052
70	0.03900	0.91867	0.04233	0.27612	0.68488	0.02437	0.94408	0.03155	0.31842	0.66961
71	0.04170	0.92312	0.03518	0.28189	0.67641	0.02627	0.94499	0.02873	0.32630	0.65531
72	0.04479	0.92510	0.03011	0.27944	0.67577	0.02845	0.94705	0.02450	0.33777	0.64525
73	0.04838	0.92463	0.02699	0.28574	0.66587	0.03096	0.94786	0.02118	0.34455	0.63127
74	0.05243	0.92442	0.02315	0.30208	0.64549	0.03376	0.94708	0.01917	0.36371	0.62170
75	0.05686	0.92246	0.02068	0.31169	0.63146	0.03669	0.94739	0.01592	0.36371	0.59960
76	0.06146	0.92091	0.01763	0.30496	0.63358	0.03972	0.94870	0.01158	0.35588	0.60439
77	0.06608	0.91903	0.01490	0.29428	0.63964	0.04298	0.94808	0.00894	0.35584	0.60118
78	0.07053	0.91513	0.01435	0.24488	0.68460	0.04655	0.94696	0.00649	0.37135	0.58211
79	0.07485	0.91189	0.01326	0.27346	0.65169	0.05047	0.94384	0.00569	0.37414	0.57540
80	0.07937	0.90914	0.01149	0.30363	0.61700	0.05476	0.94044	0.00480	0.34893	0.59631

Mortality is from Table 1; mortality-adjusted, exact-age transition probabilities are from CPS microdata samples, July 1999 through June 2007

Table 3: Transition probabilities by sex, race, Hispanic origin, and education, July 1999 through June 2007, continued

Age	Black Males—Less than High School					Black Females—Less than High School				
	Living to Dead	Inactive to Inactive	Inactive to Active	Active to Inactive	Active to Active	Living to Dead	Inactive to Inactive	Inactive to Active	Active to Inactive	Active to Active
18	0.00144	0.70883	0.28973	0.48470	0.51385	0.00046	0.74962	0.24993	0.49820	0.50134
19	0.00163	0.69970	0.29867	0.41003	0.58834	0.00051	0.70799	0.29150	0.41229	0.58720
20	0.00182	0.70370	0.29449	0.33745	0.66073	0.00056	0.70898	0.29046	0.33633	0.66311
21	0.00200	0.71279	0.28521	0.25232	0.74567	0.00062	0.72386	0.27552	0.27679	0.72259
22	0.00215	0.71490	0.28296	0.19166	0.80619	0.00068	0.70837	0.29095	0.24195	0.75737
23	0.00180	0.72832	0.26988	0.16740	0.83080	0.00149	0.72534	0.27317	0.19967	0.79884
24	0.00219	0.74096	0.25685	0.19390	0.80391	0.00199	0.77213	0.22588	0.15605	0.84196
25	0.00291	0.71935	0.27774	0.23091	0.76618	0.00236	0.80936	0.18828	0.14554	0.85210
26	0.00273	0.68364	0.31363	0.21191	0.78536	0.00235	0.74046	0.25719	0.16303	0.83461
27	0.00324	0.64582	0.35094	0.17158	0.82518	0.00243	0.68947	0.30810	0.18592	0.81165
28	0.00415	0.68449	0.31135	0.14191	0.85394	0.00193	0.69773	0.30034	0.20256	0.79551
29	0.00382	0.71439	0.28179	0.13141	0.86476	0.00174	0.72526	0.27299	0.21216	0.78610
30	0.00331	0.69185	0.30484	0.09999	0.89670	0.00130	0.73049	0.26821	0.22100	0.77770
31	0.00375	0.73154	0.26471	0.08699	0.90926	0.00184	0.76690	0.23125	0.19249	0.80567
32	0.00334	0.74952	0.24714	0.06821	0.92845	0.00227	0.75768	0.24006	0.17418	0.82356
33	0.00328	0.78167	0.21505	0.07151	0.92521	0.00209	0.76364	0.23427	0.16576	0.83214
34	0.00352	0.85612	0.14036	0.09779	0.89870	0.00202	0.76764	0.23035	0.15924	0.83875
35	0.00383	0.87812	0.11805	0.10742	0.88875	0.00250	0.77293	0.22457	0.14973	0.84777
36	0.00437	0.87953	0.11610	0.11000	0.88563	0.00256	0.78063	0.21681	0.15591	0.84153
37	0.00496	0.88621	0.10883	0.12065	0.87439	0.00271	0.80598	0.19132	0.17138	0.82591
38	0.00542	0.87673	0.11784	0.11587	0.87871	0.00286	0.84072	0.15642	0.16519	0.83195
39	0.00579	0.85179	0.14242	0.10687	0.88734	0.00327	0.86702	0.12970	0.15228	0.84444
40	0.00562	0.85848	0.13590	0.11098	0.88340	0.00396	0.87693	0.11911	0.15493	0.84112
41	0.00585	0.87292	0.12123	0.11472	0.87943	0.00427	0.86977	0.12596	0.16345	0.83228
42	0.00646	0.87634	0.11720	0.10721	0.88633	0.00435	0.85807	0.13759	0.16542	0.83024
43	0.00709	0.88749	0.10542	0.10249	0.89042	0.00509	0.85924	0.13567	0.15368	0.84124
44	0.00800	0.90803	0.08398	0.09317	0.89884	0.00525	0.86887	0.12588	0.15098	0.84377
45	0.00962	0.90856	0.08182	0.08336	0.90703	0.00541	0.87001	0.12458	0.15886	0.83573
46	0.01010	0.89608	0.09382	0.07686	0.91305	0.00594	0.87243	0.12163	0.14602	0.84804
47	0.01083	0.88982	0.09934	0.08152	0.90765	0.00682	0.87928	0.11390	0.12564	0.86754
48	0.01169	0.87803	0.11027	0.09605	0.89225	0.00672	0.87450	0.11878	0.14088	0.85241
49	0.01287	0.87008	0.11705	0.10099	0.88614	0.00737	0.87306	0.11957	0.15893	0.83370
50	0.01365	0.87615	0.11019	0.10165	0.88470	0.00790	0.88847	0.10363	0.16024	0.83186
51	0.01451	0.88303	0.10245	0.10411	0.88137	0.00823	0.90112	0.09066	0.15544	0.83633
52	0.01486	0.87805	0.10709	0.10085	0.88429	0.00888	0.89854	0.09258	0.16015	0.83097
53	0.01537	0.87975	0.10488	0.09248	0.89215	0.00932	0.90427	0.08641	0.15867	0.83200
54	0.01600	0.88564	0.09836	0.09290	0.89110	0.00100	0.91018	0.07982	0.13676	0.85325
55	0.01681	0.89150	0.09168	0.09788	0.88531	0.01048	0.90514	0.08437	0.13410	0.85542
56	0.01800	0.89876	0.08324	0.10394	0.87806	0.01134	0.91074	0.07793	0.14652	0.84215
57	0.01938	0.91762	0.06300	0.11522	0.86540	0.01162	0.92925	0.05913	0.15074	0.83764
58	0.02048	0.93338	0.04614	0.11798	0.86155	0.01246	0.94384	0.04370	0.15822	0.82932
59	0.02170	0.93951	0.03879	0.12518	0.85312	0.01328	0.94944	0.03727	0.19598	0.79074
60	0.02324	0.93298	0.04378	0.14750	0.82925	0.01417	0.94917	0.03667	0.21474	0.77110
61	0.02522	0.92682	0.04796	0.15558	0.81920	0.01509	0.95057	0.03434	0.21515	0.76976
62	0.02722	0.92719	0.04559	0.16632	0.80647	0.01661	0.95002	0.03337	0.22815	0.75524
63	0.02833	0.92655	0.04512	0.20682	0.76486	0.01734	0.94622	0.03644	0.22066	0.76200
64	0.02992	0.92443	0.04565	0.22696	0.74312	0.01818	0.94707	0.03475	0.19315	0.78867
65	0.03066	0.93042	0.03891	0.21443	0.75491	0.01906	0.95079	0.03015	0.19145	0.78949
66	0.03192	0.92690	0.04119	0.22993	0.73815	0.02007	0.94864	0.03129	0.24239	0.73753
67	0.03349	0.93076	0.03575	0.23709	0.72941	0.02082	0.94967	0.02952	0.24333	0.73585
68	0.03567	0.93238	0.03195	0.25317	0.71117	0.02290	0.95037	0.02673	0.25900	0.71810
69	0.03796	0.92957	0.03247	0.26627	0.69577	0.02445	0.95211	0.02344	0.27016	0.70538
70	0.04059	0.92937	0.03003	0.26700	0.69240	0.02644	0.95327	0.02029	0.30354	0.67001
71	0.04326	0.93029	0.02645	0.27891	0.67783	0.02840	0.95260	0.01900	0.33845	0.63315
72	0.04633	0.92904	0.02464	0.30731	0.64636	0.03058	0.95204	0.01738	0.36571	0.60370
73	0.05002	0.92648	0.02350	0.32485	0.62513	0.03258	0.95151	0.01590	0.34945	0.61797
74	0.05343	0.92575	0.02082	0.32697	0.61960	0.03525	0.95048	0.01427	0.33290	0.63184
75	0.05865	0.92344	0.01790	0.33889	0.60246	0.03797	0.95092	0.01111	0.39407	0.56796
76	0.06289	0.92132	0.01580	0.34464	0.59247	0.04010	0.95193	0.00797	0.39472	0.56519
77	0.06706	0.91835	0.01459	0.35189	0.58104	0.04388	0.94910	0.00702	0.37422	0.58190
78	0.07168	0.91444	0.01387	0.33738	0.59094	0.04760	0.94563	0.00678	0.36893	0.58347
79	0.07679	0.91061	0.01261	0.39250	0.53071	0.05122	0.94313	0.00565	0.34658	0.60220
80	0.08130	0.90829	0.01041	0.43688	0.48182	0.05594	0.93908	0.00498	0.36395	0.58012

Mortality is from Table 1; mortality-adjusted, exact-age transition probabilities are from CPS microdata samples, July 1999 through June 2007

Table 3: Transition probabilities by sex, race, Hispanic origin, and education, July 1999 through June 2007, continued

Age	Black Males—High School Degree / GED					Black Females—High School Degree / GED				
	Living to Dead	Inactive to Inactive	Inactive to Active	Active to Inactive	Active to Active	Living to Dead	Inactive to Inactive	Inactive to Active	Active to Inactive	Active to Active
18	0.00144	0.64363	0.35493	0.35707	0.64148	0.00046	0.63796	0.36158	0.30205	0.69749
19	0.00163	0.53742	0.46095	0.28995	0.70842	0.00051	0.55958	0.43991	0.25586	0.74363
20	0.00182	0.48052	0.51766	0.21777	0.78041	0.00056	0.54945	0.44999	0.22486	0.77458
21	0.00200	0.49933	0.49867	0.17048	0.82752	0.00062	0.56182	0.43756	0.20118	0.79820
22	0.00215	0.56237	0.43549	0.14398	0.85387	0.00068	0.60267	0.39665	0.17308	0.82624
23	0.00230	0.62624	0.37146	0.13854	0.85916	0.00096	0.64456	0.35448	0.15272	0.84632
24	0.00224	0.67901	0.31875	0.12960	0.86815	0.00087	0.63604	0.36310	0.15345	0.84568
25	0.00263	0.68500	0.31237	0.11490	0.88247	0.00085	0.59794	0.40121	0.17072	0.82843
26	0.00260	0.66704	0.33036	0.12041	0.87699	0.00091	0.54884	0.45025	0.16377	0.83532
27	0.00266	0.66251	0.33483	0.11198	0.88536	0.00100	0.59847	0.40053	0.13744	0.86155
28	0.00262	0.70188	0.29550	0.08890	0.90848	0.00077	0.65708	0.34216	0.11445	0.88478
29	0.00279	0.73982	0.25739	0.06032	0.93689	0.00110	0.66031	0.33859	0.11597	0.88292
30	0.00251	0.76323	0.23426	0.05368	0.94382	0.00132	0.63748	0.36120	0.12078	0.87790
31	0.00254	0.73632	0.26114	0.05886	0.93860	0.00136	0.67431	0.32434	0.11070	0.88794
32	0.00251	0.73717	0.26032	0.06496	0.93252	0.00142	0.69148	0.30711	0.10643	0.89215
33	0.00246	0.73824	0.25931	0.06847	0.92908	0.00144	0.71027	0.28829	0.09391	0.90464
34	0.00267	0.69953	0.29780	0.07085	0.92648	0.00145	0.71410	0.28445	0.09084	0.90771
35	0.00259	0.68871	0.30870	0.07056	0.92686	0.00142	0.71137	0.28721	0.09219	0.90639
36	0.00284	0.69249	0.30467	0.06905	0.92811	0.00159	0.70433	0.29408	0.08409	0.91431
37	0.00312	0.66815	0.32873	0.06778	0.92910	0.00172	0.70399	0.29429	0.07958	0.91870
38	0.00350	0.66816	0.32834	0.06427	0.93223	0.00202	0.71939	0.27859	0.07878	0.91920
39	0.00358	0.71050	0.28593	0.05964	0.93678	0.00219	0.74175	0.25607	0.07073	0.92708
40	0.00419	0.75157	0.24424	0.05928	0.93653	0.00251	0.75694	0.24055	0.06772	0.92977
41	0.00438	0.77384	0.22178	0.06306	0.93256	0.00298	0.75925	0.23778	0.07224	0.92479
42	0.00454	0.80002	0.19545	0.06740	0.92806	0.00337	0.76171	0.23493	0.07428	0.92236
43	0.00462	0.82057	0.17481	0.06900	0.92638	0.00354	0.77686	0.21959	0.08182	0.91463
44	0.00500	0.82166	0.17334	0.06564	0.92936	0.00409	0.79890	0.19701	0.08731	0.90861
45	0.00516	0.81180	0.18304	0.06132	0.93352	0.00445	0.82162	0.17393	0.08589	0.90966
46	0.00559	0.81173	0.18268	0.05725	0.93716	0.00450	0.83799	0.15751	0.08548	0.91002
47	0.00639	0.81881	0.17480	0.05210	0.94151	0.00472	0.85016	0.14512	0.08397	0.91131
48	0.00722	0.82163	0.17115	0.05318	0.93960	0.00516	0.86138	0.13345	0.07788	0.91696
49	0.00809	0.82160	0.17030	0.05706	0.93485	0.00524	0.86432	0.13044	0.07249	0.92227
50	0.00878	0.83180	0.15942	0.06074	0.93048	0.00583	0.85705	0.13712	0.06756	0.92660
51	0.01044	0.85335	0.13621	0.06555	0.92402	0.00622	0.86372	0.13006	0.06540	0.92838
52	0.01175	0.86822	0.12004	0.06993	0.91832	0.00645	0.86903	0.12452	0.06948	0.92407
53	0.01265	0.86599	0.12136	0.07230	0.91505	0.00678	0.86512	0.12810	0.07710	0.91612
54	0.01310	0.87277	0.11413	0.07612	0.91078	0.00701	0.86474	0.12825	0.09008	0.90291
55	0.01373	0.87908	0.10719	0.08439	0.90188	0.00706	0.87609	0.11685	0.10595	0.88699
56	0.01403	0.86970	0.11627	0.08840	0.89757	0.00722	0.89250	0.10028	0.11592	0.87686
57	0.01430	0.87247	0.11323	0.10304	0.88266	0.00770	0.90311	0.08919	0.12280	0.86949
58	0.01605	0.88465	0.09929	0.11631	0.86763	0.00824	0.90399	0.08777	0.13177	0.85999
59	0.01757	0.88829	0.09414	0.13127	0.85116	0.00848	0.90710	0.08443	0.14877	0.84276
60	0.01949	0.89057	0.08994	0.15037	0.83014	0.00943	0.91674	0.07383	0.16558	0.82499
61	0.02015	0.90340	0.07645	0.16728	0.81257	0.01048	0.91675	0.07277	0.18763	0.80189
62	0.02117	0.90259	0.07624	0.17628	0.80256	0.01114	0.91705	0.07181	0.22295	0.76590
63	0.02276	0.90228	0.07497	0.17676	0.80049	0.01232	0.92978	0.05790	0.24730	0.74037
64	0.02428	0.91375	0.06196	0.19692	0.77880	0.01409	0.93798	0.04793	0.26984	0.71607
65	0.02645	0.91572	0.05783	0.22284	0.75071	0.01558	0.93318	0.05123	0.30793	0.67648
66	0.02839	0.91817	0.05344	0.21463	0.75698	0.01631	0.93783	0.04585	0.27122	0.71246
67	0.02975	0.92108	0.04916	0.22706	0.74318	0.01815	0.93648	0.04536	0.28237	0.69948
68	0.03235	0.91881	0.04884	0.25260	0.71505	0.01878	0.93814	0.04308	0.29398	0.68724
69	0.03416	0.92155	0.04429	0.28188	0.68396	0.01942	0.94156	0.03902	0.29120	0.68937
70	0.03782	0.92509	0.03709	0.32130	0.64089	0.01996	0.94328	0.03676	0.29956	0.68047
71	0.04025	0.92626	0.03349	0.33375	0.62600	0.02242	0.94416	0.03342	0.29409	0.68349
72	0.04429	0.92677	0.02894	0.32181	0.63390	0.02458	0.94648	0.02894	0.26596	0.70946
73	0.04532	0.92903	0.02565	0.32661	0.62807	0.02820	0.94512	0.02667	0.27163	0.70016
74	0.05095	0.92700	0.02205	0.33917	0.60988	0.03227	0.94372	0.02401	0.27597	0.69177
75	0.05345	0.92879	0.01776	0.35012	0.59644	0.03578	0.94463	0.01959	0.27786	0.68637
76	0.05872	0.92770	0.01358	0.33109	0.61019	0.03981	0.94621	0.01399	0.29757	0.66262
77	0.06358	0.92862	0.00781	0.27533	0.66109	0.04250	0.94857	0.00893	0.32341	0.63409
78	0.06709	0.93246	0.00045	0.18414	0.74877	0.04485	0.94989	0.00526	0.31925	0.63590
79	0.07087	0.92913	0.00000	0.19024	0.73889	0.05182	0.94378	0.00441	0.26465	0.68353
80	0.07085	0.92915	0.00000	0.22032	0.70883	0.05735	0.94106	0.00160	0.20869	0.73396

Mortality is from Table 1; mortality-adjusted, exact-age transition probabilities are from CPS microdata samples, July 1999 through June 2007

Life and Worklife Expectancies, Second Edition

Table 3: Transition probabilities by sex, race, Hispanic origin, and education, July 1999 through June 2007, continued

	Black Males—Some College Education					Black Females—Some College Education				
Age	Living to Dead	Inactive to Inactive	Inactive to Active	Active to Inactive	Active to Active	Living to Dead	Inactive to Inactive	Inactive to Active	Active to Inactive	Active to Active
18	0.00144	0.70567	0.29288	0.26456	0.73400	0.00046	0.79780	0.20174	0.38802	0.61152
19	0.00163	0.69256	0.30582	0.22684	0.77153	0.00051	0.72994	0.26955	0.31423	0.68526
20	0.00182	0.67188	0.32630	0.20053	0.79765	0.00056	0.68644	0.31300	0.26976	0.72968
21	0.00200	0.65715	0.34085	0.20046	0.79754	0.00062	0.65030	0.34908	0.23759	0.76179
22	0.00215	0.66342	0.33443	0.19676	0.80110	0.00068	0.61102	0.38831	0.21242	0.78690
23	0.00275	0.66643	0.33082	0.16863	0.82862	0.00129	0.55272	0.44599	0.18679	0.81192
24	0.00237	0.63279	0.36484	0.11668	0.88096	0.00122	0.53163	0.46714	0.15542	0.84336
25	0.00195	0.54622	0.45183	0.08122	0.91683	0.00147	0.57564	0.42289	0.12579	0.87274
26	0.00151	0.49224	0.50625	0.07981	0.91867	0.00174	0.60038	0.39788	0.10728	0.89099
27	0.00123	0.50816	0.49061	0.08636	0.91240	0.00167	0.58915	0.40918	0.10218	0.89616
28	0.00042	0.58467	0.41491	0.08266	0.91692	0.00087	0.53091	0.46822	0.09546	0.90367
29	0.00056	0.64144	0.35800	0.06359	0.93585	0.00010	0.54092	0.45808	0.08582	0.91318
30	0.00102	0.62512	0.37386	0.04993	0.94905	0.00070	0.58921	0.41009	0.08421	0.91509
31	0.00166	0.58642	0.41192	0.06090	0.93744	0.00054	0.58961	0.40985	0.07962	0.91984
32	0.00202	0.59602	0.40196	0.05790	0.94008	0.00080	0.60327	0.39594	0.07849	0.92071
33	0.00231	0.62570	0.37198	0.05831	0.93937	0.00092	0.61768	0.38140	0.07647	0.92261
34	0.00268	0.67082	0.32650	0.05679	0.94054	0.00118	0.61541	0.38341	0.07122	0.92760
35	0.00261	0.71677	0.28062	0.05095	0.94644	0.00131	0.62161	0.37708	0.07016	0.92853
36	0.00243	0.69227	0.30531	0.04131	0.95626	0.00129	0.63492	0.36378	0.07197	0.92674
37	0.00254	0.66774	0.32972	0.03544	0.96202	0.00130	0.66175	0.33696	0.07131	0.92739
38	0.00252	0.63509	0.36239	0.03324	0.96423	0.00153	0.67737	0.32110	0.06961	0.92886
39	0.00283	0.61237	0.38481	0.03304	0.96413	0.00174	0.68087	0.31739	0.07028	0.92797
40	0.00318	0.62565	0.37117	0.03462	0.96220	0.00203	0.70132	0.29665	0.06889	0.92907
41	0.00338	0.67151	0.32511	0.03640	0.96022	0.00203	0.72890	0.26907	0.06572	0.93225
42	0.00365	0.71269	0.28365	0.04004	0.95631	0.00217	0.74397	0.25386	0.06322	0.93461
43	0.00430	0.74646	0.24924	0.04636	0.94934	0.00208	0.76407	0.23385	0.06200	0.93593
44	0.00505	0.77434	0.22061	0.04938	0.94557	0.00182	0.79072	0.20747	0.06483	0.93335
45	0.00583	0.78340	0.21077	0.04687	0.94731	0.00196	0.80343	0.19461	0.06668	0.93136
46	0.00694	0.80280	0.19026	0.04930	0.94376	0.00231	0.80018	0.19751	0.06837	0.92932
47	0.00775	0.80301	0.18924	0.05593	0.93631	0.00269	0.79995	0.19737	0.07429	0.92302
48	0.00840	0.79428	0.19732	0.05776	0.93383	0.00326	0.79310	0.20364	0.07642	0.92032
49	0.00824	0.81183	0.17994	0.06664	0.92513	0.00356	0.77673	0.21972	0.07204	0.92441
50	0.00874	0.83744	0.15383	0.07824	0.91302	0.00344	0.77691	0.21965	0.07250	0.92406
51	0.00807	0.85215	0.13978	0.08094	0.91099	0.00452	0.80142	0.19406	0.07930	0.91618
52	0.00792	0.86489	0.12720	0.08405	0.90803	0.00479	0.81881	0.17640	0.08051	0.91471
53	0.00923	0.86686	0.12390	0.08689	0.90387	0.00492	0.83718	0.15789	0.08655	0.90853
54	0.01089	0.85135	0.13775	0.08647	0.90264	0.00553	0.86634	0.12814	0.09589	0.89858
55	0.01215	0.83604	0.15181	0.08799	0.89985	0.00680	0.88647	0.10673	0.09833	0.89487
56	0.01493	0.81997	0.16510	0.08969	0.89537	0.00699	0.89643	0.09658	0.09993	0.89308
57	0.01711	0.82013	0.16276	0.08943	0.89346	0.00826	0.90473	0.08701	0.10129	0.89046
58	0.01595	0.84154	0.14251	0.09294	0.89111	0.00879	0.91124	0.07997	0.11172	0.87950
59	0.01528	0.86459	0.12013	0.09626	0.88846	0.00960	0.91719	0.07321	0.13359	0.85681
60	0.01515	0.88981	0.09504	0.10611	0.87875	0.01059	0.92342	0.06599	0.14821	0.84120
61	0.01615	0.90563	0.07822	0.13028	0.85357	0.01044	0.92675	0.06281	0.15748	0.83208
62	0.01507	0.91535	0.06958	0.17060	0.81434	0.00972	0.93400	0.05628	0.18905	0.80122
63	0.01843	0.91303	0.06855	0.21041	0.77116	0.01174	0.93803	0.05022	0.22266	0.76559
64	0.02114	0.88898	0.08988	0.22999	0.74886	0.01122	0.93942	0.04936	0.24818	0.74060
65	0.02499	0.86595	0.10906	0.24030	0.73471	0.01110	0.93675	0.05215	0.25026	0.73864
66	0.02730	0.89251	0.08020	0.21204	0.76066	0.01337	0.94496	0.04167	0.22724	0.75939
67	0.03129	0.88431	0.08440	0.22498	0.74373	0.01564	0.94445	0.03991	0.25830	0.72606
68	0.03263	0.88136	0.08601	0.22598	0.74140	0.01486	0.94852	0.03662	0.29263	0.69251
69	0.03673	0.88079	0.08248	0.20756	0.75570	0.01941	0.94362	0.03696	0.30448	0.67611
70	0.04089	0.88342	0.07569	0.18261	0.77650	0.02166	0.94188	0.03646	0.30337	0.67497
71	0.04477	0.90508	0.05015	0.17655	0.77868	0.02246	0.94700	0.03054	0.28981	0.68773
72	0.04448	0.92292	0.03260	0.15951	0.79601	0.02407	0.95133	0.02460	0.31996	0.65596
73	0.04950	0.92414	0.02637	0.17363	0.77687	0.02488	0.95368	0.02144	0.38091	0.59421
74	0.06015	0.91761	0.02224	0.19018	0.74966	0.02351	0.95326	0.02324	0.41653	0.55997
75	0.05951	0.90945	0.03104	0.18187	0.75862	0.02734	0.94778	0.02488	0.40390	0.56876
76	0.06170	0.91184	0.02646	0.21127	0.72703	0.03218	0.94504	0.02278	0.35547	0.61235
77	0.07534	0.90942	0.01524	0.23908	0.68558	0.03320	0.94402	0.02277	0.35492	0.61187
78	0.08136	0.89864	0.02000	0.26553	0.65311	0.04084	0.94616	0.01301	0.35011	0.60906
79	0.06892	0.90604	0.02504	0.36292	0.56816	0.04422	0.94226	0.01353	0.45258	0.50320
80	0.07616	0.89837	0.02547	0.42588	0.49796	0.04216	0.94211	0.01573	0.24986	0.70797

Mortality is from Table 1; mortality-adjusted, exact-age transition probabilities are from CPS microdata samples, July 1999 through June 2007

Table 3: Transition probabilities by sex, race, Hispanic origin, and education, July 1999 through June 2007, continued

Age	Black Males—Bachelor's and Graduate Degrees					Black Females—Bachelor's and Graduate Degrees				
	Living to Dead	Inactive to Inactive	Inactive to Active	Active to Inactive	Active to Active	Living to Dead	Inactive to Inactive	Inactive to Active	Active to Inactive	Active to Active
18										
19										
20										
21	0.00200	0.72873	0.26927	0.13974	0.85826	0.00062	0.62481	0.37457	0.05087	0.94851
22	0.00215	0.76076	0.23710	0.09828	0.89957	0.00068	0.48728	0.51205	0.09556	0.90376
23	0.00180	0.76962	0.22858	0.07202	0.92618	0.00204	0.55824	0.43972	0.12228	0.87568
24	0.00139	0.78251	0.21611	0.05655	0.94207	0.00202	0.53256	0.46542	0.08822	0.90976
25	0.00095	0.75448	0.24457	0.04934	0.94971	0.00199	0.46615	0.53186	0.06290	0.93511
26	0.00048	0.69688	0.30263	0.04780	0.95171	0.00196	0.41390	0.58413	0.06394	0.93409
27	0.00000	0.73432	0.26568	0.02636	0.97364	0.00207	0.39197	0.60596	0.06916	0.92878
28	0.00045	0.59114	0.40841	0.03177	0.96778	0.00017	0.47842	0.52142	0.06353	0.93631
29	0.00098	0.45403	0.54499	0.03938	0.95964	0.00062	0.59830	0.40108	0.04972	0.94966
30	0.00098	0.46502	0.53400	0.04800	0.95102	0.00082	0.68130	0.31788	0.04226	0.95692
31	0.00137	0.41006	0.58857	0.04021	0.95842	0.00097	0.64118	0.35785	0.05017	0.94886
32	0.00153	0.41736	0.58112	0.04020	0.95828	0.00082	0.62095	0.37823	0.04893	0.95026
33	0.00130	0.48586	0.51284	0.04145	0.95725	0.00112	0.54815	0.45073	0.04884	0.95004
34	0.00129	0.50137	0.49734	0.03502	0.96369	0.00066	0.49914	0.50020	0.04783	0.95151
35	0.00168	0.53151	0.46681	0.03318	0.96514	0.00065	0.47429	0.52506	0.04161	0.95774
36	0.00151	0.57819	0.42029	0.03302	0.96547	0.00080	0.47759	0.52161	0.03919	0.96002
37	0.00152	0.66547	0.33300	0.02620	0.97227	0.00094	0.51362	0.48543	0.04201	0.95705
38	0.00174	0.67588	0.32238	0.02627	0.97199	0.00078	0.57916	0.42007	0.04483	0.95439
39	0.00161	0.69723	0.30116	0.02948	0.96890	0.00083	0.62891	0.37025	0.04648	0.95269
40	0.00174	0.73782	0.26044	0.03024	0.96802	0.00105	0.66686	0.33209	0.04335	0.95560
41	0.00216	0.80091	0.19693	0.03089	0.96695	0.00098	0.69992	0.29910	0.03755	0.96147
42	0.00250	0.75166	0.24584	0.03128	0.96622	0.00190	0.69113	0.30697	0.03356	0.96454
43	0.00332	0.67592	0.32077	0.02614	0.97054	0.00191	0.68849	0.30960	0.02983	0.96826
44	0.00355	0.61805	0.37841	0.02085	0.97560	0.00239	0.70451	0.29310	0.02906	0.96855
45	0.00368	0.58745	0.40887	0.02282	0.97350	0.00254	0.71681	0.28065	0.03454	0.96292
46	0.00434	0.58168	0.41398	0.02774	0.96792	0.00301	0.74255	0.25444	0.03760	0.95939
47	0.00433	0.60386	0.39181	0.02894	0.96674	0.00229	0.75111	0.24660	0.04052	0.95719
48	0.00400	0.66045	0.33555	0.02698	0.96902	0.00272	0.73892	0.25836	0.04537	0.95191
49	0.00454	0.74698	0.24847	0.02853	0.96693	0.00322	0.73468	0.26210	0.04609	0.95070
50	0.00600	0.79889	0.19510	0.02395	0.97005	0.00308	0.73368	0.26324	0.04142	0.95550
51	0.00643	0.79825	0.19532	0.02031	0.97326	0.00279	0.69074	0.30647	0.03954	0.95767
52	0.00870	0.82037	0.17093	0.02966	0.96164	0.00290	0.67609	0.32101	0.03984	0.95727
53	0.00895	0.83774	0.15331	0.04233	0.94872	0.00373	0.72823	0.26804	0.03669	0.95958
54	0.00970	0.81711	0.17318	0.04868	0.94162	0.00329	0.73824	0.25847	0.04214	0.95457
55	0.01034	0.81537	0.17428	0.05135	0.93831	0.00397	0.74140	0.25464	0.05689	0.93914
56	0.01005	0.83138	0.15857	0.05488	0.93507	0.00464	0.75997	0.23539	0.06353	0.93182
57	0.01027	0.81537	0.17436	0.05574	0.93400	0.00577	0.78656	0.20767	0.06662	0.92761
58	0.01143	0.80436	0.18420	0.05687	0.93170	0.00593	0.79889	0.19518	0.08084	0.91323
59	0.01365	0.82796	0.15840	0.06712	0.91924	0.00719	0.82851	0.16430	0.11238	0.88043
60	0.01331	0.84905	0.13764	0.09793	0.88876	0.00682	0.85204	0.14114	0.14585	0.84733
61	0.01433	0.85217	0.13349	0.12718	0.85849	0.00802	0.88274	0.10924	0.16475	0.82723
62	0.01689	0.88353	0.09958	0.14252	0.84058	0.00856	0.91455	0.07689	0.18448	0.80696
63	0.01857	0.91653	0.06491	0.16935	0.81209	0.00929	0.91913	0.07158	0.18729	0.80342
64	0.01688	0.91310	0.07003	0.21334	0.76978	0.00966	0.92532	0.06502	0.17597	0.81437
65	0.01938	0.90521	0.07542	0.25276	0.72786	0.01167	0.92391	0.06442	0.18824	0.80009
66	0.02049	0.90389	0.07561	0.22245	0.75706	0.01334	0.91688	0.06977	0.22813	0.75852
67	0.02108	0.89968	0.07924	0.23638	0.74254	0.01527	0.92128	0.06345	0.23807	0.74666
68	0.02165	0.90660	0.07174	0.25067	0.72767	0.01585	0.92711	0.05705	0.26488	0.71928
69	0.02410	0.90981	0.06608	0.28516	0.69074	0.01802	0.92818	0.05380	0.28728	0.69470
70	0.02175	0.91366	0.06460	0.30718	0.67108	0.02105	0.92650	0.05244	0.32964	0.64931
71	0.02380	0.91531	0.06089	0.29724	0.67897	0.01996	0.92833	0.05171	0.36883	0.61120
72	0.02497	0.91589	0.05914	0.26436	0.71067	0.02145	0.93719	0.04136	0.38394	0.59461
73	0.03211	0.91571	0.05219	0.24101	0.72688	0.02610	0.94660	0.02729	0.39066	0.58323
74	0.03397	0.92360	0.04243	0.27631	0.68972	0.02865	0.94947	0.02188	0.40097	0.57038
75	0.03945	0.92768	0.03287	0.29454	0.66601	0.03186	0.95167	0.01647	0.40850	0.55964
76	0.04864	0.92223	0.02914	0.27139	0.67997	0.04244	0.94896	0.00860	0.37859	0.57897
77	0.04965	0.91669	0.03366	0.24879	0.70155	0.04107	0.95707	0.00186	0.36996	0.58897
78	0.05114	0.90702	0.04185	0.13607	0.81279	0.04163	0.95837	0.00000	0.45802	0.50035
79	0.05986	0.90191	0.03823	0.15590	0.78424	0.04029	0.95971	0.00000	0.50165	0.45806
80	0.07056	0.89601	0.03343	0.18498	0.74446	0.04057	0.95943	0.00000	0.49023	0.46919

Mortality is from Table 1; mortality-adjusted, exact-age transition probabilities are from CPS microdata samples, July 1999 through June 2007

Table 3: Transition probabilities by sex, race, Hispanic origin, and education, July 1999 through June 2007, continued

Age	Hispanic Males—All Education Levels					Hispanic Females—All Education Levels				
	Living to Dead	Inactive to Inactive	Inactive to Active	Active to Inactive	Active to Active	Living to Dead	Inactive to Inactive	Inactive to Active	Active to Inactive	Active to Active
18	0.00121	0.61276	0.38603	0.17916	0.81963	0.00030	0.68953	0.31016	0.29222	0.70748
19	0.00133	0.60360	0.39507	0.14480	0.85387	0.00028	0.65776	0.34196	0.23848	0.76124
20	0.00128	0.58678	0.41194	0.12313	0.87559	0.00038	0.65168	0.34795	0.20046	0.79917
21	0.00127	0.55728	0.44145	0.10915	0.88958	0.00041	0.67057	0.32901	0.18369	0.81590
22	0.00122	0.51324	0.48554	0.09283	0.90595	0.00048	0.70822	0.29130	0.17106	0.82846
23	0.00114	0.50487	0.49400	0.07432	0.92454	0.00052	0.73283	0.26665	0.16408	0.83540
24	0.00125	0.53990	0.45885	0.05822	0.94053	0.00060	0.74760	0.25180	0.15414	0.84527
25	0.00141	0.55255	0.44604	0.04942	0.94916	0.00053	0.75737	0.24210	0.14929	0.85018
26	0.00140	0.53930	0.45930	0.04487	0.95373	0.00047	0.77246	0.22706	0.14403	0.85550
27	0.00142	0.52235	0.47624	0.04270	0.95589	0.00043	0.77940	0.22017	0.14498	0.85459
28	0.00142	0.52850	0.47008	0.03762	0.96095	0.00042	0.76764	0.23194	0.14851	0.85106
29	0.00139	0.54108	0.45754	0.03006	0.96855	0.00044	0.76335	0.23622	0.14372	0.85585
30	0.00136	0.56221	0.43644	0.02716	0.97148	0.00046	0.77039	0.22915	0.13836	0.86117
31	0.00142	0.60117	0.39741	0.03103	0.96754	0.00049	0.77915	0.22035	0.13331	0.86620
32	0.00130	0.60204	0.39667	0.03152	0.96718	0.00053	0.78559	0.21388	0.12684	0.87263
33	0.00135	0.59198	0.40667	0.03268	0.96597	0.00056	0.78338	0.21606	0.12713	0.87231
34	0.00138	0.56701	0.43162	0.03135	0.96727	0.00055	0.78133	0.21812	0.12290	0.87655
35	0.00144	0.54241	0.45615	0.02804	0.97052	0.00055	0.78052	0.21892	0.11394	0.88551
36	0.00152	0.53942	0.45906	0.02637	0.97211	0.00070	0.77691	0.22239	0.10928	0.89002
37	0.00189	0.56563	0.43248	0.02571	0.97239	0.00067	0.77700	0.22233	0.10855	0.89078
38	0.00214	0.60745	0.39041	0.02514	0.97272	0.00081	0.78379	0.21540	0.10325	0.89593
39	0.00237	0.65893	0.33870	0.02699	0.97065	0.00093	0.78856	0.21050	0.09557	0.90349
40	0.00247	0.68402	0.31351	0.03013	0.96740	0.00118	0.78591	0.21291	0.09362	0.90520
41	0.00279	0.68573	0.31147	0.02981	0.96740	0.00122	0.78187	0.21691	0.09154	0.90724
42	0.00299	0.70510	0.29192	0.02911	0.96791	0.00143	0.77831	0.22026	0.08435	0.91422
43	0.00324	0.72958	0.26718	0.02926	0.96751	0.00142	0.77067	0.22791	0.07879	0.91980
44	0.00364	0.73834	0.25801	0.02739	0.96896	0.00165	0.76333	0.23502	0.07863	0.91972
45	0.00410	0.75905	0.23684	0.02764	0.96826	0.00181	0.76882	0.22937	0.07841	0.91978
46	0.00449	0.78735	0.20816	0.03083	0.96467	0.00207	0.78171	0.21622	0.07714	0.92079
47	0.00457	0.77657	0.21886	0.03087	0.96456	0.00220	0.80165	0.19615	0.07919	0.91860
48	0.00459	0.76199	0.23341	0.03355	0.96185	0.00245	0.82723	0.17032	0.08711	0.91043
49	0.00478	0.76657	0.22865	0.03839	0.95682	0.00241	0.84717	0.15042	0.09625	0.90135
50	0.00523	0.77562	0.21916	0.04168	0.95309	0.00253	0.86205	0.13541	0.10253	0.89494
51	0.00545	0.78645	0.20810	0.04548	0.94907	0.00267	0.87254	0.12480	0.10853	0.88880
52	0.00595	0.80718	0.18688	0.05094	0.94311	0.00275	0.87294	0.12431	0.10996	0.88729
53	0.00636	0.82676	0.16688	0.05342	0.94022	0.00292	0.86971	0.12736	0.10478	0.89229
54	0.00674	0.84481	0.14845	0.05250	0.94077	0.00319	0.87190	0.12491	0.09974	0.89707
55	0.00704	0.86351	0.12946	0.05279	0.94017	0.00317	0.87556	0.12127	0.09926	0.89757
56	0.00717	0.87697	0.11586	0.05511	0.93772	0.00333	0.88057	0.11609	0.10156	0.89511
57	0.00749	0.89066	0.10185	0.06318	0.92933	0.00392	0.88733	0.10875	0.10800	0.88808
58	0.00766	0.89893	0.09341	0.07275	0.91959	0.00422	0.89225	0.10353	0.12094	0.87483
59	0.00772	0.89728	0.09500	0.08799	0.90429	0.00477	0.89896	0.09627	0.13982	0.85541
60	0.00819	0.89465	0.09716	0.11561	0.87620	0.00569	0.90613	0.08818	0.15717	0.83713
61	0.00900	0.89955	0.09145	0.14050	0.85051	0.00648	0.91524	0.07828	0.18064	0.81288
62	0.00978	0.91250	0.07771	0.16746	0.82276	0.00670	0.92662	0.06668	0.20810	0.78520
63	0.01110	0.92344	0.06546	0.19876	0.79014	0.00751	0.93739	0.05510	0.22696	0.76553
64	0.01211	0.92885	0.05905	0.21814	0.76976	0.00790	0.94893	0.04317	0.23045	0.76165
65	0.01275	0.93025	0.05700	0.22815	0.75910	0.00833	0.96015	0.03153	0.25310	0.73858
66	0.01317	0.92764	0.05918	0.24194	0.74489	0.00919	0.95730	0.03351	0.25302	0.73778
67	0.01460	0.92600	0.05940	0.24161	0.74378	0.01009	0.96154	0.02837	0.26639	0.72352
68	0.01616	0.92669	0.05715	0.21784	0.76600	0.01127	0.96392	0.02481	0.27284	0.71589
69	0.01827	0.92882	0.05290	0.19999	0.78174	0.01328	0.96499	0.02173	0.27286	0.71386
70	0.02077	0.93616	0.04307	0.18225	0.79699	0.01504	0.96568	0.01929	0.27739	0.70757
71	0.02363	0.94669	0.02968	0.19491	0.78146	0.01578	0.96687	0.01735	0.29720	0.68702
72	0.02542	0.95146	0.02313	0.23375	0.74083	0.01802	0.96504	0.01694	0.29461	0.68737
73	0.02684	0.95580	0.01736	0.25625	0.71690	0.01948	0.96442	0.01609	0.26478	0.71574
74	0.02911	0.96142	0.00947	0.25848	0.71241	0.02076	0.96620	0.01303	0.25731	0.72192
75	0.03187	0.96235	0.00578	0.25737	0.71076	0.02261	0.96715	0.01024	0.24516	0.73223
76	0.03551	0.95805	0.00644	0.22012	0.74437	0.02389	0.96878	0.00733	0.24650	0.72961
77	0.03938	0.95177	0.00885	0.19016	0.77045	0.02674	0.96806	0.00521	0.25649	0.71678
78	0.04554	0.94745	0.00701	0.23634	0.71813	0.02997	0.96754	0.00250	0.29326	0.67677
79	0.05173	0.94124	0.00703	0.28659	0.66167	0.03447	0.96334	0.00219	0.26796	0.69758
80	0.05810	0.93250	0.00940	0.34131	0.60059	0.03744	0.96000	0.00256	0.22514	0.73742

Mortality is from Table 1; mortality-adjusted, exact-age transition probabilities are from CPS microdata samples, July 1999 through June 2007

Table 3: Transition probabilities by sex, race, Hispanic origin, and education, July 1999 through June 2007, continued

Age	Hispanic Males—Less than High School					Hispanic Females—Less than High School				
	Living to Dead	Inactive to Inactive	Inactive to Active	Active to Inactive	Active to Active	Living to Dead	Inactive to Inactive	Inactive to Active	Active to Inactive	Active to Active
18	0.00121	0.60926	0.38953	0.21515	0.78364	0.00030	0.76992	0.22978	0.38610	0.61360
19	0.00133	0.54884	0.44983	0.15537	0.84330	0.00028	0.74855	0.25117	0.29140	0.70832
20	0.00128	0.52079	0.47792	0.11522	0.88349	0.00038	0.75608	0.24354	0.24163	0.75800
21	0.00127	0.50193	0.49680	0.09583	0.90290	0.00041	0.77135	0.22824	0.24847	0.75112
22	0.00122	0.46282	0.53596	0.08532	0.91346	0.00048	0.81367	0.18585	0.27306	0.72646
23	0.00086	0.44713	0.55201	0.07412	0.92502	0.00043	0.82540	0.17417	0.27825	0.72132
24	0.00111	0.43318	0.56571	0.05718	0.94171	0.00041	0.82364	0.17596	0.25376	0.74584
25	0.00180	0.41799	0.58021	0.04533	0.95287	0.00028	0.82529	0.17443	0.22654	0.77319
26	0.00192	0.38590	0.61219	0.03927	0.95882	0.00017	0.82360	0.17623	0.21933	0.78051
27	0.00188	0.46022	0.53791	0.03750	0.96063	0.00024	0.81266	0.18709	0.24089	0.75886
28	0.00208	0.57250	0.42542	0.03065	0.96727	0.00038	0.78923	0.21038	0.26417	0.73545
29	0.00204	0.65818	0.33978	0.02326	0.97470	0.00052	0.77250	0.22699	0.26919	0.73029
30	0.00157	0.67138	0.32704	0.02908	0.96935	0.00060	0.77729	0.22211	0.26675	0.73265
31	0.00143	0.66818	0.33039	0.03546	0.96311	0.00069	0.78637	0.21294	0.24716	0.75215
32	0.00133	0.63315	0.36553	0.03957	0.95910	0.00058	0.78626	0.21316	0.22895	0.77047
33	0.00144	0.60006	0.39850	0.04014	0.95842	0.00050	0.79041	0.20909	0.21721	0.78229
34	0.00129	0.55782	0.44089	0.03469	0.96401	0.00050	0.79466	0.20484	0.19929	0.80021
35	0.00132	0.53572	0.46296	0.02889	0.96979	0.00057	0.79767	0.20177	0.17904	0.82040
36	0.00140	0.54261	0.45599	0.02679	0.97181	0.00069	0.80517	0.19414	0.16769	0.83161
37	0.00199	0.58336	0.41466	0.02607	0.97194	0.00068	0.81374	0.18557	0.16673	0.83258
38	0.00217	0.62544	0.37238	0.02906	0.96877	0.00087	0.82206	0.17707	0.16392	0.83521
39	0.00242	0.67708	0.32050	0.03396	0.96362	0.00105	0.82593	0.17302	0.15258	0.84637
40	0.00252	0.69879	0.29869	0.03836	0.95912	0.00130	0.81800	0.18070	0.15090	0.84780
41	0.00310	0.69025	0.30665	0.04099	0.95591	0.00156	0.79830	0.20014	0.15363	0.84481
42	0.00308	0.70572	0.29120	0.04282	0.95410	0.00181	0.78942	0.20877	0.14077	0.85742
43	0.00332	0.73632	0.26036	0.04205	0.95463	0.00175	0.77185	0.22640	0.12753	0.87072
44	0.00391	0.74786	0.24822	0.03790	0.95819	0.00175	0.75628	0.24198	0.12805	0.87020
45	0.00438	0.76454	0.23108	0.03768	0.95794	0.00194	0.76252	0.23553	0.12620	0.87186
46	0.00472	0.79731	0.19798	0.03604	0.95924	0.00200	0.78235	0.21566	0.12040	0.87761
47	0.00473	0.78149	0.21378	0.03068	0.96458	0.00230	0.80031	0.19739	0.12438	0.87332
48	0.00504	0.76080	0.23416	0.03187	0.96308	0.00302	0.82540	0.17158	0.13589	0.86109
49	0.00504	0.76392	0.23104	0.03522	0.95974	0.00325	0.84899	0.14776	0.14494	0.85181
50	0.00536	0.77307	0.22158	0.04035	0.95430	0.00333	0.86038	0.13629	0.15173	0.84494
51	0.00546	0.78432	0.21021	0.05330	0.94123	0.00352	0.87207	0.12441	0.15830	0.83818
52	0.00616	0.80465	0.18919	0.06815	0.92569	0.00320	0.87800	0.11881	0.15378	0.84302
53	0.00663	0.81550	0.17787	0.07537	0.91800	0.00309	0.87933	0.11758	0.14398	0.85293
54	0.00730	0.83275	0.15995	0.07834	0.91436	0.00349	0.88448	0.11203	0.14053	0.85598
55	0.00785	0.85502	0.13713	0.07424	0.91790	0.00354	0.89161	0.10486	0.14045	0.85601
56	0.00807	0.86464	0.12728	0.06608	0.92585	0.00371	0.89630	0.09999	0.14310	0.85319
57	0.00830	0.87994	0.11176	0.06861	0.92309	0.00467	0.90049	0.09484	0.15263	0.84270
58	0.00838	0.89856	0.09306	0.07451	0.91712	0.00502	0.90671	0.08827	0.17421	0.82077
59	0.00814	0.89436	0.09750	0.09071	0.90114	0.00563	0.91128	0.08309	0.19901	0.79536
60	0.00860	0.89252	0.09887	0.12504	0.86635	0.00667	0.91492	0.07841	0.21603	0.77731
61	0.00955	0.90019	0.09025	0.15465	0.83580	0.00759	0.92134	0.07107	0.25405	0.73836
62	0.01023	0.91121	0.07857	0.18425	0.80552	0.00771	0.93164	0.06065	0.29554	0.69675
63	0.01181	0.92623	0.06195	0.21177	0.77642	0.00850	0.94184	0.04966	0.31176	0.67974
64	0.01297	0.94038	0.04665	0.21784	0.76918	0.00866	0.95314	0.03821	0.30499	0.68635
65	0.01357	0.93173	0.05469	0.19617	0.79026	0.00891	0.96582	0.02527	0.33333	0.65777
66	0.01398	0.93995	0.04607	0.21142	0.77461	0.00989	0.96059	0.02952	0.33688	0.65323
67	0.01548	0.94301	0.04151	0.21082	0.77371	0.01070	0.96432	0.02498	0.35513	0.63416
68	0.01714	0.94530	0.03757	0.21589	0.76697	0.01203	0.96657	0.02140	0.34971	0.63826
69	0.01931	0.94663	0.03406	0.21405	0.76663	0.01451	0.96736	0.01813	0.33555	0.64993
70	0.02179	0.94608	0.03213	0.21144	0.76677	0.01621	0.96727	0.01651	0.33282	0.65097
71	0.02510	0.94577	0.02913	0.23404	0.74086	0.01666	0.96691	0.01643	0.35154	0.63180
72	0.02739	0.94981	0.02279	0.23957	0.73303	0.01898	0.96443	0.01659	0.34821	0.63281
73	0.02838	0.95678	0.01484	0.25275	0.71887	0.02013	0.96455	0.01532	0.29306	0.68682
74	0.03128	0.95557	0.01316	0.27756	0.69117	0.02072	0.96601	0.01327	0.28868	0.69060
75	0.03453	0.95131	0.01415	0.30670	0.65877	0.02273	0.96584	0.01143	0.28261	0.69466
76	0.03867	0.94954	0.01179	0.35179	0.60955	0.02476	0.96753	0.00771	0.26118	0.71406
77	0.04224	0.94715	0.01061	0.39047	0.56729	0.02767	0.96687	0.00546	0.25257	0.71975
78	0.04865	0.94112	0.01022	0.35534	0.59600	0.03215	0.96430	0.00355	0.28704	0.68081
79	0.05388	0.93517	0.01096	0.40784	0.53828	0.03686	0.96012	0.00302	0.18245	0.78068
80	0.05915	0.92635	0.01450	0.50869	0.43216	0.04020	0.95633	0.00347	0.09512	0.86468

Mortality is from Table 1; mortality-adjusted, exact-age transition probabilities are from CPS microdata samples, July 1999 through June 2007

Table 3: Transition probabilities by sex, race, Hispanic origin, and education, July 1999 through June 2007, continued

Age	Hispanic Males—High School Degree / GED					Hispanic Females—High School Degree / GED				
	Living to Dead	Inactive to Inactive	Inactive to Active	Active to Inactive	Active to Active	Living to Dead	Inactive to Inactive	Inactive to Active	Active to Inactive	Active to Active
18	0.00121	0.57215	0.42664	0.13777	0.86102	0.00030	0.48662	0.51308	0.30088	0.69882
19	0.00133	0.57738	0.42129	0.11462	0.88405	0.00028	0.51523	0.48449	0.23961	0.76011
20	0.00128	0.55676	0.44196	0.10162	0.89710	0.00038	0.54601	0.45362	0.18985	0.80978
21	0.00127	0.50957	0.48916	0.09423	0.90450	0.00041	0.58855	0.41104	0.16030	0.83929
22	0.00122	0.47133	0.52745	0.08227	0.91651	0.00048	0.66119	0.33833	0.15008	0.84944
23	0.00212	0.49589	0.50199	0.06581	0.93207	0.00043	0.71314	0.28643	0.15182	0.84775
24	0.00188	0.58752	0.41061	0.05190	0.94622	0.00062	0.72686	0.27252	0.14980	0.84958
25	0.00169	0.65452	0.34378	0.04450	0.95381	0.00050	0.72726	0.27225	0.14802	0.85149
26	0.00160	0.61010	0.38830	0.04477	0.95363	0.00039	0.75839	0.24121	0.14400	0.85561
27	0.00169	0.47030	0.52801	0.04493	0.95338	0.00040	0.79323	0.20637	0.14254	0.85707
28	0.00067	0.39901	0.60032	0.04334	0.95599	0.00054	0.79237	0.20709	0.13861	0.86085
29	0.00113	0.45416	0.54472	0.03657	0.96230	0.00049	0.78820	0.21132	0.12748	0.87203
30	0.00160	0.57417	0.42423	0.02953	0.96887	0.00062	0.79078	0.20861	0.11790	0.88148
31	0.00163	0.60618	0.39219	0.02988	0.96850	0.00076	0.79465	0.20458	0.11123	0.88801
32	0.00142	0.62207	0.37651	0.02858	0.97000	0.00081	0.80447	0.19472	0.10873	0.89046
33	0.00165	0.60677	0.39158	0.02974	0.96861	0.00075	0.79367	0.20558	0.11261	0.88665
34	0.00165	0.59725	0.40110	0.02990	0.96845	0.00065	0.78179	0.21756	0.11126	0.88808
35	0.00150	0.57402	0.42448	0.02753	0.97097	0.00060	0.76375	0.23565	0.10885	0.89056
36	0.00184	0.55254	0.44561	0.02637	0.97179	0.00063	0.73887	0.26050	0.11142	0.88795
37	0.00218	0.57177	0.42605	0.02486	0.97296	0.00056	0.72457	0.27487	0.11280	0.88664
38	0.00239	0.61579	0.38182	0.02146	0.97615	0.00095	0.72636	0.27269	0.10542	0.89363
39	0.00242	0.65779	0.33978	0.02334	0.97424	0.00099	0.73791	0.26110	0.09613	0.90288
40	0.00258	0.68618	0.31124	0.02690	0.97052	0.00137	0.75353	0.24510	0.08962	0.90901
41	0.00254	0.71138	0.28609	0.02494	0.97252	0.00141	0.77682	0.22178	0.07920	0.91940
42	0.00282	0.75795	0.23923	0.02326	0.97392	0.00150	0.78640	0.21210	0.06924	0.92927
43	0.00339	0.77146	0.22515	0.02359	0.97302	0.00136	0.79243	0.20621	0.06476	0.93388
44	0.00387	0.75471	0.24141	0.02224	0.97389	0.00177	0.78752	0.21070	0.06665	0.93158
45	0.00427	0.80150	0.19423	0.02703	0.96870	0.00188	0.78435	0.21377	0.06898	0.92914
46	0.00513	0.81958	0.17529	0.03587	0.95900	0.00228	0.78665	0.21107	0.06801	0.92970
47	0.00554	0.79359	0.20086	0.03917	0.95529	0.00228	0.80647	0.19125	0.06987	0.92785
48	0.00508	0.78804	0.20688	0.04456	0.95036	0.00201	0.82966	0.16834	0.08046	0.91754
49	0.00554	0.80198	0.19248	0.05245	0.94201	0.00193	0.85107	0.14699	0.08805	0.91002
50	0.00637	0.78088	0.21275	0.05468	0.93895	0.00178	0.88421	0.11400	0.08951	0.90871
51	0.00642	0.78760	0.20598	0.05061	0.94297	0.00183	0.89910	0.09907	0.09699	0.90118
52	0.00602	0.79950	0.19448	0.05184	0.94215	0.00244	0.89836	0.09920	0.09696	0.90060
53	0.00640	0.81286	0.18074	0.05048	0.94312	0.00287	0.89292	0.10422	0.08447	0.91266
54	0.00603	0.84126	0.15270	0.04487	0.94910	0.00296	0.88417	0.11287	0.07725	0.91979
55	0.00567	0.86560	0.12874	0.04203	0.95230	0.00301	0.87240	0.12459	0.07573	0.92126
56	0.00618	0.88242	0.11139	0.04826	0.94556	0.00309	0.86972	0.12718	0.07260	0.92431
57	0.00741	0.89626	0.09633	0.05951	0.93308	0.00308	0.87047	0.12645	0.08215	0.91477
58	0.00781	0.89869	0.09350	0.06881	0.92338	0.00332	0.87726	0.11942	0.09808	0.89860
59	0.00815	0.89911	0.09275	0.07454	0.91732	0.00367	0.89293	0.10341	0.11369	0.88265
60	0.00878	0.89650	0.09472	0.09241	0.89881	0.00422	0.90304	0.09274	0.13918	0.85660
61	0.00997	0.90597	0.08405	0.11441	0.87561	0.00475	0.91380	0.08144	0.16892	0.82633
62	0.01066	0.92786	0.06148	0.12697	0.86237	0.00496	0.92413	0.07091	0.19024	0.80481
63	0.01114	0.93427	0.05459	0.15389	0.83497	0.00621	0.92359	0.07020	0.21919	0.77460
64	0.01215	0.92621	0.06164	0.19151	0.79633	0.00694	0.92904	0.06403	0.24606	0.74700
65	0.01221	0.92151	0.06628	0.23648	0.75130	0.00746	0.94076	0.05177	0.25948	0.73305
66	0.01140	0.91619	0.07241	0.23166	0.75694	0.00804	0.94526	0.04670	0.23388	0.75808
67	0.01260	0.91249	0.07491	0.24550	0.74190	0.00843	0.95200	0.03957	0.23715	0.75442
68	0.01416	0.91374	0.07210	0.25542	0.73042	0.00931	0.95614	0.03456	0.23381	0.75688
69	0.01702	0.91194	0.07104	0.27755	0.70543	0.00947	0.96115	0.02938	0.23511	0.75543
70	0.02147	0.91576	0.06277	0.28755	0.69098	0.01160	0.96537	0.02303	0.23024	0.75816
71	0.02224	0.92099	0.05677	0.28802	0.68974	0.01354	0.96935	0.01710	0.21397	0.77249
72	0.02335	0.93040	0.04626	0.26260	0.71405	0.01601	0.96857	0.01542	0.18781	0.79618
73	0.02626	0.94388	0.02986	0.21058	0.76316	0.01713	0.96807	0.01480	0.19636	0.78651
74	0.02706	0.94856	0.02437	0.16570	0.80723	0.02152	0.96871	0.00977	0.22679	0.75169
75	0.02679	0.95962	0.01359	0.13692	0.83628	0.02328	0.97171	0.00501	0.21543	0.76129
76	0.03095	0.96826	0.00079	0.15610	0.81295	0.02158	0.97488	0.00354	0.25054	0.72788
77	0.03267	0.96695	0.00038	0.17976	0.78757	0.02499	0.97308	0.00193	0.31593	0.65908
78	0.03489	0.96511	0.00000	0.19257	0.77254	0.02569	0.97431	0.00000	0.27764	0.69666
79	0.03880	0.96120	0.00000	0.21246	0.74874	0.02767	0.97233	0.00000	0.30336	0.66897
80	0.04333	0.95667	0.00000	0.18018	0.77649	0.02912	0.97088	0.00000	0.22624	0.74464

Mortality is from Table 1; mortality-adjusted, exact-age transition probabilities are from CPS microdata samples, July 1999 through June 2007

Table 3: Transition probabilities by sex, race, Hispanic origin, and education, July 1999 through June 2007, continued

	Hispanic Males—Some College Education or More					Hispanic Females—Some College Education or More				
Age	Living to Dead	Inactive to Inactive	Inactive to Active	Active to Inactive	Active to Active	Living to Dead	Inactive to Inactive	Inactive to Active	Active to Inactive	Active to Active
18	0.00121	0.68938	0.30941	0.11550	0.88329	0.00030	0.53975	0.45995	0.13884	0.86085
19	0.00133	0.68422	0.31445	0.14587	0.85280	0.00028	0.59493	0.40479	0.17722	0.82250
20	0.00128	0.65511	0.34361	0.15814	0.84058	0.00038	0.62625	0.37337	0.18852	0.81111
21	0.00127	0.60652	0.39221	0.14205	0.85668	0.00041	0.63675	0.36283	0.17217	0.82741
22	0.00122	0.55465	0.44413	0.11430	0.88448	0.00048	0.63095	0.36857	0.14213	0.85739
23	0.00086	0.53353	0.46561	0.08609	0.91304	0.00043	0.61976	0.37981	0.12293	0.87664
24	0.00096	0.56073	0.43831	0.06750	0.93154	0.00041	0.63754	0.36205	0.11164	0.88796
25	0.00080	0.57791	0.42129	0.05969	0.93951	0.00028	0.65239	0.34734	0.11120	0.88852
26	0.00060	0.59519	0.40422	0.05083	0.94858	0.00017	0.67389	0.32594	0.10358	0.89625
27	0.00031	0.58759	0.41209	0.04555	0.95414	0.00000	0.68126	0.31874	0.09826	0.90174
28	0.00050	0.55457	0.44492	0.03858	0.96092	0.00008	0.67960	0.32032	0.10156	0.89836
29	0.00028	0.46871	0.53101	0.03032	0.96940	0.00023	0.70298	0.29679	0.09695	0.90282
30	0.00036	0.43366	0.56597	0.02155	0.97808	0.00037	0.72499	0.27464	0.08954	0.91009
31	0.00059	0.52559	0.47381	0.02629	0.97312	0.00040	0.74117	0.25843	0.08998	0.90963
32	0.00073	0.56116	0.43811	0.02463	0.97464	0.00048	0.76030	0.23922	0.08085	0.91867
33	0.00077	0.57644	0.42278	0.02652	0.97271	0.00061	0.75850	0.24089	0.08236	0.91703
34	0.00093	0.55818	0.44090	0.02862	0.97045	0.00051	0.75697	0.24252	0.08323	0.91625
35	0.00133	0.52509	0.47357	0.02737	0.97129	0.00047	0.76793	0.23160	0.07483	0.92470
36	0.00136	0.52731	0.47133	0.02570	0.97294	0.00063	0.76466	0.23471	0.06871	0.93066
37	0.00168	0.52592	0.47239	0.02612	0.97220	0.00067	0.76400	0.23533	0.06726	0.93207
38	0.00200	0.56422	0.43377	0.02240	0.97379	0.00043	0.77186	0.22771	0.06264	0.93693
39	0.00240	0.61807	0.37953	0.02299	0.97460	0.00056	0.76464	0.23480	0.05776	0.94168
40	0.00216	0.64145	0.35640	0.02446	0.97339	0.00052	0.75039	0.24909	0.05798	0.94150
41	0.00263	0.62907	0.36829	0.02248	0.97488	0.00044	0.74766	0.25190	0.05870	0.94087
42	0.00285	0.59952	0.39763	0.01957	0.97758	0.00063	0.74030	0.25907	0.05701	0.94235
43	0.00295	0.61929	0.37776	0.02047	0.97658	0.00094	0.73987	0.25919	0.05470	0.94437
44	0.00293	0.65414	0.34294	0.02043	0.97665	0.00143	0.75282	0.24576	0.05156	0.94701
45	0.00343	0.67041	0.32616	0.01750	0.97907	0.00146	0.76459	0.23395	0.05024	0.94830
46	0.00346	0.70494	0.29160	0.02130	0.97524	0.00185	0.77536	0.22279	0.05131	0.94684
47	0.00328	0.74595	0.25077	0.02468	0.97204	0.00172	0.79765	0.20063	0.05196	0.94632
48	0.00332	0.74386	0.25282	0.02702	0.96966	0.00167	0.82577	0.17256	0.05453	0.94380
49	0.00352	0.74241	0.25407	0.03098	0.96550	0.00099	0.83205	0.16696	0.06377	0.93524
50	0.00374	0.77075	0.22551	0.03334	0.96292	0.00166	0.83511	0.16323	0.07204	0.92631
51	0.00438	0.78679	0.20883	0.03280	0.96282	0.00175	0.83516	0.16310	0.07432	0.92394
52	0.00543	0.81488	0.17969	0.03140	0.96317	0.00201	0.81996	0.17802	0.07994	0.91805
53	0.00568	0.85690	0.13742	0.03154	0.96278	0.00252	0.80666	0.19082	0.08323	0.91426
54	0.00617	0.86561	0.12822	0.03039	0.96344	0.00256	0.81600	0.18143	0.07848	0.91896
55	0.00659	0.87267	0.12073	0.03749	0.95592	0.00205	0.82871	0.16924	0.07821	0.91975
56	0.00600	0.89065	0.10335	0.04887	0.94512	0.00212	0.84484	0.15304	0.08713	0.91076
57	0.00541	0.90802	0.08656	0.06000	0.93459	0.00224	0.86917	0.12859	0.08980	0.90796
58	0.00550	0.90624	0.08826	0.07338	0.92112	0.00245	0.86658	0.13097	0.09297	0.90458
59	0.00601	0.90638	0.08761	0.09209	0.90190	0.00285	0.86463	0.13252	0.10933	0.88782
60	0.00617	0.90134	0.09250	0.11685	0.87698	0.00374	0.88069	0.11557	0.11845	0.87781
61	0.00597	0.89236	0.10167	0.13790	0.85613	0.00453	0.89696	0.09851	0.11905	0.87643
62	0.00720	0.89583	0.09698	0.17078	0.82203	0.00494	0.91365	0.08141	0.12624	0.86882
63	0.00847	0.90226	0.08927	0.21266	0.77887	0.00491	0.94277	0.05232	0.13001	0.86509
64	0.00891	0.90184	0.08924	0.23834	0.75275	0.00558	0.96495	0.02946	0.11481	0.87961
65	0.01025	0.90884	0.08091	0.24057	0.74918	0.00654	0.97028	0.02319	0.12323	0.87024
66	0.01225	0.91559	0.07216	0.21551	0.77225	0.00698	0.96591	0.02711	0.16104	0.83198
67	0.01372	0.92012	0.06616	0.21494	0.77133	0.00938	0.96731	0.02331	0.17062	0.82000
68	0.01445	0.92756	0.05799	0.21086	0.77469	0.01020	0.96708	0.02272	0.19225	0.79755
69	0.01533	0.92863	0.05604	0.20832	0.77635	0.01201	0.96350	0.02450	0.20722	0.78078
70	0.01522	0.93652	0.04826	0.20185	0.78293	0.01320	0.96127	0.02554	0.22683	0.75997
71	0.01829	0.94640	0.03531	0.18731	0.79439	0.01299	0.96462	0.02239	0.27273	0.71427
72	0.01822	0.95352	0.02826	0.17714	0.80464	0.01379	0.96442	0.02179	0.29307	0.69314
73	0.01959	0.95934	0.02107	0.15695	0.82347	0.01889	0.95837	0.02275	0.26843	0.71268
74	0.01978	0.96357	0.01666	0.14028	0.83994	0.01894	0.96309	0.01797	0.21244	0.76862
75	0.02252	0.96507	0.01240	0.16564	0.81184	0.01891	0.96797	0.01312	0.17839	0.80270
76	0.02155	0.97142	0.00703	0.19465	0.78380	0.01798	0.97014	0.01188	0.20189	0.78013
77	0.02951	0.96701	0.00347	0.23557	0.73491	0.01855	0.97168	0.00977	0.20286	0.77859
78	0.03864	0.96136	0.00000	0.02571	0.93564	0.01341	0.98659	0.00000	0.33419	0.65240
79	0.05468	0.94532	0.00000	0.03601	0.90931	0.02098	0.97902	0.00000	0.35037	0.62865
80	0.06976	0.93024	0.00000	0.02409	0.90614	0.02224	0.97776	0.00000	0.37966	0.59809

Mortality is from Table 1; mortality-adjusted, exact-age transition probabilities are from CPS microdata samples, July 1999 through June 2007

Table 4: Worklife expectancies, increment-decrement methodology, by sex, race, Hispanic origin, and education, July 1999–June 2007: Males All Races

Age	All Males *			< High School			High School or GED			Some College			Bachelor Degree			Graduate Degree		
	All	Act'v	Inact	All	Act'v	Inact	All	Act'v	Inact	All	Act'v	Inact	All	Act'v	Inact	All	Act'v	Inact
18	38.6	39.3	37.9	32.4	33.0	31.9	37.9	38.3	37.0	38.9	39.6	38.1						
19	38.2	38.7	37.3	31.9	32.5	31.2	37.3	37.6	36.3	38.5	39.0	37.5						
20	37.7	38.2	36.6	31.5	32.0	30.5	36.6	36.9	35.5	37.9	38.5	36.9	41.9	42.4	40.0			
21	37.1	37.5	35.9	31.0	31.4	29.7	35.8	36.1	34.6	37.4	37.9	36.3	41.2	41.6	39.7			
22	36.5	36.8	35.2	30.4	30.8	28.9	35.1	35.3	33.7	36.8	37.2	35.7	40.5	40.7	39.2			
23	35.8	36.1	34.4	29.7	30.1	28.1	34.3	34.6	32.7	36.2	36.5	35.0	39.7	40.0	38.4	41.1	41.5	39.6
24	35.1	35.3	33.6	29.1	29.3	27.3	33.6	33.8	31.8	35.5	35.7	34.2	38.9	39.1	37.5	40.6	40.8	39.3
25	34.3	34.5	32.7	28.3	28.6	26.6	32.8	33.0	31.0	34.7	34.9	33.4	38.1	38.3	36.7	39.8	40.0	38.7
26	33.5	33.6	31.9	27.6	27.9	25.7	32.0	32.2	30.2	33.9	34.0	32.6	37.3	37.4	35.8	39.0	39.1	37.8
27	32.6	32.8	31.0	26.8	27.1	24.7	31.2	31.3	29.4	33.0	33.2	31.6	36.4	36.5	35.0	38.0	38.1	36.8
28	31.8	31.9	29.9	26.0	26.4	23.6	30.3	30.5	28.4	32.1	32.3	30.5	35.4	35.5	34.0	37.1	37.2	35.7
29	30.9	31.1	28.9	25.2	25.6	22.6	29.5	29.7	27.4	31.3	31.4	29.5	34.5	34.6	33.1	36.2	36.3	34.6
30	30.0	30.2	27.9	24.4	24.8	21.8	28.6	28.8	26.4	30.4	30.5	28.5	33.6	33.6	32.1	35.2	35.3	33.8
31	29.1	29.3	27.0	23.6	23.9	21.1	27.8	28.0	25.5	29.5	29.6	27.5	32.6	32.7	31.2	34.3	34.4	33.0
32	28.3	28.4	26.1	22.8	23.2	20.3	26.9	27.1	24.6	28.6	28.7	26.5	31.7	31.8	30.2	33.4	33.4	32.1
33	27.4	27.5	25.1	22.0	22.4	19.5	26.1	26.3	23.7	27.7	27.8	25.6	30.8	30.8	29.3	32.4	32.4	31.2
34	26.5	26.6	24.2	21.2	21.6	18.6	25.2	25.4	22.8	26.8	26.9	24.6	29.8	29.9	28.3	31.4	31.5	30.2
35	25.6	25.8	23.2	20.4	20.8	17.7	24.3	24.5	21.8	25.9	26.0	23.7	28.9	28.9	27.4	30.5	30.5	29.2
36	24.7	24.9	22.2	19.6	20.0	16.8	23.4	23.7	20.8	25.0	25.1	22.8	27.9	28.0	26.3	29.5	29.6	28.1
37	23.8	24.0	21.1	18.7	19.2	15.8	22.6	22.8	19.8	24.1	24.2	21.8	27.0	27.0	25.2	28.6	28.6	27.0
38	22.9	23.1	20.1	17.9	18.5	14.8	21.7	22.0	18.9	23.2	23.3	20.8	26.0	26.1	24.2	27.6	27.7	25.9
39	22.0	22.3	19.1	17.1	17.8	13.8	20.9	21.1	17.9	22.3	22.4	19.8	25.1	25.2	23.1	26.7	26.7	24.8
40	21.1	21.4	18.0	16.4	17.1	12.8	20.0	20.3	16.9	21.4	21.6	18.7	24.2	24.2	22.1	25.7	25.8	23.8
41	20.3	20.5	17.0	15.6	16.4	11.9	19.1	19.5	15.9	20.5	20.7	17.7	23.2	23.3	21.2	24.8	24.8	22.9
42	19.4	19.7	16.0	14.8	15.7	11.1	18.3	18.7	14.9	19.6	19.8	16.6	22.3	22.4	20.2	23.8	23.9	21.9
43	18.5	18.9	14.9	14.1	15.1	10.3	17.5	17.9	13.8	18.7	19.0	15.6	21.4	21.5	19.2	22.9	23.0	20.9
44	17.7	18.0	14.0	13.4	14.4	9.5	16.6	17.1	12.9	17.8	18.1	14.6	20.5	20.6	18.1	22.0	22.0	19.8
45	16.8	17.2	13.1	12.7	13.7	8.9	15.8	16.3	12.0	17.0	17.3	13.6	19.5	19.6	17.1	21.0	21.1	18.5
46	16.0	16.4	12.1	12.0	13.1	8.2	15.0	15.5	11.1	16.1	16.4	12.6	18.6	18.7	16.2	20.1	20.2	17.3
47	15.1	15.6	11.2	11.3	12.5	7.6	14.2	14.7	10.2	15.2	15.6	11.6	17.7	17.8	15.1	19.2	19.3	16.2
48	14.3	14.8	10.3	10.6	11.8	7.0	13.4	14.0	9.4	14.4	14.8	10.7	16.8	16.9	14.0	18.2	18.3	15.2
49	13.5	14.0	9.4	9.9	11.2	6.3	12.6	13.2	8.6	13.6	14.0	9.7	15.9	16.1	12.9	17.3	17.4	14.1
50	12.7	13.2	8.6	9.3	10.6	5.6	11.8	12.5	7.8	12.7	13.2	8.8	15.0	15.2	11.7	16.4	16.5	13.0
51	11.9	12.5	7.7	8.6	10.0	5.1	11.0	11.7	7.0	11.9	12.5	7.9	14.1	14.3	10.5	15.5	15.7	12.0
52	11.1	11.7	7.0	8.0	9.4	4.6	10.3	11.0	6.3	11.1	11.8	7.2	13.2	13.5	9.4	14.6	14.8	10.9
53	10.3	11.0	6.2	7.4	8.8	4.1	9.5	10.4	5.7	10.4	11.0	6.4	12.3	12.7	8.5	13.7	13.9	9.7
54	9.5	10.3	5.6	6.8	8.3	3.7	8.8	9.7	5.1	9.6	10.3	5.8	11.4	11.9	7.7	12.8	13.1	8.8
55	8.7	9.6	5.0	6.2	7.8	3.2	8.0	9.0	4.5	8.8	9.6	5.2	10.6	11.1	6.8	11.9	12.2	8.0
56	8.0	8.9	4.4	5.6	7.3	2.8	7.3	8.4	4.0	8.1	9.0	4.6	9.8	10.3	6.0	11.0	11.4	7.2
57	7.3	8.3	3.9	5.1	6.7	2.5	6.7	7.7	3.6	7.4	8.3	4.1	8.9	9.6	5.2	10.1	10.6	6.4
58	6.6	7.6	3.4	4.5	6.2	2.2	6.0	7.1	3.1	6.7	7.7	3.6	8.1	8.9	4.5	9.3	9.9	5.7
59	5.9	7.0	3.0	4.1	5.6	1.9	5.3	6.5	2.8	6.1	7.1	3.2	7.3	8.2	3.9	8.5	9.2	5.1
60	5.2	6.4	2.6	3.5	5.1	1.7	4.7	5.9	2.4	5.4	6.6	2.8	6.6	7.6	3.4	7.6	8.5	4.4
61	4.6	5.9	2.3	3.1	4.7	1.5	4.1	5.4	2.2	4.8	6.1	2.5	5.8	7.0	2.9	6.8	7.8	3.9
62	4.0	5.5	2.0	2.7	4.4	1.3	3.6	5.0	1.9	4.3	5.7	2.2	5.1	6.5	2.6	6.1	7.2	3.4
63	3.5	5.1	1.8	2.3	4.1	1.2	3.1	4.7	1.7	3.7	5.3	2.0	4.5	6.0	2.2	5.4	6.7	3.0
64	3.0	4.8	1.6	2.0	4.0	1.1	2.7	4.4	1.5	3.3	4.9	1.8	3.9	5.6	2.0	4.8	6.1	2.6
65	2.6	4.5	1.4	1.8	3.8	1.0	2.3	4.2	1.4	2.9	4.6	1.6	3.4	5.2	1.7	4.2	5.7	2.3
66	2.3	4.2	1.3	1.6	3.7	0.9	2.1	3.9	1.2	2.5	4.3	1.5	3.0	4.8	1.5	3.7	5.3	2.0
67	2.0	4.0	1.1	1.4	3.6	0.8	1.8	3.7	1.1	2.2	4.0	1.3	2.6	4.5	1.3	3.2	5.0	1.7
68	1.8	3.8	0.9	1.2	3.4	0.6	1.6	3.6	0.9	1.9	3.9	1.1	2.2	4.2	1.1	2.8	4.7	1.5
69	1.5	3.6	0.8	1.0	3.2	0.5	1.4	3.4	0.8	1.6	3.7	0.9	1.9	4.0	1.0	2.4	4.4	1.2
70	1.3	3.4	0.7	0.9	3.0	0.5	1.2	3.3	0.6	1.4	3.6	0.7	1.7	3.7	0.8	2.1	4.1	1.0
71	1.1	3.2	0.5	0.8	2.9	0.4	1.0	3.1	0.5	1.2	3.4	0.6	1.4	3.5	0.7	1.8	3.7	0.9
72	0.9	3.1	0.4	0.6	2.7	0.3	0.9	3.1	0.4	1.0	3.2	0.5	1.2	3.3	0.6	1.5	3.5	0.7
73	0.8	2.9	0.4	0.5	2.6	0.3	0.7	3.0	0.3	0.9	3.0	0.4	1.1	3.1	0.5	1.3	3.2	0.6
74	0.7	2.8	0.3	0.5	2.6	0.2	0.6	2.9	0.2	0.7	2.8	0.3	0.9	3.0	0.4	1.1	3.0	0.5
75	0.6	2.7	0.2	0.4	2.5	0.2	0.5	2.7	0.2	0.6	2.6	0.3	0.8	2.8	0.3	0.9	2.8	0.3

* Calculated from aggregated data, i.e., not weighted averages.

Table 4: Worklife expectancies, increment-decrement methodology, by sex, race, Hispanic origin, and education, July 1999–June 2007, continued: Females All Races

Age	All Females *			< High School			High School or GED			Some College			Bachelor Degree			Graduate Degree		
	All	Act'v	Inact	All	Act'v	Inact	All	Act'v	Inact	All	Act'v	Inact	All	Act'v	Inact	All	Act'v	Inact
18	33.1	33.8	32.4	21.8	22.5	21.2	32.5	32.9	31.7	35.5	36.1	34.7						
19	32.7	33.2	31.9	21.3	22.1	20.7	31.9	32.3	31.1	34.9	35.4	34.0						
20	32.1	32.7	31.2	20.9	21.7	20.2	31.2	31.6	30.3	34.3	34.8	33.4	35.8	36.1	34.5			
21	31.6	32.1	30.5	20.4	21.3	19.6	30.5	30.9	29.4	33.7	34.1	32.7	35.1	35.4	34.0			
22	30.9	31.4	29.7	20.0	20.8	19.0	29.8	30.3	28.5	33.1	33.5	32.0	34.3	34.5	33.1			
23	30.3	30.8	28.9	19.5	20.4	18.5	29.1	29.6	27.7	32.4	32.8	31.2	33.5	33.8	32.0	36.5	37.0	34.3
24	29.6	30.2	28.1	19.0	20.0	18.0	28.5	29.0	27.0	31.7	32.1	30.4	32.7	33.1	31.0	35.6	36.0	33.6
25	28.9	29.5	27.3	18.6	19.6	17.5	27.8	28.4	26.3	31.0	31.4	29.5	31.9	32.3	30.0	34.8	35.1	33.0
26	28.2	28.8	26.5	18.1	19.1	17.1	27.1	27.8	25.6	30.3	30.7	28.6	31.1	31.5	29.1	33.9	34.2	32.2
27	27.5	28.1	25.7	17.6	18.6	16.6	26.4	27.1	24.8	29.5	30.0	27.7	30.3	30.7	28.2	33.1	33.4	31.3
28	26.8	27.4	24.9	17.2	18.1	16.2	25.8	26.5	24.1	28.8	29.3	26.9	29.5	29.9	27.3	32.2	32.5	30.3
29	26.1	26.8	24.2	16.7	17.6	15.7	25.1	25.9	23.4	28.0	28.5	26.2	28.7	29.2	26.4	31.4	31.7	29.2
30	25.4	26.1	23.4	16.2	17.2	15.1	24.5	25.2	22.7	27.3	27.8	25.4	27.9	28.4	25.5	30.6	31.0	28.3
31	24.7	25.4	22.6	15.8	16.8	14.6	23.8	24.6	21.9	26.5	27.1	24.6	27.1	27.7	24.6	29.8	30.2	27.5
32	23.9	24.7	21.8	15.3	16.3	14.1	23.2	23.9	21.2	25.8	26.3	23.8	26.3	27.0	23.7	29.0	29.4	26.6
33	23.2	24.0	21.1	14.8	15.8	13.5	22.5	23.3	20.4	25.1	25.6	23.1	25.5	26.3	22.9	28.2	28.6	25.7
34	22.5	23.3	20.3	14.3	15.4	12.9	21.8	22.6	19.7	24.3	24.9	22.2	24.8	25.5	22.1	27.3	27.9	24.8
35	21.8	22.6	19.5	13.8	14.9	12.4	21.1	21.9	19.0	23.6	24.2	21.4	24.0	24.8	21.3	26.5	27.1	23.9
36	21.1	21.9	18.7	13.3	14.4	11.8	20.4	21.2	18.2	22.8	23.4	20.5	23.3	24.1	20.5	25.7	26.3	23.1
37	20.4	21.2	17.9	12.8	14.0	11.2	19.7	20.5	17.5	22.0	22.7	19.6	22.5	23.4	19.7	24.9	25.5	22.2
38	19.7	20.5	17.1	12.3	13.5	10.7	19.0	19.8	16.7	21.3	21.9	18.8	21.8	22.6	19.0	24.1	24.7	21.3
39	18.9	19.8	16.4	11.8	13.1	10.1	18.3	19.1	15.9	20.5	21.1	17.9	21.1	21.9	18.3	23.3	23.9	20.4
40	18.2	19.0	15.6	11.4	12.6	9.7	17.6	18.4	15.1	19.7	20.3	17.0	20.3	21.1	17.6	22.5	23.1	19.5
41	17.5	18.3	14.8	10.9	12.1	9.1	16.8	17.7	14.2	18.9	19.6	16.2	19.6	20.3	16.8	21.7	22.2	18.7
42	16.8	17.6	13.9	10.4	11.6	8.6	16.1	17.0	13.3	18.1	18.8	15.3	18.9	19.6	16.1	20.8	21.4	17.8
43	16.0	16.9	13.1	9.8	11.1	8.1	15.4	16.3	12.5	17.4	18.0	14.5	18.1	18.8	15.3	20.0	20.5	16.9
44	15.3	16.1	12.3	9.3	10.6	7.5	14.7	15.6	11.6	16.6	17.3	13.6	17.3	18.0	14.5	19.1	19.6	16.0
45	14.5	15.4	11.4	8.7	10.1	6.9	13.9	14.9	10.8	15.8	16.5	12.8	16.6	17.2	13.7	18.3	18.8	15.1
46	13.8	14.7	10.6	8.2	9.7	6.3	13.2	14.2	9.9	15.0	15.7	12.0	15.8	16.4	12.9	17.4	17.9	14.2
47	13.0	14.0	9.8	7.7	9.2	5.8	12.5	13.5	9.1	14.3	15.0	11.1	15.0	15.6	12.1	16.6	17.0	13.3
48	12.3	13.2	9.0	7.2	8.8	5.2	11.7	12.8	8.4	13.5	14.2	10.2	14.2	14.8	11.2	15.8	16.2	12.4
49	11.6	12.5	8.2	6.7	8.4	4.7	11.0	12.1	7.7	12.7	13.5	9.4	13.4	14.0	10.4	14.9	15.3	11.6
50	10.8	11.9	7.5	6.2	8.0	4.3	10.3	11.5	7.0	11.9	12.8	8.6	12.6	13.2	9.5	14.1	14.5	10.8
51	10.1	11.2	6.7	5.8	7.6	3.9	9.6	10.8	6.3	11.2	12.1	7.8	11.8	12.5	8.7	13.2	13.6	9.8
52	9.4	10.5	6.1	5.4	7.3	3.5	8.9	10.2	5.7	10.4	11.4	7.0	11.0	11.7	7.9	12.3	12.8	8.9
53	8.6	9.8	5.4	4.9	6.9	3.1	8.2	9.6	5.1	9.7	10.7	6.3	10.2	11.0	7.1	11.5	12.0	8.1
54	7.9	9.2	4.8	4.5	6.6	2.8	7.5	9.0	4.5	9.0	10.1	5.6	9.4	10.3	6.3	10.6	11.2	7.2
55	7.2	8.6	4.2	4.1	6.2	2.4	6.9	8.4	4.0	8.3	9.4	5.0	8.6	9.6	5.5	9.8	10.4	6.4
56	6.6	8.0	3.7	3.7	5.8	2.1	6.2	7.8	3.4	7.5	8.8	4.4	7.9	8.9	4.8	9.0	9.7	5.7
57	5.9	7.4	3.2	3.3	5.4	1.8	5.6	7.3	3.0	6.8	8.2	3.9	7.2	8.3	4.2	8.2	9.0	5.1
58	5.3	6.9	2.7	2.9	5.0	1.5	5.1	6.7	2.6	6.2	7.6	3.4	6.5	7.7	3.6	7.4	8.3	4.4
59	4.7	6.3	2.4	2.5	4.6	1.3	4.5	6.2	2.3	5.5	6.9	2.9	5.8	7.1	3.2	6.6	7.7	3.8
60	4.1	5.8	2.0	2.2	4.2	1.2	3.9	5.7	2.0	4.8	6.4	2.5	5.1	6.6	2.8	5.9	7.1	3.3
61	3.5	5.4	1.8	1.9	3.9	1.0	3.4	5.3	1.7	4.2	5.9	2.2	4.5	6.1	2.4	5.2	6.5	2.9
62	3.1	5.0	1.5	1.6	3.7	0.9	3.0	4.9	1.5	3.7	5.4	1.9	3.9	5.7	2.1	4.6	6.0	2.5
63	2.6	4.6	1.3	1.4	3.5	0.7	2.5	4.6	1.3	3.2	5.0	1.7	3.4	5.3	1.8	4.0	5.6	2.1
64	2.2	4.4	1.1	1.2	3.3	0.6	2.2	4.4	1.1	2.7	4.7	1.4	2.9	4.9	1.5	3.5	5.3	1.8
65	1.9	4.2	1.0	1.0	3.2	0.5	1.9	4.2	1.0	2.4	4.5	1.2	2.5	4.6	1.3	3.1	5.0	1.6
66	1.6	4.0	0.8	0.8	3.1	0.4	1.6	4.1	0.8	2.0	4.2	1.0	2.1	4.3	1.1	2.7	4.7	1.4
67	1.4	3.8	0.7	0.7	3.0	0.4	1.4	4.0	0.7	1.7	4.0	0.8	1.8	4.0	1.0	2.3	4.4	1.1
68	1.2	3.7	0.6	0.6	2.9	0.3	1.2	3.9	0.6	1.4	3.8	0.7	1.5	3.7	0.8	1.9	4.2	1.0
69	1.0	3.5	0.5	0.6	2.8	0.3	1.0	3.8	0.5	1.2	3.5	0.6	1.3	3.5	0.7	1.6	4.0	0.8
70	0.8	3.3	0.4	0.5	2.7	0.2	0.9	3.7	0.4	1.0	3.3	0.5	1.1	3.3	0.6	1.4	3.8	0.7
71	0.7	3.2	0.3	0.4	2.6	0.2	0.7	3.5	0.3	0.8	3.0	0.4	0.9	3.1	0.5	1.2	3.7	0.5
72	0.6	3.0	0.2	0.3	2.5	0.1	0.6	3.3	0.2	0.7	2.8	0.3	0.8	3.0	0.4	1.1	3.7	0.5
73	0.5	2.8	0.2	0.2	2.2	0.1	0.5	3.1	0.2	0.5	2.7	0.2	0.6	2.8	0.3	1.0	3.6	0.4
74	0.4	2.6	0.1	0.2	2.1	0.1	0.4	2.9	0.1	0.4	2.6	0.2	0.5	2.7	0.2	0.8	3.4	0.3
75	0.3	2.5	0.1	0.1	1.9	0.1	0.3	2.7	0.1	0.4	2.5	0.1	0.4	2.5	0.2	0.7	3.2	0.2

* Calculated from aggregated data, i.e., not weighted averages.

Table 4: Worklife expectancies, increment-decrement methodology, by sex, race, Hispanic origin, and education, July 1999–June 2007, continued: White Males

Age	All White Males *			< High School			High School or GED			Some College			Bachelor Degree			Graduate Degree		
	All	Act'v	Inact	All	Act'v	Inact	All	Act'v	Inact	All	Act'v	Inact	All	Act'v	Inact	All	Act'v	Inact
18	39.7	40.2	38.9	34.1	34.6	33.4	38.9	39.3	38.0	39.6	40.2	38.8						
19	39.2	39.6	38.2	33.6	34.0	32.7	38.2	38.5	37.2	39.1	39.7	38.2						
20	38.6	39.0	37.5	33.1	33.4	31.9	37.5	37.7	36.4	38.6	39.1	37.6	42.5	42.8	41.3			
21	38.0	38.3	36.7	32.5	32.8	31.1	36.8	37.0	35.5	38.0	38.5	36.9	41.5	41.9	40.4			
22	37.3	37.6	36.0	31.8	32.0	30.3	36.0	36.2	34.5	37.4	37.8	36.3	40.8	41.1	39.6			
23	36.6	36.8	35.2	31.1	31.3	29.5	35.2	35.3	33.6	36.8	37.0	35.6	40.1	40.3	38.7	41.2	41.8	40.2
24	35.8	36.0	34.4	30.3	30.5	28.6	34.4	34.5	32.6	36.1	36.2	34.8	39.3	39.4	37.8	40.9	41.1	39.8
25	35.0	35.2	33.5	29.5	29.7	27.8	33.5	33.7	31.7	35.2	35.3	34.0	38.4	38.6	36.9	40.1	40.2	39.2
26	34.2	34.3	32.6	28.8	29.0	26.9	32.7	32.8	30.9	34.4	34.5	33.1	37.6	37.7	36.0	39.2	39.3	38.2
27	33.3	33.4	31.6	27.9	28.2	25.8	31.8	32.0	30.1	33.5	33.6	32.1	36.7	36.8	35.1	38.3	38.4	37.2
28	32.4	32.5	30.6	27.1	27.4	24.6	31.0	31.1	29.1	32.6	32.7	30.9	35.8	35.9	34.1	37.3	37.4	36.1
29	31.5	31.6	29.5	26.3	26.5	23.6	30.1	30.2	28.1	31.7	31.8	29.8	34.8	34.9	33.1	36.4	36.5	35.1
30	30.6	30.7	28.4	25.4	25.7	22.8	29.2	29.4	27.0	30.8	30.9	28.7	33.9	34.0	32.1	35.4	35.5	34.2
31	29.7	29.8	27.5	24.6	24.9	22.1	28.4	28.5	26.1	29.8	29.9	27.6	33.0	33.0	31.2	34.5	34.5	33.4
32	28.8	28.9	26.6	23.8	24.1	21.3	27.5	27.6	25.1	28.9	29.0	26.7	32.0	32.1	30.3	33.5	33.6	32.5
33	27.9	28.1	25.6	23.0	23.3	20.6	26.6	26.8	24.1	28.0	28.1	25.7	31.1	31.1	29.5	32.6	32.6	31.5
34	27.0	27.1	24.7	22.2	22.5	19.7	25.7	25.9	23.0	27.1	27.2	24.8	30.1	30.2	28.6	31.6	31.6	30.5
35	26.1	26.3	23.7	21.3	21.7	18.8	24.8	25.0	22.0	26.2	26.3	23.9	29.2	29.2	27.7	30.6	30.7	29.4
36	25.2	25.4	22.6	20.5	20.8	17.8	23.9	24.2	21.0	25.3	25.4	22.9	28.2	28.3	26.7	29.7	29.7	28.3
37	24.3	24.5	21.6	19.6	20.0	16.7	23.1	23.3	20.1	24.3	24.5	21.9	27.3	27.3	25.6	28.7	28.8	27.3
38	23.4	23.6	20.5	18.8	19.2	15.6	22.2	22.4	19.1	23.5	23.6	20.8	26.3	26.4	24.6	27.8	27.8	26.3
39	22.5	22.7	19.5	17.9	18.4	14.5	21.3	21.6	18.2	22.6	22.7	19.8	25.4	25.5	23.6	26.8	26.9	25.2
40	21.6	21.8	18.4	17.1	17.7	13.4	20.4	20.7	17.2	21.7	21.8	18.8	24.5	24.5	22.5	25.9	25.9	24.2
41	20.7	20.9	17.4	16.3	17.0	12.5	19.6	19.9	16.2	20.8	20.9	17.9	23.5	23.6	21.5	24.9	25.0	23.1
42	19.8	20.1	16.4	15.4	16.3	11.6	18.7	19.0	15.2	19.9	20.1	16.9	22.6	22.7	20.5	24.0	24.0	22.0
43	18.9	19.2	15.3	14.8	15.6	10.7	17.8	18.2	14.1	19.0	19.2	15.9	21.7	21.7	19.4	23.0	23.1	20.9
44	18.1	18.4	14.3	14.0	14.9	9.9	17.0	17.4	13.1	18.1	18.3	14.9	20.7	20.8	18.2	22.1	22.1	19.7
45	17.2	17.5	13.3	13.2	14.2	9.2	16.1	16.6	12.1	17.2	17.5	13.8	19.8	19.9	17.2	21.1	21.2	18.4
46	16.3	16.7	12.4	12.5	13.5	8.4	15.3	15.8	11.3	16.4	16.6	12.8	18.9	19.0	16.3	20.2	20.3	17.2
47	15.5	15.9	11.4	11.7	12.9	7.7	14.5	15.0	10.4	15.5	15.8	11.7	18.0	18.1	15.3	19.3	19.4	16.0
48	14.6	15.1	10.5	11.0	12.2	7.0	13.6	14.2	9.6	14.6	15.0	10.7	17.0	17.2	14.2	18.3	18.4	15.0
49	13.8	14.3	9.6	10.3	11.5	6.3	12.9	13.4	8.8	13.8	14.2	9.7	16.1	16.3	13.1	17.4	17.5	14.0
50	13.0	13.5	8.7	9.7	10.9	5.6	12.0	12.7	8.0	12.9	13.4	8.8	15.2	15.4	11.9	16.5	16.6	13.0
51	12.1	12.7	7.9	8.9	10.2	5.1	11.2	11.9	7.2	12.1	12.6	7.9	14.3	14.5	10.7	15.6	15.7	11.9
52	11.3	11.9	7.1	8.2	9.6	4.6	10.5	11.2	6.4	11.2	11.8	7.1	13.4	13.7	9.7	14.7	14.9	10.9
53	10.5	11.2	6.4	7.5	9.1	4.1	9.7	10.5	5.7	10.5	11.1	6.4	12.5	12.9	8.7	13.8	14.0	9.8
54	9.7	10.4	5.7	7.0	8.5	3.7	9.0	9.8	5.1	9.7	10.4	5.7	11.7	12.1	7.8	12.9	13.2	8.9
55	8.9	9.7	5.1	6.4	8.0	3.3	8.2	9.1	4.5	8.9	9.6	5.0	10.8	11.3	6.9	12.0	12.3	8.0
56	8.2	9.0	4.5	5.8	7.4	2.9	7.4	8.4	4.0	8.1	9.0	4.5	9.9	10.5	6.1	11.1	11.5	7.2
57	7.4	8.4	3.9	5.3	6.8	2.5	6.7	7.8	3.6	7.4	8.3	4.0	9.1	9.8	5.3	10.3	10.7	6.5
58	6.7	7.7	3.5	4.7	6.3	2.2	6.0	7.1	3.1	6.7	7.7	3.5	8.3	9.1	4.5	9.4	10.0	5.8
59	6.0	7.1	3.0	4.2	5.7	1.9	5.5	6.5	2.8	6.1	7.1	3.1	7.5	8.4	3.9	8.6	9.3	5.1
60	5.3	6.5	2.7	3.7	5.1	1.7	4.8	5.9	2.4	5.4	6.6	2.7	6.6	7.7	3.3	7.9	8.6	4.5
61	4.7	6.0	2.3	3.3	4.7	1.5	4.2	5.4	2.2	4.9	6.1	2.4	5.9	7.1	2.9	7.1	7.9	4.0
62	4.0	5.6	2.1	2.7	4.4	1.3	3.5	5.0	1.9	4.2	5.7	2.1	5.2	6.6	2.5	6.4	7.3	3.5
63	3.5	5.2	1.8	2.3	4.2	1.2	3.0	4.7	1.7	3.7	5.3	1.9	4.5	6.1	2.2	5.6	6.8	3.1
64	3.1	4.8	1.6	2.1	4.0	1.1	2.7	4.4	1.5	3.3	4.9	1.8	4.0	5.7	2.0	4.9	6.2	2.7
65	2.6	4.6	1.5	1.9	3.9	1.0	2.3	4.2	1.4	2.8	4.6	1.6	3.4	5.3	1.7	4.4	5.8	2.3
66	2.3	4.3	1.3	1.6	3.8	0.9	2.1	4.0	1.2	2.4	4.2	1.4	3.0	5.0	1.5	3.8	5.4	2.0
67	2.0	4.1	1.1	1.4	3.7	0.8	1.8	3.8	1.1	2.1	4.0	1.3	2.6	4.6	1.3	3.3	5.1	1.7
68	1.8	3.9	1.0	1.3	3.5	0.7	1.7	3.6	0.9	1.9	3.8	1.1	2.3	4.3	1.1	3.0	4.8	1.5
69	1.5	3.7	0.8	1.1	3.4	0.6	1.4	3.4	0.8	1.7	3.7	0.9	1.9	4.1	1.0	2.5	4.5	1.3
70	1.3	3.5	0.7	0.9	3.2	0.5	1.2	3.3	0.6	1.4	3.5	0.8	1.6	3.8	0.8	2.1	4.2	1.1
71	1.1	3.3	0.6	0.8	3.0	0.4	1.0	3.2	0.5	1.2	3.4	0.6	1.4	3.6	0.7	1.9	3.8	0.9
72	1.0	3.2	0.5	0.7	2.9	0.3	0.9	3.1	0.4	1.1	3.2	0.5	1.3	3.4	0.6	1.6	3.5	0.7
73	0.8	3.0	0.4	0.6	2.8	0.3	0.8	3.0	0.3	0.9	3.0	0.4	1.2	3.2	0.5	1.4	3.3	0.5
74	0.7	2.9	0.3	0.5	2.7	0.2	0.6	2.9	0.2	0.8	2.8	0.3	0.9	3.1	0.4	1.0	3.0	0.4
75	0.6	2.7	0.2	0.4	2.6	0.2	0.5	2.7	0.2	0.6	2.6	0.3	0.8	2.9	0.3	0.8	2.8	0.3

* Calculated from aggregated data, i.e., not weighted averages.

Table 4: Worklife expectancies, increment-decrement methodology, by sex, race, Hispanic origin, and education, July 1999–June 2007, continued: White Females

Age	All White Females *			< High School			High School or GED			Some College			Bachelor Degree			Graduate Degree		
	All	Act'v	Inact	All	Act'v	Inact	All	Act'v	Inact	All	Act'v	Inact	All	Act'v	Inact	All	Act'v	Inact
18	33.7	34.2	32.9	22.1	22.7	21.3	32.9	33.3	32.1	36.0	36.5	35.2						
19	33.2	33.6	32.2	21.6	22.3	20.9	32.3	32.6	31.4	35.4	35.8	34.5						
20	32.6	33.0	31.5	21.1	21.9	20.3	31.6	32.0	30.5	34.7	35.1	33.7	35.7	36.1	34.7			
21	31.9	32.4	30.8	20.6	21.4	19.7	30.9	31.3	29.6	34.1	34.5	33.0	35.0	35.4	34.1			
22	31.3	31.8	29.9	20.1	20.9	19.1	30.1	30.6	28.7	33.5	33.8	32.3	34.3	34.5	33.2			
23	30.6	31.2	29.1	19.6	20.5	18.6	29.4	30.0	27.9	32.8	33.2	31.5	33.5	33.8	32.0	36.9	37.2	35.0
24	30.0	30.5	28.3	19.2	20.2	18.1	28.8	29.4	27.2	32.1	32.5	30.6	32.7	33.0	30.9	36.0	36.2	34.4
25	29.3	29.8	27.5	18.7	19.8	17.7	28.1	28.8	26.5	31.3	31.7	29.7	31.9	32.2	29.9	35.1	35.3	33.5
26	28.6	29.1	26.6	18.3	19.4	17.3	27.4	28.1	25.7	30.5	31.0	28.8	31.1	31.4	29.0	34.2	34.4	32.6
27	27.8	28.5	25.9	17.8	18.9	16.8	26.7	27.5	25.0	29.8	30.3	27.9	30.3	30.6	28.1	33.3	33.5	31.6
28	27.1	27.8	25.1	17.4	18.4	16.4	26.1	26.9	24.3	29.0	29.6	27.1	29.5	29.9	27.1	32.4	32.6	30.5
29	26.4	27.1	24.4	16.9	17.9	16.0	25.5	26.3	23.6	28.3	28.9	26.3	28.7	29.1	26.2	31.5	31.8	29.4
30	25.7	26.4	23.6	16.5	17.5	15.5	24.8	25.6	22.9	27.5	28.1	25.5	27.9	28.4	25.3	30.6	31.0	28.4
31	25.0	25.7	22.9	16.1	17.1	14.9	24.1	24.9	22.2	26.8	27.4	24.8	27.0	27.6	24.4	29.8	30.2	27.5
32	24.2	25.0	22.1	15.6	16.7	14.4	23.5	24.3	21.4	26.1	26.7	24.0	26.2	26.9	23.5	29.0	29.5	26.5
33	23.5	24.3	21.3	15.2	16.2	13.9	22.8	23.6	20.7	25.4	26.0	23.3	25.4	26.2	22.7	28.2	28.7	25.6
34	22.8	23.7	20.5	14.6	15.7	13.3	22.1	22.9	19.9	24.6	25.3	22.5	24.7	25.5	21.9	27.4	28.0	24.6
35	22.1	23.0	19.7	14.2	15.3	12.7	21.4	22.3	19.2	23.9	24.6	21.6	23.9	24.8	21.1	26.6	27.2	23.8
36	21.4	22.3	19.0	13.6	14.8	12.1	20.7	21.6	18.5	23.2	23.8	20.8	23.2	24.0	20.3	25.8	26.4	23.0
37	20.7	21.6	18.2	13.2	14.4	11.6	20.1	20.9	17.7	22.4	23.1	19.9	22.4	23.3	19.5	25.0	25.7	22.2
38	20.0	20.9	17.4	12.7	13.9	11.0	19.4	20.1	17.0	21.6	22.3	19.0	21.7	22.6	18.8	24.2	24.9	21.4
39	19.3	20.1	16.6	12.2	13.4	10.5	18.6	19.4	16.1	20.8	21.5	18.1	21.0	21.8	18.1	23.5	24.1	20.5
40	18.6	19.4	15.8	11.7	13.0	10.0	17.9	18.7	15.3	20.1	20.7	17.3	20.3	21.1	17.4	22.7	23.2	19.7
41	17.8	18.7	15.0	11.2	12.5	9.5	17.2	18.0	14.4	19.3	20.0	16.5	19.5	20.3	16.7	21.9	22.4	18.8
42	17.1	17.9	14.2	10.8	12.0	9.0	16.5	17.3	13.6	18.5	19.2	15.6	18.8	19.5	15.9	21.0	21.5	18.0
43	16.4	17.2	13.4	10.3	11.5	8.4	15.7	16.6	12.7	17.7	18.4	14.8	18.0	18.7	15.2	20.2	20.7	17.2
44	15.6	16.4	12.6	9.6	11.0	7.8	14.9	15.9	11.8	16.9	17.6	13.9	17.3	17.9	14.4	19.3	19.8	16.3
45	14.9	15.7	11.7	9.0	10.5	7.2	14.2	15.2	10.9	16.2	16.8	13.1	16.5	17.2	13.5	18.5	18.9	15.4
46	14.1	15.0	10.9	8.5	10.0	6.6	13.5	14.4	10.1	15.4	16.1	12.2	15.8	16.4	12.7	17.6	18.1	14.4
47	13.3	14.2	10.0	7.9	9.5	6.0	12.7	13.7	9.3	14.6	15.3	11.3	15.0	15.6	11.9	16.8	17.2	13.5
48	12.6	13.5	9.2	7.4	9.1	5.5	12.0	13.0	8.5	13.8	14.6	10.4	14.2	14.8	11.0	15.9	16.3	12.6
49	11.8	12.8	8.4	7.0	8.7	4.9	11.2	12.3	7.8	13.0	13.8	9.6	13.3	14.0	10.2	15.1	15.5	11.7
50	11.1	12.1	7.6	6.5	8.3	4.5	10.5	11.7	7.1	12.2	13.1	8.7	12.5	13.2	9.3	14.2	14.6	10.9
51	10.3	11.4	6.9	6.0	7.9	4.0	9.8	11.0	6.4	11.5	12.4	7.9	11.7	12.5	8.4	13.4	13.8	10.0
52	9.6	10.7	6.2	5.6	7.6	3.6	9.1	10.4	5.8	10.7	11.7	7.2	11.0	11.7	7.6	12.5	12.9	9.1
53	8.9	10.1	5.5	5.1	7.2	3.2	8.4	9.8	5.1	10.0	11.0	6.5	10.2	11.0	6.9	11.6	12.1	8.3
54	8.1	9.4	4.9	4.7	6.8	2.9	7.7	9.1	4.6	9.2	10.3	5.8	9.4	10.3	6.1	10.8	11.3	7.4
55	7.4	8.8	4.3	4.3	6.4	2.5	7.0	8.5	4.0	8.5	9.7	5.2	8.6	9.6	5.4	10.0	10.5	6.6
56	6.7	8.2	3.8	3.8	6.0	2.2	6.4	8.0	3.5	7.7	9.0	4.6	7.7	9.0	4.7	9.1	9.8	5.9
57	6.1	7.6	3.3	3.3	5.5	1.9	5.8	7.4	3.0	7.1	8.4	4.0	7.1	8.3	4.1	8.3	9.1	5.2
58	5.4	7.0	2.8	2.9	5.1	1.6	5.2	6.9	2.6	6.4	7.8	3.5	6.5	7.8	3.6	7.6	8.5	4.6
59	4.8	6.5	2.4	2.6	4.6	1.4	4.6	6.4	2.3	5.6	7.1	3.0	5.9	7.2	3.1	6.7	7.8	4.0
60	4.2	5.9	2.1	2.3	4.2	1.2	4.0	5.9	2.0	5.0	6.5	2.6	5.1	6.6	2.7	6.0	7.2	3.4
61	3.7	5.5	1.8	1.9	3.9	1.0	3.6	5.4	1.7	4.4	6.0	2.3	4.5	6.2	2.4	5.4	6.7	3.0
62	3.1	5.1	1.5	1.6	3.6	0.8	3.0	5.1	1.5	3.7	5.6	2.0	3.8	5.7	2.0	4.7	6.2	2.6
63	2.6	4.7	1.3	1.3	3.4	0.7	2.5	4.7	1.3	3.2	5.2	1.7	3.3	5.3	1.7	4.1	5.8	2.2
64	2.3	4.5	1.1	1.2	3.3	0.6	2.2	4.5	1.1	2.8	4.9	1.5	2.9	4.9	1.5	3.7	5.5	1.9
65	1.8	4.3	1.0	0.9	3.2	0.5	1.8	4.3	1.0	2.3	4.6	1.2	2.3	4.6	1.3	3.1	5.3	1.6
66	1.6	4.1	0.8	0.8	3.1	0.4	1.6	4.2	0.8	2.0	4.3	1.0	2.0	4.3	1.1	2.8	5.1	1.4
67	1.4	3.9	0.7	0.7	3.0	0.4	1.4	4.1	0.7	1.8	4.1	0.8	1.7	4.0	0.9	2.4	4.8	1.2
68	1.2	3.8	0.6	0.6	3.0	0.3	1.2	4.0	0.6	1.5	3.8	0.7	1.5	3.8	0.8	2.1	4.6	1.0
69	1.0	3.6	0.5	0.5	2.9	0.3	1.0	3.9	0.5	1.2	3.6	0.6	1.3	3.6	0.7	1.8	4.4	0.8
70	0.8	3.4	0.4	0.5	2.8	0.2	0.8	3.8	0.4	1.0	3.3	0.5	1.1	3.4	0.5	1.5	4.1	0.7
71	0.7	3.2	0.3	0.4	2.7	0.2	0.7	3.6	0.3	0.8	3.1	0.4	0.9	3.2	0.5	1.3	4.0	0.6
72	0.6	3.1	0.2	0.3	2.5	0.1	0.6	3.4	0.2	0.6	2.8	0.3	0.8	3.1	0.4	1.1	3.9	0.5
73	0.5	2.9	0.2	0.2	2.3	0.1	0.5	3.1	0.2	0.6	2.7	0.2	0.6	2.9	0.3	1.0	3.7	0.4
74	0.4	2.7	0.1	0.2	2.1	0.1	0.4	3.0	0.1	0.4	2.6	0.2	0.5	2.7	0.2	0.9	3.6	0.3
75	0.3	2.5	0.1	0.1	1.9	0.0	0.3	2.8	0.1	0.3	2.5	0.1	0.4	2.5	0.2	0.8	3.4	0.3

* Calculated from aggregated data, i.e., not weighted averages.

Table 4: Worklife expectancies, increment-decrement methodology, by sex, race, Hispanic origin, and education, July 1999–June 2007, continued: Black Males

Age	All Black Males *			< High School			High School or GED			Some College			Bachelor's or More		
	All	Act'v	Inact	All	Act'v	Inact	All	Act'v	Inact	All	Act'v	Inact	All	Act'v	Inact
18	31.8	32.3	31.4	23.5	24.0	23.2	31.8	32.2	31.3	34.7	35.3	34.0			
19	31.5	32.0	30.9	23.3	23.8	22.8	31.4	31.7	30.9	34.4	34.9	33.5			
20	31.1	31.6	30.4	23.0	23.5	22.3	30.9	31.2	30.2	34.1	34.4	33.0	38.6	38.9	37.7
21	30.6	31.1	29.7	22.7	23.3	21.8	30.3	30.6	29.5	33.1	33.8	32.4	37.1	38.3	36.0
22	30.1	30.5	29.1	22.3	22.8	21.2	29.6	30.0	28.6	32.6	33.3	31.8	36.6	37.8	35.2
23	29.6	30.0	28.3	21.7	22.3	20.6	29.0	29.3	27.7	32.3	32.7	31.2	36.4	37.2	34.5
24	29.1	29.4	27.6	21.2	21.7	20.1	28.4	28.7	26.9	31.8	32.1	30.7	35.8	36.4	33.9
25	28.4	28.8	27.0	20.7	21.1	19.6	27.8	28.1	26.2	31.1	31.4	30.1	35.2	35.7	33.4
26	27.8	28.1	26.3	20.2	20.7	19.1	27.1	27.4	25.5	30.5	30.6	29.3	34.5	34.8	32.8
27	27.1	27.4	25.5	19.7	20.2	18.5	26.5	26.8	24.7	29.7	29.8	28.4	33.8	33.9	32.1
28	26.4	26.7	24.6	19.1	19.7	17.7	25.8	26.2	23.8	28.9	29.1	27.4	32.9	33.0	31.5
29	25.7	26.0	23.7	18.5	19.2	16.9	25.2	25.6	23.0	28.1	28.3	26.4	32.0	32.1	30.9
30	24.9	25.2	22.9	17.9	18.6	16.1	24.4	24.8	22.2	27.3	27.4	25.6	31.1	31.2	30.0
31	24.1	24.4	22.1	17.3	18.0	15.1	23.7	24.1	21.6	26.5	26.6	24.8	30.2	30.3	29.1
32	23.4	23.6	21.2	16.5	17.4	14.2	23.0	23.3	20.9	25.7	25.7	23.9	29.3	29.4	28.2
33	22.6	22.9	20.4	15.7	16.8	13.2	22.2	22.5	20.2	24.9	24.9	22.9	28.4	28.5	27.1
34	21.8	22.1	19.5	15.2	16.1	12.3	21.4	21.8	19.6	24.1	24.2	21.9	27.5	27.6	26.1
35	21.0	21.4	18.7	14.4	15.6	11.8	20.7	21.0	18.8	23.3	23.4	21.1	26.6	26.7	24.9
36	20.3	20.6	17.9	14.1	15.1	11.3	19.9	20.3	18.0	22.5	22.6	20.4	25.8	25.9	23.8
37	19.5	19.9	17.0	13.4	14.6	10.9	19.2	19.5	17.2	21.6	21.7	19.6	24.9	25.0	22.5
38	18.7	19.1	16.2	13.2	14.2	10.4	18.4	18.8	16.2	20.8	20.9	18.8	24.0	24.1	21.6
39	17.9	18.4	15.2	12.6	13.8	10.0	17.6	18.1	15.2	19.9	20.0	17.9	23.1	23.3	20.6
40	17.1	17.6	14.2	12.2	13.4	9.4	16.8	17.3	14.2	19.0	19.2	16.8	22.2	22.4	19.6
41	16.4	16.9	13.3	11.5	13.0	8.8	16.1	16.6	13.3	18.2	18.4	15.6	21.3	21.5	18.8
42	15.6	16.2	12.5	11.1	12.6	8.3	15.3	16.0	12.4	17.3	17.5	14.5	20.5	20.7	18.3
43	14.9	15.5	11.7	10.8	12.2	7.7	14.7	15.3	11.7	16.5	16.8	13.5	19.6	19.8	17.7
44	14.1	14.9	11.0	10.1	11.8	7.3	14.0	14.7	11.0	15.8	16.0	12.6	18.8	18.9	16.9
45	13.4	14.2	10.3	9.6	11.4	6.9	13.3	14.0	10.3	15.1	15.3	11.8	17.9	18.0	16.0
46	12.8	13.5	9.6	9.4	10.9	6.6	12.6	13.4	9.5	14.4	14.6	11.0	17.0	17.2	15.0
47	12.1	12.8	8.9	8.9	10.4	6.2	11.9	12.7	8.8	13.7	13.9	10.3	16.2	16.3	13.7
48	11.3	12.1	8.1	8.4	9.8	5.8	11.1	12.0	8.1	13.0	13.2	9.6	15.3	15.5	12.4
49	10.6	11.5	7.4	7.9	9.4	5.4	10.5	11.3	7.4	12.3	12.5	8.9	14.4	14.7	11.0
50	9.9	10.9	6.7	7.4	9.0	4.9	9.8	10.7	6.6	11.7	11.9	8.2	13.6	13.9	9.9
51	9.4	10.2	6.1	7.1	8.6	4.5	9.1	10.1	5.9	11.1	11.4	7.6	12.8	13.1	9.1
52	8.7	9.7	5.5	6.7	8.2	4.0	8.4	9.5	5.4	10.5	10.8	7.1	11.9	12.2	8.3
53	8.0	9.1	5.0	6.3	7.8	3.6	7.8	8.9	4.9	9.9	10.2	6.6	11.1	11.5	7.7
54	7.5	8.5	4.5	5.6	7.3	3.1	7.3	8.3	4.4	9.3	9.7	6.2	10.4	10.7	7.1
55	6.7	8.0	4.1	4.9	6.9	2.7	6.4	7.8	4.0	8.7	9.1	5.7	9.6	10.0	6.5
56	6.2	7.4	3.6	4.5	6.5	2.3	6.0	7.2	3.6	8.1	8.5	5.2	8.8	9.3	5.8
57	5.7	6.9	3.2	4.1	6.1	2.0	5.6	6.7	3.2	7.5	8.0	4.6	8.1	8.6	5.3
58	5.1	6.4	2.7	3.8	5.7	1.8	5.1	6.1	2.8	6.8	7.5	4.1	7.3	7.9	4.6
59	4.6	5.9	2.4	3.4	5.3	1.6	4.5	5.7	2.5	6.2	7.0	3.6	6.5	7.2	4.0
60	4.0	5.4	2.1	3.0	4.9	1.5	4.0	5.3	2.1	5.6	6.5	3.2	5.8	6.6	3.5
61	3.6	5.0	1.9	2.6	4.6	1.3	3.6	4.9	1.9	5.1	5.9	2.9	5.2	6.0	3.0
62	2.9	4.6	1.7	2.3	4.2	1.2	2.9	4.6	1.6	4.6	5.5	2.7	4.6	5.5	2.6
63	2.6	4.3	1.5	1.9	3.9	1.1	2.5	4.3	1.4	4.1	5.1	2.5	4.1	5.1	2.3
64	2.2	4.0	1.3	1.7	3.7	1.0	2.2	3.9	1.2	3.7	4.8	2.3	3.6	4.7	2.2
65	2.0	3.8	1.2	1.5	3.6	0.8	1.9	3.6	1.0	3.3	4.6	2.1	3.2	4.4	2.0
66	1.7	3.6	1.0	1.3	3.3	0.7	1.6	3.4	0.9	3.0	4.4	1.8	2.9	4.2	1.8
67	1.5	3.4	0.9	1.1	3.2	0.6	1.3	3.1	0.7	2.7	4.2	1.6	2.6	4.0	1.6
68	1.3	3.1	0.8	1.0	3.0	0.5	1.1	2.9	0.6	2.4	4.1	1.4	2.3	3.7	1.4
69	1.1	2.9	0.6	0.9	2.8	0.5	0.9	2.6	0.5	2.2	4.0	1.1	2.1	3.5	1.3
70	1.0	2.8	0.5	0.8	2.6	0.4	0.8	2.4	0.4	2.0	3.9	0.9	1.9	3.3	1.1
71	0.8	2.7	0.4	0.6	2.5	0.3	0.7	2.3	0.3	1.6	3.7	0.6	1.7	3.3	1.0
72	0.7	2.6	0.3	0.5	2.3	0.3	0.6	2.3	0.3	1.3	3.5	0.5	1.5	3.2	0.8
73	0.6	2.4	0.3	0.4	2.2	0.2	0.5	2.2	0.2	1.1	3.2	0.4	1.3	3.1	0.7
74	0.5	2.3	0.2	0.4	2.1	0.2	0.4	2.1	0.2	0.9	3.0	0.3	1.1	2.8	0.5
75	0.4	2.2	0.2	0.3	1.9	0.1	0.4	2.1	0.1	0.8	2.7	0.2	0.9	2.7	0.4

* Calculated from aggregated data, i.e., not weighted averages.

Table 4: Worklife expectancies, increment-decrement methodology, by sex, race, Hispanic origin, and education, July 1999–June 2007, continued: Black Females

Age	All	Act'v	All Black Females * Inact	< High School			High School or GED			Some College			Bachelor's or More		
				All	Act'v	Inact	All	Act'v	Inact	All	Act'v	Inact	All	Act'v	Inact
18	31.3	31.9	30.8	21.0	21.6	20.7	31.0	31.5	30.5	32.7	33.4	32.2			
19	31.0	31.5	30.4	20.8	21.4	20.4	30.6	30.9	30.0	32.5	33.1	31.9			
20	30.6	31.1	29.9	20.5	21.1	19.9	30.0	30.4	29.3	32.2	32.7	31.5	38.2	39.0	37.0
21	30.1	30.5	29.3	20.1	20.7	19.3	29.4	29.7	28.6	31.7	32.1	31.0	37.6	38.0	36.5
22	29.6	30.0	28.7	19.6	20.3	18.8	28.7	29.1	27.8	31.2	31.6	30.4	36.9	37.1	35.9
23	29.0	29.4	28.0	19.1	19.9	18.1	28.1	28.5	27.1	30.7	30.9	29.8	36.0	36.3	35.0
24	28.3	28.7	27.3	18.6	19.4	17.4	27.4	27.8	26.4	30.0	30.3	29.1	35.4	35.6	34.4
25	27.7	28.0	26.5	18.1	18.9	16.9	26.8	27.1	25.8	29.3	29.6	28.2	34.6	34.8	33.7
26	27.0	27.3	25.8	17.6	18.2	16.5	26.1	26.4	25.1	28.6	28.9	27.5	33.8	34.0	32.9
27	26.2	26.6	25.0	17.0	17.6	16.1	25.4	25.8	24.2	27.9	28.1	26.7	33.0	33.1	32.0
28	25.5	25.8	24.2	16.4	17.0	15.5	24.7	25.1	23.4	27.1	27.4	26.0	32.2	32.3	30.9
29	24.8	25.1	23.3	15.8	16.5	14.8	24.0	24.4	22.6	26.4	26.6	25.2	31.3	31.5	29.7
30	24.0	24.4	22.5	15.3	16.0	14.3	23.2	23.7	21.9	25.6	25.8	24.2	30.4	30.6	28.7
31	23.2	23.6	21.6	14.8	15.6	13.6	22.5	23.0	21.0	24.7	25.0	23.4	29.6	29.8	28.0
32	22.5	22.9	20.8	14.3	15.1	13.1	21.9	22.3	20.2	23.9	24.2	22.5	28.7	28.9	27.3
33	21.7	22.1	20.0	13.8	14.6	12.4	21.1	21.6	19.4	23.1	23.4	21.6	27.9	28.0	26.6
34	20.9	21.3	19.2	13.2	14.1	11.8	20.4	20.9	18.7	22.3	22.6	20.8	27.0	27.1	25.8
35	20.1	20.6	18.4	12.6	13.5	11.2	19.7	20.2	17.9	21.4	21.8	19.9	26.1	26.2	24.9
36	19.4	19.8	17.5	12.1	13.0	10.6	18.9	19.5	17.1	20.6	21.0	19.0	25.2	25.3	23.9
37	18.6	19.1	16.6	11.6	12.5	9.9	18.2	18.7	16.3	19.8	20.2	18.1	24.3	24.4	22.8
38	17.8	18.3	15.7	11.1	12.1	9.3	17.4	18.0	15.4	19.1	19.4	17.2	23.4	23.6	21.6
39	17.1	17.6	14.7	10.6	11.8	8.8	16.7	17.3	14.5	18.3	18.6	16.3	22.5	22.7	20.5
40	16.3	16.9	13.9	10.2	11.3	8.3	16.0	16.6	13.7	17.5	17.9	15.3	21.6	21.8	19.5
41	15.6	16.2	13.1	9.6	10.9	8.0	15.3	15.9	12.9	16.7	17.1	14.4	20.8	21.0	18.5
42	14.8	15.5	12.3	9.3	10.5	7.5	14.4	15.2	12.1	15.9	16.4	13.5	19.9	20.1	17.6
43	14.1	14.8	11.4	8.8	10.2	7.1	13.8	14.5	11.2	15.2	15.7	12.6	19.0	19.3	16.7
44	13.4	14.2	10.6	8.4	9.8	6.6	13.1	13.9	10.4	14.4	14.9	11.7	18.2	18.4	15.7
45	12.7	13.5	9.9	7.9	9.4	6.2	12.4	13.3	9.6	13.7	14.2	11.0	17.3	17.5	14.8
46	12.0	12.9	9.2	7.6	9.1	5.7	11.7	12.8	8.8	12.8	13.5	10.3	16.4	16.7	13.9
47	11.3	12.2	8.5	7.2	8.7	5.3	11.2	12.2	8.2	12.0	12.7	9.6	15.6	15.9	13.1
48	10.7	11.6	7.8	6.6	8.2	4.9	10.6	11.7	7.5	11.4	12.1	8.9	14.8	15.0	12.4
49	10.1	11.0	7.2	6.3	7.8	4.5	9.9	11.1	6.9	10.7	11.4	8.2	13.9	14.2	11.6
50	9.4	10.4	6.5	5.8	7.5	4.1	9.3	10.5	6.4	9.9	10.7	7.3	13.1	13.4	10.8
51	8.7	9.8	5.8	5.3	7.2	3.7	8.7	9.8	5.8	9.2	10.0	6.5	12.3	12.6	10.1
52	8.0	9.1	5.2	5.0	6.9	3.3	8.0	9.2	5.2	8.4	9.4	5.7	11.4	11.7	9.1
53	7.4	8.5	4.6	4.8	6.6	3.0	7.3	8.5	4.7	7.7	8.8	4.9	10.6	10.9	8.1
54	6.7	7.9	4.0	4.5	6.3	2.6	6.5	7.9	4.2	7.1	8.2	4.2	9.7	10.1	7.2
55	6.0	7.4	3.5	4.1	6.0	2.3	5.9	7.3	3.7	6.4	7.7	3.7	8.8	9.2	6.4
56	5.4	6.8	3.0	3.5	5.6	2.0	5.5	6.8	3.3	5.9	7.2	3.2	8.0	8.5	5.5
57	4.9	6.3	2.6	3.1	5.3	1.7	4.9	6.3	2.9	5.4	6.7	2.8	7.2	7.7	4.7
58	4.4	5.8	2.3	2.8	4.9	1.5	4.5	5.9	2.6	4.8	6.2	2.5	6.4	7.0	4.0
59	3.8	5.3	2.0	2.4	4.6	1.3	4.0	5.4	2.3	4.3	5.7	2.2	5.6	6.3	3.3
60	3.4	4.9	1.7	2.2	4.4	1.2	3.5	4.9	2.0	3.9	5.2	1.9	4.9	5.8	2.8
61	2.9	4.5	1.5	2.0	4.2	1.1	3.1	4.5	1.8	3.5	4.8	1.7	4.3	5.3	2.3
62	2.4	4.2	1.3	1.8	4.1	1.0	2.5	4.1	1.6	2.9	4.4	1.5	3.7	4.9	1.9
63	2.1	3.9	1.2	1.5	3.9	0.9	2.2	3.8	1.4	2.6	4.1	1.3	3.2	4.6	1.7
64	1.8	3.7	1.0	1.4	3.8	0.7	2.0	3.6	1.2	2.2	3.8	1.2	2.7	4.3	1.4
65	1.5	3.5	0.9	1.2	3.5	0.6	1.7	3.4	1.1	1.8	3.7	1.0	2.3	3.9	1.2
66	1.3	3.3	0.8	1.0	3.2	0.6	1.5	3.4	1.0	1.5	3.5	0.9	1.9	3.5	1.1
67	1.1	3.1	0.7	0.8	3.0	0.5	1.3	3.2	0.9	1.3	3.2	0.8	1.6	3.2	0.9
68	0.9	2.9	0.6	0.7	2.8	0.4	1.1	3.1	0.7	1.2	2.9	0.7	1.3	2.9	0.7
69	0.8	2.7	0.5	0.6	2.6	0.3	1.0	3.0	0.6	1.0	2.8	0.6	1.1	2.6	0.6
70	0.7	2.5	0.4	0.5	2.4	0.3	0.8	2.9	0.5	0.9	2.7	0.5	0.8	2.3	0.5
71	0.5	2.4	0.3	0.4	2.2	0.2	0.7	2.9	0.4	0.7	2.5	0.4	0.7	2.1	0.4
72	0.4	2.3	0.2	0.3	2.1	0.2	0.6	2.8	0.3	0.6	2.3	0.3	0.5	2.0	0.2
73	0.4	2.2	0.2	0.2	2.1	0.1	0.5	2.7	0.3	0.5	2.1	0.3	0.4	1.9	0.2
74	0.3	2.1	0.1	0.2	2.0	0.1	0.4	2.5	0.2	0.5	2.0	0.3	0.3	1.8	0.1
75	0.2	2.0	0.1	0.1	1.8	0.1	0.3	2.4	0.1	0.4	2.0	0.2	0.3	1.7	0.1

* Calculated from aggregated data, i.e., not weighted averages.

Table 4: Worklife expectancies, increment-decrement methodology, by sex, race, Hispanic origin, and education, July 1999–June 2007, continued: Hispanic Males

Age	All Hispanic Males *			< High School			High School			Some College or More		
	All	Act'v	Inact	All	Act'v	Inact	All	Act'v	Inact	All	Act'v	Inact
18	39.0	39.6	38.3	38.1	38.6	37.5	39.7	40.1	38.8	40.5	41.3	39.6
19	38.6	38.9	37.6	37.7	38.0	36.9	39.1	39.4	38.1	40.0	40.6	39.0
20	38.0	38.3	36.9	37.1	37.3	36.2	38.4	38.6	37.4	39.5	39.9	38.5
21	37.3	37.5	36.2	36.4	36.6	35.4	37.7	37.9	36.6	38.9	39.2	37.9
22	36.6	36.8	35.5	35.7	35.8	34.7	37.0	37.1	35.8	38.3	38.6	37.2
23	35.9	36.0	34.6	34.9	35.0	33.9	36.2	36.3	34.8	37.6	37.8	36.4
24	35.1	35.2	33.7	34.0	34.1	33.0	35.4	35.5	33.8	36.9	37.0	35.5
25	34.2	34.3	32.8	33.2	33.2	32.1	34.6	34.7	33.0	36.1	36.2	34.6
26	33.4	33.5	32.0	32.3	32.4	31.2	33.7	33.8	32.4	35.2	35.4	33.7
27	32.5	32.6	31.1	31.4	31.5	30.0	32.9	33.0	31.7	34.4	34.5	32.9
28	31.7	31.7	30.2	30.6	30.7	28.7	32.0	32.1	30.9	33.5	33.6	32.1
29	30.8	30.9	29.2	29.7	29.8	27.7	31.1	31.2	29.7	32.6	32.7	31.4
30	29.9	30.0	28.3	28.8	28.9	26.8	30.2	30.3	28.5	31.7	31.7	30.4
31	29.0	29.1	27.3	27.9	28.0	26.1	29.3	29.4	27.6	30.7	30.8	29.2
32	28.1	28.2	26.4	27.0	27.2	25.4	28.4	28.6	26.7	29.8	29.9	28.2
33	27.2	27.3	25.6	26.2	26.3	24.6	27.6	27.7	25.8	28.9	28.9	27.3
34	26.3	26.4	24.7	25.3	25.4	23.8	26.6	26.8	25.0	27.9	28.0	26.4
35	25.4	25.5	23.8	24.4	24.5	22.8	25.8	25.9	24.1	27.0	27.1	25.6
36	24.5	24.6	22.8	23.5	23.6	21.8	24.9	25.0	23.1	26.1	26.2	24.6
37	23.6	23.7	21.7	22.6	22.7	20.7	24.0	24.1	22.0	25.2	25.3	23.6
38	22.7	22.8	20.6	21.7	21.8	19.5	23.1	23.2	20.8	24.3	24.4	22.5
39	21.8	22.0	19.5	20.8	21.0	18.5	22.2	22.3	19.6	23.4	23.5	21.4
40	20.9	21.1	18.4	19.9	20.1	17.5	21.3	21.5	18.5	22.5	22.6	20.5
41	20.0	20.2	17.5	19.1	19.3	16.6	20.4	20.6	17.4	21.6	21.7	19.6
42	19.1	19.4	16.4	18.2	18.5	15.6	19.5	19.8	16.3	20.7	20.8	18.7
43	18.3	18.6	15.4	17.4	17.7	14.6	18.6	18.9	15.4	19.8	20.0	17.6
44	17.4	17.7	14.4	16.5	16.9	13.7	17.7	18.1	14.5	18.9	19.1	16.4
45	16.5	16.9	13.5	15.7	16.1	12.8	16.8	17.3	13.5	18.0	18.2	15.3
46	15.7	16.1	12.6	14.9	15.4	11.9	16.1	16.4	12.7	17.1	17.3	14.1
47	14.9	15.3	11.8	14.1	14.6	11.2	15.3	15.7	12.1	16.2	16.5	13.0
48	14.0	14.5	11.0	13.2	13.7	10.4	14.5	14.9	11.3	15.3	15.6	12.0
49	13.2	13.7	10.1	12.4	12.9	9.5	13.8	14.2	10.5	14.4	14.8	11.0
50	12.4	12.9	9.1	11.6	12.1	8.7	13.0	13.5	9.7	13.6	14.0	9.8
51	11.6	12.1	8.2	10.7	11.4	7.8	12.3	12.8	8.9	12.7	13.2	8.8
52	10.8	11.4	7.3	10.0	10.7	7.0	11.5	12.1	7.9	11.8	12.4	7.7
53	9.9	10.7	6.4	9.1	10.0	6.2	10.6	11.5	7.0	10.9	11.7	6.8
54	9.2	10.1	5.7	8.5	9.4	5.4	10.0	10.8	6.1	10.2	10.9	6.1
55	8.5	9.4	5.0	7.8	8.8	4.7	9.2	10.1	5.4	9.4	10.1	5.5
56	7.8	8.7	4.4	7.2	8.3	4.1	8.5	9.4	4.7	8.7	9.4	4.9
57	7.1	8.0	3.9	6.5	7.6	3.6	7.8	8.7	4.2	7.9	8.7	4.4
58	6.3	7.4	3.4	5.7	7.0	3.1	7.0	8.0	3.8	7.2	8.0	4.1
59	5.7	6.7	3.1	5.2	6.3	2.8	6.3	7.4	3.4	6.5	7.3	3.7
60	5.0	6.1	2.7	4.6	5.7	2.4	5.5	6.8	3.0	5.9	6.7	3.4
61	4.5	5.6	2.4	4.1	5.3	2.1	4.8	6.2	2.6	5.3	6.2	3.1
62	3.8	5.1	2.1	3.5	4.9	1.8	4.1	5.7	2.3	4.7	5.7	2.8
63	3.2	4.8	1.8	2.9	4.6	1.5	3.6	5.2	2.2	4.2	5.3	2.5
64	3.0	4.5	1.6	2.6	4.4	1.3	3.2	4.8	2.0	3.8	5.0	2.2
65	2.6	4.3	1.4	2.3	4.3	1.1	2.8	4.4	1.8	3.4	4.9	1.9
66	2.3	4.1	1.3	1.9	4.0	0.9	2.5	4.2	1.6	3.1	4.8	1.7
67	1.9	4.0	1.1	1.6	3.8	0.8	2.2	3.9	1.4	2.7	4.7	1.4
68	1.7	4.0	0.9	1.3	3.7	0.6	1.9	3.7	1.2	2.4	4.6	1.2
69	1.4	3.8	0.7	1.1	3.5	0.5	1.7	3.5	1.0	2.1	4.5	0.9
70	1.2	3.6	0.5	0.9	3.2	0.4	1.4	3.4	0.8	1.9	4.4	0.7
71	0.9	3.3	0.3	0.7	3.0	0.3	1.2	3.5	0.6	1.6	4.4	0.5
72	0.7	3.1	0.2	0.5	2.8	0.2	0.9	3.6	0.4	1.3	4.3	0.4
73	0.5	2.9	0.2	0.4	2.6	0.2	0.8	3.8	0.3	1.2	4.2	0.2
74	0.5	2.9	0.1	0.3	2.3	0.1	0.6	3.8	0.1	1.0	4.0	0.1
75	0.4	2.8	0.1	0.3	2.1	0.1	0.6	3.5	0.1	0.8	3.6	0.1

* Calculated from aggregated data, i.e., not weighted averages.

Table 4: Worklife expectancies, increment-decrement methodology, by sex, race, Hispanic origin, and education, July 1999–June 2007, continued: Hispanic Females

Age	All Hispanic Females *			< High School			High School			Some College or More		
	All	Act'v	Inact	All	Act'v	Inact	All	Act'v	Inact	All	Act'v	Inact
18	29.3	29.9	28.7	22.4	23.2	21.9	31.4	31.7	31.0	35.9	36.5	35.3
19	28.9	29.4	28.1	22.1	23.0	21.5	30.8	31.2	30.2	35.3	35.8	34.5
20	28.4	28.9	27.4	21.7	22.6	21.0	30.2	30.6	29.4	34.7	35.1	33.8
21	27.8	28.3	26.7	21.3	22.1	20.4	29.5	30.0	28.5	34.0	34.5	33.0
22	27.2	27.8	26.0	20.8	21.7	19.9	28.8	29.4	27.6	33.4	33.8	32.3
23	26.7	27.2	25.2	20.4	21.3	19.5	28.1	28.7	26.8	32.7	33.2	31.6
24	26.1	26.6	24.6	20.0	21.0	19.1	27.4	28.1	26.1	32.0	32.5	30.7
25	25.5	26.1	23.9	19.6	20.6	18.7	26.8	27.5	25.4	31.3	31.7	29.9
26	24.9	25.5	23.3	19.2	20.1	18.3	26.1	27.0	24.7	30.6	31.0	29.1
27	24.3	24.9	22.7	18.7	19.6	17.9	25.5	26.4	24.0	29.8	30.3	28.2
28	23.7	24.3	22.1	18.3	19.1	17.5	25.0	25.8	23.4	29.1	29.5	27.4
29	23.1	23.7	21.5	17.8	18.7	17.1	24.4	25.3	22.7	28.3	28.8	26.5
30	22.5	23.1	20.8	17.4	18.3	16.6	23.8	24.7	22.1	27.6	28.1	25.7
31	21.9	22.5	20.1	17.0	17.9	16.1	23.2	24.1	21.5	26.8	27.4	24.8
32	21.3	22.0	19.5	16.6	17.5	15.6	22.6	23.4	20.9	26.1	26.7	24.0
33	20.7	21.3	18.9	16.2	17.1	15.1	22.0	22.8	20.3	25.4	26.0	23.3
34	20.1	20.7	18.2	15.6	16.7	14.5	21.4	22.1	19.7	24.6	25.2	22.5
35	19.5	20.1	17.6	15.2	16.2	14.0	20.7	21.4	19.1	23.9	24.5	21.7
36	18.8	19.5	16.9	14.7	15.8	13.4	20.1	20.7	18.5	23.2	23.8	21.0
37	18.2	18.9	16.2	14.2	15.3	12.9	19.4	20.1	17.7	22.4	23.0	20.2
38	17.6	18.2	15.5	13.7	14.8	12.3	18.7	19.4	16.9	21.7	22.3	19.4
39	16.9	17.6	14.8	13.3	14.3	11.8	18.0	18.8	16.1	20.9	21.5	18.6
40	16.3	16.9	14.1	12.7	13.7	11.3	17.3	18.1	15.2	20.1	20.7	17.9
41	15.6	16.2	13.4	12.2	13.2	10.8	16.6	17.5	14.4	19.3	19.9	17.1
42	14.9	15.6	12.7	11.7	12.6	10.3	15.9	16.8	13.6	18.6	19.1	16.2
43	14.3	14.9	12.0	11.2	12.1	9.7	15.2	16.1	12.8	17.8	18.3	15.3
44	13.5	14.2	11.2	10.5	11.4	9.0	14.5	15.3	12.0	16.9	17.5	14.3
45	12.8	13.5	10.4	9.8	10.8	8.3	13.7	14.6	11.2	16.1	16.8	13.4
46	12.1	12.8	9.5	9.2	10.3	7.6	13.0	13.9	10.3	15.4	16.0	12.5
47	11.4	12.1	8.7	8.5	9.7	6.9	12.2	13.3	9.4	14.6	15.2	11.6
48	10.7	11.5	7.9	7.9	9.1	6.2	11.5	12.6	8.6	13.8	14.5	10.8
49	10.0	10.9	7.2	7.3	8.7	5.6	10.8	12.0	7.8	13.0	13.7	10.1
50	9.4	10.3	6.6	6.8	8.2	5.1	10.1	11.5	7.1	12.3	13.0	9.4
51	8.9	9.8	6.0	6.3	7.8	4.6	9.5	10.9	6.6	11.6	12.3	8.8
52	8.3	9.2	5.5	5.8	7.4	4.2	8.9	10.4	6.1	10.9	11.6	8.1
53	7.7	8.7	5.0	5.4	7.0	3.7	8.3	9.9	5.7	10.2	11.0	7.4
54	7.1	8.2	4.5	4.8	6.6	3.3	7.8	9.3	5.2	9.5	10.3	6.7
55	6.5	7.7	3.9	4.4	6.1	2.9	7.2	8.7	4.7	8.7	9.7	5.9
56	5.9	7.1	3.4	3.9	5.6	2.5	6.5	8.0	4.2	8.0	9.1	5.2
57	5.3	6.5	3.0	3.4	5.2	2.2	5.9	7.3	3.7	7.3	8.5	4.5
58	4.7	6.0	2.6	3.0	4.7	1.9	5.3	6.7	3.2	6.7	7.9	3.9
59	4.1	5.5	2.2	2.5	4.2	1.6	4.6	6.1	2.7	6.0	7.3	3.3
60	3.6	5.0	1.9	2.2	3.9	1.4	4.0	5.6	2.3	5.4	6.9	2.7
61	3.1	4.6	1.5	1.8	3.5	1.2	3.4	5.1	2.0	4.7	6.5	2.2
62	2.6	4.2	1.3	1.5	3.2	1.0	2.9	4.7	1.7	4.1	6.1	1.7
63	2.2	4.0	1.1	1.3	3.1	0.8	2.5	4.4	1.5	3.5	5.8	1.3
64	1.9	3.8	0.9	1.1	2.9	0.7	2.1	4.1	1.3	3.0	5.4	1.0
65	1.6	3.6	0.8	1.0	2.8	0.6	1.8	4.0	1.0	2.5	5.0	0.9
66	1.4	3.4	0.7	0.8	2.7	0.5	1.6	4.0	0.9	2.1	4.5	0.8
67	1.2	3.3	0.5	0.7	2.6	0.5	1.4	3.9	0.7	1.8	4.2	0.7
68	1.0	3.2	0.5	0.6	2.6	0.4	1.1	3.8	0.5	1.5	3.9	0.6
69	0.9	3.1	0.4	0.5	2.6	0.3	1.0	3.7	0.4	1.3	3.6	0.5
70	0.8	3.0	0.3	0.5	2.6	0.3	0.8	3.7	0.3	1.1	3.4	0.5
71	0.7	2.9	0.3	0.4	2.5	0.3	0.6	3.6	0.2	0.9	3.2	0.4
72	0.6	2.9	0.2	0.3	2.6	0.2	0.4	3.5	0.2	0.8	3.1	0.3
73	0.5	2.9	0.2	0.3	2.7	0.2	0.3	3.2	0.1	0.7	3.2	0.2
74	0.4	2.9	0.1	0.3	2.7	0.1	0.2	2.9	0.1	0.5	3.3	0.2
75	0.3	2.7	0.1	0.2	2.7	0.1	0.2	2.7	0.0	0.4	3.1	0.1

* Calculated from aggregated data, i.e., not weighted averages.

Table 5: Worklife expectancies by educational attainment, conventional methodology, 2000–2006 CPS data: Males All Races

Age	All Ed Levels		<HS	HS	Some College			College Degree	Graduate Degree			Age
	Aggr't Data*	Wgt Ave**			All	No Degree	Assoc Degree		All	Masters	Phd/ Prof'l	
18	39.5	39.8	34.1	39.0	39.9	39.6	41.1					18
19	39.0	39.3	33.7	38.4	39.5	39.2	40.5	42.7				19
20	38.4	38.7	33.2	37.7	38.9	38.6	39.9	42.0				20
21	37.7	38.1	32.6	36.9	38.3	38.0	39.1	41.4	42.8	41.3		21
22	37.0	37.4	31.9	36.1	37.7	37.4	38.4	40.7	42.2	40.7	43.3	22
23	36.3	36.7	31.2	35.3	37.0	36.7	37.6	40.0	41.5	40.1	42.7	23
24	35.5	35.9	30.4	34.4	36.2	36.0	36.7	39.2	40.7	39.4	42.3	24
25	34.6	35.1	29.6	33.6	35.4	35.1	35.9	38.3	39.9	38.5	41.6	25
26	33.8	34.2	28.9	32.7	34.5	34.3	35.0	37.4	39.0	37.7	40.8	26
27	32.9	33.4	28.1	31.9	33.6	33.4	34.1	36.5	38.1	36.8	40.0	27
28	32.1	32.5	27.3	31.0	32.8	32.6	33.2	35.6	37.2	35.9	39.1	28
29	31.2	31.6	26.5	30.1	31.9	31.7	32.2	34.7	36.3	35.0	38.2	29
30	30.3	30.7	25.7	29.3	31.0	30.8	31.3	33.8	35.4	34.1	37.3	30
31	29.4	29.8	24.8	28.4	30.1	29.9	30.4	32.8	34.5	33.2	36.3	31
32	28.5	28.9	24.0	27.5	29.1	29.0	29.5	31.9	33.6	32.3	35.4	32
33	27.6	28.0	23.2	26.7	28.2	28.1	28.6	31.0	32.6	31.3	34.4	33
34	26.7	27.1	22.4	25.8	27.3	27.2	27.7	30.0	31.7	30.4	33.5	34
35	25.8	26.2	21.5	24.9	26.4	26.3	26.7	29.1	30.8	29.4	32.5	35
36	24.9	25.3	20.7	24.0	25.5	25.4	25.8	28.1	29.8	28.5	31.6	36
37	24.0	24.4	19.9	23.2	24.6	24.5	24.9	27.2	28.9	27.6	30.7	37
38	23.2	23.5	19.1	22.3	23.7	23.6	24.0	26.3	28.0	26.6	29.7	38
39	22.3	22.6	18.3	21.4	22.8	22.7	23.1	25.3	27.0	25.7	28.8	39
40	21.4	21.8	17.5	20.6	21.9	21.8	22.2	24.4	26.1	24.8	27.8	40
41	20.5	20.9	16.8	19.7	21.1	20.9	21.3	23.5	25.2	23.8	26.9	41
42	19.7	20.0	16.0	18.9	20.2	20.1	20.4	22.5	24.2	22.9	25.9	42
43	18.8	19.2	15.3	18.0	19.3	19.2	19.5	21.6	23.3	22.0	25.0	43
44	17.9	18.3	14.5	17.2	18.4	18.3	18.6	20.7	22.4	21.1	24.1	44
45	17.1	17.5	13.8	16.3	17.6	17.5	17.7	19.8	21.5	20.1	23.2	45
46	16.2	16.7	13.1	15.5	16.7	16.6	16.9	18.9	20.5	19.2	22.2	46
47	15.4	15.9	12.4	14.7	15.8	15.8	16.0	18.0	19.6	18.3	21.3	47
48	14.6	15.1	11.7	13.9	15.0	14.9	15.2	17.1	18.7	17.4	20.4	48
49	13.8	14.3	11.1	13.1	14.2	14.1	14.3	16.2	17.8	16.5	19.5	49
50	12.9	13.5	10.4	12.3	13.3	13.3	13.5	15.3	16.9	15.5	18.6	50
51	12.1	12.7	9.7	11.5	12.5	12.5	12.6	14.4	16.0	14.6	17.6	51
52	11.3	11.9	9.1	10.7	11.7	11.6	11.8	13.5	15.1	13.7	16.7	52
53	10.5	11.1	8.4	10.0	10.9	10.9	11.0	12.6	14.2	12.8	15.8	53
54	9.8	10.3	7.8	9.2	10.1	10.1	10.2	11.8	13.3	11.9	14.9	54
55	9.0	9.5	7.2	8.5	9.3	9.3	9.4	10.9	12.4	11.1	14.0	55
56	8.2	8.8	6.6	7.8	8.6	8.6	8.6	10.1	11.6	10.2	13.2	56
57	7.5	8.0	6.0	7.1	7.8	7.8	7.9	9.3	10.7	9.4	12.3	57
58	6.8	7.3	5.5	6.4	7.1	7.1	7.1	8.5	9.9	8.6	11.4	58
59	6.1	6.5	4.9	5.7	6.4	6.4	6.4	7.7	9.1	7.8	10.6	59
60	5.4	5.8	4.4	5.1	5.7	5.7	5.8	6.9	8.3	7.0	9.8	60
61	4.8	5.2	3.9	4.5	5.1	5.1	5.2	6.2	7.6	6.3	8.9	61
62	4.2	4.5	3.4	3.9	4.5	4.5	4.5	5.6	6.9	5.7	8.2	62
63	3.7	4.0	2.9	3.4	4.0	4.0	4.0	5.0	6.2	5.1	7.4	63
64	3.3	3.5	2.5	3.1	3.5	3.5	3.6	4.4	5.6	4.5	6.7	64
65	2.9	3.1	2.2	2.7	3.1	3.1	3.2	3.9	5.0	4.0	6.1	65
66	2.6	2.7	1.9	2.4	2.8	2.8	2.8	3.5	4.5	3.6	5.5	66
67	2.3	2.4	1.7	2.2	2.5	2.5	2.5	3.1	4.1	3.2	5.0	67
68	2.0	2.2	1.5	1.9	2.2	2.2	2.2	2.8	3.6	2.9	4.4	68
69	1.8	1.9	1.3	1.7	2.0	1.9	2.0	2.5	3.3	2.6	4.0	69
70	1.6	1.7	1.1	1.5	1.7	1.7	1.8	2.2	2.9	2.4	3.6	70
71	1.4	1.5	1.0	1.3	1.5	1.5	1.6	2.0	2.6	2.1	3.2	71
72	1.2	1.3	0.9	1.2	1.4	1.3	1.5	1.8	2.3	1.9	2.9	72
73	1.1	1.2	0.8	1.0	1.2	1.2	1.3	1.6	2.1	1.7	2.5	73
74	0.9	1.0	0.7	0.9	1.1	1.1	1.2	1.4	1.8	1.5	2.2	74
75	0.8	0.9	0.6	0.8	0.9	0.9	1.0	1.2	1.6	1.4	2.0	75

* Calculated from CPS data of all education levels combined. ** Weighted averages by education
Sources: Current Population Survey monthly microdata samples 2000 through 2006, and mortality data from Table 1.

Table 5: Worklife expectancies by educational attainment, conventional methodology, 2000–2006 CPS data: continued, Females All Races

Age	All Ed Levels Aggr't Data*	All Ed Levels Wgt Ave**	<HS	HS	Some College All	Some College No Degree	Some College Assoc Degree	College Degree	Graduate Degree All	Graduate Degree Masters	Graduate Degree Phd/Prof'l	Age
18	33.7	34.2	23.3	33.0	35.9	35.3	37.5					18
19	33.1	33.7	22.9	32.4	35.4	34.7	37.0	36.5				19
20	32.5	33.1	22.4	31.7	34.8	34.1	36.3	35.9				20
21	31.9	32.5	21.9	31.0	34.1	33.5	35.5	35.3	38.3	37.8		21
22	31.2	31.8	21.4	30.3	33.4	32.8	34.8	34.6	37.6	37.0	38.6	22
23	30.5	31.1	20.9	29.6	32.7	32.1	34.0	33.8	36.8	36.4	37.9	23
24	29.8	30.4	20.4	28.9	32.0	31.3	33.2	33.0	36.1	35.6	37.3	24
25	29.0	29.7	19.9	28.2	31.2	30.6	32.3	32.1	35.2	34.8	36.5	25
26	28.3	28.9	19.4	27.5	30.4	29.8	31.5	31.3	34.4	34.0	35.9	26
27	27.5	28.2	18.9	26.8	29.6	29.1	30.7	30.4	33.6	33.1	35.0	27
28	26.8	27.5	18.4	26.1	28.9	28.3	29.9	29.6	32.7	32.3	34.2	28
29	26.1	26.7	17.9	25.4	28.1	27.6	29.1	28.8	31.9	31.4	33.4	29
30	25.3	26.0	17.4	24.7	27.3	26.8	28.3	27.9	31.1	30.6	32.5	30
31	24.6	25.2	16.9	24.0	26.6	26.1	27.5	27.1	30.2	29.7	31.7	31
32	23.9	24.5	16.3	23.3	25.8	25.3	26.7	26.3	29.4	28.9	30.8	32
33	23.1	23.8	15.8	22.6	25.0	24.6	25.9	25.6	28.6	28.1	30.0	33
34	22.4	23.1	15.3	21.9	24.3	23.8	25.1	24.8	27.7	27.3	29.1	34
35	21.7	22.3	14.8	21.2	23.5	23.1	24.3	24.1	26.9	26.5	28.3	35
36	21.0	21.6	14.2	20.5	22.8	22.3	23.5	23.3	26.1	25.7	27.4	36
37	20.2	20.8	13.7	19.7	22.0	21.6	22.7	22.5	25.3	24.9	26.6	37
38	19.5	20.1	13.1	19.0	21.2	20.8	21.9	21.8	24.5	24.1	25.8	38
39	18.8	19.3	12.5	18.3	20.4	20.1	21.1	21.0	23.7	23.3	25.0	39
40	18.0	18.6	12.0	17.6	19.7	19.3	20.3	20.3	22.9	22.5	24.1	40
41	17.3	17.8	11.4	16.8	18.9	18.5	19.5	19.5	22.1	21.7	23.3	41
42	16.5	17.1	10.9	16.1	18.1	17.8	18.7	18.7	21.3	20.9	22.5	42
43	15.8	16.4	10.3	15.3	17.3	17.0	17.9	17.9	20.4	20.1	21.6	43
44	15.0	15.6	9.8	14.6	16.5	16.2	17.1	17.1	19.6	19.2	20.8	44
45	14.3	14.9	9.2	13.9	15.7	15.4	16.3	16.3	18.8	18.4	19.9	45
46	13.5	14.1	8.7	13.1	14.9	14.7	15.5	15.6	17.9	17.5	19.1	46
47	12.8	13.4	8.2	12.4	14.1	13.9	14.7	14.7	17.1	16.7	18.2	47
48	12.0	12.6	7.7	11.7	13.4	13.1	13.9	13.9	16.2	15.8	17.4	48
49	11.3	11.9	7.2	10.9	12.6	12.3	13.1	13.1	15.4	15.0	16.5	49
50	10.5	11.2	6.6	10.2	11.8	11.6	12.3	12.3	14.5	14.1	15.6	50
51	9.8	10.4	6.1	9.5	11.0	10.8	11.5	11.5	13.7	13.2	14.8	51
52	9.1	9.7	5.7	8.8	10.3	10.1	10.7	10.7	12.8	12.4	13.9	52
53	8.4	8.9	5.2	8.1	9.5	9.3	9.9	9.9	12.0	11.5	13.1	53
54	7.7	8.2	4.8	7.4	8.8	8.6	9.1	9.2	11.1	10.7	12.2	54
55	7.0	7.5	4.3	6.8	8.1	7.9	8.4	8.4	10.3	9.8	11.4	55
56	6.3	6.8	3.9	6.2	7.4	7.2	7.7	7.7	9.5	9.0	10.5	56
57	5.7	6.1	3.5	5.6	6.7	6.6	7.0	7.0	8.7	8.2	9.7	57
58	5.1	5.5	3.1	5.0	6.0	5.9	6.3	6.3	7.9	7.5	8.9	58
59	4.5	4.8	2.7	4.4	5.4	5.3	5.6	5.6	7.2	6.7	8.1	59
60	4.0	4.2	2.4	3.9	4.8	4.7	5.0	4.9	6.5	6.1	7.4	60
61	3.4	3.7	2.1	3.4	4.2	4.1	4.4	4.4	5.8	5.4	6.7	61
62	3.0	3.2	1.8	2.9	3.7	3.6	3.8	3.8	5.2	4.8	6.0	62
63	2.6	2.7	1.5	2.5	3.2	3.2	3.3	3.3	4.6	4.2	5.5	63
64	2.2	2.3	1.3	2.2	2.8	2.8	2.9	2.9	4.1	3.7	4.9	64
65	1.9	2.0	1.1	1.9	2.4	2.4	2.5	2.5	3.6	3.3	4.4	65
66	1.7	1.8	1.0	1.6	2.2	2.1	2.2	2.2	3.2	2.9	3.9	66
67	1.5	1.5	0.9	1.4	1.9	1.9	1.9	2.0	2.8	2.6	3.5	67
68	1.3	1.3	0.7	1.2	1.6	1.6	1.7	1.7	2.5	2.3	3.1	68
69	1.1	1.1	0.6	1.1	1.4	1.4	1.4	1.5	2.2	2.1	2.7	69
70	0.9	1.0	0.5	0.9	1.2	1.2	1.2	1.3	2.0	1.8	2.4	70
71	0.8	0.8	0.5	0.8	1.1	1.0	1.1	1.2	1.8	1.6	2.2	71
72	0.7	0.7	0.4	0.7	0.9	0.9	0.9	1.0	1.6	1.5	2.0	72
73	0.6	0.6	0.3	0.6	0.8	0.8	0.8	0.9	1.4	1.3	1.8	73
74	0.5	0.5	0.3	0.5	0.7	0.7	0.7	0.8	1.3	1.2	1.6	74
75	0.4	0.5	0.2	0.4	0.6	0.6	0.6	0.7	1.1	1.0	1.4	75

* Calculated from CPS data of all education levels combined. ** Weighted averages by education
Sources: Current Population Survey monthly microdata samples 2000 through 2006, and mortality data from Table 1.

Table 5: Worklife expectancies by educational attainment, conventional methodology, 2000–2006 CPS data: continued, White Males

Age	All Ed Levels		<HS	HS	Some College			College Degree	Graduate Degree		Age
	Aggr't Data*	Wgt Ave**			All	No Degree	Assoc Degree		Masters	Phd/ Prof'l	
18	40.3	40.5	35.2	39.8	40.6	40.3	41.7				18
19	39.8	39.9	34.7	39.1	40.1	39.8	41.0	43.1			19
20	39.1	39.3	34.0	38.4	39.5	39.3	40.3	42.4			20
21	38.4	38.6	33.3	37.6	38.9	38.7	39.5	41.7	41.6		21
22	37.7	37.9	32.5	36.8	38.2	38.0	38.7	41.0	41.0	43.3	22
23	36.9	37.1	31.7	35.9	37.5	37.3	37.9	40.2	40.4	42.7	23
24	36.1	36.3	30.8	35.1	36.7	36.5	37.1	39.4	39.6	42.0	24
25	35.2	35.5	30.0	34.2	35.8	35.7	36.2	38.5	38.8	41.2	25
26	34.4	34.6	29.2	33.3	35.0	34.8	35.3	37.7	37.9	40.4	26
27	33.5	33.7	28.4	32.4	34.1	33.9	34.4	36.8	37.0	39.5	27
28	32.6	32.8	27.6	31.6	33.2	33.0	33.4	35.8	36.1	38.6	28
29	31.7	31.9	26.7	30.7	32.2	32.1	32.5	34.9	35.1	37.7	29
30	30.8	31.0	25.9	29.8	31.3	31.2	31.6	34.0	34.2	36.7	30
31	29.9	30.1	25.1	28.9	30.4	30.3	30.7	33.0	33.3	35.8	31
32	29.0	29.2	24.2	28.0	29.5	29.4	29.8	32.1	32.4	34.8	32
33	28.1	28.3	23.4	27.1	28.6	28.5	28.8	31.1	31.4	33.9	33
34	27.2	27.4	22.5	26.2	27.7	27.6	27.9	30.2	30.5	32.9	34
35	26.3	26.5	21.7	25.3	26.8	26.6	27.0	29.2	29.5	31.9	35
36	25.4	25.6	20.8	24.5	25.8	25.7	26.1	28.3	28.6	31.0	36
37	24.5	24.7	20.0	23.6	24.9	24.8	25.1	27.4	27.6	30.0	37
38	23.6	23.8	19.2	22.7	24.1	23.9	24.2	26.4	26.7	29.1	38
39	22.7	22.9	18.4	21.8	23.1	23.1	23.3	25.5	25.8	28.1	39
40	21.8	22.0	17.6	20.9	22.3	22.2	22.4	24.5	24.8	27.2	40
41	20.9	21.1	16.8	20.1	21.4	21.3	21.5	23.6	23.9	26.3	41
42	20.0	20.3	16.0	19.2	20.5	20.4	20.6	22.7	23.0	25.3	42
43	19.1	19.4	15.2	18.3	19.6	19.5	19.7	21.8	22.0	24.4	43
44	18.3	18.5	14.5	17.5	18.7	18.6	18.8	20.8	21.1	23.5	44
45	17.4	17.7	13.7	16.6	17.8	17.8	17.9	19.9	20.2	22.5	45
46	16.5	16.9	13.0	15.8	16.9	16.9	17.1	19.0	19.2	21.6	46
47	15.7	16.1	12.3	15.0	16.1	16.0	16.2	18.1	18.3	20.7	47
48	14.8	15.2	11.6	14.1	15.2	15.2	15.3	17.2	17.4	19.7	48
49	14.0	14.4	10.9	13.3	14.4	14.3	14.4	16.3	16.5	18.8	49
50	13.2	13.6	10.2	12.5	13.5	13.5	13.6	15.4	15.6	17.9	50
51	12.3	12.8	9.5	11.7	12.7	12.7	12.7	14.5	14.7	17.0	51
52	11.5	12.0	8.8	10.9	11.9	11.8	11.9	13.6	13.7	16.1	52
53	10.7	11.2	8.2	10.1	11.1	11.0	11.1	12.7	12.8	15.2	53
54	9.9	10.4	7.6	9.4	10.3	10.2	10.3	11.8	11.9	14.3	54
55	9.1	9.6	6.9	8.6	9.5	9.5	9.5	11.0	11.1	13.4	55
56	8.4	8.8	6.3	7.9	8.7	8.7	8.7	10.1	10.2	12.5	56
57	7.6	8.0	5.8	7.2	7.9	8.0	7.9	9.3	9.4	11.7	57
58	6.9	7.3	5.2	6.5	7.2	7.2	7.2	8.5	8.6	10.8	58
59	6.2	6.5	4.6	5.8	6.5	6.5	6.5	7.7	7.8	10.0	59
60	5.5	5.8	4.1	5.1	5.8	5.8	5.8	6.9	7.0	9.1	60
61	4.9	5.1	3.6	4.5	5.2	5.2	5.2	6.2	6.3	8.3	61
62	4.3	4.5	3.0	3.9	4.6	4.6	4.6	5.6	5.7	7.6	62
63	3.8	4.0	2.7	3.5	4.0	4.1	4.0	5.0	5.1	6.9	63
64	3.3	3.5	2.3	3.1	3.6	3.6	3.5	4.4	4.5	6.2	64
65	2.9	3.1	2.0	2.7	3.1	3.1	3.1	3.9	4.0	5.6	65
66	2.6	2.7	1.8	2.4	2.8	2.8	2.8	3.5	3.6	5.1	66
67	2.3	2.4	1.6	2.2	2.5	2.5	2.5	3.1	3.2	4.6	67
68	2.1	2.2	1.4	1.9	2.2	2.2	2.2	2.8	2.9	4.1	68
69	1.8	1.9	1.2	1.7	2.0	2.0	2.0	2.5	2.6	3.7	69
70	1.6	1.7	1.0	1.5	1.7	1.7	1.8	2.2	2.4	3.4	70
71	1.4	1.5	0.9	1.3	1.6	1.5	1.6	2.0	2.1	3.0	71
72	1.2	1.3	0.8	1.2	1.4	1.3	1.5	1.8	1.9	2.6	72
73	1.1	1.2	0.7	1.0	1.2	1.2	1.3	1.6	1.7	2.3	73
74	0.9	1.0	0.6	0.9	1.1	1.1	1.2	1.4	1.5	2.1	74
75	0.8	0.9	0.5	0.8	0.9	0.9	1.0	1.2	1.4	1.9	75

* Calculated from CPS data of all education levels combined. ** Weighted averages by education
Sources: Current Population Survey monthly microdata samples 2000 through 2006, and mortality data from Table 1.

Table 5: Worklife expectancies by educational attainment, conventional methodology, 2000–2006 CPS data: continued, White Females

Age	All Ed Levels		<HS	HS	Some College			College Degree	Graduate Degree		Age
	Aggr't Data*	Wgt Ave**			All	No Degree	Assoc Degree		Masters	Phd/ Prof'l	
18	34.0	34.7	23.3	33.2	36.1	35.3	37.8				18
19	33.4	34.0	22.8	32.5	35.5	34.8	37.2	36.6			19
20	32.8	33.4	22.3	31.9	34.9	34.1	36.5	35.9			20
21	32.1	32.7	21.8	31.1	34.2	33.5	35.7	35.3	38.3		21
22	31.4	32.0	21.3	30.4	33.5	32.8	34.9	34.6	37.5	38.9	22
23	30.7	31.3	20.8	29.7	32.8	32.0	34.1	33.8	36.9	38.2	23
24	30.0	30.5	20.3	29.0	32.0	31.3	33.3	32.9	36.0	37.5	24
25	29.2	29.7	19.8	28.3	31.2	30.5	32.4	32.1	35.2	36.7	25
26	28.5	29.0	19.3	27.6	30.4	29.8	31.6	31.2	34.3	35.9	26
27	27.7	28.2	18.8	26.9	29.6	29.0	30.8	30.3	33.4	35.1	27
28	27.0	27.5	18.4	26.2	28.9	28.3	30.0	29.5	32.5	34.2	28
29	26.2	26.8	17.9	25.5	28.1	27.5	29.2	28.6	31.6	33.3	29
30	25.5	26.0	17.4	24.8	27.3	26.8	28.4	27.8	30.8	32.5	30
31	24.8	25.3	16.9	24.1	26.6	26.0	27.6	27.0	29.9	31.6	31
32	24.0	24.5	16.4	23.4	25.8	25.3	26.8	26.2	29.1	30.8	32
33	23.3	23.8	15.9	22.7	25.1	24.6	26.0	25.4	28.2	29.9	33
34	22.6	23.1	15.3	22.0	24.3	23.9	25.2	24.7	27.4	29.1	34
35	21.9	22.4	14.8	21.3	23.6	23.1	24.4	23.9	26.6	28.2	35
36	21.2	21.6	14.3	20.6	22.8	22.4	23.6	23.1	25.8	27.4	36
37	20.4	20.9	13.7	19.9	22.1	21.6	22.9	22.4	25.0	26.6	37
38	19.7	20.2	13.2	19.2	21.3	20.9	22.1	21.6	24.2	25.7	38
39	19.0	19.4	12.6	18.5	20.5	20.1	21.2	20.9	23.4	24.9	39
40	18.2	18.7	12.1	17.7	19.8	19.4	20.5	20.1	22.6	24.1	40
41	17.5	17.9	11.5	17.0	19.0	18.6	19.7	19.4	21.8	23.3	41
42	16.8	17.2	11.0	16.2	18.2	17.8	18.9	18.6	21.0	22.4	42
43	16.0	16.5	10.4	15.5	17.4	17.1	18.1	17.8	20.2	21.6	43
44	15.2	15.7	9.8	14.8	16.6	16.3	17.3	17.1	19.4	20.7	44
45	14.5	15.0	9.3	14.0	15.8	15.5	16.4	16.3	18.5	19.9	45
46	13.7	14.2	8.8	13.3	15.0	14.8	15.6	15.5	17.7	19.1	46
47	13.0	13.5	8.2	12.5	14.2	14.0	14.8	14.7	16.8	18.2	47
48	12.2	12.8	7.7	11.8	13.4	13.2	14.0	13.9	16.0	17.4	48
49	11.5	12.0	7.2	11.0	12.7	12.4	13.2	13.1	15.1	16.5	49
50	10.7	11.3	6.7	10.3	11.9	11.6	12.4	12.3	14.2	15.6	50
51	10.0	10.5	6.2	9.6	11.1	10.9	11.6	11.5	13.3	14.8	51
52	9.2	9.8	5.7	8.9	10.3	10.1	10.8	10.7	12.5	13.9	52
53	8.5	9.0	5.2	8.2	9.6	9.4	10.0	9.9	11.6	13.1	53
54	7.8	8.3	4.8	7.5	8.8	8.6	9.2	9.1	10.8	12.2	54
55	7.1	7.6	4.4	6.9	8.1	7.9	8.5	8.3	9.9	11.4	55
56	6.4	6.9	3.9	6.2	7.4	7.2	7.7	7.6	9.1	10.5	56
57	5.8	6.2	3.5	5.6	6.7	6.6	7.0	6.9	8.3	9.7	57
58	5.2	5.5	3.1	5.0	6.0	5.9	6.3	6.2	7.5	8.9	58
59	4.6	4.9	2.8	4.4	5.4	5.3	5.6	5.6	6.8	8.1	59
60	4.0	4.3	2.4	3.9	4.8	4.7	5.0	4.9	6.1	7.4	60
61	3.5	3.7	2.1	3.4	4.2	4.1	4.4	4.3	5.5	6.7	61
62	3.0	3.2	1.8	2.9	3.7	3.6	3.8	3.8	4.9	6.0	62
63	2.6	2.8	1.6	2.5	3.2	3.2	3.3	3.3	4.3	5.4	63
64	2.3	2.4	1.3	2.2	2.8	2.8	2.9	2.9	3.8	4.9	64
65	1.9	2.0	1.1	1.9	2.4	2.4	2.5	2.5	3.3	4.3	65
66	1.7	1.8	1.0	1.6	2.2	2.1	2.2	2.2	3.0	3.8	66
67	1.5	1.5	0.9	1.4	1.9	1.9	1.9	1.9	2.6	3.4	67
68	1.3	1.3	0.7	1.2	1.6	1.6	1.6	1.7	2.3	3.1	68
69	1.1	1.1	0.7	1.1	1.4	1.4	1.4	1.5	2.1	2.7	69
70	0.9	1.0	0.6	0.9	1.2	1.2	1.2	1.3	1.9	2.4	70
71	0.8	0.8	0.5	0.8	1.0	1.0	1.0	1.1	1.7	2.2	71
72	0.7	0.7	0.4	0.7	0.9	0.9	0.9	1.0	1.5	2.0	72
73	0.6	0.6	0.3	0.6	0.8	0.8	0.8	0.8	1.3	1.8	73
74	0.5	0.5	0.3	0.5	0.7	0.7	0.7	0.7	1.2	1.6	74
75	0.4	0.4	0.2	0.4	0.6	0.6	0.6	0.6	1.0	1.4	75

* Calculated from CPS data of all education levels combined. ** Weighted averages by education
Sources: Current Population Survey monthly microdata samples 2000 through 2006, and mortality data from Table 1.

Table 5: Worklife expectancies by educational attainment, conventional methodology, 2000–2006 CPS data: continued—Black Males and Females

Age	Black Males							Black Females							Age
	All Ed Levels		<HS	HS	Some College	College Degree	All Graduate Degrees	All Ed Levels		<HS	HS	Some College	College Degree	All Graduate Degrees	
	Aggr't Data*	Wgt Ave**						Aggr't Data*	Wgt Ave**						
18	34.0	35.1	26.7	34.2	35.8			32.9	34.0	23.6	32.3	35.7			18
19	33.4	34.6	26.4	33.7	35.4	40.0		32.3	33.5	23.3	31.8	35.3	38.6		19
20	32.8	34.1	25.9	33.1	35.0	39.5		31.7	33.0	22.9	31.2	34.8	38.2		20
21	32.3	33.5	25.5	32.5	34.4	39.0	38.8	31.1	32.5	22.3	30.6	34.3	37.7	38.3	21
22	31.7	32.9	24.9	31.8	33.9	38.3	38.4	30.5	31.8	21.8	29.9	33.6	37.1	37.6	22
23	31.0	32.2	24.3	31.1	33.2	37.6	38.0	29.8	31.1	21.3	29.2	32.9	36.3	36.8	23
24	30.3	31.5	23.7	30.4	32.6	36.9	37.5	29.1	30.4	20.8	28.5	32.2	35.6	36.0	24
25	29.6	30.8	23.1	29.6	31.8	36.1	36.9	28.4	29.7	20.2	27.8	31.5	34.8	35.2	25
26	28.9	30.0	22.5	28.9	31.0	35.3	36.1	27.7	29.0	19.7	27.1	30.7	34.0	34.4	26
27	28.1	29.2	21.8	28.1	30.2	34.4	35.2	26.9	28.2	19.1	26.4	29.9	33.2	33.6	27
28	27.3	28.4	21.2	27.4	29.4	33.4	34.3	26.1	27.5	18.6	25.6	29.2	32.4	32.8	28
29	26.5	27.6	20.5	26.6	28.5	32.5	33.4	25.4	26.7	18.0	24.9	28.4	31.5	31.9	29
30	25.7	26.8	19.9	25.8	27.6	31.6	32.5	24.6	25.9	17.4	24.1	27.6	30.6	31.0	30
31	24.9	26.0	19.3	25.0	26.7	30.7	31.6	23.8	25.2	16.9	23.4	26.7	29.7	30.1	31
32	24.1	25.1	18.6	24.2	25.8	29.8	30.7	23.1	24.4	16.3	22.7	25.9	28.8	29.2	32
33	23.3	24.3	17.9	23.4	25.0	28.9	29.8	22.3	23.6	15.7	21.9	25.1	28.0	28.3	33
34	22.4	23.5	17.3	22.6	24.1	28.0	28.9	21.5	22.8	15.1	21.2	24.2	27.1	27.4	34
35	21.6	22.7	16.5	21.8	23.2	27.0	28.0	20.7	22.0	14.5	20.4	23.4	26.2	26.6	35
36	20.8	21.8	15.9	21.0	22.4	26.1	27.1	19.9	21.3	14.0	19.7	22.6	25.3	25.7	36
37	20.0	20.9	15.3	20.2	21.5	25.2	26.2	19.2	20.5	13.4	19.0	21.8	24.5	24.8	37
38	19.2	20.0	14.7	19.4	20.7	24.3	25.3	18.4	19.7	12.7	18.2	21.0	23.6	23.9	38
39	18.4	19.2	14.1	18.6	19.8	23.4	24.4	17.6	18.9	12.2	17.5	20.2	22.7	23.0	39
40	17.6	18.4	13.5	17.8	19.0	22.5	23.5	16.9	18.1	11.6	16.7	19.4	21.9	22.1	40
41	16.8	17.6	12.8	17.1	18.1	21.6	22.6	16.1	17.4	11.0	16.0	18.5	21.0	21.2	41
42	16.0	16.8	12.3	16.3	17.3	20.7	21.7	15.4	16.6	10.5	15.2	17.7	20.1	20.3	42
43	15.3	16.0	11.7	15.6	16.5	19.8	20.8	14.6	15.8	10.0	14.5	16.9	19.3	19.4	43
44	14.5	15.2	11.1	14.8	15.7	18.9	20.0	13.9	15.1	9.5	13.8	16.1	18.4	18.5	44
45	13.8	14.5	10.6	14.1	14.9	18.1	19.1	13.1	14.3	9.0	13.1	15.3	17.5	17.6	45
46	13.1	13.8	10.1	13.3	14.1	17.3	18.3	12.4	13.6	8.5	12.4	14.5	16.7	16.7	46
47	12.3	13.1	9.5	12.6	13.4	16.4	17.4	11.7	12.8	7.9	11.7	13.7	15.9	15.8	47
48	11.6	12.4	9.0	11.9	12.6	15.6	16.5	11.0	12.1	7.4	11.0	13.0	15.0	14.9	48
49	10.9	11.6	8.5	11.2	11.9	14.7	15.6	10.3	11.4	7.0	10.3	12.2	14.2	14.1	49
50	10.2	10.9	7.9	10.5	11.2	13.9	14.8	9.6	10.7	6.5	9.6	11.5	13.3	13.2	50
51	9.5	10.2	7.4	9.8	10.5	13.1	13.9	8.9	10.0	6.0	9.0	10.8	12.5	12.3	51
52	8.9	9.5	6.9	9.1	9.8	12.2	13.1	8.2	9.3	5.6	8.3	10.1	11.7	11.5	52
53	8.2	8.9	6.4	8.5	9.1	11.5	12.3	7.6	8.3	5.2	7.7	9.4	10.9	10.6	53
54	7.6	8.2	5.8	7.9	8.4	10.8	11.5	6.9	7.6	4.7	7.0	8.7	10.0	9.7	54
55	6.9	7.5	5.3	7.3	7.7	10.1	10.7	6.3	6.9	4.2	6.5	8.0	9.2	8.9	55
56	6.3	6.9	4.9	6.7	7.1	9.4	9.9	5.7	6.3	3.8	5.9	7.4	8.4	8.1	56
57	5.8	6.2	4.4	6.1	6.4	8.7	9.1	5.1	5.7	3.4	5.3	6.8	7.6	7.3	57
58	5.2	5.6	4.0	5.5	5.8	8.0	8.4	4.6	5.0	3.0	4.8	6.1	6.9	6.5	58
59	4.6	5.0	3.5	4.9	5.2	7.3	7.7	4.0	4.5	2.7	4.2	5.5	6.2	5.8	59
60	4.1	4.5	3.1	4.4	4.6	6.6	7.0	3.5	3.9	2.4	3.7	5.0	5.5	5.1	60
61	3.6	3.9	2.8	3.9	4.1	6.0	6.3	3.0	3.4	2.1	3.2	4.4	4.9	4.5	61
62	3.1	3.4	2.4	3.4	3.6	5.5	5.7	2.6	2.9	1.8	2.8	3.9	4.3	3.9	62
63	2.8	3.0	2.1	3.0	3.2	5.1	5.1	2.3	2.5	1.6	2.4	3.4	3.8	3.4	63
64	2.4	2.7	1.9	2.7	2.9	4.7	4.6	2.0	2.2	1.4	2.1	3.0	3.4	3.0	64
65	2.2	2.4	1.7	2.4	2.5	4.3	4.1	1.7	1.9	1.2	1.8	2.7	3.0	2.6	65
66	1.9	2.1	1.5	2.1	2.3	3.9	3.7	1.5	1.7	1.0	1.6	2.4	2.7	2.3	66
67	1.7	1.9	1.3	1.9	2.0	3.7	3.3	1.3	1.4	0.9	1.4	2.2	2.4	1.9	67
68	1.5	1.7	1.2	1.8	1.8	3.4	3.0	1.1	1.3	0.8	1.2	2.0	2.2	1.7	68
69	1.4	1.5	1.0	1.6	1.6	3.2	2.7	1.0	1.1	0.6	1.1	1.8	2.0	1.5	69
70	1.2	1.4	0.9	1.5	1.4	2.9	2.3	0.9	1.0	0.5	1.0	1.7	1.9	1.3	70
71	1.1	1.2	0.7	1.4	1.3	2.7	2.0	0.7	0.9	0.5	0.9	1.5	1.7	1.2	71
72	0.9	1.1	0.6	1.3	1.2	2.5	1.7	0.7	0.8	0.4	0.8	1.4	1.6	1.1	72
73	0.8	0.9	0.5	1.2	1.0	2.3	1.5	0.6	0.7	0.3	0.7	1.3	1.5	1.0	73
74	0.7	0.8	0.5	1.1	0.9	2.1	1.3	0.5	0.6	0.3	0.6	1.2	1.4	0.8	74
75	0.6	0.7	0.4	1.0	0.8	1.9	1.1	0.5	0.5	0.3	0.5	1.1	1.4	0.7	75

* Calculated from CPS data of all education levels combined. ** Weighted averages by education
Sources: Current Population Survey monthly microdata samples 2000 through 2006, and mortality data from Table 1.

Table 5: Worklife expectancies by educational attainment, conventional methodology, 2000–2006 CPS data: continued—Hispanic Males and Females

| Age | Hispanic Males | | | | | | Hispanic Females | | | | | | Age |
| | All Ed Levels | | <HS | HS | Some College | College Degree & Higher | All Ed Levels | | <HS | HS | Some College | College Degree & Higher | |
	Aggr't Data*	Wgt Ave**					Aggr't Data*	Wgt Ave**					
18	40.2	40.9	38.7	40.9	41.9		29.3	30.1	23.1	31.5	35.9		18
19	39.5	40.4	38.3	40.3	41.4	44.7	28.9	29.7	22.7	31.0	35.4	36.9	19
20	38.7	39.7	37.6	39.6	40.8	43.8	28.3	29.2	22.3	30.4	34.8	36.5	20
21	38.0	38.9	36.8	38.8	40.1	43.0	27.7	28.6	21.8	29.7	34.1	36.0	21
22	37.2	38.1	36.0	38.0	39.5	42.2	27.1	28.0	21.3	29.0	33.5	35.4	22
23	36.4	37.3	35.1	37.1	38.7	41.4	26.5	27.4	20.9	28.4	32.8	34.7	23
24	35.5	36.5	34.3	36.3	38.0	40.6	25.9	26.8	20.4	27.7	32.0	33.9	24
25	34.7	35.6	33.4	35.4	37.1	39.7	25.2	26.2	19.9	27.1	31.3	33.1	25
26	33.8	34.7	32.5	34.5	36.3	38.8	24.6	25.6	19.5	26.4	30.6	32.3	26
27	32.9	33.8	31.6	33.6	35.4	37.9	24.0	25.0	19.0	25.8	29.8	31.5	27
28	32.0	32.9	30.7	32.8	34.6	37.0	23.4	24.4	18.6	25.2	29.0	30.7	28
29	31.1	32.1	29.8	31.9	33.7	36.1	22.8	23.7	18.1	24.5	28.3	29.9	29
30	30.2	31.1	28.9	31.0	32.7	35.1	22.2	23.1	17.7	23.9	27.6	29.1	30
31	29.3	30.2	28.0	30.1	31.8	34.2	21.5	22.5	17.2	23.2	26.8	28.3	31
32	28.4	29.3	27.1	29.2	30.9	33.3	20.9	21.9	16.7	22.6	26.1	27.6	32
33	27.5	28.4	26.3	28.3	30.0	32.3	20.3	21.2	16.2	21.9	25.4	26.8	33
34	26.6	27.5	25.4	27.4	29.1	31.4	19.6	20.6	15.7	21.2	24.6	26.0	34
35	25.7	26.6	24.5	26.5	28.2	30.5	19.0	19.9	15.2	20.6	23.9	25.3	35
36	24.8	25.7	23.6	25.6	27.3	29.5	18.3	19.3	14.6	19.9	23.1	24.5	36
37	23.9	24.8	22.7	24.7	26.4	28.6	17.7	18.6	14.1	19.2	22.4	23.7	37
38	23.0	23.9	21.8	23.8	25.5	27.7	17.0	18.0	13.5	18.5	21.6	23.0	38
39	22.1	23.0	20.9	22.9	24.6	26.8	16.3	17.3	13.0	17.8	20.8	22.2	39
40	21.2	22.2	20.0	22.0	23.7	25.9	15.6	16.6	12.4	17.1	20.1	21.4	40
41	20.4	21.3	19.2	21.2	22.8	25.0	15.0	15.9	11.8	16.4	19.3	20.6	41
42	19.5	20.4	18.3	20.3	21.9	24.1	14.3	15.2	11.3	15.7	18.5	19.8	42
43	18.6	19.6	17.5	19.5	21.0	23.2	13.6	14.5	10.7	15.0	17.7	19.0	43
44	17.8	18.7	16.6	18.6	20.1	22.4	12.9	13.8	10.1	14.3	16.9	18.2	44
45	16.9	17.8	15.8	17.8	19.2	21.5	12.2	13.0	9.5	13.6	16.2	17.5	45
46	16.1	17.0	15.0	17.0	18.4	20.6	11.5	12.3	8.9	12.9	15.4	16.6	46
47	15.3	16.2	14.2	16.2	17.6	19.7	10.8	11.6	8.3	12.2	14.6	15.8	47
48	14.4	15.4	13.4	15.3	16.8	18.8	10.2	11.0	7.8	11.4	13.9	15.0	48
49	13.6	14.6	12.6	14.5	15.9	18.0	9.5	10.3	7.2	10.7	13.1	14.2	49
50	12.8	13.8	11.8	13.7	15.1	17.1	8.8	9.6	6.6	10.1	12.3	13.4	50
51	12.0	13.0	11.1	12.9	14.3	16.2	8.2	8.9	6.1	9.4	11.6	12.6	51
52	11.2	12.2	10.3	12.1	13.5	15.4	7.5	8.2	5.6	8.8	10.8	11.8	52
53	10.5	11.4	9.5	11.4	12.7	14.6	6.9	7.5	5.1	8.2	10.1	11.0	53
54	9.7	10.6	8.8	10.6	11.9	13.8	6.3	6.9	4.6	7.5	9.5	10.2	54
55	9.0	9.8	8.1	9.9	11.1	13.0	5.8	6.3	4.1	6.9	8.8	9.4	55
56	8.3	9.1	7.4	9.1	10.3	12.2	5.2	5.7	3.7	6.4	8.1	8.7	56
57	7.5	8.3	6.7	8.4	9.5	11.4	4.7	5.1	3.2	5.8	7.4	7.9	57
58	6.8	7.5	6.1	7.7	8.8	10.6	4.1	4.6	2.9	5.2	6.7	7.2	58
59	6.2	6.8	5.5	7.0	8.1	9.8	3.6	4.0	2.5	4.5	6.0	6.6	59
60	5.5	6.1	4.8	6.3	7.3	9.0	3.1	3.5	2.2	4.0	5.5	5.9	60
61	4.9	5.4	4.2	5.7	6.7	8.3	2.7	3.0	1.9	3.5	4.9	5.2	61
62	4.3	4.8	3.6	5.1	6.0	7.6	2.4	2.6	1.6	3.1	4.5	4.7	62
63	3.8	4.3	3.1	4.6	5.4	6.9	2.1	2.3	1.4	2.7	4.1	4.1	63
64	3.3	3.8	2.7	4.2	4.9	6.3	1.8	1.9	1.1	2.4	3.7	3.6	64
65	2.9	3.3	2.3	3.8	4.5	5.7	1.5	1.7	1.0	2.1	3.3	3.2	65
66	2.6	3.0	1.9	3.5	4.0	5.2	1.3	1.4	0.8	1.9	2.9	2.8	66
67	2.3	2.6	1.7	3.2	3.6	4.8	1.1	1.3	0.7	1.7	2.7	2.6	67
68	2.0	2.4	1.4	2.9	3.3	4.4	1.0	1.1	0.6	1.5	2.5	2.3	68
69	1.8	2.1	1.3	2.7	3.0	4.0	0.9	1.0	0.5	1.3	2.3	2.0	69
70	1.6	1.9	1.1	2.5	2.7	3.7	0.7	0.8	0.4	1.2	2.0	1.8	70
71	1.4	1.7	0.9	2.3	2.5	3.4	0.6	0.7	0.4	1.1	1.8	1.6	71
72	1.3	1.5	0.8	2.1	2.4	3.0	0.6	0.6	0.3	1.0	1.6	1.4	72
73	1.1	1.4	0.7	2.0	2.3	2.7	0.5	0.6	0.3	0.9	1.5	1.3	73
74	1.1	1.2	0.6	1.9	2.1	2.5	0.4	0.5	0.2	0.8	1.3	1.2	74
75	1.0	1.1	0.6	1.9	2.0	2.2	0.4	0.4	0.2	0.8	1.2	1.1	75

* Calculated from CPS data of all education levels combined. ** Weighted averages by education
Sources: Current Population Survey monthly microdata samples 2000 through 2006, and mortality data from Table 1.

Table 6: Worklife expectancies of Never-Married, Childless Females All Races by educational attainment, conventional methodology, 2000–2006 CPS

Age	All Ed Levels		<HS	HS	Some College			College Degree	Graduate Degree			Age
	Aggr't Data*	Wgt Ave**			All	No Degree	Assoc Degree		All	Masters	Phd/ Prof'l	
18	38.4	39.9	24.1	35.5	40.0	39.2	42.0					18
19	37.7	39.3	23.5	34.8	39.3	38.5	41.2					19
20	37.0	38.5	22.9	34.0	38.5	37.8	40.4	41.2				20
21	36.2	37.8	22.3	33.2	37.8	37.0	39.5	40.4	42.0	41.8		21
22	35.4	37.0	21.6	32.4	37.0	36.2	38.7	39.6	41.1	40.9	42.1	22
23	34.7	36.2	21.1	31.6	36.2	35.5	37.8	38.7	40.3	40.0	41.4	23
24	33.8	35.3	20.5	30.8	35.4	34.7	37.0	37.9	39.4	39.2	40.6	24
25	33.0	34.5	19.9	30.0	34.5	33.8	36.1	37.0	38.6	38.3	39.8	25
26	32.1	33.7	19.3	29.2	33.7	33.0	35.2	36.1	37.7	37.4	39.0	26
27	31.3	32.8	18.7	28.4	32.8	32.1	34.3	35.2	36.8	36.5	38.1	27
28	30.4	32.0	18.1	27.6	31.9	31.3	33.4	34.3	36.0	35.6	37.2	28
29	29.6	31.1	17.5	26.8	31.1	30.4	32.5	33.4	35.0	34.6	36.3	29
30	28.7	30.2	16.9	26.0	30.2	29.5	31.6	32.5	34.1	33.7	35.4	30
31	27.8	29.4	16.4	25.2	29.3	28.7	30.7	31.6	33.2	32.8	34.5	31
32	27.0	28.6	15.8	24.5	28.4	27.8	29.8	30.7	32.3	31.9	33.6	32
33	26.1	27.5	15.3	23.7	27.5	26.9	28.9	29.7	31.3	31.0	32.6	33
34	25.2	26.7	14.7	22.9	26.7	26.1	28.0	28.8	30.4	30.0	31.7	34
35	24.4	25.7	14.2	22.1	25.8	25.2	27.1	27.9	29.5	29.1	30.7	35
36	23.5	24.6	13.7	21.3	24.9	24.4	26.3	26.9	28.5	28.1	29.8	36
37	22.7	23.8	13.2	20.6	24.1	23.5	25.4	26.0	27.6	27.2	28.9	37
38	21.8	22.9	12.7	19.8	23.2	22.6	24.5	25.1	26.6	26.2	27.9	38
39	21.0	21.8	12.1	19.1	22.4	21.8	23.6	24.2	25.7	25.3	27.0	39
40	20.1	20.9	11.6	18.3	21.5	21.0	22.8	23.2	24.7	24.4	26.1	40
41	19.3	20.2	11.0	17.6	20.7	20.2	21.9	22.3	23.8	23.4	25.2	41
42	18.5	19.2	10.5	16.9	19.8	19.3	21.0	21.4	22.9	22.5	24.3	42
43	17.7	18.3	10.0	16.1	19.0	18.5	20.1	20.5	21.9	21.5	23.3	43
44	16.9	17.7	9.5	15.4	18.1	17.7	19.3	19.6	21.0	20.6	22.4	44
45	16.1	16.8	9.1	14.7	17.3	16.9	18.4	18.7	20.1	19.7	21.5	45
46	15.3	15.9	8.6	14.0	16.5	16.1	17.6	17.8	19.1	18.8	20.5	46
47	14.5	15.1	8.2	13.3	15.7	15.3	16.7	16.9	18.2	17.8	19.6	47
48	13.7	14.5	7.8	12.5	14.9	14.5	15.9	16.1	17.3	16.9	18.7	48
49	12.9	13.7	7.4	11.8	14.1	13.7	15.1	15.2	16.3	16.0	17.8	49
50	12.2	12.8	6.9	11.1	13.3	12.9	14.2	14.3	15.4	15.1	16.8	50
51	11.4	12.1	6.5	10.3	12.5	12.1	13.5	13.5	14.5	14.2	15.9	51
52	10.6	11.3	6.0	9.7	11.8	11.4	12.7	12.7	13.6	13.3	15.0	52
53	9.9	10.6	5.6	9.0	11.0	10.7	11.9	11.8	12.7	12.5	14.1	53
54	9.2	9.8	5.1	8.3	10.3	9.9	11.1	11.0	11.8	11.6	13.2	54
55	8.4	9.1	4.7	7.7	9.5	9.2	10.4	10.2	11.0	10.8	12.3	55
56	7.7	8.5	4.3	7.0	8.8	8.5	9.7	9.4	10.1	9.9	11.4	56
57	7.1	7.5	3.8	6.4	8.1	7.7	8.9	8.7	9.3	9.1	10.5	57
58	6.4	6.8	3.4	5.8	7.4	7.1	8.3	8.0	8.5	8.4	9.6	58
59	5.8	6.2	3.1	5.2	6.7	6.3	7.6	7.3	7.8	7.7	8.8	59
60	5.2	5.5	2.8	4.7	6.0	5.6	6.9	6.6	7.1	7.0	8.1	60
61	4.6	4.9	2.5	4.1	5.3	4.9	6.3	6.0	6.4	6.3	7.3	61
62	4.1	4.3	2.2	3.7	4.7	4.3	5.6	5.4	5.9	5.7	6.7	62
63	3.6	3.8	2.0	3.3	4.2	3.8	5.0	4.8	5.3	5.2	6.2	63
64	3.2	3.4	1.7	2.9	3.7	3.4	4.5	4.3	4.9	4.7	5.7	64
65	2.9	3.0	1.5	2.6	3.3	3.1	4.0	3.9	4.4	4.2	5.2	65
66	2.6	2.7	1.4	2.3	3.1	2.9	3.5	3.5	3.9	3.8	4.7	66
67	2.3	2.4	1.2	2.0	2.7	2.6	3.1	3.2	3.5	3.4	4.3	67
68	2.1	2.1	1.1	1.8	2.4	2.2	2.8	2.9	3.1	3.0	3.8	68
69	1.8	1.9	0.9	1.6	2.1	1.9	2.4	2.7	2.8	2.8	3.3	69
70	1.6	1.7	0.8	1.4	1.8	1.7	2.1	2.5	2.6	2.5	2.9	70
71	1.5	1.5	0.7	1.3	1.6	1.5	1.9	2.4	2.3	2.3	2.5	71
72	1.3	1.3	0.6	1.1	1.5	1.3	1.7	2.3	2.0	2.0	2.1	72
73	1.2	1.3	0.6	1.1	1.3	1.2	1.5	2.2	1.8	1.8	1.8	73
74	1.1	1.2	0.5	1.0	1.2	1.1	1.4	2.1	1.5	1.6	1.6	74
75	1.0	1.0	0.4	0.9	1.1	1.0	1.3	2.0	1.3	1.4	1.4	75

* Calculated from CPS data of all education levels combined. ** Weighted averages by education
Sources: Current Population Survey monthly microdata samples 2000 through 2006, and mortality data from Table 1.

Table 7: Worklife expectancies by smoking status and educational attainment, conventional model, 2000–2003—Males All Races

Age	All Males Regardless of Smoking Status						Male Never Smokers						Male Current Smokers					
	<HS	HS	Some College No Dgr	Some College Assoc Dgr	BA Dgr	Grad Dgr	<HS	HS	Some College No Dgr	Some College Assoc Dgr	BA Dgr	Grad Dgr	<HS	HS	Some College No Dgr	Some College Assoc Dgr	BA Dgr	Grad Dgr
18	33.9	39.0	39.7	41.4			35.9	40.7	41.4	42.2			32.1	37.6	38.3	39.8		
19	33.4	38.4	39.2	40.6			35.4	40.1	40.9	41.6			31.5	36.9	37.6	38.8		
20	32.8	37.7	38.6	39.9	42.0		34.8	39.4	40.4	41.0	43.2		30.8	36.0	36.8	38.0	39.9	
21	32.1	36.9	38.1	39.2	41.3		34.2	38.7	39.9	40.3	42.4		30.0	35.2	36.1	37.1	39.0	
22	31.3	36.1	37.4	38.4	40.6	42.0	33.4	37.9	39.2	39.5	41.8	42.6	29.2	34.3	35.3	36.3	38.2	38.6
23	30.5	35.3	36.7	37.6	39.9	41.4	32.6	37.1	38.6	38.7	41.0	42.3	28.4	33.5	34.5	35.4	37.3	37.7
24	29.7	34.4	36.0	36.8	39.1	40.8	31.8	36.2	37.8	37.9	40.2	41.7	27.6	32.6	33.7	34.5	36.4	37.0
25	28.9	33.6	35.2	35.9	38.2	40.0	30.9	35.4	37.0	37.0	39.4	41.0	26.8	31.8	32.8	33.7	35.5	36.1
26	28.1	32.7	34.3	35.0	37.4	39.2	30.1	34.5	36.2	36.1	38.5	40.1	26.0	30.9	31.9	32.8	34.6	35.2
27	27.3	31.9	33.5	34.1	36.5	38.3	29.3	33.7	35.3	35.2	37.6	39.3	25.2	30.0	31.0	31.9	33.7	34.3
28	26.5	31.0	32.6	33.2	35.6	37.4	28.5	32.8	34.4	34.2	36.7	38.3	24.4	29.1	30.1	31.0	32.8	33.4
29	25.7	30.1	31.7	32.2	34.6	36.5	27.7	31.9	33.5	33.3	35.8	37.4	23.5	28.3	29.2	30.1	31.9	32.5
30	24.9	29.3	30.8	31.3	33.7	35.6	26.9	31.0	32.6	32.3	34.8	36.5	22.7	27.4	28.3	29.2	30.9	31.6
31	24.1	28.4	29.9	30.4	32.8	34.6	26.1	30.1	31.7	31.4	33.9	35.5	21.9	26.5	27.4	28.3	30.0	30.7
32	23.2	27.5	28.9	29.5	31.8	33.7	25.2	29.3	30.7	30.5	32.9	34.6	21.1	25.6	26.5	27.3	29.1	29.7
33	22.4	26.6	28.0	28.5	30.9	32.8	24.4	28.4	29.8	29.5	32.0	33.7	20.3	24.7	25.6	26.4	28.1	28.8
34	21.6	25.8	27.1	27.6	29.9	31.8	23.6	27.5	28.9	28.6	31.0	32.7	19.5	23.9	24.7	25.5	27.2	27.8
35	20.8	24.9	26.2	26.7	29.0	30.9	22.8	26.6	28.0	27.7	30.1	31.7	18.7	23.0	23.8	24.6	26.3	26.9
36	20.0	24.0	25.3	25.8	28.1	29.9	21.9	25.7	27.1	26.7	29.1	30.8	17.9	22.1	22.9	23.7	25.4	26.0
37	19.2	23.1	24.5	24.9	27.1	29.0	21.1	24.8	26.1	25.8	28.2	29.8	17.1	21.3	22.1	22.8	24.5	25.1
38	18.4	22.3	23.6	24.0	26.2	28.0	20.3	23.9	25.2	24.8	27.2	28.9	16.4	20.4	21.3	21.9	23.6	24.2
39	17.6	21.4	22.7	23.1	25.2	27.1	19.5	23.0	24.3	23.9	26.3	27.9	15.7	19.6	20.5	21.1	22.7	23.2
40	16.8	20.5	21.8	22.1	24.3	26.2	18.7	22.1	23.4	22.9	25.3	27.0	14.9	18.8	19.6	20.2	21.8	22.4
41	16.1	19.7	20.9	21.2	23.4	25.2	17.8	21.2	22.5	22.0	24.4	26.0	14.2	17.9	18.8	19.4	20.9	21.5
42	15.4	18.8	20.1	20.3	22.4	24.3	17.1	20.3	21.6	21.1	23.4	25.1	13.6	17.1	18.0	18.5	20.0	20.6
43	14.6	18.0	19.2	19.5	21.5	23.4	16.2	19.4	20.6	20.2	22.5	24.1	12.9	16.3	17.2	17.7	19.1	19.8
44	13.9	17.1	18.3	18.6	20.6	22.4	15.4	18.5	19.8	19.2	21.5	23.2	12.2	15.5	16.3	16.8	18.3	18.9
45	13.2	16.3	17.5	17.7	19.7	21.5	14.7	17.6	18.8	18.3	20.6	22.2	11.6	14.7	15.5	16.0	17.4	18.1
46	12.5	15.5	16.6	16.8	18.8	20.6	14.0	16.8	18.0	17.4	19.6	21.3	10.9	14.0	14.8	15.2	16.6	17.2
47	11.8	14.7	15.7	15.9	17.9	19.6	13.2	15.9	17.1	16.5	18.7	20.3	10.3	13.2	14.0	14.3	15.7	16.3
48	11.1	13.8	14.9	15.1	16.9	18.7	12.5	15.0	16.1	15.5	17.8	19.4	9.7	12.4	13.2	13.5	14.9	15.4
49	10.5	13.1	14.1	14.2	16.0	17.8	11.7	14.2	15.3	14.6	16.8	18.4	9.1	11.7	12.5	12.7	14.0	14.6
50	9.8	12.3	13.2	13.4	15.1	16.9	11.0	13.4	14.4	13.7	15.9	17.5	8.5	10.9	11.7	12.0	13.2	13.8
51	9.1	11.5	12.4	12.5	14.2	16.0	10.2	12.5	13.5	12.9	15.0	16.6	7.9	10.2	11.0	11.2	12.4	12.9
52	8.5	10.7	11.6	11.7	13.3	15.1	9.4	11.7	12.7	12.0	14.1	15.6	7.4	9.5	10.3	10.4	11.6	12.1
53	7.9	10.0	10.8	10.9	12.5	14.2	8.8	10.8	11.8	11.2	13.2	14.7	6.8	8.8	9.6	9.7	10.8	11.3
54	7.3	9.2	10.1	10.1	11.6	13.3	8.1	10.0	11.0	10.3	12.3	13.8	6.3	8.1	8.9	8.9	10.0	10.5
55	6.7	8.4	9.3	9.3	10.7	12.4	7.4	9.2	10.1	9.5	11.4	12.9	5.8	7.4	8.2	8.2	9.3	9.7
56	6.1	7.7	8.5	8.5	9.9	11.5	6.7	8.5	9.3	8.6	10.5	12.0	5.2	6.8	7.5	7.5	8.5	8.9
57	5.6	7.0	7.8	7.8	9.1	10.7	6.2	7.7	8.5	7.8	9.6	11.2	4.7	6.1	6.9	6.9	7.8	8.2
58	5.0	6.3	7.1	7.1	8.3	9.9	5.5	6.9	7.8	7.1	8.8	10.3	4.2	5.5	6.2	6.2	7.0	7.5
59	4.5	5.7	6.3	6.4	7.5	9.1	5.0	6.2	7.0	6.4	8.0	9.5	3.7	4.9	5.6	5.6	6.4	6.8
60	4.0	5.0	5.7	5.7	6.8	8.3	4.4	5.6	6.3	5.6	7.2	8.7	3.2	4.3	5.0	5.0	5.7	6.1
61	3.5	4.4	5.1	5.1	6.1	7.5	3.8	4.9	5.6	5.1	6.5	7.9	2.8	3.7	4.4	4.5	5.1	5.4
62	3.0	3.8	4.5	4.5	5.4	6.7	3.3	4.3	4.9	4.4	5.8	7.2	2.4	3.2	3.9	3.9	4.5	4.8
63	2.6	3.4	3.9	4.0	4.9	6.2	2.8	3.8	4.4	3.7	5.2	6.5	2.1	2.8	3.4	3.4	4.0	4.3
64	2.3	3.0	3.5	3.4	4.3	5.6	2.5	3.4	3.9	3.1	4.6	5.9	1.8	2.5	3.0	3.0	3.5	3.8
65	2.0	2.6	3.1	3.0	3.9	5.0	2.1	3.0	3.5	2.6	4.1	5.3	1.6	2.2	2.6	2.6	3.1	3.3
66	1.8	2.4	2.8	2.7	3.5	4.5	1.9	2.6	3.1	2.3	3.7	4.7	1.4	2.0	2.3	2.3	2.7	2.8
67	1.6	2.1	2.5	2.4	3.1	4.0	1.7	2.3	2.8	2.0	3.3	4.3	1.2	1.7	2.0	2.0	2.4	2.4
68	1.4	1.9	2.2	2.2	2.8	3.6	1.4	2.1	2.4	1.7	3.0	3.8	1.0	1.5	1.8	1.8	2.1	2.0
69	1.2	1.6	1.9	1.9	2.5	3.3	1.2	1.8	2.1	1.6	2.6	3.5	0.9	1.3	1.6	1.6	1.8	1.8
70	1.1	1.4	1.7	1.7	2.2	3.0	1.1	1.6	1.9	1.4	2.3	3.1	0.8	1.2	1.4	1.4	1.6	1.6
71	1.0	1.3	1.5	1.5	2.0	2.8	0.9	1.4	1.7	1.2	2.1	2.8	0.7	1.0	1.2	1.2	1.4	1.5
72	0.9	1.2	1.4	1.3	1.7	2.4	0.8	1.2	1.4	1.0	1.9	2.5	0.6	0.9	1.1	1.0	1.2	1.2
73	0.8	1.0	1.2	1.2	1.6	2.2	0.7	1.1	1.3	0.8	1.7	2.2	0.5	0.8	1.0	0.9	1.1	1.0
74	0.7	0.9	1.1	1.0	1.4	2.0	0.6	0.9	1.1	0.7	1.5	2.0	0.4	0.7	0.9	0.7	0.9	0.8
75	0.6	0.8	1.0	0.9	1.2	1.8	0.5	0.8	1.0	0.6	1.3	1.7	0.4	0.7	0.9	0.6	0.8	0.7

Sources: CPS tobacco supplements, 2000 through 2003, Bureau of the Census, and CDC, "United States Life Tables. 2004."
Note: Populations regardless of smoking status include former smokers and those not classified.

Table 7: Worklife expectancies by smoking status and educational attainment, conventional model, 2000–2003, continued—Females All Races

Age	All Females Regardless of Smoking Status						Female Never Smokers						Female Current Smokers					
	<HS	HS	Some College No Dgr	Some College Assoc Dgr	BA Dgr	Grad Dgr	<HS	HS	Some College No Dgr	Some College Assoc Dgr	BA Dgr	Grad Dgr	<HS	HS	Some College No Dgr	Some College Assoc Dgr	BA Dgr	Grad Dgr
18	23.5	33.2	35.2	37.5			23.3	33.2	35.4	37.3			24.8	34.1	35.8	38.2		
19	23.0	32.6	34.7	36.8			22.8	32.6	34.8	36.7			24.2	33.3	35.0	37.2		
20	22.5	31.9	34.1	36.1	35.9		22.3	32.0	34.2	36.1	35.8		23.5	32.5	34.2	36.3	37.4	
21	22.0	31.2	33.4	35.4	35.3		21.8	31.3	33.6	35.3	35.1		22.9	31.7	33.4	35.4	36.7	
22	21.5	30.5	32.7	34.6	34.5	37.5	21.3	30.6	32.9	34.6	34.3	37.3	22.3	30.9	32.6	34.5	35.8	37.4
23	21.0	29.8	32.0	33.8	33.7	36.8	20.8	29.9	32.2	33.8	33.5	36.5	21.7	30.1	31.8	33.6	34.9	36.7
24	20.5	29.1	31.3	33.0	32.8	36.0	20.4	29.2	31.5	33.0	32.7	35.8	21.1	29.3	31.0	32.8	34.0	35.8
25	20.0	28.3	30.5	32.2	32.0	35.2	19.9	28.5	30.8	32.2	31.9	35.0	20.5	28.5	30.1	31.9	33.1	34.9
26	19.5	27.6	29.7	31.4	31.1	34.4	19.5	27.8	30.0	31.4	31.0	34.2	19.9	27.8	29.3	31.0	32.1	34.0
27	19.0	26.9	29.0	30.5	30.3	33.6	19.0	27.1	29.2	30.6	30.2	33.4	19.4	27.0	28.5	30.2	31.2	33.1
28	18.5	26.2	28.2	29.7	29.5	32.7	18.6	26.4	28.5	29.8	29.4	32.5	18.8	26.3	27.7	29.3	30.3	32.2
29	18.0	25.5	27.4	28.9	28.6	31.9	18.1	25.7	27.7	29.0	28.5	31.7	18.2	25.6	26.9	28.4	29.3	31.3
30	17.5	24.8	26.7	28.1	27.8	31.1	17.6	25.0	27.0	28.2	27.7	30.8	17.6	24.9	26.1	27.6	28.4	30.3
31	17.0	24.1	25.9	27.3	27.0	30.2	17.1	24.2	26.2	27.4	26.9	30.0	17.0	24.1	25.3	26.8	27.5	29.3
32	16.4	23.4	25.2	26.5	26.2	29.4	16.6	23.5	25.5	26.5	26.1	29.2	16.4	23.4	24.5	25.9	26.7	28.4
33	15.9	22.7	24.4	25.7	25.4	28.6	16.1	22.8	24.7	25.7	25.4	28.4	15.8	22.6	23.7	25.0	25.8	27.5
34	15.3	22.0	23.6	24.9	24.7	27.8	15.5	22.1	23.9	24.9	24.6	27.6	15.2	21.9	22.9	24.2	24.9	26.6
35	14.8	21.2	22.9	24.1	23.9	27.0	15.0	21.4	23.2	24.1	23.9	26.8	14.5	21.1	22.2	23.3	24.0	25.7
36	14.2	20.5	22.1	23.3	23.2	26.2	14.5	20.7	22.4	23.3	23.1	26.0	13.9	20.4	21.4	22.4	23.1	24.9
37	13.7	19.8	21.4	22.5	22.4	25.4	13.9	19.9	21.6	22.5	22.3	25.1	13.3	19.6	20.7	21.6	22.2	24.0
38	13.1	19.1	20.6	21.7	21.7	24.5	13.3	19.2	20.9	21.7	21.6	24.3	12.7	18.9	19.9	20.8	21.4	23.2
39	12.5	18.4	19.8	20.9	20.9	23.7	12.8	18.5	20.1	20.9	20.8	23.5	12.2	18.2	19.1	19.9	20.5	22.4
40	11.9	17.6	19.1	20.1	20.2	22.9	12.2	17.7	19.3	20.1	20.1	22.7	11.6	17.4	18.3	19.1	19.6	21.6
41	11.4	16.9	18.3	19.2	19.4	22.1	11.6	17.0	18.6	19.3	19.4	21.8	11.0	16.7	17.5	18.3	18.7	20.7
42	10.8	16.2	17.5	18.4	18.6	21.2	11.1	16.3	17.8	18.5	18.6	21.0	10.4	15.9	16.7	17.5	17.8	19.9
43	10.3	15.4	16.7	17.6	17.8	20.4	10.5	15.5	17.0	17.7	17.8	20.2	9.9	15.2	15.9	16.7	17.0	19.0
44	9.7	14.7	15.9	16.8	17.0	19.6	10.0	14.8	16.2	16.8	17.0	19.3	9.4	14.5	15.2	15.9	16.1	18.2
45	9.1	13.9	15.2	16.0	16.2	18.7	9.4	14.0	15.4	16.0	16.2	18.4	8.8	13.7	14.4	15.1	15.3	17.3
46	8.6	13.2	14.4	15.2	15.4	17.9	8.9	13.2	14.6	15.2	15.4	17.6	8.3	13.0	13.6	14.3	14.4	16.4
47	8.1	12.4	13.6	14.3	14.6	17.0	8.3	12.5	13.8	14.3	14.6	16.7	7.8	12.3	12.9	13.5	13.6	15.5
48	7.6	11.7	12.8	13.5	13.8	16.1	7.8	11.7	13.0	13.5	13.8	15.9	7.4	11.6	12.1	12.6	12.8	14.7
49	7.1	10.9	12.1	12.7	13.0	15.3	7.3	11.0	12.2	12.6	13.0	15.0	6.9	10.9	11.4	11.8	12.0	13.9
50	6.6	10.2	11.3	11.9	12.2	14.4	6.7	10.2	11.5	11.8	12.1	14.1	6.5	10.1	10.7	11.0	11.2	13.1
51	6.1	9.5	10.5	11.1	11.4	13.5	6.2	9.5	10.7	11.0	11.3	13.2	6.0	9.5	9.9	10.2	10.5	12.2
52	5.6	8.8	9.8	10.3	10.6	12.7	5.7	8.8	9.9	10.2	10.5	12.3	5.5	8.8	9.2	9.5	9.7	11.4
53	5.2	8.1	9.1	9.5	9.8	11.8	5.2	8.1	9.1	9.4	9.8	11.4	5.1	8.1	8.5	8.8	8.9	10.5
54	4.7	7.4	8.3	8.8	9.1	10.9	4.7	7.4	8.4	8.6	9.0	10.6	4.7	7.4	7.8	8.1	8.1	9.6
55	4.2	6.7	7.6	8.0	8.3	10.1	4.2	6.8	7.7	7.9	8.2	9.7	4.3	6.7	7.1	7.4	7.4	8.8
56	3.8	6.1	7.0	7.3	7.6	9.3	3.8	6.1	7.0	7.1	7.5	8.9	3.9	6.1	6.5	6.7	6.6	7.9
57	3.4	5.5	6.3	6.6	6.9	8.5	3.4	5.5	6.3	6.4	6.7	8.1	3.5	5.5	5.8	6.0	5.9	7.2
58	3.0	4.9	5.7	5.9	6.2	7.7	3.0	4.9	5.7	5.8	6.0	7.3	3.1	4.9	5.2	5.3	5.3	6.5
59	2.7	4.3	5.0	5.3	5.5	7.0	2.6	4.3	5.0	5.1	5.3	6.6	2.8	4.4	4.7	4.6	4.6	5.8
60	2.3	3.8	4.5	4.6	4.9	6.3	2.3	3.8	4.4	4.5	4.7	5.9	2.4	3.8	4.1	4.0	4.0	5.2
61	2.0	3.3	3.9	4.1	4.3	5.6	1.9	3.2	3.9	3.9	4.1	5.1	2.1	3.3	3.6	3.4	3.4	4.5
62	1.7	2.8	3.4	3.5	3.7	5.0	1.6	2.8	3.4	3.4	3.5	4.5	1.8	2.9	3.1	2.9	2.9	3.9
63	1.5	2.4	3.0	3.0	3.2	4.4	1.4	2.4	2.9	2.9	3.0	3.9	1.6	2.5	2.7	2.5	2.5	3.3
64	1.3	2.1	2.6	2.6	2.8	3.9	1.2	2.1	2.5	2.6	2.6	3.4	1.3	2.2	2.2	2.1	2.1	2.8
65	1.1	1.8	2.2	2.3	2.5	3.4	1.0	1.8	2.2	2.2	2.2	3.0	1.1	1.9	1.9	1.8	1.8	2.3
66	1.0	1.5	1.9	2.0	2.1	3.0	0.9	1.5	1.9	1.9	1.9	2.6	1.0	1.7	1.6	1.5	1.5	2.1
67	0.8	1.3	1.7	1.8	1.9	2.6	0.8	1.3	1.7	1.7	1.7	2.2	0.8	1.4	1.4	1.2	1.3	1.9
68	0.7	1.1	1.5	1.6	1.6	2.3	0.7	1.1	1.4	1.5	1.4	1.8	0.7	1.2	1.2	1.0	1.2	1.7
69	0.6	1.0	1.2	1.4	1.4	2.0	0.6	0.9	1.2	1.3	1.2	1.6	0.6	1.1	1.0	0.7	1.0	1.6
70	0.5	0.8	1.1	1.2	1.3	1.8	0.5	0.8	1.1	1.1	1.1	1.4	0.5	0.9	0.9	0.6	0.8	1.5
71	0.5	0.7	0.9	1.0	1.1	1.6	0.4	0.7	0.9	0.9	0.9	1.2	0.4	0.7	0.7	0.4	0.7	1.3
72	0.4	0.6	0.8	0.8	1.0	1.5	0.4	0.6	0.8	0.7	0.8	1.1	0.3	0.6	0.6	0.3	0.6	1.2
73	0.3	0.5	0.6	0.7	0.9	1.3	0.3	0.5	0.7	0.6	0.7	0.9	0.3	0.5	0.5	0.2	0.5	1.2
74	0.3	0.4	0.5	0.6	0.8	1.2	0.3	0.4	0.5	0.5	0.6	0.8	0.2	0.4	0.4	0.1	0.4	1.1
75	0.2	0.4	0.5	0.5	0.7	1.1	0.2	0.3	0.4	0.4	0.5	0.6	0.2	0.4	0.3	0.1	0.3	1.0

Sources: CPS tobacco supplements, 2000 through 2003, Bureau of the Census, and CDC, "United States Life Tables. 2004."
Note: Populations regardless of smoking status include former smokers and those not classified.

Table 8: Worklife expectancies by English language proficiency and selected educational categories, Hispanics, 1990

Age	None	Poor			Good			Very Good			Only English			Age
	<HS	<HS	HS	Some College	<HS	HS	Some College	<HS	HS	Some College	<HS	HS	Some College	
18	38.3	38.5	40.3	41.5	37.2	40.8	41.5	36.0	39.7	41.7	34.2	40.4	41.0	18
19	37.6	37.9	39.5	40.8	36.8	40.3	41.0	35.6	39.1	41.1	33.7	39.7	40.4	19
20	36.8	37.2	38.8	40.1	36.2	39.6	40.4	35.0	38.4	40.5	33.2	39.0	39.8	20
21	36.0	36.4	38.0	39.4	35.5	38.8	39.8	34.4	37.7	39.9	32.5	38.2	39.1	21
22	35.1	35.6	37.2	38.7	34.8	38.1	39.1	33.7	37.0	39.2	31.8	37.5	38.5	22
23	34.3	34.7	36.4	37.9	34.0	37.3	38.4	32.9	36.2	38.5	31.1	36.7	37.7	23
24	33.5	33.9	35.6	37.1	33.2	36.5	37.6	32.2	35.3	37.7	30.3	35.8	36.9	24
25	32.7	33.1	34.7	36.2	32.4	35.7	36.8	31.4	34.5	36.9	29.6	35.0	36.1	25
26	31.9	32.3	33.9	35.4	31.7	34.8	35.9	30.8	33.6	36.0	28.9	34.1	35.2	26
27	31.1	31.5	33.0	34.5	30.9	33.9	35.0	30.0	32.8	35.1	28.2	33.2	34.3	27
28	30.2	30.6	32.2	33.7	30.1	33.1	34.1	29.2	31.9	34.3	27.4	32.3	33.4	28
29	29.5	29.8	31.4	32.8	29.3	32.2	33.3	28.5	31.0	33.4	26.7	31.4	32.5	29
30	28.6	29.0	30.5	31.9	28.5	31.3	32.4	27.7	30.2	32.5	26.0	30.6	31.6	30
31	27.9	28.3	29.7	31.1	27.8	30.5	31.5	27.1	29.3	31.6	25.3	29.7	30.7	31
32	27.1	27.4	28.8	30.3	27.0	29.6	30.6	26.3	28.4	30.8	24.6	28.8	29.8	32
33	26.3	26.6	27.9	29.4	26.2	28.7	29.7	25.5	27.5	29.8	23.9	27.9	28.9	33
34	25.5	25.7	27.1	28.5	25.3	27.8	28.8	24.7	26.7	28.9	23.1	27.0	27.9	34
35	24.6	24.8	26.3	27.7	24.4	27.0	28.0	23.9	25.8	28.1	22.3	26.2	27.1	35
36	23.8	24.0	25.4	26.9	23.6	26.1	27.1	23.1	25.0	27.2	21.5	25.3	26.2	36
37	23.0	23.1	24.6	26.1	22.8	25.3	26.3	22.3	24.2	26.4	20.8	24.5	25.3	37
38	22.2	22.3	23.8	25.2	21.9	24.4	25.4	21.5	23.3	25.5	20.0	23.6	24.5	38
39	21.3	21.5	23.0	24.4	21.1	23.6	24.5	20.7	22.5	24.6	19.2	22.7	23.6	39
40	20.6	20.7	22.2	23.6	20.3	22.8	23.7	20.0	21.7	23.8	18.5	21.9	22.8	40
41	19.8	19.9	21.5	22.8	19.5	22.0	22.9	19.2	20.9	23.0	17.8	21.2	22.0	41
42	18.9	19.0	20.7	21.9	18.6	21.2	22.1	18.3	20.1	22.1	17.0	20.3	21.1	42
43	18.1	18.1	19.9	21.1	17.8	20.4	21.2	17.6	19.2	21.3	16.2	19.5	20.2	43
44	17.3	17.3	19.2	20.4	17.0	19.6	20.4	16.8	18.4	20.4	15.5	18.7	19.4	44
45	16.4	16.5	18.4	19.6	16.2	18.8	19.6	16.0	17.6	19.6	14.8	17.9	18.5	45
46	15.6	15.7	17.7	18.8	15.4	18.0	18.8	15.2	16.8	18.8	14.1	17.1	17.7	46
47	14.8	14.9	16.9	18.0	14.6	17.2	18.0	14.4	15.9	17.9	13.4	16.3	16.8	47
48	14.0	14.1	16.1	17.2	13.8	16.3	17.1	13.6	15.1	17.1	12.6	15.4	15.9	48
49	13.2	13.3	15.3	16.3	13.0	15.5	16.3	12.8	14.2	16.2	11.9	14.6	15.0	49
50	12.4	12.5	14.5	15.5	12.2	14.6	15.5	12.0	13.4	15.3	11.2	13.8	14.2	50
51	11.7	11.7	13.7	14.7	11.5	13.8	14.7	11.3	12.6	14.5	10.5	13.0	13.4	51
52	10.9	10.9	13.0	13.9	10.7	13.0	13.9	10.5	11.8	13.7	9.8	12.1	12.5	52
53	10.2	10.1	12.2	13.1	9.9	12.2	13.0	9.8	11.0	12.9	9.1	11.3	11.7	53
54	9.4	9.4	11.4	12.4	9.2	11.4	12.3	9.0	10.2	12.1	8.4	10.5	10.9	54
55	8.7	8.6	10.6	11.6	8.4	10.6	11.4	8.3	9.5	11.2	7.7	9.7	10.1	55
56	8.0	7.9	9.9	10.9	7.6	9.9	10.6	7.5	8.7	10.5	7.0	9.0	9.3	56
57	7.3	7.2	9.1	10.1	6.9	9.1	9.8	6.8	8.0	9.6	6.4	8.2	8.5	57
58	6.6	6.6	8.3	9.3	6.2	8.4	9.0	6.1	7.2	8.9	5.7	7.5	7.7	58
59	5.9	5.9	7.6	8.5	5.5	7.7	8.2	5.5	6.5	8.1	5.1	6.8	7.0	59
60	5.2	5.2	6.8	7.8	4.9	7.0	7.5	4.8	5.8	7.3	4.5	6.1	6.2	60
61	4.6	4.6	6.1	7.0	4.3	6.3	6.8	4.3	5.1	6.6	3.9	5.5	5.5	61
62	4.0	4.0	5.5	6.2	3.7	5.6	6.2	3.7	4.5	6.0	3.5	4.9	4.9	62
63	3.5	3.5	4.9	5.5	3.2	5.0	5.5	3.3	4.0	5.4	3.0	4.3	4.3	63
64	3.0	3.0	4.3	4.9	2.8	4.5	4.9	2.9	3.5	4.9	2.6	3.9	3.8	64
65	2.6	2.6	3.8	4.3	2.4	4.0	4.4	2.5	3.2	4.5	2.3	3.5	3.3	65
66	2.2	2.3	3.4	3.7	2.1	3.6	3.9	2.3	2.9	4.1	2.0	3.2	3.0	66
67	1.9	2.0	3.0	3.2	1.9	3.2	3.4	2.0	2.6	3.7	1.8	2.9	2.7	67
68	1.6	1.8	2.6	2.7	1.7	2.8	3.0	1.8	2.4	3.3	1.6	2.7	2.4	68
69	1.4	1.6	2.3	2.2	1.5	2.5	2.6	1.6	2.2	3.0	1.4	2.5	2.2	69
70	1.2	1.4	2.0	1.9	1.3	2.3	2.3	1.5	2.0	2.7	1.2	2.3	2.1	70
71	1.0	1.2	1.7	1.6	1.2	2.0	2.0	1.3	1.8	2.4	1.1	2.2	1.9	71
72	0.9	1.0	1.5	1.4	1.1	1.7	1.7	1.2	1.6	2.1	0.9	2.0	1.7	72
73	0.7	0.9	1.2	1.2	0.9	1.5	1.4	1.1	1.5	1.8	0.9	1.8	1.5	73
74	0.6	0.8	1.1	1.1	0.9	1.3	1.1	0.9	1.3	1.6	0.8	1.6	1.3	74
75	0.5	0.7	1.0	1.0	0.8	1.2	0.9	0.9	1.2	1.5	0.7	1.5	1.2	75

Note: Calculated from aggregated data. For sources see Chapter 10.

Table 8: Worklife expectancies by English language proficiency and selected educational categories, Hispanics, 1990, continued

Age	None	Poor			Good			Very Good			Only English		
	<HS	<HS	HS	Some College	<HS	HS	Some College	<HS	HS	Some College	<HS	HS	Some College
18	20.0	23.8	26.7	28.4	24.4	31.1	34.8	23.8	32.6	37.3	22.9	32.6	37.2
19	19.6	23.4	26.3	27.8	24.0	30.5	34.2	23.4	32.0	36.7	22.4	32.0	36.6
20	19.2	22.9	25.7	27.2	23.6	29.9	33.5	22.9	31.4	36.0	21.9	31.3	35.9
21	18.8	22.4	25.2	26.7	23.1	29.3	32.9	22.5	30.7	35.3	21.4	30.6	35.2
22	18.4	21.9	24.7	26.1	22.7	28.7	32.3	22.0	30.0	34.6	20.9	29.9	34.5
23	17.9	21.4	24.2	25.5	22.2	28.1	31.6	21.5	29.4	33.9	20.5	29.2	33.7
24	17.5	20.9	23.6	24.9	21.7	27.4	30.9	21.0	28.7	33.1	20.1	28.5	33.0
25	17.1	20.4	23.1	24.3	21.2	26.8	30.3	20.6	28.0	32.3	19.7	27.8	32.1
26	16.6	19.9	22.5	23.7	20.7	26.2	29.6	20.1	27.3	31.5	19.2	27.2	31.4
27	16.2	19.3	22.0	23.2	20.2	25.5	28.9	19.6	26.7	30.8	18.8	26.5	30.6
28	15.7	18.8	21.4	22.6	19.6	24.9	28.2	19.1	26.0	30.0	18.3	25.8	29.8
29	15.3	18.3	20.8	22.0	19.1	24.3	27.5	18.6	25.3	29.2	17.8	25.1	29.0
30	14.8	17.7	20.3	21.4	18.6	23.7	26.8	18.1	24.6	28.4	17.4	24.4	28.2
31	14.3	17.2	19.8	20.9	18.1	23.0	26.1	17.6	23.9	27.6	16.9	23.6	27.4
32	13.9	16.6	19.2	20.3	17.5	22.4	25.4	17.1	23.3	26.9	16.4	23.0	26.6
33	13.4	16.1	18.7	19.7	17.0	21.8	24.7	16.6	22.6	26.1	15.9	22.3	25.9
34	12.9	15.5	18.1	19.1	16.5	21.1	24.0	16.1	21.9	25.3	15.4	21.6	25.1
35	12.4	15.0	17.6	18.6	15.9	20.5	23.4	15.5	21.2	24.6	14.8	20.9	24.4
36	12.0	14.5	17.0	18.0	15.3	19.9	22.7	15.0	20.5	23.8	14.3	20.1	23.6
37	11.5	13.9	16.5	17.4	14.8	19.2	22.0	14.4	19.8	23.1	13.8	19.4	22.8
38	11.0	13.4	15.9	16.7	14.2	18.5	21.3	13.9	19.1	22.3	13.2	18.6	22.0
39	10.5	12.8	15.3	16.1	13.6	17.8	20.5	13.3	18.3	21.5	12.7	17.9	21.2
40	10.0	12.2	14.7	15.5	13.0	17.2	19.8	12.7	17.6	20.7	12.2	17.2	20.4
41	9.5	11.7	14.1	14.9	12.4	16.5	19.1	12.2	16.9	19.9	11.7	16.4	19.6
42	9.0	11.1	13.5	14.2	11.9	15.8	18.3	11.6	16.2	19.1	11.1	15.7	18.8
43	8.5	10.6	12.9	13.6	11.3	15.1	17.6	11.1	15.4	18.3	10.6	14.9	18.0
44	8.0	10.0	12.3	12.9	10.7	14.4	16.8	10.5	14.7	17.5	10.1	14.1	17.2
45	7.5	9.5	11.6	12.3	10.2	13.6	16.0	10.0	14.0	16.7	9.5	13.4	16.4
46	7.1	8.9	11.0	11.6	9.6	12.9	15.2	9.4	13.3	15.8	9.0	12.6	15.5
47	6.6	8.4	10.3	11.0	9.1	12.2	14.5	8.9	12.5	15.0	8.5	11.9	14.7
48	6.1	7.8	9.7	10.3	8.5	11.5	13.7	8.3	11.8	14.2	8.1	11.2	14.0
49	5.7	7.3	9.1	9.7	8.0	10.9	13.0	7.8	11.1	13.4	7.6	10.5	13.2
50	5.3	6.8	8.6	9.1	7.4	10.2	12.3	7.2	10.4	12.7	7.1	9.8	12.5
51	4.9	6.3	8.0	8.5	6.9	9.5	11.5	6.7	9.7	11.9	6.7	9.1	11.7
52	4.5	5.8	7.4	7.9	6.4	8.9	10.8	6.2	9.0	11.1	6.2	8.4	11.0
53	4.1	5.3	6.9	7.3	5.9	8.2	10.1	5.7	8.3	10.3	5.8	7.8	10.3
54	3.7	4.9	6.4	6.8	5.4	7.6	9.4	5.3	7.7	9.6	5.3	7.2	9.6
55	3.3	4.4	5.8	6.2	4.9	7.0	8.7	4.8	7.1	8.8	4.9	6.6	8.9
56	2.9	4.0	5.3	5.7	4.4	6.4	8.0	4.4	6.5	8.1	4.4	6.0	8.2
57	2.6	3.6	4.9	5.1	4.0	5.8	7.3	3.9	5.9	7.5	4.0	5.4	7.6
58	2.3	3.2	4.4	4.6	3.6	5.2	6.7	3.5	5.3	6.8	3.6	4.9	6.9
59	2.0	2.8	4.0	4.1	3.2	4.6	6.0	3.1	4.8	6.1	3.2	4.3	6.3
60	1.8	2.5	3.5	3.6	2.8	4.1	5.4	2.7	4.2	5.5	2.8	3.8	5.7
61	1.5	2.1	3.2	3.2	2.4	3.7	4.8	2.4	3.7	4.9	2.5	3.3	5.2
62	1.3	1.8	2.8	2.8	2.1	3.2	4.2	2.1	3.3	4.4	2.1	2.9	4.7
63	1.1	1.5	2.5	2.4	1.8	2.9	3.8	1.8	2.9	3.8	1.8	2.5	4.2
64	0.9	1.3	2.2	2.1	1.6	2.5	3.3	1.6	2.5	3.4	1.6	2.1	3.9
65	0.7	1.1	1.9	1.8	1.4	2.3	2.9	1.4	2.2	3.0	1.4	1.8	3.5
66	0.6	1.0	1.6	1.5	1.2	2.0	2.5	1.2	2.0	2.6	1.2	1.6	3.2
67	0.5	0.8	1.3	1.4	1.0	1.8	2.2	1.0	1.8	2.3	1.0	1.4	2.9
68	0.4	0.7	1.2	1.2	0.9	1.6	1.9	0.9	1.6	2.1	0.9	1.2	2.6
69	0.4	0.6	1.0	1.1	0.8	1.4	1.7	0.8	1.4	1.9	0.8	1.1	2.5
70	0.3	0.6	0.9	0.9	0.7	1.2	1.4	0.7	1.3	1.7	0.7	0.9	2.3
71	0.3	0.5	0.9	0.8	0.6	1.1	1.3	0.6	1.2	1.5	0.7	0.8	2.1
72	0.2	0.5	0.8	0.7	0.5	1.0	1.1	0.6	1.1	1.4	0.6	0.7	1.9
73	0.2	0.4	0.8	0.6	0.5	0.9	0.9	0.5	0.9	1.2	0.5	0.6	1.7
74	0.2	0.4	0.7	0.5	0.4	0.8	0.8	0.5	0.8	1.1	0.5	0.5	1.5
75	0.2	0.3	0.6	0.5	0.4	0.7	0.7	0.4	0.8	1.1	0.4	0.5	1.4

Note: Calculated from aggregated data. For sources see Chapter 10.

Table 9: Labor force participation and unemployment rates by sex, race, age, and education, 2000 through 2006, Males of All Races

| Ages | All* | <HS | HS | Some College | | | College Degree | Masters Degree | Prof'l Degree | PhD/ Degree |
				All	No Degree	Assoc Degree				
				Labor Force Participation Rates—Males of All Races						
18 to 19	60.8%	55.2%	69.9%	57.0%	56.8%	71.0%	65.9%	64.8%	100.0%	100.0%
20 to 24	80.5%	80.9%	86.6%	74.4%	72.5%	86.6%	85.4%	81.9%	65.6%	63.4%
25 to 29	91.3%	87.6%	91.5%	91.6%	90.7%	93.9%	93.1%	91.9%	91.6%	92.8%
30 to 34	93.3%	87.5%	92.2%	94.4%	94.0%	95.4%	96.2%	95.5%	96.4%	96.0%
35 to 39	92.9%	85.5%	91.5%	94.1%	93.3%	95.6%	96.6%	96.6%	97.5%	97.2%
40 to 44	91.7%	81.1%	90.4%	93.1%	92.4%	94.3%	96.3%	96.5%	96.6%	97.3%
45 to 49	89.8%	76.0%	88.0%	90.9%	90.3%	92.1%	95.5%	96.5%	97.2%	96.5%
50 to 54	86.3%	70.9%	83.3%	86.9%	86.2%	88.4%	92.4%	94.4%	95.6%	95.8%
55 to 59	77.7%	61.6%	74.7%	78.3%	78.0%	79.1%	85.2%	85.1%	91.9%	92.0%
60 to 64	56.9%	44.2%	52.9%	58.7%	58.5%	59.2%	65.7%	64.7%	79.7%	80.1%
65 to 69	31.6%	22.9%	28.6%	32.4%	32.4%	32.6%	39.4%	37.9%	57.6%	54.6%
70 to 74	18.9%	13.0%	17.6%	19.5%	19.7%	19.1%	23.9%	23.7%	39.0%	36.1%
75 to 79	11.6%	7.7%	10.6%	13.0%	12.9%	13.5%	15.5%	14.6%	26.9%	22.2%
80+	5.7%	3.5%	5.5%	6.2%	6.0%	7.3%	8.3%	9.4%	13.6%	12.3%
18 +	75.5%	59.0%	75.3%	78.3%	76.1%	84.1%	84.5%	81.8%	83.2%	81.7%
25 to 64	87.0%	75.9%	85.4%	88.4%	87.6%	90.2%	92.4%	91.3%	94.0%	93.7%
25 +	75.7%	57.0%	74.3%	80.0%	78.2%	83.9%	84.4%	81.8%	83.3%	81.8%
				Unemployment Rates—Males of All Races						
18 to 19	15.2%	19.1%	15.0%	9.3%	9.3%	9.7%	2.0%	0.0%	0.0%	0.0%
20 to 24	9.2%	14.1%	10.4%	6.7%	6.9%	5.9%	6.0%	6.9%	5.4%	3.7%
25 to 29	5.3%	8.8%	6.5%	4.8%	5.1%	3.9%	3.0%	2.3%	3.3%	2.8%
30 to 34	4.2%	7.6%	5.2%	3.9%	4.3%	3.2%	2.4%	1.9%	1.4%	0.8%
35 to 39	3.8%	6.8%	4.7%	3.4%	3.6%	3.1%	2.3%	1.8%	0.8%	1.2%
40 to 44	3.6%	7.0%	4.1%	3.3%	3.5%	3.0%	2.5%	2.1%	0.7%	1.1%
45 to 49	3.5%	6.3%	4.0%	3.4%	3.4%	3.4%	2.5%	2.3%	0.9%	1.5%
50 to 54	3.3%	6.0%	3.7%	3.4%	3.5%	3.3%	2.5%	2.7%	0.7%	1.1%
55 to 59	3.4%	5.6%	3.5%	3.7%	3.5%	4.0%	3.1%	2.8%	0.9%	0.9%
60 to 64	3.5%	4.8%	3.5%	3.6%	3.6%	3.6%	3.4%	2.9%	1.1%	2.3%
65 to 69	3.5%	4.7%	3.6%	3.5%	3.3%	4.2%	3.3%	3.1%	1.0%	1.4%
70 to 74	3.4%	5.2%	3.3%	3.8%	3.8%	3.7%	2.6%	2.4%	1.6%	1.5%
75 to 79	3.4%	4.8%	3.4%	3.5%	3.7%	3.0%	2.2%	3.2%	1.5%	3.4%
80+%	2.3%	2.7%	2.3%	3.2%	3.6%	1.9%	2.4%	0.7%	0.0%	0.6%
18 +	4.8%	8.8%	5.6%	4.3%	4.6%	3.6%	2.8%	2.3%	1.1%	1.3%
25 to 64	3.9%	6.9%	4.6%	3.7%	3.9%	3.4%	2.6%	2.3%	1.0%	1.3%
25 +	3.9%	6.8%	4.5%	3.7%	3.8%	3.4%	2.6%	2.3%	1.1%	1.3%

*Calculated from aggregated data, i.e., not weighted averages by education

Table 9: Labor force participation and unemployment rates by sex, race, age, and education, 2000 through 2006, continued—Females of All Races

| Ages | All* | <HS | HS | Some College | | | College Degree | Masters Degree | Prof'l Degree | PhD/ Degree |
				All	No Degree	Assoc Degree				
				Labor Force Participation Rates—Females of All Races						
18 to 19	58.1%	48.4%	64.2%	60.9%	60.7%	69.1%	56.0%	52.7%	82.2%	35.2%
20 to 24	71.5%	51.9%	72.5%	72.8%	71.2%	81.7%	83.0%	79.3%	70.5%	80.1%
25 to 29	75.3%	51.2%	70.6%	78.6%	76.8%	82.7%	84.9%	85.8%	84.2%	88.3%
30 to 34	74.6%	54.5%	72.3%	77.9%	76.2%	81.0%	79.1%	83.3%	85.8%	87.3%
35 to 39	75.2%	57.9%	74.3%	79.1%	77.7%	81.5%	77.2%	81.4%	83.2%	85.7%
40 to 44	77.6%	58.0%	76.8%	81.2%	79.9%	83.2%	80.4%	85.2%	84.2%	90.2%
45 to 49	78.2%	55.0%	76.4%	81.5%	79.9%	84.1%	83.2%	89.1%	86.5%	90.0%
50 to 54	74.3%	49.4%	71.2%	78.0%	76.7%	80.4%	80.9%	88.3%	86.1%	89.4%
55 to 59	64.1%	41.1%	61.5%	68.8%	67.3%	71.8%	71.8%	78.5%	81.3%	85.7%
60 to 64	43.8%	27.1%	42.3%	50.0%	48.6%	53.0%	51.3%	58.8%	61.5%	66.6%
65 to 69	21.6%	13.2%	20.8%	26.7%	26.4%	27.4%	26.3%	31.7%	40.3%	44.5%
70 to 74	11.3%	6.9%	11.2%	14.3%	14.2%	14.5%	14.6%	18.2%	17.4%	28.6%
75 to 79	5.9%	3.6%	5.7%	7.4%	7.7%	6.6%	8.2%	12.2%	13.5%	16.8%
80+	2.3%	1.2%	2.4%	3.2%	3.0%	3.5%	3.7%	5.7%	6.7%	13.5%
18 +	60.6%	35.1%	56.7%	67.9%	65.8%	72.6%	72.8%	75.7%	77.6%	80.1%
25 to 64	72.1%	49.5%	69.3%	76.5%	74.7%	79.6%	78.7%	82.9%	83.5%	86.4%
25 +	59.5%	32.6%	54.9%	76.5%	65.0%	72.0%	72.0%	75.7%	77.6%	80.1%
				Unemployment Rates—Females of All Races						
18 to 19	12.7%	17.6%	13.6%	7.7%	7.7%	8.0%	11.6%	0.0%	0.0%	0.0%
20 to 24	8.1%	19.6%	10.0%	5.7%	5.9%	5.1%	4.8%	5.0%	2.1%	6.8%
25 to 29	5.6%	15.2%	7.4%	5.0%	5.5%	3.8%	2.6%	2.6%	2.5%	2.2%
30 to 34	4.8%	11.5%	6.1%	4.6%	5.1%	3.6%	2.5%	2.2%	1.9%	1.9%
35 to 39	4.3%	10.7%	5.0%	3.8%	4.3%	3.0%	2.5%	2.3%	1.5%	1.6%
40 to 44	3.8%	8.8%	4.3%	3.4%	3.8%	2.9%	2.5%	1.9%	1.9%	1.0%
45 to 49	3.4%	7.2%	3.6%	3.4%	3.8%	2.9%	2.5%	1.7%	1.2%	2.2%
50 to 54	3.1%	6.5%	3.2%	3.1%	3.3%	2.9%	2.5%	1.7%	2.1%	1.9%
55 to 59	3.2%	5.9%	3.2%	3.2%	3.4%	2.9%	2.6%	2.0%	1.3%	1.5%
60 to 64	3.1%	5.0%	3.0%	3.2%	3.4%	2.7%	2.4%	2.6%	2.1%	1.5%
65 to 69	3.5%	5.0%	3.1%	3.8%	4.0%	3.3%	2.9%	2.6%	2.7%	2.1%
70 to 74	3.2%	4.0%	2.9%	3.6%	3.6%	3.8%	3.1%	2.7%	2.6%	0.9%
75 to 79	3.4%	3.9%	3.3%	3.6%	3.4%	3.9%	3.0%	2.3%	4.3%	1.9%
80+%	2.1%	2.8%	1.3%	2.3%	2.4%	1.9%	2.7%	2.5%	4.5%	0.4%
18 +	4.7%	10.9%	5.4%	4.2%	4.7%	3.3%	2.7%	2.1%	1.8%	1.7%
25 to 64	4.0%	9.3%	4.5%	3.8%	4.2%	3.1%	2.5%	2.1%	1.8%	1.7%
25 +	4.0%	8.9%	4.4%	3.8%	4.2%	3.1%	2.5%	2.1%	1.8%	1.7%

*Calculated from aggregated data, i.e., not weighted averages by education

Table 9: Labor force participation and unemployment rates by sex, race, age, and education, 2000 through 2006, continued—White Males

Ages	All*	<HS	HS	Some College			College Degree	Masters Degree	Prof'l Degree	PhD/ Degree
				All	No Degree	Assoc Degree				
Labor Force Participation Rates—White Males										
18 to 19	64.1%	59.3%	72.5%	59.3%	59.1%	75.2%	73.5%	67.3%	100.0%	100.0%
20 to 24	83.1%	85.3%	89.2%	76.4%	74.4%	88.1%	86.9%	84.2%	73.4%	64.4%
25 to 29	92.9%	90.1%	93.2%	93.1%	92.4%	94.8%	93.9%	93.5%	91.5%	93.8%
30 to 34	94.3%	89.2%	93.4%	95.1%	94.7%	96.0%	96.8%	96.6%	97.6%	97.0%
35 to 39	93.9%	87.9%	92.7%	94.7%	94.1%	96.0%	96.9%	97.2%	97.8%	97.6%
40 to 44	92.8%	83.5%	91.8%	93.9%	93.3%	94.9%	96.9%	97.1%	96.5%	97.8%
45 to 49	91.1%	78.6%	89.4%	92.1%	91.5%	93.1%	95.8%	96.7%	97.5%	96.8%
50 to 54	87.4%	72.4%	84.7%	87.9%	87.2%	89.3%	93.0%	94.6%	95.7%	96.1%
55 to 59	78.7%	63.7%	75.7%	79.2%	79.1%	79.5%	85.6%	85.0%	92.1%	92.1%
60 to 64	57.6%	45.9%	53.4%	59.7%	59.5%	60.2%	65.7%	64.5%	79.9%	80.7%
65 to 69	31.8%	23.6%	29.0%	32.6%	32.8%	32.0%	39.8%	37.9%	59.1%	53.5%
70 to 74	19.1%	13.0%	17.8%	19.8%	20.0%	18.9%	24.1%	23.7%	39.2%	36.0%
75 to 79	11.8%	8.0%	10.7%	13.0%	12.8%	13.8%	15.8%	14.6%	27.1%	23.2%
80+	5.5%	3.7%	5.2%	6.2%	6.0%	7.1%	8.1%	9.3%	13.4%	12.3%
18 +	76.1%	61.1%	75.5%	78.6%	76.4%	84.4%	84.3%	81.1%	83.0%	80.8%
25 to 64	88.0%	78.4%	86.4%	89.1%	88.4%	90.7%	92.8%	91.4%	94.2%	93.9%
25 +	75.9%	58.7%	74.1%	79.9%	78.0%	84.2%	84.2%	81.1%	83.0%	80.8%
Unemployment Rates—White Males										
18 to 19	13.0%	16.1%	12.8%	8.5%	8.4%	9.4%	1.9%	0.0%	0.0%	0.0%
20 to 24	7.7%	11.4%	8.7%	5.8%	6.0%	5.0%	5.5%	7.0%	5.8%	2.6%
25 to 29	4.6%	7.3%	5.5%	4.2%	4.4%	3.6%	2.7%	2.1%	3.6%	2.6%
30 to 34	3.7%	6.8%	4.5%	3.4%	3.7%	2.9%	2.0%	1.9%	1.4%	0.8%
35 to 39	3.4%	6.0%	4.1%	3.0%	3.1%	2.7%	2.2%	1.6%	0.7%	1.2%
40 to 44	3.2%	6.3%	3.6%	3.0%	3.1%	2.8%	2.2%	2.1%	0.7%	1.2%
45 to 49	3.1%	5.3%	3.6%	3.0%	3.0%	3.1%	2.3%	2.1%	0.7%	1.1%
50 to 54	3.1%	5.4%	3.4%	3.1%	3.1%	3.1%	2.4%	2.5%	0.5%	0.9%
55 to 59	3.2%	5.2%	3.3%	3.4%	3.3%	3.6%	3.0%	2.6%	0.8%	0.8%
60 to 64	3.4%	4.4%	3.4%	3.4%	3.4%	3.5%	3.4%	2.7%	1.1%	2.3%
65 to 69	3.3%	4.3%	3.4%	3.3%	3.0%	4.1%	3.3%	3.0%	1.1%	1.0%
70 to 74	3.2%	5.0%	3.2%	3.7%	3.7%	3.8%	2.3%	2.4%	1.7%	1.2%
75 to 79	3.1%	4.2%	3.3%	3.5%	3.6%	3.0%	2.2%	3.2%	1.4%	2.9%
80+%	2.4%	2.5%	2.3%	3.3%	3.7%	2.1%	2.4%	0.5%	0.0%	0.6%
18 +	4.2%	7.6%	4.9%	3.8%	4.0%	3.3%	2.6%	2.2%	1.0%	1.2%
25 to 64	3.5%	6.1%	4.0%	3.3%	3.4%	3.1%	2.4%	2.2%	1.0%	1.2%
25 +	3.4%	6.0%	4.0%	3.3%	3.4%	3.1%	2.4%	2.2%	1.0%	1.2%

*Calculated from aggregated data, i.e., not weighted averages by education

Table 9: Labor force participation and unemployment rates by sex, race, age, and education, 2000 through 2006, continued—White Females

Ages	All*	<HS	HS	Some College			College Degree	Masters Degree	Prof'l Degree	PhD/ Degree
				All	No Degree	Assoc Degree				
Labor Force Participation Rates—White Females										
18 to 19	61.3%	51.9%	66.7%	64.2%	64.1%	70.7%	52.8%	13.5%	80.9%	35.2%
20 to 24	72.9%	51.6%	73.4%	74.4%	72.8%	82.9%	84.9%	85.3%	75.5%	82.8%
25 to 29	75.5%	49.2%	69.9%	78.4%	76.3%	82.8%	86.5%	89.1%	86.4%	90.4%
30 to 34	74.0%	53.2%	71.8%	76.6%	74.3%	80.4%	79.1%	84.5%	85.7%	88.1%
35 to 39	74.7%	57.0%	74.1%	78.5%	76.6%	81.4%	76.4%	81.0%	83.2%	86.7%
40 to 44	77.5%	58.1%	76.9%	80.8%	79.5%	82.8%	79.8%	85.1%	83.3%	90.6%
45 to 49	78.8%	54.9%	77.1%	82.0%	80.5%	84.4%	82.9%	89.0%	86.0%	90.4%
50 to 54	75.0%	49.2%	71.8%	78.7%	77.3%	81.1%	80.9%	88.5%	85.6%	89.1%
55 to 59	64.7%	41.0%	61.9%	69.1%	67.6%	72.4%	71.5%	78.6%	81.9%	84.8%
60 to 64	44.4%	27.4%	42.7%	50.1%	48.6%	53.5%	51.1%	59.1%	61.7%	68.7%
65 to 69	22.0%	13.2%	20.9%	27.1%	26.7%	28.1%	26.2%	32.4%	37.9%	41.1%
70 to 74	11.6%	7.1%	11.4%	14.3%	14.2%	14.4%	14.9%	18.7%	14.8%	30.7%
75 to 79	6.0%	3.6%	5.8%	7.4%	7.7%	6.3%	7.7%	12.6%	14.4%	16.8%
80+	2.2%	1.2%	2.2%	3.0%	2.9%	3.3%	3.4%	5.3%	5.1%	15.4%
18 +	60.0%	34.6%	55.4%	67.2%	64.9%	72.1%	72.3%	75.8%	77.1%	80.0%
25 to 64	72.1%	49.0%	69.1%	76.1%	74.2%	79.6%	78.6%	83.3%	83.4%	86.8%
25 +	58.7%	31.8%	53.5%	66.1%	63.3%	71.3%	71.3%	75.7%	77.1%	80.0%
Unemployment Rates—White Females										
18 to 19	10.6%	14.9%	11.3%	6.7%	6.7%	8.0%	9.5%	0.0%	0.0%	0.0%
20 to 24	6.6%	16.0%	8.0%	4.8%	4.9%	4.2%	4.4%	4.7%	2.3%	5.7%
25 to 29	4.6%	12.7%	6.1%	4.2%	4.7%	3.1%	2.4%	2.0%	2.6%	1.2%
30 to 34	4.1%	10.2%	5.0%	4.0%	4.6%	3.1%	2.3%	2.0%	1.8%	1.5%
35 to 39	3.8%	9.7%	4.3%	3.3%	3.7%	2.6%	2.3%	2.1%	1.6%	1.6%
40 to 44	3.3%	7.9%	3.7%	3.0%	3.3%	2.6%	2.3%	1.9%	1.8%	1.1%
45 to 49	3.1%	6.7%	3.2%	3.1%	3.5%	2.7%	2.5%	1.6%	1.3%	1.3%
50 to 54	2.8%	6.1%	2.9%	2.9%	3.0%	2.7%	2.4%	1.6%	2.3%	1.7%
55 to 59	2.9%	4.9%	3.0%	3.1%	3.3%	2.8%	2.5%	2.0%	1.2%	1.7%
60 to 64	3.0%	4.6%	2.9%	3.0%	3.2%	2.6%	2.3%	2.6%	2.2%	1.6%
65 to 69	3.1%	4.4%	2.8%	3.3%	3.4%	3.1%	2.9%	2.8%	1.7%	2.4%
70 to 74	3.1%	3.6%	2.8%	3.4%	3.3%	3.7%	2.9%	3.0%	3.6%	1.0%
75 to 79	3.2%	3.9%	3.2%	3.3%	3.4%	3.1%	3.1%	1.8%	4.5%	0.0%
80+%	1.9%	2.4%	1.4%	2.1%	2.3%	1.6%	2.3%	2.5%	6.7%	0.4%
18 +	4.1%	9.5%	4.5%	3.7%	4.1%	2.9%	2.6%	1.9%	1.8%	1.5%
25 to 64	3.5%	8.2%	3.9%	3.3%	3.7%	2.8%	2.4%	1.9%	1.8%	1.5%
25 +	3.5%	7.9%	3.8%	3.3%	3.7%	2.8%	2.4%	1.9%	1.8%	1.5%

*Calculated from aggregated data, i.e., not weighted averages by education

Table 9: Labor force participation and unemployment rates by sex, race, age, and education, 2000 through 2006, continued—Black Males

Ages	All*	<HS	HS	Some College			College Degree	All Grad Degrees
				All	No Degree	Assoc Degree		
Labor Force Participation Rates—Black Males								
18 to 19	47.9%	40.2%	59.6%	47.7%	47.5%	57.9%	61.3%	56.8%
20 to 24	70.7%	60.8%	76.4%	68.9%	67.4%	80.5%	81.2%	54.2%
25 to 29	84.6%	71.2%	83.4%	87.8%	86.9%	90.9%	92.3%	91.0%
30 to 34	88.2%	73.2%	86.4%	92.1%	91.4%	94.0%	94.6%	95.3%
35 to 39	86.7%	69.0%	85.5%	90.8%	89.7%	93.8%	95.5%	94.4%
40 to 44	83.5%	65.6%	82.7%	88.3%	87.5%	90.5%	92.2%	92.1%
45 to 49	80.3%	62.7%	79.4%	83.1%	82.3%	85.2%	91.3%	94.8%
50 to 54	76.2%	62.5%	75.1%	78.6%	77.4%	81.5%	86.0%	91.3%
55 to 59	66.2%	51.4%	66.2%	71.4%	69.8%	75.1%	77.4%	83.4%
60 to 64	45.7%	35.2%	47.2%	48.2%	47.8%	49.4%	56.3%	68.5%
65 to 69	25.2%	20.6%	24.1%	28.3%	25.5%	35.4%	35.3%	41.7%
70 to 74	15.6%	12.9%	14.8%	17.2%	14.1%	25.6%	27.3%	28.5%
75 to 79	9.6%	6.5%	13.1%	13.2%	12.6%	14.8%	14.2%	17.5%
80+	4.8%	2.1%	8.4%	6.7%	6.8%	6.5%	19.3%	10.0%
18 +	70.5%	46.7%	73.6%	77.5%	75.9%	82.6%	86.1%	82.5%
25 to 64	79.7%	60.9%	79.3%	84.4%	83.6%	86.7%	90.0%	90.1%
25 +	71.9%	45.7%	73.9%	80.4%	79.5%	82.8%	86.4%	82.7%
Unemployment Rates—Black Males								
18 to 19	30.5%	37.4%	29.4%	16.1%	16.1%	13.9%	3.1%	0.0%
20 to 24	18.7%	32.4%	19.6%	12.8%	12.8%	12.6%	7.2%	15.9%
25 to 29	10.5%	22.7%	12.2%	7.8%	8.6%	5.1%	4.1%	4.8%
30 to 34	7.7%	15.4%	8.6%	6.8%	7.5%	4.9%	4.2%	3.1%
35 to 39	7.2%	13.5%	8.7%	5.8%	5.8%	5.9%	2.8%	3.2%
40 to 44	6.8%	13.3%	7.5%	5.4%	5.7%	4.7%	4.4%	1.6%
45 to 49	6.5%	11.7%	6.9%	6.0%	6.2%	5.6%	3.9%	3.2%
50 to 54	5.7%	9.3%	5.7%	5.1%	5.5%	4.2%	3.7%	4.6%
55 to 59	5.5%	7.5%	5.4%	6.1%	5.9%	6.6%	3.1%	3.2%
60 to 64	5.2%	6.8%	4.8%	5.1%	5.4%	4.5%	5.3%	2.1%
65 to 69	5.3%	6.3%	5.8%	5.8%	6.1%	5.3%	2.4%	2.1%
70 to 74	5.2%	6.7%	5.3%	2.7%	3.5%	1.4%	4.5%	3.1%
75 to 79	6.8%	9.1%	5.2%	5.2%	5.7%	4.1%	5.6%	5.9%
80+%	3.8%	7.0%	2.2%	0.8%	1.1%	0.0%	3.9%	4.0%
18 +	9.4%	17.9%	10.3%	7.3%	7.9%	5.7%	4.0%	3.2%
25 to 64	7.3%	13.0%	8.1%	6.2%	6.6%	5.2%	3.8%	3.2%
25 +	7.2%	12.5%	8.1%	6.2%	6.6%	5.1%	3.8%	3.2%

*Calculated from aggregated data, i.e., not weighted averages by education

Table 9: Labor force participation and unemployment rates by sex, race, age, and education, 2000 through 2006, continued—Black Females

Ages	All*	<HS	HS	Some College			College Degree	All Grad Degrees
				All	No Degree	Assoc Degree		
Labor Force Participation Rates—Black Females								
18 to 19	47.3%	37.9%	55.4%	49.0%	48.8%	56.9%	73.1%	63.7%
20 to 24	68.3%	54.6%	70.6%	69.5%	68.5%	77.0%	80.4%	80.3%
25 to 29	78.8%	60.6%	75.9%	82.1%	80.7%	86.1%	89.9%	89.8%
30 to 34	80.6%	60.9%	77.1%	85.0%	84.1%	87.4%	89.4%	91.4%
35 to 39	80.3%	62.2%	77.4%	84.1%	83.8%	84.8%	89.1%	91.1%
40 to 44	79.7%	57.6%	78.0%	84.4%	83.1%	87.1%	89.7%	92.6%
45 to 49	76.3%	54.3%	74.4%	79.9%	78.2%	83.6%	88.2%	93.2%
50 to 54	71.0%	49.7%	68.8%	74.5%	74.1%	75.4%	86.4%	90.1%
55 to 59	60.7%	41.5%	59.3%	66.0%	66.3%	65.4%	78.8%	80.0%
60 to 64	40.1%	25.7%	40.7%	51.1%	50.5%	52.7%	53.8%	51.4%
65 to 69	19.4%	14.9%	19.8%	23.0%	24.0%	20.1%	25.8%	30.3%
70 to 74	10.0%	7.0%	10.8%	14.5%	15.4%	12.2%	14.0%	14.3%
75 to 79	5.5%	3.9%	5.6%	8.4%	8.2%	9.0%	11.8%	8.5%
80+	3.0%	1.5%	3.9%	7.0%	6.6%	7.8%	10.4%	4.7%
18 +	64.1%	37.1%	64.2%	73.1%	71.8%	77.0%	81.9%	79.8%
25 to 64	74.1%	51.3%	71.7%	79.6%	78.6%	81.7%	87.0%	87.5%
25 +	64.4%	35.2%	63.9%	75.0%	74.0%	77.1%	82.1%	79.8%
Unemployment Rates—Black Females								
18 to 19	25.0%	31.1%	26.4%	15.8%	15.9%	10.5%	19.4%	0.0%
20 to 24	15.9%	32.7%	18.2%	10.7%	10.9%	9.4%	7.4%	4.7%
25 to 29	10.4%	25.6%	12.4%	8.3%	8.5%	7.6%	4.0%	3.7%
30 to 34	8.2%	18.4%	10.7%	6.7%	7.1%	5.8%	3.4%	2.4%
35 to 39	7.0%	15.7%	8.2%	6.2%	6.7%	5.2%	3.0%	2.7%
40 to 44	6.5%	13.5%	7.6%	5.4%	5.8%	4.5%	4.1%	1.7%
45 to 49	5.2%	9.5%	5.6%	5.0%	5.3%	4.3%	3.4%	2.5%
50 to 54	4.8%	8.5%	4.9%	4.6%	4.9%	3.9%	3.5%	2.2%
55 to 59	4.5%	8.2%	4.7%	3.9%	4.0%	3.7%	3.3%	2.0%
60 to 64	4.2%	6.5%	3.8%	4.2%	5.1%	2.3%	2.8%	2.0%
65 to 69	6.0%	7.4%	5.3%	7.1%	7.9%	4.6%	4.3%	3.2%
70 to 74	5.1%	5.8%	4.5%	6.5%	6.4%	6.8%	5.0%	0.0%
75 to 79	5.6%	4.7%	5.4%	8.4%	5.6%	14.2%	2.5%	9.1%
80+%	4.0%	5.8%	1.1%	4.1%	3.8%	4.7%	6.0%	5.0%
18 +	8.5%	17.4%	9.9%	6.9%	7.5%	5.4%	3.8%	2.5%
25 to 64	6.8%	14.0%	7.9%	6.0%	6.4%	5.1%	3.5%	2.4%
25 +	6.8%	13.5%	7.8%	6.0%	6.4%	5.1%	3.6%	2.4%

*Calculated from aggregated data, i.e., not weighted averages by education

Table 9: Labor force participation and unemployment rates by sex, race, age, and education, 2000 through 2006, continued—Hispanic Males

| Ages | All* | <HS | HS | Some College | | | College Degree & More |
				All	No Degree	Assoc Degree	
Labor Force Participation Rates—Hispanic Males							
18 to 19	64.4%	60.8%	72.8%	60.7%	60.4%	93.1%	100.0%
20 to 24	86.2%	88.7%	89.0%	78.2%	77.2%	87.8%	86.2%
25 to 29	93.5%	93.5%	94.1%	92.3%	91.5%	93.2%	92.7%
30 to 34	94.1%	93.0%	93.9%	95.5%	95.2%	95.8%	95.4%
35 to 39	93.7%	92.8%	93.6%	94.5%	94.2%	94.6%	95.1%
40 to 44	92.1%	90.5%	91.4%	93.8%	93.6%	96.1%	96.2%
45 to 49	88.5%	85.9%	89.0%	89.8%	89.5%	93.6%	94.6%
50 to 54	83.8%	80.7%	84.9%	86.1%	86.4%	88.9%	90.8%
55 to 59	76.4%	71.7%	78.5%	79.4%	79.7%	85.0%	87.1%
60 to 64	57.9%	55.2%	54.8%	62.3%	60.8%	71.7%	71.9%
65 to 69	31.5%	26.9%	31.7%	37.8%	37.5%	48.6%	49.7%
70 to 74	16.7%	12.7%	17.9%	18.1%	17.0%	37.8%	36.1%
75 to 79	9.6%	6.8%	11.2%	13.9%	13.5%	23.2%	23.4%
80+	6.4%	3.4%	11.9%	10.6%	10.6%	17.5%	15.2%
18 +	82.9%	78.8%	85.6%	84.5%	83.4%	89.0%	88.8%
25 to 64	89.5%	87.4%	90.1%	90.8%	90.5%	92.7%	92.9%
25 +	83.5%	78.7%	85.8%	87.2%	86.9%	89.1%	89.0%
Unemployment Rates—Hispanic Males							
18 to 19	16.2%	17.7%	16.2%	11.4%	11.4%	5.8%	0.0%
20 to 24	8.1%	8.9%	8.4%	6.8%	7.0%	6.3%	7.2%
25 to 29	5.1%	5.9%	5.0%	4.8%	4.8%	3.1%	3.5%
30 to 34	4.7%	5.7%	4.5%	3.9%	3.8%	2.7%	2.3%
35 to 39	4.3%	5.4%	3.7%	3.7%	3.9%	3.6%	3.4%
40 to 44	4.4%	5.3%	4.8%	3.2%	3.1%	2.3%	2.4%
45 to 49	4.3%	5.2%	4.2%	3.6%	3.2%	2.5%	2.8%
50 to 54	4.6%	6.1%	4.0%	3.9%	4.1%	2.4%	2.4%
55 to 59	4.5%	6.4%	3.3%	3.6%	3.4%	2.5%	2.2%
60 to 64	5.9%	6.7%	4.6%	6.7%	7.7%	3.8%	4.8%
65 to 69	4.7%	6.1%	5.8%	1.3%	0.8%	3.3%	3.5%
70 to 74	5.9%	7.9%	3.7%	6.0%	6.2%	3.7%	2.4%
75 to 79	5.5%	5.2%	7.8%	2.1%	2.8%	7.8%	7.5%
80+%	4.7%	10.0%	0.0%	6.2%	8.3%	2.5%	2.2%
18 +	5.6%	6.8%	5.6%	4.7%	4.8%	3.1%	3.0%
25 to 64	4.6%	5.7%	4.4%	4.0%	4.0%	2.8%	2.8%
25 +	4.6%	5.7%	4.4%	3.9%	4.0%	2.9%	2.8%

*Calculated from aggregated data, i.e., not weighted averages by education

Table 9: Labor force participation and unemployment rates by sex, race, age, and education, 2000 through 2006, continued—Hispanic Females

| Ages | All* | <HS | HS | Some College | | | College Degree & More |
				All	No Degree	Assoc Degree	
Labor Force Participation Rates—Hispanic Females							
18 to 19	50.6%	39.9%	59.2%	58.7%	58.6%	63.9%	27.9%
20 to 24	62.9%	47.8%	66.9%	71.0%	70.1%	75.6%	77.1%
25 to 29	62.9%	46.3%	64.8%	76.3%	75.5%	78.1%	80.3%
30 to 34	64.6%	50.9%	67.0%	75.6%	75.2%	76.6%	78.4%
35 to 39	68.1%	56.1%	71.1%	77.1%	76.8%	77.9%	78.3%
40 to 44	70.5%	59.7%	72.9%	80.0%	80.2%	79.6%	80.4%
45 to 49	70.1%	58.6%	73.5%	79.0%	78.3%	80.3%	83.5%
50 to 54	63.2%	51.6%	65.5%	74.0%	74.1%	74.0%	81.6%
55 to 59	54.5%	41.7%	60.2%	67.4%	67.4%	67.5%	73.3%
60 to 64	34.9%	25.6%	40.5%	46.6%	44.0%	51.4%	56.5%
65 to 69	16.2%	11.2%	19.9%	25.3%	24.2%	27.5%	30.1%
70 to 74	8.2%	5.8%	8.8%	19.5%	18.3%	23.2%	16.3%
75 to 79	3.5%	2.3%	4.8%	8.2%	10.0%	3.8%	5.9%
80+	2.2%	0.7%	5.3%	8.0%	7.2%	9.7%	8.0%
18 +	57.9%	42.8%	62.5%	71.5%	70.6%	73.8%	75.5%
25 to 64	63.9%	50.5%	66.9%	75.4%	75.0%	76.4%	78.8%
25 +	57.5%	42.4%	62.0%	72.5%	72.0%	73.6%	75.4%
Unemployment Rates—Hispanic Females							
18 to 19	15.4%	20.6%	14.8%	9.6%	9.5%	10.6%	0.0%
20 to 24	9.4%	15.2%	9.4%	6.5%	6.6%	5.8%	4.4%
25 to 29	7.7%	13.2%	6.8%	5.6%	5.8%	5.3%	3.8%
30 to 34	6.6%	10.8%	5.8%	4.6%	5.1%	3.6%	3.9%
35 to 39	6.4%	10.5%	5.9%	4.4%	5.0%	3.1%	3.0%
40 to 44	5.8%	8.1%	5.8%	4.4%	4.8%	3.6%	3.0%
45 to 49	4.9%	7.0%	4.7%	3.9%	4.0%	3.6%	2.7%
50 to 54	5.3%	7.6%	3.9%	4.9%	5.1%	4.6%	3.1%
55 to 59	4.6%	7.0%	3.5%	3.6%	4.0%	2.6%	2.7%
60 to 64	5.0%	7.7%	3.2%	3.4%	2.9%	4.2%	3.9%
65 to 69	4.8%	6.3%	3.5%	4.8%	4.3%	5.7%	3.3%
70 to 74	6.0%	7.1%	4.8%	4.6%	4.6%	4.8%	6.0%
75 to 79	5.6%	7.2%	3.5%	5.9%	6.8%	0.0%	3.7%
80+%	0.2%	0.0%	0.6%	0.0%	0.0%	0.0%	0.0%
18 +	7.0%	10.6%	6.6%	5.2%	5.6%	4.2%	3.4%
25 to 64	6.1%	9.5%	5.5%	4.6%	4.9%	3.9%	3.3%
25 +	6.1%	9.4%	5.4%	4.6%	4.9%	3.9%	3.3%

*Calculated from aggregated data, i.e., not weighted averages by education

Table 10: Labor force participation and unemployment rates by race, age, and education, 2000 through 2006, Never-Married, Childless Females of All Races

Ages	All*	<HS	HS	Some College			College Degree	Graduate Degrees		
				All	No Degree	Assoc Degree		All	Masters	Ph.D./Prof
Labor Force Participation Rates—Never-Married, Childless Females of All Races										
18 to 19	74.4%	62.2%	78.1%	75.7%	75.3%	86.7%				
20 to 24	81.7%	62.0%	82.3%	81.1%	79.7%	87.8%	86.8%	89.4%	90.9%	79.5%
25 to 29	87.6%	60.2%	81.0%	88.7%	87.7%	90.8%	91.5%	91.9%	92.1%	90.8%
30 to 34	88.3%	55.5%	81.0%	89.0%	88.0%	90.9%	93.8%	94.8%	94.7%	95.1%
35 to 39	86.9%	55.8%	77.3%	88.4%	86.9%	90.9%	94.7%	96.0%	96.2%	95.5%
40 to 44	84.4%	52.3%	75.8%	86.6%	85.1%	89.2%	93.0%	96.2%	96.6%	94.8%
45 to 49	82.3%	46.1%	76.2%	83.9%	81.7%	87.9%	90.3%	95.3%	95.4%	95.0%
50 to 54	78.0%	48.4%	70.5%	79.1%	78.2%	80.8%	85.4%	91.2%	90.5%	93.5%
55 to 59	70.1%	41.7%	63.8%	74.3%	75.1%	72.3%	76.1%	81.5%	79.0%	89.7%
60 to 64	49.2%	27.4%	44.3%	58.4%	55.7%	65.3%	57.7%	57.7%	57.6%	57.9%
65 to 69	28.7%	17.8%	26.9%	31.4%	29.4%	37.3%	31.8%	40.0%	36.0%	53.4%
70 to 74	15.0%	7.6%	11.6%	17.3%	16.9%	18.3%	14.8%	28.0%	26.6%	33.1%
75 to 79	11.1%	5.9%	5.9%	11.7%	9.9%	16.6%	18.6%	21.5%	22.2%	14.8%
80+	6.3%	3.3%	7.4%	4.9%	4.9%	4.8%	12.0%	5.9%	5.3%	10.7%
18 +	78.8%	47.5%	72.2%	80.8%	79.4%	85.1%	88.2%	86.5%	85.8%	88.8%
25 to 64	83.7%	50.7%	75.5%	85.5%	84.2%	88.1%	90.9%	91.7%	91.5%	92.2%
25 +	78.1%	42.0%	67.5%	81.1%	79.6%	84.2%	88.6%	86.4%	85.6%	89.0%
Unemployment Rates—Never-Married, Childless Females of All Races										
18 to 19	11.1%	20.4%	10.7%	8.1%	8.3%	5.2%				
20 to 24	5.5%	14.7%	7.9%	4.8%	4.8%	4.8%	3.2%	2.8%	2.9%	2.0%
25 to 29	3.6%	13.1%	6.7%	3.9%	4.4%	2.9%	2.1%	2.0%	2.1%	1.6%
30 to 34	4.0%	11.9%	6.0%	4.3%	4.6%	3.9%	2.8%	2.8%	3.0%	2.4%
35 to 39	4.2%	14.5%	6.7%	3.9%	4.5%	3.0%	2.7%	2.2%	2.4%	1.7%
40 to 44	4.4%	8.6%	5.6%	5.6%	5.7%	5.5%	3.3%	1.8%	1.8%	1.8%
45 to 49	4.6%	11.2%	5.6%	5.5%	5.8%	5.0%	3.8%	1.9%	1.8%	2.5%
50 to 54	4.5%	7.6%	4.9%	5.6%	5.5%	5.7%	5.0%	1.6%	1.5%	1.7%
55 to 59	3.9%	4.7%	5.4%	4.2%	3.9%	5.0%	4.7%	1.6%	2.0%	0.4%
60 to 64	4.1%	5.1%	5.0%	2.9%	3.0%	2.7%	4.7%	3.5%	4.2%	1.1%
65 to 69	6.0%	8.6%	7.2%	8.9%	10.2%	5.7%	2.3%	2.4%	3.4%	0.0%
70 to 74	4.5%	0.0%	3.2%	16.7%	18.3%	12.9%	0.0%	1.3%	1.6%	0.2%
75 to 79	5.7%	7.1%	6.2%	17.6%	18.2%	16.6%	0.2%	1.2%	1.3%	0.0%
80+%	2.1%	3.5%	1.5%	0.0%	0.0%	0.0%	4.6%	0.7%	0.0%	3.2%
18 +	4.7%	12.7%	7.0%	4.8%	5.1%	4.2%	2.9%	2.2%	2.3%	1.8%
25 to 64	4.0%	10.8%	6.0%	4.5%	4.8%	4.0%	2.8%	2.1%	2.2%	1.8%
25 +	4.1%	10.6%	6.0%	4.6%	4.9%	4.0%	2.8%	2.1%	2.2%	1.8%

*Calculated from aggregated data, i.e., not weighted averages by education

Table 10: Labor force participation and unemployment rates by race, age, and education, 2000 through 2006, continued—Never-Married, Childless White Females

Ages	All*	<HS	HS	Some College			College Degree	Graduate Degrees		
				All	No Degree	Assoc Degree		All	Masters	Ph.D./Prof
Labor Force Participation Rates—Never-Married, Childless White Females										
18 to 19	76.4%	63.7%	80.0%	78.0%	77.7%	85.3%				
20 to 24	83.1%	59.9%	83.7%	82.9%	81.6%	89.0%	87.9%	90.6%	92.1%	80.5%
25 to 29	89.1%	60.0%	81.8%	90.4%	89.3%	92.5%	92.8%	93.2%	93.8%	91.1%
30 to 34	89.3%	56.9%	83.0%	89.4%	87.9%	91.9%	94.2%	95.4%	95.3%	95.5%
35 to 39	88.2%	53.5%	78.1%	89.8%	87.8%	93.1%	95.1%	96.6%	96.8%	96.0%
40 to 44	87.0%	54.0%	78.1%	88.6%	87.8%	90.0%	93.5%	96.2%	96.7%	94.6%
45 to 49	85.8%	54.5%	78.8%	85.3%	83.4%	88.5%	91.4%	95.4%	95.4%	95.5%
50 to 54	80.4%	50.5%	74.5%	78.7%	78.1%	79.8%	84.8%	91.6%	91.1%	93.0%
55 to 59	71.7%	40.1%	65.6%	75.6%	75.2%	76.6%	74.6%	80.8%	77.9%	90.0%
60 to 64	51.7%	26.9%	46.4%	58.0%	54.6%	66.8%	56.8%	59.8%	59.6%	60.5%
65 to 69	29.2%	14.2%	25.7%	32.1%	30.2%	37.5%	32.6%	40.6%	37.9%	50.1%
70 to 74	15.1%	6.9%	10.9%	18.2%	18.5%	17.6%	12.5%	28.3%	27.5%	31.1%
75 to 79	11.1%	6.3%	4.6%	11.6%	9.9%	16.3%	18.4%	21.5%	22.1%	15.9%
80+	4.8%	2.8%	5.7%	3.5%	3.8%	3.1%	9.7%	3.4%	2.7%	8.8%
18 +	80.0%	48.2%	72.7%	81.8%	80.3%	85.9%	88.7%	86.2%	85.7%	88.1%
25 to 64	85.5%	52.7%	77.4%	86.6%	85.1%	89.4%	91.5%	92.0%	92.0%	92.1%
25 +	79.1%	42.4%	67.0%	81.4%	79.6%	84.8%	88.9%	86.1%	85.4%	88.3%
Unemployment Rates—Never-Married, Childless White Females										
18 to 19	9.9%	18.1%	9.5%	7.4%	7.5%	5.3%				
20 to 24	4.7%	11.8%	6.6%	4.1%	4.2%	3.5%	3.0%	3.2%	2.6%	3.1%
25 to 29	3.1%	11.2%	5.4%	3.4%	3.9%	2.5%	2.0%	1.9%	1.9%	1.9%
30 to 34	3.5%	10.2%	4.3%	3.3%	3.7%	2.7%	2.9%	2.9%	2.6%	2.9%
35 to 39	3.4%	12.3%	4.9%	3.1%	3.3%	2.7%	2.6%	2.2%	2.2%	2.2%
40 to 44	3.8%	5.7%	4.7%	5.3%	5.6%	4.9%	2.9%	1.9%	1.7%	1.8%
45 to 49	4.1%	10.9%	4.1%	5.8%	5.9%	5.6%	3.7%	1.3%	1.9%	1.5%
50 to 54	4.0%	4.2%	4.2%	5.1%	4.8%	5.8%	5.1%	1.4%	1.9%	1.5%
55 to 59	3.7%	3.0%	4.8%	4.1%	3.9%	4.6%	4.5%	2.3%	0.5%	1.8%
60 to 64	3.6%	0.7%	5.2%	2.7%	3.4%	1.2%	4.9%	3.6%	1.2%	3.0%
65 to 69	5.3%	10.4%	5.9%	8.4%	9.4%	6.1%	1.9%	3.5%	0.0%	2.5%
70 to 74	4.5%	0.0%	3.9%	14.0%	13.5%	15.3%	0.0%	1.8%	0.2%	1.4%
75 to 79	5.7%	7.5%	4.5%	18.8%	19.3%	17.9%	0.2%	1.3%	0.0%	1.2%
80+%	2.8%	3.6%	2.0%	0.0%	0.0%	0.0%	6.1%	0.0%	4.1%	1.2%
18 +	4.1%	10.9%	5.8%	4.3%	4.5%	3.6%	2.8%	2.1%	1.9%	2.1%
25 to 64	3.5%	9.0%	4.8%	4.0%	4.3%	3.5%	2.8%	2.1%	1.9%	2.1%
25 +	3.5%	8.9%	4.8%	4.1%	4.4%	3.6%	2.7%	2.1%	1.9%	2.1%

*Calculated from aggregated data, i.e., not weighted averages by education

Table 10: Labor force participation and unemployment rates by race, age, and education, 2000 through 2006, continued—Never-Married, Childless Black and Hispanic Females

Ages	Labor Force Participation Rates						Unemployment Rates					
	All*	<HS	HS	Some College	College Degree	Grad Degree	All*	<HS	HS	Some College	College Degree	Grad Degree
Black Never-Married, Childless Females												
18 to 19	69.2%	60.1%	70.7%	74.4%			21.1%	34.6%	19.7%	14.1%		
20 to 24	80.1%	69.6%	79.4%	80.2%	87.0%	93.7%	11.1%	23.2%	14.5%	9.4%	4.1%	1.3%
25 to 34	85.3%	58.6%	77.9%	87.8%	93.8%	94.0%	6.6%	20.1%	10.6%	6.5%	2.9%	1.6%
35 to 44	78.4%	54.6%	72.1%	82.2%	93.6%	96.1%	7.3%	15.3%	9.7%	6.2%	4.4%	2.3%
45 to 54	70.1%	39.7%	67.5%	80.4%	86.1%	93.2%	6.8%	12.7%	7.2%	5.5%	5.8%	4.2%
55 to 64	53.6%	34.4%	51.5%	65.3%	77.7%	72.0%	5.0%	6.9%	6.2%	4.4%	3.1%	2.6%
65 to 74	21.4%	16.7%	25.5%	25.0%	26.7%	23.1%	8.5%	6.0%	10.2%	15.4%	4.6%	1.4%
75+	14.1%	5.1%	25.1%	20.5%	16.8%	17.3%	3.4%	5.4%	5.3%	0.0%	0.0%	1.4%
18 +	74.5%	45.1%	70.5%	80.7%	90.0%	89.3%	8.0%	17.2%	10.8%	7.3%	3.8%	2.3%
25 to 64	76.8%	46.8%	70.5%	83.1%	91.8%	92.2%	6.7%	14.7%	9.2%	6.1%	3.7%	2.4%
25 +	73.3%	40.7%	68.2%	81.2%	90.7%	89.2%	6.7%	14.2%	9.1%	6.2%	3.7%	2.3%
Hispanic Never-Married, Childless Females												
18 to 19	64.4%	48.4%	69.4%	76.8%			11.7%	20.3%	8.9%	9.0%		
20 to 24	72.7%	50.3%	77.2%	79.8%	80.5%	71.5%	6.9%	11.6%	9.0%	4.9%	2.6%	5.0%
25 to 34	78.2%	56.6%	76.0%	88.0%	90.4%	90.4%	4.7%	10.6%	4.3%	3.2%	2.7%	3.9%
35 to 44	80.4%	63.2%	76.8%	91.3%	92.0%	97.9%	6.6%	10.5%	6.8%	6.6%	4.7%	0.5%
45 to 54	72.7%	55.3%	72.5%	80.5%	89.1%	87.8%	6.6%	9.9%	7.3%	6.7%	4.0%	1.1%
55 to 64	58.2%	45.3%	57.2%	72.9%	90.6%	59.2%	2.5%	1.7%	4.2%	2.2%	2.0%	2.5%
65 to 74	19.0%	11.4%	28.1%	23.5%	40.2%	39.6%	9.4%	8.1%	5.5%	1.1%	1.2%	1.4%
75+	8.4%	1.7%	15.6%	19.9%	11.9%	3.4%	3.1%	1.1%	0.6%	0.5%	0.4%	0.3%
18 +	72.4%	51.0%	73.0%	82.8%	87.1%	86.4%	6.0%	10.7%	6.8%	4.8%	3.2%	2.7%
25 to 64	76.6%	56.8%	74.5%	87.0%	90.6%	89.1%	5.3%	9.8%	5.4%	4.3%	3.3%	2.6%
25 +	72.9%	51.4%	71.5%	85.3%	88.6%	86.8%	5.3%	9.7%	5.3%	4.5%	3.3%	2.7%

*Calculated from aggregated data, i.e., not weighted averages. Sources: see chapter 9.
Note: Sample sizes are very small during older ages.

Table 11: Labor force participation and unemployment rates by sex, age, education and smoking status, 2000 through 2003, Males of All Races

Ages	Labor Force Participation Rates						Unemployment Rates					
	All*	<HS	HS	Some College	College Degree	Grad Degree	All*	<HS	HS	Some College	College Degree	Grad Degree
All Males Regardless of Smoking Status												
18 to 19	62.1%	57.5%	72.7%	56.5%			16.4%	20.3%	16.4%	9.2%		
20 to 24	81.0%	82.6%	86.8%	74.6%	85.5%	77.3%	10.0%	16.1%	11.1%	7.2%	6.6%	6.6%
25 to 29	91.4%	87.1%	91.5%	92.1%	92.9%	92.9%	5.6%	9.5%	6.7%	4.8%	3.2%	3.0%
30 to 34	93.5%	86.8%	92.6%	94.8%	96.6%	95.9%	4.8%	8.2%	5.7%	4.6%	2.7%	2.2%
35 to 39	92.8%	84.8%	91.7%	93.9%	96.8%	96.5%	4.3%	7.5%	5.4%	3.7%	2.6%	1.8%
40 to 44	91.8%	80.5%	90.6%	93.3%	96.5%	97.4%	4.1%	8.0%	4.3%	4.0%	2.7%	2.1%
45 to 49	89.8%	75.4%	87.6%	91.2%	95.9%	96.8%	3.9%	7.2%	4.5%	3.8%	2.6%	2.1%
50 to 54	86.5%	70.9%	83.7%	86.7%	93.0%	94.6%	3.8%	6.9%	4.1%	4.1%	2.9%	1.8%
55 to 59	77.3%	60.9%	74.8%	78.6%	84.9%	87.0%	3.8%	6.7%	3.7%	3.8%	3.4%	2.4%
60 to 64	56.6%	44.2%	53.3%	58.3%	63.6%	72.1%	4.0%	6.1%	4.2%	3.8%	4.0%	2.4%
65 to 69	30.9%	22.9%	28.0%	31.7%	38.8%	44.7%	4.0%	5.1%	4.3%	3.4%	4.8%	2.4%
70 to 74	18.1%	13.0%	16.2%	19.3%	23.3%	29.1%	4.1%	4.8%	4.9%	5.0%	2.8%	2.4%
75 to 79	11.0%	7.6%	10.1%	11.1%	16.3%	17.3%	3.8%	4.1%	3.3%	4.4%	2.9%	4.4%
80+	5.7%	3.5%	5.3%	6.5%	7.7%	12.3%	1.2%	0.8%	1.0%	1.1%	2.6%	1.1%
18+	75.7%	58.7%	75.6%	78.5%	85.0%	82.6%	5.3%	10.0%	6.1%	4.7%	3.1%	2.2%
25-64	87.2%	75.4%	85.6%	88.8%	92.7%	92.5%	4.3%	7.7%	5.0%	4.1%	2.9%	2.1%
25+	75.7%	56.1%	74.4%	80.3%	85.0%	82.6%	4.3%	7.5%	4.9%	4.1%	2.9%	2.2%
Male Never Smokers												
18 to 19	59.1%	54.3%	69.5%	54.9%			14.5%	17.4%	15.3%	8.7%		
20 to 24	79.6%	82.8%	86.5%	72.6%	84.9%	71.3%	8.8%	12.4%	10.3%	7.1%	6.4%	6.0%
25 to 29	92.5%	88.8%	92.2%	93.2%	93.3%	94.0%	4.4%	7.0%	5.5%	4.2%	3.1%	2.3%
30 to 34	95.0%	88.1%	93.4%	96.2%	97.5%	96.5%	3.6%	6.0%	4.6%	3.5%	2.4%	2.0%
35 to 39	94.8%	85.0%	93.3%	96.1%	97.8%	97.4%	3.0%	4.7%	4.2%	2.7%	2.1%	1.4%
40 to 44	94.3%	84.1%	92.3%	94.8%	97.5%	98.5%	3.1%	5.7%	3.2%	3.6%	2.4%	1.6%
45 to 49	93.1%	79.3%	90.0%	94.0%	97.2%	98.2%	3.0%	7.2%	3.3%	3.1%	2.1%	1.6%
50 to 54	90.1%	75.9%	87.0%	89.4%	94.8%	95.9%	3.0%	6.1%	3.3%	3.4%	2.4%	1.7%
55 to 59	80.8%	63.9%	77.4%	80.9%	87.0%	88.0%	3.4%	7.6%	3.7%	2.6%	3.3%	2.3%
60 to 64	60.6%	48.5%	55.7%	61.8%	66.7%	72.5%	3.7%	6.1%	3.7%	3.7%	3.9%	1.8%
65 to 69	33.3%	24.1%	30.3%	33.7%	38.6%	45.8%	3.4%	6.5%	2.5%	2.8%	4.8%	1.9%
70 to 74	20.1%	12.6%	18.8%	20.6%	23.3%	32.7%	3.1%	1.2%	4.6%	3.9%	2.3%	2.8%
75 to 79	11.8%	7.9%	10.7%	12.2%	15.3%	19.6%	4.0%	3.3%	3.3%	8.3%	4.5%	1.4%
80+	4.8%	2.7%	4.9%	5.4%	7.1%	9.1%	1.4%	2.9%	1.1%	1.4%	3.3%	0.7%
18+	79.8%	62.1%	78.7%	80.9%	89.0%	86.3%	4.4%	8.5%	5.5%	4.3%	2.8%	1.8%
25-64	90.8%	79.8%	88.8%	92.1%	94.7%	94.4%	3.4%	6.2%	4.1%	3.4%	2.5%	1.8%
25+	81.2%	60.9%	78.2%	85.1%	89.2%	86.4%	3.4%	6.1%	4.0%	3.4%	2.5%	1.8%
Male Current Smokers												
18 to 19	77.3%	72.3%	85.3%	74.7%			22.4%	27.6%	19.4%	12.5%		
20 to 24	88.0%	85.2%	90.3%	86.2%	92.6%	87.0%	12.3%	19.7%	12.3%	7.9%	5.5%	11.6%
25 to 29	91.7%	87.3%	92.2%	92.9%	94.2%	93.8%	8.1%	13.2%	8.3%	6.6%	4.0%	2.3%
30 to 34	92.6%	85.6%	93.2%	94.7%	96.1%	95.0%	8.0%	12.0%	8.1%	7.2%	4.2%	4.6%
35 to 39	90.6%	83.2%	91.7%	91.8%	95.7%	97.5%	7.6%	11.9%	7.6%	6.4%	4.3%	2.4%
40 to 44	88.7%	77.9%	89.9%	91.8%	95.3%	92.0%	6.8%	11.1%	6.5%	5.5%	5.0%	5.5%
45 to 49	85.2%	72.7%	85.7%	87.5%	93.3%	94.7%	6.4%	9.0%	6.8%	5.9%	4.0%	5.1%
50 to 54	79.8%	65.5%	80.8%	81.7%	87.8%	89.6%	6.5%	7.5%	6.0%	7.3%	5.6%	4.8%
55 to 59	71.4%	59.6%	72.3%	74.9%	79.8%	80.8%	5.5%	7.3%	4.3%	6.9%	5.2%	2.8%
60 to 64	49.4%	39.1%	48.5%	55.9%	61.2%	63.5%	5.0%	6.7%	5.6%	2.4%	5.6%	3.8%
65 to 69	26.9%	21.2%	26.8%	28.9%	35.0%	39.7%	6.2%	3.3%	9.6%	7.2%	2.1%	1.9%
70 to 74	14.8%	13.5%	14.3%	15.1%	17.3%	23.8%	6.1%	9.5%	4.2%	7.8%	1.9%	1.8%
75 to 79	8.8%	4.1%	12.5%	11.2%	16.1%	6.2%	3.4%	8.3%	2.1%	4.2%	1.7%	1.6%
80+	3.8%	3.2%	4.1%	7.4%	1.8%	5.1%	2.4%	3.5%	2.3%	2.1%	1.5%	1.4%
18+	80.3%	68.3%	82.6%	83.9%	87.0%	83.6%	8.1%	13.2%	8.1%	6.6%	4.6%	4.1%
25-64	84.5%	73.8%	85.8%	87.2%	90.9%	89.1%	7.0%	10.6%	7.0%	6.3%	4.6%	4.1%
25+	79.4%	65.5%	81.4%	83.8%	86.7%	83.5%	7.0%	10.4%	7.0%	6.3%	4.5%	4.0%

*Calculated from aggregated data, i.e., not weighted averages. Sources: see chapter 9.
Note: Sample sizes are very small during older ages.

Table 11: Labor force participation and unemployment rates by sex, age, education and smoking status, 2000 through 2003, continued—Females of All Races

Ages	Labor Force Participation Rates						Unemployment Rates					
	All*	<HS	HS	Some College	College Degree	Grad Degree	All*	<HS	HS	Some College	College Degree	Grad Degree
All Females Regardless of Smoking Status												
18 to 19	59.6%	51.5%	66.5%	61.8%			13.1%	16.4%	14.0%	9.0%		
20 to 24	72.2%	52.7%	73.7%	73.6%	83.4%	81.1%	8.6%	21.3%	10.2%	6.2%	4.9%	5.1%
25 to 29	75.8%	51.1%	71.7%	79.0%	85.5%	86.2%	5.7%	15.2%	7.7%	5.0%	2.8%	2.1%
30 to 34	75.1%	56.1%	73.4%	79.1%	78.3%	82.5%	5.1%	11.1%	6.8%	4.7%	2.9%	2.4%
35 to 39	75.5%	59.2%	74.5%	79.4%	76.8%	83.7%	4.7%	12.0%	5.3%	4.0%	2.8%	2.2%
40 to 44	78.0%	59.1%	76.9%	81.5%	80.8%	86.4%	4.0%	9.5%	4.8%	3.4%	2.5%	1.9%
45 to 49	78.6%	54.8%	77.8%	81.7%	83.1%	88.1%	3.3%	8.0%	3.5%	3.1%	2.4%	1.8%
50 to 54	74.5%	49.6%	72.1%	77.6%	80.8%	89.2%	3.0%	6.5%	3.2%	2.9%	2.7%	1.3%
55 to 59	63.5%	40.5%	61.8%	68.1%	72.1%	78.6%	3.1%	5.3%	3.4%	2.8%	2.6%	2.0%
60 to 64	43.1%	26.8%	42.3%	48.6%	50.8%	61.5%	3.0%	5.0%	2.7%	3.6%	2.2%	1.4%
65 to 69	20.8%	12.7%	20.7%	25.2%	25.3%	34.0%	3.8%	5.7%	4.0%	3.2%	3.3%	2.5%
70 to 74	10.5%	6.9%	10.2%	13.8%	13.4%	16.8%	3.0%	5.3%	2.6%	2.5%	2.1%	2.1%
75 to 79	5.5%	3.6%	5.4%	6.6%	8.3%	11.4%	2.3%	2.0%	2.1%	3.2%	3.3%	2.5%
80+	2.3%	1.1%	2.2%	3.0%	4.5%	7.0%	1.6%	1.4%	0.4%	1.6%	1.8%	3.0%
18+	60.8%	35.4%	57.5%	68.2%	73.1%	76.7%	4.9%	11.4%	5.6%	4.3%	2.9%	1.9%
25-64	72.4%	49.8%	70.1%	76.8%	78.8%	83.7%	4.1%	9.6%	4.8%	3.8%	2.7%	1.9%
25+	59.7%	32.4%	55.7%	67.6%	72.3%	76.7%	4.1%	9.2%	4.7%	3.7%	2.7%	1.9%
Female Never Smokers												
18 to 19	57.2%	49.0%	63.0%	60.1%			12.3%	14.7%	13.4%	9.2%		
20 to 24	70.9%	49.5%	72.7%	71.3%	82.5%	79.2%	7.6%	19.3%	9.1%	5.8%	5.2%	5.2%
25 to 29	76.1%	47.9%	71.8%	79.0%	85.0%	86.8%	5.2%	15.4%	7.3%	4.8%	2.7%	1.9%
30 to 34	74.9%	54.1%	73.1%	78.9%	78.1%	81.8%	4.5%	10.5%	6.6%	3.9%	2.7%	2.4%
35 to 39	76.1%	58.8%	75.5%	79.6%	76.4%	84.3%	3.8%	11.5%	4.5%	3.0%	2.6%	2.2%
40 to 44	78.5%	58.3%	77.5%	82.2%	80.0%	86.5%	3.3%	8.4%	4.3%	2.5%	2.2%	1.8%
45 to 49	79.8%	56.7%	77.5%	83.1%	83.8%	89.4%	2.8%	7.2%	3.1%	2.5%	2.1%	1.8%
50 to 54	75.8%	52.1%	72.0%	79.2%	81.1%	89.4%	2.8%	7.5%	2.6%	2.6%	2.7%	1.1%
55 to 59	64.2%	40.6%	62.2%	68.7%	73.4%	79.4%	2.9%	4.8%	3.1%	2.8%	2.5%	1.8%
60 to 64	42.4%	26.5%	41.4%	47.5%	50.4%	60.5%	3.0%	5.7%	2.5%	3.4%	2.3%	1.9%
65 to 69	20.2%	11.2%	20.9%	24.2%	25.1%	33.4%	4.0%	7.3%	3.4%	4.2%	2.7%	2.7%
70 to 74	10.0%	6.4%	9.9%	14.1%	11.6%	16.2%	3.0%	5.4%	2.7%	3.2%	1.5%	0.0%
75 to 79	5.2%	3.8%	5.4%	5.8%	7.0%	8.7%	1.6%	0.9%	2.5%	1.5%	1.1%	0.8%
80+	1.4%	0.7%	1.4%	2.5%	1.9%	4.0%	1.5%	0.3%	1.8%	1.3%	1.1%	0.8%
18+	60.1%	32.9%	55.1%	67.7%	73.8%	77.8%	4.4%	10.9%	5.3%	3.9%	2.7%	1.9%
25-64	73.2%	49.4%	70.0%	77.4%	79.0%	84.3%	3.7%	9.3%	4.4%	3.2%	2.5%	1.9%
25+	59.1%	29.7%	53.0%	67.5%	73.1%	77.8%	3.6%	9.0%	4.3%	3.2%	2.5%	1.9%
Female Current Smokers												
18 to 19	76.0%	67.0%	82.4%	82.2%			17.9%	24.9%	15.2%	11.7%		
20 to 24	79.8%	61.4%	81.7%	84.1%	92.5%	93.3%	12.8%	28.3%	14.1%	7.6%	4.9%	7.7%
25 to 29	77.7%	60.1%	74.0%	83.2%	94.4%	93.8%	8.6%	19.0%	9.7%	6.4%	3.5%	5.0%
30 to 34	78.6%	62.9%	77.1%	82.5%	88.8%	93.4%	7.8%	14.3%	7.6%	7.4%	4.3%	4.2%
35 to 39	76.5%	61.4%	76.1%	80.7%	89.4%	84.0%	7.6%	15.0%	7.3%	7.0%	3.0%	3.7%
40 to 44	76.7%	57.8%	76.2%	81.9%	89.4%	88.6%	7.4%	13.9%	7.4%	6.5%	4.8%	2.9%
45 to 49	75.9%	53.2%	76.8%	81.1%	84.0%	87.4%	5.1%	9.5%	5.0%	4.8%	4.1%	0.8%
50 to 54	71.2%	47.8%	73.0%	74.9%	82.4%	90.1%	3.9%	5.7%	4.4%	3.3%	3.1%	1.1%
55 to 59	61.2%	41.4%	63.1%	67.2%	71.3%	75.6%	4.9%	6.6%	4.5%	5.7%	4.2%	1.5%
60 to 64	41.6%	29.8%	41.8%	49.5%	48.5%	62.3%	3.6%	5.5%	2.9%	3.5%	4.9%	1.8%
65 to 69	21.3%	15.3%	24.0%	24.0%	22.6%	19.7%	6.2%	7.4%	5.5%	5.1%	4.9%	3.4%
70 to 74	10.3%	6.1%	12.3%	12.7%	8.9%	9.8%	4.8%	6.9%	3.6%	4.1%	3.1%	2.8%
75 to 79	3.5%	3.2%	3.4%	3.6%	4.2%	7.8%	3.7%	2.6%	2.8%	5.1%	4.8%	3.4%
80+	2.5%	1.1%	2.4%	1.9%	4.1%	24.5%	2.5%	1.8%	0.5%	2.6%	2.7%	4.0%
18+	68.5%	48.8%	68.5%	75.8%	81.4%	79.3%	7.7%	15.6%	7.8%	6.3%	4.0%	2.6%
25-64	72.8%	53.0%	72.4%	78.5%	85.4%	85.9%	6.6%	12.4%	6.6%	6.0%	3.9%	2.5%
25+	66.8%	45.6%	66.5%	74.3%	80.4%	79.1%	6.6%	12.2%	6.5%	5.9%	3.9%	2.5%

*Calculated from aggregated data, i.e., not weighted averages. Sources: see chapter 9.
Note: Sample sizes are very small during older ages.

Table 12: Mean years to final separation, July 1999–June 2007 CPS data: Males All Races

Age	Initially Active						Initially Inactive						Age
	All*	<HS	HS	Some College	College Degree	Graduate Degrees	All*	<HS	HS	Some College	College Degree	Graduate Degrees	
18	46.7	42.7	46.0	47.3			46.7	42.7	46.0	47.3			18
19	45.7	41.8	45.1	46.4	48.8		45.7	41.8	45.1	46.4	48.8		19
20	44.8	40.9	44.2	45.5	47.9		44.8	40.9	44.1	45.5	47.9		20
21	43.9	39.9	43.2	44.5	47.0	48.6	43.9	39.9	43.2	44.5	47.0	48.6	21
22	42.9	39.0	42.3	43.6	46.0	47.7	42.9	39.0	42.3	43.6	46.0	47.7	22
23	42.0	38.0	41.3	42.7	45.1	46.8	42.0	38.0	41.3	42.7	45.1	46.8	23
24	41.1	37.1	40.4	41.7	44.2	45.8	41.1	37.1	40.4	41.7	44.2	45.8	24
25	40.1	36.1	39.4	40.8	43.2	44.9	40.1	36.1	39.4	40.8	43.2	44.9	25
26	39.2	35.2	38.5	39.8	42.3	43.9	39.2	35.2	38.5	39.8	42.3	43.9	26
27	38.2	34.3	37.6	38.9	41.3	42.9	38.2	34.2	37.6	38.9	41.3	42.9	27
28	37.3	33.3	36.6	37.9	40.3	42.0	37.3	33.3	36.6	37.9	40.3	42.0	28
29	36.3	32.4	35.7	36.9	39.3	41.0	36.3	32.3	35.6	36.9	39.3	41.0	29
30	35.4	31.5	34.7	36.0	38.4	40.0	35.4	31.4	34.7	36.0	38.4	40.0	30
31	34.4	30.5	33.8	35.0	37.4	39.0	34.4	30.5	33.7	35.0	37.4	39.0	31
32	33.5	29.6	32.8	34.1	36.4	38.0	33.5	29.5	32.8	34.1	36.4	38.0	32
33	32.5	28.7	31.9	33.1	35.4	37.1	32.5	28.5	31.8	33.1	35.4	37.1	33
34	31.6	27.8	30.9	32.2	34.5	36.1	31.5	27.6	30.9	32.1	34.5	36.1	34
35	30.6	26.8	30.0	31.2	33.5	35.1	30.6	26.6	29.9	31.2	33.5	35.1	35
36	29.7	25.9	29.0	30.3	32.5	34.1	29.6	25.6	28.9	30.2	32.5	34.1	36
37	28.8	25.0	28.1	29.3	31.6	33.1	28.7	24.7	28.0	29.3	31.6	33.1	37
38	27.8	24.1	27.2	28.4	30.6	32.2	27.7	23.7	27.0	28.3	30.6	32.2	38
39	26.9	23.2	26.2	27.4	29.7	31.2	26.7	22.7	26.0	27.3	29.6	31.2	39
40	26.0	22.3	25.3	26.5	28.7	30.3	25.8	21.7	25.1	26.4	28.7	30.2	40
41	25.1	21.5	24.4	25.6	27.7	29.3	24.8	20.7	24.1	25.4	27.7	29.3	41
42	24.1	20.6	23.5	24.7	26.8	28.3	23.8	19.7	23.1	24.4	26.7	28.3	42
43	23.2	19.8	22.6	23.7	25.8	27.4	22.8	18.7	22.1	23.4	25.8	27.3	43
44	22.3	18.9	21.7	22.8	24.9	26.4	21.8	17.8	21.1	22.4	24.8	26.4	44
45	21.4	18.1	20.8	21.9	24.0	25.5	20.8	16.8	20.1	21.4	23.8	25.4	45
46	20.5	17.3	19.9	21.0	23.0	24.5	19.8	15.9	19.1	20.5	22.8	24.4	46
47	19.6	16.5	19.0	20.1	22.1	23.6	18.8	15.0	18.1	19.4	21.8	23.4	47
48	18.8	15.7	18.1	19.2	21.2	22.6	17.8	14.0	17.1	18.4	20.8	22.4	48
49	17.9	14.9	17.3	18.3	20.2	21.7	16.8	13.1	16.1	17.3	19.8	21.4	49
50	17.0	14.2	16.4	17.4	19.3	20.8	15.8	12.2	15.1	16.3	18.7	20.4	50
51	16.2	13.4	15.6	16.6	18.4	19.8	14.8	11.3	14.1	15.3	17.6	19.3	51
52	15.3	12.7	14.7	15.7	17.5	18.9	13.8	10.5	13.2	14.3	16.6	18.2	52
53	14.5	11.9	13.9	14.9	16.6	18.0	12.9	9.7	12.2	13.3	15.5	17.2	53
54	13.7	11.3	13.1	14.1	15.7	17.1	11.9	8.9	11.3	12.4	14.5	16.1	54
55	12.9	10.6	12.3	13.2	14.8	16.1	11.0	8.1	10.4	11.4	13.4	15.1	55
56	12.1	9.9	11.5	12.5	14.0	15.2	10.1	7.4	9.6	10.5	12.4	14.1	56
57	11.3	9.2	10.7	11.7	13.1	14.4	9.2	6.7	8.8	9.7	11.4	13.1	57
58	10.5	8.6	10.0	10.9	12.3	13.5	8.4	6.1	8.0	8.8	10.5	12.0	58
59	9.8	7.9	9.2	10.1	11.5	12.6	7.6	5.5	7.2	8.1	9.6	11.1	59
60	9.1	7.3	8.5	9.4	10.8	11.8	6.9	5.0	6.5	7.3	8.7	10.2	60
61	8.4	6.7	7.8	8.7	10.0	11.0	6.3	4.5	5.9	6.7	8.0	9.2	61
62	7.8	6.2	7.2	8.1	9.3	10.2	5.6	4.1	5.3	6.1	7.2	8.4	62
63	7.2	5.8	6.7	7.5	8.7	9.5	5.1	3.7	4.8	5.5	6.6	7.6	63
64	6.7	5.4	6.2	7.0	8.1	8.8	4.6	3.3	4.3	5.0	6.0	6.8	64
65	6.2	5.2	5.8	6.4	7.5	8.1	4.1	3.0	3.8	4.5	5.4	6.1	65
66	5.8	4.9	5.3	5.9	7.0	7.5	3.7	2.7	3.4	4.0	4.9	5.5	66
67	5.4	4.6	5.0	5.5	6.5	6.9	3.2	2.4	3.0	3.5	4.4	4.9	67
68	5.0	4.3	4.6	5.0	6.1	6.5	2.8	2.1	2.6	3.1	3.9	4.3	68
69	4.7	4.0	4.4	4.7	5.8	6.1	2.5	1.8	2.2	2.6	3.5	3.8	69
70	4.4	3.8	4.1	4.5	5.4	5.6	2.1	1.6	1.9	2.3	3.1	3.3	70
71	4.1	3.5	3.9	4.2	5.0	5.1	1.9	1.4	1.6	1.9	2.8	2.9	71
72	3.9	3.3	3.7	3.9	4.7	4.6	1.6	1.2	1.4	1.6	2.4	2.5	72
73	3.6	3.1	3.5	3.5	4.4	4.2	1.4	1.0	1.2	1.4	2.2	2.2	73
74	3.5	3.1	3.5	3.3	4.2	4.1	1.2	0.9	1.0	1.2	1.9	1.9	74
75	3.3	3.0	3.4	3.1	4.0	3.8	1.0	0.8	0.8	1.0	1.7	1.6	75

*Calculated from CPS data of all education levels combined

Table 12: Mean years to final separation, July 1999–June 2007 CPS data, continued: Females All Races

Age	Initially Active						Initially Inactive						Age
	All*	<HS	HS	Some College	College Degree	Graduate Degrees	All*	<HS	HS	Some College	College Degree	Graduate Degrees	
18	46.1	40.9	45.6	47.2			46.1	40.9	45.6	47.2			18
19	45.1	39.9	44.7	46.3	47.9		45.1	39.9	44.7	46.3	47.9		19
20	44.2	38.9	43.7	45.3	46.9		44.2	38.9	43.7	45.3	46.9		20
21	43.2	37.9	42.7	44.3	45.9	45.8	43.2	37.9	42.7	44.3	45.9	45.8	21
22	42.2	36.9	41.7	43.3	45.0	44.8	42.2	36.9	41.7	43.3	45.0	44.8	22
23	41.2	36.0	40.7	42.3	44.0	43.8	41.2	36.0	40.7	42.3	44.0	43.8	23
24	40.3	35.0	39.8	41.4	43.0	42.9	40.2	35.0	39.8	41.4	43.0	42.9	24
25	39.3	34.0	38.8	40.4	42.0	41.9	39.3	34.0	38.8	40.4	42.0	41.9	25
26	38.3	33.0	37.8	39.4	41.0	40.9	38.3	33.0	37.8	39.4	41.0	40.9	26
27	37.3	32.1	36.8	38.4	40.0	39.9	37.3	32.0	36.8	38.4	40.0	39.9	27
28	36.3	31.1	35.8	37.4	39.1	39.0	36.3	31.1	35.8	37.4	39.0	38.9	28
29	35.4	30.1	34.9	36.5	38.1	38.0	35.3	30.1	34.8	36.5	38.1	38.0	29
30	34.4	29.2	33.9	35.5	37.1	37.0	34.3	29.1	33.9	35.5	37.1	37.0	30
31	33.4	28.2	32.9	34.5	36.1	36.0	33.4	28.1	32.9	34.5	36.1	36.0	31
32	32.4	27.2	31.9	33.5	35.1	35.0	32.4	27.2	31.9	33.5	35.1	35.0	32
33	31.5	26.3	31.0	32.6	34.1	34.1	31.4	26.2	30.9	32.5	34.1	34.0	33
34	30.5	25.3	30.0	31.6	33.2	33.1	30.4	25.2	29.9	31.5	33.1	33.1	34
35	29.5	24.4	29.0	30.6	32.2	32.1	29.4	24.2	28.9	30.5	32.1	32.1	35
36	28.6	23.5	28.1	29.6	31.2	31.1	28.4	23.3	28.0	29.6	31.1	31.1	36
37	27.6	22.5	27.1	28.7	30.2	30.1	27.5	22.3	27.0	28.6	30.1	30.1	37
38	26.6	21.6	26.1	27.7	29.2	29.2	26.5	21.4	26.0	27.6	29.2	29.1	38
39	25.7	20.7	25.2	26.7	28.3	28.2	25.5	20.4	25.0	26.6	28.2	28.1	39
40	24.7	19.8	24.3	25.8	27.3	27.2	24.5	19.4	24.0	25.6	27.2	27.1	40
41	23.8	18.9	23.3	24.8	26.3	26.2	23.5	18.5	23.0	24.6	26.2	26.1	41
42	22.9	18.0	22.4	23.9	25.4	25.3	22.5	17.5	22.0	23.6	25.2	25.1	42
43	21.9	17.2	21.5	22.9	24.4	24.3	21.5	16.6	20.9	22.6	24.2	24.1	43
44	21.0	16.3	20.5	22.0	23.5	23.3	20.5	15.6	19.9	21.5	23.2	23.1	44
45	20.1	15.5	19.6	21.1	22.5	22.4	19.4	14.7	18.9	20.5	22.2	22.1	45
46	19.2	14.7	18.7	20.1	21.6	21.4	18.4	13.7	17.8	19.5	21.2	21.1	46
47	18.3	13.9	17.8	19.2	20.6	20.4	17.4	12.8	16.8	18.5	20.2	20.1	47
48	17.4	13.2	17.0	18.3	19.7	19.5	16.3	11.9	15.8	17.4	19.2	19.0	48
49	16.5	12.4	16.1	17.4	18.7	18.5	15.3	11.0	14.7	16.4	18.1	18.0	49
50	15.6	11.7	15.2	16.5	17.8	17.6	14.3	10.1	13.7	15.3	17.1	16.9	50
51	14.7	11.0	14.4	15.6	16.9	16.6	13.2	9.3	12.7	14.3	16.1	15.9	51
52	13.9	10.4	13.6	14.8	16.0	15.7	12.2	8.5	11.7	13.2	15.0	14.8	52
53	13.1	9.8	12.7	13.9	15.1	14.8	11.2	7.7	10.8	12.2	13.9	13.7	53
54	12.2	9.1	11.9	13.1	14.2	13.8	10.3	7.0	9.8	11.3	12.9	12.6	54
55	11.4	8.5	11.2	12.3	13.3	12.9	9.3	6.3	8.9	10.3	11.9	11.5	55
56	10.7	8.0	10.4	11.5	12.5	12.0	8.4	5.6	8.1	9.4	10.8	10.5	56
57	9.9	7.4	9.7	10.7	11.7	11.2	7.5	5.0	7.2	8.5	9.8	9.4	57
58	9.2	6.8	9.0	9.9	10.9	10.4	6.7	4.4	6.4	7.7	8.9	8.5	58
59	8.5	6.3	8.3	9.2	10.1	9.6	6.0	3.8	5.8	6.9	8.0	7.5	59
60	7.8	5.7	7.7	8.4	9.4	8.8	5.3	3.4	5.1	6.1	7.2	6.6	60
61	7.2	5.2	7.1	7.7	8.7	8.0	4.7	3.0	4.5	5.4	6.5	5.8	61
62	6.6	4.9	6.5	7.1	8.0	7.4	4.1	2.6	4.0	4.8	5.8	5.0	62
63	6.1	4.5	6.0	6.6	7.4	6.8	3.6	2.2	3.5	4.2	5.1	4.3	63
64	5.7	4.2	5.6	6.0	6.8	6.3	3.2	1.9	3.1	3.6	4.6	3.7	64
65	5.3	4.0	5.3	5.6	6.4	5.8	2.7	1.7	2.7	3.1	4.0	3.2	65
66	5.0	3.8	5.0	5.3	5.9	5.5	2.4	1.4	2.3	2.7	3.5	2.6	66
67	4.7	3.5	4.8	4.9	5.5	5.1	2.0	1.2	2.0	2.2	3.1	2.2	67
68	4.4	3.3	4.6	4.6	5.1	4.6	1.7	1.1	1.7	1.9	2.7	1.8	68
69	4.2	3.2	4.5	4.2	4.7	4.3	1.5	0.9	1.5	1.5	2.4	1.5	69
70	3.9	3.1	4.3	3.8	4.4	4.1	1.3	0.8	1.2	1.3	2.1	1.2	70
71	3.7	2.9	4.0	3.6	4.0	4.1	1.1	0.6	1.1	1.1	1.8	0.9	71
72	3.5	2.8	3.7	3.4	3.8	4.0	0.9	0.5	0.9	0.9	1.5	0.8	72
73	3.2	2.6	3.4	3.1	3.4	4.0	0.7	0.4	0.7	0.7	1.3	0.6	73
74	3.0	2.3	3.2	3.0	3.2	3.9	0.6	0.4	0.6	0.6	1.1	0.5	74
75	2.9	2.1	3.1	3.1	3.2	3.7	0.5	0.3	0.5	0.5	1.0	0.3	75

*Calculated from CPS data of all education levels combined

Table 12: Mean years to final separation, July 1999–June 2007 CPS data, continued: White Males

Age	Initially Active						Initially Inactive						Age
	All*	<HS	HS	Some College	College Degree	Graduate Degrees	All*	<HS	HS	Some College	College Degree	Graduate Degrees	
18	47.0	43.4	46.4	47.5			47.0	43.4	46.4	47.5			18
19	46.1	42.4	45.4	46.6	49.0		46.1	42.4	45.4	46.6	49.0		19
20	45.1	41.5	44.5	45.6	48.1		45.1	41.5	44.5	45.6	48.1		20
21	44.2	40.5	43.5	44.7	47.1	48.7	44.2	40.5	43.5	44.7	47.1	48.7	21
22	43.3	39.6	42.6	43.8	46.2	47.8	43.2	39.6	42.6	43.7	46.2	47.8	22
23	42.3	38.7	41.7	42.8	45.2	46.8	42.3	38.6	41.6	42.8	45.2	46.8	23
24	41.4	37.7	40.7	41.9	44.3	45.9	41.4	37.7	40.7	41.9	44.3	45.9	24
25	40.4	36.7	39.8	40.9	43.4	45.0	40.4	36.7	39.8	40.9	43.4	45.0	25
26	39.5	35.8	38.8	40.0	42.4	44.0	39.5	35.8	38.8	40.0	42.4	44.0	26
27	38.5	34.9	37.9	39.0	41.4	43.0	38.5	34.8	37.9	39.0	41.4	43.0	27
28	37.6	33.9	36.9	38.0	40.5	42.0	37.6	33.9	36.9	38.0	40.5	42.0	28
29	36.6	33.0	36.0	37.1	39.5	41.1	36.6	32.9	35.9	37.1	39.5	41.1	29
30	35.7	32.0	35.0	36.1	38.5	40.1	35.7	32.0	35.0	36.1	38.5	40.1	30
31	34.7	31.1	34.1	35.1	37.5	39.1	34.7	31.0	34.0	35.1	37.5	39.1	31
32	33.8	30.1	33.1	34.2	36.6	38.1	33.7	30.1	33.1	34.2	36.6	38.1	32
33	32.8	29.2	32.1	33.2	35.6	37.1	32.8	29.1	32.1	33.2	35.6	37.1	33
34	31.9	28.3	31.2	32.3	34.6	36.2	31.8	28.1	31.1	32.2	34.6	36.1	34
35	30.9	27.3	30.3	31.3	33.7	35.2	30.9	27.2	30.2	31.3	33.6	35.2	35
36	30.0	26.4	29.3	30.4	32.7	34.2	29.9	26.2	29.2	30.3	32.7	34.2	36
37	29.0	25.5	28.4	29.4	31.7	33.2	28.9	25.2	28.2	29.3	31.7	33.2	37
38	28.1	24.6	27.4	28.5	30.8	32.3	28.0	24.1	27.3	28.4	30.7	32.3	38
39	27.1	23.6	26.5	27.5	29.8	31.3	27.0	23.1	26.3	27.4	29.8	31.3	39
40	26.2	22.8	25.6	26.6	28.8	30.3	26.0	22.1	25.3	26.4	28.8	30.3	40
41	25.3	21.9	24.6	25.7	27.9	29.4	25.0	21.1	24.3	25.5	27.8	29.4	41
42	24.4	21.0	23.7	24.7	26.9	28.4	24.1	20.1	23.3	24.5	26.9	28.4	42
43	23.4	20.2	22.8	23.8	26.0	27.5	23.1	19.1	22.3	23.5	25.9	27.4	43
44	22.5	19.3	21.9	22.9	25.1	26.5	22.0	18.1	21.3	22.5	24.9	26.4	44
45	21.6	18.5	21.0	22.0	24.1	25.6	21.0	17.1	20.3	21.5	23.9	25.4	45
46	20.7	17.7	20.1	21.1	23.2	24.6	20.0	16.1	19.3	20.5	22.9	24.4	46
47	19.8	16.8	19.2	20.2	22.2	23.7	19.0	15.2	18.3	19.4	21.9	23.4	47
48	19.0	16.0	18.3	19.3	21.3	22.7	18.0	14.2	17.3	18.3	20.9	22.4	48
49	18.1	15.2	17.4	18.4	20.4	21.8	17.0	13.2	16.3	17.3	19.9	21.4	49
50	17.2	14.4	16.6	17.5	19.4	20.8	16.0	12.3	15.3	16.3	18.8	20.4	50
51	16.3	13.7	15.7	16.6	18.5	19.9	14.9	11.4	14.3	15.2	17.7	19.3	51
52	15.5	12.9	14.9	15.8	17.6	19.0	14.0	10.6	13.3	14.2	16.7	18.3	52
53	14.6	12.2	14.1	14.9	16.7	18.1	13.0	9.8	12.3	13.2	15.6	17.2	53
54	13.8	11.5	13.2	14.1	15.8	17.1	12.0	9.0	11.4	12.2	14.5	16.2	54
55	13.0	10.8	12.4	13.3	14.9	16.2	11.1	8.2	10.5	11.3	13.4	15.2	55
56	12.2	10.1	11.6	12.4	14.1	15.3	10.2	7.5	9.7	10.5	12.4	14.1	56
57	11.4	9.4	10.8	11.6	13.2	14.4	9.3	6.8	8.8	9.6	11.4	13.1	57
58	10.6	8.7	10.1	10.9	12.4	13.6	8.5	6.2	8.0	8.8	10.5	12.1	58
59	9.9	8.0	9.3	10.1	11.6	12.7	7.7	5.6	7.3	8.0	9.6	11.2	59
60	9.1	7.4	8.6	9.4	10.9	11.9	7.0	5.0	6.6	7.3	8.7	10.2	60
61	8.4	6.7	7.9	8.7	10.1	11.1	6.3	4.5	5.9	6.6	8.0	9.3	61
62	7.8	6.2	7.3	8.1	9.4	10.3	5.7	4.1	5.4	6.0	7.2	8.5	62
63	7.3	5.8	6.8	7.6	8.8	9.5	5.1	3.7	4.8	5.5	6.6	7.7	63
64	6.7	5.5	6.3	7.0	8.1	8.8	4.6	3.3	4.3	4.9	6.0	6.9	64
65	6.3	5.2	5.8	6.4	7.6	8.2	4.1	3.0	3.9	4.4	5.5	6.2	65
66	5.8	4.9	5.4	5.9	7.1	7.6	3.7	2.7	3.4	4.0	4.9	5.5	66
67	5.4	4.7	5.0	5.5	6.6	7.0	3.3	2.4	3.0	3.5	4.4	4.9	67
68	5.1	4.4	4.7	5.0	6.2	6.5	2.9	2.1	2.6	3.1	4.0	4.3	68
69	4.8	4.2	4.4	4.7	5.8	6.1	2.5	1.8	2.3	2.7	3.5	3.8	69
70	4.5	3.9	4.2	4.5	5.5	5.7	2.2	1.6	2.0	2.3	3.2	3.3	70
71	4.2	3.6	4.0	4.2	5.1	5.2	1.9	1.4	1.7	1.9	2.8	2.9	71
72	3.9	3.4	3.8	3.9	4.8	4.7	1.6	1.2	1.4	1.6	2.5	2.5	72
73	3.7	3.2	3.6	3.5	4.5	4.3	1.4	1.0	1.2	1.4	2.2	2.1	73
74	3.5	3.2	3.5	3.2	4.3	4.1	1.2	0.9	1.0	1.2	2.0	1.8	74
75	3.4	3.1	3.4	3.0	4.1	3.7	1.0	0.7	0.9	1.0	1.7	1.5	75

*Calculated from CPS data of all education levels combined

Table 12: Mean years to final separation, July 1999–June 2007 CPS data, continued: White Females

Age	Initially Active						Initially Inactive						Age
	All*	<HS	HS	Some College	College or More	Graduate Degrees	All*	<HS	HS	Some College	College Degree	Graduate Degrees	
18	46.3	41.1	45.8	47.5			46.3	41.1	45.8	47.5			18
19	45.4	40.1	44.9	46.5	47.8		45.4	40.1	44.9	46.5	47.8		19
20	44.4	39.2	43.9	45.6	46.8		44.4	39.2	43.9	45.6	46.8		20
21	43.4	38.2	42.9	44.6	45.8	46.0	43.4	38.2	42.9	44.6	45.8	46.0	21
22	42.4	37.2	41.9	43.6	44.8	45.0	42.4	37.2	41.9	43.6	44.8	45.0	22
23	41.4	36.2	40.9	42.6	43.9	44.0	41.4	36.2	40.9	42.6	43.9	44.0	23
24	40.5	35.2	40.0	41.6	42.9	43.1	40.5	35.2	39.9	41.6	42.9	43.1	24
25	39.5	34.3	39.0	40.7	41.9	42.1	39.5	34.2	39.0	40.7	41.9	42.1	25
26	38.5	33.3	38.0	39.7	40.9	41.1	38.5	33.3	38.0	39.7	40.9	41.1	26
27	37.5	32.3	37.0	38.7	39.9	40.1	37.5	32.3	37.0	38.7	39.9	40.1	27
28	36.5	31.3	36.0	37.7	38.9	39.1	36.5	31.3	36.0	37.7	38.9	39.1	28
29	35.6	30.4	35.1	36.8	37.9	38.1	35.5	30.3	35.0	36.7	37.9	38.1	29
30	34.6	29.4	34.1	35.8	37.0	37.1	34.5	29.4	34.0	35.8	36.9	37.1	30
31	33.6	28.4	33.1	34.8	36.0	36.1	33.6	28.4	33.1	34.8	36.0	36.1	31
32	32.6	27.5	32.1	33.8	35.0	35.2	32.6	27.4	32.1	33.8	35.0	35.1	32
33	31.6	26.5	31.1	32.8	34.0	34.2	31.6	26.4	31.1	32.8	34.0	34.2	33
34	30.7	25.6	30.2	31.9	33.0	33.2	30.6	25.5	30.1	31.8	33.0	33.2	34
35	29.7	24.6	29.2	30.9	32.1	32.2	29.6	24.5	29.1	30.8	32.0	32.2	35
36	28.7	23.7	28.2	29.9	31.1	31.3	28.6	23.5	28.1	29.8	31.0	31.2	36
37	27.8	22.8	27.3	28.9	30.1	30.3	27.6	22.5	27.1	28.8	30.0	30.2	37
38	26.8	21.8	26.3	28.0	29.1	29.3	26.7	21.6	26.1	27.8	29.0	29.2	38
39	25.9	20.9	25.4	27.0	28.1	28.3	25.7	20.6	25.1	26.8	28.0	28.2	39
40	24.9	20.0	24.4	26.1	27.2	27.4	24.7	19.7	24.1	25.9	27.0	27.3	40
41	24.0	19.1	23.5	25.1	26.2	26.4	23.7	18.7	23.1	24.9	26.1	26.3	41
42	23.0	18.2	22.5	24.1	25.2	25.4	22.7	17.8	22.1	23.9	25.1	25.3	42
43	22.1	17.4	21.6	23.2	24.3	24.4	21.6	16.8	21.1	22.8	24.1	24.3	43
44	21.2	16.5	20.7	22.3	23.3	23.5	20.6	15.8	20.0	21.8	23.1	23.3	44
45	20.2	15.7	19.8	21.3	22.4	22.5	19.6	14.9	19.0	20.8	22.1	22.3	45
46	19.3	14.8	18.9	20.4	21.4	21.5	18.5	13.9	17.9	19.7	21.1	21.2	46
47	18.4	14.1	18.0	19.5	20.5	20.6	17.5	12.9	16.9	18.7	20.0	20.2	47
48	17.5	13.3	17.1	18.6	19.6	19.6	16.4	12.0	15.8	17.7	19.0	19.2	48
49	16.6	12.5	16.2	17.7	18.6	18.6	15.4	11.1	14.8	16.6	17.9	18.1	49
50	15.7	11.8	15.3	16.8	17.7	17.7	14.3	10.2	13.8	15.6	16.9	17.1	50
51	14.9	11.1	14.5	15.9	16.8	16.7	13.3	9.3	12.7	14.5	15.8	16.0	51
52	14.0	10.5	13.7	15.0	15.9	15.8	12.3	8.5	11.8	13.4	14.8	14.9	52
53	13.2	9.8	12.8	14.1	15.0	14.9	11.3	7.7	10.8	12.4	13.7	13.8	53
54	12.3	9.2	12.0	13.3	14.1	13.9	10.3	7.0	9.8	11.5	12.7	12.7	54
55	11.5	8.6	11.3	12.5	13.2	13.0	9.4	6.2	8.9	10.5	11.6	11.7	55
56	10.8	8.0	10.5	11.7	12.4	12.1	8.4	5.5	8.0	9.6	10.6	10.6	56
57	10.0	7.4	9.8	10.9	11.6	11.3	7.6	4.9	7.2	8.7	9.6	9.5	57
58	9.3	6.7	9.1	10.1	10.8	10.5	6.7	4.3	6.4	7.8	8.7	8.5	58
59	8.6	6.1	8.4	9.3	10.0	9.7	6.0	3.7	5.7	7.0	7.8	7.6	59
60	7.9	5.6	7.8	8.6	9.3	8.9	5.3	3.2	5.1	6.2	7.0	6.7	60
61	7.2	5.0	7.2	7.9	8.6	8.2	4.7	2.8	4.5	5.5	6.3	5.8	61
62	6.7	4.6	6.6	7.3	7.9	7.5	4.1	2.4	4.0	4.9	5.6	5.0	62
63	6.2	4.2	6.2	6.7	7.4	7.0	3.6	2.1	3.5	4.3	5.0	4.4	63
64	5.7	4.0	5.7	6.2	6.8	6.4	3.1	1.8	3.1	3.7	4.4	3.8	64
65	5.4	3.8	5.4	5.8	6.3	6.1	2.7	1.5	2.7	3.2	3.9	3.2	65
66	5.1	3.7	5.2	5.4	5.9	5.8	2.3	1.3	2.3	2.7	3.4	2.7	66
67	4.8	3.5	5.0	5.0	5.5	5.5	2.0	1.1	2.0	2.3	3.0	2.2	67
68	4.5	3.3	4.8	4.6	5.1	5.0	1.7	1.0	1.7	1.9	2.6	1.9	68
69	4.3	3.2	4.6	4.3	4.7	4.7	1.5	0.8	1.5	1.6	2.3	1.5	69
70	4.0	3.1	4.4	3.9	4.3	4.4	1.2	0.7	1.3	1.3	1.9	1.2	70
71	3.8	3.0	4.1	3.7	4.0	4.3	1.1	0.6	1.1	1.1	1.7	1.0	71
72	3.5	2.8	3.8	3.4	3.7	4.2	0.9	0.4	0.9	0.9	1.5	0.8	72
73	3.3	2.6	3.6	3.2	3.4	4.1	0.7	0.4	0.8	0.7	1.2	0.7	73
74	3.1	2.3	3.3	3.0	3.1	4.0	0.6	0.3	0.6	0.6	1.1	0.6	74
75	3.0	2.1	3.2	3.1	3.2	3.9	0.5	0.2	0.5	0.5	0.9	0.3	75

*Calculated from CPS data of all education levels combined

Table 12: Mean years to final separation, July 1999–June 2007 CPS data, continued: Black Males

Age	Initially Active					Initially Inactive					Age
	All*	<HS	HS	Some College	College or More	All*	<HS	HS	Some College	College Degree	
18	43.4	39.1	43.1	46.6		43.3	39.1	43.1	46.5		18
19	42.4	38.2	42.1	45.6	48.5	42.4	38.2	42.1	45.6	48.5	19
20	41.5	37.3	41.2	44.7	47.6	41.5	37.3	41.2	44.7	47.6	20
21	40.6	36.4	40.3	43.8	46.7	40.6	36.3	40.3	43.8	46.7	21
22	39.7	35.5	39.4	42.9	45.8	39.7	35.4	39.4	42.9	45.8	22
23	38.8	34.5	38.5	42.0	44.9	38.8	34.5	38.5	42.0	44.9	23
24	37.9	33.6	37.6	41.1	44.0	37.9	33.6	37.6	41.1	44.0	24
25	37.0	32.7	36.7	40.2	43.1	37.0	32.7	36.7	40.2	43.1	25
26	36.1	31.8	35.8	39.4	42.1	36.0	31.8	35.7	39.4	42.1	26
27	35.1	30.9	34.8	38.4	41.1	35.1	30.9	34.8	38.4	41.1	27
28	34.2	30.0	33.9	37.5	40.1	34.2	30.0	33.9	37.5	40.1	28
29	33.3	29.1	33.0	36.5	39.2	33.3	29.1	33.0	36.5	39.2	29
30	32.4	28.3	32.1	35.6	38.2	32.3	28.2	32.1	35.6	38.2	30
31	31.5	27.4	31.2	34.6	37.3	31.4	27.2	31.1	34.6	37.2	31
32	30.5	26.5	30.2	33.7	36.3	30.5	26.2	30.2	33.7	36.3	32
33	29.6	25.6	29.3	32.8	35.4	29.5	25.3	29.3	32.8	35.3	33
34	28.7	24.7	28.4	31.9	34.4	28.6	24.3	28.3	31.8	34.4	34
35	27.8	23.9	27.5	31.0	33.5	27.7	23.4	27.4	30.9	33.5	35
36	26.9	23.1	26.6	30.1	32.5	26.7	22.6	26.5	30.0	32.5	36
37	26.0	22.3	25.7	29.2	31.6	25.8	21.7	25.6	29.1	31.6	37
38	25.1	21.5	24.7	28.2	30.6	24.9	20.8	24.6	28.2	30.6	38
39	24.2	20.7	23.8	27.3	29.7	23.9	20.0	23.7	27.2	29.7	39
40	23.3	19.9	23.0	26.4	28.8	23.0	19.1	22.7	26.3	28.8	40
41	22.4	19.1	22.1	25.5	27.8	22.0	18.3	21.8	25.3	27.8	41
42	21.5	18.4	21.2	24.6	26.9	21.1	17.3	20.8	24.4	26.8	42
43	20.7	17.6	20.3	23.7	26.0	20.1	16.5	19.9	23.5	25.9	43
44	19.8	16.9	19.5	22.8	25.1	19.2	15.7	19.0	22.5	25.0	44
45	18.9	16.2	18.6	22.0	24.1	18.3	14.9	18.0	21.7	24.1	45
46	18.1	15.5	17.8	21.1	23.2	17.3	14.1	17.1	20.8	23.1	46
47	17.2	14.7	16.9	20.3	22.3	16.4	13.4	16.2	19.9	22.1	47
48	16.4	14.0	16.1	19.5	21.4	15.4	12.6	15.2	19.0	21.2	48
49	15.6	13.3	15.3	18.7	20.6	14.5	11.8	14.2	18.2	20.2	49
50	14.8	12.7	14.5	17.9	19.7	13.6	11.1	13.3	17.3	19.3	50
51	14.0	12.1	13.7	17.1	18.8	12.7	10.3	12.4	16.4	18.4	51
52	13.3	11.5	12.9	16.3	18.0	11.8	9.5	11.5	15.5	17.5	52
53	12.5	10.9	12.2	15.5	17.1	11.0	8.8	10.7	14.7	16.6	53
54	11.8	10.3	11.4	14.8	16.3	10.2	8.1	9.9	13.9	15.8	54
55	11.1	9.7	10.7	14.0	15.5	9.4	7.4	9.1	13.1	15.0	55
56	10.4	9.1	10.0	13.3	14.7	8.6	6.7	8.3	12.2	14.1	56
57	9.7	8.6	9.3	12.6	13.9	7.8	6.1	7.6	11.4	13.2	57
58	9.0	8.0	8.6	11.8	13.1	7.1	5.6	6.9	10.6	12.4	58
59	8.3	7.5	7.9	11.1	12.3	6.4	5.1	6.2	9.8	11.6	59
60	7.7	7.0	7.4	10.4	11.6	5.8	4.7	5.6	9.1	10.7	60
61	7.1	6.4	6.8	9.7	10.8	5.2	4.3	5.0	8.5	9.9	61
62	6.6	6.0	6.3	9.0	10.1	4.7	3.9	4.4	7.9	9.1	62
63	6.1	5.6	5.8	8.4	9.4	4.2	3.5	3.9	7.4	8.5	63
64	5.6	5.1	5.3	7.7	8.7	3.8	3.2	3.4	6.8	7.7	64
65	5.1	4.8	4.8	7.2	8.1	3.4	2.9	3.0	6.3	7.1	65
66	4.8	4.7	4.3	6.7	7.5	3.0	2.6	2.6	5.8	6.5	66
67	4.4	4.4	4.0	6.4	6.9	2.5	2.3	2.3	5.3	5.9	67
68	4.2	4.0	3.7	5.9	6.6	2.2	2.0	2.0	4.8	5.3	68
69	3.8	3.5	3.4	5.4	6.2	1.9	1.8	1.7	4.4	4.7	69
70	3.5	3.3	3.1	5.3	5.6	1.6	1.5	1.5	4.0	4.2	70
71	3.2	3.0	2.8	5.0	5.2	1.4	1.4	1.3	3.7	3.8	71
72	3.0	3.0	2.5	4.6	4.7	1.2	1.2	1.1	3.3	3.3	72
73	2.9	2.8	2.5	4.1	4.4	1.1	1.1	0.9	3.1	3.0	73
74	3.0	2.7	2.6	3.7	4.4	0.9	0.9	0.8	2.8	2.7	74
75	3.1	2.8	2.8	3.8	4.1	0.8	0.8	0.7	2.6	2.3	75

*Calculated from CPS data of all education levels combined

Table 12: Mean years to final separation, July 1999–June 2007 CPS data, continued: Black Females

Age	Initially Active					Initially Inactive					Age
	All*	<HS	HS	Some College	College or More	All*	<HS	HS	Some College	College Degree	
18	44.4	39.9	44.9	45.4		44.4	39.9	44.9	45.4		18
19	43.4	38.9	43.9	44.4	47.7	43.4	38.9	43.9	44.4	47.7	19
20	42.4	37.9	42.9	43.5	46.8	42.4	37.9	42.9	43.5	46.8	20
21	41.4	36.9	41.9	42.5	45.8	41.4	36.9	41.9	42.5	45.8	21
22	40.5	36.0	41.0	41.5	44.8	40.5	36.0	41.0	41.5	44.8	22
23	39.5	35.0	40.0	40.5	43.9	39.5	35.0	40.0	40.5	43.9	23
24	38.5	34.0	39.0	39.6	42.9	38.5	34.0	39.0	39.6	42.9	24
25	37.6	33.1	38.1	38.6	41.9	37.6	33.0	38.1	38.6	41.9	25
26	36.6	32.1	37.1	37.6	41.0	36.6	32.1	37.1	37.6	41.0	26
27	35.6	31.1	36.1	36.7	40.0	35.6	31.1	36.1	36.7	40.0	27
28	34.6	30.2	35.1	35.7	39.1	34.6	30.1	35.1	35.7	39.1	28
29	33.7	29.2	34.2	34.7	38.1	33.7	29.2	34.2	34.7	38.1	29
30	32.7	28.3	33.2	33.8	37.1	32.7	28.2	33.2	33.8	37.1	30
31	31.8	27.3	32.3	32.8	36.2	31.7	27.2	32.2	32.8	36.2	31
32	30.8	26.4	31.3	31.8	35.2	30.8	26.3	31.3	31.8	35.2	32
33	29.8	25.5	30.3	30.9	34.2	29.8	25.4	30.3	30.8	34.2	33
34	28.9	24.6	29.4	29.9	33.2	28.8	24.4	29.3	29.9	33.2	34
35	27.9	23.6	28.4	28.9	32.3	27.9	23.5	28.4	28.9	32.3	35
36	27.0	22.7	27.5	27.9	31.3	26.9	22.5	27.4	27.9	31.3	36
37	26.0	21.9	26.5	27.0	30.3	25.9	21.6	26.4	26.9	30.3	37
38	25.1	21.0	25.6	26.0	29.4	24.9	20.6	25.5	26.0	29.4	38
39	24.1	20.2	24.6	25.1	28.4	24.0	19.7	24.5	25.0	28.4	39
40	23.2	19.3	23.7	24.1	27.5	23.0	18.8	23.5	24.0	27.4	40
41	22.3	18.5	22.8	23.2	26.5	22.0	17.9	22.6	23.0	26.5	41
42	21.4	17.7	21.9	22.3	25.6	21.1	17.1	21.6	22.0	25.5	42
43	20.5	16.8	21.0	21.3	24.6	20.1	16.2	20.6	21.0	24.5	43
44	19.6	16.1	20.1	20.4	23.7	19.1	15.3	19.6	20.0	23.6	44
45	18.7	15.4	19.3	19.5	22.7	18.1	14.4	18.7	19.1	22.6	45
46	17.9	14.6	18.4	18.6	21.8	17.2	13.6	17.7	18.1	21.6	46
47	17.0	13.9	17.6	17.6	20.9	16.2	12.8	16.8	17.1	20.7	47
48	16.1	13.2	16.7	16.7	19.9	15.3	11.9	15.9	16.1	19.7	48
49	15.3	12.4	15.9	15.9	19.0	14.3	11.1	14.9	15.1	18.7	49
50	14.5	11.7	15.1	15.0	18.1	13.4	10.3	14.0	14.1	17.7	50
51	13.7	11.1	14.3	14.1	17.2	12.4	9.5	13.1	13.1	16.7	51
52	12.9	10.6	13.4	13.3	16.2	11.4	8.8	12.2	12.0	15.6	52
53	12.1	10.1	12.6	12.5	15.3	10.5	8.1	11.3	10.9	14.6	53
54	11.3	9.4	11.8	11.8	14.4	9.6	7.4	10.4	10.0	13.5	54
55	10.5	8.9	11.0	11.1	13.5	8.7	6.7	9.5	9.1	12.6	55
56	9.8	8.4	10.3	10.4	12.6	7.9	6.0	8.7	8.2	11.6	56
57	9.1	7.8	9.6	9.7	11.8	7.1	5.4	7.9	7.4	10.7	57
58	8.4	7.3	8.9	9.0	11.0	6.4	4.9	7.2	6.7	9.8	58
59	7.7	6.8	8.2	8.2	10.2	5.7	4.4	6.5	6.0	8.9	59
60	7.0	6.3	7.5	7.4	9.4	5.1	4.0	5.9	5.5	8.0	60
61	6.4	5.9	6.9	6.8	8.6	4.5	3.7	5.2	4.9	7.2	61
62	6.0	5.7	6.3	6.4	8.0	4.0	3.3	4.7	4.4	6.5	62
63	5.5	5.3	5.8	5.8	7.4	3.5	2.9	4.2	3.9	5.8	63
64	5.0	5.0	5.3	5.3	6.7	3.1	2.6	3.7	3.4	5.2	64
65	4.6	4.6	4.9	4.8	6.1	2.7	2.3	3.3	3.0	4.6	65
66	4.1	4.1	4.5	4.6	5.4	2.3	2.0	2.9	2.6	4.1	66
67	3.8	3.6	4.3	4.4	4.9	2.0	1.8	2.5	2.2	3.6	67
68	3.5	3.1	4.2	3.8	4.4	1.7	1.6	2.2	1.8	3.1	68
69	3.2	3.1	3.9	3.4	3.8	1.4	1.4	1.9	1.6	2.7	69
70	3.0	2.9	3.7	2.9	3.4	1.2	1.2	1.6	1.3	2.4	70
71	2.7	2.5	3.4	2.8	3.2	1.0	1.0	1.3	1.1	2.1	71
72	2.7	2.6	3.0	2.6	3.4	0.8	0.8	1.1	1.0	1.8	72
73	2.5	2.3	2.5	2.6	3.3	0.7	0.7	0.9	0.8	1.5	73
74	2.2	2.2	2.2	2.5	3.0	0.5	0.6	0.7	0.7	1.3	74
75	2.2	2.0	2.3	2.8	2.7	0.4	0.5	0.6	0.5	1.1	75

*Calculated from CPS data of all education levels combined

Table 12: Mean years to final separation, July 1999–June 2007 CPS data, continued: Hispanic Males

Age	Initially Active				Initially Inactive				Age
	All*	<HS	HS	>HS	All*	<HS	HS	>HS	
18	48.2	46.3	48.2	49.4	48.2	46.3	48.1	49.4	18
19	47.3	45.4	47.2	48.5	47.3	45.4	47.2	48.5	19
20	46.4	44.5	46.3	47.6	46.3	44.5	46.3	47.6	20
21	45.4	43.5	45.4	46.6	45.4	43.5	45.4	46.6	21
22	44.5	42.6	44.4	45.7	44.5	42.6	44.4	45.7	22
23	43.5	41.6	43.5	44.7	43.5	41.6	43.5	44.7	23
24	42.6	40.7	42.5	43.8	42.6	40.7	42.5	43.8	24
25	41.6	39.7	41.6	42.8	41.6	39.7	41.6	42.8	25
26	40.7	38.8	40.7	41.9	40.7	38.8	40.7	41.9	26
27	39.7	37.8	39.7	40.9	39.7	37.8	39.7	40.9	27
28	38.8	36.9	38.8	40.0	38.8	36.9	38.8	40.0	28
29	37.8	36.0	37.8	39.0	37.8	36.0	37.8	39.0	29
30	36.8	35.1	36.9	38.1	36.8	35.0	36.9	38.1	30
31	35.9	34.1	35.9	37.1	35.9	34.1	35.9	37.1	31
32	34.9	33.2	35.0	36.1	34.9	33.2	35.0	36.1	32
33	33.9	32.2	34.0	35.2	33.9	32.2	34.0	35.2	33
34	33.0	31.3	33.1	34.2	33.0	31.3	33.1	34.2	34
35	32.0	30.3	32.2	33.2	32.0	30.3	32.1	33.2	35
36	31.1	29.4	31.2	32.3	31.0	29.3	31.2	32.3	36
37	30.1	28.4	30.3	31.3	30.1	28.4	30.2	31.3	37
38	29.1	27.5	29.3	30.4	29.1	27.4	29.3	30.4	38
39	28.2	26.5	28.4	29.4	28.1	26.5	28.3	29.4	39
40	27.3	25.6	27.5	28.5	27.2	25.5	27.4	28.5	40
41	26.3	24.7	26.6	27.6	26.2	24.6	26.4	27.5	41
42	25.4	23.8	25.6	26.6	25.3	23.6	25.5	26.6	42
43	24.5	22.9	24.7	25.7	24.3	22.7	24.5	25.7	43
44	23.6	22.0	23.8	24.8	23.3	21.7	23.5	24.7	44
45	22.6	21.1	22.9	23.9	22.4	20.8	22.6	23.7	45
46	21.7	20.2	22.0	23.0	21.4	19.8	21.7	22.7	46
47	20.8	19.3	21.1	22.0	20.4	18.9	20.7	21.8	47
48	19.9	18.4	20.3	21.1	19.4	17.9	19.8	20.8	48
49	19.0	17.5	19.4	20.2	18.4	17.0	18.9	19.8	49
50	18.1	16.6	18.5	19.3	17.3	15.9	17.9	18.7	50
51	17.2	15.7	17.7	18.4	16.3	14.9	17.0	17.6	51
52	16.3	14.8	16.9	17.5	15.3	13.8	16.0	16.6	52
53	15.5	14.0	16.0	16.6	14.2	12.8	15.1	15.6	53
54	14.6	13.2	15.2	15.8	13.2	11.9	14.0	14.6	54
55	13.8	12.5	14.3	14.9	12.2	10.9	13.0	13.7	55
56	13.0	11.7	13.5	14.0	11.2	9.8	12.1	12.7	56
57	12.1	10.9	12.6	13.2	10.4	9.0	11.2	11.9	57
58	11.3	10.1	11.8	12.3	9.6	8.2	10.3	11.0	58
59	10.5	9.4	11.0	11.5	8.8	7.4	9.5	10.3	59
60	9.8	8.6	10.2	10.7	8.0	6.7	8.6	9.5	60
61	9.0	7.9	9.5	9.9	7.2	6.0	7.9	8.7	61
62	8.3	7.3	8.7	9.1	6.6	5.4	7.2	8.0	62
63	7.7	6.9	8.0	8.4	5.9	4.8	6.6	7.2	63
64	7.2	6.4	7.3	7.7	5.3	4.3	6.0	6.5	64
65	6.8	6.1	6.6	7.2	4.8	3.9	5.4	5.9	65
66	6.3	5.6	6.0	6.7	4.3	3.4	4.9	5.3	66
67	5.9	5.2	5.4	6.2	3.9	3.1	4.4	4.7	67
68	5.6	4.7	5.1	5.7	3.4	2.7	3.8	4.1	68
69	5.5	4.2	5.0	5.5	2.9	2.3	3.2	3.6	69
70	5.2	3.8	5.1	5.2	2.5	2.1	2.7	3.2	70
71	4.8	3.6	5.0	4.8	2.2	1.8	2.2	2.7	71
72	4.3	3.1	4.6	4.4	1.9	1.6	1.7	2.3	72
73	3.8	2.7	4.4	3.8	1.7	1.5	1.5	2.0	73
74	3.8	2.7	4.1	3.7	1.5	1.3	1.3	1.7	74
75	3.9	2.8	3.9	3.5	1.3	1.1	1.1	1.4	75

*Calculated from CPS data of all education levels combined

Table 12: Mean years to final separation, July 1999–June 2007 CPS data, continued: Hispanic Females

Age	Initially Active				Initially Inactive				Age
	All*	<HS	HS	>HS	All*	<HS	HS	>HS	
18	46.0	43.6	46.7	49.4	46.0	43.6	46.7	49.4	18
19	45.0	42.6	45.7	48.4	45.0	42.6	45.7	48.4	19
20	44.1	41.6	44.8	47.4	44.1	41.6	44.8	47.4	20
21	43.1	40.6	43.8	46.4	43.1	40.6	43.8	46.4	21
22	42.1	39.7	42.8	45.4	42.1	39.7	42.8	45.4	22
23	41.1	38.7	41.8	44.5	41.1	38.7	41.8	44.5	23
24	40.1	37.7	40.8	43.5	40.1	37.7	40.8	43.5	24
25	39.2	36.7	39.9	42.5	39.2	36.7	39.9	42.5	25
26	38.2	35.8	38.9	41.5	38.2	35.8	38.9	41.5	26
27	37.2	34.8	37.9	40.6	37.2	34.8	37.9	40.6	27
28	36.2	33.8	36.9	39.6	36.2	33.8	36.9	39.6	28
29	35.2	32.8	35.9	38.6	35.2	32.8	35.9	38.6	29
30	34.2	31.9	35.0	37.6	34.2	31.8	34.9	37.6	30
31	33.2	30.9	34.0	36.6	33.2	30.9	34.0	36.6	31
32	32.3	29.9	33.0	35.6	32.2	29.9	33.0	35.6	32
33	31.3	28.9	32.0	34.6	31.2	28.9	32.0	34.6	33
34	30.3	27.9	31.0	33.7	30.3	27.9	31.0	33.6	34
35	29.3	27.0	30.1	32.7	29.3	26.9	30.0	32.7	35
36	28.3	26.0	29.1	31.7	28.3	26.0	29.0	31.7	36
37	27.4	25.0	28.1	30.7	27.3	25.0	28.0	30.7	37
38	26.4	24.1	27.1	29.7	26.3	24.0	27.1	29.7	38
39	25.4	23.1	26.2	28.8	25.3	23.0	26.1	28.7	39
40	24.4	22.2	25.2	27.8	24.3	22.1	25.1	27.7	40
41	23.5	21.2	24.3	26.8	23.3	21.1	24.1	26.7	41
42	22.5	20.3	23.3	25.8	22.3	20.1	23.1	25.7	42
43	21.5	19.3	22.4	24.9	21.3	19.1	22.1	24.7	43
44	20.6	18.4	21.4	23.9	20.3	18.2	21.1	23.7	44
45	19.7	17.5	20.5	22.9	19.3	17.2	20.1	22.7	45
46	18.7	16.6	19.6	22.0	18.3	16.2	19.1	21.7	46
47	17.8	15.7	18.7	21.0	17.2	15.2	18.0	20.7	47
48	16.9	14.8	17.8	20.1	16.2	14.2	17.0	19.7	48
49	16.0	14.0	16.8	19.2	15.1	13.2	15.9	18.7	49
50	15.1	13.1	16.0	18.2	14.2	12.3	14.9	17.7	50
51	14.3	12.3	15.1	17.3	13.2	11.4	14.0	16.7	51
52	13.4	11.6	14.3	16.4	12.2	10.5	13.0	15.7	52
53	12.6	10.8	13.5	15.5	11.3	9.6	12.1	14.7	53
54	11.8	10.1	12.7	14.6	10.3	8.7	11.2	13.6	54
55	11.0	9.4	11.8	13.7	9.4	7.9	10.3	12.5	55
56	10.2	8.6	11.0	12.9	8.5	7.1	9.4	11.5	56
57	9.5	7.9	10.2	12.0	7.6	6.3	8.4	10.5	57
58	8.7	7.2	9.4	11.2	6.8	5.6	7.5	9.5	58
59	8.0	6.6	8.6	10.5	6.0	5.0	6.7	8.6	59
60	7.3	5.9	7.8	9.7	5.3	4.3	5.9	7.7	60
61	6.7	5.4	7.1	9.0	4.6	3.8	5.2	6.8	61
62	6.1	4.9	6.5	8.4	4.0	3.3	4.6	6.0	62
63	5.6	4.4	6.0	7.7	3.5	2.9	4.0	5.3	63
64	5.2	4.1	5.5	7.1	3.1	2.5	3.5	4.8	64
65	4.8	3.8	5.1	6.5	2.7	2.2	3.1	4.3	65
66	4.5	3.5	4.8	5.8	2.4	1.9	2.6	3.8	66
67	4.0	3.0	4.6	5.0	2.1	1.7	2.2	3.4	67
68	3.9	2.7	4.6	4.6	1.9	1.5	1.9	3.0	68
69	3.9	2.9	4.3	4.2	1.7	1.3	1.7	2.7	69
70	3.7	2.6	4.0	4.0	1.4	1.1	1.4	2.3	70
71	3.6	2.9	3.8	3.7	1.2	0.9	1.2	2.0	71
72	3.4	2.7	3.5	3.8	1.0	0.8	1.0	1.7	72
73	3.2	2.7	3.1	3.6	0.9	0.7	0.8	1.4	73
74	2.8	2.3	2.9	3.3	0.8	0.6	0.7	1.2	74
75	2.6	1.8	2.7	3.4	0.7	0.5	0.6	0.9	75

*Calculated from CPS data of all education levels combined

Appendix A

Standard Errors of Estimates

Introduction

The purpose of this appendix is to provide estimates of error associated with life and worklife measures reported in this book. Chapters 4 through 14 discuss various methods to determine expected values (means) for life and worklife expectancies. These assume fixed parameter values, i.e., that values are true and exact. However, each parameter has an associated degree of uncertainty. To estimate error in these mean life and worklife measures, we replace fixed parameter values (mortality rates, transition probabilities, and labor force participation rates) with stochastic variants. The stochastic versions of the parameter values are obtained by bootstrap and Monte Carlo methods and are used to generate a distribution of expected values which provide measures of "known error rates" for each of the life and worklife measures.

The potentially confusing aspect of uncertainty associated with life and worklife estimates, is that there are two different probability distributions (and hence sources of variability) connected to each of the life and worklife measures. The first is the distribution of *values*. For example, at a given age some members of a population will die soon while others will live for a long period. The second is the distribution of *expected values* (means) for each given life or worklife measure, i.e., the variability that would be associated with a collection of sample means randomly drawn from the entire population.

Each life and worklife measure may be modeled as a random variable. A random variable, by definition, has an associated ***probability distribution*** describing the total range of possible values the variable may have. In the case of a discrete random variable (which is often how life and worklife measures are modeled[1]), the probability distribution is the ***prob-***

ability mass function, which gives the probability that the random variable is equal to a particular value. Any summary statistic (such as the mean) that is calculated from a sample drawn from a population is itself a random variable with an associated distribution termed the ***sampling distribution***.

Consider a population of 100 marbles in a bag. The number of colored flecks per marble is counted. Appendix Figure A.1 shows a frequency distribution of the results of this count. The mean of this distribution is 9.96. The standard deviation of 0.95 is a measure of the spread in the actual *values*. The observed relative frequency of each value (i.e., the number of marbles with the same number of flecks per marble) represents the *probability distribution* and gives the *probability mass function* for any given number of flecks. For example, the exact probability of drawing a marble with say, 8 flecks is 4/100=0.04. The complete probability mass function for the number of flecks for this marble population is given in Appendix Text Table 1. The more common statistical question, however, is how much spread would be associated with samples drawn from the population. For example, how would the distributions of *expected values* of three different sample sizes: 3, 20 and 70 differ? Figure A.1 show the resulting *sampling distributions* of the sample means, given 100 replications for each sample size. The standard deviation of the sampling distribution provides us with the ***standard error*** of each estimate. Appendix Text Table 2 shows that the sample means are all very close to the true mean, but the standard deviation of the sample means decreases significantly with each increase in sample size.

In practice, the sampling distribution is rarely determined empirically due to the massive effort that would be required. Rather, the central limit theorem is used. The central limit theorem states that, given a distribution with mean μ and variance σ^2, the sampling distribution of the mean approaches a normal distribution with a mean (μ) and a variance σ^2/N as N approaches infinity *regardless of the shape of the underlying probability distribution*. This parametric approach works well for making inferences about simple sample means, but cannot be used for more complicated summary statistics.

---

1. Even though age is fundamentally a continuous variable, for demographic models there are several practical reasons to model them as discrete random variables. It is common practice to report age-specific results only for whole integer ages. Also, the level of resolution of data from which parameters (mortality and labor force participation) are calculated is often yearly data.

Appendix Text Table 1
Probability mass function for number of flecks

Value	Frequency	Probability Mass
<8	0/100	0
8	4/100	0.04
9	29/100	0.29
10	40/100	0.40
11	21/100	0.21
12	6/100	0.06
>12	0/100	0

Appendix Text Table 2
Empirical sampling distributions for 100 repeated samples of size *n*.

Sample size	Mean of sample means	sd
n=3	9.97	0.52
n=20	9.96	0.17
n=70	9.96	0.06

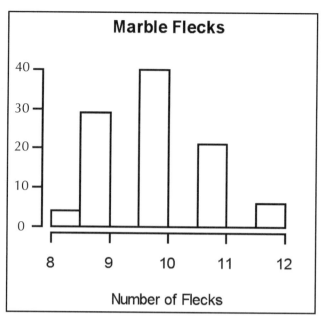

Figure A.1 *Frequency distribution of number of marble flecks in 100 marbles.*

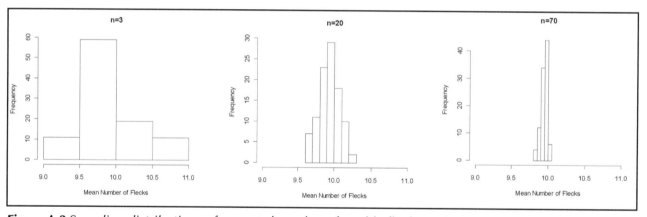

Figure A.2 *Sampling distributions of expected number of marble flecks in three different samples sizes.*

The two sources of variability associated with life and worklife measures (i.e., probability distribution and sampling distribution) are essentially the same as in the example above. The underlying *probability distribution* of possible *values* is defined by a *probability mass function* for each life and worklife measure. Probability mass functions are determined by the conditional probabilities that constitute the parameters of the demographic models, but in these relatively complicated models they can not be calculated directly. However, they can be determined using recursive formulae based on model parameters (Skoog and Ciecka 2001, 2002, 2003), or from expanded versions of the models which explicitly track all possible outcomes (see chapter 14 for an example). Nevertheless, forensic economists generally deal only with the *expected values*.

The theoretical *sampling distributions* of life and worklife measures describe the amount of spread associated with the expected values and essentially assess "known error" (per Daubert). However, because there is uncertainty at both the probability distribution and sampling distribution levels it is instructive to see how *values* and *expected values* are calculated.

All of the life and worklife models used in this book can be classified as Markov chains. The calculations involve a series of conditional probabilities or steps. Each step in the chain of calculations is a function of the preceding state and one or more transition probabilities that govern how states may change from one step to the next. A series of this type is considered to be Markovian if the state at a given step depends only on the state of the immediately preceding step and is independent of all other previous steps. That is, if it is possible to calculate the state of future step n using only information related to the current step n-1, it is a Markov chain. Life expectancy and conventional models are simple Markov chains, governed only by mortality transition probabilities and current labor force participation rates. The increment/decrement model has an additional dimension—transition between various labor force states.

Because of the stepwise nature of Markov chain models there is a broad variety of possible outcomes. Each outcome has an associated probability that can be calculated from the underlying probabilities. Thus the outcomes can be thought of as "deterministically random." That is, we use fixed probabilities to calculate life and worklife measures for a given population, so the probability of any particular event can be calculated deterministically. However, the exact outcome for any individual can not be known because each step along the chain represents a possible fork determined by the probability of survival and, in the case of the increment/decrement model, probability of transitioning into or out of the labor force. For example, there is *theoretically*[2] a small but non-zero probability that an 18 year-old individual would never enter the workforce. Let's call this probability p^i *(permanent inactivity)*. We can deterministically calculate the exact value of p^i by multiplying the probability of surviving times the probability of remaining inactive, given an initial state of inactivity for each age from 18 to death. As one would expect, this probability is extremely small (on the order of 10^{-9}) for an 18 year-old who survives to age 80. In fact, there is a $(1$-$p^i)$ chance (on the order of 0.999999999) that an 18 year-old will enter the labor force at some point between the age of 18 and death at age 80. So there's a wide range of possible outcomes for an 18 year-old individual, each with an associated probability. Taken together they comprise the probability mass function that defines the distribution which is deterministically calculated from mortality (and, in the case of increment decrement estimates, labor force transition probabilities). The practical implication is that it is impossible to predict with certainty the outcome for any individual in a Markov chain. However the *most* likely outcome is completely predictable—the expected value or mean.

In other words, even though a Markov model is inherently stochastic, the most probable path *can* be known deterministically by simply calculating the chain of conditional probabilities. It is this "most probable path" –the *expected value* or *mean* – for each life and worklife measure that constitutes the worklife estimates discussed in Chapters 4

through 14 of this book. This appendix characterizes error associated with each of these means by determining their sampling distributions. This provides measures of "known error rates" for these estimates and satisfies the requirement of Daubert. However, unlike the simple counts as in the marbles example above, the probability distributions and sampling distributions of life and worklife measures are based on complex calculations. There is no simple calculation and no option for empirical resampling. The only alternative is resampling by a Monte Carlo method as discussed below.

Methods

Sampling distributions are provided in this Appendix for the following life and worklife measures: mortality rates and life expectancies by sex, race, Hispanic origin, and educational attainment, life and worklife expectancies for smokers/non-smokers, worklife expectancies calculated by the increment/decrement and conventional models, and years to final separation calculated by the increment/decrement model. In addition, sampling distributions are provided for the underlying labor force participation rates and transition probabilities. As mentioned above, because worklife measures are calculated from complex models they require simulations to generate the sampling distributions. Skoog and Ciecka (2004) estimated "known error rates" associated with worklife expectancies calculated by the Markov increment/decrement model using the bootstrap method. But all the other sampling errors provided in this Appendix have not previously been published

We use the bootstrap and other Monte Carlo methods to generate sampling distributions of means. Bootstrap resamples were obtained by randomly drawing n bootstrap data points $(x^*_1, x^*_2, \cdots, x^*_n)$ from the population of n objects points $(x_1, x_2, \cdots, x_n)$ (Efron and Tibshirani, 1993). The number of bootstrap samples is always equal to the original sample size. The key to the bootstrap sample is that it occurs with replacement, that is, each data point is replaced before the next random draw. Thus, a particular data point from the original sample may occur in a given bootstrap resample once, several times, or not at all. This is the basis for assessing variability in the original sample.

Simple Monte Carlo simulation was used to generate random replicates of mortality rates. We could not employ bootstrap resampling for the mortality rates because we did not have the original sample data. Rather, using means and standard errors, we employed Monte Carlo sampling using a normal approximation to the binomial distribution. For ages/racial groups that lacked standard error estimates (ages 18-25) we assumed a coefficient of variation of 20% which is equal to the overall coefficients of variation for all sub-

---

2. We say theoretically, because we are using cross-sectional data to estimate longitudinal trends. This caveat is mentioned in Frasca and Winger (1989).

populations. An alternative approach would have been to use fixed standard error estimates for all subpopulations based on aggregated data for all races/education groups. Skoog and Ceicka (2004), found that modest changes in mortality rate variability caused nearly imperceptible changes in standard error estimates for years to final separation. Thus we assume that either approach would generate nearly identical results.

In each case 1000 vectors of stochastic versions of the model parameters (mortality rates, labor force transition probabilities and labor force participation rates) were generated and used to calculate 1000 expected values for each age/race/educational group. Standard errors were calculated as the square root of these sampling distribution variances.

Labor force transition probabilities were obtained from an aggregated CPS data matched set using month-in-samples 4 and 8 for July 1999 through June 2007 (see Chapter 8 for details). Labor force participation rates for the conventional model estimates were calculated from a pooled CPS data set of the seven years from January 2000 through December 2006 (see Chapter 9 for details). Smoking probabilities were obtained from the Tobacco Use Supplements of the Current Population Surveys (CPS) for the months of January and May of 2000, June and November of 2001, February of 2002, and February, June and November of 2003 (see Chapter 11 for details).

Sample sizes range from low double digits to thousands of individuals depending on age and subpopulation. In cases where there is insufficient data to estimate labor force parameters for a particular subpopulation, estimates were obtained from the same gender/educational group but for all races. For example, sample size is generally quite small for black males with a graduate degree–generally less than 100 per age. In the cases where sample size is zero, values were assumed equal to males of all races possessing a graduate degree. In addition to the rare events where sample size is zero, there are cases where the sample size is so small that the estimated probability is either 0% or 100%. Again the age-specific parameter from the "all races" equivalent to the particular gender/educational group was "borrowed" . The variability of each parameter that was obtained in this way was increased by an additional 25% to account for the fact that, on average, standard deviations for race-specific parameters are 25% larger than for the comparable "all races" educational/gender group.

We chose 1000 as our number of model simulations. The general rule of thumb is that 50 to 200 replications are adequate for estimating standard error (Efron, 1987 and Efron and Tibshirani, 1993). However, Booth and Sarkar (1998) presented findings that Monte Carlo error could influence results for replications less than 800. Chernick (1999) suggested a practical approach, i.e. start with 100 replicates and systematically increase the number of replicates to determine empirically the point at which changes in the resulting estimates are nominal. We employed Chernick's suggested practical approach on several representative subpopulations and found that standard deviation of the resulting distribution of expected values differed by no more than +/- 0.002 for bootstrap replicates greater than 500. We conservatively chose 1000 replicates to account for the fact that we did not determine a threshold of accuracy for each of the subpopulations.

Results and Conclusions

Errors associated with mortality rates and life expectancies are presented in Appendix Tables 1 and 2. These were provided to the authors by the U.S. Bureau of the Census.

Errors associated with worklife model parameters are summarized in Appendix Tables 3 through 5. Coefficients of variation generally ranged from less than 1% to 15%. Smaller subpopulations tend to exhibit higher errors in parameter estimates than aggregated samples. Also, as a general rule, standard errors tend to be lower for younger ages than for older ages. This is especially true for smaller subpopulations.

Errors associated with working life estimates are Summarized in Appendix Tables 6 through 9. For any given age/subpopulation these tend to be less than the errors associated with the underlying parameters—often by an order of magnitude. The patterns of SE by age are similar to those reported by Skoog and Ciecka, 2004. Numerically, standard errors tend to be less than or equal to a few tenths for all ages with a slight decrease by age, but as a percentage of the mean, SE's increase with increasing age.

A Final Word on Uncertainty

The CPS data from which the worklife parameters are estimated are subject to both sampling and nonsampling error (known and unknown factors). Sampling error occurs by chance any time a sample, rather than the entire population, is surveyed. In our case the data contain both year-to-year variability and age to age variability. Year to year variability arises because the data set contains samples from multiple years. Age-to-age variability arise from unknown biases and sampling errors such as inability to obtain information about all persons in the sample; differences in the interpretation of questions; inability or unwillingness of respondents to provide correct information; inability to recall information; month-in-sample effects, errors made in collecting and processing the data; errors made in estimating values for missing data; and failure to represent all sample households and all persons within sample households (BLS Handbook of Methods).

Given this variety of sources of possible error in the underlying data , the estimates of error presented in this appendix may under-estimate true error rates. The best defense against sampling and nonsampling error is to use pooled data representing multiple years. This increases the effective sample size and minimizes both known and unknown error. As discussed in Chapter 14 the data sets used in these analyses were intentionally made large enough to encompass one entire business cycle in the U.S. economy. Thus in general, we conclude that the error rates reported here make a fair representation of knowable error rates (see Skoog and Ciecka, 2004). Also, the fact that the life and worklife models tend to be robust to a modest amount of stochastic variability in mortality and labor force participation parameters increases our confidence in the use of mean values in making future predictions. However, further research in this area is warranted. For example, a sensitivity analysis that systematically increased parameter uncertainty beyond what has yet been measured would provide a more mechanistic understanding of the relationship between parameter uncertainty and model output. This would provide greater insight into the range of uncertainty in life and worklife measures, particularly for subpopulations with small sample size and potentially larger amounts of nonsampling error.

References

Booth, J. G. and S. Sarkar, 1998. "Monte Carlo Approximation of Bootstrap Variances." *Journal of the American Statistical Association,* 52: 354-357.

Chernick, M. R., 1999. *Bootstrap Methods: A Practitioner's Guide*. John Wiley & Sons, Inc.: New York.

Efron, B. and R. J. Tibhirani, 1993. *An Introduction to the Bootstrap*. Chapman & Hall: New York.

Frasca, R. R. and B. J. Winger, 1989. "An Investigation into the Median and the Mean Age of Final Separation from the Labor Force," *Journal of Forensic Economics,* 2(3), 103-14.

Kachitvichyanukul, V. and B. W. Schmeiser, 1988. "Binomial random variate generation." *Communications of the ACM*, 31, 216–222.

MacKinnon, J. G., 2002. "Bootstrap Inference in Econometrics." *Canadian Journal of Economics*, 35, 615-645.

Meyn, S.P. and R. L. Tweedie, 1993. *Markov Chains and Stochastic Stability*. Springer-Verlag: London.

R Development Core Team, 2008. *R: A Language and Environment for Statistical Computing*. R Foundation for Statistical Computing: Vienna, Austria. URL: www.r-project.org.

Appendix Table 1: Standard errors of mortality rates and expectations of remaining years of life—Males and Females of All Races

	Males of All Races												Females of All Races											
	Standard Errors of Mortality Rates						Standard Errors of Life Expectancy						Standard Errors of Mortality Rates						Standard Errors of Life Expectancy					
Age	All Educ Levels	<HS	High School	Some College	College Degree	Grad Degree	All Educ Levels	<HS	High School	Some College	College Degree	Grad Degree	All Educ Levels	<HS	High School	Some College	College Degree	Grad Degree	All Educ Levels	<HS	High School	Some College	College Degree	Grad Degree
0	0.000						0.05						0.000						0.04					
1	0.000						0.05						0.000						0.04					
2	0.000						0.05						0.000						0.04					
3	0.000						0.04						0.000						0.04					
4	0.000						0.04						0.000						0.04					
5	0.000						0.04						0.000						0.04					
6	0.000						0.04						0.000						0.04					
7	0.000						0.04						0.000						0.04					
8	0.000						0.04						0.000						0.04					
9	0.000						0.04						0.000						0.04					
10	0.000						0.04						0.000						0.04					
11	0.000						0.04						0.000						0.04					
12	0.000						0.04						0.000						0.04					
13	0.000						0.04						0.000						0.04					
14	0.000						0.04						0.000						0.04					
15	0.000						0.04						0.000						0.04					
16	0.000						0.04						0.000						0.04					
17	0.000						0.04						0.000						0.04					
18	0.000						0.04						0.000						0.04					
19	0.000						0.04						0.000						0.04					
20	0.000						0.04						0.000						0.04					
21	0.000						0.04						0.000						0.04					
22	0.000						0.04						0.000						0.04					
23	0.000						0.04						0.000						0.04					
24	0.000						0.04						0.000						0.04					
25	0.000	0.000	0.000	0.000	0.000	0.000	0.04	0.13	0.09	0.12	0.14	0.17	0.000	0.000	0.000	0.000	0.000	0.001	0.04	0.11	0.07	0.11	0.15	0.25
26	0.000	0.000	0.000	0.000	0.000	0.001	0.04	0.11	0.08	0.12	0.14	0.17	0.000	0.000	0.000	0.000	0.000	0.001	0.04	0.09	0.07	0.11	0.15	0.21
27	0.000	0.000	0.000	0.000	0.000	0.000	0.04	0.10	0.08	0.12	0.14	0.15	0.000	0.000	0.000	0.000	0.000	0.000	0.04	0.09	0.07	0.11	0.15	0.20
28	0.000	0.000	0.000	0.000	0.000	0.000	0.04	0.09	0.08	0.11	0.14	0.15	0.000	0.000	0.000	0.000	0.000	0.000	0.04	0.08	0.07	0.11	0.15	0.20
29	0.000	0.000	0.000	0.000	0.000	0.000	0.04	0.09	0.08	0.11	0.13	0.15	0.000	0.000	0.000	0.000	0.000	0.000	0.04	0.08	0.07	0.11	0.15	0.20
30	0.000	0.000	0.000	0.000	0.000	0.000	0.04	0.09	0.07	0.11	0.13	0.15	0.000	0.000	0.000	0.000	0.000	0.001	0.04	0.08	0.07	0.11	0.15	0.20
31	0.000	0.000	0.000	0.000	0.000	0.000	0.04	0.09	0.07	0.11	0.13	0.15	0.000	0.000	0.000	0.000	0.000	0.000	0.04	0.08	0.07	0.11	0.15	0.20
32	0.000	0.000	0.000	0.000	0.000	0.000	0.04	0.09	0.07	0.11	0.13	0.15	0.000	0.000	0.000	0.000	0.000	0.000	0.04	0.08	0.06	0.11	0.15	0.20
33	0.000	0.000	0.000	0.000	0.000	0.000	0.04	0.08	0.07	0.11	0.13	0.15	0.000	0.000	0.000	0.000	0.000	0.000	0.04	0.08	0.06	0.11	0.15	0.20
34	0.000	0.001	0.000	0.000	0.000	0.000	0.04	0.08	0.07	0.11	0.13	0.15	0.000	0.001	0.000	0.000	0.000	0.000	0.04	0.08	0.06	0.11	0.15	0.20
35	0.000	0.001	0.000	0.000	0.000	0.000	0.04	0.08	0.07	0.11	0.13	0.15	0.000	0.000	0.000	0.000	0.000	0.000	0.04	0.08	0.06	0.11	0.15	0.20
36	0.000	0.001	0.000	0.000	0.000	0.000	0.04	0.08	0.07	0.11	0.13	0.15	0.000	0.000	0.000	0.000	0.000	0.000	0.04	0.08	0.06	0.11	0.15	0.20
37	0.000	0.001	0.000	0.000	0.000	0.000	0.04	0.08	0.07	0.11	0.13	0.15	0.000	0.001	0.000	0.000	0.000	0.000	0.04	0.08	0.06	0.11	0.15	0.20
38	0.000	0.001	0.000	0.000	0.000	0.000	0.04	0.08	0.07	0.11	0.13	0.15	0.000	0.001	0.000	0.000	0.000	0.000	0.04	0.08	0.06	0.11	0.15	0.20
39	0.000	0.001	0.000	0.000	0.000	0.000	0.04	0.08	0.07	0.11	0.13	0.15	0.000	0.000	0.000	0.000	0.000	0.000	0.04	0.07	0.06	0.11	0.15	0.19
40	0.000	0.001	0.000	0.000	0.000	0.000	0.04	0.08	0.07	0.11	0.13	0.15	0.000	0.000	0.000	0.000	0.000	0.000	0.04	0.07	0.06	0.11	0.15	0.19
41	0.000	0.001	0.000	0.000	0.000	0.000	0.04	0.07	0.07	0.11	0.13	0.15	0.000	0.001	0.000	0.000	0.000	0.000	0.04	0.07	0.06	0.11	0.15	0.19
42	0.000	0.001	0.000	0.000	0.000	0.000	0.04	0.07	0.07	0.11	0.13	0.15	0.000	0.001	0.000	0.000	0.000	0.000	0.04	0.07	0.06	0.11	0.15	0.19
43	0.000	0.001	0.000	0.000	0.000	0.000	0.04	0.07	0.07	0.11	0.13	0.15	0.000	0.001	0.000	0.000	0.000	0.000	0.04	0.07	0.06	0.11	0.15	0.19
44	0.000	0.001	0.000	0.000	0.000	0.000	0.04	0.07	0.07	0.11	0.13	0.15	0.000	0.001	0.000	0.000	0.000	0.000	0.04	0.07	0.06	0.11	0.15	0.19
45	0.000	0.001	0.000	0.000	0.000	0.000	0.04	0.07	0.07	0.11	0.13	0.15	0.000	0.001	0.000	0.000	0.000	0.000	0.04	0.07	0.06	0.11	0.15	0.19
46	0.000	0.001	0.000	0.000	0.000	0.000	0.04	0.07	0.07	0.11	0.13	0.15	0.000	0.001	0.000	0.000	0.000	0.000	0.04	0.07	0.06	0.11	0.15	0.19
47	0.000	0.001	0.000	0.000	0.000	0.000	0.04	0.07	0.07	0.11	0.13	0.15	0.000	0.001	0.000	0.000	0.000	0.000	0.04	0.07	0.06	0.11	0.15	0.19
48	0.000	0.001	0.000	0.000	0.000	0.000	0.04	0.07	0.07	0.11	0.13	0.15	0.000	0.001	0.000	0.000	0.000	0.000	0.04	0.07	0.06	0.11	0.15	0.19
49	0.000	0.001	0.000	0.001	0.000	0.000	0.04	0.06	0.07	0.11	0.13	0.15	0.000	0.001	0.000	0.000	0.000	0.000	0.04	0.07	0.06	0.11	0.15	0.19
50	0.000	0.001	0.000	0.000	0.000	0.000	0.04	0.06	0.07	0.11	0.13	0.15	0.000	0.001	0.000	0.000	0.000	0.000	0.04	0.06	0.06	0.10	0.14	0.19
51	0.000	0.001	0.000	0.001	0.001	0.000	0.04	0.06	0.07	0.11	0.13	0.14	0.000	0.001	0.000	0.000	0.001	0.001	0.04	0.06	0.06	0.10	0.14	0.19
52	0.000	0.001	0.000	0.001	0.001	0.000	0.04	0.06	0.07	0.11	0.13	0.14	0.000	0.001	0.000	0.000	0.001	0.000	0.04	0.06	0.06	0.10	0.14	0.19
53	0.000	0.001	0.000	0.001	0.001	0.001	0.04	0.06	0.07	0.11	0.13	0.14	0.000	0.001	0.000	0.000	0.001	0.001	0.04	0.06	0.06	0.10	0.14	0.19
54	0.000	0.001	0.000	0.001	0.001	0.001	0.04	0.06	0.07	0.11	0.13	0.14	0.000	0.001	0.000	0.000	0.001	0.001	0.04	0.06	0.06	0.10	0.14	0.19
55	0.000	0.001	0.001	0.001	0.001	0.001	0.04	0.06	0.07	0.11	0.13	0.14	0.000	0.001	0.000	0.001	0.001	0.001	0.04	0.06	0.06	0.10	0.14	0.19
56	0.000	0.000	0.001	0.001	0.001	0.001	0.04	0.06	0.07	0.11	0.13	0.14	0.000	0.001	0.000	0.001	0.001	0.001	0.04	0.06	0.06	0.10	0.14	0.19
57	0.000	0.001	0.001	0.001	0.001	0.001	0.03	0.06	0.06	0.11	0.13	0.14	0.000	0.001	0.000	0.001	0.001	0.001	0.03	0.06	0.06	0.10	0.14	0.19
58	0.000	0.001	0.001	0.001	0.001	0.001	0.03	0.05	0.06	0.11	0.13	0.14	0.000	0.001	0.000	0.001	0.001	0.001	0.03	0.06	0.06	0.10	0.14	0.19
59	0.000	0.001	0.001	0.001	0.001	0.001	0.03	0.05	0.06	0.10	0.13	0.14	0.000	0.001	0.000	0.001	0.001	0.000	0.03	0.06	0.06	0.10	0.14	0.19
60	0.000	0.001	0.001	0.000	0.001	0.001	0.03	0.05	0.06	0.10	0.13	0.14	0.000	0.001	0.000	0.001	0.001	0.001	0.03	0.05	0.06	0.10	0.14	0.19
61	0.000	0.001	0.001	0.001	0.000	0.000	0.03	0.05	0.06	0.10	0.13	0.14	0.000	0.001	0.000	0.001	0.001	0.001	0.03	0.05	0.06	0.10	0.14	0.19
62	0.000	0.001	0.001	0.001	0.001	0.001	0.03	0.05	0.06	0.10	0.13	0.14	0.000	0.001	0.000	0.001	0.001	0.001	0.03	0.05	0.06	0.10	0.14	0.19
63	0.000	0.001	0.001	0.001	0.001	0.001	0.03	0.05	0.06	0.10	0.12	0.14	0.000	0.001	0.001	0.001	0.001	0.001	0.03	0.05	0.06	0.10	0.14	0.19
64	0.001	0.001	0.001	0.001	0.001	0.001	0.03	0.05	0.06	0.10	0.12	0.14	0.000	0.000	0.001	0.001	0.001	0.001	0.03	0.05	0.06	0.10	0.14	0.18
65	0.001	0.001	0.001	0.001	0.001	0.001	0.03	0.05	0.06	0.10	0.12	0.14	0.000	0.001	0.001	0.001	0.001	0.001	0.03	0.05	0.06	0.10	0.13	0.18
66	0.001	0.001	0.001	0.001	0.001	0.001	0.03	0.05	0.06	0.10	0.12	0.14	0.000	0.000	0.001	0.001	0.001	0.001	0.03	0.05	0.06	0.09	0.13	0.18
67	0.001	0.001	0.001	0.001	0.002	0.001	0.03	0.05	0.06	0.10	0.12	0.14	0.000	0.000	0.001	0.000	0.001	0.002	0.03	0.05	0.06	0.09	0.13	0.18
68	0.001	0.001	0.001	0.002	0.002	0.002	0.03	0.04	0.06	0.10	0.12	0.14	0.000	0.001	0.001	0.001	0.001	0.002	0.03	0.05	0.06	0.09	0.13	0.18
69	0.001	0.001	0.001	0.002	0.002	0.002	0.03	0.04	0.06	0.10	0.12	0.14	0.000	0.001	0.001	0.001	0.001	0.002	0.03	0.04	0.06	0.09	0.13	0.18
70	0.001	0.001	0.001	0.002	0.002	0.002	0.03	0.04	0.06	0.10	0.12	0.14	0.000	0.001	0.001	0.001	0.002	0.002	0.03	0.04	0.05	0.09	0.13	0.18
71	0.001	0.002	0.001	0.002	0.002	0.002	0.03	0.04	0.06	0.10	0.12	0.14	0.001	0.001	0.001	0.001	0.002	0.002	0.03	0.04	0.05	0.09	0.13	0.18
72	0.001	0.002	0.001	0.002	0.002	0.002	0.03	0.04	0.06	0.10	0.12	0.14	0.001	0.001	0.001	0.001	0.002	0.002	0.03	0.04	0.05	0.09	0.13	0.18
73	0.001	0.002	0.001	0.002	0.002	0.003	0.03	0.04	0.06	0.10	0.12	0.14	0.001	0.001	0.001	0.001	0.002	0.002	0.03	0.04	0.05	0.09	0.12	0.17
74	0.001	0.002	0.002	0.002	0.003	0.003	0.03	0.04	0.06	0.10	0.12	0.14	0.001	0.001	0.001	0.001	0.002	0.003	0.03	0.04	0.05	0.09	0.12	0.17
75	0.001	0.002	0.002	0.003	0.003	0.003	0.03	0.04	0.06	0.10	0.12	0.14	0.001	0.001	0.000	0.002	0.002	0.003	0.03	0.04	0.05	0.09	0.12	0.17
76	0.001	0.002	0.002	0.003	0.003	0.003	0.03	0.04	0.06	0.10	0.12	0.14	0.001	0.001	0.001	0.002	0.003	0.003	0.03	0.04	0.05	0.09	0.12	0.17
77	0.001	0.002	0.002	0.003	0.004	0.004	0.03	0.04	0.07	0.11	0.13	0.14	0.001	0.001	0.001	0.002	0.003	0.004	0.03	0.04	0.05	0.09	0.12	0.17
78	0.001	0.002	0.002	0.004	0.004	0.004	0.03	0.04	0.07	0.11	0.13	0.14	0.001	0.001	0.001	0.002	0.003	0.004	0.03	0.04	0.05	0.09	0.12	0.17
79	0.001	0.002	0.002	0.004	0.005	0.004	0.03	0.04	0.07	0.11	0.13	0.15	0.001	0.001	0.001	0.002	0.003	0.004	0.03	0.04	0.05	0.09	0.12	0.17
80	0.001	0.002	0.003	0.004	0.005	0.005	0.03	0.04	0.07	0.11	0.13	0.15	0.001	0.002	0.002	0.003	0.003	0.004	0.03	0.04	0.05	0.09	0.12	0.17
81	0.002	0.003	0.003	0.005	0.005	0.006	0.03	0.04	0.07	0.11	0.13	0.15	0.001	0.002	0.002	0.003	0.004	0.005	0.03	0.04	0.06	0.09	0.12	0.17
82	0.002	0.003	0.003	0.006	0.007	0.006	0.03	0.04	0.07	0.11	0.13	0.15	0.001	0.002	0.002	0.003	0.004	0.005	0.03	0.04	0.06	0.09	0.11	0.17
83	0.002	0.003	0.004	0.006	0.007	0.007	0.03	0.04	0.07	0.12	0.13	0.15	0.001	0.002	0.002	0.003	0.005	0.006	0.03	0.04	0.06	0.09	0.11	0.17
84	0.002	0.003	0.004	0.007	0.008	0.008	0.03	0.04	0.08	0.12	0.14	0.15	0.001	0.002	0.002	0.004	0.005	0.007	0.03	0.04	0.06	0.09	0.11	0.17
85	0.002	0.004	0.005	0.008	0.009	0.009	0.03	0.04	0.08	0.12	0.14	0.16	0.001	0.002	0.003	0.004	0.005	0.008	0.03	0.03	0.06	0.09	0.11	0.17

Source: U.S. Bureau of the Census, Demographic Statistical Methods Division, Washington, DC., unpublished tables, 1996 and 1998 from the National Mortality Longitudinal Study

Appendix Table 1: Standard errors of mortality rates and expectations of remaining years of life—White Males and Females

Age	White Males												White Females											
	Standard Errors of Mortality Rates						Standard Errors of Life Expectancy						Standard Errors of Mortality Rates						Standard Errors of Life Expectancy					
	All Educ Levels	<HS	High School	Some College	College Degree	Grad Degree	All Educ Levels	<HS	High School	Some College	College Degree	Grad Degree	All Educ Levels	<HS	High School	Some College	College Degree	Grad Degree	All Educ Levels	<HS	High School	Some College	College Degree	Grad Degree
0	0.000						0.05						0.000						0.05					
1	0.000						0.05						0.000						0.05					
2	0.000						0.05						0.000						0.04					
3	0.000						0.05						0.000						0.04					
4	0.000						0.05						0.000						0.04					
5	0.000						0.05						0.000						0.04					
6	0.000						0.05						0.000						0.04					
7	0.000						0.05						0.000						0.04					
8	0.000						0.05						0.000						0.04					
9	0.000						0.05						0.000						0.04					
10	0.000						0.04						0.000						0.04					
11	0.000						0.04						0.000						0.04					
12	0.000						0.04						0.000						0.04					
13	0.000						0.04						0.000						0.04					
14	0.000						0.04						0.000						0.04					
15	0.000						0.04						0.000						0.04					
16	0.000						0.04						0.000						0.04					
17	0.000						0.04						0.000						0.04					
18	0.000						0.04						0.000						0.04					
19	0.000						0.04						0.000						0.04					
20	0.000						0.04						0.000						0.04					
21	0.000						0.04						0.000						0.04					
22	0.000						0.04						0.000						0.04					
23	0.000						0.04						0.000						0.04					
24	0.000						0.04						0.000						0.04					
25	0.000	0.000	0.000	0.000	0.000	0.000	0.04	0.14	0.09	0.12	0.14	0.18	0.000	0.000	0.000	0.000	0.000	0.000	0.04	0.10	0.07	0.12	0.15	0.21
26	0.000	0.000	0.000	0.000	0.000	0.001	0.04	0.12	0.08	0.12	0.14	0.18	0.000	0.000	0.000	0.000	0.000	0.001	0.04	0.09	0.07	0.11	0.15	0.21
27	0.000	0.000	0.000	0.000	0.000	0.000	0.04	0.11	0.08	0.12	0.14	0.15	0.000	0.000	0.000	0.000	0.000	0.000	0.04	0.09	0.07	0.11	0.15	0.21
28	0.000	0.000	0.000	0.000	0.000	0.000	0.04	0.10	0.08	0.12	0.14	0.15	0.000	0.000	0.000	0.000	0.000	0.000	0.04	0.09	0.07	0.11	0.15	0.21
29	0.000	0.000	0.000	0.000	0.000	0.000	0.04	0.10	0.08	0.12	0.14	0.15	0.000	0.000	0.000	0.000	0.000	0.000	0.04	0.09	0.07	0.11	0.15	0.21
30	0.000	0.000	0.000	0.000	0.000	0.000	0.04	0.09	0.08	0.12	0.14	0.15	0.000	0.000	0.000	0.000	0.000	0.001	0.04	0.09	0.07	0.11	0.15	0.21
31	0.000	0.000	0.000	0.000	0.000	0.000	0.04	0.09	0.08	0.12	0.14	0.15	0.000	0.000	0.000	0.000	0.000	0.000	0.04	0.09	0.07	0.11	0.15	0.20
32	0.000	0.000	0.000	0.000	0.000	0.000	0.04	0.09	0.08	0.12	0.14	0.15	0.000	0.000	0.000	0.000	0.000	0.000	0.04	0.09	0.07	0.11	0.15	0.20
33	0.000	0.000	0.000	0.000	0.000	0.000	0.04	0.09	0.07	0.12	0.14	0.15	0.000	0.000	0.000	0.000	0.000	0.000	0.04	0.08	0.07	0.11	0.15	0.20
34	0.000	0.000	0.000	0.000	0.000	0.000	0.04	0.09	0.07	0.12	0.14	0.15	0.000	0.000	0.000	0.000	0.000	0.000	0.04	0.08	0.07	0.11	0.15	0.20
35	0.000	0.000	0.000	0.000	0.000	0.000	0.04	0.09	0.07	0.11	0.14	0.15	0.000	0.000	0.000	0.000	0.000	0.000	0.04	0.08	0.07	0.11	0.15	0.20
36	0.000	0.000	0.000	0.000	0.000	0.000	0.04	0.09	0.07	0.11	0.14	0.15	0.000	0.000	0.000	0.000	0.000	0.000	0.04	0.08	0.07	0.11	0.15	0.20
37	0.000	0.000	0.000	0.000	0.000	0.000	0.04	0.08	0.07	0.11	0.14	0.15	0.000	0.000	0.000	0.000	0.000	0.000	0.04	0.08	0.06	0.11	0.15	0.20
38	0.000	0.000	0.000	0.000	0.000	0.000	0.04	0.08	0.07	0.11	0.13	0.15	0.000	0.000	0.000	0.000	0.000	0.000	0.04	0.08	0.06	0.11	0.15	0.20
39	0.000	0.000	0.000	0.000	0.000	0.000	0.04	0.08	0.07	0.11	0.13	0.15	0.000	0.000	0.000	0.000	0.000	0.000	0.04	0.08	0.06	0.11	0.15	0.20
40	0.000	0.000	0.000	0.000	0.000	0.000	0.04	0.08	0.07	0.11	0.13	0.15	0.000	0.000	0.000	0.000	0.000	0.000	0.04	0.08	0.06	0.11	0.15	0.20
41	0.000	0.000	0.000	0.000	0.000	0.000	0.04	0.08	0.07	0.11	0.13	0.15	0.000	0.000	0.000	0.000	0.000	0.000	0.04	0.08	0.06	0.11	0.15	0.20
42	0.000	0.001	0.000	0.000	0.000	0.000	0.04	0.08	0.07	0.11	0.13	0.15	0.000	0.000	0.000	0.000	0.000	0.000	0.04	0.08	0.06	0.11	0.15	0.20
43	0.000	0.001	0.000	0.000	0.000	0.000	0.04	0.08	0.07	0.11	0.13	0.15	0.000	0.000	0.000	0.000	0.000	0.000	0.04	0.08	0.06	0.11	0.15	0.20
44	0.000	0.001	0.000	0.000	0.000	0.000	0.04	0.08	0.07	0.11	0.13	0.15	0.000	0.000	0.000	0.000	0.000	0.000	0.04	0.08	0.06	0.11	0.15	0.20
45	0.000	0.001	0.000	0.000	0.000	0.000	0.04	0.07	0.07	0.11	0.13	0.15	0.000	0.000	0.000	0.000	0.000	0.000	0.04	0.07	0.06	0.11	0.15	0.20
46	0.000	0.001	0.000	0.000	0.000	0.000	0.04	0.07	0.07	0.11	0.13	0.15	0.000	0.000	0.000	0.000	0.000	0.000	0.04	0.07	0.06	0.11	0.15	0.20
47	0.000	0.001	0.000	0.000	0.000	0.000	0.04	0.07	0.07	0.11	0.13	0.15	0.000	0.000	0.000	0.000	0.000	0.000	0.04	0.07	0.06	0.11	0.15	0.20
48	0.000	0.001	0.000	0.000	0.000	0.000	0.04	0.07	0.07	0.11	0.13	0.15	0.000	0.000	0.000	0.000	0.000	0.000	0.04	0.07	0.06	0.11	0.15	0.20
49	0.000	0.001	0.000	0.001	0.000	0.000	0.04	0.07	0.07	0.11	0.13	0.15	0.000	0.001	0.000	0.000	0.000	0.000	0.04	0.07	0.06	0.11	0.15	0.20
50	0.000	0.001	0.000	0.001	0.000	0.000	0.04	0.07	0.07	0.11	0.13	0.15	0.000	0.001	0.000	0.000	0.000	0.000	0.04	0.07	0.06	0.11	0.15	0.20
51	0.000	0.001	0.000	0.001	0.001	0.001	0.04	0.07	0.07	0.11	0.13	0.15	0.000	0.000	0.000	0.000	0.000	0.001	0.04	0.07	0.06	0.11	0.15	0.20
52	0.000	0.001	0.000	0.001	0.001	0.000	0.04	0.07	0.07	0.11	0.13	0.15	0.000	0.001	0.000	0.000	0.001	0.001	0.04	0.07	0.06	0.11	0.15	0.20
53	0.000	0.001	0.000	0.001	0.001	0.001	0.04	0.06	0.07	0.11	0.13	0.15	0.000	0.001	0.000	0.000	0.001	0.001	0.04	0.07	0.06	0.11	0.15	0.20
54	0.000	0.001	0.000	0.001	0.001	0.001	0.04	0.06	0.07	0.11	0.13	0.15	0.000	0.001	0.000	0.000	0.001	0.001	0.04	0.07	0.06	0.11	0.15	0.20
55	0.000	0.001	0.001	0.001	0.001	0.001	0.04	0.06	0.07	0.11	0.13	0.15	0.000	0.001	0.000	0.001	0.001	0.001	0.04	0.06	0.06	0.10	0.15	0.20
56	0.000	0.001	0.001	0.001	0.001	0.001	0.04	0.06	0.07	0.11	0.13	0.15	0.000	0.001	0.000	0.001	0.001	0.001	0.04	0.06	0.06	0.10	0.14	0.20
57	0.000	0.001	0.001	0.001	0.001	0.001	0.04	0.06	0.07	0.11	0.13	0.15	0.000	0.001	0.000	0.001	0.001	0.001	0.04	0.06	0.06	0.10	0.14	0.20
58	0.000	0.001	0.001	0.001	0.001	0.001	0.04	0.06	0.07	0.11	0.13	0.14	0.000	0.001	0.000	0.001	0.001	0.000	0.04	0.06	0.06	0.10	0.14	0.19
59	0.000	0.001	0.001	0.001	0.001	0.001	0.04	0.06	0.07	0.11	0.13	0.14	0.000	0.001	0.000	0.001	0.001	0.001	0.04	0.06	0.06	0.10	0.14	0.19
60	0.000	0.001	0.001	0.001	0.001	0.001	0.04	0.06	0.07	0.11	0.13	0.14	0.000	0.001	0.000	0.001	0.001	0.001	0.04	0.06	0.06	0.10	0.14	0.19
61	0.000	0.001	0.001	0.001	0.001	0.000	0.03	0.05	0.06	0.11	0.13	0.14	0.000	0.001	0.000	0.001	0.000	0.001	0.03	0.06	0.06	0.10	0.14	0.19
62	0.000	0.001	0.001	0.001	0.001	0.001	0.03	0.05	0.06	0.10	0.13	0.14	0.000	0.001	0.000	0.001	0.000	0.001	0.03	0.06	0.06	0.10	0.14	0.19
63	0.000	0.001	0.001	0.001	0.001	0.001	0.03	0.05	0.06	0.10	0.13	0.14	0.000	0.001	0.001	0.001	0.001	0.001	0.03	0.05	0.06	0.10	0.14	0.19
64	0.001	0.000	0.001	0.001	0.001	0.001	0.03	0.05	0.06	0.10	0.13	0.14	0.000	0.001	0.001	0.001	0.001	0.001	0.03	0.05	0.06	0.10	0.14	0.19
65	0.001	0.001	0.001	0.001	0.001	0.001	0.03	0.05	0.06	0.10	0.13	0.14	0.000	0.001	0.001	0.001	0.001	0.001	0.03	0.05	0.06	0.10	0.14	0.19
66	0.001	0.001	0.001	0.001	0.001	0.001	0.03	0.05	0.06	0.10	0.13	0.14	0.000	0.001	0.001	0.000	0.001	0.001	0.03	0.05	0.06	0.10	0.13	0.19
67	0.001	0.001	0.000	0.001	0.002	0.002	0.03	0.05	0.06	0.10	0.13	0.14	0.000	0.001	0.001	0.000	0.001	0.002	0.03	0.05	0.06	0.10	0.13	0.18
68	0.001	0.001	0.001	0.002	0.002	0.002	0.03	0.05	0.06	0.10	0.12	0.14	0.000	0.001	0.001	0.001	0.001	0.002	0.03	0.05	0.06	0.09	0.13	0.18
69	0.001	0.001	0.001	0.002	0.002	0.002	0.03	0.05	0.06	0.10	0.12	0.14	0.000	0.001	0.001	0.001	0.002	0.002	0.03	0.05	0.06	0.09	0.13	0.18
70	0.001	0.001	0.001	0.002	0.002	0.002	0.03	0.05	0.06	0.10	0.12	0.14	0.001	0.001	0.001	0.001	0.002	0.002	0.03	0.05	0.06	0.09	0.13	0.18
71	0.001	0.001	0.001	0.002	0.002	0.002	0.03	0.05	0.06	0.10	0.12	0.14	0.001	0.001	0.001	0.001	0.002	0.002	0.03	0.05	0.06	0.09	0.13	0.18
72	0.001	0.001	0.001	0.002	0.002	0.002	0.03	0.04	0.06	0.10	0.12	0.14	0.001	0.001	0.001	0.001	0.002	0.002	0.03	0.04	0.06	0.09	0.13	0.18
73	0.001	0.001	0.001	0.002	0.002	0.003	0.03	0.04	0.06	0.10	0.12	0.14	0.001	0.001	0.001	0.002	0.002	0.002	0.03	0.04	0.06	0.09	0.13	0.18
74	0.001	0.002	0.002	0.002	0.003	0.003	0.03	0.04	0.06	0.10	0.12	0.14	0.001	0.001	0.001	0.001	0.002	0.003	0.03	0.04	0.06	0.09	0.12	0.18
75	0.000	0.002	0.002	0.003	0.003	0.003	0.03	0.04	0.06	0.10	0.13	0.14	0.001	0.001	0.000	0.002	0.002	0.003	0.03	0.04	0.06	0.09	0.12	0.18
76	0.001	0.002	0.002	0.003	0.003	0.003	0.03	0.04	0.07	0.10	0.13	0.14	0.001	0.001	0.001	0.002	0.003	0.003	0.03	0.04	0.05	0.09	0.12	0.17
77	0.001	0.002	0.002	0.003	0.004	0.004	0.03	0.04	0.07	0.11	0.13	0.14	0.001	0.001	0.001	0.002	0.003	0.004	0.03	0.04	0.06	0.09	0.12	0.17
78	0.001	0.002	0.002	0.004	0.004	0.004	0.03	0.04	0.07	0.11	0.13	0.14	0.001	0.001	0.001	0.002	0.003	0.004	0.03	0.04	0.06	0.09	0.12	0.17
79	0.001	0.002	0.003	0.004	0.005	0.004	0.03	0.04	0.07	0.11	0.13	0.14	0.001	0.001	0.001	0.002	0.003	0.004	0.03	0.04	0.06	0.09	0.12	0.17
80	0.002	0.002	0.003	0.004	0.005	0.005	0.03	0.04	0.07	0.11	0.13	0.15	0.001	0.001	0.002	0.003	0.004	0.004	0.03	0.04	0.06	0.09	0.12	0.17
81	0.002	0.002	0.003	0.005	0.006	0.006	0.03	0.04	0.07	0.11	0.13	0.15	0.000	0.001	0.002	0.003	0.004	0.005	0.03	0.04	0.06	0.09	0.12	0.17
82	0.002	0.003	0.004	0.006	0.007	0.007	0.03	0.04	0.07	0.11	0.13	0.15	0.001	0.002	0.002	0.003	0.004	0.005	0.03	0.04	0.06	0.09	0.11	0.17
83	0.002	0.003	0.004	0.007	0.007	0.007	0.03	0.04	0.08	0.12	0.13	0.15	0.001	0.002	0.002	0.004	0.005	0.006	0.03	0.04	0.06	0.09	0.11	0.17
84	0.002	0.003	0.005	0.007	0.008	0.008	0.03	0.04	0.08	0.12	0.14	0.15	0.001	0.002	0.002	0.004	0.005	0.007	0.03	0.04	0.06	0.09	0.11	0.17
85	0.002	0.003	0.005	0.008	0.009	0.009	0.03	0.04	0.08	0.12	0.14	0.15	0.001	0.002	0.003	0.004	0.005	0.009	0.03	0.04	0.06	0.08	0.11	0.17

Source: U.S. Bureau of the Census, Demographic Statistical Methods Division, Washington, DC., unpublished tables, 1996 and 1998 from the National Mortality Longitudinal Study

Appendix Table 1: Standard errors of mortality rates and expectations of remaining years of life—Black Males and Females

Age	Black Males										Black Females									
	Standard Errors of Mortality Rates					Standard Errors of Life Expectancy					Standard Errors of Mortality Rates					Standard Errors of Life Expectancy				
	All Educ Levels	<HS	High School	Some Col-lege	BA or Higher	All Educ Levels	<HS	High School	Some Col-lege	BA or Higher	All Educ Levels	<HS	High School	Some Col-lege	BA or Higher	All Educ Levels	<HS	High School	Some Col-lege	BA or Higher
0	0.001					0.16					0.001					0.15				
1	0.000					0.16					0.000					0.15				
2	0.000					0.16					0.000					0.15				
3	0.000					0.16					0.000					0.15				
4	0.000					0.16					0.000					0.15				
5	0.000					0.16					0.000					0.15				
6	0.000					0.16					0.000					0.15				
7	0.000					0.16					0.000					0.15				
8	0.000					0.16					0.000					0.15				
9	0.000					0.16					0.000					0.15				
10	0.000					0.16					0.000					0.15				
11	0.000					0.16					0.000					0.15				
12	0.000					0.16					0.000					0.15				
13	0.000					0.16					0.000					0.15				
14	0.000					0.16					0.000					0.14				
15	0.000					0.16					0.000					0.14				
16	0.000					0.16					0.000					0.14				
17	0.000					0.16					0.000					0.14				
18	0.000					0.16					0.000					0.14				
19	0.000					0.16					0.000					0.14				
20	0.000					0.16					0.000					0.14				
21	0.000					0.15					0.000					0.14				
22	0.000					0.15					0.000					0.14				
23	0.000					0.15					0.000					0.14				
24	0.000					0.15					0.000					0.14				
25	0.000	0.001	0.001	0.001	0.000	0.15	0.33	0.36	0.59	0.64	0.000	0.000	0.000	0.001	0.002	0.14	0.36	0.32	0.56	0.68
26	0.000	0.001	0.000	0.000	0.000	0.15	0.33	0.34	0.54	0.64	0.000	0.001	0.000	0.001	0.000	0.14	0.29	0.30	0.53	0.56
27	0.000	0.001	0.001	0.001	0.000	0.15	0.32	0.34	0.54	0.64	0.000	0.000	0.000	0.001	0.001	0.14	0.26	0.30	0.53	0.56
28	0.000	0.001	0.001	0.001	0.001	0.15	0.30	0.33	0.54	0.64	0.000	0.000	0.000	0.001	0.000	0.14	0.24	0.30	0.53	0.56
29	0.000	0.001	0.001	0.001	0.000	0.15	0.29	0.33	0.54	0.64	0.000	0.001	0.001	0.000	0.001	0.14	0.24	0.30	0.53	0.56
30	0.000	0.001	0.001	0.001	0.002	0.15	0.28	0.33	0.54	0.64	0.000	0.001	0.000	0.000	0.000	0.14	0.24	0.30	0.53	0.56
31	0.000	0.001	0.001	0.001	0.001	0.15	0.27	0.33	0.54	0.63	0.000	0.001	0.000	0.000	0.001	0.14	0.23	0.30	0.53	0.56
32	0.000	0.001	0.001	0.001	0.001	0.15	0.26	0.33	0.54	0.63	0.000	0.000	0.000	0.000	0.001	0.14	0.23	0.30	0.53	0.55
33	0.001	0.001	0.001	0.001	0.001	0.15	0.26	0.32	0.54	0.63	0.000	0.001	0.000	0.001	0.001	0.14	0.23	0.30	0.53	0.55
34	0.000	0.001	0.001	0.001	0.001	0.15	0.25	0.32	0.54	0.63	0.000	0.001	0.000	0.000	0.001	0.14	0.22	0.30	0.52	0.55
35	0.001	0.001	0.001	0.000	0.001	0.15	0.25	0.32	0.54	0.63	0.000	0.001	0.000	0.001	0.000	0.14	0.22	0.30	0.52	0.55
36	0.001	0.001	0.001	0.001	0.001	0.15	0.24	0.32	0.54	0.63	0.000	0.001	0.000	0.001	0.001	0.14	0.22	0.30	0.52	0.55
37	0.001	0.001	0.001	0.001	0.001	0.15	0.24	0.32	0.54	0.63	0.000	0.001	0.001	0.001	0.001	0.14	0.21	0.30	0.52	0.55
38	0.001	0.001	0.001	0.001	0.001	0.15	0.23	0.32	0.54	0.63	0.000	0.001	0.001	0.001	0.001	0.14	0.21	0.30	0.52	0.55
39	0.001	0.001	0.000	0.001	0.001	0.15	0.23	0.32	0.54	0.63	0.000	0.001	0.001	0.001	0.001	0.14	0.21	0.29	0.52	0.55
40	0.001	0.002	0.001	0.001	0.001	0.15	0.22	0.32	0.54	0.63	0.000	0.001	0.001	0.001	0.000	0.14	0.21	0.29	0.52	0.55
41	0.001	0.001	0.001	0.001	0.001	0.15	0.22	0.32	0.54	0.63	0.000	0.000	0.001	0.001	0.001	0.14	0.20	0.29	0.52	0.55
42	0.001	0.001	0.001	0.001	0.001	0.14	0.21	0.32	0.54	0.63	0.000	0.001	0.001	0.001	0.001	0.14	0.20	0.29	0.52	0.55
43	0.001	0.002	0.001	0.001	0.002	0.14	0.21	0.32	0.54	0.63	0.001	0.001	0.001	0.001	0.001	0.14	0.20	0.29	0.52	0.55
44	0.001	0.002	0.001	0.002	0.001	0.14	0.21	0.32	0.54	0.63	0.000	0.001	0.001	0.001	0.001	0.14	0.20	0.29	0.52	0.55
45	0.001	0.002	0.000	0.002	0.002	0.14	0.20	0.32	0.54	0.63	0.001	0.001	0.001	0.001	0.000	0.14	0.20	0.29	0.52	0.55
46	0.001	0.002	0.001	0.002	0.001	0.14	0.20	0.32	0.54	0.63	0.001	0.001	0.000	0.001	0.001	0.14	0.19	0.29	0.53	0.55
47	0.001	0.002	0.001	0.002	0.001	0.14	0.20	0.32	0.54	0.63	0.001	0.001	0.000	0.001	0.002	0.14	0.19	0.29	0.53	0.55
48	0.001	0.002	0.001	0.002	0.002	0.14	0.19	0.32	0.55	0.63	0.001	0.001	0.001	0.001	0.002	0.13	0.19	0.29	0.53	0.55
49	0.001	0.002	0.002	0.002	0.000	0.14	0.19	0.32	0.55	0.63	0.001	0.001	0.001	0.001	0.001	0.13	0.18	0.29	0.53	0.55
50	0.001	0.002	0.001	0.002	0.002	0.14	0.19	0.32	0.55	0.63	0.001	0.001	0.001	0.002	0.001	0.13	0.18	0.29	0.53	0.55
51	0.001	0.002	0.002	0.002	0.002	0.14	0.18	0.32	0.55	0.63	0.001	0.001	0.001	0.001	0.002	0.13	0.18	0.29	0.53	0.55
52	0.001	0.002	0.002	0.003	0.003	0.14	0.18	0.32	0.55	0.63	0.001	0.001	0.001	0.001	0.001	0.13	0.17	0.29	0.53	0.55
53	0.001	0.002	0.002	0.002	0.003	0.14	0.17	0.32	0.55	0.63	0.001	0.001	0.001	0.002	0.001	0.13	0.17	0.29	0.53	0.55
54	0.001	0.002	0.002	0.003	0.003	0.13	0.17	0.32	0.55	0.63	0.001	0.002	0.001	0.002	0.002	0.13	0.17	0.29	0.53	0.55
55	0.001	0.002	0.002	0.004	0.003	0.13	0.17	0.32	0.55	0.63	0.000	0.002	0.002	0.002	0.003	0.13	0.17	0.29	0.53	0.54
56	0.001	0.002	0.002	0.004	0.003	0.13	0.17	0.32	0.55	0.63	0.000	0.002	0.001	0.002	0.002	0.13	0.16	0.29	0.53	0.54
57	0.002	0.002	0.002	0.005	0.005	0.13	0.16	0.32	0.56	0.63	0.000	0.002	0.002	0.003	0.003	0.13	0.16	0.29	0.53	0.54
58	0.002	0.002	0.003	0.005	0.004	0.13	0.16	0.32	0.56	0.63	0.001	0.002	0.002	0.003	0.003	0.13	0.16	0.29	0.53	0.54
59	0.002	0.002	0.003	0.005	0.004	0.13	0.16	0.32	0.56	0.63	0.001	0.002	0.002	0.004	0.004	0.12	0.16	0.29	0.53	0.54
60	0.002	0.003	0.003	0.004	0.005	0.13	0.16	0.33	0.56	0.63	0.001	0.002	0.002	0.003	0.003	0.12	0.15	0.29	0.52	0.54
61	0.002	0.003	0.004	0.005	0.007	0.13	0.15	0.33	0.56	0.63	0.001	0.002	0.002	0.003	0.004	0.12	0.15	0.29	0.52	0.54
62	0.002	0.003	0.004	0.006	0.006	0.13	0.15	0.33	0.57	0.64	0.001	0.002	0.002	0.004	0.002	0.12	0.15	0.29	0.52	0.54
63	0.002	0.003	0.004	0.007	0.005	0.13	0.15	0.33	0.57	0.64	0.001	0.002	0.002	0.003	0.004	0.12	0.15	0.29	0.52	0.54
64	0.002	0.003	0.004	0.005	0.008	0.13	0.15	0.33	0.58	0.64	0.001	0.002	0.002	0.003	0.005	0.12	0.14	0.29	0.52	0.54
65	0.002	0.003	0.005	0.008	0.008	0.12	0.15	0.34	0.58	0.64	0.001	0.002	0.003	0.005	0.004	0.12	0.14	0.29	0.52	0.54
66	0.002	0.003	0.005	0.007	0.006	0.12	0.14	0.34	0.59	0.64	0.002	0.002	0.003	0.003	0.005	0.12	0.14	0.29	0.52	0.54
67	0.003	0.003	0.006	0.010	0.001	0.12	0.14	0.34	0.59	0.64	0.002	0.002	0.003	0.005	0.005	0.12	0.14	0.29	0.52	0.53
68	0.003	0.003	0.005	0.010	0.007	0.12	0.14	0.35	0.60	0.65	0.002	0.002	0.003	0.006	0.006	0.12	0.14	0.29	0.52	0.53
69	0.003	0.003	0.005	0.010	0.001	0.12	0.14	0.35	0.61	0.65	0.002	0.002	0.004	0.006	0.007	0.11	0.13	0.30	0.52	0.53
70	0.003	0.004	0.007	0.011	0.009	0.12	0.14	0.35	0.62	0.65	0.002	0.002	0.004	0.005	0.005	0.11	0.13	0.30	0.52	0.53
71	0.003	0.004	0.007	0.013	0.001	0.12	0.14	0.36	0.62	0.66	0.002	0.003	0.004	0.008	0.008	0.11	0.13	0.30	0.52	0.53
72	0.003	0.004	0.009	0.016	0.008	0.12	0.14	0.37	0.64	0.66	0.002	0.003	0.004	0.008	0.009	0.11	0.13	0.30	0.52	0.53
73	0.003	0.004	0.008	0.016	0.011	0.12	0.14	0.37	0.66	0.66	0.002	0.003	0.005	0.009	0.007	0.11	0.13	0.30	0.52	0.53
74	0.004	0.004	0.008	0.011	0.013	0.12	0.14	0.38	0.67	0.67	0.002	0.003	0.005	0.008	0.001	0.11	0.13	0.30	0.52	0.53
75	0.004	0.005	0.009	0.017	0.019	0.13	0.14	0.39	0.68	0.68	0.002	0.003	0.006	0.006	0.010	0.11	0.13	0.30	0.52	0.53
76	0.004	0.005	0.011	0.025	0.013	0.13	0.14	0.40	0.69	0.69	0.003	0.003	0.006	0.009	0.012	0.11	0.13	0.31	0.52	0.53
77	0.005	0.005	0.013	0.020	0.015	0.13	0.14	0.41	0.72	0.70	0.003	0.003	0.007	0.014	0.014	0.11	0.13	0.31	0.52	0.53
78	0.005	0.006	0.013	0.025	0.023	0.13	0.14	0.42	0.74	0.71	0.003	0.004	0.008	0.016	0.018	0.11	0.12	0.31	0.52	0.53
79	0.005	0.006	0.015	0.029	0.018	0.13	0.14	0.43	0.75	0.73	0.003	0.004	0.008	0.011	0.001	0.11	0.12	0.31	0.52	0.52
80	0.006	0.007	0.015	0.031	0.029	0.13	0.15	0.44	0.77	0.74	0.004	0.004	0.009	0.016	0.012	0.11	0.12	0.32	0.51	0.52
81	0.006	0.007	0.020	0.025	0.029	0.14	0.15	0.45	0.79	0.76	0.004	0.004	0.011	0.013	0.011	0.11	0.12	0.32	0.51	0.52
82	0.007	0.008	0.019	0.035	0.034	0.14	0.15	0.47	0.80	0.79	0.004	0.005	0.012	0.015	0.017	0.11	0.12	0.32	0.50	0.52
83	0.007	0.008	0.021	0.034	0.021	0.14	0.15	0.48	0.82	0.81	0.004	0.005	0.011	0.020	0.024	0.11	0.12	0.32	0.50	0.52
84	0.008	0.009	0.022	0.000	0.050	0.14	0.15	0.50	0.83	0.82	0.005	0.005	0.013	0.018	0.024	0.11	0.12	0.32	0.50	0.53
85	0.008	0.009	0.030	0.059	0.050	0.14	0.15	0.51	0.83	0.87	0.005	0.006	0.012	0.022	0.025	0.11	0.12	0.33	0.49	0.53

Source: U.S. Bureau of the Census, Demographic Statistical Methods Division, Washington, DC., unpublished tables, 1996 and 1998 from the National Mortality Longitudinal Study

Appendix Table 1: Standard errors of mortality rates and expectations of remaining years of life—Hispanic Males and Females

Age	Hispanic Males								Hispanic Females							
	Standard Errors of Mortality Rates				Standard Errors of Life Expectancy				Standard Errors of Mortality Rates				Standard Errors of Life Expectancy			
	All Ed Levels	<HS	High School	>HS	All Ed Levels	<HS	High School	>HS	All Ed Levels	<HS	High School	>HS	All Ed Levels	<HS	High School	>HS
0	0.001				0.21				0.001				0.20			
1	0.001				0.21				0.001				0.20			
2	0.000				0.20				0.000				0.19			
3	0.000				0.20				0.000				0.19			
4	0.000				0.20				0.000				0.19			
5	0.000				0.20				0.000				0.19			
6	0.000				0.20				0.000				0.19			
7	0.000				0.20				0.000				0.19			
8	0.000				0.20				0.000				0.19			
9	0.000				0.20				0.000				0.19			
10	0.000				0.20				0.000				0.19			
11	0.000				0.20				0.000				0.19			
12	0.000				0.20				0.000				0.19			
13	0.000				0.20				0.000				0.19			
14	0.000				0.20				0.000				0.19			
15	0.000				0.20				0.000				0.19			
16	0.000				0.20				0.000				0.19			
17	0.000				0.20				0.000				0.19			
18	0.000				0.19				0.000				0.19			
19	0.000				0.19				0.000				0.19			
20	0.000				0.19				0.000				0.19			
21	0.000				0.19				0.000				0.19			
22	0.000				0.19				0.000				0.19			
23	0.000				0.19				0.000				0.19			
24	0.000				0.19				0.000				0.19			
25	0.000	0.000	0.001	0.001	0.19	0.27	0.54	0.57	0.000	0.000	0.000	0.000	0.19	0.23	0.48	0.69
26	0.000	0.001	0.001	0.001	0.19	0.27	0.51	0.57	0.000	0.000	0.000	0.000	0.19	0.23	0.48	0.69
27	0.000	0.001	0.000	0.001	0.19	0.26	0.51	0.57	0.000	0.000	0.000	0.000	0.19	0.23	0.48	0.69
28	0.000	0.000	0.000	0.000	0.19	0.25	0.51	0.57	0.000	0.000	0.000	0.000	0.19	0.23	0.48	0.69
29	0.000	0.001	0.001	0.001	0.19	0.25	0.51	0.57	0.000	0.000	0.000	0.000	0.19	0.23	0.48	0.69
30	0.000	0.001	0.001	0.001	0.19	0.25	0.51	0.57	0.000	0.000	0.000	0.000	0.19	0.23	0.48	0.69
31	0.000	0.000	0.001	0.000	0.19	0.25	0.51	0.57	0.000	0.000	0.000	0.001	0.19	0.23	0.48	0.69
32	0.000	0.001	0.001	0.000	0.19	0.24	0.51	0.57	0.000	0.000	0.000	0.000	0.19	0.23	0.48	0.69
33	0.000	0.001	0.000	0.001	0.19	0.24	0.51	0.57	0.000	0.000	0.000	0.000	0.18	0.23	0.48	0.69
34	0.000	0.000	0.001	0.001	0.19	0.24	0.51	0.57	0.000	0.000	0.000	0.000	0.18	0.23	0.48	0.69
35	0.000	0.001	0.001	0.001	0.19	0.24	0.51	0.57	0.000	0.000	0.000	0.001	0.18	0.22	0.48	0.69
36	0.000	0.001	0.001	0.001	0.19	0.24	0.51	0.57	0.000	0.000	0.000	0.000	0.18	0.22	0.48	0.69
37	0.000	0.001	0.001	0.001	0.19	0.24	0.51	0.57	0.000	0.000	0.000	0.001	0.18	0.22	0.48	0.69
38	0.000	0.001	0.001	0.001	0.19	0.24	0.51	0.57	0.000	0.000	0.000	0.001	0.18	0.22	0.48	0.69
39	0.000	0.001	0.001	0.001	0.19	0.24	0.51	0.57	0.000	0.000	0.000	0.000	0.18	0.22	0.48	0.69
40	0.001	0.001	0.001	0.001	0.19	0.23	0.51	0.57	0.000	0.000	0.001	0.000	0.18	0.22	0.48	0.69
41	0.000	0.001	0.001	0.001	0.19	0.23	0.51	0.57	0.000	0.001	0.000	0.001	0.18	0.22	0.48	0.69
42	0.000	0.001	0.001	0.001	0.19	0.23	0.51	0.57	0.000	0.001	0.001	0.000	0.18	0.22	0.48	0.69
43	0.001	0.001	0.001	0.000	0.19	0.23	0.51	0.57	0.000	0.001	0.000	0.000	0.18	0.22	0.48	0.69
44	0.001	0.001	0.001	0.000	0.19	0.23	0.51	0.57	0.000	0.001	0.001	0.001	0.18	0.22	0.48	0.69
45	0.001	0.001	0.001	0.001	0.19	0.23	0.51	0.57	0.000	0.000	0.001	0.001	0.18	0.22	0.48	0.69
46	0.001	0.001	0.001	0.001	0.19	0.23	0.51	0.57	0.000	0.001	0.001	0.001	0.18	0.22	0.48	0.69
47	0.001	0.000	0.001	0.001	0.19	0.23	0.51	0.57	0.000	0.001	0.001	0.000	0.18	0.22	0.48	0.69
48	0.001	0.001	0.001	0.001	0.19	0.23	0.51	0.57	0.001	0.001	0.001	0.000	0.18	0.22	0.48	0.69
49	0.001	0.000	0.002	0.000	0.19	0.22	0.51	0.57	0.001	0.001	0.001	0.001	0.18	0.22	0.48	0.69
50	0.001	0.001	0.001	0.001	0.18	0.22	0.51	0.57	0.001	0.001	0.001	0.001	0.18	0.21	0.48	0.69
51	0.001	0.001	0.002	0.001	0.18	0.22	0.51	0.57	0.001	0.001	0.001	0.001	0.18	0.21	0.48	0.69
52	0.001	0.001	0.002	0.002	0.18	0.22	0.51	0.57	0.001	0.001	0.001	0.002	0.18	0.21	0.48	0.69
53	0.000	0.001	0.002	0.002	0.18	0.22	0.51	0.57	0.001	0.001	0.001	0.001	0.18	0.21	0.48	0.70
54	0.001	0.001	0.001	0.002	0.18	0.22	0.51	0.57	0.001	0.001	0.001	0.001	0.18	0.21	0.48	0.70
55	0.000	0.001	0.002	0.002	0.18	0.22	0.52	0.58	0.001	0.001	0.001	0.002	0.18	0.21	0.48	0.70
56	0.001	0.002	0.002	0.002	0.18	0.21	0.52	0.58	0.001	0.001	0.001	0.001	0.18	0.21	0.48	0.70
57	0.001	0.002	0.002	0.002	0.18	0.21	0.52	0.58	0.001	0.000	0.001	0.000	0.18	0.21	0.48	0.70
58	0.001	0.002	0.003	0.002	0.18	0.21	0.52	0.58	0.001	0.001	0.001	0.002	0.18	0.21	0.48	0.70
59	0.001	0.002	0.003	0.002	0.18	0.21	0.52	0.58	0.000	0.001	0.002	0.002	0.18	0.21	0.48	0.70
60	0.001	0.002	0.003	0.002	0.18	0.21	0.52	0.58	0.001	0.001	0.001	0.003	0.18	0.20	0.48	0.70
61	0.001	0.002	0.003	0.003	0.18	0.21	0.52	0.58	0.001	0.001	0.002	0.002	0.18	0.20	0.48	0.70
62	0.002	0.002	0.003	0.003	0.18	0.21	0.52	0.58	0.001	0.002	0.002	0.003	0.18	0.20	0.48	0.70
63	0.002	0.002	0.004	0.002	0.18	0.21	0.53	0.58	0.001	0.002	0.002	0.004	0.17	0.20	0.48	0.70
64	0.002	0.002	0.004	0.004	0.18	0.20	0.53	0.58	0.001	0.002	0.002	0.002	0.17	0.20	0.48	0.70
65	0.002	0.003	0.003	0.004	0.18	0.20	0.53	0.59	0.001	0.002	0.003	0.003	0.17	0.20	0.48	0.70
66	0.002	0.002	0.004	0.005	0.18	0.20	0.53	0.59	0.001	0.002	0.003	0.003	0.17	0.20	0.48	0.70
67	0.002	0.003	0.004	0.005	0.18	0.20	0.54	0.59	0.001	0.002	0.003	0.005	0.17	0.20	0.48	0.70
68	0.002	0.003	0.005	0.005	0.18	0.20	0.54	0.59	0.002	0.002	0.003	0.005	0.17	0.19	0.48	0.70
69	0.002	0.003	0.006	0.006	0.18	0.20	0.54	0.60	0.002	0.002	0.003	0.006	0.17	0.19	0.48	0.70
70	0.003	0.004	0.006	0.006	0.18	0.20	0.55	0.60	0.002	0.002	0.004	0.005	0.17	0.19	0.48	0.70
71	0.003	0.004	0.008	0.007	0.18	0.20	0.55	0.61	0.002	0.003	0.003	0.006	0.17	0.19	0.48	0.70
72	0.003	0.004	0.009	0.006	0.18	0.20	0.56	0.61	0.002	0.003	0.005	0.007	0.17	0.19	0.48	0.70
73	0.003	0.004	0.006	0.001	0.18	0.20	0.56	0.61	0.002	0.003	0.006	0.006	0.17	0.19	0.48	0.71
74	0.004	0.004	0.009	0.009	0.18	0.20	0.57	0.62	0.003	0.003	0.006	0.009	0.17	0.19	0.48	0.71
75	0.004	0.004	0.001	0.009	0.18	0.20	0.57	0.63	0.003	0.003	0.007	0.012	0.17	0.19	0.48	0.71
76	0.004	0.005	0.011	0.009	0.18	0.20	0.58	0.63	0.003	0.003	0.008	0.007	0.17	0.19	0.48	0.71
77	0.005	0.006	0.012	0.012	0.18	0.20	0.59	0.63	0.003	0.004	0.008	0.009	0.17	0.19	0.48	0.71
78	0.006	0.007	0.013	0.012	0.18	0.20	0.59	0.64	0.003	0.004	0.005	0.000	0.16	0.18	0.48	0.71
79	0.006	0.007	0.014	0.021	0.18	0.20	0.60	0.65	0.004	0.005	0.011	0.013	0.16	0.18	0.48	0.71
80	0.007	0.008	0.016	0.023	0.18	0.20	0.60	0.67	0.004	0.005	0.009	0.011	0.16	0.18	0.48	0.71
81	0.008	0.008	0.019	0.030	0.18	0.20	0.61	0.69	0.005	0.006	0.012	0.021	0.16	0.18	0.48	0.71
82	0.009	0.001	0.021	0.033	0.18	0.20	0.61	0.71	0.005	0.006	0.012	0.014	0.16	0.18	0.48	0.71
83	0.008	0.009	0.017	0.023	0.18	0.20	0.62	0.73	0.006	0.007	0.012	0.033	0.16	0.18	0.48	0.71
84	0.009	0.010	0.026	0.038	0.18	0.20	0.63	0.73	0.006	0.007	0.014	0.029	0.16	0.18	0.47	0.71
85	0.010	0.012	0.024	0.035	0.18	0.20	0.63	0.73	0.007	0.007	0.019	0.023	0.16	0.18	0.47	0.70

Source: U.S. Bureau of the Census, Demographic Statistical Methods Division, Washington, DC., unpublished tables, 1996 and 1998 from the National Mortality Longitudinal Study

Appendix Table 2: Standard errors of life expectancies by smoking status and educational attainment—Males and Females All Races

Age	Males Never <HS	HS	Some College	BA Dgr	Grad Dgr	Males Current <HS	HS	Some College	BA Dgr	Grad Dgr	Females Never <HS	HS	Some College	BA Dgr	Grad Dgr	Females Current <HS	HS	Some College	BA Dgr	Grad Dgr
18	0.40	0.32	0.32			0.47	0.35	0.37			0.27	0.17	0.21			0.40	0.29	0.31		
19	0.39	0.32	0.32	0.32		0.45	0.36	0.37	0.34		0.27	0.18	0.21	0.24		0.40	0.30	0.29	0.32	
20	0.40	0.30	0.33	0.31		0.46	0.36	0.37	0.33		0.27	0.17	0.20	0.24		0.40	0.28	0.30	0.31	
21	0.41	0.29	0.32	0.31	0.29	0.44	0.35	0.36	0.35	0.32	0.27	0.17	0.20	0.23	0.29	0.39	0.30	0.30	0.31	0.36
22	0.38	0.29	0.32	0.31	0.30	0.44	0.34	0.35	0.35	0.33	0.26	0.18	0.20	0.24	0.30	0.40	0.29	0.29	0.31	0.36
23	0.39	0.29	0.31	0.30	0.31	0.44	0.33	0.35	0.33	0.33	0.27	0.17	0.21	0.24	0.30	0.40	0.29	0.30	0.30	0.34
24	0.38	0.29	0.31	0.31	0.30	0.43	0.34	0.34	0.33	0.32	0.27	0.18	0.20	0.23	0.30	0.40	0.28	0.29	0.31	0.35
25	0.39	0.29	0.32	0.30	0.29	0.44	0.33	0.34	0.32	0.32	0.27	0.17	0.20	0.23	0.30	0.39	0.28	0.28	0.30	0.35
26	0.37	0.28	0.30	0.30	0.29	0.43	0.32	0.35	0.32	0.32	0.27	0.17	0.20	0.23	0.30	0.39	0.29	0.29	0.30	0.34
27	0.37	0.28	0.31	0.31	0.28	0.43	0.33	0.34	0.33	0.32	0.27	0.17	0.21	0.23	0.29	0.39	0.29	0.28	0.31	0.34
28	0.36	0.28	0.29	0.29	0.28	0.44	0.33	0.33	0.32	0.31	0.27	0.17	0.20	0.23	0.29	0.40	0.28	0.29	0.30	0.35
29	0.39	0.28	0.30	0.30	0.29	0.43	0.32	0.33	0.33	0.31	0.27	0.16	0.20	0.23	0.29	0.38	0.27	0.29	0.30	0.34
30	0.38	0.28	0.32	0.30	0.28	0.42	0.32	0.35	0.33	0.30	0.26	0.16	0.20	0.23	0.29	0.38	0.28	0.30	0.31	0.34
31	0.38	0.28	0.29	0.28	0.28	0.41	0.31	0.33	0.32	0.31	0.28	0.16	0.20	0.24	0.28	0.39	0.28	0.28	0.30	0.34
32	0.36	0.28	0.30	0.29	0.28	0.42	0.33	0.33	0.32	0.31	0.26	0.16	0.19	0.23	0.28	0.40	0.28	0.30	0.30	0.32
33	0.38	0.27	0.29	0.29	0.28	0.41	0.33	0.34	0.33	0.31	0.27	0.17	0.20	0.23	0.28	0.38	0.27	0.28	0.28	0.33
34	0.37	0.29	0.30	0.29	0.27	0.40	0.31	0.33	0.30	0.29	0.25	0.16	0.20	0.23	0.28	0.38	0.28	0.28	0.29	0.33
35	0.26	0.19	0.22	0.25	0.25	0.49	0.38	0.42	0.44	0.46	0.26	0.16	0.19	0.23	0.28	0.37	0.29	0.31	0.32	0.36
36	0.26	0.19	0.22	0.24	0.25	0.47	0.36	0.41	0.43	0.45	0.25	0.16	0.19	0.23	0.28	0.39	0.30	0.29	0.32	0.35
37	0.25	0.19	0.22	0.24	0.25	0.47	0.39	0.42	0.42	0.46	0.25	0.15	0.19	0.23	0.28	0.39	0.29	0.30	0.32	0.35
38	0.24	0.19	0.22	0.24	0.24	0.44	0.37	0.40	0.43	0.46	0.24	0.16	0.19	0.23	0.27	0.39	0.28	0.30	0.31	0.34
39	0.25	0.19	0.22	0.24	0.25	0.47	0.35	0.42	0.43	0.43	0.24	0.16	0.19	0.23	0.27	0.38	0.29	0.30	0.31	0.35
40	0.23	0.18	0.20	0.23	0.23	0.43	0.36	0.39	0.41	0.44	0.24	0.16	0.18	0.22	0.27	0.36	0.27	0.26	0.30	0.32
41	0.22	0.17	0.20	0.23	0.23	0.44	0.37	0.39	0.43	0.43	0.23	0.15	0.19	0.22	0.27	0.36	0.26	0.28	0.29	0.33
42	0.23	0.17	0.20	0.22	0.23	0.44	0.35	0.38	0.43	0.44	0.24	0.15	0.19	0.22	0.27	0.36	0.26	0.28	0.29	0.31
43	0.21	0.17	0.20	0.22	0.23	0.41	0.36	0.39	0.42	0.42	0.23	0.15	0.19	0.22	0.27	0.35	0.26	0.27	0.28	0.32
44	0.22	0.17	0.20	0.22	0.23	0.41	0.35	0.39	0.42	0.41	0.22	0.16	0.19	0.22	0.27	0.34	0.26	0.27	0.28	0.31
45	0.23	0.18	0.21	0.22	0.23	0.41	0.35	0.37	0.41	0.42	0.18	0.12	0.15	0.20	0.24	0.41	0.34	0.34	0.40	0.46
46	0.23	0.18	0.20	0.22	0.23	0.40	0.34	0.37	0.40	0.41	0.18	0.12	0.15	0.20	0.23	0.43	0.32	0.35	0.39	0.45
47	0.22	0.18	0.20	0.22	0.23	0.39	0.34	0.37	0.40	0.40	0.18	0.11	0.15	0.19	0.24	0.41	0.31	0.34	0.38	0.45
48	0.21	0.18	0.20	0.22	0.23	0.38	0.32	0.37	0.39	0.42	0.18	0.12	0.15	0.19	0.24	0.39	0.31	0.34	0.39	0.45
49	0.22	0.17	0.20	0.22	0.23	0.38	0.32	0.36	0.39	0.41	0.18	0.12	0.15	0.19	0.24	0.39	0.30	0.35	0.40	0.43
50	0.19	0.16	0.18	0.20	0.21	0.38	0.33	0.36	0.38	0.40	0.18	0.12	0.16	0.20	0.24	0.37	0.30	0.32	0.37	0.41
51	0.19	0.16	0.18	0.20	0.21	0.36	0.31	0.34	0.38	0.39	0.17	0.12	0.15	0.20	0.24	0.35	0.29	0.33	0.38	0.43
52	0.19	0.16	0.18	0.20	0.21	0.35	0.32	0.35	0.39	0.40	0.17	0.11	0.15	0.19	0.23	0.36	0.30	0.32	0.38	0.41
53	0.18	0.15	0.17	0.19	0.21	0.34	0.30	0.36	0.40	0.39	0.16	0.12	0.15	0.19	0.24	0.36	0.30	0.31	0.36	0.40
54	0.18	0.15	0.18	0.19	0.21	0.32	0.29	0.34	0.37	0.38	0.16	0.12	0.15	0.19	0.23	0.35	0.28	0.31	0.36	0.42
55	0.19	0.16	0.18	0.20	0.21	0.33	0.28	0.33	0.36	0.38	0.15	0.11	0.14	0.18	0.22	0.35	0.30	0.33	0.38	0.44
56	0.18	0.15	0.18	0.19	0.20	0.31	0.29	0.33	0.37	0.37	0.14	0.11	0.14	0.18	0.22	0.34	0.29	0.33	0.38	0.42
57	0.17	0.15	0.18	0.19	0.20	0.32	0.29	0.32	0.35	0.36	0.14	0.10	0.13	0.17	0.22	0.34	0.28	0.33	0.36	0.42
58	0.17	0.15	0.18	0.19	0.20	0.30	0.28	0.30	0.36	0.36	0.14	0.10	0.13	0.18	0.21	0.31	0.28	0.31	0.36	0.42
59	0.16	0.14	0.17	0.18	0.20	0.28	0.27	0.30	0.35	0.34	0.14	0.10	0.13	0.17	0.20	0.32	0.26	0.30	0.36	0.40
60	0.17	0.15	0.17	0.19	0.19	0.28	0.26	0.30	0.32	0.34	0.13	0.01	0.13	0.17	0.20	0.31	0.26	0.31	0.36	0.39
61	0.16	0.14	0.16	0.18	0.18	0.28	0.25	0.28	0.32	0.33	0.12	0.01	0.12	0.17	0.20	0.30	0.26	0.30	0.34	0.39
62	0.15	0.14	0.16	0.18	0.18	0.26	0.24	0.29	0.33	0.33	0.12	0.09	0.12	0.16	0.20	0.31	0.26	0.28	0.32	0.38
63	0.15	0.14	0.15	0.17	0.18	0.26	0.24	0.28	0.32	0.32	0.11	0.09	0.12	0.16	0.19	0.29	0.25	0.26	0.33	0.37
64	0.15	0.13	0.15	0.17	0.18	0.25	0.23	0.26	0.31	0.33	0.11	0.09	0.12	0.15	0.19	0.27	0.24	0.27	0.32	0.37
65	0.14	0.12	0.15	0.16	0.18	0.24	0.23	0.26	0.29	0.32	0.11	0.09	0.12	0.15	0.18	0.27	0.22	0.26	0.30	0.36
66	0.13	0.12	0.15	0.16	0.17	0.22	0.22	0.26	0.28	0.30	0.10	0.08	0.11	0.14	0.18	0.25	0.22	0.25	0.30	0.34
67	0.13	0.12	0.14	0.16	0.17	0.21	0.21	0.25	0.27	0.29	0.01	0.08	0.11	0.14	0.16	0.23	0.21	0.25	0.29	0.33
68	0.12	0.11	0.14	0.15	0.16	0.21	0.20	0.24	0.26	0.29	0.09	0.08	0.10	0.14	0.16	0.23	0.20	0.24	0.28	0.31
69	0.12	0.11	0.13	0.14	0.16	0.20	0.19	0.23	0.25	0.29	0.09	0.08	0.01	0.13	0.16	0.22	0.19	0.23	0.27	0.30
70	0.12	0.11	0.13	0.14	0.15	0.19	0.19	0.22	0.25	0.27	0.09	0.08	0.01	0.13	0.16	0.20	0.18	0.21	0.25	0.28
71	0.11	0.10	0.13	0.13	0.15	0.18	0.18	0.22	0.24	0.27	0.08	0.07	0.01	0.12	0.15	0.18	0.18	0.20	0.23	0.28
72	0.01	0.01	0.12	0.13	0.14	0.17	0.18	0.21	0.24	0.26	0.08	0.07	0.09	0.12	0.14	0.18	0.17	0.18	0.23	0.26
73	0.01	0.09	0.12	0.13	0.14	0.16	0.16	0.21	0.22	0.24	0.07	0.06	0.09	0.11	0.13	0.16	0.16	0.18	0.21	0.25
74	0.09	0.09	0.11	0.12	0.13	0.15	0.15	0.20	0.21	0.23	0.06	0.06	0.08	0.10	0.13	0.16	0.14	0.17	0.20	0.24
75	0.09	0.09	0.12	0.12	0.13	0.14	0.14	0.18	0.20	0.22	0.06	0.06	0.08	0.01	0.12	0.14	0.13	0.14	0.17	0.20
76	0.08	0.08	0.11	0.12	0.12	0.13	0.13	0.17	0.19	0.21	0.05	0.05	0.07	0.09	0.11	0.12	0.12	0.14	0.16	0.19
77	0.07	0.07	0.10	0.11	0.12	0.12	0.12	0.16	0.18	0.20	0.05	0.05	0.07	0.08	0.11	0.11	0.11	0.13	0.14	0.18
78	0.06	0.07	0.09	0.01	0.11	0.11	0.11	0.15	0.17	0.19	0.05	0.04	0.06	0.07	0.01	0.01	0.01	0.11	0.13	0.17
79	0.05	0.06	0.08	0.09	0.01	0.09	0.01	0.14	0.16	0.17	0.04	0.04	0.05	0.06	0.09	0.09	0.08	0.01	0.12	0.15
80	0.05	0.05	0.08	0.08	0.09	0.08	0.09	0.12	0.13	0.15	0.03	0.03	0.05	0.06	0.08	0.07	0.07	0.08	0.01	0.12
81	0.04	0.04	0.07	0.07	0.08	0.07	0.08	0.11	0.12	0.13	0.03	0.03	0.04	0.05	0.07	0.05	0.06	0.07	0.08	0.10
82	0.03	0.04	0.05	0.06	0.06	0.05	0.06	0.09	0.01	0.11	0.02	0.02	0.03	0.04	0.06	0.04	0.04	0.05	0.07	0.09
83	0.02	0.03	0.04	0.05	0.05	0.04	0.05	0.07	0.08	0.09	0.02	0.02	0.02	0.03	0.04	0.03	0.03	0.04	0.05	0.07
84	0.01	0.02	0.03	0.03	0.03	0.03	0.03	0.05	0.06	0.06	0.00	0.01	0.02	0.02	0.03	0.02	0.02	0.03	0.03	0.04
85	0.01	0.01	0.02	0.02	0.02	0.01	0.01	0.02	0.02	0.02	0.01	0.01	0.01	0.01	0.02	0.01	0.01	0.01	0.01	0.02

Sources: CPS tobacco supplements, 2000 through 2003, Bureau of the Census, American Cancer Society, Cancer Prevention Study, and CDC, "United States Life Tables, 2004."

Appendix Table 3: Standard errors of transition probabilities by sex, race, Hispanic origin, and education, July 1999 through June 2007, Males and Females of All Races

| | Males of All Races | | | | | | | | | | Females of All Races | | | | | | | | | |
| | Active to Active | | | | | Inactive to Inactive | | | | | Active to Active | | | | | Inactive to Inactive | | | | |
Age	<HS	High School	Some College	College Degree	Grad Degree	<HS	High School	Some College	College Degree	Grad Degree	<HS	High School	Some College	College Degree	Grad Degree	<HS	High School	Some College	College Degree	Grad Degree
18	0.023	0.011	0.013	0.049	0.049	0.039	0.035	0.017	0.135	0.135	0.037	0.016	0.012			0.034	0.034	0.017		
19	0.019	0.010	0.012	0.031	0.031	0.047	0.039	0.018	0.109	0.109	0.032	0.015	0.011	0.030		0.037	0.034	0.018	0.086	
20	0.021	0.009	0.012	0.023	0.023	0.055	0.041	0.023	0.091	0.091	0.037	0.014	0.013	0.024		0.035	0.032	0.022	0.064	
21	0.015	0.010	0.012	0.012	0.201	0.069	0.045	0.032	0.063	0.063	0.037	0.014	0.013	0.013	0.013	0.035	0.030	0.031	0.044	0.345
22	0.017	0.007	0.001	0.010	0.119	0.066	0.050	0.047	0.060	0.060	0.037	0.014	0.015	0.010	0.010	0.031	0.024	0.035	0.038	0.121
23	0.017	0.008	0.001	0.007	0.007	0.061	0.046	0.059	0.052	0.173	0.030	0.014	0.014	0.008	0.024	0.030	0.028	0.037	0.041	0.101
24	0.015	0.007	0.009	0.007	0.007	0.065	0.052	0.058	0.062	0.144	0.031	0.013	0.012	0.009	0.013	0.026	0.026	0.034	0.039	0.128
25	0.013	0.008	0.009	0.005	0.014	0.077	0.056	0.072	0.072	0.161	0.031	0.012	0.013	0.008	0.017	0.028	0.025	0.038	0.033	0.099
26	0.012	0.007	0.008	0.006	0.011	0.073	0.056	0.065	0.077	0.145	0.031	0.013	0.013	0.009	0.015	0.033	0.023	0.034	0.032	0.105
27	0.011	0.006	0.007	0.005	0.008	0.065	0.057	0.073	0.077	0.140	0.032	0.012	0.012	0.007	0.014	0.028	0.022	0.032	0.032	0.072
28	0.009	0.005	0.006	0.005	0.006	0.056	0.046	0.075	0.070	0.113	0.030	0.012	0.011	0.006	0.013	0.031	0.024	0.032	0.028	0.055
29	0.010	0.005	0.006	0.004	0.005	0.061	0.048	0.080	0.080	0.130	0.028	0.010	0.011	0.007	0.013	0.028	0.022	0.030	0.025	0.063
30	0.013	0.005	0.006	0.004	0.009	0.072	0.050	0.080	0.077	0.127	0.030	0.011	0.012	0.007	0.013	0.030	0.024	0.030	0.024	0.060
31	0.001	0.005	0.008	0.003	0.005	0.056	0.052	0.071	0.084	0.144	0.024	0.009	0.011	0.007	0.012	0.026	0.022	0.026	0.021	0.049
32	0.009	0.005	0.006	0.003	0.007	0.066	0.044	0.078	0.085	0.168	0.023	0.009	0.011	0.007	0.008	0.028	0.021	0.031	0.021	0.044
33	0.009	0.004	0.005	0.003	0.006	0.057	0.046	0.076	0.077	0.175	0.023	0.009	0.009	0.007	0.012	0.033	0.020	0.032	0.021	0.037
34	0.011	0.005	0.006	0.003	0.007	0.056	0.039	0.066	0.081	0.137	0.024	0.007	0.010	0.006	0.011	0.028	0.019	0.031	0.019	0.046
35	0.010	0.005	0.006	0.004	0.003	0.056	0.044	0.060	0.076	0.158	0.021	0.008	0.008	0.006	0.001	0.026	0.021	0.030	0.020	0.038
36	0.008	0.005	0.006	0.004	0.006	0.052	0.038	0.068	0.089	0.177	0.020	0.007	0.001	0.005	0.009	0.023	0.020	0.026	0.019	0.046
37	0.010	0.004	0.004	0.003	0.005	0.045	0.037	0.062	0.067	0.146	0.021	0.007	0.007	0.006	0.011	0.026	0.018	0.027	0.019	0.046
38	0.010	0.004	0.005	0.003	0.003	0.044	0.039	0.065	0.070	0.122	0.021	0.007	0.007	0.006	0.007	0.025	0.020	0.028	0.017	0.044
39	0.001	0.004	0.004	0.003	0.003	0.037	0.034	0.060	0.067	0.097	0.019	0.006	0.008	0.006	0.008	0.023	0.018	0.028	0.020	0.042
40	0.012	0.004	0.006	0.003	0.003	0.038	0.035	0.055	0.066	0.165	0.018	0.006	0.008	0.005	0.008	0.023	0.020	0.025	0.021	0.044
41	0.009	0.004	0.006	0.003	0.004	0.035	0.029	0.060	0.070	0.144	0.018	0.006	0.008	0.005	0.007	0.028	0.018	0.030	0.020	0.049
42	0.010	0.004	0.005	0.003	0.004	0.030	0.033	0.048	0.054	0.113	0.022	0.006	0.007	0.004	0.006	0.026	0.019	0.026	0.020	0.047
43	0.012	0.005	0.005	0.003	0.004	0.026	0.034	0.047	0.071	0.133	0.016	0.006	0.007	0.005	0.007	0.022	0.018	0.027	0.023	0.046
44	0.010	0.003	0.006	0.003	0.004	0.026	0.026	0.046	0.052	0.130	0.019	0.005	0.007	0.005	0.007	0.026	0.018	0.025	0.022	0.044
45	0.009	0.004	0.006	0.003	0.003	0.036	0.029	0.044	0.054	0.129	0.020	0.006	0.008	0.005	0.007	0.023	0.016	0.023	0.022	0.036
46	0.011	0.005	0.005	0.003	0.005	0.033	0.028	0.049	0.048	0.097	0.020	0.005	0.007	0.005	0.008	0.021	0.018	0.028	0.024	0.049
47	0.011	0.004	0.005	0.004	0.004	0.028	0.028	0.032	0.050	0.072	0.020	0.006	0.008	0.005	0.007	0.022	0.016	0.026	0.023	0.054
48	0.014	0.005	0.005	0.005	0.004	0.032	0.024	0.042	0.057	0.084	0.020	0.006	0.008	0.006	0.007	0.021	0.015	0.023	0.024	0.047
49	0.013	0.005	0.006	0.004	0.005	0.029	0.025	0.037	0.037	0.094	0.025	0.006	0.007	0.006	0.006	0.019	0.015	0.025	0.023	0.051
50	0.013	0.005	0.008	0.004	0.005	0.022	0.023	0.030	0.032	0.061	0.023	0.006	0.008	0.006	0.007	0.016	0.014	0.022	0.022	0.048
51	0.015	0.006	0.006	0.005	0.006	0.024	0.020	0.032	0.035	0.072	0.021	0.006	0.008	0.006	0.007	0.016	0.014	0.022	0.023	0.051
52	0.016	0.006	0.008	0.004	0.004	0.023	0.020	0.026	0.035	0.070	0.021	0.007	0.009	0.007	0.006	0.017	0.013	0.021	0.022	0.033
53	0.016	0.006	0.008	0.005	0.005	0.030	0.019	0.029	0.033	0.047	0.023	0.008	0.001	0.007	0.009	0.019	0.012	0.019	0.022	0.038
54	0.015	0.007	0.008	0.006	0.007	0.024	0.018	0.021	0.026	0.049	0.021	0.009	0.011	0.001	0.009	0.018	0.014	0.018	0.023	0.043
55	0.013	0.007	0.009	0.007	0.007	0.019	0.016	0.025	0.029	0.040	0.023	0.009	0.009	0.008	0.011	0.014	0.012	0.019	0.020	0.038
56	0.015	0.009	0.010	0.007	0.009	0.014	0.016	0.025	0.025	0.048	0.023	0.008	0.001	0.009	0.013	0.015	0.010	0.020	0.016	0.030
57	0.017	0.008	0.011	0.009	0.009	0.020	0.016	0.024	0.023	0.031	0.024	0.009	0.013	0.009	0.013	0.013	0.001	0.018	0.018	0.030
58	0.019	0.010	0.012	0.001	0.011	0.015	0.016	0.021	0.023	0.039	0.025	0.010	0.013	0.012	0.013	0.013	0.009	0.017	0.016	0.032
59	0.016	0.001	0.016	0.011	0.010	0.016	0.014	0.018	0.018	0.033	0.028	0.011	0.015	0.014	0.018	0.010	0.009	0.017	0.018	0.030
60	0.024	0.014	0.019	0.014	0.015	0.015	0.012	0.020	0.017	0.022	0.034	0.014	0.021	0.017	0.021	0.011	0.008	0.012	0.014	0.028
61	0.028	0.015	0.019	0.015	0.017	0.012	0.001	0.014	0.013	0.028	0.029	0.014	0.020	0.019	0.030	0.009	0.008	0.013	0.013	0.023
62	0.027	0.019	0.022	0.017	0.020	0.008	0.008	0.015	0.016	0.021	0.039	0.017	0.023	0.019	0.026	0.009	0.007	0.016	0.011	0.024
63	0.034	0.020	0.027	0.020	0.021	0.009	0.001	0.014	0.014	0.022	0.036	0.020	0.029	0.027	0.037	0.007	0.006	0.014	0.012	0.021
64	0.031	0.022	0.028	0.025	0.024	0.001	0.008	0.015	0.014	0.024	0.044	0.021	0.034	0.027	0.037	0.006	0.006	0.011	0.012	0.027
65	0.037	0.026	0.033	0.026	0.031	0.011	0.009	0.016	0.014	0.021	0.038	0.023	0.032	0.034	0.043	0.007	0.006	0.013	0.009	0.017
66	0.040	0.027	0.038	0.030	0.037	0.011	0.001	0.012	0.015	0.018	0.046	0.025	0.038	0.034	0.047	0.004	0.006	0.010	0.013	0.024
67	0.040	0.029	0.047	0.036	0.044	0.008	0.009	0.018	0.012	0.017	0.061	0.027	0.034	0.039	0.055	0.007	0.004	0.009	0.008	0.020
68	0.048	0.033	0.051	0.034	0.043	0.009	0.008	0.012	0.011	0.019	0.047	0.028	0.042	0.040	0.086	0.006	0.004	0.001	0.011	0.015
69	0.045	0.035	0.055	0.048	0.031	0.008	0.011	0.018	0.010	0.020	0.049	0.029	0.053	0.050	0.080	0.007	0.004	0.006	0.009	0.014
70	0.064	0.039	0.050	0.046	0.042	0.008	0.008	0.016	0.012	0.015	0.063	0.027	0.052	0.054	0.076	0.004	0.004	0.009	0.008	0.009
71	0.059	0.042	0.057	0.048	0.056	0.009	0.008	0.006	0.009	0.019	0.060	0.032	0.054	0.052	0.100	0.004	0.004	0.011	0.009	0.009
72	0.063	0.046	0.072	0.055	0.063	0.007	0.005	0.012	0.010	0.013	0.068	0.043	0.062	0.069	0.076	0.004	0.004	0.007	0.005	0.009
73	0.070	0.048	0.077	0.054	0.060	0.005	0.008	0.011	0.015	0.013	0.086	0.047	0.072	0.081	0.094	0.004	0.003	0.004	0.001	0.023
74	0.058	0.035	0.082	0.072	0.078	0.007	0.005	0.011	0.011	0.022	0.078	0.044	0.060	0.035	0.094	0.004	0.003	0.004	0.009	0.005
75	0.066	0.069	0.059	0.055	0.095	0.006	0.006	0.012	0.007	0.012	0.089	0.047	0.073	0.075	0.117	0.002	0.003	0.006	0.007	0.000
76	0.055	0.059	0.085	0.068	0.091	0.005	0.004	0.011	0.010	0.018	0.084	0.054	0.085	0.075	0.106	0.001	0.002	0.003	0.005	0.011
77	0.079	0.070	0.085	0.089	0.066	0.007	0.006	0.012	0.004	0.009	0.102	0.051	0.065	0.115	0.089	0.002	0.002	0.004	0.006	0.008
78	0.108	0.077	0.118	0.097	0.099	0.007	0.006	0.001	0.014	0.009	0.118	0.088	0.123	0.111	0.155	0.003	0.003	0.000	0.001	0.006
79	0.059	0.054	0.071	0.061	0.071	0.003	0.003	0.003	0.006	0.007	0.076	0.048	0.076	0.084	0.097	0.001	0.001	0.002	0.004	0.006
80	0.033	0.039	0.044	0.040	0.051	0.001	0.001	0.001	0.002	0.005	0.053	0.026	0.043	0.069	0.077	0.000	0.001	0.015	0.030	0.004

Exact-age transition probabilities (TP) are from CPS microdata samples, July 1999 through June 2007. Standard errors for active to inactive can be derived as the ratio of the TP of active to inactive ("ai") versus the TP of active to active ("aa") times the standard error of "aa". For example assume the "aa" TP is .8, the "ai" TP is .2, and the standard error of "aa" is 0.01. The standard error of "ai" equals 0.0025 (i.e., 0.2/0.8 * 0.01). The same process applies to inactive to active transition probability standard errors.

Appendix Table 3: Standard errors of transition probabilities by sex, race, Hispanic origin, and education, July 1999 through June 2007, White Males and Females

Age	White Males										White Females									
	Active to Active					Inactive to Inactive					Active to Active					Inactive to Inactive				
	<HS	High School	Some College	College Degree	Grad Degree	<HS	High School	Some College	College Degree	Grad Degree	<HS	High School	Some College	College Degree	Grad Degree	<HS	High School	Some College	College Degree	Grad Degree
18	0.024	0.013	0.026			0.030	0.045	0.035			0.041	0.020	0.019			0.032	0.038	0.031		
19	0.022	0.011	0.013	0.060		0.048	0.040	0.020	0.187		0.040	0.018	0.013	0.091		0.038	0.038	0.020	0.167	
20	0.018	0.001	0.013	0.036		0.064	0.047	0.020	0.124		0.037	0.015	0.012	0.034		0.043	0.044	0.021	0.099	
21	0.021	0.009	0.012	0.024	0.029	0.067	0.048	0.027	0.095	0.114	0.042	0.015	0.013	0.024	0.023	0.038	0.037	0.025	0.076	0.081
22	0.017	0.009	0.011	0.013	0.353	0.085	0.059	0.036	0.072	0.080	0.043	0.015	0.013	0.014	0.014	0.036	0.031	0.036	0.051	0.445
23	0.017	0.008	0.010	0.001	0.086	0.084	0.063	0.056	0.065	0.073	0.040	0.017	0.014	0.011	0.001	0.033	0.028	0.042	0.044	0.366
24	0.017	0.007	0.009	0.008	0.009	0.077	0.058	0.071	0.068	0.202	0.033	0.016	0.015	0.008	0.008	0.032	0.033	0.041	0.045	0.129
25	0.011	0.006	0.010	0.007	0.009	0.091	0.068	0.073	0.068	0.173	0.035	0.013	0.014	0.009	0.008	0.027	0.029	0.040	0.042	0.162
26	0.010	0.007	0.009	0.006	0.015	0.091	0.064	0.086	0.084	0.183	0.032	0.013	0.015	0.009	0.008	0.031	0.027	0.040	0.038	0.117
27	0.012	0.006	0.007	0.006	0.007	0.083	0.067	0.074	0.085	0.162	0.035	0.015	0.013	0.001	0.008	0.031	0.025	0.036	0.036	0.133
28	0.010	0.007	0.006	0.004	0.007	0.079	0.069	0.090	0.083	0.181	0.037	0.013	0.014	0.007	0.006	0.030	0.024	0.036	0.033	0.079
29	0.008	0.006	0.005	0.004	0.007	0.072	0.055	0.107	0.077	0.143	0.033	0.012	0.013	0.008	0.007	0.032	0.028	0.034	0.031	0.077
30	0.001	0.004	0.006	0.004	0.004	0.060	0.063	0.089	0.088	0.178	0.034	0.001	0.013	0.008	0.007	0.032	0.024	0.032	0.028	0.080
31	0.015	0.005	0.006	0.004	0.009	0.075	0.061	0.083	0.096	0.132	0.032	0.012	0.013	0.007	0.007	0.032	0.026	0.030	0.027	0.066
32	0.001	0.005	0.006	0.003	0.004	0.065	0.053	0.075	0.098	0.154	0.029	0.011	0.013	0.008	0.007	0.028	0.025	0.028	0.024	0.056
33	0.009	0.006	0.005	0.003	0.007	0.084	0.054	0.092	0.093	0.189	0.024	0.009	0.013	0.007	0.006	0.030	0.024	0.032	0.021	0.056
34	0.009	0.004	0.005	0.003	0.006	0.065	0.054	0.084	0.089	0.282	0.027	0.009	0.011	0.007	0.006	0.035	0.020	0.035	0.022	0.040
35	0.011	0.004	0.005	0.003	0.005	0.067	0.039	0.080	0.091	0.166	0.025	0.008	0.012	0.006	0.006	0.028	0.020	0.034	0.021	0.047
36	0.009	0.004	0.006	0.004	0.003	0.061	0.042	0.069	0.080	0.182	0.024	0.008	0.009	0.006	0.006	0.028	0.024	0.034	0.021	0.032
37	0.007	0.004	0.006	0.003	0.005	0.061	0.045	0.071	0.091	0.187	0.022	0.008	0.001	0.006	0.005	0.026	0.021	0.027	0.020	0.049
38	0.009	0.004	0.005	0.003	0.006	0.059	0.039	0.062	0.071	0.168	0.025	0.008	0.008	0.006	0.005	0.029	0.021	0.029	0.020	0.052
39	0.010	0.004	0.005	0.003	0.004	0.051	0.043	0.068	0.078	0.139	0.024	0.008	0.008	0.006	0.005	0.029	0.022	0.028	0.019	0.044
40	0.001	0.004	0.005	0.003	0.003	0.045	0.035	0.061	0.077	0.118	0.021	0.006	0.008	0.006	0.005	0.023	0.020	0.031	0.021	0.044
41	0.012	0.004	0.005	0.004	0.004	0.039	0.042	0.067	0.070	0.152	0.020	0.006	0.008	0.005	0.004	0.026	0.023	0.026	0.022	0.050
42	0.009	0.004	0.005	0.003	0.004	0.043	0.034	0.066	0.077	0.149	0.021	0.007	0.009	0.005	0.004	0.034	0.019	0.031	0.022	0.048
43	0.010	0.003	0.006	0.003	0.004	0.040	0.037	0.060	0.063	0.120	0.022	0.007	0.007	0.004	0.004	0.030	0.021	0.030	0.020	0.050
44	0.012	0.005	0.005	0.003	0.005	0.034	0.038	0.058	0.076	0.146	0.018	0.006	0.007	0.006	0.005	0.025	0.021	0.028	0.025	0.051
45	0.001	0.003	0.006	0.003	0.003	0.029	0.028	0.049	0.052	0.145	0.022	0.005	0.008	0.005	0.004	0.029	0.020	0.028	0.024	0.049
46	0.011	0.004	0.006	0.003	0.003	0.042	0.031	0.052	0.059	0.135	0.024	0.006	0.009	0.005	0.004	0.027	0.018	0.027	0.025	0.042
47	0.013	0.005	0.005	0.003	0.005	0.036	0.033	0.056	0.053	0.099	0.023	0.005	0.007	0.005	0.005	0.024	0.019	0.030	0.026	0.056
48	0.010	0.004	0.005	0.004	0.003	0.032	0.028	0.035	0.058	0.088	0.023	0.006	0.008	0.005	0.004	0.025	0.016	0.028	0.026	0.059
49	0.011	0.005	0.005	0.004	0.005	0.035	0.027	0.043	0.064	0.080	0.023	0.007	0.008	0.006	0.005	0.026	0.017	0.026	0.023	0.049
50	0.013	0.005	0.006	0.004	0.005	0.032	0.027	0.049	0.043	0.100	0.028	0.007	0.008	0.006	0.004	0.021	0.017	0.026	0.023	0.059
51	0.012	0.006	0.007	0.004	0.005	0.024	0.024	0.032	0.038	0.067	0.025	0.007	0.008	0.006	0.005	0.020	0.015	0.024	0.023	0.049
52	0.016	0.006	0.006	0.005	0.006	0.029	0.026	0.038	0.041	0.066	0.025	0.006	0.008	0.006	0.005	0.019	0.015	0.023	0.025	0.056
53	0.017	0.006	0.008	0.005	0.004	0.027	0.023	0.029	0.038	0.078	0.026	0.007	0.009	0.008	0.006	0.020	0.016	0.023	0.023	0.032
54	0.017	0.007	0.008	0.005	0.005	0.032	0.020	0.030	0.038	0.054	0.021	0.008	0.011	0.008	0.006	0.021	0.013	0.020	0.023	0.044
55	0.015	0.007	0.008	0.006	0.007	0.025	0.020	0.023	0.026	0.050	0.022	0.001	0.011	0.001	0.007	0.021	0.014	0.019	0.024	0.044
56	0.013	0.008	0.009	0.006	0.008	0.022	0.017	0.027	0.030	0.043	0.024	0.009	0.001	0.008	0.007	0.015	0.013	0.021	0.021	0.038
57	0.016	0.009	0.011	0.008	0.009	0.016	0.017	0.027	0.027	0.046	0.024	0.008	0.010	0.001	0.008	0.019	0.011	0.021	0.018	0.034
58	0.018	0.009	0.012	0.001	0.001	0.025	0.017	0.023	0.024	0.035	0.026	0.001	0.014	0.011	0.008	0.014	0.011	0.021	0.018	0.029
59	0.018	0.010	0.012	0.011	0.011	0.017	0.018	0.023	0.026	0.040	0.027	0.012	0.014	0.013	0.010	0.015	0.009	0.019	0.017	0.033
60	0.018	0.011	0.016	0.010	0.012	0.019	0.014	0.020	0.019	0.035	0.029	0.011	0.015	0.015	0.011	0.013	0.009	0.018	0.019	0.033
61	0.028	0.016	0.019	0.015	0.014	0.016	0.013	0.021	0.018	0.024	0.040	0.015	0.021	0.017	0.014	0.014	0.008	0.012	0.015	0.029
62	0.032	0.018	0.019	0.014	0.018	0.011	0.011	0.015	0.014	0.029	0.032	0.015	0.022	0.020	0.017	0.009	0.009	0.014	0.013	0.023
63	0.033	0.020	0.021	0.018	0.020	0.010	0.009	0.016	0.015	0.021	0.050	0.018	0.023	0.020	0.016	0.011	0.007	0.016	0.013	0.023
64	0.035	0.021	0.029	0.022	0.021	0.010	0.001	0.015	0.017	0.022	0.042	0.021	0.031	0.030	0.024	0.007	0.007	0.015	0.012	0.022
65	0.035	0.023	0.030	0.026	0.027	0.011	0.009	0.013	0.013	0.026	0.054	0.022	0.031	0.032	0.024	0.007	0.006	0.012	0.013	0.029
66	0.042	0.025	0.037	0.028	0.032	0.012	0.009	0.018	0.012	0.024	0.042	0.024	0.034	0.035	0.027	0.008	0.006	0.013	0.009	0.019
67	0.042	0.030	0.040	0.030	0.038	0.011	0.010	0.011	0.017	0.019	0.060	0.027	0.041	0.038	0.029	0.003	0.005	0.012	0.012	0.007
68	0.042	0.030	0.050	0.038	0.046	0.001	0.011	0.018	0.010	0.018	0.069	0.028	0.035	0.040	0.034	0.008	0.005	0.010	0.009	0.022
69	0.053	0.033	0.051	0.039	0.045	0.001	0.007	0.013	0.011	0.021	0.056	0.028	0.044	0.038	0.035	0.006	0.004	0.011	0.012	0.014
70	0.054	0.038	0.055	0.043	0.034	0.009	0.011	0.020	0.011	0.018	0.060	0.030	0.053	0.051	0.042	0.006	0.004	0.007	0.008	0.016
71	0.066	0.041	0.052	0.050	0.043	0.009	0.009	0.016	0.012	0.017	0.066	0.025	0.055	0.056	0.045	0.005	0.004	0.010	0.009	0.001
72	0.060	0.043	0.060	0.050	0.055	0.010	0.007	0.006	0.001	0.021	0.067	0.034	0.054	0.058	0.049	0.004	0.004	0.012	0.009	0.008
73	0.068	0.049	0.080	0.059	0.063	0.008	0.005	0.013	0.011	0.014	0.066	0.043	0.067	0.068	0.053	0.005	0.004	0.007	0.004	0.011
74	0.067	0.050	0.076	0.058	0.062	0.005	0.008	0.012	0.016	0.013	0.085	0.044	0.076	0.091	0.073	0.004	0.003	0.002	0.010	0.028
75	0.068	0.037	0.084	0.066	0.080	0.007	0.006	0.013	0.011	0.021	0.084	0.047	0.069	0.039	0.053	0.002	0.003	0.005	0.010	0.005
76	0.072	0.070	0.066	0.052	0.105	0.006	0.006	0.013	0.008	0.013	0.097	0.048	0.074	0.080	0.070	0.002	0.003	0.006	0.007	0.000
77	0.064	0.059	0.091	0.071	0.094	0.005	0.005	0.011	0.012	0.018	0.094	0.057	0.086	0.085	0.066	0.000	0.002	0.003	0.005	0.012
78	0.081	0.070	0.088	0.092	0.069	0.008	0.006	0.012	0.005	0.010	0.121	0.051	0.069	0.125	0.087	0.002	0.002	0.004	0.005	0.010
79	0.109	0.077	0.117	0.093	0.106	0.007	0.007	0.006	0.015	0.011	0.136	0.093	0.125	0.112	0.093	0.003	0.003	0.000	0.001	0.006
80	0.061	0.056	0.072	0.061	0.076	0.003	0.003	0.003	0.006	0.008	0.095	0.050	0.071	0.092	0.074	0.001	0.001	0.003	0.004	0.005

Exact-age transition probabilities (TP) are from CPS microdata samples, July 1999 through June 2007. Standard errors for active to inactive can be derived as the ratio of the TP of active to inactive ("ai") versus the TP of active to active ("aa") times the standard error of "aa". For example assume the "aa" TP is .8, the "ai" TP is .2, and the standard error of "aa" is 0.01. The standard error of "ai" equals 0.0025 (i.e., 0.2/0.8 * 0.01). The same process applies to inactive to active transition probability standard errors.

Appendix Table 3: Standard errors of transition probabilities by sex, race, Hispanic origin, and education, July 1999 through June 2007, Black Males and Females

Age	Black Males								Black Females							
	Active to Active				Inactive to Inactive				Active to Active				Inactive to Inactive			
	<HS	High School	Some College	BA and Higher	<HS	High School	Some College	BA and Higher	<HS	High School	Some College	BA and Higher	<HS	High School	Some College	BA and Higher
18	0.066	0.067	0.080		0.051	0.070	0.069		0.089	0.060	0.070		0.063	0.061	0.052	
19	0.081	0.047	0.054	0.063	0.060	0.073	0.058	0.169	0.010	0.050	0.046	0.119	0.078	0.074	0.042	0.173
20	0.075	0.042	0.042	0.095	0.080	0.087	0.055	0.138	0.077	0.043	0.042	0.035	0.093	0.078	0.054	0.180
21	0.071	0.029	0.047	0.145	0.112	0.084	0.079	0.109	0.083	0.040	0.040	0.125	0.071	0.062	0.063	0.172
22	0.051	0.043	0.050	0.096	0.115	0.079	0.010	0.193	0.088	0.037	0.038	0.056	0.109	0.079	0.071	0.144
23	0.076	0.030	0.035	0.082	0.115	0.108	0.120	0.207	0.073	0.033	0.046	0.041	0.097	0.056	0.092	0.136
24	0.076	0.035	0.043	0.034	0.098	0.096	0.134	0.128	0.060	0.038	0.036	0.024	0.068	0.082	0.091	0.122
25	0.101	0.026	0.022	0.027	0.117	0.099	0.131	0.212	0.050	0.040	0.025	0.027	0.087	0.080	0.079	0.185
26	0.089	0.036	0.054	0.020	0.182	0.109	0.226	0.187	0.077	0.037	0.031	0.030	0.089	0.075	0.117	0.130
27	0.062	0.040	0.030	0.028	0.133	0.106	0.154	0.269	0.071	0.028	0.031	0.033	0.121	0.079	0.123	0.174
28	0.087	0.018	0.034	0.031	0.149	0.083	0.141	0.308	0.079	0.029	0.025	0.017	0.012	0.066	0.092	0.158
29	0.082	0.016	0.024	0.018	0.069	0.099	0.149	0.165	0.077	0.035	0.025	0.018	0.115	0.075	0.102	0.135
30	0.056	0.023	0.026	0.022	0.175	0.089	0.176	0.200	0.078	0.030	0.032	0.016	0.109	0.087	0.099	0.112
31	0.016	0.021	0.022	0.027	0.168	0.085	0.123	0.171	0.083	0.024	0.026	0.018	0.097	0.076	0.106	0.115
32	0.087	0.023	0.038	0.018	0.103	0.125	0.208	0.281	0.062	0.023	0.022	0.022	0.061	0.074	0.103	0.174
33	0.039	0.021	0.027	0.018	0.092	0.103	0.161	0.220	0.052	0.026	0.022	0.011	0.093	0.060	0.137	0.132
34	0.061	0.017	0.018	0.023	0.136	0.086	0.203	0.094	0.070	0.020	0.023	0.017	0.113	0.058	0.099	0.117
35	0.066	0.024	0.033	0.018	0.034	0.105	0.110	0.121	0.080	0.018	0.027	0.015	0.105	0.071	0.101	0.119
36	0.081	0.025	0.022	0.008	0.084	0.104	0.125	0.355	0.063	0.027	0.021	0.018	0.092	0.067	0.083	0.091
37	0.021	0.020	0.025	0.023	0.098	0.080	0.204	0.100	0.044	0.017	0.022	0.017	0.063	0.070	0.114	0.114
38	0.063	0.020	0.008	0.003	0.047	0.106	0.184	0.161	0.072	0.020	0.023	0.018	0.062	0.053	0.109	0.109
39	0.050	0.019	0.016	0.013	0.096	0.085	0.123	0.075	0.062	0.019	0.022	0.016	0.051	0.057	0.122	0.076
40	0.050	0.019	0.018	0.021	0.061	0.075	0.162	0.193	0.058	0.017	0.021	0.019	0.070	0.067	0.081	0.125
41	0.062	0.017	0.028	0.011	0.110	0.060	0.098	0.214	0.048	0.018	0.026	0.012	0.057	0.058	0.093	0.106
42	0.046	0.017	0.029	0.021	0.004	0.066	0.157	0.144	0.051	0.025	0.022	0.011	0.050	0.064	0.089	0.083
43	0.051	0.022	0.021	0.003	0.051	0.084	0.102	0.116	0.068	0.017	0.018	0.012	0.063	0.063	0.074	0.088
44	0.040	0.020	0.026	0.015	0.042	0.063	0.065	0.186	0.049	0.021	0.020	0.016	0.046	0.051	0.070	0.107
45	0.042	0.017	0.025	0.018	0.052	0.069	0.115	0.154	0.030	0.023	0.022	0.014	0.054	0.048	0.065	0.091
46	0.029	0.014	0.023	0.009	0.046	0.069	0.079	0.163	0.046	0.018	0.027	0.018	0.047	0.036	0.056	0.077
47	0.042	0.018	0.025	0.017	0.076	0.050	0.096	0.123	0.056	0.021	0.025	0.015	0.055	0.053	0.072	0.093
48	0.040	0.021	0.026	0.015	0.044	0.086	0.060	0.113	0.043	0.020	0.027	0.012	0.058	0.058	0.087	0.067
49	0.080	0.016	0.029	0.012	0.072	0.050	0.130	0.136	0.053	0.020	0.032	0.017	0.048	0.039	0.068	0.114
50	0.049	0.022	0.034	0.012	0.064	0.065	0.062	0.078	0.059	0.022	0.021	0.021	0.051	0.037	0.090	0.092
51	0.034	0.015	0.049	0.017	0.067	0.059	0.080	0.057	0.071	0.015	0.027	0.013	0.027	0.048	0.076	0.073
52	0.038	0.025	0.016	0.023	0.043	0.039	0.051	0.105	0.055	0.020	0.031	0.011	0.003	0.048	0.060	0.076
53	0.047	0.023	0.035	0.019	0.053	0.039	0.053	0.162	0.037	0.022	0.036	0.016	0.049	0.041	0.058	0.077
54	0.049	0.025	0.033	0.035	0.071	0.051	0.125	0.059	0.060	0.029	0.026	0.019	0.051	0.041	0.065	0.056
55	0.051	0.026	0.039	0.025	0.046	0.059	0.065	0.104	0.051	0.031	0.039	0.026	0.037	0.034	0.053	0.057
56	0.047	0.029	0.028	0.033	0.042	0.042	0.064	0.104	0.038	0.034	0.037	0.030	0.033	0.039	0.057	0.073
57	0.045	0.037	0.041	0.023	0.038	0.047	0.091	0.085	0.069	0.028	0.036	0.036	0.025	0.028	0.049	0.046
58	0.046	0.031	0.030	0.037	0.021	0.057	0.115	0.098	0.055	0.034	0.032	0.031	0.039	0.027	0.048	0.102
59	0.059	0.049	0.050	0.034	0.027	0.025	0.052	0.144	0.074	0.035	0.026	0.035	0.022	0.035	0.009	0.048
60	0.037	0.031	0.058	0.044	0.028	0.058	0.073	0.065	0.073	0.046	0.065	0.041	0.013	0.039	0.062	0.052
61	0.069	0.053	0.061	0.054	0.030	0.050	0.075	0.016	0.071	0.053	0.077	0.064	0.025	0.025	0.015	0.038
62	0.085	0.048	0.132	0.073	0.044	0.029	0.031	0.043	0.061	0.055	0.059	0.063	0.026	0.020	0.038	0.065
63	0.047	0.061	0.101	0.055	0.010	0.022	0.040	0.127	0.082	0.065	0.091	0.058	0.014	0.034	0.045	0.046
64	0.105	0.054	0.126	0.080	0.022	0.037	0.045	0.026	0.071	0.081	0.077	0.075	0.024	0.022	0.038	0.013
65	0.081	0.086	0.128	0.099	0.021	0.024	0.090	0.026	0.064	0.063	0.143	0.056	0.016	0.017	0.033	0.034
66	0.076	0.124	0.179	0.090	0.029	0.035	0.086	0.082	0.097	0.086	0.128	0.110	0.016	0.030	0.052	0.001
67	0.083	0.099	0.136	0.143	0.022	0.032	0.049	0.021	0.096	0.107	0.095	0.119	0.014	0.026	0.027	0.077
68	0.168	0.125	0.059	0.104	0.018	0.016	0.079	0.092	0.128	0.102	0.173	0.157	0.015	0.017	0.025	0.032
69	0.117	0.128	0.216	0.041	0.030	0.030	0.015	0.032	0.120	0.108	0.113	0.170	0.018	0.022	0.012	0.030
70	0.109	0.181	0.068	0.209	0.018	0.024	0.022	0.095	0.097	0.113	0.178	0.196	0.025	0.020	0.008	0.029
71	0.215	0.156	0.062	0.119	0.018	0.031	0.121	0.075	0.204	0.184	0.200	0.174	0.005	0.017	0.028	0.040
72	0.118	0.182	0.072	0.218	0.019	0.030	0.008	0.011	0.118	0.132	0.357	0.060	0.014	0.024	0.006	0.023
73	0.176	0.246	0.333	0.230	0.019	0.026	0.015	0.010	0.199	0.286	0.079	0.201	0.005	0.012	0.036	0.037
74	0.171	0.235	0.394	0.142	0.006	0.001	0.014	0.013	0.106	0.248	0.239	0.251	0.013	0.010	0.038	0.007
75	0.127	0.145	0.101	0.062	0.021	0.007	0.013	0.063	0.296	0.226	0.072	0.208	0.007	0.004	0.005	0.009
76	0.210	0.080	0.073	0.064	0.026	0.007	0.015	0.047	0.228	0.194	0.091	0.190	0.009	0.022	0.007	0.007
77	0.123	0.353	0.108	0.070	0.019	0.006	0.014	0.088	0.107	0.068	0.108	0.284	0.009	0.018	0.004	0.006
78	0.099	0.295	0.109	0.269	0.017	0.007	0.015	0.005	0.164	0.063	0.082	0.347	0.009	0.003	0.005	0.049
79	0.136	0.094	0.147	0.093	0.009	0.008	0.190	0.012	0.233	0.107	0.156	0.114	0.011	0.004	0.001	0.002
80	0.193	0.065	0.090	0.206	0.008	0.003	0.003	0.044	0.133	0.237	0.095	0.175	0.002	0.001	0.003	0.011

Exact-age transition probabilities (TP) are from CPS microdata samples, July 1999 through June 2007. Standard errors for active to inactive can be derived as the ratio of the TP of active to inactive ("ai") versus the TP of active to active ("aa") times the standard error of "aa". For example assume the "aa" TP is .8, the "ai" TP is .2, and the standard error of "aa" is 0.01. The standard error of "ai" equals 0.0025 (i.e., 0.2/0.8 * 0.01). The same process applies to inactive to active transition probability standard errors.

Appendix Table 3: Standard errors of transition probabilities by sex, race, Hispanic origin, and education, July 1999 through June 2007, Hispanic Males and Females

Age	Hispanic Males						Hispanic Females					
	Active to Active			Inactive to Inactive			Active to Active			Inactive to Inactive		
	<HS	High School	More than HS	<HS	High School	More than HS	<HS	High School	More than HS	<HS	High School	More than HS
18	0.035	0.042	0.031	0.050	0.079	0.079	0.070	0.054	0.049	0.043	0.069	0.074
19	0.033	0.024	0.066	0.082	0.091	0.061	0.067	0.044	0.040	0.060	0.072	0.059
20	0.023	0.030	0.114	0.105	0.097	0.064	0.054	0.031	0.033	0.054	0.064	0.052
21	0.033	0.025	0.111	0.111	0.108	0.078	0.059	0.038	0.032	0.048	0.068	0.064
22	0.022	0.024	0.036	0.129	0.132	0.093	0.061	0.032	0.030	0.048	0.065	0.060
23	0.026	0.016	0.044	0.148	0.147	0.102	0.059	0.038	0.023	0.043	0.047	0.083
24	0.018	0.020	0.035	0.145	0.111	0.116	0.047	0.041	0.031	0.040	0.060	0.072
25	0.012	0.013	0.030	0.149	0.149	0.135	0.044	0.030	0.021	0.035	0.055	0.071
26	0.015	0.018	0.024	0.138	0.205	0.168	0.043	0.031	0.025	0.039	0.051	0.073
27	0.016	0.016	0.023	0.161	0.165	0.010	0.047	0.033	0.019	0.038	0.042	0.077
28	0.013	0.016	0.023	0.124	0.110	0.147	0.056	0.032	0.025	0.040	0.059	0.070
29	0.008	0.013	0.021	0.130	0.130	0.154	0.050	0.025	0.022	0.040	0.050	0.069
30	0.011	0.012	0.008	0.147	0.119	0.139	0.041	0.026	0.018	0.038	0.041	0.056
31	0.016	0.008	0.015	0.153	0.126	0.161	0.046	0.033	0.020	0.041	0.054	0.061
32	0.011	0.017	0.011	0.125	0.129	0.165	0.038	0.025	0.022	0.037	0.050	0.059
33	0.014	0.011	0.019	0.155	0.150	0.184	0.034	0.023	0.020	0.035	0.051	0.058
34	0.001	0.016	0.010	0.109	0.152	0.189	0.035	0.031	0.018	0.041	0.048	0.055
35	0.011	0.013	0.012	0.122	0.109	0.115	0.036	0.029	0.025	0.036	0.055	0.058
36	0.009	0.007	0.016	0.137	0.222	0.146	0.034	0.022	0.015	0.038	0.051	0.055
37	0.001	0.012	0.025	0.101	0.136	0.153	0.029	0.026	0.015	0.032	0.065	0.061
38	0.014	0.013	0.016	0.133	0.195	0.148	0.031	0.028	0.018	0.044	0.064	0.060
39	0.012	0.008	0.023	0.104	0.135	0.201	0.035	0.026	0.016	0.043	0.065	0.054
40	0.015	0.009	0.002	0.116	0.080	0.137	0.029	0.022	0.017	0.035	0.050	0.072
41	0.016	0.018	0.021	0.088	0.139	0.170	0.028	0.022	0.014	0.041	0.062	0.083
42	0.016	0.011	0.014	0.102	0.121	0.191	0.034	0.022	0.020	0.049	0.059	0.070
43	0.015	0.006	0.012	0.126	0.139	0.170	0.032	0.016	0.017	0.051	0.056	0.069
44	0.015	0.014	0.009	0.071	0.045	0.225	0.025	0.025	0.018	0.046	0.086	0.064
45	0.012	0.011	0.003	0.080	0.142	0.105	0.028	0.021	0.016	0.054	0.054	0.065
46	0.013	0.016	0.009	0.091	0.112	0.010	0.035	0.030	0.015	0.040	0.078	0.105
47	0.020	0.027	0.016	0.078	0.015	0.150	0.031	0.020	0.018	0.043	0.066	0.063
48	0.008	0.016	0.018	0.076	0.134	0.060	0.034	0.025	0.020	0.043	0.065	0.083
49	0.014	0.020	0.007	0.137	0.108	0.185	0.034	0.032	0.018	0.040	0.026	0.059
50	0.019	0.025	0.023	0.069	0.106	0.112	0.044	0.040	0.025	0.033	0.057	0.043
51	0.014	0.027	0.017	0.081	0.124	0.118	0.038	0.028	0.029	0.041	0.051	0.088
52	0.028	0.028	0.028	0.082	0.092	0.053	0.040	0.036	0.032	0.034	0.032	0.054
53	0.030	0.007	0.013	0.061	0.127	0.110	0.042	0.035	0.027	0.037	0.056	0.100
54	0.031	0.029	0.018	0.079	0.125	0.059	0.032	0.036	0.036	0.038	0.039	0.068
55	0.028	0.014	0.022	0.102	0.045	0.095	0.041	0.025	0.027	0.042	0.062	0.069
56	0.022	0.024	0.015	0.033	0.019	0.065	0.047	0.047	0.029	0.032	0.065	0.070
57	0.022	0.034	0.056	0.047	0.107	0.083	0.046	0.026	0.039	0.035	0.050	0.081
58	0.030	0.039	0.042	0.055	0.078	0.045	0.060	0.043	0.048	0.029	0.063	0.052
59	0.038	0.051	0.052	0.064	0.086	0.068	0.060	0.060	0.035	0.037	0.045	0.071
60	0.032	0.036	0.042	0.057	0.050	0.097	0.078	0.050	0.061	0.028	0.050	0.090
61	0.050	0.044	0.066	0.055	0.015	0.064	0.082	0.064	0.065	0.032	0.042	0.056
62	0.066	0.086	0.081	0.039	0.060	0.080	0.084	0.087	0.064	0.023	0.035	0.017
63	0.057	0.079	0.085	0.031	0.025	0.081	0.099	0.095	0.060	0.018	0.032	0.027
64	0.073	0.080	0.142	0.014	0.036	0.011	0.084	0.106	0.084	0.022	0.054	0.010
65	0.053	0.123	0.127	0.034	0.061	0.082	0.133	0.135	0.069	0.013	0.045	0.041
66	0.101	0.135	0.130	0.029	0.032	0.083	0.092	0.113	0.073	0.008	0.025	0.019
67	0.075	0.142	0.144	0.036	0.091	0.057	0.123	0.197	0.240	0.004	0.010	0.010
68	0.135	0.220	0.035	0.034	0.066	0.064	0.194	0.114	0.157	0.018	0.011	0.008
69	0.060	0.166	0.035	0.020	0.009	0.001	0.089	0.227	0.175	0.024	0.035	0.082
70	0.242	0.123	0.034	0.013	0.080	0.081	0.229	0.200	0.042	0.016	0.006	0.006
71	0.131	0.104	0.040	0.015	0.011	0.010	0.122	0.033	0.228	0.014	0.024	0.024
72	0.194	0.050	0.042	0.017	0.011	0.052	0.166	0.039	0.234	0.004	0.005	0.016
73	0.361	0.181	0.055	0.009	0.006	0.008	0.136	0.369	0.050	0.013	0.017	0.078
74	0.323	0.200	0.050	0.025	0.010	0.001	0.209	0.058	0.064	0.014	0.004	0.007
75	0.190	0.044	0.069	0.008	0.007	0.001	0.364	0.055	0.047	0.005	0.004	0.006
76	0.084	0.083	0.067	0.008	0.008	0.007	0.112	0.057	0.062	0.003	0.004	0.005
77	0.245	0.072	0.066	0.007	0.005	0.009	0.352	0.413	0.061	0.001	0.003	0.004
78	0.130	0.089	0.070	0.034	0.007	0.006	0.129	0.062	0.069	0.012	0.003	0.004
79	0.135	0.094	0.094	0.009	0.008	0.009	0.146	0.114	0.094	0.003	0.004	0.001
80	0.232	0.248	0.056	0.003	0.003	0.004	0.093	0.229	0.062	0.001	0.002	0.003

Exact-age transition probabilities (TP) are from CPS microdata samples, July 1999 through June 2007. Standard errors for active to inactive can be derived as the ratio of the TP of active to inactive ("ai") versus the TP of active to active ("aa") times the standard error of "aa". For example assume the "aa" TP is .8, the "ai" TP is .2, and the standard error of "aa" is 0.01. The standard error of "ai" equals 0.0025 (i.e., 0.2/0.8 * 0.01). The same process applies to inactive to active transition probability standard errors.

Appendix Table 4: Standard errors of increment-decrement worklife expectancies by sex, race, Hispanic origin, and education: Males and Females of All Races

Age	Males of All Races — Standard errors of increment-decrement worklife expectancies										Females of All Races — Standard errors of increment-decrement worklife expectancies									
	< HS		HS or GED		Some College		BA		Grad Degree		< HS		HS or GED		Some College		BA		Grad Degree	
	Act'v	Inact	Act'v	Inact	Act'v	Inact	Act'v	Inact	Act'v	Inact	Act'v	Inact	Act'v	Inact	Act'v	Inact	Act'v	Inact	Act'v	Inact
18	0.34	0.34	0.18	0.20	0.26	0.26					0.37	0.37	0.22	0.22	0.28	0.28				
19	0.33	0.34	0.18	0.19	0.24	0.25	0.24	0.37			0.36	0.37	0.21	0.22	0.27	0.28	0.39	0.44		
20	0.33	0.34	0.17	0.19	0.24	0.24	0.21	0.31			0.36	0.36	0.21	0.22	0.27	0.28	0.29	0.33		
21	0.32	0.35	0.17	0.19	0.24	0.24	0.20	0.26	0.40	0.36	0.36	0.36	0.21	0.21	0.27	0.28	0.25	0.28	0.45	0.59
22	0.32	0.35	0.17	0.20	0.23	0.25	0.19	0.23	0.41	0.32	0.35	0.35	0.20	0.21	0.27	0.28	0.23	0.25	0.39	0.79
23	0.31	0.36	0.17	0.21	0.23	0.25	0.18	0.22	0.34	0.30	0.35	0.35	0.20	0.21	0.27	0.28	0.22	0.25	0.37	0.59
24	0.31	0.36	0.16	0.21	0.23	0.26	0.18	0.21	0.28	0.34	0.34	0.34	0.20	0.21	0.27	0.28	0.22	0.25	0.36	0.50
25	0.31	0.37	0.16	0.22	0.23	0.26	0.18	0.21	0.26	0.33	0.34	0.33	0.20	0.21	0.26	0.28	0.22	0.24	0.35	0.47
26	0.30	0.39	0.16	0.21	0.23	0.27	0.18	0.22	0.25	0.34	0.33	0.33	0.19	0.21	0.26	0.28	0.21	0.24	0.35	0.45
27	0.30	0.40	0.16	0.22	0.23	0.27	0.18	0.23	0.25	0.34	0.33	0.33	0.19	0.21	0.26	0.28	0.21	0.24	0.35	0.44
28	0.29	0.41	0.16	0.22	0.23	0.29	0.18	0.24	0.24	0.35	0.32	0.32	0.19	0.21	0.26	0.27	0.21	0.24	0.34	0.42
29	0.29	0.40	0.16	0.22	0.23	0.30	0.18	0.24	0.24	0.33	0.32	0.32	0.19	0.20	0.25	0.27	0.21	0.24	0.34	0.41
30	0.29	0.40	0.16	0.22	0.22	0.31	0.18	0.25	0.24	0.32	0.31	0.31	0.18	0.20	0.25	0.27	0.21	0.24	0.34	0.41
31	0.29	0.40	0.15	0.23	0.22	0.32	0.18	0.25	0.24	0.30	0.31	0.31	0.18	0.20	0.25	0.27	0.20	0.24	0.33	0.40
32	0.28	0.39	0.15	0.23	0.22	0.32	0.18	0.25	0.24	0.32	0.31	0.31	0.18	0.20	0.24	0.27	0.20	0.23	0.33	0.39
33	0.28	0.40	0.15	0.23	0.22	0.33	0.18	0.25	0.24	0.35	0.30	0.31	0.17	0.19	0.24	0.27	0.20	0.23	0.33	0.38
34	0.27	0.40	0.15	0.23	0.22	0.32	0.18	0.24	0.24	0.37	0.30	0.31	0.17	0.19	0.24	0.27	0.20	0.23	0.33	0.38
35	0.27	0.40	0.15	0.23	0.22	0.31	0.18	0.24	0.24	0.35	0.29	0.30	0.17	0.19	0.23	0.27	0.20	0.23	0.32	0.38
36	0.27	0.39	0.15	0.24	0.22	0.31	0.18	0.24	0.24	0.37	0.29	0.29	0.16	0.19	0.23	0.27	0.19	0.23	0.32	0.39
37	0.26	0.38	0.15	0.24	0.22	0.33	0.18	0.26	0.24	0.40	0.28	0.29	0.16	0.19	0.23	0.27	0.19	0.22	0.32	0.39
38	0.26	0.38	0.14	0.24	0.22	0.33	0.18	0.26	0.24	0.40	0.27	0.29	0.16	0.19	0.23	0.27	0.19	0.22	0.32	0.39
39	0.26	0.38	0.14	0.24	0.22	0.34	0.18	0.26	0.24	0.37	0.26	0.28	0.16	0.19	0.22	0.27	0.19	0.22	0.32	0.40
40	0.26	0.37	0.14	0.24	0.22	0.34	0.18	0.26	0.24	0.38	0.26	0.28	0.16	0.19	0.22	0.27	0.19	0.22	0.31	0.40
41	0.25	0.36	0.14	0.24	0.22	0.34	0.18	0.26	0.24	0.42	0.25	0.27	0.15	0.19	0.22	0.27	0.19	0.22	0.31	0.41
42	0.25	0.36	0.14	0.25	0.21	0.35	0.18	0.27	0.24	0.43	0.25	0.27	0.15	0.19	0.22	0.28	0.19	0.22	0.31	0.42
43	0.25	0.35	0.14	0.25	0.21	0.34	0.18	0.27	0.24	0.44	0.24	0.26	0.15	0.19	0.22	0.27	0.19	0.22	0.31	0.41
44	0.24	0.34	0.14	0.25	0.21	0.34	0.18	0.29	0.24	0.47	0.24	0.26	0.15	0.19	0.21	0.27	0.19	0.22	0.31	0.41
45	0.23	0.34	0.13	0.24	0.21	0.34	0.18	0.29	0.24	0.51	0.23	0.25	0.14	0.19	0.21	0.27	0.19	0.23	0.31	0.41
46	0.23	0.34	0.13	0.24	0.21	0.33	0.18	0.30	0.24	0.52	0.23	0.24	0.14	0.18	0.21	0.27	0.19	0.23	0.30	0.42
47	0.23	0.33	0.13	0.24	0.21	0.34	0.18	0.30	0.24	0.49	0.23	0.23	0.14	0.18	0.21	0.27	0.18	0.23	0.30	0.43
48	0.22	0.31	0.13	0.23	0.21	0.33	0.18	0.31	0.24	0.46	0.22	0.22	0.14	0.17	0.20	0.27	0.18	0.23	0.30	0.44
49	0.22	0.30	0.13	0.22	0.21	0.34	0.17	0.31	0.24	0.47	0.22	0.21	0.14	0.17	0.20	0.27	0.18	0.23	0.30	0.43
50	0.21	0.28	0.13	0.22	0.20	0.33	0.17	0.29	0.24	0.48	0.22	0.20	0.13	0.16	0.20	0.26	0.18	0.23	0.30	0.43
51	0.20	0.26	0.13	0.21	0.20	0.31	0.17	0.29	0.24	0.47	0.21	0.19	0.13	0.16	0.20	0.25	0.18	0.23	0.30	0.42
52	0.20	0.25	0.12	0.20	0.20	0.30	0.17	0.29	0.24	0.48	0.20	0.18	0.13	0.15	0.19	0.25	0.18	0.22	0.29	0.41
53	0.19	0.23	0.12	0.19	0.20	0.29	0.17	0.28	0.24	0.45	0.19	0.17	0.13	0.14	0.19	0.24	0.18	0.21	0.29	0.39
54	0.18	0.22	0.12	0.18	0.20	0.28	0.17	0.27	0.24	0.40	0.19	0.16	0.13	0.14	0.19	0.23	0.18	0.21	0.29	0.39
55	0.17	0.20	0.12	0.16	0.20	0.26	0.17	0.25	0.24	0.38	0.18	0.15	0.12	0.13	0.19	0.21	0.17	0.20	0.29	0.38
56	0.17	0.17	0.12	0.15	0.19	0.25	0.17	0.24	0.24	0.35	0.18	0.13	0.12	0.12	0.19	0.20	0.17	0.19	0.29	0.35
57	0.16	0.15	0.12	0.14	0.19	0.23	0.17	0.22	0.24	0.34	0.17	0.12	0.12	0.10	0.18	0.19	0.17	0.18	0.29	0.33
58	0.16	0.14	0.11	0.13	0.19	0.22	0.17	0.21	0.23	0.31	0.17	0.11	0.11	0.09	0.18	0.18	0.17	0.17	0.29	0.32
59	0.15	0.12	0.11	0.12	0.19	0.20	0.17	0.19	0.23	0.30	0.16	0.01	0.11	0.09	0.18	0.16	0.17	0.16	0.29	0.30
60	0.15	0.11	0.11	0.11	0.19	0.19	0.17	0.17	0.23	0.27	0.16	0.09	0.11	0.08	0.18	0.15	0.17	0.15	0.29	0.29
61	0.15	0.10	0.11	0.01	0.19	0.17	0.17	0.16	0.23	0.24	0.16	0.08	0.11	0.07	0.18	0.14	0.17	0.13	0.29	0.27
62	0.15	0.09	0.11	0.09	0.19	0.16	0.17	0.15	0.23	0.23	0.16	0.07	0.11	0.07	0.18	0.13	0.18	0.13	0.29	0.25
63	0.15	0.08	0.12	0.08	0.19	0.15	0.18	0.14	0.23	0.21	0.16	0.06	0.12	0.06	0.19	0.12	0.18	0.12	0.29	0.23
64	0.16	0.08	0.12	0.08	0.20	0.14	0.18	0.13	0.23	0.20	0.16	0.06	0.12	0.06	0.19	0.11	0.18	0.11	0.30	0.22
65	0.16	0.08	0.12	0.08	0.20	0.14	0.18	0.12	0.24	0.19	0.17	0.05	0.12	0.05	0.19	0.10	0.19	0.10	0.31	0.20
66	0.17	0.07	0.13	0.07	0.20	0.13	0.19	0.12	0.24	0.18	0.17	0.05	0.13	0.05	0.19	0.09	0.19	0.09	0.33	0.18
67	0.17	0.07	0.13	0.07	0.21	0.12	0.19	0.11	0.24	0.16	0.18	0.04	0.14	0.04	0.19	0.08	0.19	0.09	0.34	0.17
68	0.17	0.06	0.13	0.06	0.22	0.11	0.19	0.01	0.24	0.15	0.19	0.04	0.14	0.04	0.19	0.07	0.19	0.08	0.36	0.15
69	0.18	0.05	0.13	0.06	0.22	0.10	0.20	0.09	0.23	0.14	0.18	0.03	0.14	0.03	0.20	0.07	0.20	0.07	0.39	0.13
70	0.18	0.05	0.14	0.06	0.22	0.09	0.20	0.08	0.22	0.12	0.19	0.03	0.14	0.03	0.20	0.06	0.20	0.06	0.39	0.11
71	0.19	0.04	0.14	0.05	0.22	0.08	0.20	0.07	0.22	0.11	0.19	0.02	0.14	0.03	0.20	0.05	0.20	0.05	0.40	0.01
72	0.19	0.04	0.15	0.04	0.22	0.06	0.20	0.07	0.23	0.10	0.19	0.02	0.14	0.02	0.21	0.05	0.20	0.05	0.42	0.09
73	0.19	0.03	0.15	0.03	0.22	0.06	0.21	0.06	0.23	0.09	0.19	0.02	0.15	0.02	0.21	0.03	0.21	0.04	0.39	0.08
74	0.19	0.03	0.15	0.03	0.21	0.05	0.20	0.06	0.24	0.08	0.18	0.01	0.15	0.01	0.21	0.03	0.20	0.04	0.39	0.08
75	0.17	0.02	0.14	0.02	0.19	0.04	0.20	0.04	0.24	0.07	0.16	0.01	0.13	0.01	0.20	0.02	0.17	0.03	0.36	0.04

Mortality rates are from Table I and transitions probabilities are from Table II using CPS microdata from July 1999 through June 2007.

Appendix Table 4: Standard errors of increment-decrement worklife expectancies by sex, race, Hispanic origin, and education: White Males and Females

Age	White Males — Standard errors of increment-decrement worklife expectancies										White Females — Standard errors of increment-decrement worklife expectancies									
	< HS		HS or GED		Some College		BA		Grad Degree		< HS		HS or GED		Some College		BA		Grad Degree	
	Act'v	Inact	Act'v	Inact	Act'v	Inact	Act'v	Inact	Act'v	Inact	Act'v	Inact	Act'v	Inact	Act'v	Inact	Act'v	Inact	Act'v	Inact
18	0.37	0.38	0.19	0.22	0.27	0.27					0.40	0.40	0.25	0.26	0.31	0.31				
19	0.37	0.38	0.18	0.20	0.25	0.26	0.27	0.42			0.39	0.39	0.24	0.25	0.30	0.30	0.43	0.45		
20	0.36	0.39	0.18	0.21	0.25	0.25	0.23	0.35			0.38	0.38	0.23	0.25	0.30	0.30	0.32	0.35		
21	0.36	0.40	0.18	0.21	0.24	0.25	0.22	0.29	0.52	0.43	0.38	0.38	0.22	0.25	0.30	0.30	0.28	0.30	0.51	0.66
22	0.35	0.41	0.18	0.22	0.24	0.25	0.21	0.26	0.54	0.35	0.37	0.38	0.22	0.24	0.30	0.30	0.26	0.28	0.45	0.84
23	0.35	0.41	0.17	0.22	0.24	0.26	0.20	0.25	0.38	0.33	0.37	0.37	0.22	0.24	0.29	0.31	0.25	0.28	0.42	0.78
24	0.34	0.41	0.17	0.23	0.24	0.27	0.20	0.25	0.31	0.37	0.36	0.37	0.21	0.23	0.29	0.31	0.25	0.28	0.41	0.58
25	0.34	0.42	0.17	0.24	0.24	0.27	0.20	0.25	0.28	0.35	0.36	0.36	0.21	0.23	0.29	0.31	0.24	0.28	0.40	0.53
26	0.34	0.43	0.17	0.24	0.24	0.28	0.20	0.27	0.27	0.36	0.36	0.36	0.21	0.23	0.28	0.31	0.24	0.28	0.40	0.50
27	0.34	0.44	0.17	0.24	0.24	0.29	0.20	0.27	0.27	0.36	0.36	0.36	0.21	0.23	0.28	0.31	0.24	0.28	0.40	0.49
28	0.33	0.44	0.17	0.25	0.23	0.32	0.20	0.28	0.26	0.38	0.36	0.36	0.20	0.22	0.28	0.31	0.24	0.28	0.39	0.48
29	0.33	0.44	0.17	0.25	0.23	0.35	0.20	0.29	0.26	0.37	0.35	0.36	0.20	0.22	0.27	0.30	0.24	0.27	0.39	0.48
30	0.33	0.43	0.16	0.26	0.23	0.36	0.20	0.30	0.26	0.36	0.35	0.35	0.20	0.22	0.27	0.30	0.23	0.27	0.39	0.47
31	0.33	0.43	0.16	0.26	0.23	0.36	0.20	0.31	0.26	0.33	0.34	0.34	0.20	0.22	0.27	0.30	0.23	0.27	0.38	0.46
32	0.32	0.43	0.16	0.26	0.23	0.37	0.20	0.31	0.26	0.34	0.34	0.34	0.19	0.22	0.26	0.30	0.23	0.26	0.38	0.46
33	0.32	0.44	0.16	0.27	0.23	0.38	0.20	0.29	0.26	0.40	0.33	0.33	0.19	0.22	0.26	0.30	0.23	0.26	0.37	0.46
34	0.32	0.44	0.16	0.27	0.23	0.37	0.20	0.28	0.26	0.50	0.32	0.32	0.19	0.22	0.26	0.30	0.22	0.26	0.37	0.44
35	0.32	0.44	0.16	0.26	0.23	0.37	0.20	0.28	0.26	0.42	0.32	0.32	0.19	0.21	0.26	0.30	0.22	0.25	0.37	0.44
36	0.31	0.45	0.16	0.27	0.23	0.37	0.20	0.27	0.26	0.41	0.31	0.31	0.18	0.21	0.25	0.30	0.22	0.25	0.36	0.44
37	0.31	0.45	0.16	0.27	0.23	0.38	0.20	0.29	0.26	0.42	0.31	0.31	0.18	0.21	0.25	0.30	0.22	0.25	0.36	0.44
38	0.31	0.46	0.16	0.27	0.23	0.38	0.20	0.28	0.26	0.43	0.31	0.31	0.17	0.21	0.25	0.31	0.22	0.25	0.35	0.44
39	0.30	0.46	0.16	0.27	0.23	0.39	0.20	0.29	0.26	0.40	0.31	0.31	0.17	0.21	0.25	0.31	0.21	0.25	0.35	0.44
40	0.30	0.45	0.16	0.27	0.23	0.39	0.20	0.29	0.26	0.40	0.30	0.30	0.17	0.21	0.24	0.31	0.21	0.25	0.35	0.44
41	0.29	0.45	0.15	0.28	0.22	0.40	0.20	0.30	0.26	0.42	0.30	0.30	0.16	0.21	0.24	0.31	0.21	0.25	0.34	0.45
42	0.29	0.44	0.15	0.28	0.22	0.41	0.20	0.31	0.26	0.47	0.30	0.30	0.16	0.21	0.24	0.31	0.21	0.25	0.34	0.45
43	0.28	0.44	0.15	0.28	0.22	0.40	0.20	0.32	0.26	0.49	0.29	0.29	0.16	0.21	0.23	0.31	0.21	0.24	0.34	0.45
44	0.27	0.42	0.15	0.29	0.22	0.39	0.20	0.35	0.26	0.57	0.28	0.28	0.15	0.21	0.23	0.31	0.21	0.25	0.34	0.46
45	0.26	0.42	0.15	0.28	0.22	0.38	0.20	0.34	0.26	0.61	0.28	0.28	0.15	0.21	0.23	0.31	0.21	0.25	0.34	0.46
46	0.26	0.42	0.15	0.28	0.22	0.37	0.20	0.34	0.26	0.61	0.28	0.28	0.15	0.20	0.23	0.31	0.21	0.25	0.33	0.46
47	0.25	0.40	0.15	0.27	0.22	0.39	0.20	0.33	0.26	0.57	0.27	0.27	0.15	0.20	0.22	0.30	0.20	0.25	0.33	0.46
48	0.25	0.39	0.14	0.26	0.21	0.38	0.20	0.34	0.26	0.54	0.26	0.26	0.15	0.19	0.22	0.30	0.20	0.25	0.33	0.46
49	0.24	0.38	0.14	0.25	0.21	0.38	0.19	0.35	0.26	0.53	0.26	0.26	0.14	0.19	0.22	0.29	0.20	0.25	0.33	0.45
50	0.24	0.35	0.14	0.25	0.21	0.38	0.19	0.33	0.26	0.54	0.25	0.25	0.14	0.18	0.21	0.29	0.20	0.25	0.33	0.45
51	0.23	0.32	0.14	0.24	0.21	0.34	0.19	0.31	0.26	0.54	0.24	0.24	0.14	0.17	0.21	0.28	0.20	0.25	0.33	0.43
52	0.23	0.31	0.13	0.23	0.21	0.33	0.19	0.31	0.26	0.54	0.23	0.23	0.14	0.16	0.21	0.27	0.20	0.25	0.33	0.43
53	0.22	0.28	0.13	0.21	0.21	0.30	0.19	0.30	0.25	0.52	0.22	0.22	0.13	0.15	0.21	0.26	0.20	0.24	0.33	0.41
54	0.21	0.26	0.13	0.19	0.20	0.29	0.19	0.29	0.25	0.45	0.21	0.21	0.13	0.15	0.20	0.24	0.20	0.24	0.33	0.41
55	0.20	0.23	0.13	0.18	0.20	0.27	0.19	0.27	0.25	0.41	0.20	0.20	0.13	0.14	0.20	0.23	0.20	0.23	0.33	0.39
56	0.19	0.20	0.13	0.16	0.20	0.26	0.19	0.26	0.25	0.39	0.20	0.20	0.13	0.13	0.19	0.22	0.20	0.22	0.33	0.38
57	0.19	0.18	0.12	0.15	0.19	0.24	0.19	0.24	0.25	0.37	0.19	0.19	0.13	0.12	0.19	0.21	0.20	0.20	0.32	0.35
58	0.18	0.17	0.12	0.14	0.19	0.22	0.19	0.23	0.25	0.35	0.19	0.19	0.13	0.10	0.19	0.19	0.19	0.19	0.32	0.34
59	0.18	0.15	0.12	0.12	0.19	0.20	0.19	0.21	0.24	0.32	0.18	0.18	0.13	0.09	0.19	0.18	0.19	0.18	0.32	0.32
60	0.17	0.13	0.12	0.11	0.19	0.19	0.18	0.18	0.24	0.30	0.18	0.18	0.12	0.09	0.19	0.16	0.19	0.17	0.32	0.31
61	0.17	0.12	0.12	0.10	0.19	0.17	0.19	0.17	0.24	0.26	0.18	0.18	0.13	0.08	0.19	0.15	0.19	0.16	0.33	0.29
62	0.18	0.10	0.12	0.01	0.19	0.16	0.19	0.15	0.24	0.25	0.17	0.17	0.13	0.07	0.19	0.14	0.19	0.14	0.33	0.27
63	0.18	0.01	0.12	0.09	0.19	0.15	0.19	0.15	0.24	0.23	0.18	0.18	0.13	0.07	0.19	0.13	0.20	0.13	0.34	0.26
64	0.18	0.09	0.13	0.09	0.20	0.14	0.19	0.14	0.24	0.21	0.19	0.19	0.13	0.06	0.20	0.12	0.20	0.12	0.35	0.25
65	0.18	0.09	0.13	0.08	0.20	0.13	0.19	0.13	0.25	0.20	0.20	0.20	0.13	0.06	0.20	0.11	0.21	0.11	0.37	0.23
66	0.19	0.08	0.13	0.08	0.20	0.13	0.19	0.12	0.25	0.19	0.21	0.21	0.14	0.05	0.20	0.10	0.21	0.01	0.40	0.20
67	0.19	0.07	0.14	0.07	0.21	0.12	0.20	0.12	0.25	0.17	0.23	0.23	0.15	0.05	0.21	0.09	0.21	0.09	0.41	0.18
68	0.20	0.07	0.14	0.07	0.22	0.11	0.20	0.10	0.26	0.15	0.23	0.23	0.15	0.04	0.20	0.08	0.21	0.08	0.43	0.17
69	0.21	0.06	0.14	0.06	0.22	0.10	0.21	0.01	0.25	0.14	0.21	0.21	0.15	0.04	0.21	0.07	0.21	0.07	0.45	0.15
70	0.22	0.06	0.15	0.06	0.23	0.01	0.21	0.09	0.24	0.13	0.21	0.21	0.15	0.03	0.21	0.06	0.22	0.06	0.42	0.13
71	0.22	0.05	0.16	0.05	0.23	0.08	0.22	0.08	0.24	0.11	0.21	0.21	0.14	0.03	0.22	0.06	0.22	0.06	0.43	0.12
72	0.22	0.04	0.16	0.04	0.23	0.06	0.22	0.07	0.24	0.10	0.20	0.20	0.15	0.02	0.21	0.05	0.22	0.05	0.44	0.11
73	0.21	0.04	0.16	0.03	0.23	0.06	0.22	0.07	0.24	0.09	0.19	0.19	0.15	0.02	0.22	0.03	0.22	0.04	0.42	0.11
74	0.21	0.03	0.15	0.03	0.22	0.05	0.22	0.06	0.24	0.08	0.18	0.18	0.15	0.02	0.22	0.02	0.23	0.04	0.41	0.10
75	0.20	0.02	0.14	0.02	0.20	0.05	0.20	0.05	0.24	0.07	0.17	0.17	0.14	0.01	0.22	0.02	0.18	0.03	0.37	0.05

Mortality rates are from Table I and transitions probabilities are from Table II using CPS microdata from July 1999 through June 2007.

Appendix Table 4: Standard errors of increment-decrement worklife expectancies by sex, race, Hispanic origin, and education: Black Males and Females

Age	Black Males — Standard errors of increment-decrement worklives								Black Females — Standard errors of increment-decrement worklives							
	< HS		HS or GED		Some College		BA +		< HS		HS or GED		Some College		BA +	
	Act'v	Inact	Act'v	Inact	Act'v	Inact	Act'v	Inact	Act'v	Inact	Act'v	Inact	Act'v	Inact	Act'v	Inact
18	1.05	1.04	0.60	0.59	0.74	0.75			0.89	0.88	0.56	0.56	0.69	0.70		
19	1.04	1.04	0.59	0.59	0.71	0.72	0.76	0.78	0.88	0.87	0.55	0.55	0.67	0.68	0.67	0.73
20	1.04	1.04	0.58	0.59	0.70	0.71	0.75	0.77	0.86	0.87	0.54	0.55	0.67	0.67	0.60	0.67
21	1.03	1.04	0.57	0.59	0.70	0.71	0.74	0.76	0.86	0.86	0.54	0.54	0.67	0.67	0.58	0.63
22	1.02	1.03	0.57	0.60	0.69	0.72	0.70	0.78	0.85	0.86	0.53	0.54	0.66	0.67	0.55	0.60
23	1.02	1.03	0.56	0.60	0.67	0.73	0.67	0.79	0.84	0.85	0.53	0.54	0.66	0.67	0.54	0.59
24	1.01	1.02	0.55	0.61	0.66	0.73	0.63	0.77	0.82	0.83	0.53	0.55	0.66	0.67	0.52	0.59
25	1.00	1.03	0.54	0.61	0.66	0.73	0.61	0.79	0.81	0.82	0.53	0.54	0.65	0.67	0.52	0.60
26	0.98	1.03	0.53	0.61	0.65	0.77	0.60	0.78	0.81	0.81	0.52	0.54	0.65	0.67	0.51	0.59
27	0.96	1.01	0.53	0.62	0.64	0.74	0.60	0.80	0.80	0.81	0.52	0.54	0.65	0.67	0.51	0.60
28	0.96	1.01	0.51	0.62	0.64	0.72	0.60	0.79	0.79	0.79	0.51	0.54	0.64	0.67	0.50	0.59
29	0.94	0.99	0.51	0.62	0.63	0.72	0.59	0.72	0.78	0.80	0.51	0.54	0.64	0.68	0.50	0.58
30	0.93	1.02	0.50	0.62	0.63	0.70	0.59	0.74	0.76	0.79	0.50	0.54	0.64	0.68	0.50	0.56
31	0.92	1.04	0.50	0.62	0.63	0.67	0.59	0.76	0.75	0.77	0.50	0.54	0.63	0.68	0.49	0.55
32	0.92	1.01	0.49	0.62	0.63	0.72	0.58	0.78	0.73	0.75	0.49	0.54	0.63	0.68	0.49	0.56
33	0.89	1.01	0.49	0.60	0.62	0.77	0.58	0.75	0.72	0.75	0.49	0.53	0.63	0.70	0.49	0.54
34	0.87	1.01	0.48	0.58	0.62	0.83	0.58	0.69	0.70	0.76	0.48	0.52	0.62	0.68	0.49	0.53
35	0.85	0.94	0.48	0.58	0.61	0.80	0.58	0.73	0.69	0.74	0.48	0.52	0.62	0.68	0.49	0.54
36	0.82	0.94	0.47	0.57	0.60	0.82	0.57	0.79	0.67	0.71	0.47	0.52	0.61	0.68	0.49	0.54
37	0.77	0.92	0.47	0.57	0.60	0.88	0.57	0.66	0.65	0.68	0.46	0.52	0.61	0.71	0.49	0.57
38	0.77	0.87	0.46	0.59	0.59	0.85	0.57	0.65	0.64	0.67	0.46	0.52	0.60	0.72	0.49	0.58
39	0.74	0.87	0.45	0.60	0.59	0.80	0.57	0.65	0.62	0.65	0.45	0.52	0.60	0.73	0.48	0.59
40	0.73	0.83	0.45	0.60	0.59	0.81	0.57	0.74	0.61	0.64	0.44	0.53	0.59	0.72	0.48	0.61
41	0.70	0.83	0.44	0.60	0.59	0.77	0.57	0.79	0.60	0.61	0.44	0.52	0.59	0.72	0.48	0.60
42	0.66	0.73	0.44	0.61	0.58	0.80	0.57	0.77	0.59	0.60	0.43	0.53	0.58	0.72	0.48	0.59
43	0.64	0.71	0.43	0.61	0.58	0.77	0.56	0.74	0.58	0.59	0.42	0.52	0.57	0.70	0.48	0.59
44	0.62	0.69	0.42	0.60	0.57	0.74	0.56	0.75	0.55	0.57	0.42	0.52	0.56	0.69	0.47	0.61
45	0.60	0.68	0.41	0.60	0.57	0.75	0.56	0.77	0.52	0.56	0.41	0.51	0.56	0.68	0.47	0.62
46	0.59	0.66	0.40	0.59	0.57	0.73	0.56	0.80	0.52	0.54	0.40	0.50	0.55	0.67	0.47	0.62
47	0.60	0.66	0.40	0.58	0.56	0.73	0.56	0.82	0.52	0.52	0.39	0.50	0.54	0.67	0.47	0.63
48	0.59	0.63	0.39	0.59	0.56	0.72	0.55	0.86	0.51	0.50	0.38	0.48	0.53	0.67	0.46	0.62
49	0.59	0.62	0.39	0.55	0.56	0.74	0.55	0.87	0.51	0.46	0.37	0.45	0.52	0.67	0.46	0.63
50	0.53	0.59	0.39	0.54	0.55	0.70	0.55	0.84	0.50	0.43	0.37	0.44	0.51	0.67	0.46	0.61
51	0.49	0.57	0.38	0.52	0.54	0.70	0.55	0.83	0.49	0.40	0.36	0.43	0.51	0.64	0.45	0.59
52	0.48	0.52	0.38	0.49	0.52	0.69	0.55	0.84	0.46	0.39	0.36	0.42	0.50	0.61	0.45	0.58
53	0.48	0.50	0.37	0.48	0.51	0.69	0.54	0.85	0.44	0.39	0.36	0.39	0.49	0.60	0.45	0.57
54	0.47	0.48	0.37	0.47	0.51	0.70	0.54	0.74	0.44	0.37	0.35	0.37	0.48	0.57	0.44	0.56
55	0.45	0.41	0.36	0.45	0.50	0.64	0.54	0.73	0.43	0.32	0.34	0.34	0.47	0.54	0.44	0.54
56	0.42	0.36	0.36	0.42	0.49	0.63	0.53	0.72	0.42	0.29	0.33	0.33	0.46	0.51	0.43	0.53
57	0.40	0.32	0.36	0.40	0.49	0.63	0.52	0.69	0.43	0.26	0.32	0.30	0.45	0.46	0.42	0.50
58	0.39	0.28	0.35	0.38	0.49	0.61	0.52	0.68	0.41	0.25	0.32	0.29	0.45	0.43	0.41	0.49
59	0.40	0.26	0.35	0.34	0.50	0.52	0.52	0.66	0.41	0.21	0.32	0.28	0.46	0.39	0.40	0.42
60	0.39	0.25	0.34	0.33	0.50	0.49	0.52	0.56	0.39	0.19	0.32	0.26	0.47	0.38	0.40	0.39
61	0.40	0.24	0.34	0.29	0.50	0.45	0.52	0.52	0.37	0.18	0.31	0.24	0.47	0.34	0.40	0.36
62	0.39	0.23	0.34	0.25	0.51	0.41	0.51	0.52	0.36	0.17	0.31	0.22	0.47	0.32	0.39	0.34
63	0.38	0.19	0.35	0.22	0.49	0.41	0.51	0.53	0.35	0.15	0.31	0.22	0.49	0.30	0.38	0.30
64	0.40	0.18	0.35	0.21	0.48	0.41	0.52	0.45	0.33	0.14	0.32	0.21	0.49	0.28	0.37	0.26
65	0.38	0.17	0.36	0.19	0.48	0.40	0.52	0.44	0.33	0.12	0.32	0.20	0.52	0.26	0.37	0.25
66	0.40	0.16	0.37	0.18	0.50	0.38	0.52	0.44	0.33	0.11	0.34	0.19	0.52	0.24	0.37	0.24
67	0.42	0.14	0.35	0.16	0.46	0.34	0.53	0.41	0.32	0.01	0.40	0.18	0.50	0.19	0.37	0.24
68	0.45	0.13	0.36	0.14	0.43	0.33	0.53	0.42	0.31	0.01	0.44	0.16	0.51	0.16	0.38	0.19
69	0.39	0.13	0.37	0.14	0.51	0.30	0.54	0.36	0.33	0.09	0.46	0.15	0.46	0.15	0.37	0.17
70	0.40	0.11	0.39	0.12	0.42	0.30	0.59	0.35	0.34	0.08	0.50	0.13	0.48	0.14	0.40	0.16
71	0.46	0.01	0.36	0.11	0.46	0.31	0.53	0.29	0.40	0.06	0.54	0.11	0.56	0.14	0.40	0.15
72	0.40	0.09	0.39	0.10	0.56	0.18	0.57	0.22	0.36	0.05	0.52	0.09	0.66	0.13	0.38	0.12
73	0.40	0.08	0.47	0.08	0.70	0.13	0.57	0.20	0.37	0.04	0.58	0.07	0.46	0.13	0.49	0.10
74	0.39	0.07	0.48	0.05	0.72	0.11	0.42	0.20	0.34	0.04	0.51	0.06	0.49	0.11	0.48	0.07
75	0.35	0.07	0.40	0.03	0.41	0.10	0.27	0.20	0.46	0.03	0.45	0.05	0.32	0.06	0.39	0.06

Mortality rates are from Table I and transitions probabilities are from Table II using CPS microdata from July 1999 through June 2007.

Appendix Table 4: Standard errors of increment-decrement worklife expectancies by sex, race, Hispanic origin, and education: Hispanics Males and Females

Age	Hispanic Males Standard errors of inc-dec worklives						Hispanic Females Standard errors of inc-dec worklives					
	< HS		HS or GED		> HS		< HS		HS or GED		> HS	
	Act'v	Inact	Act'v	Inact	Act'v	Inact	Act'v	Inact	Act'v	Inact	Act'v	Inact
18	0.53	0.53	0.69	0.71	0.65	0.68	0.60	0.58	0.79	0.79	0.77	0.78
19	0.52	0.53	0.68	0.69	0.63	0.65	0.57	0.56	0.78	0.79	0.76	0.76
20	0.52	0.53	0.67	0.69	0.62	0.64	0.55	0.55	0.78	0.78	0.75	0.76
21	0.52	0.53	0.67	0.69	0.62	0.64	0.55	0.54	0.77	0.78	0.75	0.76
22	0.51	0.53	0.67	0.71	0.62	0.64	0.54	0.53	0.77	0.78	0.74	0.75
23	0.51	0.54	0.66	0.71	0.61	0.65	0.53	0.53	0.76	0.77	0.74	0.75
24	0.51	0.54	0.66	0.71	0.61	0.67	0.52	0.52	0.76	0.77	0.74	0.75
25	0.50	0.55	0.66	0.73	0.61	0.68	0.51	0.51	0.76	0.77	0.73	0.75
26	0.50	0.56	0.66	0.73	0.61	0.69	0.51	0.51	0.75	0.77	0.73	0.76
27	0.50	0.60	0.66	0.70	0.60	0.66	0.51	0.50	0.75	0.77	0.72	0.76
28	0.50	0.60	0.66	0.69	0.60	0.66	0.51	0.50	0.74	0.77	0.72	0.76
29	0.50	0.61	0.66	0.72	0.60	0.66	0.50	0.49	0.74	0.77	0.71	0.76
30	0.50	0.61	0.66	0.74	0.60	0.67	0.49	0.49	0.74	0.77	0.71	0.75
31	0.50	0.60	0.66	0.75	0.60	0.70	0.49	0.48	0.73	0.76	0.71	0.74
32	0.50	0.58	0.66	0.75	0.60	0.72	0.48	0.48	0.73	0.75	0.70	0.74
33	0.50	0.58	0.66	0.74	0.60	0.71	0.47	0.47	0.72	0.75	0.70	0.74
34	0.50	0.56	0.66	0.75	0.60	0.70	0.47	0.47	0.72	0.75	0.70	0.74
35	0.50	0.56	0.66	0.76	0.60	0.67	0.46	0.47	0.72	0.75	0.70	0.74
36	0.50	0.60	0.66	0.83	0.60	0.69	0.46	0.46	0.71	0.75	0.70	0.73
37	0.50	0.61	0.66	0.80	0.60	0.71	0.45	0.46	0.71	0.75	0.70	0.74
38	0.50	0.64	0.66	0.87	0.60	0.75	0.45	0.46	0.70	0.75	0.69	0.74
39	0.50	0.64	0.66	0.87	0.60	0.79	0.44	0.45	0.70	0.75	0.69	0.73
40	0.49	0.65	0.65	0.89	0.60	0.78	0.43	0.45	0.69	0.75	0.68	0.74
41	0.49	0.65	0.65	0.95	0.60	0.80	0.43	0.44	0.69	0.76	0.68	0.74
42	0.49	0.67	0.65	0.95	0.60	0.82	0.42	0.44	0.69	0.75	0.68	0.74
43	0.48	0.70	0.65	0.99	0.60	0.83	0.41	0.43	0.68	0.76	0.68	0.74
44	0.48	0.65	0.65	0.98	0.60	0.90	0.41	0.43	0.67	0.77	0.67	0.75
45	0.48	0.65	0.65	1.02	0.60	0.85	0.40	0.42	0.67	0.76	0.67	0.77
46	0.48	0.66	0.64	1.00	0.60	0.84	0.40	0.41	0.67	0.76	0.67	0.79
47	0.47	0.65	0.64	0.97	0.60	0.87	0.39	0.40	0.66	0.75	0.67	0.77
48	0.47	0.66	0.63	0.99	0.60	0.89	0.39	0.40	0.66	0.73	0.66	0.77
49	0.47	0.69	0.63	0.99	0.59	0.97	0.39	0.39	0.65	0.70	0.66	0.76
50	0.46	0.65	0.62	1.00	0.59	0.93	0.39	0.38	0.64	0.69	0.65	0.75
51	0.46	0.66	0.61	0.99	0.59	0.91	0.38	0.37	0.62	0.66	0.65	0.76
52	0.46	0.65	0.60	0.94	0.59	0.84	0.37	0.35	0.61	0.64	0.64	0.74
53	0.45	0.63	0.59	0.94	0.58	0.84	0.36	0.34	0.60	0.63	0.63	0.74
54	0.44	0.63	0.59	0.89	0.58	0.79	0.35	0.32	0.59	0.60	0.62	0.71
55	0.43	0.61	0.58	0.75	0.58	0.79	0.35	0.30	0.57	0.59	0.61	0.70
56	0.41	0.50	0.58	0.72	0.58	0.74	0.34	0.27	0.57	0.57	0.61	0.69
57	0.41	0.46	0.58	0.73	0.58	0.71	0.33	0.25	0.56	0.52	0.61	0.67
58	0.41	0.44	0.58	0.66	0.56	0.66	0.33	0.23	0.56	0.49	0.61	0.63
59	0.40	0.42	0.58	0.60	0.56	0.65	0.32	0.21	0.56	0.45	0.60	0.61
60	0.40	0.38	0.57	0.52	0.55	0.63	0.32	0.19	0.55	0.42	0.61	0.58
61	0.41	0.34	0.57	0.47	0.54	0.58	0.31	0.17	0.55	0.40	0.60	0.47
62	0.42	0.30	0.57	0.46	0.53	0.55	0.31	0.15	0.58	0.37	0.60	0.38
63	0.42	0.27	0.56	0.44	0.53	0.51	0.29	0.14	0.59	0.35	0.60	0.35
64	0.43	0.25	0.55	0.43	0.54	0.47	0.29	0.13	0.62	0.33	0.61	0.33
65	0.46	0.24	0.56	0.43	0.54	0.46	0.32	0.12	0.66	0.28	0.62	0.32
66	0.49	0.22	0.57	0.41	0.54	0.43	0.29	0.11	0.71	0.23	0.63	0.30
67	0.50	0.20	0.57	0.41	0.56	0.37	0.30	0.11	0.80	0.19	0.66	0.29
68	0.53	0.17	0.66	0.36	0.59	0.33	0.38	0.11	0.80	0.17	0.56	0.29
69	0.51	0.13	0.64	0.30	0.38	0.28	0.40	0.10	0.85	0.17	0.52	0.30
70	0.62	0.11	0.60	0.29	0.31	0.28	0.49	0.08	0.74	0.12	0.49	0.23
71	0.57	0.01	0.55	0.16	0.33	0.18	0.43	0.07	0.57	0.10	0.60	0.22
72	0.62	0.09	0.52	0.01	0.38	0.15	0.44	0.05	0.62	0.07	0.54	0.21
73	0.74	0.08	0.62	0.06	0.42	0.09	0.46	0.05	0.76	0.06	0.32	0.21
74	0.69	0.07	0.55	0.04	0.25	0.05	0.52	0.04	0.45	0.03	0.23	0.11
75	0.50	0.05	0.30	0.03	0.18	0.04	0.58	0.02	0.38	0.02	0.17	0.05

Mortality rates are from Table I and transitions probabilities are from Table II using CPS microdata from July 1999 through June 2007.

Appendix Table 5: Labor force participation rates and their standard errors by educational attainment, conventional methodology, Males of All Races

	Males of All Races: Labor Force Participation Rates									Males of All Races: Standard Errors of Labor Force Participation Rates									
Age	<HS	HS	Some College			College Degree	Graduate Degree			<HS	HS	Some College			College Degree	Graduate Degree			Age
			All	No Degree	Assoc Degree		All	Masters	Phd/Prof'l			All	No Degree	Assoc Degree		All	Masters	Phd/Prof'l	
18	46.2%	68.8%	56.5%	56.2%	71.9%					0.27%	0.34%	0.61%	0.62%	4.42%					18
19	50.8%	75.8%	63.4%	62.3%	80.4%	71.7%				0.42%	0.31%	0.34%	0.34%	2.01%	4.67%				19
20	63.5%	78.4%	66.1%	64.8%	81.7%	78.7%				0.49%	0.29%	0.29%	0.31%	1.09%	3.19%				20
21	75.3%	83.0%	69.6%	68.0%	83.8%	82.8%	71.1%	76.5%		0.46%	0.28%	0.30%	0.31%	0.75%	1.51%	6.21%	9.14%		21
22	80.8%	86.3%	74.2%	72.3%	86.5%	85.3%	77.6%	81.9%		0.43%	0.26%	0.30%	0.33%	0.67%	0.58%	4.00%	4.89%		22
23	83.7%	88.0%	79.1%	77.0%	88.4%	86.8%	82.6%	85.6%	73.6%	0.43%	0.24%	0.29%	0.33%	0.56%	0.39%	2.38%	2.32%	5.83%	23
24	85.3%	89.2%	84.0%	82.3%	90.4%	88.3%	86.0%	88.3%	79.8%	0.41%	0.24%	0.27%	0.34%	0.40%	0.31%	1.47%	1.49%	4.13%	24
25	86.1%	90.1%	87.9%	86.5%	92.3%	90.1%	88.3%	89.7%	84.7%	0.39%	0.24%	0.28%	0.35%	0.45%	0.29%	0.91%	0.94%	2.12%	25
26	86.9%	90.9%	90.2%	89.0%	93.4%	91.8%	90.4%	90.9%	89.5%	0.41%	0.24%	0.24%	0.30%	0.40%	0.27%	0.71%	0.70%	1.55%	26
27	87.5%	91.2%	91.4%	90.4%	93.7%	93.1%	91.9%	91.9%	91.7%	0.38%	0.24%	0.25%	0.30%	0.41%	0.24%	0.60%	0.74%	1.02%	27
28	87.7%	91.5%	92.6%	91.9%	94.1%	94.1%	92.6%	92.5%	93.1%	0.37%	0.22%	0.22%	0.29%	0.40%	0.21%	0.44%	0.57%	0.65%	28
29	88.0%	91.7%	93.2%	92.7%	94.4%	94.9%	93.6%	93.2%	94.6%	0.39%	0.23%	0.22%	0.29%	0.36%	0.21%	0.38%	0.47%	0.62%	29
30	87.8%	91.9%	93.8%	93.3%	94.8%	95.5%	94.3%	94.0%	95.5%	0.40%	0.21%	0.20%	0.24%	0.34%	0.21%	0.38%	0.48%	0.58%	30
31	87.6%	91.9%	94.1%	93.5%	95.1%	95.9%	95.0%	94.8%	95.7%	0.37%	0.21%	0.20%	0.25%	0.30%	0.18%	0.32%	0.40%	0.51%	31
32	87.6%	92.1%	94.3%	93.8%	95.4%	96.2%	95.6%	95.5%	96.2%	0.40%	0.20%	0.19%	0.23%	0.31%	0.17%	0.29%	0.37%	0.47%	32
33	87.4%	92.0%	94.3%	93.7%	95.5%	96.5%	96.2%	96.1%	96.4%	0.37%	0.21%	0.21%	0.27%	0.32%	0.17%	0.27%	0.30%	0.51%	33
34	87.0%	91.9%	94.3%	93.6%	95.7%	96.6%	96.5%	96.4%	96.6%	0.37%	0.20%	0.19%	0.23%	0.28%	0.17%	0.24%	0.26%	0.42%	34
35	86.7%	91.7%	94.0%	93.3%	95.5%	96.6%	96.8%	96.8%	96.8%	0.40%	0.20%	0.19%	0.25%	0.30%	0.18%	0.26%	0.31%	0.43%	35
36	86.5%	91.5%	94.0%	93.2%	95.5%	96.6%	96.9%	96.8%	97.1%	0.40%	0.20%	0.20%	0.26%	0.27%	0.17%	0.23%	0.29%	0.44%	36
37	85.7%	91.3%	94.0%	93.2%	95.5%	96.5%	96.9%	96.6%	97.3%	0.41%	0.22%	0.22%	0.27%	0.32%	0.15%	0.19%	0.23%	0.37%	37
38	85.0%	91.1%	93.8%	93.0%	95.3%	96.4%	97.0%	96.6%	97.5%	0.40%	0.20%	0.19%	0.25%	0.27%	0.17%	0.24%	0.35%	0.29%	38
39	84.3%	90.9%	93.7%	92.9%	95.1%	96.5%	96.9%	96.4%	97.7%	0.42%	0.20%	0.19%	0.24%	0.26%	0.17%	0.24%	0.31%	0.30%	39
40	83.2%	90.7%	93.6%	92.9%	94.6%	96.4%	96.8%	96.3%	97.7%	0.39%	0.19%	0.20%	0.25%	0.30%	0.17%	0.23%	0.30%	0.34%	40
41	82.3%	90.5%	93.4%	92.7%	94.6%	96.3%	96.7%	96.5%	97.2%	0.43%	0.20%	0.19%	0.26%	0.31%	0.15%	0.23%	0.31%	0.30%	41
42	81.1%	90.3%	93.0%	92.3%	94.3%	96.2%	96.7%	96.5%	96.9%	0.45%	0.19%	0.20%	0.26%	0.30%	0.16%	0.21%	0.26%	0.35%	42
43	79.8%	90.0%	92.6%	91.9%	94.0%	96.2%	96.7%	96.7%	96.9%	0.44%	0.21%	0.21%	0.27%	0.30%	0.19%	0.23%	0.27%	0.45%	43
44	78.8%	89.7%	92.2%	91.4%	93.7%	95.9%	96.8%	96.9%	96.8%	0.48%	0.20%	0.20%	0.28%	0.29%	0.19%	0.24%	0.29%	0.41%	44
45	78.0%	89.3%	91.7%	90.9%	93.4%	95.7%	96.8%	96.8%	96.8%	0.49%	0.21%	0.22%	0.28%	0.33%	0.18%	0.21%	0.27%	0.33%	45
46	76.6%	88.6%	91.3%	90.5%	92.8%	95.6%	96.7%	96.7%	97.0%	0.50%	0.22%	0.22%	0.29%	0.35%	0.19%	0.21%	0.28%	0.35%	46
47	76.0%	87.9%	90.8%	90.2%	92.1%	95.4%	96.6%	96.5%	97.0%	0.53%	0.23%	0.23%	0.29%	0.36%	0.19%	0.21%	0.26%	0.32%	47
48	75.8%	87.3%	90.3%	89.8%	91.4%	95.0%	96.2%	96.1%	96.7%	0.52%	0.25%	0.23%	0.28%	0.39%	0.19%	0.21%	0.29%	0.31%	48
49	74.7%	86.4%	89.6%	89.1%	90.5%	94.6%	96.0%	95.9%	96.3%	0.56%	0.25%	0.25%	0.30%	0.41%	0.20%	0.22%	0.31%	0.33%	49
50	73.6%	85.4%	88.7%	88.3%	89.7%	93.9%	95.6%	95.5%	96.1%	0.52%	0.25%	0.24%	0.30%	0.43%	0.22%	0.25%	0.32%	0.38%	50
51	72.3%	84.4%	87.8%	87.2%	89.0%	93.2%	95.2%	95.0%	95.8%	0.55%	0.28%	0.26%	0.32%	0.44%	0.23%	0.24%	0.30%	0.39%	51
52	70.8%	83.2%	86.8%	86.1%	88.3%	92.3%	94.8%	94.4%	95.6%	0.61%	0.29%	0.29%	0.35%	0.46%	0.27%	0.24%	0.32%	0.37%	52
53	68.5%	81.8%	85.5%	84.7%	87.3%	91.2%	94.0%	93.3%	95.2%	0.61%	0.33%	0.29%	0.38%	0.49%	0.27%	0.26%	0.34%	0.38%	53
54	66.5%	80.0%	84.0%	83.0%	86.2%	89.9%	92.9%	91.8%	94.7%	0.61%	0.34%	0.30%	0.37%	0.50%	0.28%	0.27%	0.35%	0.39%	54
55	64.9%	78.2%	82.4%	81.5%	84.3%	88.6%	91.5%	89.9%	93.8%	0.64%	0.33%	0.33%	0.41%	0.55%	0.32%	0.30%	0.42%	0.44%	55
56	63.1%	76.4%	80.4%	79.8%	81.8%	87.1%	89.8%	87.7%	93.1%	0.62%	0.36%	0.36%	0.44%	0.61%	0.35%	0.35%	0.48%	0.51%	56
57	61.2%	74.5%	78.2%	77.9%	78.9%	85.1%	87.7%	85.1%	91.9%	0.64%	0.38%	0.38%	0.45%	0.66%	0.38%	0.41%	0.56%	0.51%	57
58	59.5%	72.2%	75.5%	75.3%	75.8%	82.6%	85.4%	82.4%	90.4%	0.65%	0.40%	0.41%	0.49%	0.76%	0.41%	0.41%	0.57%	0.55%	58
59	57.7%	69.5%	72.7%	72.8%	72.5%	79.7%	82.7%	78.9%	88.7%	0.67%	0.40%	0.43%	0.53%	0.81%	0.45%	0.49%	0.65%	0.61%	59
60	54.0%	65.0%	69.0%	69.2%	68.4%	76.0%	79.2%	74.5%	86.3%	0.62%	0.42%	0.49%	0.59%	0.89%	0.55%	0.55%	0.75%	0.76%	60
61	49.3%	59.3%	64.2%	64.2%	64.0%	71.1%	74.9%	69.7%	82.9%	0.64%	0.43%	0.54%	0.65%	0.97%	0.58%	0.57%	0.78%	0.75%	61
62	44.3%	53.0%	58.9%	58.9%	59.0%	65.9%	70.8%	64.7%	79.8%	0.62%	0.46%	0.56%	0.64%	1.08%	0.63%	0.66%	0.90%	0.89%	62
63	38.9%	46.1%	52.9%	52.8%	53.1%	60.1%	66.2%	59.4%	76.0%	0.64%	0.46%	0.61%	0.69%	1.15%	0.69%	0.71%	0.97%	1.01%	63
64	33.1%	39.8%	46.7%	46.9%	46.2%	54.5%	61.1%	53.8%	71.1%	0.58%	0.46%	0.61%	0.72%	1.18%	0.72%	0.77%	1.00%	1.10%	64
65	29.1%	35.1%	41.4%	41.4%	41.2%	49.2%	56.4%	48.8%	66.6%	0.54%	0.44%	0.56%	0.68%	1.15%	0.71%	0.77%	0.98%	1.17%	65
66	26.1%	31.9%	36.9%	37.1%	36.4%	44.6%	51.6%	43.3%	61.9%	0.50%	0.43%	0.58%	0.69%	1.12%	0.74%	0.84%	1.06%	1.22%	66
67	23.5%	28.9%	32.8%	32.8%	32.7%	39.7%	46.2%	37.9%	56.5%	0.51%	0.46%	0.57%	0.69%	1.16%	0.79%	0.84%	1.12%	1.23%	67
68	20.5%	26.5%	29.4%	29.5%	29.2%	35.5%	41.4%	33.5%	51.2%	0.53%	0.45%	0.64%	0.72%	1.24%	0.79%	0.86%	1.10%	1.42%	68
69	18.2%	24.2%	26.2%	26.4%	25.5%	31.7%	38.2%	30.3%	48.1%	0.50%	0.46%	0.62%	0.71%	1.28%	0.77%	0.88%	1.05%	1.49%	69
70	16.6%	22.2%	23.8%	24.1%	23.0%	29.1%	35.6%	28.5%	44.5%	0.43%	0.46%	0.61%	0.70%	1.21%	0.72%	0.86%	1.04%	1.36%	70
71	14.7%	20.1%	21.4%	21.7%	20.5%	26.5%	32.7%	26.0%	41.5%	0.43%	0.43%	0.60%	0.71%	1.02%	0.71%	0.90%	1.09%	1.40%	71
72	13.1%	17.9%	19.5%	19.6%	19.0%	24.0%	30.0%	23.7%	37.9%	0.43%	0.42%	0.59%	0.66%	1.17%	0.76%	0.93%	1.20%	1.43%	72
73	11.8%	16.2%	17.9%	17.8%	18.2%	21.9%	27.4%	21.3%	35.1%	0.41%	0.42%	0.56%	0.67%	1.16%	0.74%	0.87%	0.96%	1.41%	73
74	10.7%	14.9%	17.0%	16.5%	18.5%	20.8%	24.1%	18.8%	30.9%	0.39%	0.41%	0.59%	0.63%	1.31%	0.74%	0.81%	1.04%	1.27%	74
75	9.6%	13.1%	15.6%	15.2%	16.8%	18.7%	21.2%	16.0%	27.6%	0.33%	0.40%	0.55%	0.57%	1.27%	0.70%	0.82%	1.03%	1.36%	75

Sources: Current Population Survey monthly microdata samples 2000 through 2006.

Appendix Table 5: Labor force participation rates and their standard errors by educational attainment, conventional methodology, Females of All Races

Age	Females of All Races: Labor Force Participation Rates									Females of All Races: Standard Errors of Labor Force Participation Rates									Age
	<HS	HS	Some College All	No Degree	Assoc Degree	College Degree	Grad All	Masters	Phd/Prof'l	<HS	HS	Some College All	No Degree	Assoc Degree	College Degree	Grad All	Masters	Phd/Prof'l	
18	44.4%	62.9%	60.2%	60.0%	67.0%					0.32%	0.34%	0.52%	0.50%	3.99%	6.97%				18
19	45.5%	67.0%	65.6%	64.9%	75.9%	68.4%				0.52%	0.34%	0.30%	0.31%	1.87%	4.90%				19
20	49.5%	68.5%	67.3%	66.4%	77.6%	78.4%				0.58%	0.35%	0.27%	0.27%	0.97%	2.79%				20
21	51.0%	71.0%	69.8%	68.5%	79.9%	81.4%	73.9%	74.0%		0.61%	0.36%	0.26%	0.28%	0.73%	1.14%	4.91%	6.50%		21
22	51.8%	72.1%	72.6%	71.0%	81.2%	82.8%	78.6%	79.3%		0.61%	0.36%	0.28%	0.32%	0.64%	0.44%	3.43%	3.78%		22
23	51.3%	71.8%	74.7%	72.9%	82.1%	83.8%	80.6%	81.9%	71.7%	0.62%	0.35%	0.30%	0.35%	0.53%	0.34%	1.66%	1.64%	5.2%	23
24	51.3%	71.5%	77.2%	75.2%	83.1%	84.5%	82.8%	83.7%	78.1%	0.64%	0.38%	0.31%	0.38%	0.53%	0.30%	1.05%	1.13%	3.4%	24
25	51.3%	70.8%	78.5%	76.5%	83.5%	85.0%	84.1%	85.3%	79.3%	0.62%	0.39%	0.32%	0.39%	0.56%	0.30%	0.78%	0.88%	2.6%	25
26	51.1%	70.5%	78.6%	76.6%	83.1%	85.0%	85.2%	85.9%	82.9%	0.62%	0.37%	0.32%	0.37%	0.53%	0.31%	0.61%	0.69%	1.5%	26
27	51.0%	70.3%	78.4%	76.4%	82.5%	84.8%	85.5%	85.8%	85.0%	0.65%	0.37%	0.33%	0.42%	0.55%	0.32%	0.56%	0.62%	1.4%	27
28	51.7%	70.2%	78.4%	76.5%	82.2%	84.0%	85.7%	85.8%	86.1%	0.62%	0.39%	0.31%	0.39%	0.52%	0.32%	0.48%	0.59%	1.0%	28
29	52.0%	70.4%	78.1%	76.3%	81.6%	82.8%	85.3%	85.1%	86.5%	0.64%	0.36%	0.32%	0.39%	0.49%	0.32%	0.50%	0.59%	0.9%	29
30	52.4%	71.0%	77.9%	76.0%	81.4%	81.6%	85.0%	84.4%	87.7%	0.64%	0.35%	0.31%	0.39%	0.53%	0.31%	0.51%	0.59%	1.0%	30
31	53.7%	71.6%	77.9%	76.2%	81.1%	80.0%	84.2%	83.6%	87.1%	0.61%	0.35%	0.32%	0.43%	0.50%	0.34%	0.46%	0.55%	0.9%	31
32	54.5%	71.9%	77.8%	76.2%	80.8%	78.7%	83.9%	83.3%	86.5%	0.61%	0.35%	0.31%	0.40%	0.50%	0.34%	0.48%	0.56%	0.9%	32
33	55.1%	72.2%	77.8%	76.2%	80.5%	77.9%	83.5%	82.8%	86.5%	0.59%	0.34%	0.33%	0.40%	0.49%	0.36%	0.49%	0.58%	1.0%	33
34	55.7%	72.7%	77.9%	76.3%	80.7%	77.3%	83.0%	82.3%	86.1%	0.59%	0.33%	0.32%	0.40%	0.47%	0.35%	0.48%	0.54%	0.9%	34
35	56.4%	73.2%	78.3%	76.8%	80.8%	76.7%	82.4%	81.7%	85.2%	0.60%	0.33%	0.31%	0.40%	0.47%	0.35%	0.48%	0.57%	0.9%	35
36	57.0%	73.7%	78.6%	77.0%	81.2%	76.8%	82.2%	81.6%	84.5%	0.62%	0.32%	0.30%	0.39%	0.47%	0.36%	0.50%	0.57%	0.9%	36
37	57.6%	74.1%	79.0%	77.5%	81.5%	76.9%	82.0%	81.4%	84.4%	0.57%	0.31%	0.29%	0.38%	0.46%	0.36%	0.52%	0.61%	1.0%	37
38	58.1%	74.8%	79.6%	78.2%	82.0%	77.1%	82.3%	81.7%	84.5%	0.59%	0.31%	0.29%	0.38%	0.44%	0.35%	0.51%	0.60%	1.0%	38
39	58.0%	75.4%	80.2%	78.8%	82.4%	77.6%	83.1%	82.6%	85.0%	0.59%	0.29%	0.28%	0.36%	0.44%	0.36%	0.48%	0.58%	0.9%	39
40	58.5%	75.9%	80.4%	79.1%	82.6%	78.4%	83.9%	83.5%	85.7%	0.57%	0.28%	0.26%	0.35%	0.41%	0.33%	0.47%	0.54%	0.8%	40
41	58.4%	76.3%	80.7%	79.6%	82.6%	79.3%	84.6%	84.2%	86.5%	0.61%	0.29%	0.27%	0.36%	0.42%	0.36%	0.45%	0.55%	0.8%	41
42	58.0%	76.7%	81.1%	79.7%	83.3%	80.2%	85.5%	85.2%	86.7%	0.59%	0.29%	0.28%	0.35%	0.44%	0.33%	0.46%	0.52%	0.9%	42
43	57.5%	77.0%	81.3%	79.8%	83.7%	80.9%	86.1%	86.2%	86.9%	0.59%	0.27%	0.27%	0.35%	0.41%	0.32%	0.47%	0.53%	0.9%	43
44	57.5%	76.9%	81.4%	79.9%	83.9%	81.7%	86.5%	86.7%	86.8%	0.58%	0.28%	0.26%	0.35%	0.40%	0.33%	0.42%	0.47%	1.0%	44
45	56.3%	76.8%	81.6%	80.0%	84.1%	82.5%	87.0%	87.3%	86.6%	0.58%	0.28%	0.25%	0.33%	0.38%	0.31%	0.40%	0.49%	0.9%	45
46	55.3%	76.7%	81.5%	79.9%	84.2%	82.9%	87.7%	88.3%	86.8%	0.58%	0.29%	0.27%	0.35%	0.40%	0.33%	0.44%	0.51%	0.9%	46
47	55.0%	76.4%	81.3%	79.7%	84.0%	83.2%	88.4%	89.1%	87.5%	0.60%	0.29%	0.27%	0.37%	0.44%	0.31%	0.41%	0.47%	0.9%	47
48	54.4%	75.9%	80.8%	79.1%	83.4%	83.2%	88.7%	89.3%	87.5%	0.61%	0.29%	0.28%	0.37%	0.43%	0.32%	0.39%	0.42%	0.9%	48
49	52.9%	75.1%	80.3%	78.7%	82.8%	82.8%	89.0%	89.5%	87.9%	0.66%	0.29%	0.29%	0.36%	0.43%	0.33%	0.35%	0.39%	0.9%	49
50	52.0%	74.1%	79.6%	78.1%	82.2%	82.2%	89.2%	89.5%	88.7%	0.63%	0.30%	0.29%	0.38%	0.44%	0.36%	0.37%	0.41%	0.9%	50
51	50.9%	72.8%	78.9%	77.4%	81.5%	81.7%	88.8%	89.1%	88.2%	0.63%	0.31%	0.29%	0.36%	0.49%	0.37%	0.38%	0.41%	0.8%	51
52	49.4%	71.2%	77.9%	76.5%	80.4%	80.9%	88.2%	88.3%	87.8%	0.62%	0.32%	0.31%	0.40%	0.50%	0.38%	0.37%	0.43%	0.8%	52
53	48.1%	69.2%	76.6%	75.2%	79.1%	79.8%	87.5%	87.4%	87.9%	0.64%	0.32%	0.31%	0.41%	0.52%	0.40%	0.43%	0.45%	0.9%	53
54	46.8%	67.4%	74.8%	73.4%	77.6%	78.1%	86.0%	85.8%	87.1%	0.63%	0.33%	0.34%	0.42%	0.55%	0.41%	0.39%	0.44%	0.9%	54
55	45.0%	65.8%	73.3%	71.7%	76.3%	76.2%	84.3%	83.9%	85.9%	0.64%	0.35%	0.37%	0.47%	0.60%	0.44%	0.44%	0.48%	0.9%	55
56	43.0%	63.7%	71.3%	69.7%	74.5%	74.2%	82.5%	81.8%	85.4%	0.64%	0.35%	0.38%	0.46%	0.67%	0.48%	0.51%	0.56%	1.1%	56
57	41.2%	61.6%	69.0%	67.3%	72.4%	72.1%	79.5%	78.5%	83.8%	0.59%	0.36%	0.38%	0.47%	0.66%	0.49%	0.54%	0.62%	1.1%	57
58	39.1%	59.3%	66.6%	65.0%	69.9%	69.2%	76.1%	75.0%	80.7%	0.59%	0.36%	0.42%	0.50%	0.69%	0.55%	0.58%	0.67%	1.2%	58
59	36.7%	56.7%	64.0%	62.2%	67.8%	66.5%	73.2%	71.9%	78.3%	0.61%	0.39%	0.45%	0.55%	0.75%	0.57%	0.66%	0.76%	1.3%	59
60	34.0%	52.5%	59.8%	58.0%	63.6%	62.4%	69.2%	67.9%	73.8%	0.60%	0.39%	0.46%	0.56%	0.82%	0.66%	0.74%	0.79%	1.6%	60
61	30.6%	47.9%	55.2%	53.6%	58.7%	57.3%	64.4%	63.2%	69.3%	0.56%	0.39%	0.49%	0.60%	0.91%	0.68%	0.82%	0.93%	1.6%	61
62	27.3%	42.9%	50.5%	49.1%	53.7%	51.8%	59.9%	58.8%	64.5%	0.56%	0.39%	0.50%	0.58%	0.90%	0.73%	0.89%	0.95%	1.9%	62
63	23.1%	37.4%	44.8%	43.6%	47.5%	45.9%	54.4%	53.1%	59.8%	0.50%	0.40%	0.52%	0.64%	0.97%	0.75%	0.98%	1.03%	2.2%	63
64	20.0%	32.0%	39.1%	38.4%	40.8%	40.3%	48.7%	47.1%	54.3%	0.47%	0.36%	0.51%	0.63%	0.97%	0.74%	0.97%	1.15%	2.1%	64
65	17.6%	28.2%	35.0%	34.5%	36.3%	35.4%	43.5%	41.5%	51.3%	0.40%	0.35%	0.52%	0.62%	0.94%	0.72%	0.99%	1.11%	2.3%	65
66	15.4%	24.4%	31.0%	30.5%	32.1%	30.9%	39.0%	36.7%	46.8%	0.40%	0.36%	0.52%	0.60%	0.94%	0.75%	1.05%	1.14%	2.4%	66
67	13.6%	21.1%	27.2%	27.0%	27.7%	26.6%	34.3%	31.7%	42.7%	0.40%	0.36%	0.53%	0.66%	1.01%	0.70%	1.07%	1.14%	2.6%	67
68	12.3%	18.7%	24.6%	24.5%	24.9%	23.6%	30.3%	27.9%	37.6%	0.34%	0.32%	0.51%	0.61%	1.00%	0.74%	1.03%	1.15%	2.3%	68
69	10.9%	16.5%	22.2%	22.0%	22.5%	20.9%	27.0%	24.9%	33.8%	0.37%	0.30%	0.51%	0.60%	0.96%	0.71%	1.05%	1.22%	2.4%	69
70	9.2%	14.6%	19.3%	19.1%	19.6%	18.4%	23.8%	22.0%	29.8%	0.33%	0.29%	0.48%	0.58%	0.85%	0.70%	1.01%	1.11%	2.0%	70
71	8.3%	12.9%	16.9%	16.8%	17.1%	16.5%	21.3%	19.7%	27.1%	0.29%	0.29%	0.46%	0.54%	0.89%	0.68%	1.04%	1.18%	2.7%	71
72	7.1%	11.5%	14.5%	14.4%	14.8%	14.8%	19.3%	18.2%	24.1%	0.25%	0.27%	0.44%	0.52%	0.86%	0.61%	1.05%	1.11%	2.5%	72
73	6.0%	10.2%	12.6%	12.6%	12.6%	13.1%	18.3%	17.2%	23.7%	0.27%	0.25%	0.44%	0.50%	1.04%	0.68%	1.06%	1.14%	2.7%	73
74	5.2%	8.8%	11.1%	11.1%	11.1%	11.7%	16.8%	15.8%	21.0%	0.24%	0.25%	0.41%	0.47%	0.82%	0.66%	1.04%	1.11%	2.8%	74
75	4.6%	7.5%	9.8%	9.8%	9.7%	10.8%	15.4%	14.7%	19.0%	0.22%	0.23%	0.35%	0.43%	0.65%	0.59%	1.02%	1.16%	2.4%	75

Sources: Current Population Survey monthly microdata samples 2000 through 2006.

Appendix Table 5: Labor force participation rates and their standard errors by educational attainment, conventional methodology, White Males

| Age | White Males: Labor Force Participation Rates | | | | | | | | White Males: Standard Errors of Labor Force Participation Rates | | | | | | | | Age |
| | | | Some College | | | | | | | | Some College | | | | | | |
	<HS	HS	All	No Degree	Assoc Degree	College Degree	Masters	Phd/ Prof'l	<HS	HS	All	No Degree	Assoc Degree	College Degree	Masters	Phd/ Prof'l	
18	49.9%	71.6%	58.8%	58.5%	75.7%				0.30%	0.38%	0.68%	0.71%	4.88%				18
19	54.7%	78.4%	65.5%	64.4%	82.0%				0.45%	0.31%	0.37%	0.36%	2.26%				19
20	67.8%	80.9%	68.1%	66.7%	83.4%	80.5%			0.49%	0.30%	0.32%	0.33%	1.18%	3.25%			20
21	80.1%	85.7%	71.4%	69.8%	85.5%	84.5%	79.5%		0.48%	0.29%	0.31%	0.33%	0.77%	1.65%	8.83%		21
22	85.2%	88.9%	76.1%	74.1%	88.0%	86.9%	83.9%		0.42%	0.26%	0.32%	0.35%	0.71%	0.64%	5.89%		22
23	87.5%	90.4%	80.9%	78.8%	90.0%	88.2%	86.4%	77.5%	0.42%	0.25%	0.31%	0.34%	0.55%	0.40%	2.60%	7.06%	23
24	88.7%	91.6%	85.8%	84.0%	91.8%	89.4%	89.7%	81.4%	0.41%	0.23%	0.28%	0.35%	0.40%	0.32%	1.62%	4.32%	24
25	89.2%	92.3%	89.8%	88.5%	93.4%	91.2%	91.7%	86.0%	0.36%	0.23%	0.27%	0.34%	0.40%	0.29%	1.08%	2.25%	25
26	89.6%	92.8%	91.9%	90.9%	94.4%	92.7%	92.7%	89.6%	0.37%	0.23%	0.24%	0.30%	0.40%	0.28%	0.72%	1.69%	26
27	90.1%	93.0%	92.9%	92.2%	94.6%	93.8%	93.6%	92.0%	0.37%	0.22%	0.23%	0.28%	0.42%	0.24%	0.59%	1.12%	27
28	90.0%	93.2%	94.0%	93.5%	95.0%	94.8%	94.2%	93.7%	0.36%	0.21%	0.23%	0.28%	0.38%	0.22%	0.56%	0.74%	28
29	90.0%	93.3%	94.4%	94.1%	95.2%	95.6%	94.7%	95.6%	0.38%	0.22%	0.22%	0.27%	0.36%	0.21%	0.52%	0.60%	29
30	89.6%	93.3%	94.8%	94.4%	95.6%	96.1%	95.2%	96.5%	0.38%	0.21%	0.19%	0.23%	0.32%	0.20%	0.45%	0.52%	30
31	89.4%	93.2%	94.9%	94.5%	95.8%	96.5%	95.9%	96.9%	0.38%	0.21%	0.20%	0.25%	0.32%	0.18%	0.37%	0.46%	31
32	89.2%	93.3%	95.1%	94.6%	96.0%	96.8%	96.5%	97.3%	0.42%	0.21%	0.19%	0.25%	0.30%	0.17%	0.35%	0.46%	32
33	89.2%	93.2%	95.0%	94.5%	96.0%	96.9%	96.9%	97.4%	0.38%	0.22%	0.20%	0.26%	0.31%	0.16%	0.29%	0.45%	33
34	88.9%	93.1%	95.0%	94.4%	96.1%	96.9%	97.1%	97.3%	0.37%	0.20%	0.19%	0.25%	0.28%	0.16%	0.25%	0.30%	34
35	88.8%	92.9%	94.7%	94.1%	95.7%	96.9%	97.4%	97.5%	0.39%	0.19%	0.19%	0.25%	0.30%	0.18%	0.34%	0.48%	35
36	88.6%	92.7%	94.6%	94.0%	95.8%	96.9%	97.4%	97.7%	0.41%	0.20%	0.20%	0.27%	0.30%	0.19%	0.26%	0.46%	36
37	88.1%	92.6%	94.6%	93.9%	95.9%	96.8%	97.2%	97.7%	0.41%	0.21%	0.21%	0.28%	0.34%	0.16%	0.24%	0.31%	37
38	87.2%	92.3%	94.4%	93.7%	95.7%	96.8%	97.4%	97.8%	0.39%	0.20%	0.20%	0.27%	0.26%	0.17%	0.28%	0.33%	38
39	86.6%	92.1%	94.3%	93.7%	95.5%	97.1%	97.0%	98.0%	0.42%	0.20%	0.18%	0.25%	0.28%	0.16%	0.29%	0.31%	39
40	85.5%	92.1%	94.3%	93.6%	95.5%	97.0%	96.9%	97.8%	0.40%	0.20%	0.20%	0.26%	0.31%	0.16%	0.28%	0.37%	40
41	84.6%	91.9%	94.1%	93.4%	95.2%	96.9%	97.0%	97.2%	0.44%	0.20%	0.20%	0.25%	0.31%	0.16%	0.35%	0.28%	41
42	83.4%	91.8%	93.8%	93.1%	94.9%	96.8%	97.0%	97.0%	0.45%	0.20%	0.20%	0.26%	0.30%	0.17%	0.28%	0.41%	42
43	82.5%	91.5%	93.5%	92.9%	94.6%	96.7%	97.0%	97.1%	0.44%	0.20%	0.21%	0.28%	0.30%	0.19%	0.27%	0.48%	43
44	81.6%	91.1%	93.2%	92.6%	94.4%	96.4%	97.1%	97.0%	0.48%	0.20%	0.22%	0.27%	0.30%	0.18%	0.27%	0.37%	44
45	80.8%	90.7%	92.7%	92.1%	94.0%	96.2%	97.1%	97.1%	0.50%	0.22%	0.21%	0.26%	0.34%	0.18%	0.29%	0.33%	45
46	79.2%	90.1%	92.4%	91.8%	93.6%	96.0%	96.9%	97.4%	0.51%	0.22%	0.22%	0.28%	0.34%	0.19%	0.29%	0.33%	46
47	78.5%	89.4%	92.0%	91.4%	93.1%	95.8%	96.6%	97.3%	0.55%	0.23%	0.23%	0.31%	0.36%	0.21%	0.28%	0.32%	47
48	78.0%	88.7%	91.4%	90.8%	92.4%	95.4%	96.2%	97.0%	0.59%	0.26%	0.23%	0.29%	0.37%	0.21%	0.28%	0.34%	48
49	76.8%	87.8%	90.6%	90.2%	91.5%	95.0%	96.0%	96.5%	0.56%	0.27%	0.24%	0.30%	0.43%	0.20%	0.28%	0.36%	49
50	75.5%	86.7%	89.8%	89.3%	90.8%	94.4%	95.6%	96.3%	0.56%	0.25%	0.25%	0.30%	0.43%	0.21%	0.34%	0.37%	50
51	74.1%	85.7%	88.8%	88.2%	90.0%	93.7%	95.0%	96.0%	0.62%	0.28%	0.27%	0.33%	0.47%	0.24%	0.30%	0.42%	51
52	72.3%	84.5%	87.8%	87.1%	89.2%	92.9%	94.6%	95.8%	0.65%	0.30%	0.29%	0.38%	0.46%	0.26%	0.33%	0.38%	52
53	70.0%	83.2%	86.5%	85.7%	88.3%	91.8%	93.5%	95.3%	0.69%	0.33%	0.30%	0.38%	0.49%	0.25%	0.36%	0.40%	53
54	68.2%	81.5%	85.0%	84.1%	86.9%	90.6%	92.1%	94.8%	0.65%	0.35%	0.31%	0.39%	0.53%	0.27%	0.36%	0.39%	54
55	66.8%	79.5%	83.3%	82.6%	85.0%	89.2%	90.2%	94.0%	0.71%	0.34%	0.34%	0.43%	0.58%	0.31%	0.43%	0.46%	55
56	65.2%	77.4%	81.3%	80.8%	82.4%	87.6%	87.9%	93.2%	0.69%	0.36%	0.36%	0.46%	0.64%	0.37%	0.47%	0.50%	56
57	63.3%	75.5%	79.0%	78.9%	79.1%	85.5%	85.0%	92.1%	0.72%	0.40%	0.39%	0.49%	0.74%	0.40%	0.59%	0.56%	57
58	61.5%	72.9%	76.3%	76.5%	75.9%	82.9%	82.3%	90.7%	0.68%	0.41%	0.42%	0.48%	0.78%	0.43%	0.64%	0.62%	58
59	59.7%	70.1%	73.5%	73.8%	72.8%	80.0%	78.7%	89.0%	0.72%	0.42%	0.48%	0.56%	0.92%	0.49%	0.71%	0.70%	59
60	55.7%	65.7%	69.9%	70.3%	68.9%	76.1%	74.6%	86.5%	0.72%	0.44%	0.53%	0.63%	0.98%	0.58%	0.80%	0.79%	60
61	50.8%	60.0%	65.1%	65.3%	64.5%	71.2%	69.7%	83.3%	0.69%	0.48%	0.57%	0.65%	0.99%	0.62%	0.84%	0.85%	61
62	46.0%	53.4%	59.9%	59.8%	60.1%	66.1%	64.8%	80.2%	0.68%	0.50%	0.56%	0.71%	1.15%	0.70%	0.90%	1.01%	62
63	40.2%	46.5%	53.9%	53.5%	54.7%	60.4%	59.8%	76.7%	0.68%	0.50%	0.64%	0.73%	1.23%	0.71%	1.00%	1.12%	63
64	34.3%	40.0%	47.6%	47.6%	47.5%	54.6%	54.5%	71.6%	0.71%	0.50%	0.64%	0.74%	1.28%	0.78%	1.05%	1.19%	64
65	29.9%	35.4%	42.0%	42.1%	41.8%	49.5%	49.5%	67.5%	0.63%	0.45%	0.65%	0.70%	1.26%	0.73%	1.02%	1.16%	65
66	27.0%	32.3%	37.4%	37.7%	36.6%	45.0%	44.2%	62.5%	0.57%	0.47%	0.61%	0.71%	1.20%	0.77%	1.13%	1.31%	66
67	24.1%	29.2%	33.1%	33.3%	32.3%	40.1%	38.5%	56.7%	0.57%	0.49%	0.62%	0.76%	1.19%	0.81%	1.16%	1.33%	67
68	20.9%	26.9%	29.6%	30.1%	28.3%	35.8%	33.8%	51.1%	0.59%	0.48%	0.65%	0.76%	1.25%	0.82%	1.18%	1.42%	68
69	18.5%	24.6%	26.3%	26.8%	24.6%	32.1%	30.7%	48.3%	0.55%	0.48%	0.63%	0.77%	1.33%	0.81%	1.14%	1.47%	69
70	16.8%	22.4%	23.9%	24.4%	22.4%	29.3%	28.7%	44.3%	0.49%	0.48%	0.63%	0.74%	1.25%	0.72%	1.06%	1.42%	70
71	14.7%	20.2%	21.5%	22.0%	19.8%	26.7%	26.1%	41.5%	0.48%	0.43%	0.62%	0.71%	1.06%	0.76%	1.11%	1.45%	71
72	13.1%	18.0%	19.6%	19.9%	18.7%	24.1%	24.0%	38.1%	0.45%	0.46%	0.60%	0.70%	1.26%	0.82%	1.21%	1.53%	72
73	11.9%	16.4%	18.0%	18.0%	18.1%	22.3%	21.3%	35.3%	0.43%	0.45%	0.58%	0.66%	1.21%	0.79%	1.03%	1.54%	73
74	10.9%	15.0%	17.1%	16.6%	18.6%	21.1%	18.6%	31.2%	0.42%	0.42%	0.63%	0.69%	1.38%	0.72%	1.07%	1.38%	74
75	9.8%	13.2%	15.6%	15.3%	16.9%	19.1%	16.3%	27.9%	0.37%	0.41%	0.57%	0.62%	1.31%	0.72%	1.08%	1.39%	75

Sources: Current Population Survey monthly microdata samples 2000 through 2006.

Appendix Table 5: Labor force participation rates and their standard errors by educational attainment, conventional methodology, White Females

| | White Females: Labor Force Participation Rates | | | | | | | | White Females: Standard Errors of Labor Force Participation Rates | | | | | | | | |
| | | | Some College | | | | | | | | Some College | | | | | | |
Age	<HS	HS	All	No Degree	Assoc Degree	College Degree	Masters	Phd/Prof'l	<HS	HS	All	No Degree	Assoc Degree	College Degree	Masters	Phd/Prof'l	Age
18	48.1%	65.6%	63.5%	63.3%	69.2%				0.35%	0.35%	0.57%	0.58%	4.44%				18
19	48.7%	69.3%	68.2%	67.6%	77.6%				0.61%	0.38%	0.32%	0.34%	2.00%				19
20	51.7%	70.4%	69.7%	68.8%	79.2%	80.4%			0.67%	0.40%	0.29%	0.30%	0.98%	3.01%			20
21	51.6%	72.5%	71.9%	70.7%	81.2%	83.4%	78.1%		0.70%	0.39%	0.28%	0.31%	0.76%	1.28%	7.45%		21
22	51.5%	73.1%	74.3%	72.7%	82.6%	84.7%	85.9%		0.69%	0.40%	0.31%	0.34%	0.69%	0.45%	4.19%		22
23	50.6%	72.4%	76.0%	74.2%	83.1%	85.7%	87.3%	76.2%	0.72%	0.41%	0.33%	0.39%	0.57%	0.34%	1.75%	6.1%	23
24	50.3%	71.6%	78.2%	76.2%	84.0%	86.3%	88.4%	83.4%	0.72%	0.41%	0.33%	0.43%	0.56%	0.31%	0.91%	3.4%	24
25	49.8%	70.6%	79.1%	76.9%	84.2%	86.8%	89.6%	83.6%	0.66%	0.41%	0.36%	0.44%	0.56%	0.31%	0.81%	2.8%	25
26	49.2%	70.0%	78.8%	76.6%	83.6%	86.7%	90.0%	86.0%	0.72%	0.44%	0.35%	0.44%	0.57%	0.31%	0.65%	1.4%	26
27	48.9%	69.5%	78.3%	76.0%	82.7%	86.4%	89.1%	87.2%	0.69%	0.44%	0.36%	0.46%	0.56%	0.33%	0.60%	1.5%	27
28	49.7%	69.4%	77.9%	75.7%	82.1%	85.3%	88.6%	87.6%	0.69%	0.43%	0.37%	0.46%	0.55%	0.34%	0.56%	1.1%	28
29	50.2%	69.5%	77.4%	75.1%	81.5%	83.8%	87.5%	86.9%	0.70%	0.43%	0.36%	0.47%	0.56%	0.36%	0.63%	1.0%	29
30	50.7%	70.3%	76.9%	74.5%	81.1%	82.2%	86.2%	87.9%	0.69%	0.40%	0.37%	0.48%	0.59%	0.35%	0.58%	1.2%	30
31	52.3%	70.9%	76.7%	74.4%	80.6%	80.3%	85.0%	87.3%	0.73%	0.40%	0.35%	0.47%	0.53%	0.36%	0.58%	1.1%	31
32	53.1%	71.3%	76.5%	74.2%	80.3%	78.8%	84.4%	86.7%	0.69%	0.40%	0.36%	0.48%	0.56%	0.38%	0.63%	0.9%	32
33	53.8%	71.6%	76.6%	74.4%	80.2%	77.6%	83.5%	86.9%	0.67%	0.38%	0.37%	0.46%	0.56%	0.39%	0.60%	1.1%	33
34	54.3%	72.1%	76.8%	74.7%	80.3%	77.0%	82.6%	86.7%	0.71%	0.39%	0.36%	0.47%	0.54%	0.38%	0.62%	1.0%	34
35	55.3%	72.7%	77.4%	75.5%	80.4%	76.2%	81.6%	85.4%	0.66%	0.38%	0.35%	0.46%	0.52%	0.38%	0.61%	1.0%	35
36	55.9%	73.3%	77.8%	75.8%	81.1%	76.1%	81.2%	84.9%	0.66%	0.35%	0.32%	0.42%	0.49%	0.40%	0.63%	1.1%	36
37	56.7%	73.9%	78.4%	76.4%	81.4%	76.1%	80.9%	84.6%	0.66%	0.35%	0.32%	0.42%	0.51%	0.40%	0.70%	1.1%	37
38	57.2%	74.6%	79.0%	77.2%	81.8%	76.2%	81.2%	84.5%	0.67%	0.34%	0.32%	0.44%	0.46%	0.38%	0.64%	1.1%	38
39	57.5%	75.3%	79.5%	77.8%	82.1%	76.7%	81.9%	84.7%	0.67%	0.32%	0.32%	0.42%	0.50%	0.38%	0.63%	1.1%	39
40	58.2%	76.1%	79.8%	78.2%	82.2%	77.8%	83.0%	85.5%	0.64%	0.32%	0.30%	0.39%	0.44%	0.36%	0.62%	0.9%	40
41	58.6%	76.4%	80.2%	78.9%	82.2%	78.8%	83.8%	86.1%	0.64%	0.31%	0.30%	0.39%	0.45%	0.35%	0.58%	1.0%	41
42	58.2%	76.8%	80.7%	79.3%	82.9%	79.6%	84.9%	86.0%	0.69%	0.30%	0.30%	0.40%	0.44%	0.37%	0.58%	0.9%	42
43	57.9%	77.3%	81.1%	79.6%	83.3%	80.4%	85.7%	86.1%	0.68%	0.30%	0.28%	0.39%	0.47%	0.34%	0.55%	1.0%	43
44	57.8%	77.5%	81.4%	79.8%	83.8%	81.2%	86.1%	86.2%	0.67%	0.31%	0.29%	0.39%	0.43%	0.38%	0.52%	1.1%	44
45	56.4%	77.3%	81.8%	80.4%	84.1%	82.0%	87.0%	86.2%	0.68%	0.31%	0.30%	0.38%	0.43%	0.34%	0.52%	1.0%	45
46	55.3%	77.3%	81.9%	80.4%	84.3%	82.5%	87.9%	86.5%	0.68%	0.30%	0.29%	0.39%	0.44%	0.37%	0.56%	0.9%	46
47	55.0%	77.1%	81.8%	80.3%	84.2%	82.8%	88.6%	87.4%	0.73%	0.32%	0.30%	0.38%	0.46%	0.35%	0.51%	1.0%	47
48	54.2%	76.6%	81.4%	79.9%	83.8%	82.9%	89.2%	87.4%	0.72%	0.32%	0.30%	0.40%	0.44%	0.34%	0.44%	0.9%	48
49	52.9%	75.6%	81.0%	79.5%	83.3%	82.6%	89.6%	87.7%	0.72%	0.32%	0.31%	0.45%	0.49%	0.38%	0.41%	0.9%	49
50	52.1%	74.6%	80.2%	78.8%	82.7%	82.1%	89.6%	88.2%	0.72%	0.33%	0.31%	0.43%	0.48%	0.38%	0.41%	1.0%	50
51	50.8%	73.4%	79.5%	78.0%	82.0%	81.6%	89.1%	87.8%	0.73%	0.34%	0.31%	0.41%	0.51%	0.40%	0.43%	0.9%	51
52	49.1%	71.9%	78.6%	77.2%	81.0%	80.8%	88.4%	87.4%	0.74%	0.34%	0.34%	0.44%	0.54%	0.41%	0.45%	0.9%	52
53	47.9%	69.9%	77.2%	75.8%	79.7%	79.7%	87.6%	87.5%	0.74%	0.33%	0.36%	0.46%	0.55%	0.40%	0.49%	1.0%	53
54	46.5%	68.2%	75.4%	74.0%	78.1%	78.0%	85.9%	87.0%	0.73%	0.37%	0.38%	0.46%	0.62%	0.44%	0.47%	1.0%	54
55	44.8%	66.5%	73.8%	72.1%	77.0%	75.8%	84.1%	86.0%	0.75%	0.37%	0.39%	0.48%	0.65%	0.48%	0.49%	1.1%	55
56	42.9%	64.3%	71.7%	70.0%	75.1%	73.7%	82.0%	85.5%	0.76%	0.40%	0.41%	0.51%	0.68%	0.53%	0.64%	1.1%	56
57	41.1%	62.0%	69.3%	67.6%	72.9%	71.7%	78.5%	83.7%	0.70%	0.38%	0.42%	0.51%	0.67%	0.53%	0.64%	1.2%	57
58	39.2%	59.6%	66.9%	65.1%	70.7%	68.9%	74.8%	80.8%	0.68%	0.40%	0.45%	0.57%	0.75%	0.59%	0.68%	1.3%	58
59	36.9%	56.9%	64.2%	62.1%	68.7%	66.3%	71.6%	78.1%	0.69%	0.40%	0.47%	0.58%	0.84%	0.64%	0.81%	1.4%	59
60	34.1%	52.7%	60.0%	58.0%	64.3%	62.2%	67.7%	73.8%	0.67%	0.41%	0.50%	0.64%	0.86%	0.71%	0.87%	1.7%	60
61	30.7%	48.1%	55.3%	53.6%	59.3%	57.2%	62.9%	70.0%	0.66%	0.42%	0.53%	0.60%	0.96%	0.73%	0.97%	1.7%	61
62	27.7%	43.2%	50.7%	49.1%	54.1%	51.6%	59.0%	65.9%	0.58%	0.42%	0.54%	0.65%	1.00%	0.79%	1.02%	2.1%	62
63	23.4%	37.8%	45.0%	43.7%	48.0%	45.6%	53.6%	60.8%	0.58%	0.41%	0.54%	0.64%	1.03%	0.81%	1.14%	2.3%	63
64	20.2%	32.3%	39.5%	38.7%	41.2%	39.9%	48.0%	54.6%	0.55%	0.40%	0.56%	0.69%	1.01%	0.81%	1.20%	2.4%	64
65	17.9%	28.4%	35.4%	34.8%	37.0%	35.1%	42.4%	50.8%	0.48%	0.38%	0.56%	0.65%	1.00%	0.76%	1.20%	2.5%	65
66	15.5%	24.7%	31.5%	30.8%	33.1%	30.6%	37.7%	45.2%	0.47%	0.37%	0.55%	0.65%	1.02%	0.80%	1.24%	2.5%	66
67	13.6%	21.3%	27.7%	27.4%	28.5%	26.5%	32.6%	40.1%	0.48%	0.36%	0.56%	0.70%	1.10%	0.79%	1.33%	2.6%	67
68	12.3%	18.8%	25.0%	24.8%	25.5%	23.7%	28.8%	36.0%	0.41%	0.35%	0.56%	0.67%	1.08%	0.77%	1.27%	2.4%	68
69	11.0%	16.7%	22.5%	22.3%	23.0%	21.1%	25.8%	33.1%	0.42%	0.32%	0.55%	0.65%	0.99%	0.77%	1.25%	2.6%	69
70	9.3%	14.9%	19.4%	19.3%	19.7%	18.6%	22.8%	29.9%	0.38%	0.30%	0.50%	0.60%	0.93%	0.77%	1.24%	2.3%	70
71	8.4%	13.1%	17.0%	17.0%	17.1%	16.8%	20.3%	27.5%	0.34%	0.31%	0.49%	0.58%	0.91%	0.73%	1.25%	2.6%	71
72	7.3%	11.6%	14.5%	14.5%	14.8%	14.9%	18.6%	24.1%	0.30%	0.30%	0.45%	0.55%	0.91%	0.68%	1.17%	2.8%	72
73	6.3%	10.4%	12.5%	12.5%	12.5%	13.1%	17.4%	24.1%	0.32%	0.27%	0.50%	0.54%	1.12%	0.74%	1.18%	3.1%	73
74	5.5%	8.9%	10.9%	10.9%	10.8%	11.7%	15.9%	21.3%	0.29%	0.27%	0.41%	0.49%	0.81%	0.72%	1.21%	2.7%	74
75	4.9%	7.6%	9.6%	9.7%	9.5%	10.6%	14.7%	18.7%	0.25%	0.24%	0.38%	0.44%	0.66%	0.59%	1.24%	2.9%	75

Sources: Current Population Survey monthly microdata samples 2000 through 2006.

Appendix Table 5: Labor force participation rates and their standard errors by educational attainment, conventional methodology, Black Males

Age		Black Males: Labor Force Participation Rates					Black Males: Std Errors of Labor Force Participation				Age
	<HS	HS	Some College	College Degree	Graduate Degree	<HS	HS	Some College	College Degree	Graduate Degree	
18	37.3%	58.1%	47.0%			0.69%	1.11%	1.88%			18
19	46.1%	66.3%	55.8%			1.05%	0.96%	1.21%			19
20	52.6%	68.9%	60.0%	73.0%		1.30%	0.90%	1.06%	12.40%		20
21	59.1%	72.5%	63.8%	77.2%		1.46%	0.92%	1.10%	5.66%		21
22	67.0%	76.3%	69.1%	81.0%	66.1%	1.48%	0.96%	0.97%	3.01%	5.37%	22
23	64.1%	78.0%	74.5%	83.2%	39.8%	1.58%	0.92%	1.06%	1.93%	7.78%	23
24	65.7%	79.6%	80.1%	85.5%	58.6%	1.66%	0.83%	1.01%	1.51%	9.66%	24
25	68.6%	80.8%	83.1%	87.8%	94.7%	1.62%	0.87%	0.94%	1.34%	3.05%	25
26	72.5%	81.9%	86.1%	90.3%	82.5%	1.64%	0.88%	0.80%	1.14%	3.96%	26
27	71.8%	82.5%	87.0%	91.9%	88.1%	1.79%	0.88%	0.91%	1.04%	2.89%	27
28	72.8%	83.4%	88.5%	93.3%	92.2%	1.80%	0.88%	0.82%	0.88%	2.05%	28
29	70.8%	84.1%	89.1%	93.8%	95.6%	1.98%	0.83%	0.83%	0.89%	1.40%	29
30	71.1%	85.0%	90.4%	94.3%	88.9%	1.89%	0.69%	0.78%	0.81%	2.43%	30
31	75.5%	86.1%	90.8%	94.2%	93.8%	1.78%	0.76%	0.64%	0.95%	1.68%	31
32	71.9%	86.3%	91.8%	94.7%	97.9%	1.90%	0.74%	0.62%	0.81%	0.83%	32
33	70.5%	86.1%	91.9%	95.0%	96.0%	1.74%	0.70%	0.77%	0.77%	1.13%	33
34	77.1%	86.3%	91.4%	95.8%	96.1%	1.49%	0.73%	0.61%	0.63%	1.07%	34
35	67.6%	86.0%	90.9%	96.2%	92.8%	1.82%	0.77%	0.71%	0.71%	1.50%	35
36	72.0%	85.4%	91.0%	96.1%	91.5%	1.79%	0.73%	0.81%	0.61%	1.79%	36
37	66.3%	85.1%	90.9%	95.6%	94.9%	1.88%	0.81%	0.70%	0.62%	1.39%	37
38	71.7%	84.9%	90.5%	94.6%	96.9%	1.59%	0.75%	0.73%	0.86%	0.95%	38
39	67.4%	84.3%	90.4%	93.8%	95.5%	1.67%	0.73%	0.66%	0.82%	1.23%	39
40	70.6%	83.6%	89.9%	93.3%	93.2%	1.62%	0.71%	0.75%	0.97%	1.39%	40
41	63.9%	83.0%	89.4%	92.9%	91.6%	1.63%	0.75%	0.78%	0.90%	1.56%	41
42	64.7%	82.2%	88.6%	91.7%	96.5%	1.65%	0.81%	0.81%	0.81%	1.07%	42
43	68.1%	81.4%	87.2%	92.0%	94.5%	1.61%	0.76%	0.78%	0.87%	1.68%	43
44	61.1%	80.9%	86.1%	91.4%	89.9%	1.54%	0.84%	0.77%	1.23%	1.97%	44
45	59.2%	80.7%	85.6%	91.2%	93.3%	1.51%	0.77%	0.98%	0.95%	1.37%	45
46	64.3%	79.5%	84.2%	91.0%	94.0%	1.70%	0.81%	0.94%	1.09%	1.19%	46
47	64.5%	79.0%	82.9%	91.7%	98.1%	1.64%	0.88%	0.86%	0.96%	0.76%	47
48	63.9%	78.4%	82.9%	91.2%	93.9%	1.61%	0.94%	1.05%	0.98%	1.44%	48
49	61.9%	77.7%	82.4%	91.3%	95.4%	1.71%	0.93%	1.02%	0.96%	1.09%	49
50	60.7%	76.7%	80.8%	89.5%	89.9%	1.62%	0.95%	0.98%	1.13%	1.65%	50
51	63.2%	76.1%	80.0%	87.8%	91.5%	1.68%	0.92%	0.97%	1.28%	1.42%	51
52	65.2%	75.2%	79.0%	85.8%	94.1%	1.54%	1.05%	1.21%	1.62%	1.21%	52
53	63.9%	73.1%	77.3%	83.2%	91.5%	1.52%	1.13%	1.17%	1.58%	1.48%	53
54	59.6%	70.7%	75.8%	80.5%	89.7%	1.71%	1.15%	1.18%	1.71%	1.59%	54
55	52.6%	69.8%	74.4%	79.0%	89.4%	1.71%	1.17%	1.35%	1.87%	1.72%	55
56	52.9%	68.6%	72.8%	77.8%	84.4%	1.63%	1.24%	1.35%	1.81%	2.08%	56
57	51.9%	66.6%	71.2%	77.1%	81.6%	1.64%	1.31%	1.50%	2.15%	2.51%	57
58	51.8%	65.4%	68.2%	75.8%	78.4%	1.56%	1.37%	1.73%	2.22%	2.70%	58
59	47.9%	63.5%	64.6%	73.0%	79.3%	1.68%	1.47%	1.79%	2.27%	2.62%	59
60	45.2%	57.9%	59.4%	68.3%	76.9%	1.67%	1.42%	1.98%	2.80%	2.87%	60
61	40.3%	52.3%	54.5%	62.6%	72.0%	1.66%	1.50%	2.13%	3.00%	2.89%	61
62	35.8%	47.4%	48.2%	55.8%	66.2%	1.57%	1.49%	2.08%	3.13%	3.28%	62
63	29.5%	41.9%	42.1%	49.8%	62.1%	1.61%	1.49%	2.26%	3.68%	3.60%	63
64	27.0%	36.3%	37.0%	44.6%	58.9%	1.45%	1.57%	2.28%	3.66%	4.32%	64
65	23.6%	31.7%	33.7%	41.9%	49.7%	1.31%	1.47%	1.97%	3.23%	4.03%	65
66	22.5%	27.7%	30.8%	38.9%	43.7%	1.20%	1.64%	2.06%	3.47%	3.65%	66
67	19.4%	24.5%	27.7%	36.3%	37.8%	1.34%	1.56%	2.29%	3.79%	3.82%	67
68	18.4%	22.1%	25.8%	34.0%	43.4%	1.23%	1.51%	2.38%	4.33%	4.20%	68
69	17.4%	19.6%	23.3%	30.9%	35.5%	1.26%	1.60%	2.31%	4.29%	4.11%	69
70	16.3%	18.8%	21.3%	30.6%	34.5%	1.22%	1.73%	2.30%	3.57%	4.55%	70
71	14.0%	17.8%	20.1%	30.6%	33.4%	1.10%	1.59%	2.75%	3.53%	4.34%	71
72	12.6%	16.0%	18.1%	28.9%	34.3%	1.05%	1.56%	2.65%	4.09%	5.22%	72
73	11.0%	14.6%	16.4%	25.7%	21.7%	1.21%	1.72%	2.68%	5.12%	4.20%	73
74	9.7%	14.5%	16.0%	25.6%	12.7%	1.08%	1.54%	2.53%	5.97%	3.43%	74
75	8.0%	14.2%	15.1%	20.0%	16.0%	0.90%	1.70%	2.12%	3.96%	4.01%	75

Sources: Current Population Survey monthly microdata samples 2000 through 2006.

Appendix Table 5: Labor force participation rates and their standard errors by educational attainment, conventional methodology, Black Females

Age	Black Females: Labor Force Participation Rates					Black Females: Std Errors of Labor Force Participation					Age
	<HS	HS	Some College	College Degree	Graduate Degree	<HS	HS	Some College	College Degree	Graduate Degree	
18	32.3%	53.8%	48.6%			0.76%	0.99%	1.49%			18
19	35.9%	60.5%	56.9%			1.18%	0.91%	0.92%			19
20	44.0%	62.6%	60.1%	76.8%		1.36%	0.93%	0.88%	9.81%		20
21	50.8%	66.7%	64.3%	79.8%		1.38%	0.90%	0.82%	3.95%		21
22	54.3%	69.8%	68.7%	80.6%	81.6%	1.34%	0.98%	0.84%	1.60%	5.51%	22
23	55.6%	71.0%	73.0%	82.6%	83.6%	1.57%	0.91%	0.89%	1.22%	5.82%	23
24	56.3%	72.3%	76.5%	84.4%	85.5%	1.42%	0.96%	0.80%	1.14%	3.56%	24
25	58.1%	73.6%	78.8%	86.1%	87.4%	1.48%	0.95%	0.80%	1.16%	2.96%	25
26	59.4%	74.8%	80.0%	87.5%	89.2%	1.61%	0.93%	0.81%	1.02%	1.88%	26
27	60.3%	75.3%	81.4%	89.5%	89.4%	1.58%	0.90%	0.83%	0.89%	1.69%	27
28	60.4%	75.5%	82.6%	89.6%	90.3%	1.65%	0.83%	0.78%	0.94%	1.44%	28
29	60.6%	75.9%	82.8%	89.5%	91.1%	1.63%	0.90%	0.74%	0.83%	1.62%	29
30	60.3%	76.6%	83.8%	89.5%	91.0%	1.56%	0.86%	0.70%	0.94%	1.42%	30
31	60.5%	76.7%	84.5%	89.1%	90.4%	1.73%	0.85%	0.77%	0.92%	1.12%	31
32	61.3%	76.8%	84.8%	88.9%	90.8%	1.65%	0.85%	0.69%	0.84%	1.39%	32
33	61.6%	77.4%	84.5%	89.5%	90.6%	1.57%	0.82%	0.70%	0.95%	1.49%	33
34	62.2%	77.7%	84.4%	89.5%	90.1%	1.59%	0.83%	0.68%	0.85%	1.44%	34
35	62.9%	77.5%	84.0%	88.8%	90.4%	1.63%	0.77%	0.76%	0.85%	1.42%	35
36	62.8%	77.4%	84.0%	89.4%	91.0%	1.65%	0.77%	0.82%	0.92%	1.39%	36
37	62.2%	77.6%	84.0%	89.1%	91.2%	1.60%	0.79%	0.72%	0.92%	1.25%	37
38	62.3%	77.7%	85.0%	88.7%	91.4%	1.54%	0.79%	0.66%	0.80%	1.37%	38
39	60.4%	78.0%	85.1%	88.7%	92.0%	1.56%	0.79%	0.70%	0.96%	1.28%	39
40	59.0%	77.5%	85.2%	89.2%	92.5%	1.43%	0.77%	0.63%	0.88%	1.36%	40
41	57.6%	77.6%	84.7%	88.9%	92.2%	1.62%	0.72%	0.71%	1.01%	1.17%	41
42	57.1%	77.8%	84.2%	89.4%	92.4%	1.46%	0.82%	0.68%	0.85%	0.98%	42
43	55.5%	77.4%	83.6%	89.5%	93.4%	1.44%	0.76%	0.75%	0.90%	1.45%	43
44	56.1%	76.2%	83.0%	89.5%	93.6%	1.56%	0.79%	0.74%	0.87%	1.26%	44
45	55.7%	76.0%	81.6%	89.1%	93.0%	1.50%	0.76%	0.73%	0.92%	0.85%	45
46	54.5%	75.4%	80.8%	89.0%	92.9%	1.52%	0.77%	0.80%	1.02%	1.02%	46
47	53.9%	74.3%	79.8%	88.2%	92.7%	1.42%	0.82%	0.88%	1.01%	1.22%	47
48	53.8%	73.3%	78.1%	87.8%	91.0%	1.56%	0.88%	0.85%	1.11%	1.53%	48
49	51.6%	72.8%	77.4%	87.4%	90.4%	1.65%	0.89%	0.88%	1.09%	1.26%	49
50	50.0%	71.7%	76.9%	86.9%	89.6%	1.52%	0.89%	0.91%	1.04%	1.35%	50
51	50.1%	70.5%	75.8%	86.5%	90.0%	1.46%	0.95%	0.91%	1.22%	1.15%	51
52	49.8%	68.6%	74.6%	86.0%	89.8%	1.50%	0.97%	0.97%	1.27%	1.30%	52
53	49.2%	66.6%	73.3%	85.5%	89.0%	1.52%	1.00%	1.03%	1.18%	1.19%	53
54	48.2%	64.5%	71.1%	84.3%	86.8%	1.47%	1.06%	1.11%	1.31%	1.23%	54
55	47.0%	62.7%	69.9%	83.0%	85.2%	1.48%	1.12%	1.14%	1.42%	1.83%	55
56	44.6%	60.9%	67.9%	81.3%	83.2%	1.53%	1.10%	1.32%	1.68%	2.11%	56
57	41.2%	59.4%	65.9%	79.6%	80.4%	1.47%	1.01%	1.26%	1.92%	2.03%	57
58	37.5%	57.3%	64.2%	76.1%	77.4%	1.45%	1.16%	1.40%	2.02%	2.04%	58
59	35.3%	54.7%	63.1%	72.4%	74.8%	1.55%	1.19%	1.45%	2.25%	2.12%	59
60	32.6%	50.7%	59.5%	67.5%	68.9%	1.40%	1.22%	1.49%	2.53%	2.51%	60
61	28.8%	46.1%	56.3%	62.0%	61.3%	1.41%	1.28%	1.64%	2.69%	3.03%	61
62	25.8%	41.1%	51.7%	54.7%	51.8%	1.34%	1.27%	1.78%	2.99%	3.11%	62
63	23.4%	35.5%	44.4%	47.1%	44.4%	1.15%	1.26%	1.73%	3.24%	3.24%	63
64	21.2%	30.3%	37.3%	42.0%	38.3%	1.10%	1.26%	1.75%	2.76%	3.31%	64
65	18.5%	27.3%	32.1%	36.7%	34.2%	1.03%	1.14%	1.54%	2.64%	3.50%	65
66	16.8%	23.3%	27.0%	32.3%	32.5%	1.09%	1.13%	1.66%	3.03%	3.51%	66
67	15.4%	20.1%	23.4%	26.8%	30.2%	0.93%	1.22%	1.82%	2.82%	3.28%	67
68	13.4%	18.2%	21.6%	23.1%	24.6%	0.90%	1.06%	1.92%	3.12%	3.95%	68
69	11.6%	15.7%	20.0%	19.6%	19.5%	0.89%	1.08%	1.81%	2.64%	2.85%	69
70	9.8%	13.2%	18.4%	17.7%	16.6%	0.78%	1.12%	1.57%	2.25%	2.67%	70
71	8.5%	12.4%	16.1%	16.1%	15.1%	0.81%	0.88%	1.81%	2.70%	2.49%	71
72	7.0%	10.9%	14.5%	15.0%	14.7%	0.63%	1.01%	1.62%	2.18%	3.41%	72
73	5.6%	8.9%	13.6%	14.7%	13.9%	0.73%	1.10%	1.73%	2.90%	4.03%	73
74	4.8%	8.8%	12.8%	14.2%	14.0%	0.55%	0.89%	1.88%	2.81%	3.87%	74
75	4.3%	7.7%	11.3%	14.0%	14.5%	0.49%	0.75%	1.70%	2.92%	3.24%	75

Sources: Current Population Survey monthly microdata samples 2000 through 2006.

Appendix Table 5: Labor force participation rates and their standard errors by educational attainment, conventional methodology, Hispanic Males

Age	Hispanic Males: Labor Force Participation				Hispanic Males: Std Errors of LF Participation				Age
	<HS	HS	Some College	BA or More	<HS	HS	Some College	BA or More	
18	47.6%	66.6%	60.1%		0.64%	0.97%	1.65%		18
19	58.1%	77.4%	67.0%		0.73%	0.78%	1.07%		19
20	74.2%	84.6%	69.6%	88.0%	0.64%	0.69%	0.99%	4.00%	20
21	84.5%	86.4%	73.2%	85.9%	0.59%	0.65%	0.95%	3.01%	21
22	88.8%	89.9%	77.5%	85.9%	0.51%	0.58%	0.91%	1.97%	22
23	90.9%	91.9%	81.8%	87.5%	0.46%	0.50%	0.87%	1.64%	23
24	92.0%	92.2%	86.0%	89.0%	0.44%	0.50%	0.79%	1.44%	24
25	92.7%	92.8%	88.8%	89.8%	0.39%	0.47%	0.67%	1.14%	25
26	93.2%	94.3%	90.9%	91.3%	0.39%	0.43%	0.65%	0.91%	26
27	93.5%	94.0%	92.3%	92.5%	0.42%	0.46%	0.69%	0.95%	27
28	93.5%	94.9%	93.4%	93.1%	0.36%	0.40%	0.60%	0.82%	28
29	93.6%	94.6%	94.2%	93.6%	0.39%	0.41%	0.54%	0.79%	29
30	93.4%	94.5%	95.1%	94.6%	0.42%	0.40%	0.50%	0.70%	30
31	93.1%	93.9%	95.3%	94.9%	0.37%	0.43%	0.47%	0.64%	31
32	93.0%	93.4%	95.4%	95.3%	0.44%	0.45%	0.49%	0.57%	32
33	93.2%	94.6%	95.4%	95.7%	0.41%	0.45%	0.57%	0.65%	33
34	93.1%	93.2%	95.0%	95.5%	0.39%	0.49%	0.59%	0.56%	34
35	93.2%	93.0%	94.4%	95.6%	0.40%	0.50%	0.52%	0.64%	35
36	93.2%	94.4%	94.5%	95.4%	0.41%	0.44%	0.58%	0.75%	36
37	93.0%	93.0%	94.6%	94.9%	0.45%	0.51%	0.69%	0.55%	37
38	92.6%	94.6%	94.1%	94.6%	0.41%	0.45%	0.50%	0.79%	38
39	92.3%	93.3%	94.2%	95.3%	0.48%	0.52%	0.56%	0.78%	39
40	91.7%	93.1%	94.3%	95.3%	0.47%	0.48%	0.69%	0.65%	40
41	91.3%	92.2%	94.0%	95.5%	0.53%	0.54%	0.55%	0.49%	41
42	90.7%	91.1%	93.7%	96.0%	0.57%	0.59%	0.66%	0.56%	42
43	89.8%	91.1%	93.5%	96.4%	0.53%	0.61%	0.64%	0.71%	43
44	88.9%	89.0%	92.3%	96.0%	0.62%	0.69%	0.67%	0.63%	44
45	88.0%	89.0%	91.6%	95.4%	0.69%	0.75%	0.88%	0.65%	45
46	86.4%	90.8%	91.1%	95.5%	0.72%	0.71%	1.07%	0.80%	46
47	85.7%	89.4%	89.9%	94.9%	0.81%	0.81%	0.93%	0.89%	47
48	85.3%	87.2%	89.7%	93.8%	0.79%	0.88%	0.84%	0.75%	48
49	84.3%	88.3%	89.3%	93.4%	0.81%	0.94%	1.02%	0.88%	49
50	83.8%	87.2%	88.7%	93.0%	0.77%	0.88%	1.04%	0.98%	50
51	82.7%	87.4%	87.0%	91.6%	0.91%	0.91%	1.17%	1.00%	51
52	80.9%	84.3%	86.2%	90.8%	0.99%	1.11%	1.18%	1.04%	52
53	78.8%	81.0%	84.8%	89.6%	1.04%	1.43%	1.45%	1.13%	53
54	77.3%	82.8%	84.0%	88.5%	1.07%	1.25%	1.43%	1.30%	54
55	75.3%	80.6%	82.5%	88.3%	1.09%	1.35%	1.47%	1.50%	55
56	73.3%	81.1%	81.0%	88.1%	1.17%	1.41%	1.59%	1.56%	56
57	71.7%	80.7%	78.8%	87.5%	1.23%	1.47%	1.75%	1.44%	57
58	69.3%	75.5%	76.8%	86.3%	1.33%	1.59%	2.03%	1.75%	58
59	67.4%	73.4%	74.1%	83.6%	1.37%	1.65%	2.09%	1.99%	59
60	64.7%	67.5%	70.3%	79.1%	1.40%	1.83%	2.17%	2.52%	60
61	60.2%	60.7%	66.2%	75.6%	1.43%	2.08%	2.54%	2.90%	61
62	55.3%	53.7%	62.2%	72.2%	1.55%	2.21%	2.80%	2.57%	62
63	49.9%	47.6%	55.5%	69.1%	1.58%	2.22%	2.95%	3.17%	63
64	43.0%	42.4%	50.8%	65.7%	1.54%	2.20%	2.87%	3.11%	64
65	36.4%	39.1%	45.8%	63.1%	1.47%	2.35%	3.05%	3.44%	65
66	32.5%	34.6%	42.2%	57.6%	1.56%	2.37%	3.70%	3.45%	66
67	27.8%	31.0%	36.9%	49.7%	1.36%	2.20%	3.33%	3.64%	67
68	23.5%	28.0%	33.5%	45.9%	1.55%	2.18%	3.38%	4.05%	68
69	20.0%	25.7%	29.0%	43.2%	1.43%	2.23%	3.26%	3.59%	69
70	17.8%	23.4%	24.4%	38.3%	1.47%	2.23%	3.42%	3.93%	70
71	14.0%	20.3%	21.2%	36.8%	1.37%	2.30%	2.72%	4.52%	71
72	12.6%	15.7%	18.2%	35.9%	1.17%	2.23%	2.53%	3.78%	72
73	10.8%	14.6%	15.9%	32.7%	0.97%	1.96%	3.22%	4.08%	73
74	9.0%	13.5%	15.4%	32.9%	1.18%	2.62%	3.21%	3.99%	74
75	8.3%	14.4%	15.7%	28.6%	0.96%	2.11%	2.95%	4.21%	75

Sources: Current Population Survey monthly microdata samples 2000 through 2006.

Appendix Table 5: Labor force participation rates and their standard errors by educational attainment, conventional methodology, Hispanic Females

Age	Hispanic Females: Labor Force Participation				Hispanic Females: Std Errors of LF Participation				Age
	<HS	HS	Some College	BA or More	<HS	HS	Some College	BA or More	
18	33.8%	57.4%	58.1%		0.71%	0.96%	1.48%		18
19	37.3%	61.9%	63.5%		0.93%	0.91%	1.02%		19
20	44.1%	63.8%	65.5%	69.7%	1.03%	0.93%	0.86%	4.00%	20
21	47.4%	65.9%	68.0%	74.0%	1.03%	0.89%	0.85%	3.01%	21
22	48.1%	66.7%	70.7%	77.1%	0.96%	0.87%	0.83%	1.97%	22
23	47.8%	66.5%	73.0%	78.9%	0.97%	0.89%	0.91%	1.64%	23
24	47.7%	65.9%	75.1%	79.2%	0.97%	0.88%	0.88%	1.44%	24
25	47.2%	65.0%	76.3%	79.4%	0.88%	0.89%	0.90%	1.14%	25
26	46.5%	64.7%	77.2%	80.4%	0.84%	0.86%	0.91%	0.91%	26
27	46.3%	65.1%	76.5%	80.3%	0.88%	0.93%	0.94%	0.95%	27
28	46.8%	65.2%	76.6%	79.8%	0.90%	0.90%	0.92%	0.82%	28
29	47.4%	65.3%	75.9%	79.8%	0.89%	0.91%	1.02%	0.79%	29
30	48.1%	66.1%	75.5%	79.9%	0.88%	0.85%	0.95%	0.70%	30
31	50.1%	66.6%	75.4%	78.8%	0.89%	0.89%	0.98%	0.64%	31
32	51.1%	66.7%	76.0%	78.4%	0.85%	0.92%	0.95%	0.57%	32
33	51.9%	67.1%	75.5%	78.1%	0.84%	0.91%	0.96%	0.65%	33
34	52.2%	68.1%	75.5%	78.4%	0.87%	0.93%	0.97%	0.56%	34
35	53.3%	69.0%	76.1%	77.9%	0.87%	0.92%	1.03%	0.64%	35
36	54.2%	69.8%	76.5%	78.2%	0.90%	0.91%	1.02%	0.75%	36
37	55.9%	70.7%	77.0%	78.3%	0.93%	0.86%	0.99%	0.55%	37
38	56.9%	71.8%	78.5%	78.5%	0.88%	0.92%	0.90%	0.79%	38
39	58.0%	72.5%	80.0%	78.6%	0.93%	0.95%	1.02%	0.78%	39
40	59.0%	73.0%	80.3%	79.2%	0.89%	0.92%	0.93%	0.65%	40
41	59.5%	72.5%	79.8%	80.0%	0.92%	0.90%	0.95%	0.49%	41
42	60.0%	72.7%	79.7%	80.4%	0.90%	0.91%	1.02%	0.56%	42
43	60.3%	73.1%	79.3%	81.4%	0.95%	1.00%	1.19%	0.71%	43
44	60.7%	73.4%	79.0%	81.9%	0.97%	1.05%	1.09%	0.63%	44
45	60.1%	73.2%	78.4%	82.9%	0.97%	0.98%	1.10%	0.65%	45
46	59.7%	74.3%	78.5%	83.2%	0.99%	1.07%	1.08%	0.80%	46
47	58.8%	73.8%	78.8%	83.5%	1.04%	1.08%	1.25%	0.89%	47
48	57.9%	72.2%	78.5%	83.5%	1.05%	1.11%	1.18%	0.75%	48
49	56.4%	70.4%	77.3%	82.8%	1.11%	1.20%	1.22%	0.88%	49
50	55.3%	68.7%	77.0%	82.2%	1.10%	1.16%	1.28%	0.98%	50
51	53.6%	66.7%	75.5%	81.6%	1.13%	1.27%	1.49%	1.00%	51
52	51.7%	65.1%	74.2%	81.6%	1.15%	1.26%	1.65%	1.04%	52
53	50.3%	63.2%	71.3%	81.1%	1.19%	1.44%	1.69%	1.13%	53
54	49.2%	62.4%	69.6%	80.0%	1.16%	1.48%	1.68%	1.30%	54
55	46.9%	61.6%	69.6%	77.7%	1.22%	1.52%	1.80%	1.50%	55
56	44.5%	61.5%	69.6%	75.8%	1.27%	1.55%	1.78%	1.56%	56
57	42.2%	60.3%	67.3%	73.3%	1.25%	1.61%	1.70%	1.44%	57
58	39.1%	59.4%	66.0%	69.9%	1.24%	1.53%	1.97%	1.75%	58
59	35.4%	56.6%	62.5%	68.4%	1.33%	1.71%	2.24%	1.99%	59
60	32.2%	51.7%	55.1%	65.6%	1.26%	1.81%	2.27%	2.52%	60
61	28.7%	45.4%	49.2%	61.3%	1.17%	1.79%	2.52%	2.90%	61
62	26.1%	40.7%	46.2%	56.5%	1.18%	1.72%	2.47%	2.57%	62
63	22.4%	34.9%	41.0%	51.2%	1.17%	1.83%	2.67%	3.17%	63
64	19.4%	29.7%	36.2%	44.8%	1.16%	1.91%	3.06%	3.11%	64
65	17.4%	25.9%	34.2%	38.9%	0.96%	1.78%	3.07%	3.44%	65
66	14.0%	22.6%	30.9%	33.6%	0.93%	1.75%	2.90%	3.45%	66
67	11.5%	20.0%	25.9%	30.1%	1.08%	1.77%	2.83%	3.64%	67
68	9.8%	17.1%	25.2%	26.5%	0.73%	1.71%	2.91%	4.05%	68
69	8.3%	15.1%	24.9%	24.7%	0.94%	1.80%	3.52%	3.59%	69
70	6.7%	13.3%	22.1%	23.4%	0.81%	1.23%	3.41%	3.93%	70
71	6.7%	11.2%	23.2%	19.0%	0.63%	1.61%	3.21%	4.52%	71
72	6.1%	9.1%	20.4%	16.3%	0.68%	1.49%	2.59%	3.78%	72
73	5.3%	8.3%	15.3%	15.3%	0.87%	1.05%	4.24%	4.08%	73
74	5.0%	6.5%	12.0%	12.0%	0.81%	1.58%	2.76%	3.99%	74
75	4.0%	5.4%	11.8%	10.0%	0.55%	1.21%	1.63%	4.21%	75

Sources: Current Population Survey monthly microdata samples 2000 through 2006.

Appendix Table 6: Conventional model worklife expectancy standard errors by educational attainment, Males and Females of All Races

Age	Males of All Races									Females of All Races									Age
	<HS	HS	Some College			College Degree	Graduate Degree			<HS	HS	Some College			College Degree	Graduate Degree			
			All	No Degree	Assoc Degree		All	Masters	Phd/Prof'l			All	No Degree	Assoc Degree		All	Masters	Phd/Prof'l	
18	0.05	0.07	0.05	0.05	0.08					0.04	0.05	0.04	0.04	0.07					18
19	0.05	0.07	0.05	0.05	0.07	0.08				0.04	0.05	0.04	0.04	0.06	0.07				19
20	0.04	0.07	0.05	0.05	0.07	0.07				0.04	0.05	0.04	0.04	0.05	0.05				20
21	0.04	0.07	0.05	0.05	0.06	0.06	0.10	0.13		0.04	0.05	0.04	0.04	0.05	0.05	0.01	0.11		21
22	0.04	0.07	0.05	0.05	0.06	0.06	0.08	0.09	0.14	0.04	0.05	0.03	0.04	0.05	0.05	0.08	0.09	0.18	22
23	0.04	0.07	0.05	0.05	0.06	0.06	0.07	0.08	0.11	0.04	0.05	0.03	0.04	0.05	0.04	0.08	0.08	0.15	23
24	0.04	0.07	0.05	0.05	0.06	0.06	0.06	0.07	0.09	0.04	0.05	0.03	0.04	0.05	0.04	0.07	0.08	0.14	24
25	0.04	0.07	0.04	0.04	0.06	0.05	0.06	0.07	0.08	0.04	0.04	0.03	0.04	0.05	0.04	0.07	0.08	0.13	25
26	0.04	0.07	0.04	0.04	0.06	0.05	0.06	0.07	0.08	0.04	0.04	0.03	0.04	0.05	0.04	0.07	0.07	0.13	26
27	0.04	0.07	0.04	0.04	0.06	0.05	0.06	0.07	0.08	0.04	0.04	0.03	0.04	0.05	0.04	0.07	0.07	0.13	27
28	0.04	0.06	0.04	0.04	0.06	0.05	0.06	0.07	0.08	0.04	0.04	0.03	0.04	0.05	0.04	0.07	0.07	0.13	28
29	0.04	0.06	0.04	0.04	0.06	0.05	0.06	0.07	0.08	0.04	0.04	0.03	0.04	0.05	0.04	0.07	0.07	0.13	29
30	0.03	0.06	0.04	0.04	0.06	0.05	0.05	0.06	0.07	0.04	0.04	0.03	0.04	0.05	0.04	0.07	0.07	0.13	30
31	0.03	0.06	0.04	0.04	0.06	0.05	0.05	0.06	0.07	0.04	0.04	0.03	0.04	0.05	0.04	0.06	0.07	0.12	31
32	0.03	0.06	0.04	0.04	0.06	0.05	0.05	0.06	0.07	0.04	0.04	0.03	0.04	0.05	0.04	0.06	0.07	0.12	32
33	0.03	0.06	0.04	0.04	0.06	0.05	0.05	0.06	0.07	0.03	0.04	0.03	0.04	0.05	0.04	0.06	0.07	0.12	33
34	0.03	0.06	0.04	0.04	0.06	0.05	0.05	0.06	0.07	0.03	0.04	0.03	0.03	0.05	0.04	0.06	0.07	0.12	34
35	0.03	0.06	0.04	0.04	0.06	0.05	0.05	0.06	0.07	0.03	0.04	0.03	0.03	0.05	0.04	0.06	0.07	0.12	35
36	0.03	0.06	0.04	0.04	0.06	0.05	0.05	0.06	0.07	0.03	0.04	0.03	0.03	0.05	0.04	0.06	0.07	0.12	36
37	0.03	0.05	0.04	0.04	0.06	0.05	0.05	0.06	0.07	0.03	0.04	0.03	0.03	0.05	0.04	0.06	0.07	0.12	37
38	0.03	0.05	0.04	0.04	0.06	0.05	0.05	0.06	0.07	0.03	0.04	0.03	0.03	0.05	0.04	0.06	0.07	0.12	38
39	0.03	0.05	0.04	0.04	0.06	0.05	0.05	0.06	0.07	0.03	0.04	0.03	0.03	0.05	0.04	0.06	0.07	0.12	39
40	0.03	0.05	0.04	0.04	0.06	0.05	0.05	0.06	0.07	0.03	0.03	0.03	0.03	0.04	0.04	0.06	0.07	0.12	40
41	0.03	0.05	0.04	0.04	0.06	0.05	0.05	0.06	0.07	0.03	0.03	0.03	0.03	0.04	0.04	0.06	0.06	0.12	41
42	0.03	0.05	0.04	0.04	0.06	0.04	0.05	0.06	0.07	0.03	0.03	0.03	0.03	0.04	0.04	0.06	0.06	0.12	42
43	0.03	0.04	0.04	0.04	0.06	0.04	0.05	0.06	0.07	0.03	0.03	0.03	0.03	0.04	0.04	0.06	0.06	0.12	43
44	0.03	0.04	0.04	0.04	0.06	0.04	0.05	0.06	0.07	0.03	0.03	0.03	0.03	0.04	0.04	0.06	0.06	0.12	44
45	0.03	0.04	0.04	0.04	0.05	0.04	0.05	0.06	0.07	0.03	0.03	0.03	0.03	0.04	0.04	0.06	0.06	0.12	45
46	0.03	0.04	0.03	0.04	0.05	0.04	0.05	0.06	0.07	0.03	0.03	0.03	0.03	0.04	0.04	0.06	0.06	0.12	46
47	0.03	0.04	0.03	0.04	0.06	0.04	0.05	0.06	0.07	0.03	0.03	0.03	0.03	0.04	0.04	0.06	0.06	0.12	47
48	0.03	0.03	0.03	0.04	0.05	0.04	0.05	0.06	0.07	0.03	0.03	0.03	0.03	0.04	0.04	0.06	0.06	0.12	48
49	0.03	0.03	0.03	0.04	0.05	0.04	0.05	0.06	0.07	0.03	0.02	0.03	0.03	0.04	0.04	0.06	0.06	0.12	49
50	0.03	0.03	0.03	0.03	0.05	0.04	0.05	0.06	0.07	0.03	0.02	0.03	0.03	0.04	0.04	0.06	0.06	0.12	50
51	0.03	0.03	0.03	0.03	0.05	0.04	0.05	0.06	0.07	0.02	0.02	0.02	0.03	0.04	0.04	0.06	0.06	0.12	51
52	0.03	0.03	0.03	0.03	0.05	0.04	0.05	0.06	0.07	0.02	0.02	0.02	0.03	0.04	0.04	0.05	0.06	0.12	52
53	0.03	0.03	0.03	0.03	0.05	0.04	0.05	0.06	0.07	0.02	0.02	0.02	0.03	0.04	0.04	0.05	0.06	0.12	53
54	0.03	0.03	0.03	0.03	0.05	0.04	0.05	0.06	0.07	0.02	0.02	0.02	0.03	0.04	0.04	0.05	0.06	0.11	54
55	0.02	0.02	0.03	0.03	0.05	0.04	0.05	0.06	0.07	0.02	0.02	0.02	0.03	0.04	0.04	0.05	0.06	0.11	55
56	0.02	0.02	0.03	0.03	0.05	0.04	0.05	0.06	0.07	0.02	0.02	0.02	0.03	0.04	0.04	0.05	0.06	0.11	56
57	0.02	0.02	0.03	0.03	0.05	0.04	0.05	0.06	0.07	0.02	0.02	0.02	0.03	0.04	0.03	0.05	0.06	0.11	57
58	0.02	0.02	0.03	0.03	0.05	0.04	0.05	0.06	0.07	0.02	0.02	0.02	0.03	0.04	0.03	0.05	0.06	0.11	58
59	0.02	0.02	0.03	0.03	0.05	0.04	0.04	0.05	0.07	0.02	0.02	0.02	0.03	0.04	0.03	0.05	0.06	0.11	59
60	0.02	0.02	0.03	0.03	0.05	0.04	0.04	0.05	0.07	0.02	0.01	0.02	0.03	0.04	0.03	0.05	0.06	0.11	60
61	0.02	0.02	0.03	0.03	0.05	0.04	0.04	0.05	0.07	0.02	0.01	0.02	0.02	0.04	0.03	0.05	0.06	0.11	61
62	0.02	0.02	0.03	0.03	0.05	0.04	0.04	0.05	0.06	0.01	0.01	0.02	0.02	0.04	0.03	0.05	0.06	0.11	62
63	0.02	0.02	0.02	0.03	0.05	0.03	0.04	0.05	0.06	0.01	0.01	0.02	0.02	0.04	0.03	0.05	0.05	0.11	63
64	0.02	0.02	0.02	0.03	0.05	0.03	0.04	0.05	0.06	0.01	0.01	0.02	0.02	0.03	0.03	0.05	0.05	0.11	64
65	0.02	0.02	0.02	0.02	0.05	0.03	0.04	0.05	0.06	0.01	0.01	0.02	0.02	0.03	0.03	0.05	0.05	0.11	65
66	0.02	0.02	0.02	0.02	0.05	0.03	0.04	0.05	0.06	0.01	0.01	0.02	0.02	0.03	0.03	0.05	0.05	0.11	66
67	0.01	0.01	0.02	0.02	0.05	0.03	0.04	0.05	0.06	0.01	0.00	0.02	0.02	0.03	0.03	0.04	0.05	0.10	67
68	0.01	0.01	0.02	0.02	0.05	0.03	0.04	0.05	0.06	0.01	0.01	0.02	0.02	0.03	0.03	0.04	0.05	0.10	68
69	0.01	0.01	0.02	0.02	0.05	0.03	0.04	0.05	0.06	0.01	0.01	0.02	0.02	0.03	0.02	0.04	0.05	0.10	69
70	0.01	0.01	0.02	0.02	0.05	0.03	0.04	0.05	0.06	0.01	0.01	0.01	0.02	0.03	0.02	0.04	0.05	0.01	70
71	0.01	0.01	0.02	0.02	0.05	0.03	0.04	0.05	0.06	0.01	0.01	0.01	0.02	0.03	0.02	0.04	0.04	0.01	71
72	0.01	0.01	0.02	0.02	0.05	0.03	0.04	0.04	0.06	0.01	0.01	0.01	0.02	0.03	0.02	0.04	0.04	0.01	72
73	0.01	0.01	0.02	0.02	0.05	0.03	0.03	0.04	0.06	0.01	0.01	0.01	0.01	0.03	0.02	0.04	0.04	0.09	73
74	0.01	0.01	0.02	0.02	0.05	0.03	0.03	0.04	0.05	0.01	0.01	0.01	0.01	0.02	0.02	0.04	0.04	0.09	74
75	0.00	0.01	0.02	0.02	0.04	0.03	0.03	0.04	0.05	0.01	0.01	0.01	0.01	0.02	0.02	0.04	0.04	0.09	75

Sources: Current Population Survey monthly microdata samples 2000 through 2006.

Appendix Table 6: Conventional model worklife expectancy standard errors by educational attainment, White Males and Females

Age	White Males									White Females									Age
			Some College			College Degree	Graduate Degree					Some College			College Degree	Graduate Degree			
	<HS	HS	All	No Degree	Assoc Degree		All	Masters	Phd/Prof'l	<HS	HS	All	No Degree	Assoc Degree		All	Masters	Phd/Prof'l	
18	0.05	0.04	0.05	0.05	0.09					0.05	0.03	0.04	0.04	0.08					18
19	0.05	0.04	0.05	0.05	0.08	0.09				0.05	0.03	0.04	0.04	0.06	0.08				19
20	0.05	0.04	0.05	0.05	0.07	0.07				0.05	0.03	0.04	0.04	0.06	0.06				20
21	0.05	0.04	0.05	0.05	0.07	0.06	0.11	0.13		0.05	0.03	0.04	0.04	0.06	0.05	0.10	0.12		21
22	0.05	0.04	0.05	0.05	0.07	0.06	0.09	0.01	0.15	0.05	0.03	0.04	0.04	0.06	0.05	0.09	0.09	0.21	22
23	0.05	0.04	0.04	0.05	0.07	0.06	0.07	0.08	0.13	0.05	0.03	0.04	0.04	0.06	0.05	0.07	0.08	0.16	23
24	0.05	0.04	0.04	0.05	0.07	0.06	0.07	0.07	0.10	0.05	0.03	0.04	0.04	0.06	0.05	0.07	0.08	0.15	24
25	0.05	0.03	0.04	0.05	0.07	0.06	0.07	0.07	0.09	0.05	0.03	0.04	0.04	0.06	0.05	0.07	0.07	0.14	25
26	0.05	0.03	0.04	0.05	0.07	0.05	0.07	0.07	0.09	0.05	0.03	0.04	0.04	0.06	0.05	0.07	0.07	0.14	26
27	0.05	0.03	0.04	0.05	0.07	0.05	0.06	0.07	0.08	0.04	0.03	0.04	0.04	0.05	0.05	0.07	0.07	0.14	27
28	0.05	0.03	0.04	0.05	0.07	0.05	0.06	0.07	0.08	0.04	0.03	0.04	0.04	0.05	0.05	0.07	0.07	0.14	28
29	0.05	0.03	0.04	0.04	0.07	0.05	0.06	0.07	0.08	0.04	0.03	0.04	0.04	0.05	0.05	0.07	0.07	0.14	29
30	0.05	0.03	0.04	0.04	0.06	0.05	0.06	0.07	0.08	0.04	0.03	0.04	0.04	0.05	0.05	0.07	0.07	0.14	30
31	0.05	0.03	0.04	0.04	0.06	0.05	0.06	0.06	0.08	0.04	0.03	0.04	0.04	0.05	0.05	0.07	0.07	0.14	31
32	0.04	0.03	0.04	0.04	0.06	0.05	0.06	0.06	0.08	0.04	0.03	0.04	0.04	0.05	0.05	0.07	0.07	0.14	32
33	0.04	0.03	0.04	0.04	0.06	0.05	0.06	0.06	0.08	0.04	0.02	0.04	0.04	0.05	0.05	0.07	0.07	0.14	33
34	0.04	0.03	0.04	0.04	0.06	0.05	0.06	0.06	0.08	0.04	0.02	0.03	0.04	0.05	0.05	0.07	0.07	0.13	34
35	0.04	0.03	0.04	0.04	0.06	0.05	0.06	0.06	0.08	0.04	0.02	0.03	0.04	0.05	0.05	0.07	0.07	0.13	35
36	0.04	0.03	0.04	0.04	0.06	0.05	0.06	0.06	0.08	0.04	0.02	0.03	0.04	0.05	0.04	0.07	0.07	0.13	36
37	0.04	0.03	0.04	0.04	0.06	0.05	0.06	0.06	0.08	0.04	0.02	0.03	0.04	0.05	0.04	0.07	0.07	0.13	37
38	0.04	0.03	0.04	0.04	0.06	0.05	0.06	0.06	0.08	0.04	0.02	0.03	0.04	0.05	0.04	0.06	0.07	0.13	38
39	0.04	0.03	0.04	0.04	0.06	0.05	0.06	0.06	0.08	0.04	0.02	0.03	0.04	0.05	0.04	0.06	0.07	0.13	39
40	0.04	0.03	0.04	0.04	0.06	0.05	0.05	0.06	0.08	0.04	0.02	0.03	0.04	0.05	0.04	0.06	0.07	0.13	40
41	0.04	0.03	0.04	0.04	0.06	0.05	0.05	0.06	0.08	0.04	0.02	0.03	0.03	0.05	0.04	0.06	0.07	0.13	41
42	0.04	0.03	0.04	0.04	0.06	0.05	0.05	0.06	0.08	0.04	0.02	0.03	0.03	0.05	0.04	0.06	0.07	0.13	42
43	0.04	0.03	0.04	0.04	0.06	0.05	0.05	0.06	0.08	0.03	0.02	0.03	0.03	0.05	0.04	0.06	0.07	0.13	43
44	0.04	0.03	0.04	0.04	0.06	0.05	0.05	0.06	0.08	0.03	0.02	0.03	0.03	0.05	0.04	0.06	0.07	0.13	44
45	0.04	0.03	0.04	0.04	0.06	0.05	0.05	0.06	0.08	0.03	0.02	0.03	0.03	0.05	0.04	0.06	0.07	0.13	45
46	0.04	0.03	0.04	0.04	0.06	0.05	0.05	0.06	0.07	0.03	0.02	0.03	0.03	0.05	0.04	0.06	0.06	0.13	46
47	0.03	0.03	0.04	0.04	0.06	0.05	0.05	0.06	0.07	0.03	0.02	0.03	0.03	0.05	0.04	0.06	0.06	0.13	47
48	0.03	0.03	0.04	0.04	0.06	0.05	0.05	0.06	0.07	0.03	0.02	0.03	0.03	0.05	0.04	0.06	0.06	0.13	48
49	0.03	0.03	0.03	0.04	0.06	0.04	0.05	0.06	0.07	0.03	0.02	0.03	0.03	0.05	0.04	0.06	0.06	0.13	49
50	0.03	0.02	0.03	0.04	0.06	0.04	0.05	0.06	0.07	0.03	0.02	0.03	0.03	0.05	0.04	0.06	0.06	0.13	50
51	0.03	0.02	0.03	0.04	0.06	0.04	0.05	0.06	0.07	0.03	0.02	0.03	0.03	0.05	0.04	0.06	0.06	0.13	51
52	0.03	0.02	0.03	0.04	0.06	0.04	0.05	0.06	0.07	0.03	0.02	0.03	0.03	0.05	0.04	0.06	0.06	0.13	52
53	0.03	0.02	0.03	0.04	0.06	0.04	0.05	0.06	0.07	0.03	0.02	0.03	0.03	0.05	0.04	0.06	0.06	0.12	53
54	0.03	0.02	0.03	0.03	0.06	0.04	0.05	0.06	0.07	0.03	0.02	0.03	0.03	0.05	0.04	0.06	0.06	0.12	54
55	0.03	0.02	0.03	0.03	0.06	0.04	0.05	0.06	0.07	0.02	0.02	0.03	0.03	0.05	0.04	0.06	0.06	0.12	55
56	0.03	0.02	0.03	0.03	0.06	0.04	0.05	0.06	0.07	0.02	0.02	0.03	0.03	0.05	0.04	0.06	0.06	0.12	56
57	0.02	0.02	0.03	0.03	0.06	0.04	0.05	0.06	0.07	0.02	0.02	0.03	0.03	0.04	0.04	0.06	0.06	0.12	57
58	0.02	0.02	0.03	0.03	0.06	0.04	0.05	0.06	0.07	0.02	0.02	0.02	0.03	0.04	0.04	0.06	0.06	0.12	58
59	0.02	0.02	0.03	0.03	0.06	0.04	0.05	0.05	0.07	0.02	0.02	0.02	0.03	0.04	0.04	0.06	0.06	0.12	59
60	0.02	0.02	0.03	0.03	0.06	0.04	0.05	0.05	0.07	0.02	0.01	0.02	0.03	0.04	0.03	0.05	0.06	0.12	60
61	0.02	0.02	0.03	0.03	0.06	0.04	0.05	0.05	0.07	0.02	0.01	0.02	0.03	0.04	0.03	0.05	0.06	0.12	61
62	0.02	0.02	0.03	0.03	0.06	0.04	0.05	0.05	0.07	0.02	0.01	0.02	0.02	0.04	0.03	0.05	0.06	0.12	62
63	0.02	0.02	0.03	0.03	0.06	0.04	0.04	0.05	0.07	0.02	0.01	0.02	0.02	0.04	0.03	0.05	0.06	0.12	63
64	0.02	0.02	0.03	0.03	0.05	0.04	0.04	0.05	0.07	0.01	0.01	0.02	0.02	0.04	0.03	0.05	0.06	0.12	64
65	0.02	0.02	0.02	0.03	0.05	0.03	0.04	0.05	0.07	0.01	0.01	0.02	0.02	0.04	0.03	0.05	0.05	0.11	65
66	0.02	0.02	0.02	0.03	0.05	0.03	0.04	0.05	0.07	0.01	0.01	0.02	0.02	0.04	0.03	0.05	0.05	0.11	66
67	0.02	0.02	0.02	0.03	0.05	0.03	0.04	0.05	0.07	0.01	0.01	0.02	0.02	0.03	0.03	0.05	0.05	0.11	67
68	0.01	0.02	0.02	0.02	0.05	0.03	0.04	0.05	0.06	0.01	0.00	0.02	0.02	0.03	0.03	0.05	0.05	0.11	68
69	0.01	0.01	0.02	0.02	0.05	0.03	0.04	0.05	0.06	0.00	0.01	0.02	0.02	0.03	0.03	0.05	0.05	0.11	69
70	0.01	0.01	0.02	0.02	0.05	0.03	0.04	0.05	0.06	0.01	0.01	0.01	0.02	0.03	0.02	0.04	0.05	0.10	70
71	0.01	0.01	0.02	0.02	0.05	0.03	0.04	0.05	0.06	0.01	0.01	0.01	0.02	0.03	0.02	0.04	0.05	0.10	71
72	0.01	0.01	0.02	0.02	0.05	0.03	0.04	0.05	0.06	0.01	0.01	0.01	0.02	0.03	0.02	0.04	0.04	0.10	72
73	0.01	0.01	0.02	0.02	0.05	0.03	0.04	0.05	0.06	0.01	0.01	0.01	0.02	0.03	0.02	0.04	0.04	0.10	73
74	0.01	0.01	0.02	0.02	0.05	0.03	0.04	0.05	0.06	0.01	0.01	0.01	0.01	0.02	0.02	0.04	0.04	0.01	74
75	0.00	0.01	0.02	0.02	0.05	0.03	0.04	0.05	0.06	0.01	0.01	0.01	0.01	0.02	0.02	0.04	0.04	0.09	75

Sources: Current Population Survey monthly microdata samples 2000 through 2006.

Appendix Table 6: Conventional model worklife expectancy standard errors by educational attainment, Black Males and Females

Age	Black Males					Black Females					Age
	<HS	HS	Some College	College Degree	Graduate Degree	<HS	HS	Some College	College Degree	Graduate Degree	
18	0.14	0.12	0.17			0.11	0.09	0.13			18
19	0.14	0.12	0.17			0.11	0.09	0.13			19
20	0.14	0.12	0.17	0.26		0.11	0.09	0.13	0.19		20
21	0.14	0.12	0.17	0.23		0.11	0.09	0.13	0.18		21
22	0.14	0.12	0.17	0.22	0.28	0.11	0.09	0.13	0.17	0.20	22
23	0.13	0.12	0.17	0.22	0.27	0.11	0.09	0.13	0.17	0.20	23
24	0.13	0.12	0.17	0.22	0.26	0.11	0.09	0.13	0.17	0.19	24
25	0.13	0.12	0.17	0.22	0.24	0.11	0.09	0.13	0.17	0.19	25
26	0.13	0.12	0.16	0.22	0.24	0.11	0.09	0.12	0.16	0.18	26
27	0.13	0.11	0.16	0.21	0.24	0.10	0.09	0.12	0.16	0.18	27
28	0.13	0.11	0.16	0.21	0.24	0.10	0.09	0.12	0.16	0.18	28
29	0.13	0.11	0.16	0.21	0.24	0.10	0.08	0.12	0.16	0.18	29
30	0.12	0.11	0.16	0.21	0.24	0.10	0.08	0.12	0.16	0.18	30
31	0.12	0.11	0.16	0.21	0.23	0.01	0.08	0.12	0.16	0.17	31
32	0.12	0.11	0.16	0.21	0.23	0.01	0.08	0.12	0.16	0.17	32
33	0.12	0.11	0.15	0.21	0.23	0.09	0.08	0.12	0.15	0.17	33
34	0.12	0.11	0.15	0.21	0.23	0.09	0.08	0.12	0.15	0.17	34
35	0.11	0.10	0.15	0.21	0.22	0.09	0.08	0.12	0.15	0.17	35
36	0.11	0.10	0.15	0.20	0.22	0.09	0.08	0.12	0.15	0.17	36
37	0.11	0.10	0.15	0.20	0.22	0.09	0.08	0.12	0.15	0.17	37
38	0.10	0.10	0.14	0.20	0.22	0.09	0.08	0.12	0.15	0.17	38
39	0.10	0.10	0.14	0.20	0.22	0.08	0.08	0.12	0.15	0.17	39
40	0.10	0.01	0.14	0.20	0.22	0.08	0.07	0.11	0.15	0.17	40
41	0.10	0.01	0.14	0.20	0.22	0.08	0.07	0.11	0.15	0.16	41
42	0.01	0.01	0.14	0.20	0.21	0.08	0.07	0.11	0.15	0.16	42
43	0.09	0.09	0.14	0.20	0.21	0.08	0.07	0.11	0.15	0.16	43
44	0.09	0.09	0.14	0.19	0.21	0.08	0.07	0.11	0.15	0.16	44
45	0.09	0.09	0.14	0.19	0.21	0.07	0.07	0.11	0.15	0.16	45
46	0.08	0.09	0.13	0.19	0.21	0.07	0.07	0.11	0.15	0.16	46
47	0.08	0.09	0.13	0.19	0.20	0.07	0.07	0.11	0.15	0.16	47
48	0.08	0.09	0.13	0.19	0.20	0.07	0.07	0.11	0.15	0.16	48
49	0.08	0.09	0.13	0.19	0.20	0.06	0.07	0.11	0.14	0.16	49
50	0.07	0.08	0.13	0.19	0.20	0.06	0.07	0.10	0.14	0.16	50
51	0.07	0.08	0.12	0.18	0.20	0.06	0.06	0.10	0.14	0.16	51
52	0.07	0.08	0.12	0.18	0.19	0.06	0.06	0.10	0.14	0.16	52
53	0.07	0.08	0.12	0.18	0.19	0.05	0.06	0.10	0.14	0.16	53
54	0.06	0.08	0.12	0.18	0.19	0.05	0.06	0.01	0.14	0.15	54
55	0.06	0.08	0.12	0.17	0.19	0.05	0.06	0.01	0.13	0.15	55
56	0.06	0.07	0.11	0.17	0.19	0.05	0.06	0.09	0.13	0.15	56
57	0.05	0.07	0.11	0.17	0.19	0.04	0.06	0.09	0.13	0.15	57
58	0.05	0.07	0.11	0.17	0.18	0.04	0.06	0.09	0.13	0.15	58
59	0.05	0.07	0.10	0.17	0.18	0.04	0.05	0.09	0.13	0.15	59
60	0.05	0.07	0.10	0.17	0.18	0.04	0.05	0.09	0.13	0.14	60
61	0.04	0.07	0.01	0.17	0.17	0.03	0.05	0.08	0.12	0.14	61
62	0.04	0.06	0.09	0.16	0.17	0.03	0.05	0.08	0.12	0.14	62
63	0.04	0.06	0.09	0.16	0.17	0.03	0.05	0.08	0.11	0.14	63
64	0.04	0.06	0.09	0.15	0.16	0.03	0.05	0.08	0.11	0.14	64
65	0.04	0.06	0.08	0.15	0.16	0.03	0.05	0.08	0.11	0.13	65
66	0.03	0.06	0.08	0.15	0.15	0.03	0.04	0.07	0.11	0.13	66
67	0.03	0.06	0.08	0.15	0.15	0.02	0.04	0.07	0.10	0.12	67
68	0.03	0.06	0.08	0.14	0.14	0.02	0.04	0.07	0.10	0.12	68
69	0.03	0.06	0.08	0.14	0.14	0.02	0.04	0.07	0.01	0.12	69
70	0.03	0.06	0.07	0.13	0.14	0.02	0.04	0.06	0.09	0.11	70
71	0.03	0.06	0.07	0.13	0.13	0.02	0.04	0.06	0.09	0.11	71
72	0.02	0.05	0.07	0.13	0.13	0.02	0.04	0.06	0.09	0.11	72
73	0.02	0.05	0.06	0.13	0.12	0.02	0.04	0.06	0.09	0.11	73
74	0.02	0.05	0.06	0.12	0.11	0.02	0.04	0.06	0.08	0.10	74
75	0.02	0.05	0.06	0.11	0.11	0.02	0.04	0.06	0.08	0.10	75

Sources: Current Population Survey monthly microdata samples 2000 through 2006.

Appendix Table 6: Conventional model worklife expectancy standard errors by educational attainment, Hispanic Males and Females

Age	Hispanic Males				Hispanic Females				Age
	<HS	HS	Some College	BA or More	<HS	HS	Some College	BA or More	
18	0.12	0.15	0.17		0.08	0.10	0.15		18
19	0.12	0.15	0.17		0.08	0.10	0.15		19
20	0.12	0.15	0.17	0.21	0.08	0.10	0.15	0.19	20
21	0.11	0.15	0.17	0.21	0.08	0.10	0.15	0.18	21
22	0.11	0.15	0.17	0.20	0.08	0.10	0.15	0.17	22
23	0.11	0.15	0.17	0.20	0.08	0.10	0.15	0.17	23
24	0.11	0.15	0.17	0.20	0.08	0.01	0.15	0.17	24
25	0.11	0.15	0.17	0.20	0.08	0.01	0.15	0.17	25
26	0.11	0.15	0.17	0.20	0.07	0.01	0.15	0.17	26
27	0.11	0.15	0.16	0.20	0.07	0.01	0.15	0.17	27
28	0.11	0.14	0.16	0.20	0.07	0.01	0.15	0.17	28
29	0.11	0.14	0.16	0.20	0.07	0.01	0.15	0.17	29
30	0.11	0.14	0.16	0.20	0.07	0.01	0.15	0.17	30
31	0.10	0.14	0.16	0.20	0.07	0.01	0.15	0.17	31
32	0.10	0.14	0.16	0.20	0.07	0.01	0.15	0.17	32
33	0.10	0.14	0.16	0.19	0.07	0.09	0.15	0.17	33
34	0.10	0.14	0.16	0.19	0.07	0.09	0.15	0.17	34
35	0.10	0.14	0.16	0.19	0.07	0.09	0.15	0.17	35
36	0.01	0.14	0.16	0.19	0.07	0.09	0.15	0.17	36
37	0.01	0.14	0.16	0.19	0.07	0.09	0.15	0.17	37
38	0.01	0.14	0.15	0.19	0.07	0.09	0.15	0.17	38
39	0.01	0.14	0.15	0.19	0.06	0.09	0.15	0.16	39
40	0.09	0.14	0.15	0.19	0.06	0.09	0.15	0.16	40
41	0.09	0.14	0.15	0.19	0.06	0.09	0.15	0.16	41
42	0.09	0.13	0.15	0.19	0.06	0.09	0.15	0.16	42
43	0.09	0.13	0.15	0.19	0.06	0.09	0.15	0.16	43
44	0.09	0.13	0.15	0.19	0.06	0.09	0.15	0.16	44
45	0.09	0.13	0.15	0.19	0.06	0.09	0.14	0.16	45
46	0.09	0.13	0.15	0.19	0.06	0.09	0.14	0.16	46
47	0.09	0.13	0.15	0.19	0.06	0.09	0.14	0.16	47
48	0.09	0.13	0.15	0.19	0.06	0.09	0.14	0.16	48
49	0.08	0.13	0.15	0.19	0.05	0.09	0.14	0.16	49
50	0.08	0.13	0.15	0.19	0.05	0.08	0.14	0.16	50
51	0.08	0.13	0.15	0.18	0.05	0.08	0.14	0.16	51
52	0.08	0.13	0.15	0.18	0.05	0.08	0.14	0.16	52
53	0.08	0.12	0.14	0.18	0.05	0.08	0.14	0.16	53
54	0.08	0.12	0.14	0.18	0.05	0.08	0.14	0.16	54
55	0.08	0.12	0.14	0.18	0.05	0.08	0.14	0.16	55
56	0.07	0.12	0.14	0.18	0.05	0.08	0.14	0.16	56
57	0.07	0.12	0.14	0.18	0.04	0.07	0.14	0.15	57
58	0.07	0.12	0.14	0.18	0.04	0.07	0.13	0.15	58
59	0.07	0.12	0.14	0.17	0.04	0.07	0.13	0.15	59
60	0.06	0.11	0.14	0.17	0.04	0.07	0.13	0.15	60
61	0.06	0.11	0.13	0.17	0.04	0.07	0.13	0.14	61
62	0.06	0.11	0.13	0.17	0.04	0.06	0.13	0.14	62
63	0.06	0.11	0.13	0.17	0.03	0.06	0.13	0.14	63
64	0.05	0.10	0.12	0.16	0.03	0.06	0.13	0.13	64
65	0.05	0.10	0.12	0.16	0.03	0.06	0.12	0.13	65
66	0.05	0.01	0.12	0.16	0.03	0.05	0.12	0.12	66
67	0.05	0.01	0.11	0.15	0.03	0.05	0.12	0.12	67
68	0.04	0.09	0.11	0.15	0.02	0.05	0.11	0.11	68
69	0.04	0.09	0.11	0.14	0.02	0.05	0.11	0.11	69
70	0.04	0.09	0.10	0.14	0.02	0.04	0.10	0.10	70
71	0.04	0.09	0.01	0.13	0.02	0.04	0.01	0.01	71
72	0.04	0.09	0.01	0.12	0.02	0.04	0.09	0.09	72
73	0.03	0.09	0.09	0.12	0.02	0.04	0.09	0.09	73
74	0.03	0.09	0.09	0.11	0.02	0.03	0.08	0.08	74
75	0.03	0.08	0.08	0.11	0.01	0.03	0.08	0.07	75

Sources: Current Population Survey monthly microdata samples 2000 through 2006.

Appendix Table 7: Standard errors of worklife expectancies for never-married, childless females by educational attainment, conventional methodology
Never-married, childless females of all races

Age	<HS	HS	Some College			College Degree	Graduate Degree			Age
			All	No Degree	Assoc Degree		All	Masters	Phd/Prof'l	
18	0.20	0.13	0.15	0.17	0.29					18
19	0.20	0.13	0.14	0.17	0.27	0.25				19
20	0.20	0.13	0.14	0.17	0.26	0.22				20
21	0.19	0.13	0.14	0.17	0.26	0.21	0.22	0.27		21
22	0.19	0.13	0.14	0.17	0.26	0.21	0.19	0.21	0.38	22
23	0.19	0.13	0.14	0.17	0.26	0.21	0.18	0.21	0.36	23
24	0.19	0.13	0.14	0.17	0.27	0.21	0.18	0.21	0.35	24
25	0.19	0.13	0.14	0.17	0.26	0.21	0.18	0.21	0.35	25
26	0.19	0.13	0.14	0.17	0.26	0.21	0.18	0.21	0.35	26
27	0.19	0.13	0.14	0.17	0.26	0.21	0.18	0.21	0.34	27
28	0.19	0.13	0.14	0.17	0.26	0.21	0.18	0.20	0.35	28
29	0.18	0.13	0.14	0.17	0.26	0.21	0.18	0.21	0.35	29
30	0.18	0.13	0.14	0.17	0.26	0.21	0.18	0.21	0.35	30
31	0.18	0.13	0.14	0.17	0.26	0.21	0.18	0.20	0.35	31
32	0.18	0.13	0.14	0.17	0.26	0.21	0.18	0.21	0.35	32
33	0.18	0.13	0.14	0.17	0.26	0.21	0.18	0.21	0.35	33
34	0.17	0.13	0.14	0.17	0.26	0.21	0.18	0.21	0.35	34
35	0.17	0.13	0.14	0.17	0.26	0.21	0.18	0.21	0.34	35
36	0.17	0.13	0.14	0.17	0.26	0.21	0.18	0.21	0.35	36
37	0.17	0.12	0.14	0.17	0.26	0.21	0.17	0.20	0.35	37
38	0.16	0.12	0.14	0.17	0.26	0.21	0.18	0.20	0.35	38
39	0.16	0.12	0.14	0.17	0.26	0.21	0.18	0.20	0.34	39
40	0.16	0.12	0.14	0.17	0.26	0.21	0.18	0.21	0.35	40
41	0.16	0.12	0.14	0.17	0.26	0.21	0.18	0.21	0.34	41
42	0.16	0.12	0.14	0.17	0.26	0.21	0.18	0.20	0.34	42
43	0.16	0.12	0.14	0.17	0.26	0.21	0.18	0.20	0.34	43
44	0.15	0.12	0.14	0.17	0.26	0.21	0.17	0.20	0.35	44
45	0.15	0.12	0.14	0.17	0.26	0.21	0.18	0.20	0.35	45
46	0.15	0.12	0.14	0.17	0.26	0.21	0.18	0.20	0.35	46
47	0.14	0.12	0.14	0.17	0.26	0.21	0.18	0.20	0.34	47
48	0.14	0.12	0.14	0.17	0.26	0.21	0.18	0.21	0.34	48
49	0.14	0.12	0.14	0.16	0.26	0.21	0.18	0.20	0.34	49
50	0.14	0.12	0.14	0.16	0.26	0.21	0.18	0.20	0.34	50
51	0.13	0.12	0.13	0.16	0.26	0.21	0.17	0.20	0.34	51
52	0.13	0.11	0.13	0.16	0.26	0.21	0.18	0.20	0.34	52
53	0.13	0.11	0.13	0.16	0.26	0.21	0.17	0.20	0.35	53
54	0.12	0.11	0.13	0.16	0.26	0.21	0.18	0.21	0.35	54
55	0.12	0.11	0.13	0.16	0.26	0.21	0.18	0.20	0.34	55
56	0.12	0.11	0.13	0.16	0.26	0.21	0.18	0.20	0.35	56
57	0.11	0.11	0.13	0.16	0.25	0.20	0.18	0.20	0.35	57
58	0.11	0.11	0.13	0.15	0.25	0.20	0.18	0.20	0.34	58
59	0.11	0.11	0.13	0.15	0.25	0.20	0.18	0.20	0.35	59
60	0.10	0.10	0.13	0.15	0.25	0.20	0.18	0.20	0.34	60
61	0.01	0.10	0.12	0.15	0.24	0.20	0.18	0.19	0.34	61
62	0.01	0.10	0.12	0.14	0.24	0.20	0.17	0.20	0.33	62
63	0.09	0.01	0.12	0.14	0.23	0.20	0.17	0.19	0.33	63
64	0.09	0.09	0.12	0.14	0.23	0.20	0.17	0.19	0.33	64
65	0.08	0.09	0.12	0.13	0.22	0.20	0.17	0.19	0.33	65
66	0.08	0.09	0.11	0.13	0.21	0.20	0.17	0.19	0.32	66
67	0.08	0.09	0.11	0.13	0.20	0.19	0.16	0.18	0.31	67
68	0.07	0.09	0.10	0.12	0.19	0.18	0.16	0.18	0.30	68
69	0.07	0.08	0.01	0.11	0.18	0.18	0.15	0.17	0.28	69
70	0.06	0.08	0.09	0.11	0.18	0.18	0.15	0.17	0.27	70
71	0.06	0.08	0.09	0.01	0.16	0.18	0.15	0.17	0.26	71
72	0.06	0.08	0.08	0.09	0.15	0.18	0.14	0.16	0.24	72
73	0.05	0.08	0.08	0.09	0.15	0.18	0.14	0.16	0.23	73
74	0.05	0.08	0.07	0.08	0.13	0.18	0.13	0.16	0.22	74
75	0.05	0.08	0.07	0.08	0.13	0.18	0.13	0.15	0.21	75

Sources: Current Population Survey monthly microdata samples 2000 through 2006, and mortality data from Table 1.

Appendix Table 8: Standard errors of worklife expectancies by smoking status and educational attainment—Males All Races

Age	All Males Regardless of Smoking Status						Male Never Smokers						Male Current Smokers					
	<HS	HS	No Dgr	Assoc Dgr	BA Dgr	Grad Dgr	<HS	HS	No Dgr	Assoc Dgr	BA Dgr	Grad Dgr	<HS	HS	No Dgr	Assoc Dgr	BA Dgr	Grad Dgr
18	0.12	0.08	0.12	0.27			0.19	0.13	0.17	0.32			0.19	0.14	0.22	0.35		
19	0.13	0.08	0.11	0.19	0.17		0.19	0.12	0.17	0.26	0.23		0.19	0.13	0.20	0.29	0.30	
20	0.12	0.08	0.11	0.18	0.16		0.19	0.12	0.17	0.25	0.22		0.19	0.13	0.20	0.29	0.30	
21	0.12	0.08	0.11	0.17	0.13	0.35	0.19	0.12	0.17	0.24	0.17	0.39	0.19	0.13	0.20	0.29	0.30	0.50
22	0.12	0.08	0.11	0.17	0.12	0.28	0.18	0.12	0.17	0.24	0.16	0.36	0.19	0.13	0.20	0.28	0.27	0.50
23	0.12	0.08	0.11	0.17	0.12	0.18	0.18	0.12	0.17	0.24	0.16	0.25	0.19	0.13	0.19	0.28	0.27	0.43
24	0.12	0.08	0.11	0.17	0.12	0.16	0.18	0.12	0.17	0.24	0.16	0.21	0.19	0.13	0.19	0.28	0.27	0.42
25	0.12	0.08	0.11	0.17	0.12	0.15	0.18	0.12	0.17	0.24	0.16	0.20	0.18	0.12	0.19	0.28	0.27	0.39
26	0.12	0.07	0.11	0.17	0.12	0.15	0.18	0.12	0.17	0.24	0.16	0.19	0.18	0.12	0.19	0.28	0.27	0.39
27	0.12	0.07	0.11	0.17	0.12	0.15	0.18	0.12	0.17	0.24	0.16	0.19	0.18	0.12	0.19	0.27	0.26	0.38
28	0.12	0.07	0.11	0.17	0.12	0.14	0.18	0.12	0.17	0.24	0.16	0.19	0.18	0.12	0.19	0.27	0.26	0.38
29	0.12	0.07	0.11	0.17	0.12	0.14	0.18	0.12	0.17	0.24	0.16	0.19	0.18	0.12	0.19	0.27	0.26	0.37
30	0.12	0.07	0.11	0.17	0.11	0.14	0.18	0.12	0.16	0.24	0.16	0.19	0.18	0.12	0.19	0.27	0.26	0.37
31	0.11	0.07	0.11	0.17	0.11	0.14	0.18	0.12	0.17	0.24	0.16	0.19	0.18	0.12	0.19	0.27	0.26	0.36
32	0.11	0.07	0.11	0.17	0.11	0.14	0.18	0.11	0.17	0.24	0.16	0.19	0.18	0.12	0.19	0.27	0.26	0.36
33	0.11	0.07	0.11	0.17	0.11	0.14	0.18	0.11	0.17	0.24	0.16	0.19	0.17	0.12	0.18	0.27	0.26	0.36
34	0.11	0.07	0.11	0.17	0.11	0.14	0.18	0.11	0.17	0.24	0.16	0.19	0.17	0.12	0.18	0.27	0.26	0.36
35	0.11	0.07	0.11	0.17	0.11	0.14	0.17	0.11	0.17	0.24	0.16	0.19	0.17	0.12	0.18	0.27	0.26	0.36
36	0.11	0.07	0.11	0.17	0.11	0.14	0.17	0.11	0.17	0.24	0.16	0.19	0.17	0.12	0.18	0.27	0.26	0.36
37	0.11	0.07	0.11	0.17	0.11	0.14	0.17	0.11	0.17	0.24	0.16	0.19	0.16	0.12	0.18	0.27	0.26	0.36
38	0.11	0.07	0.11	0.17	0.11	0.14	0.17	0.11	0.17	0.24	0.16	0.19	0.16	0.12	0.18	0.27	0.26	0.35
39	0.11	0.07	0.10	0.17	0.11	0.14	0.17	0.11	0.16	0.24	0.16	0.19	0.16	0.12	0.18	0.27	0.26	0.35
40	0.11	0.07	0.10	0.17	0.11	0.14	0.16	0.11	0.17	0.24	0.16	0.19	0.16	0.12	0.18	0.27	0.26	0.36
41	0.11	0.07	0.11	0.17	0.11	0.14	0.16	0.11	0.17	0.24	0.16	0.19	0.16	0.12	0.18	0.27	0.26	0.35
42	0.11	0.07	0.10	0.17	0.11	0.14	0.16	0.11	0.17	0.24	0.16	0.19	0.15	0.12	0.18	0.27	0.26	0.36
43	0.10	0.07	0.10	0.17	0.11	0.14	0.16	0.11	0.17	0.24	0.16	0.19	0.15	0.12	0.18	0.28	0.26	0.36
44	0.10	0.07	0.10	0.17	0.11	0.14	0.16	0.11	0.17	0.24	0.16	0.19	0.15	0.12	0.18	0.28	0.26	0.35
45	0.10	0.07	0.10	0.17	0.11	0.14	0.16	0.11	0.17	0.24	0.16	0.19	0.15	0.12	0.18	0.28	0.26	0.35
46	0.01	0.07	0.10	0.17	0.11	0.14	0.16	0.11	0.17	0.24	0.16	0.19	0.14	0.12	0.18	0.28	0.26	0.35
47	0.01	0.07	0.10	0.17	0.11	0.14	0.15	0.11	0.17	0.24	0.16	0.19	0.14	0.12	0.18	0.28	0.26	0.35
48	0.09	0.07	0.10	0.17	0.11	0.14	0.15	0.11	0.17	0.24	0.16	0.19	0.14	0.12	0.18	0.29	0.26	0.35
49	0.09	0.07	0.10	0.17	0.11	0.14	0.15	0.11	0.17	0.24	0.16	0.19	0.14	0.12	0.18	0.29	0.26	0.35
50	0.09	0.07	0.10	0.17	0.11	0.14	0.15	0.11	0.17	0.24	0.16	0.19	0.14	0.12	0.19	0.29	0.26	0.35
51	0.09	0.06	0.10	0.17	0.11	0.14	0.15	0.11	0.17	0.25	0.16	0.19	0.13	0.12	0.19	0.29	0.26	0.35
52	0.09	0.06	0.10	0.17	0.11	0.14	0.15	0.11	0.17	0.25	0.16	0.19	0.13	0.12	0.19	0.30	0.26	0.35
53	0.08	0.06	0.10	0.17	0.11	0.14	0.14	0.11	0.17	0.25	0.16	0.19	0.13	0.12	0.19	0.30	0.26	0.35
54	0.08	0.06	0.10	0.17	0.11	0.14	0.14	0.11	0.17	0.25	0.16	0.19	0.13	0.12	0.19	0.30	0.26	0.35
55	0.08	0.06	0.10	0.17	0.11	0.14	0.14	0.11	0.16	0.25	0.16	0.19	0.12	0.12	0.19	0.31	0.27	0.35
56	0.08	0.06	0.10	0.17	0.11	0.14	0.13	0.11	0.16	0.25	0.16	0.19	0.12	0.12	0.19	0.31	0.27	0.35
57	0.07	0.06	0.10	0.17	0.11	0.14	0.13	0.11	0.16	0.25	0.16	0.19	0.12	0.12	0.19	0.32	0.27	0.35
58	0.07	0.06	0.01	0.17	0.11	0.14	0.13	0.11	0.16	0.25	0.16	0.19	0.11	0.12	0.19	0.32	0.27	0.36
59	0.07	0.06	0.01	0.17	0.11	0.14	0.12	0.10	0.16	0.24	0.16	0.19	0.11	0.12	0.19	0.32	0.27	0.36
60	0.07	0.06	0.01	0.17	0.11	0.14	0.11	0.10	0.16	0.24	0.16	0.19	0.11	0.12	0.19	0.32	0.27	0.36
61	0.06	0.06	0.01	0.16	0.11	0.14	0.11	0.01	0.16	0.24	0.16	0.18	0.10	0.11	0.19	0.32	0.27	0.36
62	0.06	0.06	0.01	0.16	0.11	0.14	0.10	0.01	0.15	0.23	0.16	0.18	0.01	0.11	0.19	0.32	0.27	0.36
63	0.06	0.05	0.09	0.16	0.11	0.14	0.01	0.01	0.15	0.23	0.15	0.18	0.09	0.11	0.18	0.32	0.27	0.36
64	0.05	0.05	0.09	0.15	0.10	0.13	0.09	0.09	0.15	0.23	0.15	0.18	0.09	0.11	0.18	0.32	0.26	0.35
65	0.05	0.05	0.09	0.15	0.01	0.13	0.09	0.09	0.14	0.22	0.15	0.18	0.09	0.11	0.18	0.31	0.24	0.35
66	0.05	0.05	0.08	0.14	0.01	0.13	0.08	0.09	0.14	0.22	0.14	0.17	0.09	0.11	0.17	0.31	0.24	0.33
67	0.04	0.05	0.08	0.14	0.09	0.13	0.08	0.08	0.14	0.21	0.14	0.17	0.08	0.11	0.16	0.29	0.24	0.32
68	0.04	0.05	0.08	0.14	0.09	0.13	0.07	0.08	0.13	0.20	0.13	0.17	0.08	0.10	0.15	0.29	0.24	0.31
69	0.04	0.04	0.08	0.13	0.09	0.12	0.07	0.08	0.12	0.19	0.13	0.17	0.07	0.01	0.14	0.27	0.23	0.30
70	0.04	0.04	0.07	0.13	0.09	0.12	0.06	0.07	0.12	0.19	0.13	0.16	0.07	0.01	0.14	0.26	0.23	0.30
71	0.03	0.04	0.07	0.13	0.08	0.12	0.06	0.07	0.12	0.18	0.12	0.16	0.06	0.09	0.13	0.26	0.22	0.30
72	0.03	0.04	0.07	0.12	0.08	0.12	0.05	0.07	0.11	0.16	0.12	0.16	0.06	0.08	0.13	0.26	0.21	0.30
73	0.03	0.04	0.06	0.12	0.08	0.11	0.05	0.07	0.10	0.16	0.12	0.16	0.06	0.08	0.13	0.20	0.21	0.28
74	0.03	0.04	0.06	0.12	0.07	0.11	0.05	0.06	0.10	0.16	0.11	0.16	0.06	0.08	0.12	0.22	0.21	0.27
75	0.03	0.03	0.06	0.11	0.07	0.11	0.05	0.06	0.09	0.16	0.11	0.15	0.04	0.08	0.12	0.18	0.20	0.26

Sources: CPS tobacco supplements, 2000 through 2003, Bureau of the Census, and CDC, "United States Life Tables. 2004."
Note: Populations regardless of smoking status include former smokers and those not classified (only for the CPS tobacco supplements above).

Appendix Table 8: Standard errors of worklife expectancies by smoking status and educational attainment—Females of All Races

Age	All Females Regardless of Smoking Status						Female Never Smokers						Female Current Smokers					
			Some College		BA Dgr	Grad Dgr			Some College		BA Dgr	Grad Dgr			Some College		BA Dgr	Grad Dgr
	<HS	HS	No Dgr	Assoc Dgr			<HS	HS	No Dgr	Assoc Dgr			<HS	HS	No Dgr	Assoc Dgr		
18	0.15	0.09	0.12	0.25			0.20	0.12	0.15	0.29			0.27	0.16	0.25	0.35		
19	0.14	0.09	0.12	0.18	0.31		0.20	0.12	0.15	0.23	0.35		0.26	0.16	0.24	0.35	0.44	
20	0.14	0.09	0.12	0.17	0.18		0.20	0.12	0.15	0.22	0.21		0.26	0.16	0.24	0.36	0.35	
21	0.14	0.08	0.12	0.17	0.15	0.21	0.19	0.11	0.15	0.22	0.17	0.24	0.26	0.16	0.24	0.35	0.36	0.50
22	0.14	0.08	0.12	0.16	0.14	0.21	0.19	0.11	0.15	0.22	0.17	0.24	0.26	0.16	0.24	0.34	0.33	0.50
23	0.14	0.08	0.12	0.16	0.14	0.19	0.19	0.11	0.15	0.22	0.16	0.23	0.26	0.16	0.24	0.34	0.33	0.49
24	0.14	0.08	0.12	0.16	0.14	0.19	0.19	0.11	0.15	0.21	0.16	0.22	0.25	0.16	0.24	0.34	0.33	0.49
25	0.13	0.08	0.12	0.16	0.14	0.18	0.18	0.11	0.15	0.21	0.16	0.21	0.25	0.15	0.23	0.34	0.33	0.49
26	0.13	0.08	0.11	0.16	0.14	0.18	0.18	0.11	0.15	0.21	0.16	0.21	0.25	0.15	0.23	0.34	0.33	0.49
27	0.13	0.08	0.11	0.16	0.13	0.18	0.18	0.10	0.14	0.21	0.16	0.21	0.24	0.15	0.23	0.34	0.33	0.48
28	0.13	0.08	0.11	0.16	0.13	0.18	0.18	0.10	0.14	0.21	0.16	0.21	0.24	0.15	0.23	0.34	0.33	0.47
29	0.13	0.08	0.11	0.15	0.13	0.18	0.18	0.10	0.14	0.21	0.16	0.21	0.23	0.15	0.22	0.33	0.32	0.47
30	0.12	0.07	0.11	0.15	0.13	0.17	0.17	0.01	0.14	0.21	0.16	0.21	0.23	0.15	0.22	0.33	0.32	0.47
31	0.12	0.07	0.11	0.15	0.13	0.17	0.17	0.01	0.14	0.21	0.16	0.21	0.22	0.15	0.22	0.33	0.32	0.47
32	0.12	0.07	0.11	0.15	0.13	0.17	0.17	0.01	0.14	0.21	0.16	0.21	0.22	0.14	0.22	0.33	0.32	0.47
33	0.12	0.07	0.11	0.15	0.13	0.17	0.17	0.01	0.14	0.21	0.16	0.20	0.21	0.14	0.22	0.33	0.32	0.47
34	0.12	0.07	0.11	0.15	0.13	0.17	0.17	0.01	0.14	0.20	0.16	0.20	0.21	0.14	0.22	0.33	0.32	0.47
35	0.11	0.07	0.11	0.15	0.13	0.17	0.16	0.01	0.14	0.21	0.16	0.20	0.21	0.14	0.22	0.32	0.32	0.46
36	0.11	0.07	0.10	0.15	0.13	0.17	0.16	0.09	0.14	0.20	0.16	0.20	0.20	0.14	0.22	0.32	0.31	0.46
37	0.11	0.07	0.10	0.15	0.13	0.17	0.16	0.09	0.14	0.20	0.16	0.20	0.20	0.14	0.22	0.32	0.31	0.46
38	0.11	0.07	0.10	0.15	0.13	0.17	0.15	0.09	0.14	0.20	0.16	0.20	0.20	0.14	0.22	0.32	0.31	0.45
39	0.11	0.07	0.10	0.15	0.13	0.17	0.15	0.09	0.14	0.20	0.16	0.20	0.20	0.14	0.22	0.32	0.31	0.45
40	0.11	0.07	0.10	0.15	0.13	0.16	0.15	0.09	0.14	0.20	0.16	0.19	0.20	0.14	0.22	0.32	0.31	0.44
41	0.10	0.07	0.10	0.14	0.13	0.16	0.14	0.09	0.13	0.20	0.15	0.19	0.19	0.13	0.21	0.32	0.31	0.44
42	0.10	0.06	0.10	0.14	0.12	0.16	0.14	0.09	0.13	0.20	0.15	0.19	0.19	0.13	0.21	0.32	0.31	0.44
43	0.10	0.06	0.10	0.14	0.13	0.16	0.14	0.09	0.13	0.20	0.15	0.19	0.19	0.13	0.21	0.32	0.31	0.44
44	0.01	0.06	0.10	0.14	0.12	0.16	0.13	0.08	0.13	0.20	0.15	0.19	0.19	0.13	0.21	0.33	0.31	0.43
45	0.01	0.06	0.01	0.14	0.12	0.16	0.13	0.08	0.13	0.20	0.15	0.19	0.18	0.13	0.21	0.33	0.31	0.43
46	0.09	0.06	0.01	0.14	0.12	0.16	0.13	0.08	0.13	0.20	0.15	0.19	0.18	0.13	0.21	0.33	0.31	0.43
47	0.09	0.06	0.01	0.14	0.12	0.16	0.13	0.08	0.13	0.20	0.15	0.19	0.17	0.13	0.21	0.33	0.31	0.43
48	0.09	0.06	0.01	0.14	0.12	0.16	0.12	0.08	0.13	0.20	0.15	0.19	0.17	0.13	0.21	0.33	0.31	0.43
49	0.09	0.06	0.01	0.14	0.12	0.16	0.12	0.08	0.13	0.19	0.15	0.19	0.16	0.13	0.21	0.33	0.31	0.43
50	0.08	0.06	0.09	0.14	0.12	0.16	0.11	0.08	0.13	0.19	0.15	0.19	0.16	0.12	0.20	0.33	0.31	0.43
51	0.08	0.06	0.09	0.14	0.12	0.16	0.11	0.08	0.13	0.19	0.15	0.19	0.16	0.12	0.20	0.33	0.31	0.43
52	0.08	0.06	0.09	0.14	0.12	0.16	0.11	0.07	0.13	0.19	0.15	0.19	0.15	0.12	0.20	0.33	0.31	0.43
53	0.08	0.06	0.09	0.14	0.12	0.16	0.10	0.07	0.12	0.19	0.15	0.19	0.15	0.12	0.20	0.33	0.31	0.43
54	0.07	0.06	0.09	0.13	0.12	0.16	0.01	0.07	0.12	0.19	0.15	0.19	0.14	0.12	0.20	0.33	0.31	0.43
55	0.07	0.05	0.09	0.13	0.12	0.16	0.01	0.07	0.12	0.19	0.14	0.19	0.14	0.12	0.20	0.33	0.31	0.43
56	0.07	0.05	0.09	0.13	0.12	0.16	0.09	0.07	0.12	0.18	0.14	0.19	0.13	0.12	0.20	0.32	0.30	0.43
57	0.06	0.05	0.09	0.13	0.12	0.16	0.08	0.07	0.12	0.18	0.14	0.19	0.13	0.12	0.20	0.32	0.30	0.43
58	0.06	0.05	0.09	0.13	0.12	0.16	0.08	0.06	0.12	0.18	0.14	0.19	0.12	0.11	0.19	0.32	0.30	0.42
59	0.06	0.05	0.08	0.13	0.11	0.16	0.07	0.06	0.11	0.18	0.14	0.19	0.12	0.11	0.19	0.32	0.29	0.41
60	0.05	0.05	0.08	0.13	0.11	0.15	0.07	0.06	0.11	0.17	0.13	0.18	0.12	0.11	0.19	0.32	0.28	0.41
61	0.05	0.04	0.08	0.12	0.11	0.15	0.06	0.06	0.11	0.17	0.13	0.18	0.11	0.11	0.19	0.32	0.28	0.40
62	0.05	0.04	0.08	0.12	0.10	0.15	0.06	0.05	0.10	0.16	0.12	0.17	0.10	0.10	0.18	0.30	0.28	0.39
63	0.04	0.04	0.07	0.11	0.10	0.15	0.05	0.05	0.10	0.15	0.12	0.17	0.01	0.01	0.17	0.29	0.27	0.39
64	0.04	0.04	0.07	0.11	0.01	0.14	0.05	0.05	0.01	0.15	0.11	0.17	0.09	0.09	0.17	0.29	0.26	0.35
65	0.04	0.04	0.07	0.11	0.09	0.14	0.04	0.05	0.09	0.14	0.11	0.16	0.09	0.09	0.16	0.28	0.24	0.33
66	0.03	0.03	0.07	0.10	0.09	0.14	0.04	0.04	0.09	0.13	0.10	0.16	0.08	0.09	0.16	0.23	0.24	0.30
67	0.03	0.03	0.06	0.09	0.09	0.13	0.04	0.04	0.09	0.12	0.01	0.15	0.08	0.08	0.15	0.22	0.22	0.29
68	0.03	0.03	0.06	0.09	0.08	0.13	0.04	0.04	0.08	0.12	0.09	0.14	0.08	0.08	0.15	0.19	0.21	0.28
69	0.03	0.03	0.05	0.08	0.08	0.12	0.03	0.03	0.07	0.11	0.09	0.14	0.07	0.07	0.14	0.18	0.20	0.26
70	0.02	0.03	0.05	0.08	0.08	0.12	0.03	0.03	0.07	0.11	0.08	0.13	0.06	0.07	0.13	0.16	0.18	0.26
71	0.02	0.02	0.05	0.07	0.07	0.11	0.03	0.03	0.07	0.01	0.08	0.12	0.06	0.06	0.13	0.14	0.17	0.26
72	0.02	0.02	0.05	0.07	0.07	0.11	0.03	0.03	0.06	0.09	0.07	0.12	0.05	0.06	0.11	0.11	0.16	0.26
73	0.02	0.02	0.04	0.06	0.07	0.11	0.02	0.03	0.06	0.08	0.07	0.11	0.05	0.05	0.11	0.08	0.15	0.19
74	0.02	0.02	0.04	0.05	0.06	0.10	0.02	0.03	0.05	0.07	0.06	0.11	0.05	0.05	0.10	0.08	0.15	0.20
75	0.02	0.02	0.04	0.05	0.06	0.01	0.02	0.02	0.05	0.06	0.06	0.11	0.05	0.04	0.01	0.04	0.13	0.21

Sources: CPS tobacco supplements, 2000 through 2003, Bureau of the Census, and CDC, "United States Life Tables. 2004."
Note: Populations regardless of smoking status include former smokers and those not classified (only for the CPS tobacco supplements above).

Appendix Table 9: Standard errors of mean years to final separation, July 1999 - June 2007 CPS data: Males and Females All Races

Age	Males of All Races										Females of All Races									
	Initially Active					Initially Inactive					Initially Active					Initially Inactive				
	<HS	HS	Some College	College Degree	Graduate Degrees	<HS	HS	Some College	College Degree	Graduate Degrees	<HS	HS	Some College	College Degree	Graduate Degrees	<HS	HS	Some College	College Degree	Graduate Degrees
18	0.26	0.19	0.33			0.26	0.19	0.33			0.33	0.19	0.28			0.33	0.19	0.28		
19	0.26	0.19	0.33	0.32		0.26	0.19	0.33	0.32		0.33	0.19	0.28	0.31		0.33	0.19	0.28	0.31	
20	0.26	0.19	0.33	0.32		0.26	0.19	0.33	0.32		0.33	0.19	0.28	0.31		0.33	0.19	0.28	0.31	
21	0.26	0.19	0.33	0.32	0.41	0.26	0.19	0.33	0.32	0.41	0.33	0.19	0.28	0.31	0.56	0.33	0.19	0.28	0.31	0.56
22	0.26	0.19	0.33	0.32	0.41	0.26	0.19	0.33	0.32	0.41	0.33	0.19	0.28	0.31	0.56	0.33	0.19	0.28	0.31	0.56
23	0.26	0.19	0.33	0.32	0.41	0.26	0.19	0.33	0.32	0.41	0.33	0.19	0.28	0.31	0.56	0.33	0.19	0.28	0.31	0.56
24	0.26	0.19	0.33	0.32	0.41	0.26	0.19	0.33	0.32	0.41	0.33	0.19	0.28	0.31	0.56	0.33	0.19	0.28	0.31	0.56
25	0.26	0.19	0.33	0.32	0.41	0.26	0.19	0.33	0.32	0.41	0.33	0.19	0.28	0.31	0.56	0.33	0.19	0.28	0.31	0.56
26	0.26	0.20	0.33	0.32	0.41	0.26	0.20	0.33	0.32	0.41	0.33	0.19	0.28	0.31	0.56	0.33	0.19	0.28	0.31	0.56
27	0.26	0.20	0.33	0.32	0.41	0.27	0.20	0.33	0.32	0.41	0.33	0.19	0.28	0.31	0.56	0.33	0.19	0.28	0.31	0.56
28	0.27	0.20	0.33	0.32	0.41	0.27	0.20	0.33	0.32	0.41	0.33	0.19	0.28	0.31	0.56	0.33	0.19	0.28	0.31	0.56
29	0.27	0.20	0.33	0.32	0.41	0.27	0.20	0.33	0.32	0.41	0.33	0.19	0.28	0.31	0.56	0.33	0.19	0.28	0.31	0.56
30	0.27	0.20	0.33	0.32	0.41	0.27	0.20	0.33	0.32	0.41	0.33	0.19	0.28	0.31	0.56	0.33	0.19	0.28	0.31	0.56
31	0.27	0.20	0.33	0.32	0.41	0.27	0.20	0.33	0.32	0.41	0.33	0.19	0.28	0.31	0.56	0.33	0.19	0.28	0.31	0.57
32	0.27	0.20	0.33	0.32	0.41	0.27	0.20	0.33	0.32	0.41	0.33	0.19	0.28	0.31	0.57	0.33	0.19	0.28	0.31	0.57
33	0.27	0.20	0.33	0.32	0.41	0.27	0.20	0.34	0.32	0.41	0.33	0.19	0.28	0.31	0.57	0.33	0.19	0.28	0.31	0.57
34	0.27	0.20	0.34	0.32	0.41	0.27	0.20	0.34	0.32	0.41	0.32	0.19	0.28	0.31	0.57	0.33	0.19	0.28	0.31	0.57
35	0.27	0.20	0.34	0.32	0.41	0.27	0.20	0.34	0.32	0.41	0.32	0.19	0.28	0.31	0.57	0.33	0.19	0.28	0.31	0.57
36	0.27	0.20	0.34	0.32	0.41	0.28	0.20	0.34	0.32	0.41	0.32	0.19	0.28	0.31	0.57	0.33	0.19	0.28	0.31	0.57
37	0.27	0.20	0.34	0.32	0.41	0.28	0.20	0.34	0.32	0.41	0.32	0.19	0.28	0.31	0.57	0.33	0.19	0.28	0.31	0.57
38	0.27	0.20	0.34	0.32	0.41	0.28	0.20	0.34	0.32	0.41	0.32	0.19	0.28	0.31	0.57	0.33	0.20	0.28	0.31	0.57
39	0.27	0.20	0.34	0.32	0.41	0.29	0.20	0.34	0.32	0.41	0.32	0.19	0.28	0.31	0.57	0.33	0.20	0.29	0.31	0.57
40	0.27	0.20	0.34	0.32	0.41	0.30	0.20	0.34	0.32	0.41	0.32	0.19	0.28	0.31	0.57	0.33	0.20	0.29	0.31	0.57
41	0.27	0.20	0.34	0.32	0.41	0.30	0.21	0.34	0.32	0.41	0.31	0.19	0.28	0.31	0.57	0.33	0.20	0.29	0.32	0.57
42	0.27	0.20	0.34	0.32	0.42	0.31	0.21	0.34	0.32	0.42	0.31	0.19	0.28	0.31	0.57	0.33	0.20	0.29	0.32	0.57
43	0.27	0.20	0.34	0.32	0.42	0.32	0.21	0.35	0.33	0.42	0.31	0.19	0.28	0.31	0.57	0.33	0.20	0.29	0.32	0.58
44	0.27	0.20	0.34	0.33	0.42	0.32	0.21	0.35	0.33	0.42	0.31	0.19	0.28	0.31	0.57	0.33	0.20	0.30	0.32	0.58
45	0.26	0.20	0.34	0.33	0.42	0.33	0.22	0.36	0.33	0.42	0.30	0.19	0.28	0.31	0.57	0.33	0.21	0.30	0.32	0.58
46	0.26	0.20	0.34	0.33	0.42	0.34	0.22	0.36	0.33	0.42	0.30	0.19	0.28	0.31	0.57	0.34	0.21	0.30	0.32	0.58
47	0.26	0.20	0.34	0.33	0.42	0.34	0.23	0.37	0.33	0.42	0.29	0.19	0.28	0.31	0.57	0.34	0.21	0.31	0.32	0.59
48	0.26	0.20	0.34	0.33	0.42	0.34	0.23	0.37	0.34	0.43	0.29	0.19	0.28	0.31	0.57	0.34	0.21	0.31	0.33	0.60
49	0.26	0.20	0.34	0.33	0.42	0.34	0.24	0.38	0.34	0.43	0.28	0.19	0.28	0.31	0.57	0.33	0.22	0.31	0.33	0.60
50	0.25	0.20	0.34	0.33	0.42	0.35	0.24	0.39	0.35	0.44	0.28	0.19	0.27	0.31	0.57	0.33	0.22	0.32	0.33	0.61
51	0.25	0.20	0.34	0.33	0.42	0.35	0.25	0.40	0.35	0.44	0.27	0.18	0.27	0.31	0.57	0.33	0.22	0.32	0.34	0.61
52	0.25	0.20	0.34	0.33	0.42	0.34	0.25	0.41	0.36	0.45	0.27	0.18	0.27	0.31	0.57	0.32	0.22	0.33	0.34	0.62
53	0.25	0.20	0.34	0.33	0.42	0.34	0.26	0.42	0.37	0.46	0.26	0.18	0.27	0.31	0.57	0.32	0.22	0.33	0.35	0.63
54	0.24	0.20	0.34	0.33	0.42	0.34	0.26	0.43	0.38	0.48	0.25	0.18	0.27	0.31	0.57	0.31	0.22	0.34	0.35	0.64
55	0.24	0.20	0.34	0.33	0.42	0.33	0.26	0.43	0.38	0.49	0.24	0.18	0.26	0.31	0.56	0.30	0.22	0.34	0.35	0.65
56	0.23	0.20	0.34	0.33	0.43	0.32	0.26	0.43	0.39	0.49	0.23	0.17	0.26	0.31	0.56	0.29	0.22	0.34	0.36	0.66
57	0.23	0.20	0.34	0.33	0.43	0.31	0.26	0.44	0.40	0.50	0.23	0.17	0.26	0.30	0.56	0.28	0.21	0.33	0.36	0.66
58	0.22	0.20	0.34	0.33	0.43	0.30	0.26	0.43	0.40	0.51	0.22	0.17	0.25	0.30	0.56	0.26	0.21	0.33	0.36	0.66
59	0.22	0.20	0.33	0.33	0.43	0.29	0.25	0.43	0.40	0.51	0.22	0.17	0.25	0.30	0.55	0.25	0.20	0.32	0.36	0.67
60	0.22	0.19	0.33	0.33	0.42	0.28	0.25	0.43	0.40	0.51	0.21	0.16	0.25	0.29	0.55	0.24	0.20	0.31	0.36	0.66
61	0.21	0.19	0.33	0.32	0.42	0.27	0.24	0.42	0.40	0.51	0.20	0.16	0.25	0.29	0.54	0.22	0.19	0.31	0.35	0.66
62	0.21	0.19	0.32	0.32	0.42	0.26	0.24	0.41	0.39	0.51	0.20	0.16	0.24	0.29	0.53	0.21	0.18	0.30	0.34	0.65
63	0.21	0.19	0.32	0.32	0.42	0.25	0.23	0.40	0.39	0.51	0.20	0.15	0.24	0.28	0.53	0.19	0.18	0.29	0.33	0.64
64	0.20	0.19	0.31	0.32	0.42	0.23	0.22	0.39	0.38	0.51	0.19	0.15	0.24	0.27	0.52	0.18	0.17	0.27	0.32	0.63
65	0.20	0.19	0.31	0.31	0.41	0.22	0.21	0.37	0.37	0.50	0.19	0.15	0.23	0.27	0.51	0.17	0.16	0.26	0.31	0.61
66	0.19	0.18	0.31	0.31	0.41	0.21	0.21	0.36	0.36	0.49	0.18	0.15	0.23	0.26	0.50	0.16	0.15	0.25	0.30	0.58
67	0.19	0.18	0.30	0.30	0.40	0.20	0.20	0.35	0.35	0.48	0.19	0.15	0.23	0.26	0.48	0.14	0.14	0.23	0.29	0.56
68	0.19	0.18	0.29	0.30	0.40	0.19	0.19	0.33	0.34	0.47	0.18	0.15	0.22	0.25	0.48	0.13	0.14	0.22	0.27	0.53
69	0.19	0.17	0.29	0.30	0.39	0.18	0.18	0.32	0.33	0.46	0.19	0.15	0.22	0.25	0.48	0.12	0.13	0.20	0.26	0.50
70	0.19	0.17	0.28	0.29	0.38	0.17	0.17	0.30	0.32	0.44	0.20	0.16	0.22	0.24	0.48	0.11	0.12	0.19	0.24	0.47
71	0.19	0.17	0.28	0.28	0.36	0.17	0.17	0.29	0.31	0.42	0.19	0.16	0.22	0.24	0.49	0.10	0.11	0.17	0.23	0.44
72	0.20	0.17	0.27	0.28	0.35	0.16	0.16	0.27	0.30	0.40	0.19	0.16	0.22	0.24	0.49	0.09	0.10	0.16	0.21	0.41
73	0.21	0.17	0.27	0.27	0.34	0.15	0.15	0.25	0.29	0.38	0.20	0.15	0.22	0.24	0.50	0.09	0.01	0.14	0.20	0.39
74	0.20	0.18	0.26	0.27	0.33	0.14	0.14	0.24	0.27	0.36	0.20	0.16	0.23	0.23	0.51	0.08	0.09	0.13	0.19	0.36
75	0.20	0.18	0.26	0.27	0.33	0.13	0.13	0.22	0.26	0.34	0.20	0.17	0.24	0.24	0.49	0.07	0.08	0.12	0.17	0.33

Mortality rates are from Table I and transitions probabilities are from Table II using CPS microdata from July 1999 through June 2007.

Appendix Table 9: Standard errors of mean years to final separation, July 1999 - June 2007 CPS data: White Males and Females

Age	White Males										White Females										Age
	Initially Active					Initially Inactive					Initially Active					Initially Inactive					
	<HS	HS	Some College	College Degree	Graduate Degrees	<HS	HS	Some College	College Degree	Graduate Degrees	<HS	HS	Some College	College Degree	Graduate Degrees	<HS	HS	Some College	College Degree	Graduate Degrees	
18	0.30	0.21	0.32			0.30	0.21	0.32			0.35	0.21	0.29			0.35	0.21	0.29			18
19	0.30	0.21	0.32	0.34		0.30	0.21	0.32	0.34		0.35	0.21	0.29	0.33		0.35	0.21	0.29	0.33		19
20	0.30	0.21	0.32	0.34		0.30	0.21	0.32	0.34		0.35	0.21	0.29	0.33		0.35	0.21	0.29	0.33		20
21	0.30	0.21	0.32	0.34	0.41	0.30	0.21	0.32	0.34	0.41	0.35	0.21	0.29	0.33	0.59	0.35	0.21	0.29	0.33	0.59	21
22	0.30	0.21	0.32	0.34	0.41	0.30	0.21	0.32	0.34	0.41	0.35	0.21	0.29	0.33	0.59	0.35	0.21	0.29	0.33	0.59	22
23	0.30	0.21	0.32	0.34	0.41	0.30	0.21	0.32	0.34	0.41	0.35	0.21	0.29	0.33	0.59	0.35	0.21	0.29	0.33	0.59	23
24	0.30	0.21	0.32	0.34	0.41	0.30	0.21	0.32	0.34	0.41	0.35	0.21	0.29	0.33	0.59	0.35	0.21	0.29	0.33	0.59	24
25	0.30	0.21	0.32	0.34	0.41	0.30	0.21	0.32	0.34	0.41	0.35	0.21	0.29	0.33	0.59	0.35	0.21	0.29	0.33	0.59	25
26	0.30	0.21	0.32	0.34	0.41	0.30	0.21	0.32	0.34	0.41	0.35	0.21	0.29	0.33	0.60	0.35	0.21	0.29	0.33	0.60	26
27	0.30	0.21	0.32	0.34	0.41	0.30	0.21	0.32	0.34	0.41	0.35	0.21	0.29	0.33	0.60	0.35	0.21	0.29	0.33	0.60	27
28	0.30	0.21	0.32	0.34	0.41	0.30	0.21	0.32	0.34	0.41	0.35	0.21	0.29	0.33	0.60	0.35	0.21	0.29	0.33	0.60	28
29	0.30	0.21	0.32	0.34	0.41	0.31	0.21	0.32	0.34	0.41	0.35	0.21	0.29	0.33	0.60	0.35	0.21	0.29	0.33	0.60	29
30	0.30	0.21	0.32	0.34	0.41	0.31	0.21	0.32	0.34	0.41	0.35	0.21	0.29	0.33	0.60	0.35	0.21	0.29	0.33	0.60	30
31	0.31	0.21	0.32	0.34	0.41	0.31	0.21	0.32	0.34	0.41	0.35	0.21	0.29	0.33	0.60	0.35	0.21	0.29	0.33	0.60	31
32	0.31	0.21	0.33	0.34	0.41	0.31	0.21	0.33	0.34	0.41	0.35	0.21	0.29	0.33	0.60	0.35	0.21	0.29	0.33	0.60	32
33	0.31	0.21	0.33	0.34	0.41	0.31	0.21	0.33	0.34	0.41	0.35	0.21	0.29	0.33	0.60	0.35	0.21	0.29	0.33	0.60	33
34	0.31	0.21	0.33	0.34	0.41	0.31	0.21	0.33	0.34	0.41	0.35	0.21	0.29	0.33	0.60	0.35	0.21	0.29	0.33	0.60	34
35	0.31	0.21	0.33	0.34	0.41	0.31	0.21	0.33	0.34	0.41	0.34	0.21	0.29	0.33	0.60	0.35	0.21	0.29	0.33	0.60	35
36	0.31	0.21	0.33	0.35	0.41	0.32	0.22	0.33	0.35	0.41	0.34	0.21	0.29	0.33	0.60	0.35	0.21	0.29	0.33	0.60	36
37	0.31	0.21	0.33	0.35	0.41	0.32	0.22	0.33	0.35	0.41	0.34	0.21	0.29	0.33	0.60	0.35	0.21	0.29	0.33	0.60	37
38	0.31	0.21	0.33	0.35	0.41	0.32	0.22	0.33	0.35	0.41	0.34	0.21	0.29	0.33	0.60	0.35	0.21	0.29	0.33	0.60	38
39	0.31	0.22	0.33	0.35	0.41	0.33	0.22	0.33	0.35	0.41	0.34	0.21	0.29	0.33	0.60	0.35	0.21	0.29	0.34	0.60	39
40	0.31	0.22	0.33	0.35	0.41	0.34	0.22	0.33	0.35	0.41	0.34	0.21	0.29	0.33	0.60	0.35	0.21	0.30	0.34	0.60	40
41	0.31	0.22	0.33	0.35	0.42	0.35	0.22	0.34	0.35	0.42	0.33	0.21	0.29	0.33	0.60	0.35	0.21	0.30	0.34	0.60	41
42	0.31	0.22	0.33	0.35	0.42	0.36	0.23	0.34	0.35	0.42	0.33	0.21	0.29	0.33	0.60	0.35	0.22	0.30	0.34	0.60	42
43	0.30	0.22	0.33	0.35	0.42	0.37	0.23	0.34	0.35	0.42	0.33	0.21	0.29	0.33	0.60	0.36	0.22	0.30	0.34	0.61	43
44	0.30	0.22	0.33	0.35	0.42	0.38	0.23	0.35	0.35	0.42	0.33	0.21	0.29	0.33	0.60	0.36	0.22	0.30	0.34	0.61	44
45	0.30	0.22	0.33	0.35	0.42	0.39	0.24	0.35	0.35	0.42	0.32	0.20	0.29	0.33	0.60	0.36	0.22	0.31	0.34	0.61	45
46	0.30	0.22	0.33	0.35	0.42	0.40	0.25	0.36	0.36	0.42	0.32	0.20	0.29	0.33	0.60	0.36	0.23	0.31	0.34	0.61	46
47	0.30	0.22	0.33	0.35	0.42	0.40	0.25	0.36	0.36	0.43	0.31	0.20	0.29	0.33	0.60	0.36	0.23	0.32	0.35	0.61	47
48	0.29	0.22	0.33	0.35	0.42	0.41	0.26	0.37	0.36	0.43	0.31	0.20	0.28	0.33	0.60	0.36	0.23	0.32	0.35	0.62	48
49	0.29	0.22	0.33	0.35	0.42	0.41	0.26	0.38	0.37	0.44	0.30	0.20	0.28	0.33	0.60	0.36	0.24	0.32	0.35	0.62	49
50	0.29	0.22	0.33	0.35	0.42	0.42	0.26	0.39	0.37	0.45	0.29	0.20	0.28	0.33	0.60	0.36	0.24	0.33	0.36	0.63	50
51	0.29	0.22	0.33	0.35	0.42	0.42	0.27	0.40	0.38	0.45	0.29	0.20	0.28	0.33	0.60	0.35	0.24	0.33	0.36	0.64	51
52	0.28	0.22	0.33	0.35	0.42	0.41	0.27	0.41	0.39	0.46	0.28	0.20	0.28	0.33	0.60	0.35	0.24	0.34	0.37	0.64	52
53	0.28	0.22	0.33	0.35	0.42	0.41	0.28	0.42	0.40	0.48	0.27	0.19	0.28	0.33	0.60	0.34	0.24	0.34	0.37	0.65	53
54	0.28	0.22	0.33	0.35	0.42	0.40	0.28	0.42	0.40	0.49	0.26	0.19	0.27	0.33	0.60	0.33	0.24	0.34	0.38	0.66	54
55	0.27	0.22	0.33	0.36	0.42	0.39	0.28	0.43	0.41	0.50	0.25	0.19	0.27	0.33	0.60	0.32	0.24	0.34	0.39	0.67	55
56	0.27	0.21	0.33	0.36	0.42	0.37	0.28	0.43	0.42	0.51	0.24	0.19	0.27	0.32	0.60	0.31	0.24	0.34	0.39	0.68	56
57	0.26	0.21	0.33	0.36	0.42	0.36	0.28	0.43	0.42	0.51	0.24	0.18	0.27	0.32	0.60	0.30	0.23	0.34	0.39	0.68	57
58	0.26	0.21	0.33	0.35	0.42	0.34	0.28	0.43	0.43	0.51	0.23	0.18	0.26	0.32	0.59	0.28	0.23	0.34	0.39	0.69	58
59	0.25	0.21	0.32	0.35	0.42	0.33	0.27	0.42	0.43	0.52	0.22	0.18	0.26	0.31	0.59	0.26	0.22	0.33	0.39	0.69	59
60	0.25	0.21	0.32	0.35	0.42	0.32	0.27	0.42	0.43	0.52	0.22	0.18	0.26	0.31	0.58	0.25	0.21	0.32	0.39	0.69	60
61	0.25	0.21	0.31	0.35	0.42	0.30	0.26	0.41	0.42	0.52	0.21	0.18	0.25	0.31	0.58	0.23	0.20	0.32	0.38	0.69	61
62	0.24	0.21	0.31	0.35	0.42	0.29	0.25	0.40	0.42	0.52	0.21	0.17	0.25	0.30	0.57	0.22	0.19	0.31	0.37	0.69	62
63	0.24	0.21	0.31	0.34	0.41	0.28	0.25	0.39	0.42	0.52	0.20	0.17	0.25	0.30	0.57	0.20	0.19	0.29	0.35	0.68	63
64	0.24	0.20	0.30	0.34	0.41	0.26	0.24	0.38	0.41	0.51	0.20	0.17	0.24	0.29	0.56	0.19	0.18	0.28	0.34	0.66	64
65	0.23	0.20	0.29	0.34	0.41	0.25	0.23	0.36	0.40	0.50	0.20	0.17	0.24	0.29	0.55	0.17	0.17	0.27	0.33	0.64	65
66	0.23	0.19	0.29	0.33	0.40	0.24	0.22	0.35	0.39	0.49	0.20	0.16	0.24	0.28	0.54	0.16	0.16	0.25	0.31	0.62	66
67	0.22	0.19	0.28	0.33	0.39	0.23	0.22	0.33	0.38	0.48	0.21	0.16	0.23	0.28	0.54	0.15	0.15	0.24	0.30	0.60	67
68	0.22	0.19	0.28	0.32	0.39	0.22	0.21	0.32	0.37	0.47	0.21	0.16	0.23	0.27	0.54	0.14	0.14	0.23	0.28	0.57	68
69	0.22	0.18	0.27	0.31	0.38	0.21	0.20	0.30	0.36	0.45	0.23	0.17	0.23	0.27	0.54	0.12	0.13	0.21	0.26	0.54	69
70	0.22	0.18	0.27	0.31	0.37	0.19	0.19	0.29	0.35	0.43	0.23	0.17	0.22	0.26	0.55	0.11	0.12	0.19	0.25	0.51	70
71	0.23	0.18	0.27	0.30	0.35	0.18	0.18	0.27	0.34	0.42	0.21	0.17	0.23	0.25	0.55	0.10	0.12	0.18	0.23	0.48	71
72	0.23	0.18	0.27	0.30	0.34	0.17	0.17	0.25	0.33	0.40	0.21	0.16	0.23	0.25	0.53	0.09	0.11	0.16	0.22	0.45	72
73	0.23	0.18	0.26	0.29	0.33	0.16	0.16	0.24	0.31	0.38	0.21	0.16	0.23	0.25	0.54	0.08	0.10	0.15	0.20	0.42	73
74	0.23	0.18	0.26	0.29	0.33	0.15	0.15	0.22	0.30	0.36	0.20	0.16	0.23	0.25	0.55	0.08	0.09	0.13	0.19	0.39	74
75	0.23	0.18	0.26	0.29	0.32	0.14	0.14	0.20	0.28	0.34	0.20	0.17	0.25	0.25	0.54	0.07	0.09	0.12	0.18	0.36	75

Mortality rates are from Table I and transitions probabilities are from Table II using CPS microdata from July 1999 through June 2007.

Appendix Table 9: Standard errors of mean years to final separation, July 1999 - June 2007 CPS data: Black Males and Females

Age	Black Males								Black Females								Age
	Initially Active				Initially Inactive				Initially Active				Initially Inactive				
	<HS	HS	Some College	BA Plus	<HS	HS	Some College	BA Plus	<HS	HS	Some College	BA Plus	<HS	HS	Some College	BA Plus	
18	0.70	0.49	1.17		0.70	0.49	1.17		0.75	0.57	0.78		0.75	0.57	0.78		18
19	0.70	0.49	1.17	0.94	0.70	0.49	1.17	0.94	0.75	0.57	0.78	0.85	0.75	0.57	0.78	0.85	19
20	0.70	0.49	1.17	0.94	0.70	0.49	1.17	0.94	0.75	0.57	0.78	0.85	0.75	0.57	0.78	0.85	20
21	0.70	0.49	1.17	0.94	0.70	0.49	1.17	0.94	0.75	0.57	0.78	0.85	0.75	0.57	0.78	0.85	21
22	0.70	0.49	1.17	0.94	0.70	0.49	1.17	0.94	0.75	0.57	0.78	0.85	0.75	0.57	0.78	0.85	22
23	0.71	0.49	1.18	0.95	0.71	0.49	1.18	0.95	0.75	0.57	0.78	0.85	0.75	0.57	0.78	0.85	23
24	0.71	0.50	1.18	0.95	0.71	0.50	1.18	0.95	0.75	0.57	0.78	0.85	0.75	0.57	0.78	0.85	24
25	0.71	0.50	1.18	0.95	0.71	0.50	1.18	0.95	0.75	0.57	0.78	0.85	0.75	0.57	0.78	0.85	25
26	0.71	0.50	1.18	0.95	0.71	0.50	1.18	0.95	0.75	0.57	0.78	0.85	0.75	0.57	0.78	0.85	26
27	0.71	0.50	1.19	0.96	0.71	0.50	1.19	0.96	0.75	0.57	0.78	0.85	0.75	0.57	0.78	0.85	27
28	0.71	0.50	1.19	0.96	0.71	0.50	1.19	0.96	0.75	0.57	0.78	0.86	0.75	0.57	0.78	0.86	28
29	0.71	0.50	1.19	0.96	0.72	0.50	1.19	0.96	0.75	0.57	0.78	0.86	0.75	0.57	0.78	0.86	29
30	0.72	0.50	1.20	0.96	0.72	0.50	1.20	0.96	0.75	0.57	0.78	0.86	0.75	0.57	0.78	0.86	30
31	0.72	0.50	1.20	0.96	0.73	0.50	1.20	0.96	0.75	0.57	0.78	0.86	0.75	0.57	0.78	0.86	31
32	0.72	0.50	1.20	0.96	0.73	0.51	1.20	0.96	0.75	0.57	0.79	0.86	0.76	0.57	0.79	0.86	32
33	0.72	0.51	1.20	0.96	0.74	0.51	1.20	0.96	0.75	0.57	0.79	0.86	0.76	0.57	0.79	0.86	33
34	0.71	0.51	1.20	0.96	0.75	0.51	1.20	0.96	0.75	0.57	0.79	0.86	0.76	0.57	0.79	0.86	34
35	0.71	0.51	1.21	0.96	0.77	0.51	1.21	0.96	0.75	0.57	0.79	0.86	0.76	0.57	0.79	0.86	35
36	0.71	0.51	1.21	0.96	0.77	0.51	1.21	0.96	0.75	0.57	0.79	0.86	0.76	0.57	0.79	0.86	36
37	0.71	0.51	1.21	0.96	0.78	0.51	1.21	0.96	0.74	0.57	0.79	0.86	0.77	0.58	0.79	0.86	37
38	0.70	0.51	1.22	0.97	0.78	0.52	1.22	0.97	0.74	0.57	0.79	0.86	0.77	0.58	0.79	0.86	38
39	0.69	0.51	1.22	0.97	0.78	0.52	1.22	0.97	0.73	0.57	0.79	0.86	0.78	0.58	0.80	0.86	39
40	0.69	0.51	1.22	0.97	0.78	0.52	1.23	0.97	0.73	0.57	0.79	0.86	0.78	0.58	0.80	0.87	40
41	0.68	0.51	1.23	0.97	0.78	0.53	1.23	0.97	0.72	0.57	0.79	0.87	0.78	0.59	0.80	0.87	41
42	0.67	0.51	1.23	0.97	0.78	0.54	1.24	0.98	0.72	0.57	0.79	0.87	0.77	0.59	0.81	0.87	42
43	0.66	0.52	1.23	0.98	0.78	0.55	1.24	0.98	0.71	0.57	0.79	0.87	0.77	0.60	0.82	0.87	43
44	0.65	0.52	1.24	0.98	0.79	0.56	1.25	0.98	0.71	0.57	0.79	0.87	0.77	0.60	0.83	0.87	44
45	0.64	0.52	1.24	0.98	0.79	0.57	1.26	0.98	0.70	0.57	0.79	0.87	0.77	0.61	0.83	0.88	45
46	0.63	0.51	1.25	0.98	0.79	0.58	1.27	0.99	0.68	0.57	0.79	0.87	0.77	0.62	0.84	0.88	46
47	0.62	0.51	1.25	0.99	0.79	0.59	1.28	1.00	0.67	0.57	0.79	0.87	0.77	0.63	0.85	0.89	47
48	0.61	0.51	1.26	0.99	0.78	0.60	1.29	1.00	0.66	0.57	0.78	0.88	0.77	0.64	0.86	0.90	48
49	0.61	0.51	1.26	0.99	0.77	0.61	1.31	1.02	0.65	0.56	0.78	0.88	0.76	0.64	0.86	0.90	49
50	0.61	0.51	1.27	1.00	0.77	0.63	1.33	1.03	0.64	0.56	0.77	0.88	0.75	0.64	0.87	0.91	50
51	0.60	0.50	1.28	1.00	0.77	0.64	1.34	1.04	0.63	0.56	0.77	0.88	0.74	0.65	0.89	0.92	51
52	0.59	0.50	1.28	1.00	0.76	0.65	1.37	1.06	0.62	0.55	0.76	0.88	0.73	0.66	0.90	0.93	52
53	0.57	0.50	1.29	1.01	0.76	0.66	1.39	1.07	0.60	0.55	0.75	0.88	0.72	0.65	0.91	0.94	53
54	0.56	0.49	1.29	1.02	0.75	0.67	1.41	1.08	0.58	0.55	0.75	0.88	0.71	0.65	0.92	0.96	54
55	0.56	0.49	1.29	1.02	0.73	0.67	1.42	1.09	0.56	0.54	0.73	0.88	0.69	0.65	0.93	0.97	55
56	0.55	0.48	1.29	1.03	0.71	0.66	1.43	1.10	0.55	0.54	0.71	0.88	0.67	0.65	0.93	0.99	56
57	0.53	0.48	1.30	1.03	0.69	0.65	1.45	1.11	0.54	0.53	0.70	0.87	0.65	0.64	0.93	0.99	57
58	0.52	0.47	1.30	1.04	0.67	0.64	1.47	1.13	0.52	0.53	0.68	0.87	0.62	0.63	0.91	0.99	58
59	0.50	0.47	1.31	1.04	0.65	0.63	1.49	1.14	0.51	0.51	0.67	0.86	0.60	0.62	0.89	0.99	59
60	0.49	0.46	1.31	1.05	0.62	0.61	1.52	1.15	0.49	0.51	0.66	0.85	0.57	0.61	0.87	0.99	60
61	0.49	0.45	1.32	1.05	0.59	0.59	1.53	1.16	0.49	0.50	0.66	0.84	0.54	0.59	0.83	0.99	61
62	0.48	0.44	1.33	1.06	0.57	0.57	1.53	1.18	0.47	0.49	0.66	0.83	0.51	0.58	0.80	0.98	62
63	0.48	0.43	1.33	1.06	0.55	0.54	1.52	1.19	0.45	0.48	0.64	0.82	0.48	0.56	0.76	0.96	63
64	0.47	0.42	1.34	1.06	0.52	0.51	1.51	1.19	0.43	0.46	0.62	0.80	0.46	0.53	0.72	0.94	64
65	0.46	0.41	1.34	1.05	0.50	0.48	1.49	1.19	0.42	0.45	0.61	0.78	0.43	0.51	0.68	0.92	65
66	0.47	0.40	1.33	1.05	0.48	0.45	1.47	1.19	0.40	0.44	0.59	0.77	0.41	0.49	0.63	0.89	66
67	0.45	0.40	1.32	1.04	0.45	0.43	1.45	1.19	0.39	0.42	0.59	0.75	0.39	0.46	0.59	0.87	67
68	0.45	0.40	1.32	1.03	0.43	0.40	1.45	1.17	0.39	0.42	0.56	0.74	0.37	0.43	0.55	0.83	68
69	0.46	0.37	1.28	1.01	0.41	0.36	1.45	1.15	0.38	0.44	0.53	0.73	0.35	0.40	0.50	0.80	69
70	0.48	0.36	1.27	0.97	0.39	0.33	1.43	1.13	0.38	0.46	0.54	0.72	0.33	0.37	0.45	0.76	70
71	0.44	0.36	1.26	0.94	0.37	0.30	1.42	1.11	0.37	0.47	0.50	0.71	0.31	0.34	0.42	0.73	71
72	0.44	0.38	1.22	0.95	0.35	0.27	1.41	1.07	0.38	0.50	0.51	0.69	0.28	0.31	0.38	0.70	72
73	0.49	0.36	1.20	0.90	0.33	0.24	1.40	1.02	0.42	0.53	0.56	0.66	0.26	0.28	0.35	0.66	73
74	0.43	0.39	1.22	0.89	0.31	0.20	1.39	0.98	0.39	0.52	0.66	0.60	0.25	0.25	0.30	0.63	74
75	0.43	0.47	1.27	0.86	0.28	0.17	1.36	0.94	0.40	0.57	0.48	0.62	0.23	0.22	0.26	0.59	75

Mortality rates are from Table I and transitions probabilities are from Table II using CPS microdata from July 1999 through June 2007.

Appendix Table 9: Standard errors of mean years to final separation, July 1999 - June 2007 CPS data: Hispanic Males and Females

Age	Hispanic Males						Hispanic Females						Age
	Initially Active			Initially Inactive			Initially Active			Initially Inactive			
	<HS	HS	>HS	<HS	HS	>HS	<HS	HS	>HS	<HS	HS	>HS	
18	0.62	0.67	0.72	0.62	0.67	0.72	0.65	0.74	0.92	0.65	0.74	0.92	18
19	0.62	0.67	0.72	0.62	0.67	0.72	0.65	0.74	0.92	0.65	0.74	0.92	19
20	0.62	0.67	0.72	0.62	0.67	0.72	0.65	0.74	0.92	0.65	0.74	0.92	20
21	0.62	0.67	0.72	0.62	0.67	0.72	0.65	0.74	0.92	0.65	0.74	0.92	21
22	0.62	0.67	0.72	0.62	0.67	0.72	0.65	0.74	0.92	0.65	0.74	0.92	22
23	0.62	0.67	0.72	0.62	0.67	0.72	0.65	0.74	0.92	0.65	0.74	0.92	23
24	0.62	0.67	0.72	0.62	0.67	0.72	0.65	0.74	0.92	0.65	0.74	0.92	24
25	0.62	0.67	0.72	0.62	0.67	0.72	0.65	0.74	0.92	0.65	0.74	0.92	25
26	0.62	0.67	0.72	0.62	0.67	0.72	0.65	0.74	0.92	0.65	0.74	0.92	26
27	0.62	0.68	0.72	0.62	0.68	0.72	0.65	0.74	0.92	0.65	0.74	0.92	27
28	0.62	0.68	0.73	0.62	0.68	0.73	0.65	0.74	0.92	0.65	0.74	0.92	28
29	0.63	0.68	0.73	0.63	0.68	0.73	0.65	0.74	0.92	0.65	0.74	0.92	29
30	0.63	0.68	0.73	0.63	0.68	0.73	0.65	0.74	0.92	0.65	0.74	0.92	30
31	0.63	0.68	0.73	0.63	0.68	0.73	0.65	0.74	0.92	0.65	0.74	0.92	31
32	0.63	0.68	0.73	0.63	0.68	0.73	0.65	0.74	0.92	0.65	0.74	0.92	32
33	0.63	0.68	0.73	0.63	0.68	0.73	0.65	0.74	0.92	0.65	0.74	0.93	33
34	0.63	0.68	0.73	0.63	0.68	0.73	0.65	0.74	0.92	0.65	0.74	0.93	34
35	0.63	0.68	0.73	0.63	0.68	0.73	0.65	0.74	0.93	0.65	0.74	0.93	35
36	0.63	0.68	0.73	0.63	0.69	0.73	0.65	0.74	0.93	0.65	0.74	0.93	36
37	0.63	0.69	0.73	0.63	0.69	0.73	0.65	0.74	0.93	0.65	0.74	0.93	37
38	0.64	0.69	0.73	0.64	0.69	0.73	0.65	0.74	0.93	0.65	0.75	0.93	38
39	0.64	0.69	0.73	0.64	0.69	0.73	0.65	0.74	0.93	0.65	0.75	0.93	39
40	0.64	0.69	0.73	0.64	0.70	0.74	0.65	0.74	0.93	0.66	0.75	0.93	40
41	0.64	0.69	0.74	0.64	0.70	0.74	0.65	0.74	0.93	0.66	0.75	0.93	41
42	0.64	0.69	0.74	0.65	0.71	0.74	0.65	0.74	0.93	0.66	0.76	0.93	42
43	0.64	0.69	0.74	0.65	0.72	0.75	0.65	0.74	0.93	0.66	0.76	0.94	43
44	0.64	0.69	0.74	0.66	0.72	0.75	0.65	0.74	0.93	0.66	0.77	0.94	44
45	0.64	0.70	0.74	0.67	0.74	0.75	0.64	0.73	0.93	0.66	0.77	0.94	45
46	0.65	0.70	0.75	0.68	0.76	0.76	0.64	0.73	0.93	0.66	0.78	0.95	46
47	0.65	0.70	0.75	0.68	0.77	0.78	0.64	0.73	0.93	0.67	0.79	0.96	47
48	0.65	0.70	0.75	0.69	0.78	0.79	0.64	0.73	0.93	0.67	0.79	0.96	48
49	0.65	0.70	0.75	0.71	0.80	0.80	0.63	0.72	0.93	0.68	0.81	0.97	49
50	0.65	0.70	0.75	0.72	0.80	0.83	0.63	0.72	0.92	0.68	0.82	0.98	50
51	0.65	0.70	0.75	0.73	0.83	0.84	0.62	0.71	0.92	0.69	0.83	0.99	51
52	0.65	0.70	0.75	0.76	0.85	0.89	0.61	0.70	0.92	0.69	0.83	1.00	52
53	0.65	0.70	0.75	0.78	0.87	0.93	0.60	0.69	0.91	0.68	0.82	1.01	53
54	0.65	0.69	0.75	0.80	0.88	0.95	0.59	0.67	0.91	0.67	0.82	1.02	54
55	0.65	0.68	0.74	0.81	0.89	0.97	0.57	0.66	0.90	0.67	0.81	1.03	55
56	0.64	0.68	0.74	0.81	0.91	1.00	0.56	0.65	0.89	0.66	0.80	1.05	56
57	0.63	0.68	0.74	0.82	0.91	1.01	0.55	0.64	0.88	0.64	0.79	1.06	57
58	0.62	0.67	0.73	0.81	0.91	1.01	0.54	0.63	0.87	0.63	0.78	1.07	58
59	0.61	0.67	0.73	0.80	0.91	1.00	0.53	0.62	0.85	0.61	0.76	1.07	59
60	0.61	0.66	0.72	0.78	0.89	0.98	0.52	0.61	0.84	0.58	0.74	1.06	60
61	0.61	0.66	0.70	0.77	0.87	0.95	0.50	0.61	0.81	0.56	0.71	1.05	61
62	0.60	0.64	0.69	0.74	0.85	0.92	0.49	0.60	0.80	0.54	0.68	1.02	62
63	0.59	0.63	0.67	0.71	0.82	0.88	0.48	0.59	0.78	0.51	0.64	0.98	63
64	0.58	0.63	0.65	0.68	0.79	0.84	0.46	0.59	0.75	0.48	0.60	0.94	64
65	0.57	0.60	0.62	0.65	0.76	0.79	0.44	0.59	0.73	0.46	0.56	0.90	65
66	0.56	0.59	0.60	0.62	0.72	0.74	0.43	0.61	0.71	0.43	0.52	0.85	66
67	0.55	0.58	0.57	0.59	0.68	0.70	0.42	0.63	0.69	0.40	0.46	0.80	67
68	0.56	0.57	0.54	0.56	0.63	0.64	0.39	0.67	0.69	0.37	0.40	0.75	68
69	0.56	0.56	0.52	0.52	0.58	0.58	0.39	0.74	0.70	0.35	0.36	0.70	69
70	0.57	0.60	0.52	0.49	0.52	0.52	0.43	0.75	0.62	0.32	0.32	0.64	70
71	0.55	0.59	0.38	0.46	0.45	0.45	0.42	0.80	0.57	0.29	0.29	0.59	71
72	0.61	0.57	0.33	0.43	0.41	0.40	0.49	0.72	0.52	0.26	0.24	0.51	72
73	0.58	0.54	0.33	0.41	0.30	0.31	0.44	0.58	0.59	0.24	0.21	0.45	73
74	0.62	0.53	0.37	0.38	0.25	0.27	0.45	0.63	0.52	0.21	0.17	0.39	74
75	0.71	0.62	0.40	0.36	0.22	0.21	0.48	0.77	0.34	0.19	0.15	0.34	75

Mortality rates are from Table I and transitions probabilities are from Table II using CPS microdata from July 1999 through June 2007.

References

Abraham, Katherine G., and Henry S. Farber, "Job Duration, Seniority, and Earnings," *American Economic Review* 78(), 1987, 278-97.

Alter, George C. and William E. Becker, "Estimating lost future earnings using the new worklife tables" *Monthly Labor Review* 108(2), 1985, 39-42.

American Cancer Society, personal communication, June 29, 1998.

Baker, David T., and Robert H. Sims, "Worklife Tables," *Trial* 22(6), 1986, 10.

Baker, Wm. Gary, and Michael K. Seck, *Determining Economic Loss in Injury and Death Cases*, Colorado Springs, Shepard's McGraw Hill, 1987.

Barnow, Burt S., "The employment rate of people with disabilities," *Monthly Labor Review* 131(11), 2008, 44-50.

Bell, Edward B. and Allan J. Taub, "Expected Worklife, Transition Probabilities and the Size of an Award," *Journal of Forensic Economics* 11(2), 1998, p 91-102.

Berman, Jay and Janet Pfleeger, "Which industries are sensitive to business cycles," *Monthly Labor Review* 120(2), 1997, 19-25.

Bell, Felicitie C., Alice H. Wade, and Stephen C. Goss, *Life Tables for the United States Social Security Area 1900-2080*, Actuarial Study No. 107, U.S. Department of Health and Human Services, Social Security Administration, SSA Pub. No. 11-11536, August 1992.

———, and Michael L. Miller, *Life Tables for the United States Social Security Area 1900-2080*, Actuarial Study No. 120, U.S. Department of Health and Human Services, Social Security Administration, SSA Pub. No. 120, August 2005.

Best, John R. and Balkrishna D. Kale, "Older workers in the 21st century: active and educated, a case study," *Monthly Labor Review* 119(6), 1996, 18-28.

Boudreaux, Kenneth J., "A further adjustment needed to estimate lost earning capacity," *Monthly Labor Review* 106(10), 1983, 30-31.

Brault, Matthew, "Disability Status and the Characteristics of People in Group Quarters: A Brief Analysis of Disability Prevalence Among the Civilian Noninstitutionalized and Total Populations in the American Community Survey," Bureau of the Census, February 2008 at www.census.gov/hhes/www/disability/GQdisability.pdf.

———, and Sharon Stern, *Evaluation Report Covering Disability*, U.S. Bureau of the Census, 2006 American Community Survey Content Test Report P.4, January 3, 2007.

Brookshire, Michael L., "An Agenda for Future Research in Forensic Economics," *Journal of Forensic Economics* 4(3), 1991, 287-96.

————, and William E. Cobb, "The Life-Participation-Employment Approach to Worklife Expectancies in Personal Injury and Wrongful Death Cases," *For the Defense,* July 1983, 20-25.

————, William E. Cobb and Anthony M. Gamboa, "Work-life of the Partially Disabled," *Trial* 23(3), 1987, 44-47.

————, and Frank Slesnick, "A 1996 Study of 'Prevailing Practice' in Forensic Economics," *Journal of Forensic Economics* 10(1), 1997, 1-28.

————, Michael Luthy, and Frank Slesnick, "2006 Survey of Forensic Economists: Their Methods, Estimates, and Perspectives," *Journal of Forensic Economics* 19(1), 2006, 29-59.

Capozza, Dennis R., Alice Nakamura and Gregory Bloss, "Work History in Female Earnings Loss," *Journal of Forensic Economics* 2(3), 1989, 55-68.

Cattann, Peter, "The diversity of Hispanics in the U.S. work force," *Monthly Labor Review* 116(8), 1993, 3-15.

Chirikos, Thomas N. and Gilbert Nestel, "Occupational Differences in the Ability of Men to Delay Retirement," *The Journal of Human Resources*, 26(1), 1991, 1-26.

Ciecka, James, "A Survey of the Structure and Duration of Time Periods for Lost Earnings Calculations," *Journal of Legal Economics* 4(2), 1994, 39-50.

————, and Jerry Goldman, "A Markov Process Model For Worklife Expectancies of Smokers and Nonsmokers," *Journal of Forensic Economics* 8(1), 1995, 1-12.

————, and Thomas Donley, "A Logit Model of Labor Force Participation," *Journal of Forensic Economics* 9(3), 1996, 261-82.

————, and Peter Ciecka, "Life Expectancy and the Properties of Survival Data," *Litigation Economics Digest* 1(2), 1996, 19-33.

————, Seth Epstein and Jerry Goldman. "Updated Estimates of Work-Life Expectancies Based on the Increment-Decrement Model," *Journal of Legal Economics*, 1995, 5(1): 1-34.

————, Thomas Donley and Jerry Goldman, "A Markov Process Model of Work-Life Expectancies Based on Labor Market Activity in 1992-93," *Journal of Legal Economics*, 1995, 5(3): 17-41.

————, Thomas Donley and Jerry Goldman, 'Errata to "A Markov Process Model of Work-Life Expectancies Based on Labor Market Activity in 1992-93,"' *Journal of Legal Economics*, 1996, 6(1): 81-85.

————, Thomas Donley and Jerry Goldman, "Regarding Median Years to Retirement and Worklife Expectancy," *Journal of Forensic Economics* 10(3), 1997, 297-310.

————, Thomas Donley and Jerry Goldman, "A Markov Process Model of Work-Life Expectancies Based on Labor Market Activity in 1994-95," *Journal of Legal Economics*, 1997, 7(1): 2-25.

————, Thomas Donley and Jerry Goldman, "A Markov Process Model of Work-Life Expectancies Based on Labor Market Activity in 1997-98," *Journal of Legal Economics*, 2000, 9(3): 33-66.

————, Thomas Donley, Seth Epstein, and Jerry Goldman, "Work Life Expectancies of Nonsmokers, Light Smokers, and Heavy Smokers," *Litigation Economics Digest*, 1998, 3(2): 151-162.

–––, and Gary Skoog, "An Essay on the New Worklife Expectancy Tables and the Continuum of Disability," *Journal of Forensic Economics*, 2001, 14(2), 135-140.

Clauterie, Terrence M., "Review: The New Worklife Expectancy Tables: 1998," *Journal of Legal Economics*, 1998, 7(3): 75-76.

Cohany, Sharon R., and Emy Sok, "Trends in labor force participation of married mothers of infants," *Monthly Labor Review* 130(2), 2007, 9-16.

Conference Board, The, "U.S. Leading Economic Indicators and Related Composite Indexes for September 2008," U.S. Business Cycle Indicators, released October 20, 2008, at website www.conference-board.org/pdf_free/economics/bci/LEI1008.pdf.

Corcione, Frank P, book review of. *The New Worklife Expectancy Tables: Revised for 1995 For Persons With and Without Disability by Gender and Level of Education*, by A. M. Gamboa, Jr., Vocational Econometrics, Inc. 1995, in *Journal of Forensic Economics*, 8(3), 1995, 295-97.

–––, "Response to Andrew Gluck Regarding the New Worklife Expectancy Tables," *Journal of Forensic Economics*, 9(3), 1996, 339-42.

––– and Robert J. Thornton. "Female Work Experience: Voluntary Versus Involuntary Labor Force Activity," *Journal of Forensic Economics*, 4(2), 1991, 163-74.

Costo, Stephanie L., "Trends in retirement plan coverage over the last decade," *Monthly Labor Review* 129(2), 2006, 58-64.

Deaton, Angus and Christina Paxson, "Mortality, Education, Income, and Inequality among American Cohorts," NBER Working Paper No. 7140, 1999.

Doll R, Peto R, Wheatley K., Gray R, and Sutherland I, "Mortality in relation to smoking : 40 years observations on male British doctors," *British Medical Journal*, 309, 1994, 901-911.

Duleep, Harriet O, "Measuring Socioeconomic Mortality Differentials Over Time," *Demography* 29(2), 1989, 345-51.

Eck, James R., W. Gary Baker and Reed W. Davis, "Valuation of Structured Settlements: Should a Life Annuity Be Valued as Certain to Life Expectancy or Mortality Adjusted," *Journal of Forensic Economics* 2(1), 1988, 117-22.

Ettner, Susan L., "The Impact of 'Parent Care' on Female Labor Supply Decisions," *Demography* 32(1), 1995, 63-80.

Ezzati, Majid, Ari B. Friedman, Sandeep C. Kulkarni and Christopher J. J. Murray, "The Reversal of Fortunes: Trends in County Mortality and Cross-Country Mortality Disparities in the United States," PLoS Medicine, http://medicine.plos-journals.org/perlserv, June, 2008, pp 1-15.

Feldman, Jacob J., Diane M. Makuc, Joel C. Kleinman, and Joan Cornoni-Huntley, "National Trends in Educational Differentials in Mortality," *American Journal of Epidemiology* 129(5), 1989, 919-33.

Finch, John L., "Worklife estimates should be consistent with known labor force participation," *Monthly Labor Review* 105(6), 1983, 34-36.

Fjeldsted, Boyd L., "The Significance of the Distinction Between a Life Annuity and An Annuity Certain for a Term Equal to Life Expectancy: A Note," *Journal of Forensic Economics* 7(1), 1993, 125-27.

Foster, Edward and Gary R. Skoog, "The Markov Assumption for Worklife Expectancy," *Journal of Forensic Economics* 17(2) 2004, 167-183.

Frasca, Ralph and Lawrence Hadley, "The LPE Method Has Major Flaws," *Trial* 2(3) 1989, 56-59.

——— and Bernard Winger, "An Investigation into the Median and the Mean Age of Final Separation from the Labor Force," *Journal of Forensic Economics* 2(3) 1989, 103-14.

Fullerton, Howard N. and James J. Byrne, "Length of Working Life for Men and Women, 1970, Bureau of Labor Statistics, *Monthly Labor Review*, 99(2), 1976, 31-35.

Fullerton, Howard N.. Jr., "Labor force 2006: slowing down and changing composition," *Monthly Labor Review* 120(11), 1977, 23-38.

Funderburk, Dale R., "Worklife Tables: Are They Reliable," *Trial* 22(2), 1986, 44-48.

———, "An Analysis of Railroad Worklife Tables," *Journal of Forensic Economics* 2(1), 1988, 63-72.

Gamboa, A. M., Jr, *The New Worklife Expectancy Tables: Revised for 1995 For Persons With and Without Disability by Gender and Level of Education*, Vocational Econometrics, Inc. 1995.

———, *The New Worklife Expectancy Tables: Revised for 2005 For Persons With and Without Disability by Gender and Level of Education*, Vocational Econometrics, Inc. 2006.

———, and David S. Gibson, *The New Worklife Expectancy Tables: Revised for 2006 by Gender and Level of Educational Attainment, and Level of Disability*, Vocational Econometrics, Inc. 2006.

———, John P. Tierney, and Gwendolyn H. Holland, "Worklife Expectancy and Disability," *Journal of Forensic Economics* 2(2), 1989, 29-32.

Gardner, Jennifer M. "The 1990-91 recession: how bad was the labor market," *Monthly Labor Review* 117(6), 1994, 3-11.

Gibson, David S., "Daubert, Disability, and Worklife Expectancies," circulated to VEI subscribers, 2001, available for download at www.vocecon.com/daubertwle.pdf.

Gendell, Murray, "Older workers: increasing their labor force participation and hours of work," *Monthly Labor Review* 131(2), 2008, 41-54.

Gibson, David S., and John P. Tierney, "Disability and Worklife Expectancy Tables: A Response," *Journal of Forensic Economics*, Fall 2000, 13(3), 309-318.

Gluck, Andrew, "Regarding the New Worklife Expectancy Tables," *Journal of Forensic Economics* 9(3), 1996, 335-37.

Goldman, William, Stephen Antczak and Laura Freeman, "Woman and jobs in recessions: 1969-92," *Monthly Labor Review* 116(7), 1993, 26-35.

Grenier, Giles, "The Effect of Language Characteristics on the Wages of Hispanic American Males," *Journal of Labor Economics* 19(1), 1984, 35-52.

Gruber, J. and B. C. Madrian, "Health Insurance and Job Mobility: The Effects of Public Policy on Job-Lock," *Industrial Labor Relations Review* 48(1), 1994, 86-102.

Hale, Thomas W., "The Lack of a Disability Measure in Today's Current Population Survey," *Monthly Labor Review*, 123(6), 2001, 38-40.

Hall, Robert E., "The Importance of Lifetime Jobs in the U.S. Economy," *American Economic Review* 72, 1982, 716-24

Han, Wen-Jui, Christopher J. Ruhm, Jane Waldfogel and Elizabeth Washbrook, "The timing of mothers' employment after childbirth," *Monthly Labor Review* 131(6), 2008, 15-27.

Hayghe, Howard V., "Developments in women's labor force participation," *Monthly Labor Review* 120(9), 1997, 41-46.

Heckman, James, J. and Robert J. Willis, "A Beta-logistic Model for the Analysis of Sequential Labor Force Participation by Married Women," *The Journal of Political Economy* 85(1), 1977, 27-58.

Herz, Diane E., "Work after early retirement: an increasing trend among men," *Monthly Labor Review* 118(4), 1995, 13-20.

——— and Phillip L. Rones, "Institutional barriers to employment of older workers," *Monthly Labor Review* 112(4), 1989, 14-21.

Hill, Elizabeth T., "The labor force participation of older women: retired? working? both?" *Monthly Labor Review* 125(9), 2002, 39-48.

Hipple, Steven, "Self-employment in the United States: an update," *Monthly Labor Review* 127(7), 2004, 13-23.

Horner, Stephen M. and Frank Slesnick, "The Valuation of Earning Capacity: Definition, Measurement and Evidence," *Journal of Forensic Economics* 12(1), 1999, 13-32.

Horrigan, Michael W. and James P. Markey, "Recent gains in women's earnings: better pay or longer hours?" *Monthly Labor Review* 113(7), 1993, 11-17.

Hummer, Robert, A., Charles B. Nam, and Richard Rogers, "Adult Mortality Differentials Associated with Cigarette Smoking in the United States," *Population Research and Policy Review*, 17(3), 1998, 285-304.

Hunt, Tamorah, Joyce Pickersgill, and Herbert Rutemiller, "Median Years to Retirement and Worklife Expectancy," *Journal of Forensic Economics* 10(2), 1997, 171-215.

———, "Regarding Median Years to Retirement and Worklife Expectancy: Reply to Ciecka, Donley and Goldman," *Journal of Forensic Economics*, 1997, 10(3), 311-25.

Iams, Howard M. and John L. McCoy, "Predictors of Mortality Among Newly Retired Workers." *Social Security Bulletin* 54(3), 1991, 2-10.

Iribarren, Carlos, Irene S. Tekawa, Stephen Sidney, and Gary Friedman, "Effect of Cigar Smoking on the Risk of Cardiovascular Disease, Chronic Obstructive Pulmonary Disease, and Caner in Men," *New England Journal of Medicine*, 340(23), 1999, 1773-80.

Jennings, William and Penelope Mercurio-Jennings, "A Critique of the Joint Probability of Life, Participation, and Employment Approach," *Journal of Legal Economics*, 1998, 8(1): 61-70.

Johnson, Norman, "Life Tables for All Races and Hispanics by Educational Level," U.S. Bureau of the Census, Demographic Statistical Methods Division, Washington, DC., unpublished tables, 1996 and 1998.

Karoly, Lynn A. and Julie Zissimopoulos, "Self-employment among older U.S. workers," *Monthly Labor Review* 127(7), 2004, 24-47.

Kitagawa, Evelyn M. and Philip M. Hauser, *Differential Mortality in the United States: A Study in Socioeconomic Epidemiology,* Cambridge, Mass.: Harvard University Press, 1973.

Krueger, Kurt V, "Tables of Inter-year Labor Force Status of the U.S. Population (1998-2004) to Operate the Markov Model of Worklife Expectancy," *Journal of Forensic Economics* 17(3), 2004: 313-381.

———, Gary R Skoog, and James E. Ciecka "Worklife in a Markov Model with Full-time and Part-time Activity," *Journal of Forensic Economics* 19(1), 2006: 61-82.

Kunst, Anton E. and Johan P. Mackenbach, "The Size of Mortality Differences Associated with Educational Level in Nine Industrialized Countries," *American Journal of Public Health* 84(6), 1994, 932-37.

Landsea, William F., "Worklife—Definitions and Impact on Methodology," *Journal of Legal Economics*, 1991, 1(1),: 51-61.

Leibowitz, Arleen and Jacob Alex Klerman, "Explaining Changes in Married Mother's Employment Over Time," *Demography* 32(3), 1995, 265-78.

Lettau, Michael K. and Thomas C. Buchmueller, "Comparing benefit cost for full and part-time workers" *Monthly Labor Review* 122(3), 1999, 30-35.

Levine, Phillip B., "CPS contemporaneous and retrospective unemployment compared," *Monthly Labor Review* 116(8), 1993, 33-39.

Lew, Edward A. and Lawrence Garfinkel, "Differences in Mortality and Longevity by Sex, Smoking Habits and Health Status," *Transactions of the Society of Actuaries* 39, 1987, 19-37.

Lin, CC, Rogot E., Johnson, NJ., Sorlie, PD. and Arias, E., "A further study of life expectancy by socioeconomic factors in the National Longitudinal Mortality Study," *Ethn Dis* 13(s), 2003, 240-7

Lleras-Muney, Adriana, "The Relationship Between Education and Adult Mortality in the United States," NBER Working Paper No. W8986, 2002.

Long, James E. and Ethel B. Jones, "Labor Force Entry and Exit by Married Women: A Longitudinal Analysis," *Review of Economics and Statistics* 62(1) 1980, 1-6.

Loprest, Pamela, Kalman Rupp and Steven H. Sandell, "Gender, Disabilities, and Employment in the Health and Retirement Study," *Journal of Human Resources* 30 Supplement, 1995, S293-311.

Mansur, Khandaker and Bac Tran, "Latent Class Models for Analysis of Response Error and Rotation Group Bias in the Current Population Survey," presentation at Joint Statistical Meeting, 2004.

Marion, Peter A., Douglas C. Doll, Melvin C. McFall and Abbott M. Webber, "Report of the Task Force on Smoker/Non-Smoker Mortality," Society of Actuaries, March 1, 1983, Itasca, Illinois.

McManus, Walter S,. William Gould, and Finis Welch, "Earnings of Hispanic Men: the Role of English Language Proficiency," *Journal of Labor Economics* 1(2), 1983, 101-30.

Meisenheimer, Joseph R., "How do immigrants fare in the U.S. labor market?" *Monthly Labor Review* 115(12),1992, 3-19.

Millimet, Daniel L, Michael Nieswiadomy, Hang Ryu, and Daniel Slottje, "Estimating Worklife Expectancy: An Econometric Approach," *Journal of Econometrics*, 2003, 113, 83-113.

Mosisa, Abraham, "Labor force characteristics of second-generation Americans," *Monthly Labor Review* 129(9), 2006, 10-19.

——— and Hipple, Steven, "Trends in labor force participation in the United States," *Monthly Labor Review* 129(10), 2006, 35-57.

Monheit, A. C. and P. F. Cooper, "Health Insurance and Job Mobility: Theory and Evidence," *Industrial Labor Relations Review* 48(1), 1994, 68-85.

Nakamura, Alice and Masao "Predicting Female Labor Supply: Effects of Children and Recent Work Experience," *Journal of Human Resources* 29(2), 1994, 304-27.

National Bureau of Economic Research, Public Information Office, Business Cycle Expansions and Contractions, at www.nber.org/cycles.html.

National Cancer Institute, *Changes in Cigarette-Related Disease Risks and Their Implication for Prevention and Control*, Washington, D.C.: National Institutes of Health, 1997, NIH Pub. No. 97-4213.

National Health Interview Surveys, "Percentage of adults who were current, former, or never smokers, overall and by sex, race, Hispanic origin, age, and education, National Health Interview Surveys, selected years—United States, 1965-1994," unpublished spreadsheet, 1998.

———, "Percentage of adults 18 years and older by cigarette smoking status and number of cigarettes smoked per day by current smokers, overall and by sex, race, Hispanic origin, United States, National Health Interview Surveys, 1987, 1988, 1990, 1991 (combined)," unpublished spreadsheet, 1998.

Pappas, Gregory, Susan Queen, Wilbur Hadden and Gail Fisher, "The Increasing Disparity in Mortality Between Socioeconomic Groups in the United States, 1960 and 1986," *The New England Journal of Medicine* 329(2), 1993, 103-9.

Peeters, Anna, Jan Barendregt, Frans Willekens, Johan Machenback, Abdullah Mamun, and Luc Bonneux, "Obesity in Adulthood and Its Consequences for Life Expectancy: A Life-Table Analysis," *Annals of Internal Medicine*, 138(1), 2003, 24-32.

Peracchi, Franco and Finis Welch. "Trends in Labor Force Transitions of Older Men and Women," *Journal of Labor Economics* 12(2), 1994, 210-42.

Peto, Richard, Alan D. Lopez, Jillian Boreham, Michael Thun and Clark Heath, Jr., "Mortality from tobacco in developed countries: indirect estimation from national vital statistics," *The Lancet* 339(5), 1992, 1268-1278.

Piette, Michael J. and Janet R. Thornton, "Using New Labor Force Participation Rates When Computing Economic Damage and Loss: A Methodological Note," *Journal of Legal Economics* 4(2), 1994, 81-88.

Principal Mortality Tables, Old and New, Tillinghast-Towers Perrin Company, St. Louis, MO, 1987.

Reimers, Cordelia, "Is the Average Age of Retirement Changing?" *Journal of the American Statistical Association*, 71(355), 1976, 552-58.

Richards, Hugh, "Female Worklife Capacity by Education and Occupation," *Journal of Forensic Economics* 10(3), 1997, 255-77.

——— and Richard J. Solie, "Worklife Estimates by Occupation," *Journal of Forensic Economics* 9(1), 1996, 287-96.

——— and Ronald Barry, "U.S. Life Tables for 1990 by Sex. Race. and Education," *Journal of Forensic Economics* 11(1), 1998, 9-26.

———, "Worklife Expectancies: Increment-decrement Less Accurate than Conventional," *Journal of Forensic Economics* 13(3), 2000, 271-289.

Rogers, Richard G. and Eve Powell-Griner, "Life Expectancies of Cigarette Smokers and Nonsmokers in the United States," *Social Sciences Medicine* 32(10), 1991, 1151-1159.

Rogot, Eugene, Paul D. Sorlie, Norman J. Johnson, and Catherine A. Schmitt, *A Mortality Study of 1.3 Million Persons by Demographic. Social and Economic Factors: 1979-1985 Follow-Up,* Bethesda, MD. National Institutes of Health. NIH publication 92-3297, 1992.

———. Paul D. Sorlie, and Norman J. Johnson, "Life Expectancy by Employment Status. Income. and Education in the National Longitudinal Mortality Study," *Public Health Reports* 107(4), 1992, 457-61.

Romans, Thomas and Frederick G. Gloss, "The Estimation of Retirement Age in Calculation of Earnings Loss," *Journal of Legal Economics* 3(2), 1993, 25-32.

Rones, Phillip L., Jennifer M. Gardner and Randy E. Ilg, "Trends in hours of work since the mid-1970s," *Monthly Labor Review* 120(4), 1997, 3-14.

———. "Can the Current Population Survey be used to identify the disabled?," *Monthly Labor Review* 104(6), 1981, 37-38.

Rydqewski, Leo G., William G. Deming and Phillip L. Rones, "Seasonal employment falls over past three decades," *Monthly Labor Review* 116(7), 1993, 3-14.

Schechter, Evan S., "Work While Receiving Disability Benefits: Additional Findings From the New Beneficiary Followup Survey," *Social Security Bulletin* 60(1), 1997, 3-17.

Schieren, George A. "Median Worklife, Mean Age at Final Separation, or Transition Probabilities to Calculate Expected Lost Earnings," *Journal of Forensic Economics* 7(1), 1993, 103-9.

Schur, Lisa A., "Dear End Jobs of a Path to Economic Well Being? The Consequences of Non-Standard Work Among People with Disabilities," *Behavioral Sciences and the Law*, November-December 2002, 601-20.

———, "Barriers of Opportunities? The Causes of Contingent and Part-Time Work Among People with Disabilities," *Industrial Relations*, October 2003, 589-622.

Shaw, Katherine "Persistence of Female Labor Supply: Empirical Evidence and Implications," *Journal of Human Resources* 29(2), 1994, 348-78.

Skoog, Gary, "The Markov (Increment-Decrement) Model of Labor Force Activity: New Results Beyond Worklife Expectancies," *Journal of Forensic Economics* 11(1), 2001, 1-21.

———, "The Markov (Increment-Decrement) Model of Labor Force Activity: Extended Tables of Central Tendency, Variation, and Probability Intervals," *Journal of Forensic Economics* 11(1), 2001a, 23-87.

———, and James Ciecka, "Worklife Expectancies of Railroad Workers," *Journal of Forensic Economics* 11(3), 1998, 237-252.

———, and James Ciecka, "A Markov (Increment-Decrement) Model of Labor Force Activity: New Results Beyond Worklife Expectancies," *Journal of Legal Economics* 11(1), 2001a, 1-21.

———, and James Ciecka, "A Markov (Increment-Decrement) Model of Labor Force Activity: Extended Tables of Central Tendency, Variation, and Probability Intervals," *Journal of Legal Economics* 11(1), 2001b, 23-87.

———, and James Ciecka, "Probability Mass Functions for Labor Market Activity Induced by the Markov (Increment-Decrement) Model of Labor For Activity," *Economic Letters* 77(3), 2002, 425-431.

———, and James Ciecka, "Probability Mass Functions for Years to Final Separation from the Labor Force Induced by the Markov Model," *Journal of Forensic Economics* 16(1), 2003, 51-86.

———, and James Ciecka, "Reconsidering and Extending the Conventional/Demographic and LPE Models: the *LPd* and *Lpi* Restricted Markov Models," *Journal of Forensic Economics* 17(1), 2004, 47-94.

———, and James Ciecka, "Parameter Uncertainty in the Estimation of the Markov Model of Labor Force Activity: Known Error Rates Satisfying Dauber," *Litigation Economics Review* 6(2), 2004, 1-27.

———, and James Ciecka, "Worklife Expectancies via Competing Risks/Multiple Decrement Theory with an Application to Railroad Workers," *Journal of Forensic Economics* 19(3), 2006a, 243-260.

———, and James Ciecka, "Allocation of Worklife Expectancy and the Analysis of Front and Uniform Loading with Nomograms," *Journal of Forensic Economics* 19(3), 2006b, 261-296.

Slesnick, Frank and Robert Thornton, "Life Expectancies for Persons with Medical Risks," *Journal of Forensic Economics* 7(2), 1994, 197-207.

Smith, Shirley J., *Tables of Working Life, The Increment-Decrement Model*, Bulletin 2135, US Department of Labor, Bureau of Labor Statistics, November 1982.

———, "New worklife estimates reflect changing profile of labor force," *Monthly Labor Review* 105(3), 1983, 3-11.

———, "Labor force participation rates are not the relevant factor," *Monthly Labor Review* 105(6), 1983, 36-38.

———, "Estimated annual hours of labor force activity," *Monthly Labor Review* 106(2), 1983, 13-22.

———, "Using the appropriate worklife estimate in court proceedings," *Monthly Labor Review* 106(10), 1983, 31-32.

———, "Estimating lost future earnings using the new worklife tables: a comment," *Monthly Labor Review* 108(2), 1985, 42.

———, *Worklife Estimates: Effects of Race and Education*, Bulletin 2254, US Department of Labor, Bureau of Labor Statistics, February 1986.

Snyder, Stephen, William Evans, and Stephen Snyder, "The Impact of Income on Mortality: Evidence from the Social Security Notch," NBER Working Paper No. W9197, 2002.

Sorlie, Paul D., Eric Backlund, and Jacob B. Keller, "US Mortality by Economic, Demographic, and Social Characteristics: The National Longitudinal Mortality Study." *American Journal of Public Health* 85(7), 1995, 949-56.

Spizman, Lawrence, M., "Work-Life Expectancy for the Self-Employed," *The Earnings Analyst* 1, 1998, 81-89.

Steenland, Kyle, Jane Henley, and Michael Thun, "All-Cause and Cause-specific Death Rates by Educational Status for Two Million People in Two American Cancer Society Cohorts, 1959-1996," *American Journal of Epidemiology*, 156(1), 2002, 11-21.

Stern, Steve, "Measuring the Effect of Disability on Labor Force Participation," *The Journal of Human Resources* 24(3), 1989, 361-95.

Suyderhoud, Jack P. and Richard L. Pollock, "Current Versus Ultimate Life Expectancies: Perceptions and Implications," *Journal of Forensic Economics* 4(1), 1990, 101-15.

Tainer, Evelina, "English Language Proficiency and the Determination of Earnings among Foreign-Born Men," *The Journal of Human Resources* 23(4), 1988, 108-22.

Thornton, Robert and Frank Slesnick, "New Estimates of Life Expectancies for Persons with Medical Risks," *Journal of Forensic Economics* 10(3), 1997, 285-90.

Thun, Michael J., Cathy A. Day-Lally, Eugenia E. Calle, W. Dana Flanders, and Clark W. Heath, Jr., "Excess Mortality among Cigarette Smokers: Changes in a 20-Year Interval," *American Journal of Public Health* 85(9), 1995, 1223-1230.

———, Louis F. Apicella, and S. Jane Henley, "Smoking vs Other Risk Factors as the Cause of Smoking-Attributable Deaths, Confounding in the Courtroom" *JAMA*. 2000;284:706-712.

Toossi, Mitra, "A new look at long-term labor force projections to 2050," *Monthly Labor Review*, 129(11), 2006, 19-40.

———, "Labor force projections to 2016: more workers in their golden years," *Monthly Labor Review*, 130(11), 2007, 33-52.

Topel, Robert H., "Job Mobility, Search, and Earnings Growth: A Reinterpretation of Human Capital Earnings Functions," *Research in Labor Economics,* Volume 8, Part A (Greenwich, CT: JAI Press Inc., 1986), 199-233.

———, and Michael P. Ward, "Job Mobility and the Careers of Young Men," *The Quarterly Journal of Economics* 62, 1992, 439-79.

Townsend, Jules A., "Date of Injury or Date of Trial: A Comment on Work Life Expectancy Calculations," *Litigation Economics Digest* 2(2), 1997, 169-71.

U.S. Bureau of the Census, "1990 Census of Population and Housing 5% Public Use Microdata Samples," CD-ROM, CD90-PUMSA1 through 7, Data User Services Division. Washington, DC., August 1993 and December 1995.

———,, Current Population Surveys, Tobacco Use Supplement, Microdata CD-ROM, September 1992, January 1993, and May 1993, Data User Services Division, Washington, DC.

———,, *Education in the United States, 1990 Census of the Population*, Washington, DC., U.S. Government Printing Office, Census publication 1990 CP-3-4, 1994.

———, "Earning by Education and Occupation," Subject Summary Tape File (SSTF) 22A, CD-ROM, CD90SSTF22A, Data User Services Division, Washington, DC., October 1994.

———, Current Population Reports, P60-197, "Money Income in the United States: 1997," U.S. Government Printing Office, Washington, DC, September 1998.

U.S. Department of Labor, Bureau of Labor Statistics, "Labor force status of the civilian non institutional population by age, sex, race, Hispanic origin, and years of school completed," unpublished data, 1980 and 1990.

———, "Length of Working Life for Men and Women, 1970," Special Labor Force Report 187 (Revised) (1977).

———, "Perspectives on Working Women: A Databook," Bulletin 2080, (1980), 34.

———, PINC-04. Educational attainment—people 18 years old and over by total money earnings in 2007, age race, Hispanic origin, and sex, at website http://pubdb3.cen-sus.gov/macro/032008/perinc/toc.htm.

U.S. Department of Health, Education, and Welfare, *Reducing the Health Consequences of Smoking: 25 Years of Progress: A Report of the Surgeon General, 1989*, DHHS Publication No. (CDC) 89-8411, Rockville, MD, 1989.

———, Center for Disease Control, "Cigarette Smoking Among Adults—United States, 2004," MMWR, November 11, 2005, at www.cdc.gov/MMWR/preview/mmwrhtml/mm5444a2.htm.

———, Center for Disease Control, Smoking and Tobacco Use, "Cigarette Smoking-Related Mortality," September 2006 at www.cdc.gov/tobacco/data_statistics/fact_sheets/fast_facts/index.htm.

U.S. Department of Health and Human Services, National Center for Health Statistics, *Vital Statistics of the United States, 1990, Life Tables,* Volume II, Section 6. DHHS Publication No. (PHS)94-1104, Hyattsville, MD, 1994.

———, National Center for Health Statistics, *United States Life Tables, 2000,* National Vital Statistics Report Volume 51, Number 3, December 19, 2002.

———, National Center for Health Statistics, *United States Life Tables, 2004,* National Vital Statistics Report Volume 56, Number 9, December 28, 2007.

Williams, Donald R., "Women's part-time employment: a gross flow analysis," *Monthly Labor Review* 118(4), 1995, 36-44.

Yelin, Edward H. and Patricia P. Katz, "Labor force trends of persons with and without disabilities," *Monthly Labor Review* 117(10), 1994, 36-42.

About the Editors

Hugh Richards graduated from Oberlin College (1967) with a major in geology, the University of Washington (1981) with a M.F.A. in filmmaking, and the University of Alaska, Fairbanks (1987) with a M.S. in resource economics. He currently resides in Fairbanks, Alaska, where he is a consulting forensic economist. Hugh is married to Jamila, a pianist who grew up in Prague, and is the delighted sixty-four-year-old father of Juanito, our Guatemala miracle brought home for Christmas 2007.

Michael Donaldson holds a BA from Western State College of Colorado (1989) and a Ph.D. in computer simulation modeling from University of California, Davis (1995). He currently resides in Fairbanks, Alaska, where he and his wife Catherine are raising two boys. Michael is a consultant specializing in data acquisition and analysis and also teaches science at the Institute for Science and Mathematics, home of the famed "Mad Scientist Workshops."

Index

Future Damage and Present Value Calculator

by Steve Weintraub

Released annually with the most recent figures!

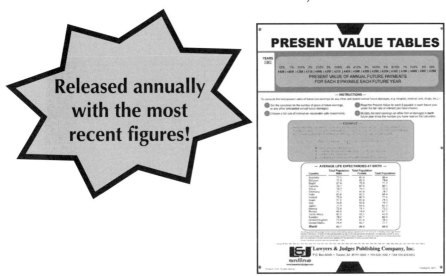

Side 1

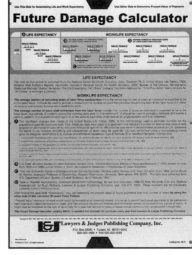

Side 2

Our Future Damage and Present Value Calculator contains several different settings for determining your client's worklife expectancy. It is lightweight and travels easily in a briefcase, so that you can access worklife tables on-the-go. It is updated annually with the most recent figures.

The Future Damage Calculator breaks down human life expectancies and years of participation in the labor force by sex, age, education level and ethnicity. You will find this information invaluable when determining potential earnings prior to final retirement. Whatever type of case you are working on, you will find the information you need without wasting hours on research. Ideal for use in trial, research, settlement conferences, and structured settlement offers.

This calculator contains the average life expectancies for over twenty countries: United States, Canada, Afghanistan, Australia, Brazil, China, Cuba, Dominican Republic, El Salvador, Germany, India, Iran, Iraq, Israel, Italy, Japan, North Korea, Mexico, Pakistan, Philippines, Russia, South Africa, the United Kingdom, and Vietnam as well as a worldwide average life expectancy. The new calculator also reflects annual changes in life expectancies for the male and female populations, as well as the total population size, of the countries listed. All life expectancy data is updated yearly with the most recent figures.

The flip side of the calculator provides the Present Value Tables sorted by a wide range of interest rates showing the present value of future lost earnings or any other anticipated annual future damages. The calculator contains expanded Present Value Tables including 7 and 7.5 percent, which are important for calculating worker's compensation claims.

Due to the popularity of this product we offer generous quantity discounts, so be sure to ask everyone in the office before ordering. We also offer this product on our L&J Standing Order Plan. Call us at 520-323-1500 for more information!

Product Code: 0615 • 8.5x11 • Slide Calculator